6 —

The Poet's Manual
and Rhyming Dictionary

The Poet's Manual
and Rhyming Dictionary

by FRANCES STILLMAN

Based on *The Improved Rhyming Dictionary*

by JANE SHAW WHITFIELD

Thomas Y. Crowell, Publishers
Established 1834
New York

Contents

Introduction   vii

How to Use the Rhyming Dictionary   xvii

Abbreviations Used in This Book   xviii

THE POET'S MANUAL

Chapter I   Rhythm and Meter; The Stanza   3

Chapter II   Rhyme and Rhyme Patterns   32

Chapter III   Traditional Forms in Poetry   41

Chapter IV   New Ways in Verse; Rhyme   80

Chapter V   New Ways in Rhythm: Free Verse and Modernist-Traditional Forms   88

Chapter VI   The Content of Poetry   97

Chapter VII   Style   112

RHYMING DICTIONARY

Ā (ay)   Single (Masculine) Rhymes   127

    Double (Feminine) Rhymes   133

    Triple Rhymes   147

Ä (ah)   Single (Masculine) Rhymes   152

    Double (Feminine) Rhymes   156

    Triple Rhymes   161

Ă (cab)   Single (Masculine) Rhymes   162

    Double (Feminine) Rhymes   167

    Triple Rhymes   180

Ē (bee)	Single (Masculine) Rhymes	187
	Double (Feminine) Rhymes	193
	Triple Rhymes	201
Ĕ (heh)	Single (Masculine) Rhymes	204
	Double (Feminine) Rhymes	209
	Triple Rhymes	222
Ī (eye)	Single (Masculine) Rhymes	229
	Double (Feminine) Rhymes	234
	Triple Rhymes	242
Ĭ (bib)	Single (Masculine) Rhymes	245
	Double (Feminine) Rhymes	251
	Triple Rhymes	263
Ō (oh)	Single (Masculine) Rhymes	272
	Double (Feminine) Rhymes	276
	Triple Rhymes	283
Ŏ (bob)	Single (Masculine) Rhymes	286
	Double (Feminine) Rhymes	290
	Triple Rhymes	298
Ô (awe)	Single (Masculine) Rhymes	304
	Double (Feminine) Rhymes	306
	Triple Rhymes	308
OO (good)	Single (Masculine) Rhymes	309
	Double (Feminine) Rhymes	311
	Triple Rhymes	312
OI (boy)	Single (Masculine) Rhymes	313
	Double (Feminine) Rhymes	315
	Triple Rhymes	317
OU (how)	Single (Masculine) Rhymes	318
	Double (Feminine) Rhymes	320
	Triple Rhymes	323
Ū (you)	Single (Masculine) Rhymes	324
	Double (Feminine) Rhymes	328
	Triple Rhymes	334
Ŭ (tub)	Single (Masculine) Rhymes	337
	Double (Feminine) Rhymes	342
	Triple Rhymes	353

APPENDIXES

I Publication	359
II Markets for Poetry and Verse	369
Index	381

Introduction

To a certain extent a poet is born, not made — the reverse of this statement is equally true. The gifts of the poet are innate, but the imagination and inspiration that belong to the poet are only half the story. The poet's art must be learned. The techniques of versewriting comprise a real craft, and a major preoccupation of any poet must be the development of his skill in handling them. The wit who said that genius is 10 per cent inspiration and 90 per cent perspiration perhaps erred in his proportions; but in the case of poetry it is true that an important part of the poet's effort must be devoted to technical questions which have as much to do with hard work as with inspiration.

This book has a threefold purpose. First, it is designed to serve as a reference book in the field of prosody, or the handling of language in poetry; the complete index will enable the reader to find any term or the full treatment of any branch of the subject without difficulty. Second, if read consecutively, the text presents a full course in prosody, from the basic traditional meters through the newest modern developments, that should help the versewriter to improve his writing through the systematic study of the technical resources of his art. Third, the rhyming dictionary, the most extensive available, will enable the versewriter to find the rhymes he needs quickly and easily. In addition, an appendix on publication gives practical guidance for the submission of verse to periodicals and a directory of periodicals that publish poetry.

Defining a few of the terms in which versewriting is usually discussed will make it possible to begin a consideration of the subject.

Verse is composition in words that employs deliberate patterns of sound in its language. These patterns may follow the rules of regular or mixed *meter* or the loose cadences of *free verse*. Verse is almost always divided into *lines* and a line is also sometimes called a verse, though we will not use the term in this way. The lines are often organized into *stanzas*, which are also sometimes loosely called verses. Verse frequently employs the device of *rhyme* to heighten its effectiveness.

Poetry is, of course, verse — although not all verse is poetry. Poetry employs the same battery of techniques as verse, but it transcends verse in a way that has escaped definition, despite numerous attempts by philosophers and poets to pin it down. Poetry seems to partake of the miraculous, as does all great art; it adds up to more than the sum of its parts.

Meter in English is the organized system of writing verse that patterns language by causing an accented syllable to occur at regular intervals of one out of every two or three in the succession of words in a line.

Free verse is verse that is not written according to the rules of meter.

The *line* is a unit of language in a poem, a group of words that stand together and usually appear in one line of type, though it may, if it is long, run over into a second or even a third line or more. Four lines of varying length from Walt Whitman's "Out of the Cradle Endlessly Rocking" may serve as an example:

Out of the cradle endlessly rocking,
Out of the mocking-bird's throat, the musical shuttle,
Out of the Ninth-month midnight,
Over the sterile sands and the fields beyond, where the child leaving his bed
    wander'd alone, bareheaded, barefoot . . . .

The *stanza* is a group of lines that belong together; it is set off from other stanzas by an extra space between the last line of one stanza and the first line of the next.

Rhyme is the chiming of the same or similar sounds at the ends of lines in a poem.

Prosody refers to the whole field of the handling of language in poetry and verse; the foregoing terms — meter, free verse, the line, the stanza, and rhyme — are all included in it. *Versification* is a major subclassification in prosody; it deals specifically with the science of meter and rhyme in traditional verse composition.

As we shall see in considering verse forms used in English, during the development of prosody throughout the centuries many ways of approaching the writing of poetry bave appeared in different parts of the world. These varied possibilities all lie open to the poet of today, who searches everywhere for elements capable of increasing the expressiveness of his art. The twentieth century has added to poetic techniques in ways comparable to the innovations in modern music. Modern poets continue to develop finer distinctions of accent and stress, a widening of the scale, a sure and highly differentiated use of dissonance, and time sequences which afford new rhythmic expressiveness. This spirit of technical inventiveness and daring in modern prosody constantly exerts pressure upon the boundaries of poetry in an effort to enlarge them. Many such attempts fail, but some succeed — an understanding of this aim is necessary to the comprehension of many contemporary poems.

It will be useful here to describe briefly the main kinds of verse, since they should be borne in mind as general background to any study of poetry and poetic forms. We will return to them from a different viewpoint in Chapter VI, in discussing the kinds of subject matter used in the various kinds of poetry.

EPIC POETRY

Epic poetry has been considered in all countries and in all times to be the highest form of poetic achievement because it relates heroic events on a grand scale. An epic is a very long poem, the action of which takes place on a national or supranational level, often with the supernatural playing a part. Homer's *Iliad* and *Odyssey* are the prototypes and at the same time the ideal of the epic form. Milton's *Paradise Lost* and *Paradise Regained* are the major examples of the epic in English. *Beowulf*, an ancient Anglo-Saxon poem of unknown date and authorship, is the oldest epic in the history of English literature.

The invocation that begins Milton's *Paradise Lost* is a good example of epic style. The subject is stated in the first lines, as it was in the classical epics of Homer and Virgil, and Milton invokes the Muse — characteristically mingling the classical concept of the Muse with Judaeo-Christian theology — to sing of it.

> Of Man's First Disobedience, and the Fruit
> Of that forbidden Tree, whose mortal tast
> Brought Death into the World, and all our woe,
> With loss of *Eden*, till one greater Man
> Restore us, and regain the blissful Seat,
> Sing Heav'nly Muse, that on the secret top
> Of *Oreb*, or of *Sinai*, didst inspire
> That Shepherd, who first taught the chosen Seed,
> In the beginning how the Heav'ns and Earth
> Rose out of *Chaos*: or if *Sion* Hill
> Delight thee more, and Siloa's Brook that flow'd
> Fast by the Oracle of God; I thence
> Invoke thy aid to my adventrous Song,
> That with no middle flight intends to soar
> Above th'Aonian Mount, while it pursues
> Things unattempted yet in Prose or Rhime.
> And chiefly Thou O Spirit, that dost prefer
> Before all Temples th'upright heart and pure,
> Instruct me, for Thou know'st; Thou from the first
> Wast present, and with mighty wings outspread
> Dove-like satst brooding on the vast Abyss
> And mad'st it pregnant: What in me is dark
> Illumine, what is low raise and support;
> That to the highth of this great Argument
> I may assert Eternal Providence,
> And justifie the ways of God to man.

First, note that Milton intends to try "things unattempted yet in Prose or Rhime." This is a definite statement of his intention to make innovations not only in subject matter but also in poetic technique, a double aim which modern poets share. Second, the theme is truly epic in nature and scope; the scene is the universe, the protagonist is man, and Milton's high purpose is nothing less than to "justifie the ways of God to men." This single example serves to illustrate some of the most salient characteristics of the epic form.

NARRATIVE POETRY

Narrative poetry tells a story on a smaller, more human scale than does the epic. A long narrative poem is often a novel in verse. A romance tells a legendary tale of chivalry; the French *Romance of the Rose* is an example from the Middle Ages, and in more modern times Tennyson wrote a romance in his verse treatment of the Arthurian legends, *The Idylls of the King*. A shorter narrative poem may be linked to the novella, or a short story in verse. *The Canterbury Tales*, by Chaucer, includes traditional and folk tales taken from many sources, supposedly related by a group of pilgrims whose motivation and situation in life are cleverly revealed by the poet in the telling.

A ballad is a short narrative poem, lyrical in mood and style, which was originally meant to be sung while dancing. In recent years, with the revival of folk music, the ballad has come back into its own as song. The early ballads were anonymous and grew out of traditional folk stories; they are full of quaint, archaic turns of speech and are often actually in dialect, some of the best known being Scottish ballads. The modern literary ballad frequently imitates the folk ballad in tone and flavor. "Barbara Allen" and "Sir Patrick Spens" are examples of the early folk ballad, while Stephen Vincent Benét's "Ballad of William Sycamore" is a good modern example.

DRAMATIC POETRY

Dramatic poetry uses the direct discourse of its characters to tell its story or set forth its situation. Drama was always written in poetry in classical times, although Aristophanes introduced some prose passages into his plays, as Shakespeare was to do much later. However, it was not until comparatively modern times that the drama began to be written entirely in prose.

As for shorter dramatic forms in poetry, the dramatic monologues of Browning are classics of their type. Certain ballads are also written in dramatic form, usually in question and answer dialogue. Such a ballad, in which the dialogue is held between a dead man and his living friend, is A. E. Housman's "Is My Team Ploughing."

IS MY TEAM PLOUGHING

' Is my team ploughing,
  That I was used to drive
And hear the harness jingle
  When I was man alive? '

Ay, the horses trample,
  The harness jingles now;
No change though you lie under
  The land you used to plough.

' Is football playing
  Along the river shore,
With lads to chase the leather,
  Now I stand up no more? '

Ay, the ball is flying,
  The lads play heart and soul,
The goal stands up, the keeper
  Stands up to keep the goal.

' Is my girl happy,
  That I thought hard to leave,
And has she tired of weeping
  As she lies down at eve? '

Ay, she lies down lightly,
  She lies not down to weep:
Your girl is well contented.
  Be still, my lad, and sleep.

' Is my friend hearty,
  Now I am thin and pine,
And has he found to sleep in
  A better bed than mine? '

Yes, lad, I lie easy,
  I lie as lads would choose;
I cheer a dead man's sweetheart,
  Never ask me whose.
                    —A. E. Housman

DESCRIPTIVE POETRY

Descriptive poetry is primarily devoted to the presentation of scenes, persons, and objects. In it, the thing described is the main point; the poem seeks to do no more than paint a picture. A short descriptive poem has no difficulty in keeping strictly within its thematic bounds; the very length of the longer poem makes it inevitable that the author's feelings and opinions should enter the picture, but these must in all cases remain subordinate to the main pictorial theme. "The Deserted Village," by Oliver Goldsmith, is a famous example. It begins by setting the nostalgic scene that is to give way before the ruin brought upon the English countryside by disastrous politico-economic conditions.

> Sweet Auburn, loveliest village of the plain,
> Where health and plenty cheared the labouring swain,
> Where smiling spring its earliest visit paid,
> And parting summer's lingering blooms delayed,
> Dear lovely bowers of innocence and ease,
> Seats of my youth, where every sport could please,
> How often have I loitered o'er thy green,
> Where humble happiness endeared each scene!

DIDACTIC POETRY

Didactic poetry is objective in its aim to teach. What is taught may be a body of knowledge, as in Lucretius' *De Rerum Natura* (*On the Nature of Things*), a long Latin poem in six books that instructs the reader in a complete system of cosmology. Such poetry may be a fully developed moral treatise, as is Pope's *Essay on Man*; or it may be a simple set of facts, as in the nursery rhymes detailing the number of days in each month or the order of the kings of England.

LYRIC POETRY

The word lyric originally meant "suitable to sing to the music of the lyre." Lyric is still used to mean the words to a song, and its musical connotations still signify that a lyric poem should be musical and graceful.

Lyric poetry is subjective in its approach, expressing the feelings, thoughts, and visions of the poet himself directly and often very personally. Palgrave, the editor of the famous *Golden Treasury*, said that the lyric poem turns on a single thought, feeling, or situation, and is characterized by brevity, the coloring of human passion, and rapidity of movement. The following is a lyric about poets which lingers in the memory.

ODE

> We are the music-makers,
>   And we are the dreamers of dreams,
> Wandering by lone sea-breakers,
>   And sitting by desolate streams;

World losers and world forsakers,
  On whom the pale moon gleams:
Yet we are the movers and shakers
  Of the world for ever, it seems.

With wonderful deathless ditties
We build up the world's great cities,
  And out of a fabulous story
  We fashion an empire's glory:
One man with a dream, at pleasure,
  Shall go forth and conquer a crown;
And three with a new song's measure
  Can trample an empire down.

We, in the ages lying
  In the buried past of the earth,
Built Nineveh with our sighing,
  And Babel itself with our mirth;
And o'erthrew them with prophesying
  To the old of the new world's worth;
For each age is a dream that is dying,
  Or one that is coming to birth.
                    —A. W. E. O'Shaughnessy

SATIRICAL VERSE

Satirical verse holds up some abuse or folly of man or society to the derision of its audience, often with the aim of improving conditions by exposing them and by calling down upon them the censure of an aroused audience. Satire is as ancient as the vices and weaknesses of mankind which it attacks. When directed against an individual, it can be pitilessly destructive of a career or a reputation.

Satire, in verse as in prose, employs all the devices of scornful wit. It may be written in the form of narrative, dramatic, descriptive, or lyric poetry. Some famous examples of satire are the plays of Aristophanes, Molière, and Ben Jonson, *The Dunciad*, by Alexander Pope, and *Don Juan*, by Lord Byron.

OCCASIONAL VERSE

The poet laureate of England holds the one public office in the Western world whose main function is to produce occasional verse. It is an old and respected tradition that the official poet should produce a poem in honor of various important occasions, such as the Queen's birthday. Good poetry, unfortunately, is not always produced to order, but sometimes it is. Kipling's "Recessional", written to celebrate the sixtieth anniversary of Queen Victoria's reign, is an example.

RECESSIONAL
June 22, 1897

God of our fathers, known of old—
    Lord of our far-flung battle line—
Beneath whose awful hand we hold
    Dominion over palm and pine—
Lord God of Hosts, be with us yet,
Lest we forget, lest we forget!

                .   .   .   .

For heathen heart that puts her trust
    In reeking tube and iron shard—
All valiant dust that builds on dust,
    And guarding calls not Thee to guard—
For frantic boast and foolish word,
Thy Mercy on Thy people, Lord!

                        —Rudyard Kipling

Greeting card verse is an ubiquitous kind of mass-produced occasional verse that has enjoyed great popularity but little esteem.

LIGHT AND HUMOROUS VERSE

Light and humorous verse are the effervescence of poetry. Often serious at bottom, they take the comic view of life as opposed to the tragic; they aim to amuse (and sometimes edify) the reader, to make him smile or even laugh. Although the comic muse has apparently been downgraded in recent years, with a concurrent critical tendency to assign "importance" only to modern poetry of serious or tragic significance, the best light and humorous verse should not be underrated—it will last as long as anything in English poetry.

Vers de société is the name of a kind of light verse which comments on the social whirl and the various predicaments of individuals who are caught up in it.

Nonsense verse is a special variety of humorous verse which does not seem to make sense, but which often has method in its madness. Lewis Carroll was supreme in this genre, and the poems of Edward Lear have been beloved by generations of children and adults.

Parody, in verse as in prose, is a comic or satirical imitation of another piece of writing that exaggerates its style and subject matter in a sort of *reductio ad absurdum*, playing especially upon any weakness in structure or content of the original.

Some parodies have become better known than the poems that they imitate, and in certain extreme cases the original has been practically forgotten and the parody remembered as a humorous poem in its own right. "Father William," by Lewis Carroll, is an example of this. How many people are aware that it is a parody of a poem by Robert Southey, and who is familiar with Southey's bathetic original? "Father William" is a deliciously nonsensical piece of verse that can be appreciated without reference to any other.

However, parody is best understood when the original is known, and some of the most hilarious effects can only be fully grasped by one conversant with the solemnities of the work being parodied.

Dialect verse derives much of its humor from its use of dialect, combined with the exploitation of the country or folksy locales in which dialect flourishes. A rude or shrewd bucolic humor is often an element; in such verse the " smooth " sins of the sophisticated world are often shown up in implied or explicit contrast to the simple world.

Macaronic verse is written in a ludicrously jumbled and distorted combination of several languages. A sort of cross between dialect verse and macaronic verse is the *foreign admixture* type, which exploits the dialectical mixed usages of a foreign group, such as the German-Americans.

TRANSLATION

Finally, the translation of poetry from other languages must be mentioned as a separate poetic activity, although it obviously does not fit into the same classificatory framework as the other kinds of poetry listed here.

A translation may, in fact, be of any "kind" of poetry. Ideally, it should reproduce the poem from another language complete with all the equivalent nuances of expression, all the turns of thought as well as phrase, and all the devices of prosody of the original. The best known translated work in English, much of which was in poetry in the original languages, is the Bible.

The translator has a dual responsibility, both to do justice to the original work in all the subtleties of the original language, and to render it by doing justice to the potentialities of his own language. It is inadvisable to attempt translation into a language to which one is not native. The ideal direction in translating poetry is *from* a foreign language, which of course one must know extremely well in order to understand all the nuances of the original work, *into* one's own language, whose idioms and expressions one knows creatively as one can never know any other.

How to Use the
Rhyming Dictionary

1. The reader should look for rhymes under the vowel sound of the rhyme he seeks. For example, if he wishes a rhyme for "hat," he should look under Ă, whereas for "hate" he should look under Ā.

2. The vowel sounds upon which the rhymes depend are given in alphabetical order. If the reader is searching for a vowel sound that puzzles him, he should consult the table of contents. Otherwise, the running heads at the top of each page will tell him which rhyme sounds he has before him.

3. Three chapters are devoted to every vowel sound: one each for single rhymes, double rhymes, and triple rhymes. For example, under Ā, one finds in the first section "ate, bait, date, etc."; in the second section, "able, Babel, fable, gable, cable, etc."; in the third section, "fadedness, jadedness."

4. Consonant sounds within each classification occur in alphabetical order, listed according to their actual sound rather than spelling. Thus "c" is listed under either "k" or "s". "Ch" occurs third in the list. "X" is listed under "ks," its actual phonetic combination of sounds, and "qu" is listed under "k" or "kw" for the same reason.

5. Within the entry for each rhyme, the words are alphabetized according to the sound that immediately precedes the rhyme sound, as in "at, bat, chat, fat, gat, hat, cat, etc." or "acrobat, pussycat, Krazy Kat, diplomat, etc."

6. Within each entry, the words are arranged in numbered groups according to the number of syllables they contain. Therefore, if one needs a word of one syllable to complete a line, he need look no farther than the words following the numeral "1." If he needs three syllables, he looks only at the words that follow the number "3." He might also choose a one- or two-syllable word for the rhyme and qualify it with an adjective of one or two syllables, thus arriving at the desired three syllables.

7. Imperfect rhymes appear in italics; they are words which would be perfect rhymes if the accent fell on the rhyme sound, but it does not. Imperfect rhymes are often used in modern poetry.

8. In cases where regional pronunciations vary, words have been included

that may not seem rhymes according to every reader's pronunciation. This may be true in particular for words ending in "r," since this sound is pronounced variously or not at all, and often modifies the pronunciation of the preceding vowel. The user of the book should not use a rhyme that does not rhyme *for him*. He should, however, remember that it rhymes for some people, and that is why it appears in the list. The same word appears in more than one place if it has more than one pronunciation that rhymes with other words.

9. Cross references are made to entries that may contain additional rhymes. References to other sections may be rapidly found by turning to the indicated vowel sound and the section of one-, two-, or three-syllable rhymes. It has been necessary to give general cross references between the entire sections Ŏ (bob), Ô (awe), and Ä (ah), since some people pronounce entries in parts of these sections in precisely the same way, whereas others make a distinction between them.

10. Separate entries are made for nouns taking "s" or "es" in the plural and verbs in the third person singular of the present tense in the following cases: (1) if there are additional words that rhyme, as in "bays" and "raise"; (2) if the number of syllables is different, as in "ace" and "aces," causing the entry to occur in a different section; (3) if only part of the initial entry can take an "s" ending and it has seemed desirable to sort out the words that can. Unless one of these conditions is present, the user will find nouns entered only in their singular form and no separate indication of the third person singular form of verbs in the present tense.

ABBREVIATIONS

Ar.	Arabic	exc.	except	loc.	local
Aram.	Aramaic	F.	French	N.	north
arch.	archaic	G.	German	obs.	obsolete
coll.	colloquial	Gr.	Greek	Pg.	Portuguese
D.	Dutch	Heb.	Hebrew	Pol.	Polish
dial.	dialect	Hind.	Hindustani	Russ.	Russian
e.g.	*exempli gratia* [L.], for example	Ir.	Ireland	Sp.	Spanish
		It.	Italian	Scot.	Scotland
Eng.	England	Jap.	Japanese	Tag.	Tagalog
etc.	et cetera	L.	Latin		

The Poet's Manual
and Rhyming Dictionary

The Poet's Manual

I

Rhythm and Meter; The Stanza

Rhythm, the most basic element of the technique of versification, is a temporal phenomenon: it can only occur with the passage of time, as one event (a movement, a note in music, a syllable of poetry) succeeds another. Rhythm is present when the intervals required by the events, or the intervals that space the emphases upon certain events in the chain, are regular.

The world and universe as we know them seem to be made up of both temporal and spatial extension. Visual art (painting, sculpture) is primarily spatial, whereas music, literature, and the dance are primarily temporal, depending upon a succession of sounds, concepts, or movements.

The human use of rhythm as an element of play reaches back into the early ages of mankind, and we do not know much about it; we can only ascertain that rhythm and the rhythmic movements of dancing are a natural expression of the most primitive peoples. As Darcy says in *Pride and Prejudice*, "Every savage can dance." As in the case of most primitive elements in human nature, the simple impulse toward rhythm appears very early in the individual's life — every baby likes to be rocked, and, if nobody else will do it, even rocks himself.

The universality of rhythm in the world, in the turning of our terrestrial globe, the regular movements of the planets in their orbits, and the alternation of day and night, is too obvious to need extended comment. Sound, light, and energy move in waves. In the living individual, the pulse of the heartbeat, though seldom consciously thought of, pervades the entire being. It would seem, in fact, that all the natural, nonvolitional motions of life and matter are characterized by rhythm.

It is therefore probably not surprising that the earliest literature of mankind should have been rhythmic, and that poetry should come, historically, before prose. The epics, sagas, and songs that were handed down by word of mouth among preliterate people may have been strongly rhythmic because they were closer to the roots of mankind than modern literature. There were, however, also two good logical reasons why an oral literature should be composed in verse: the rhythm helped to hold the attention of the listener and it assisted the memory of the bard who sang, spoke, or chanted the poem.

Writings concerning the sacred mysteries of religion, which seek to interpret the underlying rhythm of the universe in terms of revelation and direct experience, usually express their message in poetry or strongly rhythmic prose. On a lower plane, practitioners of magic arts have traditionally used incantation as an instrument — incantation in the sense of the rhythmic invocation of the powers of darkness. The incantatory language of poetry, in its broadest meaning, is merely considered to be rhythmic expression, but all rhythmic language possesses some of the qualities of magical incantation or religious chanting in its ability to affect the listener on a nonrational level. This strange power of poetry undoubtedly contributes to making memorable some of the noblest passages in all literature.

To go from the sublime to the ridiculous, modern advertisers, too, are aware of the penetrating power of rhythmic language. Songs and jingles are constantly used to impress the name of some product upon both the conscious and subconscious mind of the listener, and thus to influence him — in this case, to the specific action of buying the advertiser's wares. The public is urged to

> Double your pleasure, double your fun,
> With Doublemint, Doublemint, Doublemint gum!

Or to

> See the U. S. A.
> In your Chevrolet!

Advertising verse is usually on a very simple level, resembling the nursery rhyme in its dependence on a strong beat and on rhyming. If the ultimate in advertising, the subliminal message unseen by the conscious eye, ever is used in earnest, rhythm will undoubtedly be combined with it to reinforce its direct appeal to the subconscious mind.

Rhythm, it is evident, is a potent element in many kinds of activities, including literature. In poetry it is of prime importance, being a major stylistic instrument of poetic form. Therefore in poetry it has developed far beyond the expression of the primitive rhythmic urge, and has been analyzed and systematized in the science of prosody.

Within the general concept of rhythm in poetry, meter is, as we have already seen, the name of the regular system of the alternation of accented and unaccented syllables in English and of long and short syllables in the classical languages. The word "meter" comes from the Greek *metron*, meaning meter or measure.

By accent (called tonic accent in English) we mean the mechanical emphasis that is usually placed upon one syllable in every two or three in spoken English. It is indicated in the dictionary by an accent mark (′) placed before, after, or over the accented syllable. Another way to show it is by using capital letters, as in EMphasis, CONcert, WILLingness, imAGinAtion. This difference in accent from syllable to syllable exists, of course, not only in poetry but in all speech. There are also variations in the strength of the accent. For example, in the word

DIFference the first syllable, DIF, receives a strong or primary accent. The second syllable, fer, is unaccented, and many people do not even pronounce it separately. The third syllable, ence, may receive a weak or secondary accent, if the speaker wishes or if the meter requires it in verse, as in Wordsworth's line "The DIF | ferENCE | to ME." In this line there are six syllables, and the second, fourth, and sixth are accented; each accented syllable is preceded by an unaccented one, forming a definite rhythmic pattern. "Difference" could also fit into another pattern in which it would be pronounced "DIF-fer-ence," as in "TELL me the | DIFference, | TELL it me | TRUTHfully." Here the pattern is in groups of three syllables with the accent on the first.

In comparing English meter with that of Latin and Greek, the English-speaking person is at a disadvantage because he cannot imagine a poetic rhythm based upon quantity, or relative length of syllables. Unless he has made a special study of phonetics he is hardly conscious of what is long and what is short in English.

What is a long syllable in English? It is a syllable which takes measurably longer to pronounce than a short one because it contains a long vowel or a lengthy combination of consonants. Every English vowel has a long and a short pronunciation, and sometimes more than one. For example, the letter "a" has two long pronunciations, "ay" as in "make" and "ah" as in "father," and a short pronunciation which is like the "a" sound in "hat." The first "e" in "fever" is long, while the "e" in "met" is short. A syllable is also said to be long if it contains a time-consuming combination of consonants; for example, "breath" takes longer to say than "bet," although the two words contain the same short vowel sound.

It was upon comparable distinctions between long and short syllables that the Greeks and Romans based their meters in poetry. We have seen that English, as compared to the classical languages, has a strong tonic accent, which *Webster's Third New International Dictionary* defines as "the relative phonetic prominence (as from greater stress or higher pitch) of a spoken syllable or word." The accented syllable in English is usually spoken a fraction of a tone higher than the unaccented one, as well as with slightly more force. However, tonic accent is not at all the same thing as the meaningful emphasis normally placed upon the most important part of a clause or sentence. The placing of accent is a mechanical linguistic phenomenon that occurs naturally and, for all practical purposes, automatically, whereas the placing of emphasis is a rational interpretation meant to show the importance of a unit of meaning. Tonic accent is only the tick-tock of our linguistic clockwork as it goes along; it underlies all larger means of expressiveness in English.

It should be said at once that although conventional English versification is based upon patterns of tonic accent the relative length of syllables plays an important part in the music of English poetry — a part that is, however, not at all systematized, although it colors the work of all important poets.

As we have seen, although the English-speaking person is unable to read Latin and Greek poetry aloud as it should be read, he knows that quantity was the determinant in the meters of classical antiquity that have so deeply influenced English versification. The basic patterns and relationships are the same in the four major meters, with the substitution in English of an accented syllable for the long syllable of Latin or Greek and an unaccented syllable for a short one. The classical system of prosody lies historically at the root of our own, and it is customary to accept Greek poetry as the common ancestor of the poetry of the entire Western world. Nevertheless, as will be seen, another and very powerful poetic stream contributed to making English poetry what it is today.

In Greek, the oldest and most frequently employed meter was the one that is least used in English — *dactylic* meter. This is composed of units (each called a dactyl) of three syllables of which the first and most important is accented in English and long in Greek and Latin. The so-called epic verse was the line containing six such units; a metric unit is called a foot, so it should be said that this line has six feet. The six-foot line has a specific name that will be included later in the description of the terminology of meter; it is *hexameter*. An example of the epic line in English may be taken from the beginning of Longfellow's *Evangeline:*

THIS is the | FORest pri | MEval. The | MURmuring | PINES and the | HEMlocks
BEARDed with | MOSS and in | GARments | GREEN, indis | TINCT in the | TWIlight....

The epic verse in dactylic hexameter may be represented in a sort of metrical algebra borrowed from the dot-dash of wireless telegraphy as:

$$—\cdot\cdot \quad | \quad —\cdot\cdot \quad | \quad —\cdot\cdot \quad | \quad —\cdot\cdot \quad | \quad —\cdot\cdot \quad | \quad —\cdot\cdot$$

It may be counted, as a piano teacher counts the beats in music for a child, as:

ONE and a | TWO and a | THREE and a | FOUR and a | FIVE and a | SIX and.

Note that the final foot has only two syllables instead of three. When the poet leaves out an unaccented syllable that is called for by the meter at the end of a line, the line is "truncated." In this case, the device provides a split second's pause which serves to mark line division when the poem is read aloud rather than seen on the page, for the Greek epic grew up in an oral tradition. All poetry, as a matter of fact, is composed primarily for the ear rather than for the eye, and the poet or critic with impeccable taste in poetry is often said to have a "good ear."

Homer's *Odyssey* and *Iliad* are composed in dactylic hexameters. These great epics were repeated orally from memory long before they were written down, and their sonorous beauty and power in the original language have moved generations of heroes more modern than those described in the epics. It is only very ancient tradition that gives us the name of Homer as the author of the two greatest epics of classical literature, and no proof has ever been found that such a man as the blind poet ever existed. The two epics are thought to have emerged in their final shape some time between the twelfth and the ninth centuries B.C.

Next in popularity to dactylic meter in ancient Greece was *iambic*, which was very often employed by the lyric poets who followed Homer. The island of Lesbos was traditionally considered the birthplace of lyric poetry in Greece, for it was there that "burning Sappho loved and sung," as Byron wrote in "The Isles of Greece." Actually, Lesbos was the center of a school of lyric poetry, and Sappho was a leading member of the poetic movement there. The few of Sappho's lyrics that have been preserved strike a sympathetic chord in the modern reader because of their personal content and their sparely beautiful diction. It is interesting to note that Sappho was the first woman poet to become famous in the Western world. There were a few women poets very early in China and Japan, but it was many centuries before another than Sappho became well known in Europe.

Greek culture and learning were transported to Italy by Greek scholar-slaves, and Greek poetry became the model for the Latin. The meter of Greek drama (which usually had been written in short iambic lines) was borrowed and used freely and imaginatively by Latin dramatists. At the same time that the dactylic hexameter became the dominant measure in Latin epic and narrative poetry, a generation of younger lyricists were using all the technical resources of Greek lyric poetry. (The polished verse of the lyric poets Catullus and Horace has been a major influence on English poets through the centuries.) Virgil's great literary pic, *The Aeneid*, whose lines are in the classical "epic verse," was written at the peak of the Augustan age, which saw the supreme flowering of Roman civilization. It is interesting to note that in later centuries Virgil's *Aeneid* was used in prophecy and soothsaying in the *sortes Vergilianae* (Virgilian lots), much as the Bible has been traditionally used in such popular magic. Especially during the Middle Ages, the poet Virgil became widely known as a folk figure, a necromancer, and a superhuman being. Dante represented Virgil as his guide in the nether world in his great epic *The Divine Comedy*. Thus the relationship between poetry and magic in the long, slow currents of popular myth is shown in the evolution of Virgil's fame.

By the early Middle Ages, Latin poetry had evolved into a more popular art, and its mood and cadences had changed. Meter based on accent rather than quantity was used in the student songs and lyrics which were spread over southern Europe by the wandering scholars. Rhyme, as we shall see later in discussing the history of that phenomenon, had made its appearance and had caught on with the public; it added a lilt to the songs and made them easy to remember.

Modern versification was born. The poetry of Provence, France, Italy, and Spain derived from popular Latin verse and adopted its beat. The new use of the combination of accentual rhythm and rhyme in lyric and narrative poetry was more elastic and varied in its music than the formal, unrhymed quantitative system of classical times, although it too had reflected mood in its choice of language.

Rhyme, in particular, now contributed to stanza forms of surpassing loveliness, elaboration, and sensitivity.

Meanwhile, the inhabitants of the Germanic lands to the north had been developing their own kind of poetry, which depended not at all upon classical models or the wellsprings of classical inspiration. High and Low German, Icelandic, and Anglo-Saxon epics and sagas were written in lines of two sections, each containing two strongly stressed syllables; thus there were four strong stresses to the line. Of these, sometimes all four, usually three, or at the very least two, were alliterative; that is, they began with the same sound. A late example, taken from William Langland's *The Vision of Piers Plowman*, will serve to give an idea of how this kind of poetry went.

> In a somer seson, whan soft was the sonne,
> I shope me into shroudes, as I a shepe were;
> In habit as a heremite unholy of works
> Went wide in this world, wondres to here.

An analysis of these lines shows the stressed syllables and the alliteration, as well as the two sections in each line.

> In a SOMer SEson | whan SOFT was the SONne,
> I SHOPe me into SHROUDes, | as I a SHEPe WERe;
> In HABite as an HERemite | unHOly of WORKS
> Went WIDe in this WORLD, | WONdres to HERe.

Note that accent as we know it is not the determinant in these lines; what counts is the strong stressing of the four main syllables, and no account is taken of any weak or secondary accents which may also be present. The number of syllables between stresses, or the total number in the line, is unimportant. (The lines quoted here contain from twelve to fifteen syllables.) This kind of strongly stressed alliterative poetry many centuries later influenced the prosody of one of the most important modern English poets, Gerard Manley Hopkins, who has had a profound effect on much contemporary poetry.

Saint Godric, who died in 1170, is said to have been the first poet in England to rebel against the ancient Anglo-Saxon forms. Only three fragments of his verse survive, but these show clearly that he had deserted the conventions of Anglo-Saxon alliterative prosody and written lines in recognizable metrical feet. The Norman conquest of England had occurred in 1066, and it is likely that Godric experienced Norman influence during his lifetime; it was to be expected that the impact of Norman French and Latin scholarship would produce a revulsion against the powerful but rude Anglo-Saxon poetics.

The Normans brought to England a new stream of civilization stemming from the Latin-rooted cultures of southern Europe, and gradually the Norman French and Anglo-Saxon languages began that fusion which was to become, in time, modern English. Not until the fourteenth century did a great poet emerge in the rapidly evolving English language. This was Chaucer, who was dubbed "the father of English poetry" by Dryden some three centuries later. Chaucer's prosody was very much like modern English versification. However, in country places far from the dynamic center of London, especially in the north, the old ways persisted. They were revived to a certain extent in Chaucer's day in Langland's *Vision of Piers Plowman* (quoted earlier), but though they continued well into the fifteenth century the old prosody never seriously threatened to regain its sway.

Chaucer, an accomplished cosmopolite, used French stanza forms in his versions of the French *Romance of the Rose* and other works, but his most remarkable technical resource, which he used with great freedom in his *Canterbury Tales*, was the iambic pentameter line. This line was to become even more basic to English poetry than the so-called epic verse, the dactylic hexameter, was to the ancients. Chaucer rhymed his iambic pentameters in heroic couplets in the Prologue and in many of the tales of his magnum opus. (An outline of meters and lines, including iambic pentameter, follows this historical sketch.)

After Chaucer, only a few minor poets, among them King James I of Scotland, William Dunbar, and John Skelton, as well as the unknown author of the remarkable morality play called *Everyman,* figure in literary history until the mid-and late sixteenth century, when English poetry burst into perhaps its greatest flowering with Sir Philip Sidney, Edmund Spenser, William Shakespeare, Christopher Marlowe, Ben Jonson, and other poets and dramatists. English poetry, the most characteristic art and the greatest vehicle of expression for people of the English tongue, then came into its own.

One of the most important changes which marked the centuries between Chaucer and Shakespeare, and which perhaps more than any other epitomized the division between the late Middle Ages and the modern era, was the invention of printing in Europe in about 1440 and the rapid dissemination of its techniques. The Gutenberg Bible, generally accepted as the first book to be printed from movable type, was published in Mainz, Germany, in about 1454. William Caxton, the first English printer, set up his print shop in London in 1477. The change-over from the scarce, handwritten manuscript book available only to a wealthy few to the mechanically produced printed book available to many made a great difference in literature. For the first time literature could be known and appreciated by the masses of the people.

METER

The meters used in English versification are relatively few, but they can hardly be called simple in the multitude of ways they are used in the living poetry of the language. An outline of these meters is nevertheless not difficult to master, for the meters depend only upon patterns of two or three syllables each. Poetry and poetic meters are sometimes, in nineteenth-century poetry and elsewhere, referred to as "numbers." The reason for this will become obvious as the meters are outlined, for versification, like music, is at base a sort of mathematics of sound.

IAMBIC METER

First and most important in English versification is iambic (pronounced eye-AM-bik) meter. One iambic foot — called an iamb (EYE-amb) or iambus (eye-AM-bus) — is a unit of two syllables, the second of which is accented. An iamb may be expressed as ·— or ti-TUM. An example of a single iamb is the phrase "a CHILD." An iambic line from Oscar Wilde's "Ballad of Reading Gaol" is:

> He DID | not WEAR | his SCAR | let CLOAK

It may be counted as:

> And ONE | and TWO | and THREE | and FOUR.

TROCHAIC METER

Trochaic (tro-KAY-ik) meter also has a unit of two syllables, but in this case the accent falls on the first syllable of the pair. One trochaic foot is called a trochee (TRO-key) and may be expressed —· or TUM-ty; an example is the word "CHILDish." The following illustration of a trochaic line is from Longfellow's "Psalm of Life":

> TELL me | NOT, in | MOURNful | NUMbers
> ONE and | TWO and | THREE and | FOUR and.

ANAPESTIC METER

Anapestic (an-a-PEST-ik or AN-a-PEST-ik) meter has a unit of three syllables, with the accent upon the third. One foot of anapestic meter is called an anapest (AN-a-pest or AN-a-PEST). It may be expressed as ··— or ti-ti-TUM. This example of an anapestic line is from Byron's "The Destruction of Sennacherib":

> And the SHEEN | of their SPEARS | was like STARS | on the SEA
> And a ONE | and a TWO | and a THREE | and a FOUR.

DACTYLIC METER

Dactylic (dak-TIL-ik) meter also has a unit of three syllables, but in this case the accent is on the first syllable. One dactylic foot is called a dactyl (DAK-til) and may be expressed —·· or TUM-ti-ty. An example of a dactyl is "VERily."

The beginning of Longfellow's *Evangeline* has already been quoted as an example of the classical epic verse, which was composed of six dactylic feet.

THIS is the | FORest pri | MEval. The | MURmuring | PINES and the | HEMlocks
ONE and a | TWO and a | THREE and a | FOUR and a | FIVE and a | SIX and

THE MONOSYLLABIC FOOT

In English two accented syllables seldom occur side by side, since it is impossible to pronounce two juxtaposed accents with perfect smoothness. In that case a shift in accent often occurs; in other cases there is a slight but measurable pause between the two, or a dragging out and diphthongizing of the first accented syllable of the pair that practically makes it into two syllables. Whenever two accented syllables appear side by side in a line in English poetry, at least one of them is likely to compose a monosyllabic foot, in which a pause takes the place of an unaccented syllable.

The line from Masefield's "Sea Fever" "And all I ask is a tall ship and a star to steer her by," is an example. It scans as:

and ALL | i ASK | is a TALL — SHIP | and a STAR | to STEER | her BY.

The fourth foot is monosyllabic, with a rest between "tall" and "ship." This pattern is fairly common in the ballad line.

CLASSICAL METERS

The following are classical meters used in Greek and Latin poetry and especially adapted to the needs of a language whose quantitative system of rhythm in prosody differentiates between long and short syllables. A few of these meters are often considered by critics and analysts to be present in English poetry, and the verse-writer should therefore be aware of their existence. However, for practical purposes of composition, the writer need not try to use them. Iambic, trochaic, anapestic, and dactylic meters are the only meters necessary in approaching the writing of English verse. This is all the more true when one considers that a basic principle of English verse is that there is only one accent to the metrical foot.

SPONDAIC METER

Spondaic (spon-DAY-ik) meter is made up of feet having two long syllables. One foot is called a spondee (spon-DEE). Because the spondee has two long syllables, there is frequently a confusion in English when a foot with these specifications occurs. In English one of the two long syllables is inevitably accented, and the foot is thus an iamb or a trochee. However, the fact that the syllables are noticeably long confuses some people and leads them to think mistakenly that they are both accented. An example of such a line, whose interpretation is often disputed, is from Shelley's "Ode to the West Wind":

> o WILD | West WIND | thou BREATH | of AU | tumn's BE | ing.

The first six syllables of the line are long, and if English were a language in which meter depended upon quantity instead of accent the first three feet would be spondaic. Nevertheless, it is clear that "wild," "wind," and "breath" receive accents, and that "o," "West," and "thou" do not.

One can think of the spondee as a metrical foot in English prosody only if one admits quantity as well as accent to be a determinant of meter. Any attempt to mix these two principles, however, results in chaos; it is far better to keep them separate and to consider that the true spondee is not found in English poetry.

AMPHIBRACHIC METER

Amphibrachic (am-fih-BRAK-ik) meter contains units of three syllables in which the middle syllable is long in Latin and accented in English, while the first and third syllables are respectively short or unaccented. One foot is called an amphibrach (AM-fih-brak) and may be represented as ·—· or ti-TUM-ty. An example of an amphibrachic line is:

> There WAS a | young LAdy | of BROOKlyn
> a ONE and | a TWO and | a THREE and.

The divisions between feet, however, may with equal logic be differently placed:

> There WAS | a young LA | dy of BROOK | lyn
> a ONE | and a TWO | and a THREE | and.

The second example, because of this simple change, is in mixed iambic and anapestic meter. Thus it is apparent that amphibrachic meter and iambic-anapestic are interchangeable in this and similar cases, and the poet may think of the line in either way.

THE PAEON

The paeon is a foot containing four syllables, one long and the other three short, which occurs in four patterns according to the placement of the long syllable. The so-called first paeon (—···) may occur singly in English as one accented syllable followed by three unaccented ones, but it is very rare. An example is "SHAD-ow-i-ness." The second, third, and fourth paeons occur practically never in English in a line of poetry, since the four syllables would fall into units different from the paeon, or a secondary accent would come into play.

OTHER CLASSICAL METERS

Other classical meters, which do not occur at all in English, are the amphimacer (also sometimes called the Cretic), pyrrhic, tribrach, epitrite, molossus, bacchius, and antibacchius.

Compared to the complications inherent in classical meters, the English apparatus of four major meters based upon groups of either two or three syllables seems simple indeed. However, the manipulation of English meters allows for highly subtle effects, and they are actually no more simple to use than was the Greek system.

LINES ACCORDING TO LENGTH

MONOMETER

Monometer (mo-NOM-e-ter) is the name of a line containing one metrical foot in any meter.

Iambic monometers are like the following in pattern:*

I told	i TOLD
a lie	a LIE
as bold	as BOLD
as I	as I
could dare	could DARE
to try.	to TRY.

Trochaic monometers sound like this:

Once a	ONCE a
turtle,	TURtle,
name of	NAME of
Myrtle,	MYRtle,
wandered	WANdered
sadly	SADly
down to	DOWN to
Hadley....	HADley....

Anapestic monometers:

In a branch	in a BRANCH
Of a tree....	of a TREE....

*Unsigned examples have been furnished by the author and have no pretensions to be other than pieces of meter.

Dactylic monometers:

Children are   CHILDren are
Slumbering....   SLUMbering....

ACCENT LINES

Seldom is an entire poem written in lines as short as monometer; usually the line of this length is used as a tail line, refrain, or accent line, as is the fifth line of the following example from " I Am a Parcel of Vain Strivings Tied," by Thoreau:

I am a parcel of vain strivings tied
By a chance bond together,
Dangling this way and that, their links
Were made so loose and wide,
Methinks
For milder weather.

DIMETER

Dimeter (DIM-e-ter) is the name of the two-foot line. An example of *iambic dimeter* is the phrase "and so to bed," and an example of verse in iambic dimeter can easily be constructed upon it:

And so to bed: And SO | to BED:
The world grows still.   The WORLD | grows STILL.
Now sleeps the will,   Now SLEEPS | the WILL,
That urgent will   That UR | gent WILL
Within your head.   WithIN | your HEAD.

Trochaic dimeter goes:

Up the hillsides,   UP the | HILLsides,
Down the valleys,   DOWN the | VALLeys,
All a-gallop   ALL a- | GALLop
Passed our moments.   PASSED our | MOments.

Anapestic dimeter goes (with apologies to Byron for breaking his line, from "The Destruction of Sennacherib," in two):

The Assyrian came down   The AsSYR | ian came DOWN
Like the wolf on the fold.... Like the WOLF | on the FOLD....

Dactylic dimeter:

Glimmering, shimmering,   GLIM | mering, | SHIMmering,
Shone all the heavenly   SHONE all the | HEAVenly
Lights of the universe.   LIGHTS of the | Universe.

TRIMETER

Trimeter (TRIM-e-ter) is the name of the three-foot line. This example of *iambic trimeter* is "The Only News I Know," by Emily Dickinson.

The only news I know	The ON | ly NEWS | i KNOW
Is bulletins all day	Is BULL | eTINS | all DAY
From Immortality.	From IM | morTAL | itY.
The only shows I see	The ON | ly SHOWS | i SEE
Tomorrow and Today,	ToMORR | ow AND | toDAY,
Perchance Eternity.	PerCHANCE | eTER | niTY.

Trochaic trimeter goes this way:

Riding up the hillsides,	RIDing | UP the | HILLsides,
Posting down the valleys,	POSTing | DOWN the | VALLeys,
All aglow with loving	ALL a | GLOW with | LOVing
Passed our golden moments.	PASSED our | GOLDen | MOments.

Anapestic trimeter:

In the glow of the lowering sun
We would turn on the trail to the hills.

In the GLOW \| of the LOW \| ering SUN \|
We would TURN \| on the TRAIL \| to the HILLS.

Dactylic trimeter:

Turning and galloping wearily,
Homeward we rode through the wilderness.

TURNing and \| GALLoping \| WEARily, \|
HOMEward we \| RODE through the \| WILderness.

TETRAMETER

Tetrameter (te-TRAM-e-ter) is the name of the four-foot line; an example of *iambic tetrameter* may be taken from Tennyson's "In Memoriam."

And bats went round in fragrant skies,
   And wheel'd or lit the filmy shapes
   That haunt the dusk, with ermine capes
And woolly breasts and beaded eyes....

And BATS \| went ROUND \| in FRA \| grant SKIES,
   And WHEEL'D \| or LIT \| the FILM \| y SHAPES
   That HAUNT \| the DUSK, \| with ER \| mine CAPES
And WOOL \| ly BREASTS \| and BEAD \| ed EYES....

Longfellow's *Hiawatha* is in *trochaic tetrameter:*

> BY the | SHORES of | GIT | chee | GUMee,
> BY the | SHINing | BIG sea | WAter....

This example of *anapestic tetrameter* is from Byron's "The Destruction of Sennacherib":

> The Assyrian came down like the wolf on the fold,
> And his cohorts were gleaming in purple and gold;
> And the sheen of their spears was like stars on the sea....

> The asSYR | ian came DOWN | like the WOLF | on the FOLD,
> And his CO | horts were GLEAM | ing in PUR | ple and GOLD;
> And the SHEEN | of their SPEARS | was like STARS | on the SEA....

Dactylic tetrameter:

> Down in the valleys of beautiful fantasy,
> Up in the hills with the mountain folk lingering....

> DOWN in the | VALLeys of | BEAUtiful | FANtasy,
> UP in the | HILLS with the | MOUNTain folk | LINgering....

PENTAMETER

Pentameter (pen-TAM-e-ter) is the name of the five-foot line. *Iambic pentameter* is the most widely used poetic line in English; it is the "heroic line" used by Shakespeare and other dramatists, by Chaucer in *The Canterbury Tales* and by Milton in *Paradise Lost*. An example taken from Edward Fitzgerald's translation of the *Rubáiyát of Omar Khayyám* is as follows:

> A Book of Verses underneath the Bough,
> A Jug of Wine, a Loaf of Bread— and Thou
>   Beside me singing in the Wilderness—
> Oh, Wilderness were Paradise enow!

> a BOOK | of VER | ses UN | derNEATH | the BOUGH,
> a JUG | of WINE, | a LOAF | of BREAD | —and THOU
>   BeSIDE | me SING | ing IN | the WIL | derNESS—
> oh WIL | derNESS | were PAR | aDISE | eNOW!

Trochaic pentameter goes:

> In the crested wavelets on the surface
> Swam with horrid ease the shining serpents,
> Swam and glistened like an evil omen.

> IN the | CRESTed | WAVElets | ON the | SURface
> SWAM with | HORrid | EASE , the | SHINing | SERpents,
> SWAM and | GLISTened | LIKE an | EVil | Omen.

Anapestic pentameter:

At the crests of the waves where the serpents were swimming along.
At the CRESTS | of the WAVES | where the SER | pents were SWIM | ming aLONG.

Dactylic pentameter:

Bring to the banquet the hardened and battle-scarred warriors,
Give them the garlands that justly should deck out their weariness.

BRING to the | BANquet the | HARDened and | BATtle-scarred | WARriors,
GIVE them the | GARlands that | JUSTly should | DECK out their | WEARiness.

HEXAMETER

Hexameter (hex-AM-e-ter) is the name of the six-foot line. The "epic verse" of Greek and Latin is the dactylic hexameter, which has already been cited; French and certain other languages use iambic hexameter as the standard poetic and dramatic line, as iambic pentameter is used in English. The languages in which the longer line is standard are inflected languages, with grammatical endings added to most words, as contrasted with English, in which words are likely to be monosyllabic. Naturally, it requires a longer line to say the same thing in the inflected languages than in English.

The *iambic hexameter* is also called the *alexandrine*. It is sometimes used in English to vary the movement of a stanza composed in the main of iambic pentameter lines, as Spenser used it in the last line of his famous stanza form and a few writers (for example, Fulke Greville, in "Caelica") have used it in extended blank verse or heroic couplets. It is characterized by a slow and stately movement. One of Spenser's hexameter lines that end each stanza of *The Faerie Queene* is:

Did now but freshly spring, and silken blossoms beare.
Did NOW | but FRESH | ly SPRING, | and SILK | en BLOS | soms BEARE.

T. S. Eliot wrote in "The Love Song of J. Alfred Prufrock":

For I have known them all already, known them all....
For I | have KNOWN | them ALL | alREAD | y, KNOWN | them ALL....

Trochaic hexameter is very seldom used, but goes like this:

Down the clustered stairways, down descending ever,
Never pausing, never ending downward tending....

DOWN the | CLUSTered | STAIRways, | DOWN de | SCENDing | EVer.
NEVer | PAUSing, | NEVer | ENDing | DOWNward | TENDing....

Anapestic hexameter (illustrated here by a line from Karl Shapiro's "Buick") is also rare:

As a sloop with a sweep of immaculate wings on her delicate spine....

As a SLOOP | with a SWEEP | of imMAC | ulate WINGS | on her DEL | icate SPINE....

Dactylic hexameter has been used in English mainly in imitation of the epic line of Latin and Greek poetry. The first lines of Longfellow's *Evangeline* have already been cited; here is another line from the same poem:

Faint was the air with the odorous breath of magnolia blossoms....

FAINT was the | AIR with the | Odorous | BREATH of mag | NOLia | BLOSSoms....

HEPTAMETER

Heptameter (hep-TAM-e-ter) is the name of the seven-foot line. It is frequently called the ballad line, since it is often used in that form of poetry. In ballads the line, used in couplets, has a break (or caesura) after the fourth foot; it is usually broken into two lines of four and three feet.

Iambic heptameter is illustrated here by a line from Thomas Hardy's "The Lacking Sense":

With nevermore this too remorseful air upon her face....

With NEV | erMORE | this TOO | reMORSE | ful AIR | upON | her FACE....

An example of a ballad line with a strong break after the fourth foot is the following, from "Captain Stratton's Fancy," by Masefield:

Oh some are fond of Spanish wine, and some are fond of French....

Oh SOME | are FOND | of SPAN | ish WINE, || and SOME | are FOND | of FRENCH....

Trochaic heptameter goes:

Down the clustered stairways, still descending ever downward....

DOWN the | CLUSTered | STAIRways, | STILL de | SCENDing | EVer | DOWNward....

A ballad line in trochaic heptameter might go:

Down the lustrous stair of heaven Emmaline came running....

DOWN the | LUStrous | STAIR of | HEAVen || EMma | LINE came | RUNning....

Anapestic heptameter:

Like a horn on a hill that has never thus echoed before is the beat of my heart....

Like a HORN | on a HILL | that has NEV | er thus ECH | oed beFORE |
is the BEAT | of my HEART....

A ballad line in anapestic heptameter (printed in two lines in Poe's "Annabel Lee," from which it is borrowed) is:

For the moon never beams without bringing me dreams of the beautiful
Annabel Lee....

For the MOON | never BEAMS | without BRING | ing me DREAMS ||
of the BEAU | tiful ANN | abel LEE....

Dactylic heptameter:

> Down in the valley of Avon so peaceful, so perilous, waited young Willoughby.
>
> DOWN in the | VALLey of | AVon so | PEACEful, so | PERilous, | WAITed
>   young | WILLoughby.

A slight rewriting of the line places a break after the fourth foot of the line and makes possible a natural split into two parts, as in the ballad line:

> Down in the valley of Avon so perilous waited the treacherous Willoughby.
>
> DOWN in the | VALLey of | AVon so | PERilous || WAITed the |
>   TREACHerous | WILLoughby.

OCTAMETER

Octameter (ok-TAM-e-ter) is the name of the eight-foot line; it is the longest line included in the system of nomenclature of lines, although longer lines occur. The longer the line, the stronger is its tendency to break into two sections which might as well be printed in two lines instead of one. The poet who chooses to write very long lines does so because he considers the mid-line break less strong than the break between lines and wishes his line to be read as a unit, with only minor pauses, no matter how long the line may be.

Iambic octameter goes:

> A kestrel flew with swing of wings above against the slatey skies;
> The breathless wonder of its flight was mirrored in your sky-gray eyes.
>
> a KES | trel FLEW | with SWING | of WINGS | aBOVE | aGAINST |
>   the SLATE | y SKIES;
> the BREATH | less WON | der OF | its FLIGHT | was MIR | rored IN |
>   your SKY | -gray EYES.

Trochaic octameter is illustrated by this line from "The Raven," by Poe:

> Then, methought, the air grew denser, perfumed from an unseen censer....
>
> THEN, me | THOUGHT, the | AIR grew | DENSer | PERfumed | FROM
>   an | UNseen | CENSer....

Lines in anapestic or dactylic octameter are, of course, possible; but with three syllables to the foot, and eight feet to the line, the total would be twenty-four syllables, enough to make the line too unwieldy. In "The Destruction of Sennacherib" Byron might have written, but did not:

> The Assyrian came down like the wolf on the fold, and his
>   cohorts were gleaming in purple and gold.

Obviously this line is too long, and is better stated in two lines, as Byron wrote it.

There are no standard designations for lines longer than octameter. Such longer lines are sometimes used, but seldom or never in sustained passages of overlong lines; rather, they occur singly or in short groups as a means of expressing mood by lengthening and weighting the passage.

IRREGULAR METERS

After studying the outline of the formal meters of English verse, and then reading with attention a variety of passages from some of the greatest poetry ever written, the reader perceives that meters are seldom slavishly followed or written with perfect regularity. They provide a kind of skeleton framework upon which the poet may construct his poem as he pleases. Variations in the rhythm are not only permitted, but enhance the movement of the line. However, much practice is necessary before the beginning versewriter can control his medium with a sure touch, and before he knows just how far he can go in introducing variations without ruining the sound-line of his poem.

Mixed meters are very frequently used, and in this connection it should be noted that iambic and anapestic meters mix readily and smoothly, as do trochaic and dactylic; they may be called compatible meters. The first pair are alike in having the last syllable of the foot accented, which gives a rising motion to their music; the second pair have the accent on the first syllable, which gives a falling or downward movement. In mixing compatible meters, a regular, wavelike motion can be sustained without interruption, with the unaccented syllables between the accented crests varying between one and two. Mixed iambic and anapestic meter is seen in the following line from "My Lost Youth," by Long-fellow:

> The sunrise gun, with its hollow roar....

> The SUN | rise GUN | with its HOL | low ROAR....
>   (iamb)   (iamb)   (anapest)   (iamb)

Mixed trochaic and dactylic meter goes:

> Out of the darkness voices of mystery
> Come to me from forgotten centuries.

> OUT of the | DARKness | VOIces of | MYStery
>   (dactyl)   (trochee)   (dactyl)   (dactyl)

> COME to | ME from for | GOTten | CENturies.
>   (trochee)   (dactyl)   (trochee)   (dactyl)

ACCENT METER

Accent meter is the loose pattern in which various combinations of metrical feet are used; its only requirement in regular forms is that each line should contain a given number of accents. Ballads, for example, are frequently written in accent meter, with four accents in lines one and three of the quatrain and three accents in lines two and four. The mixture of metrical feet may be completely irregular, and may include monosyllabic feet composed of a pause and an accented syllable. An example is a quatrain from "Sir Patrick Spens," a Scottish ballad of unknown authorship.

> O long, long will the ladies stand
>> With their gold combs in their hair,
> Waiting for their own dear lords,
>> For they'll see them no mair.

o LONG, | LONG | will the LA | dies STAND
(iamb)　　*(monosyl-*　　*(anapest)*　　*(iamb)*
　　　　　　labic foot)

　　with their GOLD, | COMBS | in their HAIR,
　　(anapest)　　　*(mono foot)*　　*(anapest)*

WAITing | FOR their | OWN dear | 　LORDS,
(trochee)　　*(trochee)*　　*(trochee)*　　*(trochee* with final
　　　　　　　　　　　　　　　　　　weak syllable omitted)

　　For THEY'LL | see THEM | no MAIR.
　　(iamb)　　　*(iamb)*　　　*(iamb)*

In some modern poems in accent meter the lines are of varying lengths, with no stanza pattern. Such a poem is Part I of W. H. Auden's "In Memory of W. B. Yeats."

> Far from his illness
> The wolves ran on through the evergreen forests....

FAR from his | ILLness
(dactyl)　　　*(trochee)*

The WOLVES | ran ON | through the EV | ergreen FOR | ests....
(iamb)　　　*(iamb)*　　*(anapest)*　　　*(anapest)*

Accent meter thus is seen to be a strongly rhythmic mixture of meters. There are never more than two unaccented syllables between accents (except in the rare cases where the first paeon is used). It is unlike Anglo-Saxon poetics, in which the number of unaccented syllables and secondary accents does not count at all, but every line has four strong alliterated stresses. Accent meter is metrical and varied, whereas the Anglo-Saxon line is nonmetrical and monotonous.

SPRUNG RHYTHM

Sprung rhythm is the name which Gerard Manley Hopkins (1844-89) gave to his system of metrics, which was essentially accent meter. Hopkins used stylistic devices (alliteration, a preponderance of Anglo-Saxon vocabulary, deliberate use of archaic or provincial turns of phrase, and inversion of natural order) to suggest the power of Anglo-Saxon poetry, which he said had a strong influence on him. The word "sprung," he said, connoted for him something like "abrupt." He wrote: "The essence of sprung rhythm [is that] one stress makes one foot." This is hardly a new idea in English prosody, in which one accent always makes one foot. Nevertheless, the total effect which Hopkins obtained in his poetry was new, and it has had great influence since its tardy publication in 1918. Instead of the intense musicality of most poetry in accent meter, Hopkins deliberately sought the sense of halt, or impediments to smoothness. He did not hesitate to write such lines as the one in "Pied Beauty" which goes:

With SWIFT, | — SLOW; | — SWEET, | — SOUR; | aDAZZ | le, DIM.

A more conventional poet would have filled the pauses with syllables (With swift and slow; with sweet and sour; adazzle, dim), but Hopkins did not want things to go that easily in his poems.

Sprung rhythm, then, is Gerard Manley Hopkins' own name for the kind of accent meter he used. Its individuality was due not to Hopkins' metrical theories, but to his style.

FREE VERSE

Free verse (or *vers libre*, the French term) is poetry that uses the rhythms of prose, or cadenced language, rather than the regular beat of a system of meters. It is seldom or never rhymed in perfect rhyme, though it may be written in regular stanza forms. Refrains and repetitions are often used in free verse.

In Chapter V, "New Ways in Rhythm," free verse will be considered in detail.

SCANSION

To scan a line is to analyze and identify its metrical pattern, just as we have been doing in this chapter with examples of the various meters. Each syllable may be marked with an accent or a nonaccent, or the accented syllables may be capitalized as in our examples. Scansion may also be accomplished mentally, by identifying the meter at sight. Scansion is the act or art of scanning, however it is done. Any piece of writing or speech, in poetry or in prose, can be scanned to determine its meter, if any, or its rhythm.

The accents in a line are not all of the same value, and no actor or reader, for example, would ever give Shakespeare's line "The quality of mercy is not strained," from *Merchant of Venice*, exactly the same accent on each of the five accented syllables of the iambic pentameter pattern. "Qual," "mer," and "strained" receive strong accents, while "ty" and "is" receive lighter ones. However, the line scans in the regular iambic pentameter pattern of:

The QUAL | iTY | of MER | cy IS | not STRAINED.

Natural pronunciation is often slightly distorted by the poet to conform with the metrical pattern, or the metrical pattern is distorted by the words the poet chooses to use. This practice has been consecrated by the usage of the greatest poets. In this case, there is a contrapuntal scansion — the regular metrical pattern which the reader expects, and against which the poet is writing, and the actual pattern of natural pronunciation. In this metrical counterpoint, two things remain constant — the correct number of syllables in the line and the correct number of accents. For example, the first line of Shakespeare's Sonnet xxx is "When to the sessions of sweet silent thought." It has ten syllables, as the iambic pentameter line must. Since a sonnet often begins with a trochee in the first foot and the rest of the line in iambic meter, let us scan the line in that regular pattern:

WHEN to | the SESS | ions OF | sweet SI | lent THOUGHT.

Can the line be read with anything approaching this pattern? Certainly some kind of compromise must be reached between perfectly regular scansion and natural reading in such a case.

METER AND MOOD

The music of poetry, in which meter plays a large part, is important in conveying the mood and color of a composition, and the various meters are traditionally associated with certain moods.

Iambic meter is perhaps the only one (in English) that is virtually unlimited in its gamut, though it must be added that it lacks the extreme swing of some other meters. Since it is the most natural English meter, it may be used in a number of ways, according to the style and diction of the poet. It is the most malleable metrical instrument.

Trochaic meter has a tripping movement as it is generally used, and goes with a swing in the ballad. It seldom conveys the seriousness or solemnity which can be attained with iambic meter.

Anapestic meter is galloping and gay. It seems to fit poems of riding or other violent movement. When the Assyrian comes down like a wolf on the fold in Byron's famous poem, the meter aids immeasurably in conveying the swoop and glitter of the attack.

Dactylic meter has a slower movement and a dying fall; it usually gives a pervasive impression of sadness and melancholy, as in Longfellow's *Evangeline*.

Mood is also expressed by the time value or quantity of the syllables, but here we are immediately in less definite territory. In general, short vowels and short syllables are lighter and gayer than long ones; long syllables are the more solemn.

CAESURA

A device of prosody that is related as closely to meaning as to verse technique is the caesura. As used in modern poetry, the caesura is a break in the flow of sound within a line caused by a break in meaning — the end of one sentence and the beginning of another, for example — that occasions a rhetorical pause in the reading of the line. It comes preferably at about the middle of the line, but it may come near either end. The use of caesura adds variety to the music of the line and the entire poem.

Various kinds of caesura may be distinguished.

1. A *feminine caesura* follows an unaccented (or short, in classical prosody) syllable, as in Wordsworth's lines from "The World":

> The world is too much with us: || late and soon
> Getting and spending, || we lay waste our powers.

2. A *lyric caesura* is a feminine caesura that follows an unaccented syllable required by the meter, as in the example cited above.

3. An *epic caesura* is a feminine caesura that follows an extra unaccented syllable (i. e., not required by the meter) that is crowded into the iambic line under cover of the caesural pause, as in this example from Shakespeare's *Antony and Cleopatra:*

> I'll not sleep neither. || This mortal house I'll ruin....

4. A *masculine caesura* follows an accented syllable, as in these lines from "The Lotos-Eaters," by Tennyson:

> Let us alone. || Time driveth onward fast.
> And in a little while our lips are dumb.
> Let us alone. || What is it that will last?

THE LINE

The *end-stopped line* is a line of poetry that expresses a complete thought, without spilling over grammatically into the next line. These lines from Pope's "Essay on Criticism" are an example:

> A little learning is a dangerous thing;
> Drink deep, or taste not the Pierian spring....

Enjambment (from the French *enjambement*, an encroachment) is the running on of one line into the next to complete the meaning, as in these lines from Wordsworth's "The World":

> The world is too much with us: late and soon
> Getting and spending, we lay waste our powers.

In *run-on verse*, the thought runs on in a series of lines, no one of which expresses a complete thought; the lines are characterized by enjambment.

THE STANZA

Within a poem a stanza is a division containing one or more lines which is separated by spacing from other similar units. Occasionally, stanzas may be numbered, but usually spacing is sufficient to differentiate them from one another.

The stanza may be defined according to the number of lines it contains. Most lyric poems are made up of a group of stanzas of the same length, but this is not always so. Often a poet may prefer to use stanzas of irregular length, corresponding to paragraphs in prose, the lines being grouped solely according to the logic of their content. Regular stanza forms, however, may continue the thought from one stanza to another. The stanza in this case is a conventional device, rather than a logical unit of thought. A fresh thought may be started in mid-stanza if desired.

On the other hand, one stanza may constitute a complete poem.

THE ONE-LINE STANZA

A stanza containing only one line is sometimes used singly, but it is extremely rare to find an entire poem built of separate one-line stanza units. The interpolated one-line stanza is extremely effective as a kind of shock tactic; its contrast with the rest of the poem and its brevity make it effective as a unit.

THE COUPLET

The couplet is a stanza of two lines. The term may also refer to a rhyme unit that is not set off as a separate stanza.

The commonest use of the couplet is in connected heroic verse, as a vehicle of narrative poetry. Chaucer used the heroic couplet in *The Canterbury Tales*, and Dryden and Pope used the later version of the form in the "closed" heroic couplet, which came to a full stop at the end and permitted no lines to run on from couplet to couplet.

An example of the heroic couplet may be taken from Browning's dramatic monologue "My Last Duchess":

> That's my last Duchess painted on the wall,
> Looking as if she were alive. I call
> That piece a wonder, now: Fra Pandolf's hands
> Worked busily a day, and there she stands.

The closed heroic couplet is seen in Alexander Pope's *Essay on Man:*

> Know then thyself, presume not God to scan;
> The proper study of Mankind is Man.
> Plac'd on this isthmus of a middle state,
> A Being darkly wise, and rudely great....

In English, the couplet as a stanza is less popular than in connected verse, but there are a fair number of lyric poems in which it is used. Robert Frost occasionally wrote in couplet stanza form, as in "The Tuft of Flowers":

> I went to turn the grass once after one
> Who mowed it in the dew before the sun.
>
> The dew was gone that made his blade so keen
> Before I came to view the leveled scene.

Another example comes from Swinburne's "A Lyke-Wake Song":

> Fair of face, full of pride,
> Sit ye down by a dead man's side.
>
> Ye sang songs a' the day:
> Sit down at night in the red worm's way.
>
> Proud ye were a' day long:
> Ye'll be but lean at evensong.
>
> . . . . .
> Gold hair and glad grey een,
> Nae man kens if you have been.

THE DISTICH

The distich is a two-line stanzaic unit in Greek prosody; more specifically, it was the two-line unit in dactylic hexameter that was the vehicle of Greek elegiac poetry. The term was borrowed from Greek and extended all over the Middle East, as well as Europe; but "distich" is not the common designation of the two-line stanza in English prosody. When the term is met in the title of a poem in English, the poem is very likely a translation or adaptation from some other language. The distich is usually a self-contained sense unit, and is often of an epigrammatic nature.

1

O my moon-lovely love, I've seen this miracle:
The moon come down to me, dressed as a woman.

2

If you love truly, lose yourself in love.
You wish to be yourself? Ah, faithless one!
—Saadi (1194–1291, Persia)
English version by F. S.

THE TRIPLET OR TERCET

The unit of three lines of verse may be called either a triplet or a tercet, except that the term "tercet" is invariably used to refer to either a three-line stanza in the *terza rima* form or to the 2 three-line groups which compose the sestet of the Italian sonnet. (These forms and others mentioned below will be treated in Chapter III, "Traditional Forms.") The following example is from Charles Lamb's "The Old Familiar Faces":

I have had playmates, I have had companions,
In my days of childhood, in my joyful school-days—
All, all are gone, the old familiar faces.

I have been laughing, I have been carousing,
Drinking late, sitting late, with my bosom cronies—
All, all are gone, the old familiar faces.

THE QUATRAIN

The quatrain is a stanza containing four lines of verse, and is the most popular stanza form in English lyric poetry. A typical lyric quatrain begins "Never Seek to Tell Thy Love" by William Blake:

Never seek to tell thy love
Love that never told can be;
For the gentle wind does move
Silently, invisibly.

Other quatrains frequently used are the ballad stanza and the sapphic.

THE QUINTET OR CINQUAIN

The quintet or cinquain is a stanza containing five lines. (The term "quintain" for the five-line stanza is now obsolete, but may sometimes be found in very old treatises on prosody.) The five-line stanza is illustrated by this passage from Coleridge's "The Rime of the Ancient Mariner":

> Beyond the shadow of the ship,
> I watched the water-snakes:
> They moved in tracks of shining white,
> And when they reared, the elfish light
> Fell off in hoary flakes.

> Within the shadow of the ship
> I watched their rich attire:
> Blue, glossy green, and velvet black,
> They coiled and swam; and every track
> Was a flash of golden fire.

A specific meaning of the word "cinquain" is the five-line poem of that name, the form of which was invented by Adelaide Crapsey. (See Chapter III.)

THE SESTET, SEXTET, OR SEXTAIN

The stanza of six lines is called a sestet, a sextet, or a sextain — rarely, a sexain. It has always been a popular length for the stanzas of longer poems. Shakespeare used it in his long narrative poem *Venus and Adonis*, and his version is often called the Venus and Adonis stanza. (See Chapter III.)

An example of a six-line stanza is the following from "To Lucasta, going beyond the Seas," by Richard Lovelace:

> If to be absent were to be
>   Away from thee;
>   Or that when I am gone
>   You or I were alone;
> Then, my Lucasta, might I crave
> Pity from blustering wind or swallowing wave.

Another famous example is from "The Blessèd Damozel," by Dante Gabriel Rossetti:

> The blessèd damozel lean'd out
>   From the gold bar of Heaven;
> Her eyes were deeper than the depth
>   Of waters stilled at even;
> She had three lilies in her hand,
>   And the stars in her hair were seven.

The term "sestet" has a specific meaning. It is invariably used to mean the last six lines of the Italian sonnet.

THE SEPTET

The septet is a stanza unit of seven lines. It, too, has always been popular in longer poems, and one of its variations, called rhyme royal, was used by Chaucer and Shakespeare, among others. One of the numerous possible variations of the seven-line stanza, from "Night," by Shelley, follows:

> Swiftly walk o'er the western wave,
> Spirit of night!
> Out of the misty eastern cave,—
> Where, all the long and lone daylight,
> Thou wovest dreams of joy and fear
> Which make thee terrible and dear,—
> Swift be thy flight!

THE OCTAVE

A stanza of eight lines is called an octave, as is the division of the first eight lines of the Italian sonnet. The term "octet" also exists, but is used only in the specific sense of the first eight lines of the sonnet form as an alternative to the more common term, "octave."

The following lines from Sir Walter Scott's "Brignall Banks" are an example of an eight-line stanza:

> O Brignall banks are wild and fair,
> And Greta woods are green,
> And you may gather garlands there,
> Would grace a summer queen;
> And as I rode by Dalton Hall,
> Beneath the turrets high,
> A Maiden on the castle wall
> Was singing merrily:— ....

THE NINE-LINE STANZA

Edmund Spenser is the most famous writer of the nine-line stanza in English; he used his own version of it throughout his unfinished epic, *The Faerie Queene*. Keats also used Spenserian stanzas, as have many other poets since Spenser's day. However, there are many other versions of the nine-line stanza, one of which, from "A Runnable Stag" by John Davidson, is reproduced here:

> When the pods went pop on the broom, green broom,
> And apples began to be golden-skinn'd,
> We harbored a stag in the Priory coomb,
> And we feather'd his trail up-wind, up-wind,

> We feather'd his trail up-wind—
> A stag of warrant, a stag, a stag,
> A runnable stag, a kingly crop,
> Brow, bay and tray and three on top,
> A stag, a runnable stag.

THE TEN-LINE STANZA

Many variations of this form have been used, notably by Keats in several of his odes, and also by Thomas Chatterton, among others. The following example is from Keats' "Ode to a Nightingale":

> Thou wast not born for death, immortal bird!
> No hungry generations tread thee down;
> The voice I hear this passing night was heard
> In ancient days by emperor and clown:
> Perhaps the self-same song that found a path
> Through the sad heart of Ruth, when, sick for home,
> She stood in tears amid the alien corn;
> The same that ofttimes hath
> Charmed magic casements, opening on the foam
> Of perilous seas, in faery lands forlorn.

STANZAS OF MORE THAN TEN LINES

Keats used an eleven-line stanza in several of his odes, and many poets have used even longer stanzas in odes and in other long poems. The twelve-line stanza appears in the second stanza of Keats' "Ode to Psyche," and the other stanzas of that poem are even longer. The fourteen-line stanza, specifically a poem resembling a sonnet, but without the sonnet's strict structure, is called the quatorzain. Fourteen-line stanzas, including the sonnet, are often called "fourteeners" in English.

DIVISIONS IN LONG POEMS

Epics or long narrative poems may be divided into "books" or "cantos," and these larger sections are sometimes broken up into shorter numbered or unnumbered sections. Within the sections, the poetry may be written in stanzas, as is that of Spenser's *Faerie Queene*, in heroic couplets, in blank verse (unrhymed metrical lines, usually in iambic pentameter in English), in free verse (unrhymed, cadenced, but not metrical lines), or even in some combination of these forms.

ARE STANZAS NECESSARY?

Certainly there is much poetry that is not written in stanza form at all, but in a series of lines broken only into sections of various lengths corresponding to chapters in prose. If the poet wishes, a short poem may be composed in any number of consecutive lines without any stanza arrangement whatever. However, the vast majority of lyric poems are written in stanzas, which serve a definite structural purpose. One can only conclude that if stanzas are not always necessary they are nevertheless usually desirable.

II

Rhyme and Rhyme Patterns

Rhyme in verse is the repetition, in the lines of a poem, of the same end sound or sounds. Rhyme is composed of the last accented vowel in a line and any consonants and unaccented syllables that may follow it. A different consonantal sound must precede the rhyme sound each time it recurs. Thus the end sound "ay" allows as rhymes bay, day, lay, may, and nay or neigh — but not both. "Eater" may be rhymed with beater, cheater, heater, and liter. The repetition of sound must not extend forward to the initial consonant sound, for then the effect would be one of total repetition or identity rather than rhyme.

The word "rhyme" is also spelled rime, and the latter was originally the correct spelling, since the word is derived from the Provençal *rim*. The usual English spelling of rhyme comes from a false identification of it with rhythm, which came originally from the Greek *rhythmos*. The concept of rhyme was unknown to the Greeks, and rhyme was not used in classical poetry.

Rhyme first came into use in the church Latin of North Africa around A.D. 200 in certain hymns and chants. By the fourth century, rhymed sacred poetry had spread more widely and had become a real stylistic movement in church liturgy.

During the Dark and Middle Ages, rhyme, as well as alliteration and assonance, was a major element in popular poetry, both in the Latin of student songs and in verse in the emerging modern languages of Provence, France, and Italy. By the fourteenth century, rhyme had become universally accepted in the poetry of Europe, except in Spain. Even in the north, the old, alliterative verse conventions had given way to the new fashions. All over Europe troubadours and minnesingers were entertaining people with their melodic and charming poems in the vernacular, that is, in the modern languages as opposed to Latin, which was still the *lingua franca*, the common language of scholars, of the Church, and of diplomacy.

In the sixteenth century, blank verse, that is, unrhymed metrical verse, came into use in Italy and England, though Italy soon went back to rhymed forms, under the French influence. In England, rhymed verse had found a modern rival; heroic blank verse would continue to be used as a major vehicle of the longer poetic forms in English. Rhyme, however, is an integral part of many traditional poetic forms, and it seems unlikely that it will ever vanish entirely from the sonnet, the ballad, or the simple lyric.

Rhyme proper, or perfect rhyme, continues to be what it has always been, the regular chime of identical terminal sounds in lines of poetry. Professor Gilbert Highet calls it "the most obvious of poetic devices based on sound," and, indeed, it does seem so at first glance — just as the wheel must have seemed an obvious concept as soon as it was discovered. There are, however, other phonic devices more ancient than rhyme, and one must, therefore, consider them to have been, at least historically, more obvious. The figure of speech called *onomatopoeia*, the imitation in sound of the thing described, is perhaps the most obvious of all phonic devices. Every student who has ever studied Greek is familiar with Aristophanes' famous onomatopoeic chorus in his satirical play *The Frogs*. That this is an absolutely basic phonic device, one might almost say phonic impulse, is clear when one reflects that it is one of the earliest resources of the very small child when he first learns to speak. "Quack-quack" and "bow-wow" are the names of creatures who inhabit the child's world. Onomatopoeia is also widespread among primitive peoples and in primitive languages, and is the ancestor of many words in our own vocabulary.

Alliteration and assonance, too, were widely used long before the device of rhyme was invented. The Chinese were far ahead of the Western world in the use of rhyme, for many of the ancient poems in the anthology called the "Book of Songs" (dated before 500 B.C.) use rhyme in regular patterns.

Perhaps rhyme is first of all a musical device. It delights the ear as music does, especially as it is used in popular songs and ballads. That it is a mnemonic device is equally true. In nursery rhymes and lyric and narrative poetry of an oral tradition, it assists the memory. Rhymes concerning such matters as the number of days in the months or the succession of the kings of England have been memorized by children as far back as the memory of mankind reaches, and many an adult still mumbles to himself "thirty days hath..." when in doubt about a date.

That rhyme also has a structural and even substantive function in poetry is less often realized. It serves to bind together the unit in which it is used, to intensify the logical connections and the unity of meaning. When used with great skill, it is a device that seems not to be imposed from without, but dictated from within. A group of rhyming lines seem bound together in an almost magical way that enhances both the sense and the music.

A succession of rhymes seems to assist the progression of thought, differentiating one unit from another and providing a technical transition. A strong contrast in the rhyme sounds can contribute to the contrast of ideas. Interlocked rhyming, on the other hand, contributes to an interlocking of ideas.

Finally, there is the sheer intellectual pleasure in the skillful use of rhyme, just as in any exercise of virtuosity — a pleasure shared by poet and reader alike, as in music such a pleasure is shared by performer and listener. The play of rhyming is an intellectual play, and, from serious poetry to the patter songs of W. S. Gilbert, it contributes to the pleasures of poetry and verse.

KINDS OF RHYME

The designation of certain forms in grammar or prosody as "masculine" or "feminine" does not mean that these forms have anything to do with sex, but is a purely formal usage of nomenclature. Usually the designation masculine is given to the so-called strong concept, and feminine to the weak.

A line ending on an accented syllable is considered to have a strong ending, and therefore the rhyme of a single accented syllable is called masculine rhyme. Examples are Ann, ban, can, Dan, fan, etc. Lines in iambic or anapestic meter ordinarily end with a stressed syllable and are most likely to use masculine rhyme, but an extra syllable or syllables may be added at the end of such a line. If a line in trochaic or dactylic meter ends with a masculine rhyme, it means that one or two weak syllables have to be omitted at the end, and the line ends with a truncated foot.

Rhyme which includes an accented syllable followed by a weak, or unaccented, syllable is called feminine rhyme. Examples are early, burly, curly, and surly. Two-syllable rhyme is also sometimes called trochaic rhyme, because its accentual pattern is trochaic, and a perfect trochaic line, if rhymed, must have feminine or trochaic rhyme.

Rhyme which includes an accented syllable followed by two weak or unaccented syllables is three-syllable or dactylic rhyme, since its accentual pattern is that of the dactyl, and a perfect dactylic line must end in that way. It is also sometimes considered to come under the general heading of feminine rhyme, since if ending with one weak syllable makes a rhyme feminine, two must make it even more so. Examples are verily-merrily and pillager-villager.

In actual practice, both masculine and feminine rhymes may be used with any meter. Three-syllable rhyme, however, can only be used when the meter of the poem is in three-syllable units, that is, in dactylic or anapestic meter. If the music of a poem is iambic or trochaic, the last syllable of a three-syllable word would receive a secondary accent, and the rhyme would be made upon that final syllable. For example:

> They LAUGHED and DANCED so MERRiLY
> That THEY forGOT the RAGing SEA.

The same last word can be fitted into several meters and rhyme schemes.

> They LAUGHED and DANCED so MERriLY (iambic)
>
> They were LAUGHing and DANCing so MERrily (anapestic)
>
> LAUGHing and DANCing so MERrily (dactylic).

Though the use of rhymes of various length permits great variety in the music of a poem, in general it must be said that rhymes in English tend to be masculine rather than feminine, because of the nature of the language. A masculine rhyme gives the lines more strength than does the constant resolution of lines on a weak syllable. In that respect English is more fortunate than Italian and certain other languages, in which, because of the prevalence in their vocabularies of weak, inflected endings, most rhymes are feminine.

SPELLING RHYMES

Spelling rhymes are rhymes in which the terminal sounds are spelled alike but not pronounced alike. Often such sounds were actually at some time in the past pronounced in the same way, but, as the language developed and time passed, changes in pronunciation came about, and the two endings no longer rhyme.

For example, Chaucer rhymed "houres" with "youres"; in Chaucer's day the two were both pronounced with the "oo" sound still heard in modern "your."

Spelling rhymes are not considered perfect rhymes, but certain pairs of words have so often been rhymed in this way that their use has become accepted practice; for example, "move" and "love." In this case, only the final "v" consonantal sound is the same, and the actual effect is called consonant rhyme. Perfect rhymes for these words are move-behoove and love-above, in which both the vowel sound and the final consonant are the same. Such similarly spelled pairs as "bough" and "though" would not under any circumstances be paired, since the end sound in each is a simple vowel sound, and the two words involve two absolutely different sounds.

Shakespeare wrote, in Sonnet CXVI:

> Let me not to the marriage of true minds
> Admit impediments. Love is not *love*
> Which alters when it alteration finds,
> Or bends with the remover to *remove*.

And here is John Donne, in "Song":

> Go and catch a falling star,
>   Get with child a mandrake *root*,
> Tell me where all past years are,
>   Or who cleft the Devil's *foot;*
>
> Teach me to hear mermaids singing,
> Or to keep off envy's stinging,
>   And *find*
>   What *wind*
> Serves to advance an honest *mind*.

MOOD IN RHYME

It is well known that certain vowel and consonant sounds are associated with certain moods, though it is impossible to establish the distinctions with scientific accuracy. The relative length of syllables has something to do with it, as well as the particular qualities of the various sounds. The sensitivity of the poet is, in the last analysis, the final authority in this field.

If the mood of a line is dependent on the relative length of the syllables and the choice of certain vowels and consonants, it is also true that the mood of a passage or of an entire poem may be established and maintained by the choice of certain sounds as rhymes.

Listen to the beginning of Milton's great elegy "Lycidas."

> Yet once more, O ye laurels, and once more
> Ye myrtles brown, with ivy never sere,
> I come to pluck your berries harsh and crude,
> And with forced fingers rude
> Shatter your leaves before the mellowing year.
> Bitter constraint, and sad occasion dear,
> Compels me to disturb your season due:
> For Lycidas is dead, dead ere his prime....

No poet has ever had a keener ear than Milton for the mood in sound, and his long, strong rhymes in the beginning of this poem toll out with a noble sorrow.

Now hear Sir W. S. Gilbert in mock heroic mood, as he starts out in the vein of "Roll on, thou deep and dark blue ocean, Roll!"

TO THE TERRESTRIAL GLOBE
by a Miserable Wretch

> Roll on, thou ball, roll on!
> Through pathless realms of space
>   Roll on!
> What though I'm in sorry case?
> What though I cannot meet my bills?
> What though I suffer toothache's ills?
> What though I swallow countless pills?
>   Never *you* mind!
>   Roll on!
>
> Roll on, thou ball, roll on!
> Through seas of inky air
>   Roll on!
> It's true I have no shirts to wear;
> It's true my butcher's bill is due;
> It's true my prospects all look blue—

But don't let that unsettle you:
Never *you* mind!
Roll on!

[It rolls on.]
—Sir W. S. Gilbert

Gilbert began with a rolling, solemn rhyme, but in the fifth line he changed to a short syllable for his rhyme, thereby achieving a contrast and a transition to the querulous funniness of his personal situation. In the second stanza, having established his intentions in the first, he was long and solemn in his rhymes throughout.

The following poem by Longfellow is a good example of the suiting of the sound of the words, and especially of the rhyme words, to the subject

SNOW-FLAKES

Out of the bosom of the air
    Out of the cloud-folds of her garments shaken,
Over the woodlands brown and bare,
    Over the harvest-fields forsaken,
        Silent, and soft, and slow
        Descends the snow.

Even as our cloudy fancies take
    Suddenly shape in some divine expression,
Even as the troubled heart doth make
    In the white countenance confession,
        The troubled sky reveals
        The grief it feels.

This is the poem of the air
    Slowly in silent syllables recorded;
This is the secret of despair,
    Long in its cloudy bosom hoarded,
        Now whispered and revealed
        To wood and field.
            —Henry Wadsworth Longfellow

The whole poem whispers softly. The long syllables of the rhymes seem to make the snow fall slowly, while the feminine rhymes of the second and fourth lines slow up the movement even further. The actual content of the poem is slight, but the mood it conveys is one that is recognized by many readers.

ODD AND GROTESQUE RHYMES

In light and humorous verse, in which the poet is communicating light and humorous ideas, the rhyme can often be made to contribute directly to the effect desired. The element of incongruity is frequently used, for example, by such a poet as Ogden Nash. His technique is to bend the language as far as it will go, and then a little further, for a rhyme. The wilder the rhyme, the more likely it is to have more than one syllable, so feminine and three-syllable rhymes abound in light verse.

The inverted spelling rhyme is one ready source of humor; that is, the device of spelling rhymes all alike, whatever the accepted English spelling may be. The following anonymous verse makes use of this device.

THE INDIAN

There once were some people called Sioux
Who spent all their time making shioux
Which they colored in various hioux;
    Don't think they just made them to ioux
    Oh! no, they just sold them for bioux.

Nash and other contemporary humorists use the inverted spelling-rhyme fairly constantly as a source of humor. Not all languages have spelling as irrational as English, so it may be said that this kind of rhyming is rather specially found in English and American verse.

RHYME SCHEMES

It takes two lines to establish a rhyme. From that simple statement onward it will be seen that rhymes generally come in some sort of pattern. The simplest, of course, is that in which two successive lines rhyme; it is called rhymed couplets.

In the algebra of rhyming, each new terminal sound which is to rhyme is indicated by a letter of the alphabet, with "a" indicating the first rhyme sound, "b" the second, and so on. A couplet such as the following, which begins the general prologue to Chancer's *Canterbury Tales:*

Whan that Aprill with his shoures soote	(a)
The droght of March hath perced to the roote	(a)

rhymes a-a, and the poem then proceeds with b-b, and so forth:

And bathed every vein in swich licour	(b)
Of which vertu engendred is the flour....	(b)

A triplet may be rhymed a-a-a, the second stanze b-b-b, and so forth. Various stanza forms and various fixed verse forms have set rhyme schemes. For example, the ballad stanza (this sample is taken from "Sir Patrick Spens") usually rhymes:

O lang, lang may the ladies stand,	—
Wi thair gold kems in thair hair,	(a)
Waiting for thair ain deir lords,	—
For they'll se thame na mair.	(a)

A more sophisticated quatrain from "With Rue My Heart Is Laden," by A. E. Housman, rhymes a-b-a-b:

> With rue my heart is laden   (a)
> For golden friends I had,   (b)
> For many a rose-lipt maiden   (a)
> And many a lightfoot lad.   (b)

RANDOM RHYME

Rhyme may also occur at the ends of lines in no set or regular pattern, often mixed with unrhymed lines, seemingly at the whim of the poet. Such random rhyme is frequently used in modern poetry, and gives an impression of great freedom and flexibility.

INTERNAL AND INITIAL RHYME

Rhyme may occur elsewhere than at the ends of lines. It is frequently used in a pattern of internal or inner rhyme that usually comes at the middle and at the end of a long line. It may also occur in a regular pattern in the first words of two or more lines, in which case it is called initial rhyme.

Internal and initial rhyme may be mixed and may occur at random, without any regular pattern of intervals between rhymes. Random internal rhyme, random initial rhyme, and random mixed internal and initial rhyme are all possible.

A good example of internal rhyme is found in Poe's "The Raven," which employs a regular pattern of internal and end rhyme.

> Open here I flung the *shutter*, when, with many a flirt and *flutter*,
> In there stepped a stately Raven of the saintly days of yore;
> Not the least obeisance *made he*; not a minute stopped or *stayed he*;
> But with mien of lord or *lady*, perched above my chamber door—
> Perched upon a bust of Pallas just above my chamber door—
> Perched, and sat, and nothing more.

Initial rhyme produces quite a different effect from internal rhyme, being characterized by a spare, rather mannered music that tends to slow up rather than speed the verse. An example of initial rhyme is found in the following lyric, in which the first words of the quatrains rhyme.

PORTRAIT OF MARY

> *Mary* sweeps the grate again,
> Mary cleans the stair;
> Against the dust in spate again
> She binds her mop of hair.

Chary with the words she speaks,
   It's seldom she lets fall
A sound— but like a bird she speaks,
   Like a grackle's call.

Wary of the light that falls
   In trembling bunches, green as grapes,
She drags the pictures off the walls,
   She beats the rugs and drapes.

Mary, midst the green of springtime,
   Mary with her darkling ways—
This is all she's seen of springtime,
   This is all her praise.
                                                                —F. S.

Internal and initial rhyme occurring at random in modern poetry is more likely to be in the new modulations of near-rhyme than in perfect rhyme; therefore this subject will be considered in Chapter IV, "New Ways in Verse Rhyme." One example of random internal rhyme may be given here, in this excerpt from T. S. Eliot's "Burnt Norton":

Words move, music moves,
Only in time; but that which is only living
Can only die. Words, after *speech, reach....*

CROSS RHYME

Cross rhyme is rhyme that matches the end of one line with the middle of the next, or vice versa.

And he shall *go* where time lies still and frozen
Beneath eternal *snow.*

RHYME PATTERNS

In standard English prosody, after the Anglo-Saxon ways had fallen into disuse and up to fairly recent times, poetry was either rhymed in a system of perfect rhymes or written in blank verse without any rhyme at all, but within the framework of regular meter. Modern poetry still uses all the devices of conventional prosody, but has added rich new resources to it, so that the range of poetic virtuosity is more dazzling than ever.

Some modern uses of near rhyme will be discussed in detail together with the new ways of using loose rhyme schemes and random rhyme mixed with nonrhyme.

III

Traditional Forms in Poetry

Poetry inevitably partakes of the genius of the language in which it is written. In doing so, it shares the curse of Babel which has separated the tribes of men; but at the same time it is in many ways international. All art, including poetry, is of universal interest and tends to leap over artificial and natural boundaries.

Nowhere is this fact more apparent than in the study of the traditional forms in which poetry has been written throughout the centuries, and in which it is still being written. These forms come from many periods and many sources— from Greek and Latin, early English, French, Italian, German, and other modern European languages, and from Japanese. Their appearance in English reflects the fact that poets in the past have more often than not had a classical education and have taken an interest in other languages and other cultures.

However, beyond the education and interest of the individual poet, the whole history of England and of the English language enters into the picture. It was natural enough for Chaucer, for example, to be influenced by the forms of French poetry, as well as by Latin and Italian, because in his day the schools in London were still conducted in French, as a result of the Norman conquest two centuries earlier. Latin was the main subject studied. In consequence, Geoffrey Chaucer was trilingual. With such a background in Latin and French, he can have had little difficulty in reading the Italian of Dante and Boccaccio as well.

The tradition of classical education has endured in England to the present day, and English schoolboys are taught not only how to read Latin, but how to write it, and write it well. The works of Latin poets have thus had great influence in English poetry and have indirectly influenced all English and American poets, whether or not they happened to be classical scholars.

TRADITIONAL STANZA FORMS

TERZA RIMA

This three-line stanza form was the vehicle which Dante used to write *The Divine Comedy* (*ca.* 1300). This form may be written in any meter, but iambic

41

pentameter is preferred in English. Terza rima stanzas are chain rhymed a-b-a, b-c-b, c-d-c, etc., and end with an extra line or a couplet rhyming with the middle line of the last tercet. An example in English is Shelley's "Ode to the West Wind," from which the beginning section is given here:

O wild West Wind, thou breath of Autumn's being,	(a)
Thou, from whose unseen presence the leaves dead	(b)
Are driven, like ghosts from an enchanter fleeing,	(a)
Yellow, and black, and pale, and hectic red,	(b)
Pestilence stricken multitudes: O thou	(c)
Who chariotest to their dark wintry bed	(b)
The winged seeds, where they lie cold and low,	(c)
Each like a corpse within its grave, until	(d)
Thine azure sister of the Spring shall blow	(c)
Her clarion o'er the dreaming earth, and fill	(d)
(Driving sweet buds like flocks to feed in air)	(e)
With living hues and odours plain and hill:	(d)
Wild spirit, which art moving everywhere;	(e)
Destroyer and preserver; hear, oh hear!	(e)

THE BALLAD STANZA

The ballad stanza is a quatrain in which the first and third lines contain four metrical feet (in regular or accent meter), while the second and fourth lines contain three feet. The second and fourth lines rhyme. The following is an example by an anonymous poet.

> The twelvemonth and a day being up,
>   The dead began to speak:
> "Oh who sits weeping on my grave,
>   And will not let me sleep?"

THE RUBAI

The rubai (plural rubais or rubaiyat) is a quatrain rhymed a-a-b-a. Edward Fitzgerald, the great translator of Omar Khayyám, wrote it in iambic pentameter.

> The Moving Finger writes; and, having writ,
> Moves on: nor all your Piety nor Wit
>   Shall lure it back to cancel half a Line,
> Nor all your Tears wash out a Word of it.

THE SAPPHIC

The sapphic, perhaps the most famous of classical stanzas, was used by the Greek lyric poet Sappho, for whom it is named. Like other Greek poetry, it is

unrhymed. The first three lines are in trochaic pentameter except for the third
foot, which must be a dactyl. The fourth line has two feet, a dactyl and a trochee.

S A P P H I C S

> All the night sleep came not upon my eyelids,
> Shed not dew, nor shook nor unclosed a feather,
> Yet with lips shut close and with eyes of iron
> Stood and beheld me.
>
> Then to me so lying awake a vision
> Came without sleep over the seas and touched me,
> Softly touched mine eyelids and lips; and I too,
> Full of the vision,
>
> Saw the white, implacable Aphrodite,
> Saw the hair unbound and the feet unsandalled
> Shine as fire of sunset on western waters;
> Saw the reluctant
>
> Feet, the straining plumes of the doves that drew her,
> Looking always, looking with necks reverted,
> Back to Lesbos, back to the hills whereunder
> Shone Mitylene.
>
> —Algernon Charles Swinburne

The last stanza of the above selection can be analyzed as follows:

FEET, the | STRAINing | PLUMES of the | DOVES that | DREW her,
   (trochee)   *(trochee)*   *(dactyl)*   *(trochee)*   *(trochee)*
LOOKing | ALways, | LOOKing with | NECKS re | VERTed
   (trochee)   *(trochee)*   *(dactyl)*   *(trochee)*   *(trochee)*
BACK to | LESbos, | BACK to the | HILLS where | UNder
   (trochee)   *(trochee)*   *(dactyl)*   *(trochee)*   *(trochee)*
   SHONE Mityl | ENe.
     (dactyl)   *(trochee)*

THE VENUS AND ADONIS STANZA

The so-called Venus and Adonis stanza was used by Shakespeare in his narrative poem of that name. It has six lines, and an a-b-a-b-c-c rhyme scheme. Shakespeare wrote it in iambic pentameter, and other poets have occasionally used
shorter lines. It is similar to the ottava rima stanza (see below), which has six
instead of four alternately rhymed lines before the final couplet.

The following example, from "Wrestling Jacob," by Charles Wesley, is written
in iambic tetrameter.

> I need not tell Thee who I am,
> My misery or sin declare,

> Thyself hast called me by my name,
>   Look on Thy hands, and read it there;
> But who, I ask Thee, who art Thou?
> Tell me Thy name, and tell me now.

RHYME ROYAL

This seven-line stanza form, usually written in iambic pentameter in English, rhymes a-b-a-b-b-c-c. It was used by Chaucer in the late fourteenth century and Shakespeare in the sixteenth, and has been used by many other English poets since then. Chaucer used it in his long narrative poem *Troilus and Criseyde*:

And therewithal he heng adown his heed,	(a)
And fil on knees, and sorwfully he sighte.	(b)
What mighte he seyn? He felt he nas but deed,	(a)
For wroth was she that sholde his sorwes lighte.	(b)
But natheles, whan that he speken mighte,	(b)
Than seide he thus, "God woot that of this game,	(c)
Whan al is wist, than am I nought to blame."	(c)

OTTAVA RIMA

Ottava rima is an eight-line stanza with an a-b-a-b-a-b-c-c rhyme scheme. Invented in Italy in the fourteenth century, it was used by Boccaccio in two epic poems in 1340 and 1347. Byron's *Don Juan* (1819–24), the best-known poem in ottava rima in English, strikes the mock-heroic, almost burlesque note that later came to be connected with the form.

The English winter— ending in July,	(a)
To recommence in August— now was done.	(b)
'Tis the postilion's paradise: wheels fly;	(a)
On roads, east, south, north, west, there is a run.	(b)
But for post-horses who finds sympathy?	(a)
Man's pity's for Himself, or for his son,	(b)
Always premising that said son at college	(c)
Has not contracted much more debt than knowledge.	(c)

THE SICILIAN OCTAVE

This eight-line Italian stanza form, which may also constitute an entire poem in one stanza, is like ottava rima in the first six lines, rhyming a-b-a-b-a-b, but instead of ending with a rhymed couplet it ends with another a-b pair of lines. Thus the entire eight lines are in alternating rhymes, a-b-a-b-a-b-a-b.

Edmund Spenser (1552–99) developed his stanza form mainly from ottava rima, although it also has a resemblance to rhyme royal, the rhyme scheme of the first six lines being the same. The Italian narrative poets, who wrote in ottava rima, were Spenser's models, and he was also familiar with Chaucer's work in rhyme royal. His stanza has nine lines, one more than ottava rima and two more than rhyme royal; it uses interlocking rhyme (perhaps suggested by rhyme royal) and has a long last line that gives it a stately and meditative flavor. The first eight lines are in iambic pentameter, and the ninth line is an alexandrine; the rhyme scheme is a-b-a-b-b-c-b-c-c. The following example is from Spenser's *Faerie Queene:*

Both roofe, and floore, and walls were all of gold,	(a)
But overgrowne with dust and old decay,	(b)
And hid in darkness, that none could behold	(a)
The hew thereof: for vew of cherefull day	(b)
Did never in that house it selfe display,	(b)
But a faint shadow of uncertain light;	(c)
Such as a lamp, whose light does fade away;	(b)
Or as the moone, cloathéd with clowdy night,	(c)
Does shew to him that walkes in feare and sad affright.	(c)

John Keats, early in the nineteenth century, used the Spenserian stanza with notable success. The following example is from "The Eve of St. Agnes":

St. Agnes' Eve — Ah, bitter cold it was!
The owl, for all his feathers, was a-cold:
The hare limped trembling through the frozen grass,
And silent was the flock in wooly fold;
Numb were the Beadsman's fingers, while he told
His rosary, and while his frosted breath
Like pious incense from a censer old,
Seemed taking flight for heaven, without a death,
Past the sweet Virgin's picture, while his prayer he saith.

TRADITIONAL POEM FORMS

The Italian sonnet — also called the Petrarchan sonnet after the poet Petrarch (1304–74), its first major practitioner — is a lyric poem containing fourteen lines in iambic pentameter with a set rhyme scheme. Apparently the form developed after long experimentation from a kind of "little song" (*sonetto* in Italian and *sonet* in Provençal, from Latin *sonus*, meaning sound). The Italian poet Guittone of Arezzo, who died in 1294, established its rules. Its structure falls into two parts, the octave, or first eight lines, and the sestet, or last six. The octave states and develops the proposition, whatever the subject of the poem may be. The sestet contains its solution. Thus there is a major break in the movement at the end of the eighth line and a strong progression in the solution of the last six. There are also minor thought divisions between the fourth and fifth lines (between the two quatrains of the octave), and between the eleventh and twelfth lines (between the two tercets that make up the sestet). The rhyme scheme is a-b-b-a, a-b-b-a, c-d-e, c-d-e.

The rhyme scheme of the first eight lines is not supposed to be changed, according to the rules, but one variation is traditionally permitted in the sestet; it may also be rhymed c-d-c, d-c-d. In using this alternative rhyme pattern, the poet should be careful to have the movement of his sestet fall into two equal parts, that is, two tercets. The last six lines should not be allowed to contain sense groups of two lines each, or of four and two.

In actual practice in English many more variations of the rhyme scheme of the Italian sonnet have been used by great poets than the foregoing remarks would suggest. However much the purist may insist upon the rules and the original pattern of the Italian sonnet, it is hard to find a completely regular model in English. If the rhyme scheme of the octave conforms to the pattern and a break comes, as scheduled, between the fifth and sixth lines, the sestet is sure to be rhymed in an unorthodox way or to fall into couplets.

The following example is a perfect Italian sonnet. It contains minor breaks between the fourth and fifth lines and the eleventh and twelfth and a major break between the octave and the sestet. Its rhyme scheme is entirely regular.

THE SONNET

What is a sonnet? 'Tis the pearly shell	(a)
That murmurs of the far-off murmuring sea;	(b)
A precious jewel carved most curiously;	(b)
It is a little picture painted well.	(a)
What is a sonnet? 'Tis the tear that fell	(a)
From a great poet's hidden ecstasy;	(b)
A two-edged sword, a star, a song— ah me!	(b)
Sometimes a heavy-tolling funeral bell.	(a)
This was the flame that shook with Dante's breath;	(c)
The solemn organ whereon Milton played,	(d)
And the clear glass where Shakespeare's shadow falls:	(e)
A sea this is— beware who ventureth!	(c)
For like a fiord the narrow floor is laid	(d)
Mid-ocean deep sheer to the mountain walls.	(e)

—Richard Watson Gilder

Wordsworth's most famous sonnet, "The World," has the second rhyme scheme in the sestet, c-d-c, d-c-d, but it falls into three couplets rather than into two tercets, as it would strictly be supposed to do.

THE WORLD

The world is too much with us; late and soon,	(a)
Getting and spending, we lay waste our powers;	(b)
Little we see in nature that is ours;	(b)
We have given our hearts away, a sordid boon!	(a)
The sea that bares her bosom to the moon;	(a)
The winds that will be howling at all hours,	(b)
And are up-gather'd now like sleeping flowers;	(b)
For this, for everything, we are out of tune;	(a)
It moves us not. —Great God! I'd rather be	(c)
A Pagan suckled in a creed outworn;	(d)
So might I, standing on this pleasant lea,	(c)
Have glimpses that would make me less forlorn;	(d)
Have sight of Proteus rising from the sea;	(c)
Or hear old Triton blow his wreathed horn.	(d)

—William Wordsworth

Wordsworth varied the rhyme scheme of the sestet still further in other sonnets, rhyming it c-d-e, d-c-e; c-d-d, e-c-e; c-d-c, d-e-e; c-d-d, c-d-c; etc. He also varied the rhyme scheme of the octave occasionally, making it a-b-b-a, a-c-c-a. The only one of these changes that did violence to the spirit of the Italian sonnet was that in which the last two lines were rhymed as a couplet. This version of the rhyme scheme ends the sonnet as a Shakespearean sonnet ends, on a pithy, climactic two-line unit that is welded together by the rhyme. The music of the normal Italian sonnet is slower than this, more cumulative, and more meditative.

THE MILTONIC SONNET

John Milton (1608-74) wrote the Italian sonnet without the sharp break between the octave and the sestet required by the original rules of the form. The break in Milton's sonnet comes anywhere from the middle of the eighth line to the end of the ninth. In his most famous sonnet, "On His Blindness," the break comes after the second foot of the eighth line.

ON HIS BLINDNESS

When I consider how my light is spent,
E'er half my days, in this dark world and wide,
And that one Talent which is death to hide
Lodg'd with me useless, though my Soul more bent
To serve therewith my Maker, and present
My true account, least he returning chide,

Doth God exact day-labour, light deny'd,
I fondly ask; But patience to prevent
That murmur, soon replies, God doth not need
Either man's work or his own gifts, who best
Bear his milde yoak, they serve him best, his State
Is Kingly, Thousands at his bidding speed
And post o'er Land and Ocean without rest:
They also serve who only stand and waite.
                                                          —John Milton

THE ENGLISH OR SHAKESPEAREAN SONNET

The Italian sonnet form was introduced into England early in the sixteenth century by Sir Thomas Wyatt and Henry Howard, Earl of Surrey. The native English form was soon developed by Sir Philip Sidney, Michael Drayton, Samuel Daniel, William Shakespeare, and others. It bears Shakespeare's name not because he was the first to write it, but because his sonnets in this pattern are the most famous in all English literature. Possibly one could also argue that it was in his hands that the form came to full maturity.

As in the Italian sonnet, the rhyme scheme is the determining factor in the movement of the Shakespearean sonnet. It is rhymed in quatrains for the first twelve lines and concludes with a couplet: a-b-a-b, c-d-c-d, e-f-e-f, g-g. The break in thought between the octave and the sestet of the traditional Italian sonnet is usually retained, but the epigrammatic force of the final couplet is so strong that there is a tendency to place a major turn of meaning between the twelfth and thirteenth lines as well; sometimes, as in the example that follows, the latter becomes the main division in the thought of the poem. In any case, the final couplet is likely to sum up the message or give a surprising or striking twist to the conclusion. It introduces, in its tight-knit succinctness, a note that is entirely different from the music of the Italian sonnet. Shakespeare's Sonnet xxx is a good example of the way in which he handled the form.

XXX

When to the sessions of sweet silent thought	(a)
I summon up remembrance of things past,	(b)
I sigh the lack of many a thing I sought,	(a)
And with old woes new wail my dear time's waste:	(b)
Then can I drown an eye, unused to flow,	(c)
For precious friends hid in death's dateless night,	(d)
And weep afresh love's long-since-cancell'd woe,	(c)
And moan th' expense of many a vanish'd sight:	(d)
Then can I grieve at grievances foregone,	(e)
And heavily from woe to woe tell o'er	(f)
The sad account of fore-bemoaned moan,	(e)

Which I new pay as if not paid before.   (f)
But if the while I think on thee, dear friend,   (g)
All losses are restored and sorrows end.   (g)
                    —William Shakespeare

The thought of this sonnet has natural divisions at the end of each quatrain.

Quatrain 1. When I start remembering things, I sigh over many lacks and old woes.

Quatrain 2. Then I can weep for vanished friends, old loves, and old sights.

Quatrain 3. Then I can grieve anew over old grievances, and go over old woes and old moans as if I had never bemoaned them before.

Couplet. However, if I think of you, dear friend, all those old losses and sorrows vanish.

The content of the three quatrains builds up to the final contrasting thought, which is thereby thrown into high relief. By building the sonnet in this manner the device of rhyme is used structurally to give each segment of the thought a heightened unity. The tight couplet rhyming of the final couplet makes its message more intense and compact than that of the three preceding quatrains.

The striking quality of Shakespeare's final couplets is apparent even when they are seen alone, without the quatrains which lead up to them, as is shown in these excerpts from Sonnets LXXIII, LXXXVII, and XCIV.

This thou perceiv'st, which makes thy love more strong
To love that well which thou must leave ere long.

Thus have I had thee, as a dream doth flatter
In sleep a King; but waking, no such matter.

For sweetest things turn sourest by their deeds;
Lilies that fester smell far worse than weeds.

The Shakespearean sonnet employs seven rhyme sounds instead of the four or five of the Italian sonnet. This increase in the number of rhyme sounds gives the Shakespearean sonnet more variety and elasticity than the earlier form, and there is a far wider range of possible rhymes that may be used. In it no one rhyme is employed more than twice, whereas in the Italian sonnet the poet must use the same two rhymes four times in the first eight lines.

SPENSER'S SONNET

The English sonnet now called Shakespearean was already in use when Spenser began to write sonnets. We know from Spenser's works that he was enamored of interlocking rhyme schemes, for he used them in his early "Shepheard's Calender"; in the sonnets that make up the "Amoretti," a group of love sonnets written in honor of his betrothed, Elizabeth Boyle; and in the stanza form that he invented for his masterpiece, *The Faerie Queene*. In movement, his sonnet form is essentially like the English or Shakespearean sonnet, but its rhyme scheme is a-b-a-b, b-c-b-c, c-d-c-d, e-e. The rhymes "b" and "c" are used four times each, and the other three rhymes each appear twice. This is exactly the same proportion as in the Italian sonnet, although the rhymes appear in a different order from those of the earlier form and it is "b" and "c" that are most frequent.

The advantages of including more rhymes in the English or Shakespearean sonnet are thrown away in Spenser's version of it. To balance losing this advantage, the quatrains are more closely linked by the interlocking rhyme. Apparently, few poets have considered this desirable, for Spenser's sonnet form has been little used. The following sonnet is an example.

WHILST IT IS PRIME

Fresh Spring, the herald of love's mighty king,	(a)
In whose cote-armour richly are displayd	(b)
All sorts of flowers, the which on earth do spring,	(a)
In goodly colours gloriously arrayd—	(b)
Goe to my love, where she is carelesse layd,	(b)
Yet in her winters bowre not well awake;	(c)
Tell her the joyous time will not be staid	(b)
Unlesse she doe him by the forelock take;	(c)
Bid her therefore her selfe soone ready make	(c)
To wayt on Love amongst his lovely crew;	(d)
Where every one, that misseth then her make,	(c)
Shall be by him amearst with penance dew.	(d)
Make hast, therefore, sweet love, whilest it is prime;	(e)
For none can call againe the passed time.	(e)

—Edmund Spenser

OTHER SONNET FORMS

The *tailed sonnet* is an odd sonnet form embellished by added lines, systematically arranged, and usually shorter than the basic iambic pentameter sonnet line, in the form of "tails," as in tail rhyme. This form was especially used in Italy.

The *curtal sonnet* is a short, or curtailed, sonnet form, usually having eleven lines rhyming a-b-a, a-b-a, d-b-c-d-c. Sometimes it is ten lines long and rhymes a-b-a-b-a, d-b-c-d-c. Properly speaking, of course, the curtal sonnet is not really a sonnet at all.

SONNET SEQUENCES

Sequences of sonnets, variations on a theme or on related themes, have always been considered major poetical works. Spenser wrote such a sequence in his "Amoretti" and Shakespeare in his "Sonnets." Occasionally a sonnet sequence has been used as a vehicle for narrative poetry, as in William Ellery Leonard's moving autobiographical poem "Two Lives." Elizabeth Barrett Browning's sonnet sequence *Sonnets from the Portuguese* is second only to Shakespeare's sonnets in popularity. Her sonnets, like Christina Rossetti's, are in the Italian form.

A "sonnet of sonnets" is a sequence of fifteen sonnets built on the opening sonnet. In this form, a new sonnet is written around each line of the opening sonnet, with the theme line used either to begin or to end it. Christina Rossetti, in her "Monna Innominata," produced such a sonnet sequence, using the Italian form.

Almost every poet has written sonnets at some time in his career, and occasionally a writer becomes obsessed by the form. A physician named Merrill Moore wrote at least one sonnet a day for most of his adult life, winding up with so many thousands of sonnets that the reader is discouraged even before he begins reading any of them. Dr. Moore wrote nothing but sonnets, a preoccupation that cannot fail to seem excessive.

THE BALLADE

The ballade first appeared in Provençal literature, stemming from the Italian *canzone di ballo,* or dancing song. It was in France, however, that it developed as the form we know, reaching its height in the fourteenth century. It came into English from French models during that early period, Froissart in particular probably influencing Chaucer. The most famous ballade writer wrote in the next century; he was François Villon, the vagabond poet whose tragic life has stirred imaginations for centuries. The rules of the ballade form were enunciated rather late in its history, in 1493, by Henri de Croi in his *L'Art et science de rhètorique.*

There are three kinds of ballade, containing, respectively, stanzas of eight, ten, or seven lines. A ballade consists of three stanzas and an envoi that is usually half as long as the stanza. The distinguishing feature of the ballade is a refrain that appears four times — as the last line of each stanza and of the envoi. This refrain must add to the meaning of the poem each time it is used, rather than being simply a combination of musical syllables, as in a song. The envoi should take the form of an address to the poet's patron or to someone concerned in the subject of the ballade.

The Eight-Line Stanza

The eight-line stanza ballade contains three eight-line stanzas and a four-line envoi, totaling twenty-eight lines. According to de Croi's rules, it had to be written in eight-syllable lines, as if the correspondence of the number of syllables in the line and the number of lines in the stanza gave it some kind of mystical unity. However, this rule is not strictly observed in English.

Only three rhyme sounds are used in this ballade form, and therefore terminal sounds with many possible rhymes must be selected. Rhyme "a" appears six times, "b" fourteen times, and "c" five times, not counting repetitions. The rhyme scheme is a-b-a-b-b-c-b-C (the capital letter signifies the repeated refrain) three times, followed by b-c-b-C in the envoi.

A BALLADE FOR LOST CHILDHOOD

The fireflies needled through the night	(a)
Across the grass; the purple air	(b)
Was full of pinetrees, and the tight	(a)
And frustrate knot of my despair—	(b)
Despair that I was always there,	(b)
Not otherwhere nor otherwhen,	(c)
Not glamorous, nor old, nor fair—	(b)
Ah life! to have it all again!	(C)
How sharp the woe! How sad the plight	(a)
Of one who had so much to bear!	(b)
To be a child was utter blight,	(a)
And no one knew or seemed to care	(b)
That there was nothing worth a dare,	(b)
That all was tame, and I was ten,	(c)
Penned in, cooped up, and straight of hair.	(b)
Ah life! to have it all again!	(C)
The lake was small and blackly bright.	(a)
We swam all day amidst its glare,	(b)
Above its depths of deepest fright	(a)
Afraid, and falsely debonair.	(b)
Our mother played at solitaire	(b)
In evening's glow. The children then	(c)
Raced aimlessly around her chair.	(b)
Ah life! to have it all again!	(C)

Envoi

Dear friends, despite our luckless share	(b)
Of woes that filled our youthful ken,	(c)
Let's cry, from out our adult snare,	(b)
Ah life! to have it all again!	(C)

—F. S.

The Ten-Line Stanza

The ten-line-stanza ballade is usually written in iambic pentameter and has as its rhyme-scheme a-b-a-b-b-c-c-d-c-D, repeated three times, and an envoi of c-c-d-c-D; thus it has a total of thirty-five lines. The envoi may contain an extra line, c-c-d-c-c-D, bringing the grand total up to thirty-six lines. Originally this ballade form had to be written in lines of ten syllables, but this rule is no longer strictly observed in English.

A Ballad of François Villon
PRINCE OF ALL BALLAD-MAKERS

Bird of the bitter bright grey golden morn	(a)
Scarce risen from the dusk of dolorous years,	(b)
First of us all and sweetest singer born	(a)
Whose far shrill note the world of new men hears	(b)
Cleave the cold shuddering shade as twilight clears;	(b)
When song new-born put off the old world's attire	(c)
And felt its tune on her changed lips expire,	(c)
Writ foremost on the roll of time that came	(d)
Fresh girt for service of the latter lyre,	(c)
Villon, our sad bad glad mad brother's name!	(D)

Alas the joy, the sorrow, and the scorn,
   That clothed thy life with hopes and sins and fears,
And gave thee stones for bread and tares for corn
    And plume-plucked gaol-birds for thy starveling peers
    Till death clipt close their flight with shameful shears;
Till shifts came short and loves were hard to hire,
When lilt of song nor twitch of twangling wire
   Could buy thee bread or kisses; when light fame
Spurned like a ball and haled through brake and briar,
   Villon, our sad bad glad mad brother's name!

Poor splendid wings so frayed and soiled and torn!
   Poor kind wild eyes so dashed with light quick tears!
Poor perfect voice, most blithe when most forlorn,
    That rings athwart the sea whence no man steers
    Like joy-bells crossed with death-bells in our ears!
What far delight has cooled the fierce desire
That like some ravenous bird was strong to tire
   On that frail flesh and soul consumed with flame,
But left more sweet than roses to respire,
   Villon, our sad bad glad mad brother's name?

Envoi

Prince of sweet songs made out of tears and fire,	(c)
A harlot was thy nurse, a God thy sire;	(c)
Shame soiled thy song, and song assoiled thy shame.	(d)
But from thy feet now death has washed the mire,	(c)
Love reads our first at head of all our quire,	(c)
Villon, our sad bad glad mad brother's name.	(D)

        —Algernon Charles Swinburne

The Ballade Royal

The ballade royal was used by Chaucer in his "Ballade of Good Counsel." This ballade form is written in rhyme royal, a seven-line stanza with an a-b-a-b-b-c-C rhyme scheme. It may employ either iambic tetrameter or iambic pentameter. Chaucer's ballade is in iambic pentameter. It has four stanzas, the fourth replacing the envoi of the first two ballade forms. The last line of each stanza is the repeated refrain. There are twenty-eight lines.

BALLADE OF GOOD COUNSEL

Flee from the crowd and dwell with truthfulness;
   Suffice thee with thy goods, tho' they be small:
To hoard brings hate, to climb brings giddiness;
   The crowd has envy, and success blinds all;
   Desire no more than to thy lot may fall;
Work well thyself to counsel others clear,
And Truth shall make thee free, there is no fear!

Torment thee not all crooked to redress,
   Nor put thy trust in fortune's turning ball;
Great peace is found in little busy-ness;
   And war but kicks against a sharpened awl;
   Strive not, thou earthen pot, to break the wall;
Subdue thyself, and others thee shall hear;
And Truth shall make thee free, there is no fear!

What God doth send, receive in gladsomeness;
   To wrestle for this world foretells a fall.
Here is no home, here is but wilderness:
   Forth, pilgrim, forth; up, beast, and leave thy stall!
   Know thy country, look up, thank God for all:
Hold the high way, thy soul the pioneer,
And Truth shall make thee free, there is no fear!

Therefore, poor beast, forsake thy wretchedness;
   No longer let the vain world be thy stall.
His mercy seek who in his mightiness
   Made thee of naught, but not to be a thrall.
   Pray freely for thyself and pray for all
Who long for larger life and heavenly cheer;
And Truth shall make thee free, there is no fear!
            —Geoffrey Chaucer
            (Modern version by Henry Van Dyke.)

OTHER BALLADE FORMS

The *double ballade* has six stanzas instead of three, and the stanzas may be of either eight or ten lines. An envoi may be added or omitted, as the author desires. The rhyme scheme is exactly the same as in the single ballade form.

The *double-refrain ballade* is exactly like the traditional eight-line-stanza ballade, except that it has two refrain lines instead of one in each stanza. The fourth and eighth lines are both refrains, and recur in the same spot in each stanza. The rhyme scheme is the same as that of the regular eight-line-stanza ballade, except for the envoi, which rhymes in two couplets, b-B, c-C, with the first refrain appearing as the second line and the second refrain as the fourth line.

THE BALLAD OF PROSE AND RHYME

When the ways are heavy with mire and rut	(a)
In November fogs, in December snows,	(b)
When the North wind howls, and the doors are shut,—	(a)
There is place and enough for the pains of prose;	(B)
But whenever a scent from the whitethorn blows,	(b)
And the jasmine-stars at the casement climb,	(c)
And a Rosalind-face at the lattice shows,	(b)
Then hey!— for the ripple of laughing rhyme!	(C)
When the brain gets dry as an empty nut,	(a)
Then the reason stands on its squarest toes,	(b)
When the mind (like a beard) has a "formal cut,"—	(a)
There is place and enough for the pains of prose;	(B)
But whenever the May-blood stirs and glows,	(b)
And the young year draws to the "golden prime,"	(c)
And Sir Romeo sticks in his ear a rose,—	(b)
Then hey!— for the ripple of laughing rhyme!	(C)
In a theme where the thoughts have a pedant-strut,	(a)
In a changing quarrel of "Ayes" and "Noes,"	(b)
In a starched procession of "If" and "But,"—	(a)
There is place and enough for the pains of prose;	(B)
But whenever a soft glance softer grows	(b)
And the light hours dance to the trysting-time,	(c)
And the secret is told "that no one knows,"—	(b)
Then hey!— for the ripple of laughing rhyme!	(C)

Envoy

In the work-a-day world,— for its needs and woes,	(b)
There is place enough for the pains of prose;	(B)
But whenever the May-bells clash and chime,	(c)
Then hey!— for the ripple of laughing rhyme!	(C)

—Austin Dobson

THE CHANT ROYAL

The chant royal, an elaboration of the ballade form, was invented in France in the medieval period and used for serious, stately, and often religious themes. The form was not introduced into England until the revival of interest in French forms of the latter part of the nineteenth century.

The chant royal has five stanzas of eleven lines each and an envoi of five lines. The rhyme scheme, which includes five rhymes, is a-b-a-b-c-c-d-d-e-d-E for five stanzas, with the last line of each stanza as the refrain. A five-line envoi that rhymes d-d-e-d-E follows. The total is sixty lines.

The following example of the form, by Austin Dobson, has an envoi of seven lines instead of five, rhyming c-c-d-d-e-d-E, and thus lengthening the poem by two lines.

THE DANCE OF DEATH
(After Holbein)
"Contra vim Mortis
Non est medicamen in hortis."

He is the despots' Despot. All must bide,	(a)
Later or soon, the message of his might;	(b)
Princes and potentates their heads must hide,	(a)
Touched by the awful sigil of his right;	(b)
Beside the Kaiser he at eve doth wait	(c)
And pours a potion in his cup of state;	(c)
The stately Queen his bidding must obey;	(d)
No keen-eyed Cardinal shall him affray;	(d)
And to the Dame that wantoneth he saith—	(e)
"Let be, Sweet-heart, to junket and to play."	(d)
There is no King more terrible than Death.	(E)

The lusty Lord, rejoicing in his pride,
He draweth down; before the armèd Knight
With jingling bridle-rein he still doth ride;
He crosseth the strong Captain in the fight;
The Burgher grave he beckons from debate;
He hales the Abbot by his shaven pate,
Nor for the Abbess' wailing will delay;
No bawling Mendicant shall say him nay;
E'en to the pyx the Priest he followeth,
Nor can the Leech his chilling finger stay. .
There is no King more terrible than Death.

All things must bow to him. And woe betide
The Wine-bibber,— the Roisterer by night;
Him the feast-master, many bouts defied,

Him 'twixt the pledging and the cup shall smite;
Woe to the Lender at usurious rate,
The hard Rich Man, the hireling Advocate;
Woe to the Judge that selleth Law for pay;
Woe to the Thief that like a beast of prey
With creeping tread the traveller harryeth:—
These, in their sin, the sudden sword shall slay··
There is no King more terrible than Death.

He hath no pity,— nor will be denied.
When the low hearth is garnished and bright,
Grimly he flingeth the dim portal wide,
And steals the Infant in the Mother's sight;
He hath no pity for the scorned of fate:—
He spares not Lazarus lying at the gate,
Nay, nor the Blind that stumbleth as he may;
Nay, the tired Ploughman,— at the sinking ray,—
In the last furrow,— feels an icy breath,
And knows a hand hath turned the team astray··
There is no King more terrible than Death.

He hath no pity. For the new-made Bride,
Blithe with the promise of her life's delight,
That wanders gladly by her Husband's side,
He with the clatter of his drum doth fright;
He scares the Virgin at the convent grate;
The Maid half-won, the Lover passionate;
He hath no grace for weakness and decay:
The tender Wife, the Widow bent and gray,
The feeble Sire whose footstep faltereth,—
All these he leadeth by the lonely way··
There is no King more terrible than Death.

Envoy

Youth, for whose ear and monishing of late,	(c)
I sang of prodigals and lost estate,	(c)
Have thou thy joy of living and be gay;	(d)
But know not less that there must come a day,—	(d)
Aye, and perchance e'en now it hasteneth,—	(e)
When thine own heart shall speak to thee and say,—	(d)
There is no King more terrible than Death.	(E)

—Austin Dobson

THE TRIOLET

The triolet is a slight, eight-line poem in which the first two lines are repeated as a refrain in the last two lines, while the first line reappears also in the middle of the poem as line four. These refrain lines should be identical in sound, if not in meaning; they may contain plays upon words and even puns, though this is not mandatory, and a triolet in which the lines are repeated as a simple refrain can be very satisfactory. The triolet was originally used as a vehicle for serious poetry, but it is now considered a light form that should not be required to carry too deep or complicated a meaning. A long poem called *The Cléomadés*, by the French trouvère Adenès Le Roi (1258–97), contains the first known triolet. The rhyme scheme, with the refrain lines in capital letters, is A-B-a-A-a-b-A-B. The lines are usually short in length, and the poem is frequently written in mixed meter.

THE TOWN DWELLER

The country is charming,	(A)
but I stay in town	(B)
and find nature alarming.	(a)
"The country is charming	(A)
now," friends say, disarming	(a)
me. "Won't you come down?"	(b)
The country is charming,	(A)
but I stay in town.	(B)

ROSE FEVER

Go, lovely rose!	(A)
I think you'll drive me mad.	(B)
Kerchoo! the mischief grows—	(a)
Blow, lovely nose!	(A)
I've nothing now but woes,	(a)
And all the joys I had	(b)
Go. —Lovely rose,	(A)
I think you'll drive me mad.	(B)

—F. S.

The second of these "Triolets of a Country-Hater" is not regular, since the fourth line is not quite a repetition of the first—but it sounds sufficiently similar to get in under the wire.

THE RONDEL

The rondel was invented in France in the fourteenth century and was widely used in the late medieval period; rondels were written in English as early as the fifteenth century and revived in the nineteenth. The form contains fourteen lines and two rhymes. As in the triolet, there is a two-line refrain, but in the rondel it is repeated three times in its entirety. The first and second, seventh and eighth, and thirteenth and fourteenth lines are the same. The rhyme scheme is A-B-b-a-a-b-A-B-a-b-b-a-A-B, or sometimes A-B-a-b-b-a-A-B-a-b-a-b-A-B. The following is a rondel of fourteen lines.

A RONDEL

A rondel is something to write	(A)
As a matter of trial and error.	(B)
Ballads are sometimes much fairer	(b)
And sonnets are good to indite,	(a)
But if you are wakeful at night,	(a)
And sleep becomes rarer and rarer,	(b)
A rondel is something to write	(A)
As a matter of trial and error.	(B)
While the children are screaming with fright,	(a)
And the house is shaking with terror,	(b)
And a bear is brought in by a bearer	(b)
And sits there sharing your light,	(a)
A rondel is something to write	(A)
As a matter of trial and error.	(B)

—F. S.

Sometimes the rondel contains only thirteen lines and omits one of the two refrain lines at the end; it may use either the first or the second refrain line as the thirteenth and final line of the poem.

THE WANDERER

Love comes back to his vacant dwelling,—	(A)
The old, old Love that we knew of yore!	(B)
We see him stand by the open door,	(b)
With his great eyes sad, and his bosom swelling.	(a)
He makes as though in our arms repelling,	(a)
He fain would lie as he lay before;—	(b)
Love comes back to his vacant dwelling,	(A)
The old, old Love that we knew of yore!	(B)
Ah, who shall help us from over-spelling	(a)
That sweet, forgotten, forbidden lore!	(b)
E'en as we doubt in our heart once more,	(b)
With a rush of tears to our eyelids welling,	(a)
Love comes back to his vacant dwelling.	(A)

—Austin Dobson

THE CHAUCERIAN ROUNDEL

The Chaucerian roundel, as written by Chaucer in the fourteenth century, was influenced by the French rondel form and is really a kind of rondel. It is

constructed with the first line repeated as a refrain at the end of the second and
third stanzas. It has ten lines in all, and the rhyme scheme is A-b-b, a-b-A, a-b-b-A.

THE CITY SQUARE

There's something in the city square	(A)
That, if it's looked at, melts away	(b)
Into the dazzle of the day.	(b)
It acts as if it were not there—	(a)
We never see it, though we say,	(b)
"There's *something* in the city square!"	(A)
A glint of sun on curling hair,	(a)
A skirl of pipes that dance and play—	(b)
Does Pan still linger there today?	(b)
There's something in the city square...	(A)

—F. S.

THE RONDELET

The rondelet, or little rondel, is a poem of seven lines with a rhyme scheme
A-b-A-a-b-b-A. The refrain (line A) should be shorter than the other lines and
is usually written in iambic dimeter, while the second, fourth, fifth, and sixth
lines are in iambic tetrameter.

THE OLD MAN

And there he is!	(A)
He still survives his mounting ills,	(b)
And there he is!	(A)
That harsh and granite heart of his,	(a)
Intolerant of other wills,	(b)
Still counts the beats like dollar bills—	(b)
And there he is!	(A)

—F. S.

THE RONDEAU

The rules governing the rondeau form were laid down in France in the early
sixteenth century. The rondeau is a lyric poem of fifteen lines written in three
stanzas of uneven length, with a refrain ending the second and third stanzas.
The refrain is a fragment taken from the beginning of the first line, and may
consist of a phrase or a clause, or even, as in the following example, a single word.

CHILDREN AT NIGHT

Children at night, we lie there numb with fear;	(a)
A great black shadow threatens to come near	(a)

And blot us out, annihilate us quite.   (b)
Its darkness is denial of all sight,   (b)
And from the door it broods and seems to leer.   (a)

At first there's nothing different to hear,   (a)
But then a muffled pounding strikes the ear—   (a)
  Why can't we scream aloud, or light a light,   (b)
    Children?   (R)

What holds us rigid as it slithers near?   (a)
We close our eyes against what may appear,   (a)
  Or dive beneath the covers, hold them tight   (b)
  Against the ghoulish troll who rules the night,   (b)
In whose dark kingdom we're no longer dear   (a)
  Children.   (R)

                                        —F. S.

THE TEN-LINE RONDEAU

There is also a ten-line rondeau arranged in two stanzas, each ending in a
one-word refrain which repeats the first word of the poem. The rhyme scheme
is a-b-b-a-a-b-R, a-b-b-a-R. The refrain is not counted as a line, since it is invariably composed of just one word in this form.

JOURNEYS

Journeys are always far, though they be near,   (a)
  And they are always difficult to make—   (b)
  A parting is required, a little break,   (b)
If one but go to there, deserting here,   (a)
And leave one's treasures, grown absurdly dear—   (a)
  Oh, it is always dangerous to take   (b)
    Journeys!   (R)

One feels foreboding, packs pathetic gear,   (a)
  And then all night lies tossing, wide awake,   (b)
  And thinks how, even though for your sweet sake,   (b)
It's hard to go away, hard not to fear   (a)
    Journeys.   (R)

                                        —F. S.

THE ROUNDEL

The roundel is an English form that the poet Swinburne derived in the nineteenth century from the rondeau. It is a lyric poem of eleven lines, with the first
part of the first line repeated as a refrain in the fourth and eleventh lines. The

refrain may rhyme (B) as in the example that follows, but this is not a requirement of the form. The rhyme scheme, therefore, may be either a-b-a-B, b-a-b,
a-b-a-B, or, without a rhyme at the end of the refrain, a-b-a-R, b-a-b, a-b-a-R.

Swinburne used his invention as freely as others have used the sonnet. "A Century of Roundels," dedicated by the poet to Christina Rossetti, is a roundel
sequence that is well worth reading and rereading.

A DIALOGUE

I

Death, if thou wilt, fain would I plead with thee:	(a)
Canst thou not spare, of all our hopes have built,	(b)
One shelter where our spirits fain would be,	(a)
Death, if thou wilt?	(B)
No dome with suns and dews impearled and gilt,	(b)
Imperial: but some roof of wildwood tree,	(a)
Too mean for Sceptre's heft or swordblade's hilt.	(b)
Some low sweet roof where love might live, set free	(a)
From change and fear and dreams of grief and guilt;	(b)
Canst thou not leave life even thus much to see,	(a)
Death, if thou wilt?	(B)

II

Man, what art thou to speak and plead with me?
What knowest thou of my workings, where and how
What things I fashion? Nay, behold and see,
    Man, what art thou?

The fruits of life, and blossoms of thy bough,
What are they but my seedlings? Earth and sea
Bear nought but when I breathe on it must bow.

Bow thou down too before me: though thou be
Great, all the pride shall fade from off thy brow,
When Time and strong Oblivion ask of thee,
    Man, what art thou?

III

Death, if thou be or be not, as was said,
Immortal; if thou make us nought, or we
Survive: thy power is made but of our dread,
    Death, if thou be.

Thy might is made out of our fear of thee:
Who fears thee not, hath plucked from off thy head
The crown of cloud that darkens earth and sea.

Earth, sea and sky, as rain and vapour shed
Shall vanish; all the shows of them shall flee:
Then shall we know full surely, quick or dead,
  Death, if thou be.
                    —Algernon Charles Swinburne

THE KYRIELLE

The kyrielle is a medieval French form whose name is derived from a part of the church liturgy, the *kyrie eleison,* which is characterized by frequent repetition, as in a refrain, of the sentence "Lord, have mercy upon us." The kyrielle is written in couplets that are often paired in quatrains, and has a refrain in the second line of the couplet or the fourth line of the quatrain; this refrain may be composed of as little as a single word or as much as a whole line. The poem rhymes a-A, a-A, etc., if it is in couplets, or a-a-b-B, c-c-b-B, etc., if in quatrains. The latter may also be rhymed a-b-a-B, c-b-c-B, etc. The lines are usually in iambic tetrameter throughout.

The words to many hymns are in this rather simple form, though it is by no means confined to religious poetry.

A LENTEN HYMN

With broken heart and contrite sigh,
A trembling sinner, Lord, I cry:
Thy pard'ning grace is rich and free:
O God, be merciful to me.

I smite upon my troubled breast,
With deep and conscious guilt opprest,
Christ and His cross my only plea:
O God, be merciful to me.

Far off I stand with tearful eyes,
Nor dare uplift them to the skies;
But Thou dost all my anguish see:
O God, be merciful to me.

Nor alms, nor deeds that I have done,
Can for a single sin atone;
To Calvary alone I flee:
O God, be merciful to me.

And when, redeemed from sin and hell,
With all the ransomed throng I dwell,
My raptured song shall ever be,
God has been merciful to me.
                    —Thomas Campion (1567–1620)

THE LAI

The lai (virelai or virelay) is a medieval French lyric form of obscure origin, possibly connected with the Provençal *ley*; it was revived in the seventeenth century. The lai is composed in units of three lines: a rhymed couplet in lines of five syllables, and a third line, containing only two syllables, which rhymes not with the preceding couplet but with the other short tail lines in the stanza. The stanza may be of any length desired, so long as it is a multiple of these three lines; the poem may contain any number of stanzas.

Sound the trumpet song!	(a)
Let it float along	(a)
The way.	(b)
It's the heady, strong	(a)
Beat that can't go wrong	(a)
Today.	(b)

A similar arrangement of lines and rhymes has long been popular in English poetry, but the strict limitation of the length of the lines to five and two syllables has seldom been observed.

The lyric form called the lai should not be confused with the *lay* (sometimes also called the lai) which was a medieval type of short narrative poem, usually written in octosyllabic verse (iambic tetrameter) and dealing with such subjects as the Arthurian legends. Macauley's "Lays of Ancient Rome" are an example of this latter form.

The *virelai ancien* is a medieval form whose complications make it even harder to write than the lai, for it uses interlocking rhyme. The long lines of the second stanza must rhyme with the short lines of the first stanza, the long lines of the third stanza with the short lines of the second, and so forth. In the last stanza, to round things off, the long lines rhyme with the short lines of the previous stanza, while the short lines must rhyme with the long lines of the first stanza. The stanzas in the virelai ancien are always of the same length. The lines are sometimes longer than five syllables, and the third line of the basic triplet may be of the same length as the rest, instead of being a very short line. The rhyme scheme (which may, of course, be longer than this sample) is a-a-b-a-a-b, b-b-c-b-b-c, c-c-a-c-c-a.

NIGHTMARE

Step by step, the stair	(a)
Climbs in empty air,	(a)
Gleaming starkly white;	(b)
Jagged fragments — bare	(a)
Ruined walls — are there	(a)
In the moonlit night.	(b)

I climb on in fright,   (b)
And the lantern light   (b)
   Glimmers far below;   (c)
Pressing toward the height,   (b)
Knowledge fails, and sight   (b)
   Dims and seems to go.   (c)

On that broken bow,   (c)
Trembling in the glow,   (c)
   I am poised up where   (a)
Dream and nightmare know   (c)
Airy overthrow,   (c)
   Asking, do I dare?   (a)

             —F. S.

The *virelai nouveau* is a form of the lai characterized by the use of a double refrain. The poem opens with a rhymed couplet containing two refrain lines. These lines are then used alternately, one at a time, at the end of each stanza up to the last one, where they both appear at the end but in reverse order. All lines are of the same length. Only two rhyme sounds are used in the poem. The stanzas need not be of any set length, and the position of the two rhymes is variable. For example, the stanzas might go A^1-A^2-a-b-a-b-b-A^1, b-b-a-b-b-A^2, a-a-b-a-b-A^1, b-b-a-b-b-A^2, a-b-a-A^2-A^1. After the opening couplet, the stanzas are built upon units of three lines, until the end, when the opening couplet again appears. The following example has a rhyme scheme that goes A^1-A^2-a-a-a-b-a-A^1, a-b-a-b-a-b-b-a-A^2, a-a-b-a-b-a-b-a-A^1, a-b-a-b-a-b-a-b-a-a-a-a-a-a-A^2, a-b-a-A^2-A^1.

JULY

Good-bye to the Town! — good-bye!   (A^1)
Hurrah! for the sea and the sky!   (A^2)
In the street the flower-girls cry;   (a)
In the street the water-carts ply: (a)
And a fluter, with features awry,   (a)
Plays fitfully, "Scots, who hae"—   (b)
And the throat of the fluter is dry;   (a)
Good-bye to the Town! Good-bye!   (A^1)

And over the rooftops nigh   (a)
Comes a waft like a dream of the May;   (b)
And a lady-bird lit on my tie;   (a)
And a cockchafer came with the tray;   (b)
And a butterfly (no one knows why)   (a)
Mistook my Aunt's cap for a spray;   (b)
And "next door" and "over the way"   (b)
The neighbors take wing and fly: (a)
Hurrah! for the sea and the sky!   (A^2)

To Buxton, the waters to try,—   (a)
To Buxton goes old Mrs. Bligh;   (a)
And the Captain to Homburg and play   (b)
Will carry his cane and his eye;   (a)
And even Miss Morgan Lefay   (b)
Is flitting — to far Peckham Rye;   (a)
And my Grocer has gone — in a "Shay,"   (b)
And my Tailor has gone — in a "Fly";   (a)
Good-bye to the Town! — Good-bye!   (A¹)

And it's O for the sea and the sky,   (a)
And it's O for the boat and the bay,   (b)
For the white foam whirling by   (a)
And the sharp, salt edge of the spray!   (b)
For the wharf where the black nets fry,   (a)
And the wrack and the oarweed sway!   (b)
For the stroll when the moon is high   (a)
To the nook by the Flag-house gray!   (b)
For the *risus ab angulo* shy   (a)
From the Some-one we designate "Di!"   (a)
For the moment of silence— the sigh!   (a)
"How I dote on a Moon!" "So do I!"   (a)
For the token we snatch on the sly   (a)
(With nobody there to say Fie!)   (a)
Hurrah! for the sea and the sky!   (A²)

So Phyllis, the fawn-footed, hie   (a)
For a hansom. Ere close of the day,   (b)
Between us a "world" must lie,—   (a)
Hurrah! for the sea and the sky!   (A²)
Good-bye to the Town! — GOOD-BYE!   (A¹)

—Austin Dobson

THE VILLANELLE

The villanelle was originally a round song sung by farm laborers; the name comes from the Latin *villa*, or farm. The medieval French villanelles were irregular, but in the sixteenth century the form became fixed as we know it today. It is written in tercets rhymed a-b-a until the last stanza. The first stanza furnishes the two refrains, A¹-b-A², and the succeeding stanzas repeat these two lines alternately in the third line of the tercet as the refrain a-b-A¹, a-b-A², etc. Each refrain line must be repeated the same number of times. Then, in the last stanza, a quatrain, they are repeated together, a-b-A¹-A². The poem is frequently composed of five tercets and a closing quatrain, but may have three, five, seven, nine, or any odd number of tercets, as desired.

THE REVENANT

I heard fine pebbles rake my pane,	(A¹)

I heard fine pebbles rake my pane, (A^1)
And rose from sleep to stare below   (b)
Where no one stood, tonight, again, (A^2)

No shadowed shape in wind and rain   (a)
Where once you flung reminders, so   (b)
I heard fine pebbles rake my pane— (A^1)

And yet my eyes went searching, fain   (a)
To see some huddle stir and go   (b)
Where no one stood, tonight, again. (A^2)

And suddenly I thought the grain   (a)
Of stone stood up and seemed to grow;   (b)
I heard fine pebbles rake my pane, (A^1)

And lion-gold, your heavy mane   (a)
Of hair one moment caught the glow   (b)
Where no one stood, tonight, again. (A^2)

So fell a fancy filled my brain   (a)
I turned and whispered hoarsely, "No!"   (b)
I heard fine pebbles rake my pane (A^1)
Where no one stood, tonight, again. (A^2)

—F. S.

The popularity of the villanelle has revived somewhat among modern poets, perhaps because it lends itself very well to the creation of mood. W. H. Auden, among other poets, has used it with memorable success.

THEME WITH VARIATIONS

The theme with variations has numerous poetic possibilities. The theme may be original, as is the first quatrain of the rondeau redoublé, or it may be a well-known passage used line by line to set off a chain reaction in successive stanzas of a new poem. If the theme is original rather than borrowed, it is usually developed in a serious way, though this is not an invariable rule. If the theme is borrowed, it is frequently developed in a surprising, odd, or humorous way.

THE RONDEAU REDOUBLE

The rondeau redoublé is a theme with variations with some features of the rondeau. It states its four refrain lines as the first quatrain. Then these four lines are used successively as the last lines of the four following quatrains. A sixth and final quatrain follows, containing no repetition of previous lines, but tailed in a fifth short line by the beginning phrase or clause from the first line. Thus there are twenty-five lines — six quatrains and a tail line. The same two rhymes must be used throughout; the rhyme scheme is A^1-B^1-A^2-B^2, b-a-b-A^1, a-b-a-B^1, b-a-b-A^2, a-b-a-B^2, a-b-a-b-T. The example that follows is in iambic pentameter.

DEATH THAT TOOK FAIR HELEN

Oh Death that took fair Helen, you who wait	(A^1)
Down every twisted passageway we wend,	(B^1)
We'll see your unknown visage, soon or late—	(A^2)
The passageway will turn, and reach an end.	(B^2)
And are you enemy, or are you friend?	(a)
Along the walls are pictured scenes that state	(b)
The beauty that all living might portend,	(b)
On Death that took fair Helen, you who wait!	(A^1)
And we mistake the scenes for real, and prate	(a)
Of what we hope, or how our life will trend,	(b)
Taking for granted there is something great	(a)
Down every twisted passageway we wend.	(B^1)
We do not know what waits around each bend,	(b)
And wish our passageways were clear and straight—	(a)
But whether they go upward or descend,	(b)
We'll see your unknown visage, soon or late.	(A^2)
And sometime when we're gay, inebriate	(a)
Of life itself, and hear our bards commend	(b)
The upward way, and celebrate man's fate,	(a)
The passageway will turn, and reach an end.	(B^2)
What gods are there we might propitiate?	(a)
How guard the passageway, and how defend	(b)
The right to keep on going? — we who hate	(a)
And fear your scythe with every breath we spend,	(b)
Oh Death that took fair Helen?	(R)

—F. S.

CHAIN RHYMING AND CHAIN VERSE

The Italian terza rima stanza, which we have seen at the beginning of the section on traditional stanza forms, chain-rhymes from stanza to stanza as follows: a-b-a, b-c-b, c-d-c, d-e-d, e-f-e-f or e-f-e, f-f. When a terza rima poem contains fourteen lines in iambic pentameter and rhymes a-b-a, b-c-b, c-d-c, d-e-d, e-e, it is called a terza rima sonnet. The charm and individuality of the terza rima form depends in the main upon its chain-rhyming. As a vehicle of serious poetry terza rima has been outstanding.

Many other chain-rhyming effects are possible in addition to terza rima. We have seen one example in the virelai ancien. It is possible to chain-rhyme quatrains, cinquains, and even longer stanzas. All that is necessary is to carry over a rhyme from one stanza to the next in a regular pattern, as, for example, in quatrains, a-a-b-a, b-b-c-b, c-c-d-c, d-d-a-d.

In addition to chain rhyme, there are other possibilities of linkage between stanzas in repetition of a word, a phrase, or an entire line, often between the last line of one verse and the first line of the next. The sestina is thus linked in chain repetition from stanza to stanza.

The following is an example of a poem that repeats the last line of each stanza in the first line of the next in an unusually effective way.

THE CENTAURS

Playing upon the hill three centaurs were!
They lifted each a hoof! They stared at me!
And stamped the dust!

They stamped the dust! They snuffed upon the air!
And all their movements had the fierce glee
Of power, and pride, and lust!

Of power and pride and lust! Then, with a shout,
They tossed their heads, and wheeled, and galloped round,
In furious brotherhood!

In furious brotherhood! Around, about,
They charged, they swerved, they leaped! Then, bound on bound,
They raced into the wood!

—James Stephens

THE PANTOUM

The pantoum (or pantum) is a verse form of Malay origin, coming from the literature of Southeast Asia and the East Indies. It first came to the attention of European writers around 1820, when the German poet Adelbert von Chamisso, having discovered the form, wrote three examples. Victor Hugo included a pantoum in *Les Orientales* (1829) and other French authors also became interested. The first European writers of the pantoum, among them Théodore de Banville, retained the Malay division of its subject matter, keeping natural scenery (or background) in the first two lines of each quatrain, and human action (or foreground) in the third and fourth lines. Charles Baudelaire, however, departed from this pattern and considered the subject as a unified one, as have later writers. Austin Dobson introduced the form in English.

The pantoum is written in interlinked quatrains, usually rhyming a-b-a-b, in which the second and fourth lines of each stanza become the first and third lines of the next; in the last stanza, the form comes full circle as the hitherto unrepeated first and third lines of the first stanza are used, in reverse order, as the second and fourth lines. Thus the poem begins and ends with the same line.

The line repetitions of the pantoum are capable of contributing to very different moods, from the querulous humor of Austin Dobson's "In Town," through the light, rather tinkling improvisations of a love poem in the oriental manner, to a mood of obsessive and threatening horror in a pantoum that has not yet been written.

CLOTHES

I have a hard time with my clothes,
  They are either too long or too short,
They're big or they're small — heaven knows,
  They are always of quite the wrong sort!

They are either too long or too short,
  They are hopeless as soon as they're home,
They are always of quite the wrong sort
  No matter how far I may roam.

They are hopeless as soon as they're home,
  And no matter how much I complain,
No matter how far I may roam,
  They continue to give me a pain.

No matter how much I complain,
  There is no one to help me about them—
They continue to give me a pain,
  And I wish I could get on without them!

There is no one to help me about them,
  They're big or they're small — heaven knows,
I wish I could get on without them!
  I have a hard time with my clothes.

                                        —F. S.

THE SESTINA

The sestina is an unrhymed form which was invented sometime toward the end of the thirteenth century by the famous Provençal troubadour Arnaud Daniel. It was admired and used by Dante and Petrarch in Italy, but was not much used in France and England before the nineteenth century. It is composed in six stanzas of six lines each in blank verse, followed by a three-line envoi, or *tornada*, as the refrain of a poem was called in Provençal.

Instead of rhyme, the sestina uses word repetition; the end word of each line of the first stanza is repeated in different order, in each of the following stanzas and the envoi. Originally, the end words were supposed to have a feminine ending. The end word in the last line of each stanza becomes the end word in the first line of the next stanza, a device that links the stanzas in a chain of repetition. The arrangement of repetition is as follows:

Stanza I.   1-2-3-4-5-6
Stanza II.   6-1-5-2-4-3
Stanza III. 3-6-4-1-2-5
Stanza IV.   5-3-2-6-1-4
Stanza V.   4-5-1-3-6-2
Stanza VI.   2-4-6-5-3-1.

The envoi contains inner repetition, as well as terminal repetition. The first line has word 2 in the middle and 5 at the end. The second line has word 4 in the middle and 3 at the end, while the third line has word 6 in the middle and 1 at the end.

GROWING UP

Once I plucked berries, ripened in the sun,
Grown wild beside a little meadow spring—
The red-flushed berries smelling wild and warm,
And busy insects buzzing through the air,
My father at my side; while over yonder
And down a little hill, the swamp began.

Those sunlit days were when my life began,
My conscious life, awareness like a sun
Almost too bright to bear, that here and yonder
Were plants in earth that lived, knew how to spring
To life's implicit rendezvous with air,
Plants that would bear as long as they were warm.

What was it kindled, made the meadow warm,
What kindled hearts, and what, since all began,
Made fuel for burning out of common air?
Like a young pagan then I hailed the sun,
Bowed down my head beside the meadow spring,
And closed my eyes against the darkness yonder—

How like a spell the word still echoes— yonder!
I soon had fled the near, the dear, the warm,
The memories beside the meadow spring;
My father dead, with whom my life began,
I hid in swamps, protected from the sun,
Breathing a strange, contaminated air.

And there, entrapped in stinking, moldy air,
I saw that one could never get to yonder,
But it receded, under moon or sun,
The swampy dark was cold, and nothing warm
Had touched my nightmare since my flight began.
I was alone, and had forgotten spring,

Or so I thought. But still some trace of spring
Was mingled in my mind. A gust of air
Blew through the swamp, and suddenly began
To sweep the poisons out. I saw, just yonder,
Through lowering trees, a vision bright and warm—
My childhood meadow in a burst of sun.

My dear, beside the meadow spring, not yonder,
In sparkling air we built a dwelling warm,
And there began a life with love our sun.

—F. S.

THE RHYMED SESTINA

Some writers in English have not been satisfied with the original sestina form,
and have sought to make it more melodious through the addition of rhyming.
Since the system of repetition provided by the traditional sestina form would
produce couplet rhyming in some stanzas, which was considered undesirable,
the system was changed sufficiently to avoid that calamity. Swinburne used a
rhyme scheme of a-b-a-b-a-b, b-a-b-a-b-a, in alternating stanzas, which provided
against couplet rhyming.

Swinburne's rhymed sestina shown here has the following pattern of word
repetition:

Stanza I.	1-2-3-4-5-6
Stanza II.	6-1-4-3-2-5
Stanza III.	5-6-1-4-3-2
Stanza IV.	2-5-6-1-4-3
Stanza V.	3-2-1-6-5-4
Stanza VI.	4-3-2-5-6-1
Envoi.	1 – – 4
	2 – – 3
	5 – – 6.

SESTINA

I saw my soul at rest upon a day	1
As the bird sleeping in the nest of night,	2
Among soft leaves that give the starlight way	3

To touch its wings but not its eyes with light;	4
So that it knew as one in visions may,	5
And knew not as men waking, of delight.	6
This was no measure of my soul's delight;	6
It had no power of joy to fly by day,	1
Nor part in the large lordship of the light;	4
But in a secret moon-beholden way	3
Had all its will of dreams and pleasant night,	2
And all the love and life that sleepers may.	5
But such life's triumph as men waking may	5
It might not have to feed its faint delight	6
Between the stars by night and sun by day,	1
Shut up with green leaves and a little light	4
Because its way was as a lost star's way.	3
A world's not wholly known of day or night.	2
All loves and dreams and sounds and gleams of night	2
Made it all music that such minstrels may,	5
And all they had they gave it of delight;	6
But in the full face of the fire of day	1
What place shall be for any starry light,	4
What part of heaven in all the wide sun's way?	3
Yet the soul woke not, sleeping by the way,	3
Watched as a nursling of the large-eyed night,	2
And sought no strength nor knowledge of the day,	1
Nor closer touch conclusive of delight,	6
Nor mightier joy nor truer than dreamers may,	5
Nor more of song than they, nor more of light.	4
For who sleeps once and sees the secret light	4
Whereby sleep shows the soul a fairer way	3
Between the rise and rest of day and night,	2
Shall care no more to fare as all men may	5
But be it place of pain or of delight,	6
There shall he dwell, beholding night as day.	1
Song, have thy day and take thy fill of light	1-4
Before the night be fallen across thy way;	2-3
Sing while he may, man hath no long delight.	5-6

—Algernon Charles Swinburne

THE ODE

The Greek ode was not characterized by a set stanza form, and, of course, had no rhyme scheme, since the Greeks did not use rhyme. However, it did have a set progression of stanzas.

The *Pindaric ode*, so called because it was written by the Theban poet Pindar (*ca.* 518–442 B.C.), consisted of a succession of stanzas patterned upon the first three, called the strophe, the antistrophe, and the epode. The poet constructed these stanzas freely, in any pattern he wished, then repeated the pattern of the three stanzas to the end of the poem.

This pattern of three stanzas originated with the choral performance of the ode in Greece. The chorus moved up one side of the orchestra chanting the strophe, and then came down the other side chanting the antistrophe. Then they came to a standstill and chanted the epode before the audience. This continued for each group of strophe, antistrophe, and epode, until the end.

Modern poets in writing the Pindaric ode usually use rhyme, and construct any kind of stanza they may wish. The only requirement is that the pattern of the first three stanzas be followed throughout.

The *Horatian (or stanzaic) ode* is written in a succession of stanzas that follow the pattern set in the first stanza; the Latin poet Horace (65–8 B.C.) used this form. Keats, in his "Ode to a Nightingale," invented a ten-line stanza in iambic pentameter except for the eighth line, which is in iambic trimeter; the rhyme scheme is a-b-a-b-c-d-e-c-d-e.

My heart aches and a drowsy numbness pains	(a)
My sense, as though of hemlock I had drunk,	(b)
Or emptied some dull opiate to the drains	(a)
One minute past, and Lethe-wards had sunk:	(b)
'Tis not through envy of thy happy lot,	(c)
But being too happy in thine happiness,—	(d)
That thou, light-winged Dryad of the trees,	(e)
In some melodious plot	(c)
Of beechen green, and shadows numberless,	(d)
Singest of summer in full throated ease.	(e)

The *irregular ode* is a modern invention and has no pattern at all; the stanzas are of varying forms and lengths, as in Wordsworth's "Ode: Intimations of Immortality."

COUNTING SYLLABLES

From the Japanese come a group of forms that depend not on devices of meter and rhyme, but on maintaining a strict limitation of the number of syllables in each line.

The inspiration behind this syllable-counting method of writing poetry is allusively imagistic. In the Japanese poem, what is not said is almost more important than what is. One simple image, drawn with great economy, can suggest a universe.

THE HAIKU

The haiku is a poem of three lines containing seventeen syllables in all; the three lines contain, respectively, five, seven, and five syllables. No consideration of meter or rhyme enters into the technique of such a poem — only the rather stark progression of syllables adding up to an image that implies far more than it says.

> Against the gold screen
> A silken dress flutters. Whose?
> Ah, the autumn wind!
> > —Buson (18th century)

> The grasshoppers' cry
> Does not reveal how very
> Soon they are to die.
> > —Basho (17th century)

Many translators have rendered the haiku in couplets, but it seems to others that the special "threeness" of the tercet should be preserved. There is a pattern of starts and pauses in any poem, and to change the number of lines is to destroy that pattern. Especially in the haiku, there is a concluding concept in the third line which gains in suggestiveness by its brevity.

THE TANKA

The tanka is a poem of five lines containing thirty-one syllables. The first three lines are exactly like those of the haiku, and there are two additional lines of seven syllables each. In translating tankas into English, poets sometimes, almost in spite of themselves, add the elements of meter and rhyme. However, the conventions of Western prosody do not apply in this kind of Japanese poetry, and the originals of these poems are without either rhyme or meter.

> Why was it fated
> That in one brief night of love
> Your heart was sated,
> While mine was made your captive
> For as long as I shall live?
> —Empress Kwokamu-Innobetto (12th century)
> (English version by F. S.)

> Since I have loved you
> I compare my former thoughts
> To those I have now,

And realize that I then
Had no ideas at all.
                    —Atsutada (10th century)
                    (English version by F. S.)

THE NAGA-UTA

Longer lyric poems in alternating lines of five and seven syllables are also possible. After any given number of repetitions of the combination of five and seven,
the poem ends with an extra seven-syllable line. The following is an example
of this form.

My desire is great
To look upon your dear face,
My longing is great
To speak, and hear you answer.
I must, nonetheless,
Give up these two cherished hopes,
For if it so chanced
They came to know, at my house,
Or they heard next door
That you and I had conversed
A while together,
I should be punished greatly
For my imprudence.

That my good reputation
Be lost, is nothing—
But that surely, without it
You'd not love me any more.
                    —Anonymous (16th century)
                    (English version by F. S.)

THE CINQUAIN

An American poet, Adelaide Crapsey, invented a form dependent upon the
count of syllables which she called the cinquain. Its lines contain, respectively,
two, four, six, eight, and two syllables, and are in a prevailingly iambic meter.
Her verse in this form is akin in spirit to that of the imagists, who have been
influenced by the use of the image in Japanese poetry. Adelaide Crapsey's cinquain has been a very popular form, and is still being widely used. Other poets
have used varying combinations of numbered syllables in their lines and have
claimed to invent forms in this system. However, none but the cinquain has
attained universal recognition.

THE WARNING

Just now,
Out of the strange
Still dusk — as strange, as still—
A white moth flew. Why am I grown
So cold?

         —Adelaide Crapsey

THE ENGLYN

Although the use of syllable-count forms of verse in English stems in the main from the Japanese, it would be a mistake to think that they were the only nation ever to use such a method in poetry.

For example, in Welsh poetry — and the Welsh, in their native Celtic language, have a long bardic tradition — there is a form called the englyn that consists of thirty syllables. In quatrain form, the lines have, respectively, ten, six, seven, and seven syllables. The sixth syllable of the first line announces the rhyme, and the last syllable of the succeeding three lines rhymes with it. (The final syllable of the first line is without rhyme.)

The content of this form of verse is usually epigrammatic.

THE LOVER PASSES AT TWILIGHT

The dusk was like a pond, a stagnant pool.
Suddenly my heart donned
black garments, while your face swanned
whitely toward some fool beyond.

         —F. S.

SYLLABLE COUNT IN MODERN VERSE

The illustrious contemporary poet Marianne Moore bases the form of her poetry upon the count of syllables. Her complicated lines depend almost without exception upon this device. Instead of writing her line in traditional meters (which also involve using a certain number of syllables), she dispenses with meter and retains syllable count as the determinant of the lines in her stanzaic patterns.

Marianne Moore's poems are arranged in complicated but regular stanza forms, though they read like prose. Their technical basis — the count of syllables — is not immediately apparent.

PREDOMINANTLY HUMOROUS FORMS

THE LIMERICK

Of uncertain origin, the limerick is a five-line verse rhymed a-a-b-b-a, in which the first, second, and fifth lines contain three feet (one iamb and two anapests), while the third and fourth lines contain two beats (usually two anapests). It is usually epigrammatic.

There ONCE was a MAN from NanTUCKet	(a)
Who KEPT all his CASH in a BUCKet;	(a)
But his DAUGHTer named NAN	(b)
Ran aWAY with a MAN,	(b)
And AS for the BUCKet, NanTUCKet.	(a)

But he followed the pair to Pawtucket,
The man and the girl with the bucket;
   And he said to the man
   He was welcome to Nan,
But as for the bucket, Pawtucket.

                 —Anonymous

Can anyone imagine a serious poem written in limericks? There is something comic about the very rhythm and arrangement of the lines. The above example repeats the place name, which is mentioned factually in the first line, with a pun on it in the last line. It is safe to say that the majority of limericks have first lines ending in a place name — usually the protagonist's place of origin. "There was a young lady of Lynn," "There was an old man of Canarsie," or "There was a young man of Benares" are all fine beginnings of limericks. The further adventures of the persons mentioned in these first lines all have something to do with clever rhyming on the names of their towns.

One large group of limericks simply repeats the name of the place instead of introducing a new rhyme in the last line, which relieves the writer of having to find more than one rhyme for it. Edward Lear, one of the most famous of limerick writers, who did much to popularize the form, almost always wrote his limericks in this style.

There was a young lady of Portugal
Whose ideas were excessively nautical;
   She climbed up a tree
   To examine the sea,
But declared she would never leave Portugal.

                 —Edward Lear

Modern limerick writers, however, generally prefer to introduce a new rhyme in the last line. The pattern most often used now, however, is the following:

An epicure, dining at Crewe,
Found quite a large mouse in his stew.
   Said the waiter, "Don't shout
   And wave it about,
Or the rest will be wanting one too!"

                 —Anonymous

THE CLERIHEW

The clerihew is named in honor of its inventor, Edmund Clerihew Bentley. It is a humorous, pseudo-biographical quatrain, rhymed as two couplets, with lines of uneven length more or less in the rhythm of prose. It is short and pithy, and often contains or implies a moral reflection of some kind. The name of the individual who is the subject of the quatrain usually supplies the first line.

LOUIS XVI

The Sixteenth Louis
Exclaimed, "Phooey!"
Then, "Heavens! What was that I said?
I must have lost my head."

—F. S.

THE LITTLE WILLIE

The Little Willie is named in honor of its original protagonist. It is a humorous quatrain usually written in mixed iambic and anapestic tetrameter and rhymed in two couplets, a-a-b-b. Originally it detailed some horrendous mishap that befell Little Willie, together with its completely logical but often grisly consequences. Little Willie was an *enfant terrible* of truly staggering proportions, and after every disaster he was resurrected to participate in the next quatrain as if he had never been felled in the last.

The Little Willie is now written about all members of the family, and Willie himself need not figure in it at all. The subject matter, however, remains the same — disaster and its surprising but inevitable consequences.

Little Willie hid, and stayed,
In a cornerstone that was being laid.
In a thousand years, won't they feel silly
When they open it up and out jumps Willie!

When our apartment's ceiling fell
Father merely muttered, "Well!"
Mother, polite through thick and thin
Thanked the neighbors for dropping in.

IV

New Ways in Verse; Rhyme

Seldom in history is the dividing line between one period and another clear-cut. It almost never happens that suddenly and simultaneously everybody stops doing something in the old way and begins doing it in the new. Instead the new current runs along beside the old for a while, before one becomes dominant or the two become inextricably mingled.

In the history of poetry, new currents begin with new poets, and the two poetic revolutions that began in the nineteenth century were set off by two American poets who were very different from one another. Poe's influence was felt primarily in France, where his theories were instrumental in the formation of the symbolist movement that reached its height in the 1870s and 1880s. From France, this movement in its turn influenced modern poetry in England and in America very strongly in the twentieth century, producing the modernist movement of which T. S. Eliot may be considered the head. The stream of change started by Poe had to do with "pure" poetry, poetry divorced from logic and meaning, the effect of a poem as pure sound.

The other important new voice from America was Walt Whitman's, that "barbaric yawp" which was heard around the world as surely as the revolutionary shot at Concord of which Emerson wrote. Whitman's stream of change abolished the old rules of polite prosody, as well as polite restrictions upon the subject matter of poetry. As a young man, Whitman wrote in traditional forms, but he soon threw away the rules and began to write the free-verse poems in his ever-expanding book, *Leaves of Grass*. He wrote poems whose long, resounding free-verse lines were reminiscent in their music of the Bible. He piled length upon length to achieve amazing climaxes. The general reading public, a public that loved verse and was enthusiastic about the works of Longfellow and Tennyson, was horrified by Whitman's temerity in daring to call his works poetry. Longfellow's *Hiawatha* was published in the same year as *Leaves of Grass*, to loud critical hosannas and great public appreciation. As succeeding editions of Whitman's book appeared, always enlarged, the public was welcoming installments of *The Idylls of the King* from Tennyson. Robert Browning, too, was a popular idol. No one but Whitman himself suspected that his barbaric yawp was the voice of the future.

Another American poet was writing at that time whose technical innovations were of startling originality, but her work was not published (except for a few poems) or noticed until the twentieth century. It is only comparatively recently that Emily Dickinson's works have appeared in definitive editions and she has been recognized both at home and abroad as the major poet she indubitably was.

During the period just before the First World War free verse took the center of the poetic stage and stayed there for several decades. Traditional verse forms, however, were never completely abandoned, and many modern poets were writing poems of great lyric grace and originality. As the century has progressed, traditional forms have returned increasingly to favor, with a difference in their use that stamps them as being unmistakably of the present time.

At present, then, both traditional-modern and free-verse forms are used side by side. It is not only the techniques of versification, but also the diction, structure, and content of poetry that have changed.

Almost all poets agree that it is much more difficult to write irregular or free verse than to write in the strict forms of traditional prosody. Traditional forms, they say, are a help in organizing the poem. They give it shape and definition. Even the use of rhyme, and the search for fresh rhymes, may suggest new insights into the subject matter of the poem.

On the other hand, the poet writing free verse has no "handle" to grasp. The free-verse poem must have its own interior logic, for there is no external pattern to help it along. The poem must create its own form, and this is not easy to achieve.

In general, poets feel that it is important to serve an apprenticeship working in the traditional forms of poetry before going on to the more complicated free forms. Working in traditional forms that have in themselves a certain structure and movement helps the young poet to gain a feeling for these indispensable elements of poetry. His apprenticeship will give him assurance in handling the verse line as a unit and in manipulating the musical elements of poetry. It will assist him in developing his "ear" and his subtle sense of definition of structure.

NEW WAYS IN RHYME

NEAR-RHYME

All the devices that are close to rhyme and may be substituted for it in a poem can be classified as near-rhyme. This classification includes imperfect rhyme, unaccented rhyme, dissonant rhyme, vowel rhyme, consonant rhyme, and consonance, together with their subgroups. Repetition also sometimes takes the place of rhyme.

Beyond these devices of near-rhyme and repetition there is only nonrhyme—the total absence of rhyme found in blank verse and free verse. Forms that lack rhyme as a unifying element must be held together by means of content, stylistic devices, and rhythm.

As we have seen, rhyme and near-rhyme are powerful instruments in achieving subtle unity and development in a poem and are also sources of much musical delight for both poet and reader. There is more near-rhyme than is apparent to the untrained eye in free verse, and it is often this subtle, hidden rhyme which, unrecognized by the reader, contributes more than any other single element to the unity of the poem.

IMPERFECT RHYME

In this rhyming dictionary, the term "imperfect rhyme" means the imperfect chiming of accented and unaccented syllables which would be perfect rhymes if both were accented. Imperfect rhyme, or accented-unaccented coupling, can be one of the most effective devices of contemporary versification. It is one kind of intentional flatting of the rhyme. Examples are the pairs ring-striking, spot-parrot, and burn-bittern.

> And cave men stagger up, and leave their dens,
> And hear the sea-borne song of distant sirens.

UNACCENTED RHYME

Unaccented rhyme can occur only when the line terminates with a feminine or three-syllable end word. In this case, the accented syllables that are ordinarily the rhyme sounds are completely different, but they are followed by an unaccented syllable (or syllables) that would make a perfect rhyme if it were accented.

In his "Elegy for Jane," Theodore Roethke concludes with this couplet:

> I, with no rights in this matter,
> Neither father nor lover.

The unaccented rhyme on "er" gives the effect of a rhyming echo to the lines, and the dissonance of the initial nonrhyme is thus resolved.

HALF-RHYME

Half-rhyme is a feminine or three-syllable rhyme in which the accented syllable rhymes, but the following one or two unaccented syllables are different. Examples are cover-shovel, wily-piling, wilderness-building.

These three kinds of near-rhyme depend to an important degree on accent.

The next categories of near-rhyme, on the other hand, depend on the consonant and vowel sounds that make up the rhyme.

DISSONANT RHYME

Dissonant rhyme is illustrated by such a pair as bite-strike. The long "i" sound is the same, but the terminal consonants miss. Both are unvoiced explosives, that is, simple breath explosions in which the vocal chords do not take part. "P" is the third consonant in this group. Because these consonants are similar, unschooled rhymers frequently misrhyme them at random. However, when this "fault" is practiced as a regular dissonant rhyme system, it produces an effect of its own that can be very successful.

In order to use a dissonant rhyme system, the poet should know something about the science of phonetics. He should know not only that "t," "k," and "p" belong together as unvoiced explosive consonants, but that their opposite numbers, the voiced explosives, are "d," hard "g," and "b." "S" and "sh" are unvoiced sibilants, whereas "z" and "zh" are voiced; "f" and "th" (as in "thing") are unvoiced, but their opposite numbers "v" and "th" (as in "that") are voiced; and "l," "m," "n," and "r" are similar in being voiced liquid continuants. The various consonant groups may be used together as rhyme variants, or they may appear in regular patterns with their opposites. The writer must be careful to use dissonant rhyme *as a system*, for a single dissonant rhyme will inevitably seem like a mistake.

Imperfect dissonant rhyme, unaccented dissonant rhyme, and half-dissonant rhyme are all possible. The first would couple an accented-unaccented pair of dissonant rhymes, such as wend-deterrent; the second, a pair of unaccented dissonant rhymes, such as second-mordant; and the third, a pair of two- or three-syllable words of which the first syllables are accented and in dissonant rhyme while the syllables that follow are unrelated, as in wending-center.

ASSONANCE AND VOWEL RHYME

Assonance is the repetition of the same vowel sound in neighboring words in a line (or in several lines) of a poem or prose. It is used to intensify the mood or the music of the passage.

"The fleeing Greeks received me peacefully" is a line composed mainly of "ee" sounds; seven of the ten syllables of the line are constructed upon that vowel sound. It is a rather extreme example of assonance.

When assonance occurs at the ends of lines in place of rhyme — that is, when the terminal sounds are composed of the same accented vowel or vowels plus a random mixture of consonants — the result is called vowel rhyme. For example, lines ending in time, ripe, and vile have nothing in common but the "i" sound of their vowel rhyme. The following is from Karl Shapiro's "The Dome of Sunday":

> A silent clatter in the high-speed eye
> Spinning out photo circulars of sight.

E. L. Mayo, in "The Pool," wrote a quatrain in which all four lines end with vowel rhyme:

She sees the falling leaves, the dying leaves	(a)
That cling there still; above	(b)
Through the brown horror of the boughs she sees	(a)
The empty, arching skull.	(b)

Half-vowel rhyme is an effect that may be used in a poem, but imperfect and unaccented vowel rhyme may not, for the simple reason that all unaccented vowels have a strong tendency to be reduced to the ubiquitous "uh" sound of the "schwa" in phonetics. This means simply that unaccented vowels are not differentiated sufficiently to be effective in rhyme patterns.

Examples of half-vowel rhyme would be such pairs as capping-lambent and ogre-opening.

ALLITERATION AND CONSONANT RHYME

Alliteration is the repetition of the same consonant sound, usually at the beginning of words in a series which appear near each other, in the same line or group of lines in poetry or prose. Alliteration may also occur with the repetition of a consonant sound used in the middle of polysyllabic words, or at the ends of words.

Alliteration as a musical effect in poetry is very ancient indeed, having been used by the Anglo-Saxons as one of the main principles of their prosody. In modern verse it has been more loosely used than by the Anglo-Saxons, and often very persuasively. It is a device that can become vitiated through overuse, and too much alliteration is almost *ipso facto* suspect. Swinburne, for example, used it to such an extent that it almost became a vice. One sometimes suspects, no doubt unfairly, that he did not care what he said, so long as it alliterated! For example, this quatrain from "By the North Sea" sounds very lovely, but means little:

> A land that is lonelier than ruin,
> A sea that is stranger than death:
> Far fields that a rose never blew in,
> Wan waste where the winds lack breath....

Consonant rhyme is the effect achieved when the same consonant recurs at the end of the last accented syllable in each line of a rhyme pattern but the vowel or vowels before it are different. If the rhyme is feminine or three-syllable, the unaccented syllable or syllables should be identical, as in perfect feminine or three-syllable rhyme.

Emily Dickinson, who was far ahead of her time in technique and who employed many of the devices of near-rhyme, used consonant rhyme in many of her poems. (Her rather hidebound friend and critic, Thomas Wentworth Higginson, went so far as to "correct" it as a fault in many of her poems that he edited. Among her numerous consonant rhymes are the pairs gate-mat and one-stone in "The Soul Selects Her Own Society," design-maintain, wind-God, and plan-unknown in "Four Trees upon a Solitary Acre," and gone-down and despair-more in "The Auctioneer of Parting."

Consonant rhyme is particularly effective in feminine rhyming. John Crowe Ransom, in "Bells for John Whiteside's Daughter," rhymes body-study, window-shadow, little-scuttle, and ready-study.

Theodore Roethke wrote, in "My Papa's Waltz,"

> The whiskey on your breath
> Could make a small boy *dizzy*;
> But I hung on like death:
> Such waltzing was not *easy*.

An example of imperfect consonant rhyme occurs in "Elegy for Jane," by the same author:

> I remember the neckcurls, limp and damp as ten*drils*,
> And her quick look, a sidelong pickerel *smile*.

Unaccented-consonant rhyme and half-consonant rhyme are also sometimes used. An example of the first would be tendrils-tumbles, and of the second, easy-sizzling.

CONSONANCE

Consonance, or the use of identical consonant sounds both at the beginning and end of a word, is often used in place of rhyme, and is a very successful device. For example, one might end lines with lack, lake, lick, like, lock, luck, look, and Luke. Consonance is particularly effective in the irregular patterns of contemporary poetry, either used throughout or mixed with other kinds of rhyme, with which it fits perfectly. The vowel sounds, in consonance, seem to modulate from one key to another as they change, giving a musical quality to the lines that no other device gives.

> Faded and brown are the autumn leaves
> Falling across our lives and loves.

Imperfect consonance, unaccented consonance, and half-consonance are all possible. In imperfect consonance, the accented-unaccented coupling of imperfect rhyme would give such a pair as lack-childlike. Unaccented consonance would give melancholic-childlike, and half-consonance would give signer-sanest.

REPETITION

There is one other device akin to rhyme that can take over its function when used deliberately — that is repetition.

In ordinary rhyming, repetition is to be avoided like the plague, for it is considered a mistake if one merely repeats, instead of varying, the initial consonant sound of the rhyme. However, like other verbal devices traditionally considered to be "faults," repetition can be extremely effective when used with design and skill.

In such a traditional form as the sestina, repetition takes over the function of rhyme entirely. In the complicated pattern of repeated words it is notable that the last line of one stanza and the first line of the next always repeat their final word, in a sort of chain.

ANALYSIS OF A POEM

If we analyze Carl Sandburg's poem "Grass," we see that many of the devices just outlined are important in building the free-verse lines into a unified poem.

In the first stanza, which has three lines, the first line begins with an assonantal group of words, "*Pile* the bodies *high*," and so does the second, "*Shovel* them *under*." The second line ends, "and let me work," which is linked in dissonant rhyme with the second stanza. The third line of the first stanza introduces another piece of assonance, "I *am* the gr*a*ss," with the "I" sound echoing the assonance of the first line; it then goes on to return to the assonance of the previous line in "*cov*er," which is actually a half-rhyme with "Shovel."

Now let us look at the first three lines together:

> Pile the bodies high at Austerlitz and Waterloo,
> Shovel them under and let me work—
> I am the grass; I cover all.

The two assonantal phrases that begin the first two lines have been commented upon. In addition, "Austerlitz" (with the first syllable pronounced in the anglicized fashion in which we say "Austria") and "Waterloo" have great parallelism of sound. "Au" is the same sound as in "Wa(ter)," "ter" occurs in both words, and the final syllable in both cases begins with an "l."

"Pile them high" recurs in the first two lines of the next stanza, and the terminal sounds of the first four lines of this stanza are "burg-dun-work-ductor." Not only are "burg" and "work" dissonant rhymes, but the hard "g" and "k" are voiced and unvoiced variations of the same sound. "Dun" and "ductor" are related by assonance, and thus are vowel rhymes. As we have seen, "work" is repeated from the first stanza and it will be repeated in the last line of the poem. Meanwhile, the second stanza ends with a couplet in short, four-syllable lines. The first is "What pl*ace* is th*is*?" in which the final sibilants of the second and fourth words are alliterative and also link the line in consonant rhyme with what is to come in the next stanza. The last line of the second stanza is "Where are we now?" — a departure from the previous sound patterns.

> And pile them high at Gettysburg,
> And pile them high at Ypres and Verdun.
> Shovel them under and let me work.
> Two years, ten years, and passengers ask the conductor:
> What place is this?
> Where are we now?

The final couplet of the poem is both brief and repetitive. "I am the grass" is repeated from the beginning of the third line, and echoes the final consonant in "place" and "this" above. The final line, "Let me work," is the third occurrence of that brief prayer.

> I am the grass.
> Let me work.

Analysis thus reveals the complex technical unity of sound which welds this poem into a unit far beyond its unity of meaning. Even in the seventh line, when the poet writes "Two years, ten years," his logic is musical rather than substantive; "One year, ten years," or "Three years, ten years," would not have had the inevitability of sound (furnished by alliteration) that makes the phrase memorable. It is not the exact number of years, but the sound of the number, which is important here.

Not all free-verse poems are held together by a unifying principle of near-rhyme, assonance, alliteration, and repetition. However, this is one way in which free verse can use the resources of the modern manipulation of sound values.

These modern ways of handling sound values are perhaps even more important in traditional-modern verse, which uses them in the time-honored way in regular rhyme patterns as well as in loose and irregular patterns.

V

New Ways in Rhythm: Free Verse
and Modernist-Traditional Forms

ACCENT AND STRESS

The difference between the metrical systems of traditional versification and the more modern practices of irregular and free verse may perhaps be epitomized by the difference between the words "accent" and "stress."

Accent, as we have seen, occurs in a fairly arbitrary way in our tonic-accented language. If one takes any word of two syllables, one realizes that it has to have an accent either on the first or the second syllable. It is either a ti-TUM word or a TUM-ti word, an iamb or a trochee. However, when such a two-syllable word is put into a line of verse, it may lose its accent altogether and become just ti-ti, its accent being taken over by a strongly accented syllable just preceding or following it. The word "running," is a trochee when taken alone, but, in an anapestic line like "We reQUIRE running WATer, and BATHtubs and SHOWers," it falls unaccented into the shadow between "reQUIRE" and "WATer." This is about the extent of the elasticity and variability of accent in our system of accent meters.

As we have seen in discussing the basic meters of traditional English versification, these patterns of accent have nothing to do with sense or meaning, although they may intensify a mood through the special characteristics of their movement. *Stress*, on the other hand, is related to meaning. In reading a poem aloud, one inevitably stresses certain words or groups of words that are important to the meaning of the line. It is in this sense that one can make a distinction between stress, which follows meaning, and accent, which determines the mechanical pattern of the language.

Traditional verse is composed in accent patterns, as well as in meaningful stress groups; free and irregular verse is composed only according to the rhythms of the latter.

It has been said that free verse is written in "the rhythms of speech" or "the rhythms of prose." By this is meant only that the lines are not composed to fit the pattern of mechanical scansion. It does not mean that they sound exactly like ordinary speech or ordinary prose, for they do not. The poet has cadenced them in a particular way, complete with the starts and stops that belong to separation into lines. How important these cadences are can be realized only when one tries to break up a piece of real prose into lines and present it as poetry. Even if prose is imaginative and "poetic," like that of Thomas Wolfe, it cannot be made into poetry by a typographical trick.

Real poetry, whatever its prosodic stance, happens as poetry. The poem by Carl Sandburg that was analyzed at the end of the last chapter cannot be thought of otherwise than as a poem. Just as an experiment, let us write it as prose.

GRASS

Pile the bodies high at Austerlitz and Waterloo, shovel them under and let me work — I am the grass; I cover all.

And pile them high at Gettysburg and pile them high at Ypres and Verdun. Shovel them under and let me work. Two years, ten years, and passengers ask the conductor: What place is this? Where are we now?

I am the grass. Let me work. — Carl Sandburg

Is anybody fooled by the paragraphing? Can anybody read this passage aloud otherwise than as Sandburg wrote it, in lines of poetry? I think not. Every line has the completeness of a phrase in music as the poem is read aloud, and merely running them together in a paragraph cannot destroy their integrity as lines or the poem's integrity as a poem.

THE PAUSE: STARTS AND STOPS

The pauses that mark the starts and stops of lines are an integral part of a poem. Just as the empty space that surrounds or is enclosed by sculpture is an important element in the composition, so the pauses that mark the stops and starts of poetry serve to punctuate and define the flow of sound. A poet who tends to write lines that flow along without any pause would do well to consider breaking up his lines somewhat. Using the sharp, short declarative sentence to climax or punctuate a flow of longer, more complex statements is one useful way to accomplish this.

BALANCED FREE VERSE

Although "Grass" is recognizably written in Sandburg's idiom and his own tone of voice, it is composed in the same kind of free verse that Whitman wrote, and the same kind in which much of the Bible is written. The main emphasis in this kind of free verse is on neither the beginning nor the end of the line, but is balanced.

The longer lines of this poem each contain two stress groups, while the short lines contain one. The stress groups, moreover, are balanced within themselves; each begins and ends with an important word.

The first verse of Whitman's "When Lilacs Last in the Dooryard Bloom'd" displays these same characteristics.

> When lilacs last in the dooryard bloom'd,
> And the great star early | droop'd in the western sky in the night,
> I mourn'd, | and yet shall mourn with ever-returning spring.
> Ever-returning spring, | trinity sure to me you bring,
> Lilac blooming perennial | and drooping star in the west,
> And thought of him I love.

Here again the lines are in balance, the four long lines in two stressed parts, and the shorter lines at beginning and end in one. Each line ends as strongly as it begins. Like a phrase in music, each line is spoken, as it were, on one breath, and the pause at the end coincides with the drawing of another breath. Poetry, like music, is conceived in human terms, as song to be sung (or spoken) by the human voice. There is just so much breath available to handle a phrase, but within that range the phrase may be short or long, dramatic or meditative.

Whitman often built up to a climax by making his lines longer and longer, and let sheer weight add to the intensity. Even his long lines, however, are notable for their balance, and for the fact that they end as strongly as they begin.

END STRESS: THE RISING LINE

It is impossible to be categorical about the matter of where stress falls in a stress group, but certain free-verse poetry tends to let a rising line predominate, that is, a line which culminates with the principal stress at or toward the end of the line.

When a poem is written for the most part in lines with this rising movement, an affirmative mood and a definite unity of rhythm are attained. H. D. (Hilda Doolittle) wrote, in a free-verse poem called "Song":

> You are as GOLD
> as the half-ripe GRAIN
> that merges to GOLD again.

Notice how the voice, in reading these lines, rises to emphasis at or near the end of the line. This end stress, combined with the shortness of the lines, seems to give a hard, sculptural quality to this and other poems by H. D. Such a poem could be diagrammed as a wave motion beginning low and working up to the crest toward the end, then down to the beginning of the next line or wave.

FRONT STRESS: THE FALLING LINE

Many other free-verse poets tend to write a line that begins with a strong stress and tails off with lesser stresses and connectives, while the next line once more begins with an emphatic word or idea.

Marianne Moore wrote, in "In Distrust of Merits," that the world was fighting a blind man:

> who cannot see that the enslaver is
> enslaved; the hater, harmed. O shining O
> firm star, O tumultuous
> ocean....

Notice how the line ends usually on an adjective or some other weak word, and the next line begins on the strong idea — the point to which the end of the previous line led.

Hardly any poet writes poems made up completely of rising or falling lines, for contrasts and turns usually need to be introduced to vary the movement. A few lines, however, may be given as an extreme example of the rhythm of the falling line:

> WHO would wish to go to the
> ASYLUM that stands so bleakly and a-
> LONE upon the
> HILL?
> WHO but the
> HELPless ones,
> LOST ones wandering, thinking perhaps
> ANYwhere will
> DO?

Richard Wilbur, in his poem "Juggler," begins with mainly front-stressed lines in two stanzas, then passes to a transitional stanza in which he accomplishes a turn, and ends with two stanzas in mainly end-stressed lines. The form of this poem is singularly appropriate to the subject, leaving at the end, as it were, all balls caught, as the audience applauds.

The wave motion of free verse, progressing as it does in units of phrases or lines, is a larger motion than that of traditional meter; actually, however, the traditional poem is made up of stress groups, as well, superimposed upon the tick-tock of its patterned syllables.

Some writers and critics hold that the introduction of so-called temporal prosody, that is, writing in patterns of long and short syllables as the ancients did, is the operative principle of the new systems of writing verse in English. Insofar as the meaningful stress group takes a certain shorter or longer length of time, a certain amount of breath, to read, temporal considerations are certainly relevant. Various writers find that longer or shorter stress groups fit their personal modes of expression, or fit certain subjects.

No one, however, would seriously suggest that an English line should be scanned according to syllable length, as one scans a line of Latin poetry. Such scanning is just another tick-tock system, from syllable to syllable. The operative principle of the new poetry is phrasing, as in music; the stress group makes up the unified line or part of a line that is said or sung on a breath and the starts and stops that punctuate these phrases. This is not to say that the meaningful stress group does not include a certain number of secondary accents, in addition to the main stress or stresses, just as a phrase of music is written in measures.

MODERNIST IRREGULAR FORMS

If Whitman and the Bible together gave rise to the strong free-verse current in American and world poetry, it may equally be said that Poe and the symbolists whom he influenced (though they misunderstood his theories) were the progenitors of the modernist movement in poetry.

This school of thought did not discard the accustomed classical English prosody, as did Whitman, even though they, too, considered it somewhat outworn. They determined to use and to build upon the old structures. It is interesting to note that, in the main, this group adopted and made fashionable an attitude of world-weariness and despair well adapted to an old and well-worn method, even though they sometimes modified that method almost to unrecognizability. They considered themselves the end products of an era, the oversophisticated and degenerate last flowers of a Western world that was surely going into eclipse. Whitman and his school, in contrast, had affirmed a new and positive view of the world as good, a belief in the brotherhood of man and the importance of the individual, and, in Whitman's case, a somewhat strident but refreshing patriotism.

These two attitudes do not match invariably with the two streams of modern prosody, but it is interesting to note how in general they sorted themselves out.

One of the great precursors of modern irregular forms in poetry was Matthew Arnold's "Dover Beach," certainly one of the most beautiful, most pessimistic, and most influential poems in English.

DOVER BEACH

The sea is calm tonight.
The tide is full, the moon lies fair
Upon the straits; —on the French coast the light
Gleams and is gone; the cliffs of England stand
Glimmering and vast, out in the tranquil bay.
Come to the window, sweet is the night air!

Only, from the long line of spray
Where the sea meets the moon-blanched land,
Listen! you hear the grating roar
Of pebbles which the waves draw back, and fling,
At their return, up the high strand,
Begin, and cease, and then again begin,
With tremulous cadence slow, and bring
The eternal note of sadness in.

Sophocles long ago
Heard it on the Aegaean,...

—Matthew Arnold

The lines are irregular in length, and scan as slightly irregular iambic meter. The rhyme is perfect rhyme (except for "breath"-"Faith" and "roar"- "drear," occurring later), but the rhyme pattern is irregular. If the poem were contemporary, it is certain that the actual rhymes would be fresher and more unexpected. Arnold did not hesitate to use the time-honored old rhyme groups that were a little tired even then.

T. S. Eliot was born in the year that Matthew Arnold died, so the space of time between the poets is not long. Although Eliot writes in another period and another key, the music of his early masterpiece, "The Love Song of J. Alfred Prufrock," reminds one of "Dover Beach." Here, too, the lines are uneven in length, but in general scan as mixed iambic meter. The rhyme pattern is also irregular, though it begins in rhymed couplets, with two unrhymed lines interpolated in stanza one. The rhymes are somewhat more interesting in themselves than Arnold's, though in the main they are monosyllabic and not unexpected. However, such wry pairs as "ices"-"crisis" do much to lift the average.

This poem, like "Dover Beach," has an elegiac tone. The first lines, "The sea is calm tonight," and "Let us go, then, you and I," though quite different in meaning, have a strange equivalence in temporal quality. Eliot's counterpoint couplet,

In the room the women come and go
Talking of Michelangelo

somehow reminds one of Arnold's "Sophocles long ago...."

Eliot's poem, of course, is really completely different from "Dover Beach," and yet one cannot miss a sort of family resemblance. Of the two, Eliot's poem is the more hopeless. Arnold at least implied that love might console him for the hopelessness of the world by being "true." Prufrock, who has "seen them all already, seen them all," does not mourn the great tragedy of a faithless, war-torn world, but the personal-psychological resignation of a sensitive but ineffectual individual. At least part of the difference between the two poems may be accounted for by the fact that Freud had burst upon the world during the lapse of time between them, and his view of the human psyche had narrowed and turned inward the poet's view.

Eliot was soon to lead a movement back to a kind of religious orthodoxy, so that the thought of one branch of the traditional-modernist movement as well as its method may be said to flow back into the channels of the historic affirmations of the Western world. Yet perhaps even the Christianity of this group is an overintellectualized, nondynamic system, at the opposite pole from Vachel Lindsay's naïvely enthusiastic revival chant in "General William Booth Enters into Heaven."

However, one should not carry the parallelism of moral viewpoint and method too far. Such a hedonistic poet as Dylan Thomas was a writer in the traditional-modernist fashion, though he was a new romantic rather than a new classicist. Dylan Thomas was drunk with rhythm and the music of words, and used all the devices of meter, phrase, rhyme, and near-rhyme to the utmost. In the first stanza of "The Force That through the Green Fuse Drives the Flower," the rhymes are "flower" - "trees" - "destroyer" - "rose" - "fever." Thus, the first, third, and fifth lines are linked in unaccented rhyme, while the second and fourth lines are in consonance ("trees" and "rose"). The poem scans as regular iambic meter — five-line stanzas in iambic pentameter, except for the third line, which is in iambic dimeter. After four such stanzas, the poet ends with a couplet in iambic pentameter and in consonant rhyme. The stanza pattern of the poem is quite traditional, while the rhyme is modernist. The diction is the element above all others that reveals the contemporary nature of the poem. (See Chapter VII.)

To sum up, the modernist irregular forms are written: (1) In lines of uneven length and mixed meters; (2) with irregular rhyme occurrences in no set pattern, but without all lines necessarily rhyming; and using the resources of near rhyme, (3) with stanzas either of set lengths or of irregular lengths corresponding to paragraphs.

Modernist irregular poetry is usually strongly lyrical in its effect, combining discipline with a sense of freedom. The unexpected occurs in it with a pleasurable surprise or shock effect, but it does not spoil the musicality of the poem.

Because its irregularity lends itself to strong contrasts and surprises, the possibilities of dramatic effect are enhanced in the modernist irregular forms. If one of the main delights in reading poetry in traditional forms lies in the expectation of what comes next in a known pattern, it is equally delightful in the modernist irregular forms to be faced with the unexpected turn or the surprising solution.

MODERNIST USE OF TRADITIONAL FORMS

The modern tendency in using traditional forms has been to expand their boundaries through the use of the rhyme variants included in near-rhyme by employing modern stress-group rhythms and by distorting the forms themselves. Modern poets have used all traditional forms, almost without exception, and many have written with equal success in both free verse and traditional patterns. Ezra Pound is an outstanding example of this versatility.

The traditional-modernist poet usually displays great technical virtuosity in handling set forms; his polished writing reflects his pleasure in its many-faceted play. On the one hand, he has available the battery of traditional forms— sonnets, villanelles, sestinas, and the rest. On the other hand, he has the resources of modern prosody — near-rhyme and stress-group rhythm. The rhyming of any traditional set form may include any of the variations provided by near-rhyme in its pattern. The meter of the lines may be colored or modified by the stress-group concept of rhythm, though in the set forms how far the poet goes in this direction is necessarily limited.

Further distortion of the set forms is sometimes attempted, but too much distortion so changes the form that its usefulness is destroyed. For example, the short-line sonnets that some writers have tried to write may turn out to be pleasant poems, but they have lost the mood and movement of the sonnet form. On the other hand, it is possible to write a free-verse villanelle, preserving its tercet stanza form and the repetition of the first and third lines in regular pattern, but using stress-group rhythm and omitting rhyme entirely. It is surprising that this distortion of the villanelle still retains much of the charm of the form; it is still recognizably a villanelle. This is possible because the device of line repetition is extremely powerful in its cohesive effect. The following is an example of a free-verse villanelle.

MELVIN

Small boy following small girl home, kicking leaves
Heaped red and brown and crackling in the gutters,
I remember you well, I remember your name, Melvin.

And in the autumn sunlight, somewhere in a midwest city,
Is there another like you in the burnt-out afternoon,
Small boy following small girl home, kicking leaves?

Where is the small girl, whose name I have forgotten
Or mislaid somewhere? She has gone irretrievably, but
I remember you well, I remember your name, Melvin.

You whom I have never seen again across many years
Are transfixed in my mind, trapped in time's terrible lava,
Small boy following small girl home, kicking leaves.

It is as if you had never lived anywhere else
But that sunlit city, that sunlit year, full of the smells of home.
I remember you well, I remember your name, Melvin.

And as I look back down the long track from there to here
I cannot see you behind me, but I know you are there,

Small boy following small girl home, kicking leaves.
I remember you well, I remember your name, Melvin.

—F. S.

For the writer of poetry, as well as for the connoisseur, it is always pleasurable
to discover that it is possible to do something with a form that one has never
done before and that comes off rather well. There is room for considerable ingenuity in this field of adapting traditional forms to modernist ways. At the same
time, however, many attempts at originality fall very flat. The trained taste
and trained ear, here as elsewhere, are an indispensable part of the poet's equipment.

VI

The Content of Poetry

How does the content of poetry differ from that of other literature, if at all? A key word in this question is "literature," which is here taken to mean written composition that possesses qualities of style and thought that make it an enduring part of the cultural heritage of a society. Literature may teach moral lessons by example, and it may impart wisdom, but it has no immediate practical application. It is a vehicle for the distilled essence of life itself, and its usefulness and its delight consist in its almost magical ability to widen and intensify experience.

Literature may be written either in poetry or in prose. What makes an author decide to write his masterpiece in one instead of the other? Do certain subjects lend themselves better to prose expression, and others to poetry? Or is it the author's natural bent as a writer that decides the question?

Most literature is written in prose probably for one main reason: poets are in the minority among authors. If the author is a poet, however, and if he wishes to write whatever work he has in mind in poetry, there is no reason why he cannot do so. The subject matter of poetry is no more limited than that of literature in general.

A work written as poetry, however, is different from a work written as prose, and not only because it is expressed within the conventions of verse form. Poetry's method of handling its subject differs from that of prose. Prose is definitive and exhaustive, whereas poetry is suggestive and selective. Prose develops a subject completely and logically, proceeding sensibly from point A to point B, whereas poetry may leap from A to Z, implying everything in between. Prose walks the whole distance, whereas poetry may leap or fly. Poetry, in short, is not versified prose, but another method of locomotion entirely.

In addition to being selective, poetry is likely to make its point in terms of images or symbols. Through the brief juxtaposition of two images a poem may say or suggest what a prose piece would take several pages and a hundred times more words to make clear. Images and symbols, of course, also appear in prose works, but usually they are a subordinate element; seldom or never do the image and the symbol form the main vocabulary of a prose piece, as is so often the case with poetry.

TRUTH IN POETRY

The poet's true vision must always be the subject of poetry, whatever the poem is about, since the major justification of poetry, as of all literature, is that it enlarges life. A genuine insight or moment of illumination is shared by the poet, and because of its truth it is the equivalent — sometimes more than the equivalent — of actual experience for the reader. The poet may sometimes discover or work out this truth in the act of writing his poem. This process has been the subject of considerable thought and analysis on the part of both poets and philosophers, and has never been fully explained — but whatever it is, it has a good deal to do with the matter of getting at truth.

Wordsworth's definition of poetry as "emotion recalled in tranquillity" is of interest in its emphasis on the element of recollection, for the experience of many writers has shown that the poem which is composed when the emotion it expresses is at its height is likely to be a failure. At the moment when love or grief has actually transported the poet, he is least likely to be able to write about it well, to transmute it into a work of art. It is not until a little distance has provided perspective that he can recreate his emotion in a good poem. In short, too close an involvement in the subject is likely to spoil its rendering, for a certain detachment is necessary in creating a work of art. Wordsworth was phrasing a profound truth about poetic creation, even though as a definition of poetry his statement seems inadequate.

Nothing shows up more surely in would-be poetry than a lack of truth, whether the falseness or pose be deliberate or involuntary on the part of the poet. Oddly enough, the ersatz is more apparent in poetry than in prose, for poetry is so highly wrought and so stripped down to essentials that there is nowhere to hide. The very verbiage of prose can camouflage with cleverness a false premise or a basic emptiness and insincerity.

Allen Tate writes, in "Three Types of Poetry," one of the essays in *On the Limits of Poetry*, "Although *The Divine Comedy* is allegorical, it would not be one of the great poems of all time if Dante had not believed its structure of action to be true."

Concerning the communicated truth of Thomas Hardy's poetry, Ezra Pound wrote: "No man can read Hardy's poems collected but that his own life, and forgotten moments of it, will come back to him, in a flash here and an hour there. Have you a better test of true poetry?"

Pound was speaking of the shock of recognition that constitutes the impact of a great work of art on the beholder, and he saw it in terms of correspondence with the recollection of the reader's own life. His statement is deeply sincere, but, however touching, it seems too narrow a definition of the recognition which is the response to art. Even without any previous analogous experience, the reader may experience that stab of recognition which says, "This is it! This is how it is!" Sometimes the poem seems like a revelation of something remembered from a former life, or what the French call the feeling of *dejà vu* (already seen), even though nothing in it in any way resembles a past experience of the reader. Actually, though, the distilled essence of life in a work of art, and especially in a poem, can be recognized simply by the touchstone of the life within us. If the poem is alive and true, it arouses a response in us; we carry around a sort of inner tuning fork, if we will listen to it, which can detect true pitch. What this means to the poet is simply that he must examine what he says very carefully, and make sure of its truth.

> O! 'tis an easy thing
>   To write and sing
> But to write true, unfeigned verse
> Is very hard!...

Thus wrote Henry Vaughan, one of the metaphysical poets of seventeenth-century England, who deeply understood, as all good poets must, the difficulty of the search for truth and its expression in poetry. William Butler Yeats held that writing facile verse was the greatest temptation a poet has, and the greatest mistake he can make.

The writer, then, must wrestle with reality and imagination to be sure of what he himself knows and thinks. This search for truth cannot be guaranteed to produce poetry, but without it the effort is hopeless. The beginning writer must question himself: what do I know, what have I experienced, what have I seen with acute vision, that could be used in the writing of a poem?

This is what Sir Philip Sidney's Muse was talking about when she said to him, "Fool! look in thy heart and write!" One caution and one piece of encouragement must be added. Let the fledgling poet, in looking into his own heart, beware of sentimentality; and let him use his mind fearlessly and to the utmost.

IS ANY SUBJECT BARRED?

Is any subject barred from poetry? This is a foolish question, but it is so often posed that one might as well ask it and get it over. The answer is no, nothing is barred, providing it can be made into a poem.

THEMES

The theme is the general field of meaning within which a particular poem takes up its subject. The great themes upon which poets write have not changed much in the last four centuries or so, although in different periods different themes tend to come to the fore. Love and death are the two greatest universal themes, with time and nature running a close second. Religion and philosophical reflection, human nature, personal loneliness, nostalgia, hope, hopelessness, and frustration, all are frequent themes of poetry. The power of poetry itself is a theme. Social criticism may be written straightforwardly, in a spirit of high moral earnestness and indignation, or it may be written (animated by the same motives) as satire. The celebration of national and heroic greatness may be the theme of an epic. The world, the flesh, and the devil may be one or several themes.

In our time, the themes that relate to psychological insights and analysis, such as personal loneliness and frustration, have been emphasized more than during any other period. During the 1930s, there was an attempt to make social protest the main theme of serious poetry, but, although much passion and ink were expended, not much poetry resulted. Probably the writers of the 1930s were too close to their subject during that decade of economic depression and social ferment to attain the necessary perspective.

The theme of love has been used by poets of ancient and modern times, in Orient and Occident. It is a universal theme, for everybody loves at one time or another, briefly or enduringly, happily or unhappily. It is a wonder there is anything fresh to be said about it, and yet just as no two individuals in the world are exactly alike, no two loves are alike either, if the poet has the courage and vision to express himself truly instead of in a stereotype. Though many poems have been written in a time of war to the distant object of the poet's love, such a poem as Karl Shapiro's "V-Letter" is true and individual. His affirmation of the wholeness of his love, his touching use of unexpected and nostalgic common imagery ("As groceries in a pantry gleam and smile | Because they are important weights | Bought with the metal minutes of your pay"), and his matter-of-fact courage, combine to make one of the most moving poems to come out of the last war.

Some of Shakespeare's sonnets are about the power of love to raise and make whole, some are about the power of poetry to immortalize the beloved; the theme of the first is love, the second, poetry.

"Gather ye rosebuds, while ye may" is not really about picking roses, but about seizing time on the wing. "My Last Duchess," a dramatic poem, is on the theme of human nature, contrasting calculating coldness and wickedness with innocence. T. S. Eliot's "Preludes" interprets his early world, in particular his native city, and re-creates its mood of vulgarity and emptiness. E. M. Forster characterized the modern mood of threatening despair (in *Howard's End*) as "panic and emptiness," and this, too, is the theme of much contemporary poetry.

Often a poet has favorite themes that run through his work and may be seen to develop and change as he grows in power. Some themes seem to be more important at certain ages — the experience of war, for example, is likely to be a young man's theme, though the older man can recollect and interpret it. Young poets have an often regrettable tendency to tackle tragic themes about which they know little; an overwhelming *Weltschmerz*, the terrible sadness of the universe, is likely to be felt with all the poignancy of youth, but to be too generalized a feeling, with little or no experience to back it up.

THE SUBJECTS OF POETRY

The first way of thinking of the subjects of poetry is in relation to the kinds of poetry and the kinds of writing. Subject matter in general is usually considered to fall into classifications suited to narrative, descriptive, and expository writing. Narrative subjects, in poetry, are those of the epic, the narrative poem, and the poetic drama. Descriptive poetry, besides occurring incidentally in other forms, exists as a separate classification. To call lyric poetry expository seems at first glance inappropriate; yet its subject matter is a special kind of exposition, the setting forth and the explanation or illustration of personal insights of all kinds.

EPIC SUBJECTS

The epic subject is usually narrative, and the main quality necessary for it is sheer size — largeness of concept, of the scale of action, of the moral stature of the personae (or cast of characters), and of the sweep of the total work. An epic usually relates not one, but several strands of narrative, in which supernatural or religious elements may play a part. However, this is not true of all epics. Lucretius' *De Rerum Natura* has been classified as a didactic epic, and without doubt Ezra Pound's *Cantos* constitute the most famous contemporary epic in English. Thomas Hardy's *Dynasts* is a dramatic epic; Samuel Butler's *Hudibras*, a satirical epic. The single element that all epics have in common is vastness of size and scope.

Few poets in all history have conceived of subjects on an epic scale or been able to handle vast materials of myth, history, and religion in a memorable manner, and these — among them Homer, Dante, Milton, and Goethe — stand out in a special way. Poetic drama alone seems to be equal to the epic form in establishing a poet among the great, and few critics would cavil at a judgment placing Shakespeare at the very peak.

As to the public attitude toward the epic, there has for some time been an impression in the air that this form gets but little appreciation in our time. However, this seems to be a negative illusion. Excellent new translations of the world's great epics in other languages continue to appear in English and to sell in large quantities. Unfortunately, people seem to have lost the habit of reading poetry, and would sooner read Homer in a good prose translation than read Pound's *Cantos*, Spenser's *Faerie Queene*, or Milton's *Paradise Lost* in the beauty of the original English poetry.

The greatness of a poet is still judged, by and large, according to the size as well as the importance of his total work, and an epic remains the biggest and greatest single work, in scope and form, that a poet can undertake. It therefore seems likely that ambitious poets will continue to undertake to write epics in the future, as they have in the past.

NARRATIVE SUBJECTS

The difference between epic poetry and narrative poetry is mainly one of size of the material and the vision, as well as of the finished work. Narrative poetry is on a lesser scale than the epic, but it still may be a "big" form. It, too, tells a story or tale. At its largest, it may be composed of a collection of stories; Chaucer's *Canterbury Tales* reveals a large cross section of English society in the fourteenth century in the course of relating a series of narratives gathered from various sources. Narrative poetry may take the form of a novel in verse, such as Stephen Vincent Benét's *Western Star*, or a historical narrative such as the same author's *John Brown's Body*. It may be a narrative poem of medium length, such as Longfellow's *Evangeline*, or as short as "Home Burial," by Robert Frost. It may take the form of a ballad, as does "La Belle Dame Sans Merci," by Keats. If the poet has a story to relate, he may choose the appropriate form and manner and tell it in poetry.

Because the handling of narrative material in poetry is more selective than in prose, every image or incident has heightened significance. In general, though, the building of the narrative is the same in outline, whatever the medium. Both character and incident are important. After an introductory passage, the plot must be developed, must mount to a crisis, and must be resolved in a denouement.

It was not long ago that narrative poetry was read as eagerly by members of the general public as novels are today. It kept its popularity all through the nineteenth century, up to the time of the First World War. Even more recently, such poets as Robinson Jeffers and Edwin Arlington Robinson published book-length narrative poems that were fairly widely read. At the present time, lengthy and ambitious narrative poetry seems to be in temporary eclipse, but this trend could be reversed at any time by the appearance of an outstanding work in this form.

ALLEGORY

Allegory in narrative poetry reached the height of its popularity in the Middle Ages, when religious and moral meanings were usual not only in stories and story-poems but in pictorial art as well. In allegory, a set of characters is symbolical of a set of meanings, and may even apply to sets of meanings on two levels simultaneously, as in the moral and political allegory of Spenser's *The Faerie Queene*. The setting and the action may also have an underlying significance or represent something else in terms of the allegorical story underneath the surface. Allegory is an organized, broad, and essentially simple use of sets of symbols in a way quite different from that in which the symbol is used in modern literature. As used in an older period it was often an example of the riddle interest that has always existed to a greater or lesser extent in poetry.

THE MATERIAL OF POETIC DRAMA

Narrative subjects in poetry may be handled in dramatic form as well as in direct narrative. For presentation on the stage, the dramatic subject of classical drama used to be required to conform to the three unities of action, time, and place. The three unities as a principle were never rigorously applied in English drama, except in an experimental way by Jonson and Dryden, but inherent in the idea of stage presentation in a single performance is a certain limitation in the scope of the material, even if this limitation is not strictly defined. The classical Chinese drama, which goes on for days, can present material of novelistic or epic length that a single performance precludes. Shakespeare's historical plays are the single exception in English poetic drama to the built-in limitations of the single performance, for they form a continuous series of epic length and scope.

Another difference between the main current of poetry and the poetic drama is that a play in verse which is intended for production rather than for quiet reading alone (the latter is called "closet drama") must be clear enough and simple enough in texture to be understood at first hearing — at a single performance. This somewhat limits the subtlety of the poetry. Christopher Fry's contemporary poetic drama is an excellent example of what can be done by the poet in this area.

DIDACTIC SUBJECTS

Poetry is no longer used for the purely didactic subject, although the didactic element, in the sense of the pointing of morals, occurs incidentally in lyric and other forms of verse. In its largest sense, the aim of all literature is in part didactic. However, the direct teaching of lessons and imparting of information is now confined to textbooks, encyclopedias, technical manuals, and other practical guides.

DESCRIPTIVE SUBJECTS

Extended description, without the element of narrative, has a class of poetry all its own — descriptive poetry — but it is a limited category. Descriptive passages, that is, the description of nature, people, and phenomena, are an integral part of the narrative technique, for without them understanding of the personae and the setting of the action would be lacking and much of the interest of the story would be lost. Brief descriptive poems are frequently classed as lyrics, for they are likely to contain a subcurrent of subjective feeling which takes them out of the purely descriptive category.

It is often forgotten that although descriptive writing, important as it is, is usually a subordinate element in creative literature, it is a major form in scientific writing, much of which has a purely descriptive function.

Description is an important element in the creation of the image and the symbol in literature. It is usually concerned with sensory impressions rendered with truth and vividness to recreate the object described in the mind of the reader with a heightened sense of reality.

SUBJECTS OF LYRIC POETRY

The subjects of lyric poetry are of the widest range and diversity. They are not large in the sense that they require extremely long treatment, but they may be subjects whose implications widen to eternity. Philosophical reflections, flashes of incisive vision or understanding, subjective emotional reactions, all colored and animated by the transforming power of the imagination — these and many more come under the general heading of lyric poetry. In general, lyric writing is a very special kind of exposition — the explanation of a mood or feeling or the development of a personal idea. It may and usually does include other kinds of writing, in particular, descriptive passages; it sometimes includes dialogue or seems to be spoken as a monologue.

Kinds of lyric poetry that are defined in terms of their verse form have been treated in Chapter III. There are also certain kinds that are designated partly or wholly according to their subject matter.

Ode and Elegy

Two such kinds of lyric poetry are the ode and the elegy, although, as we have seen in Chapter III, certain kinds of odes are also distinguished according to verse form. The ode is said to be a "lyrical poem of exalted emotions"; its exaltation is invariably connected with the praise or celebration of the subject to which the ode is dedicated. The elegy, which is also written in an elevated tone, is a poem of lament for someone (or something) dead and gone.

The first stanza of Keats' "Ode to a Nightingale," already cited in Chapter III as an example of the stanzaic (or Horatian) ode, shows very well the ecstatic and exalted tone of the form.

Charles Mills Gayley writes in *Methods and Materials of Literary Criticism*, "The ideal content [of the ode] ... is highly imaginative and varied, whether the purpose be the celebration of some occasion or merely the development of an idea."

The Epitaph

The epitaph is another lyric form that is distinguished according to its subject matter; it deals with and sums up a completed life. Originally it was meant as a funerary inscription, but it has been developed extensively as a literary form since the earliest times. Many of the lyrics in the *Greek Anthology*, for example, are epitaphs. Sometimes the epitaph is epigrammatic, humorous, or satirical in nature, and sometimes it is dramatic and moving, as are the lyrics in *The Spoon River Anthology*, by Edgar Lee Masters.

The Epigram

The epigram is a brief lyric poem that deals with a single subject in a pithy, witty way; its content may be said to be wit. In general, it summarizes or epitomizes its subject — puts it into a nutshell or characterizes it in an unforgettable way. Like all wit, it appeals to the mind rather than to the emotions. With the epigram, we verge on the territory of the satirical or light and humorous manner in verse. An example is the following quatrain.

SURGEONS MUST BE VERY CAREFUL

Surgeons must be very careful
When they take the knife!
Underneath their fine incisions
Stirs the Culprit — *Life!*
—Emily Dickinson

VIEWPOINT AND MANNER

There is a considerable class of poetry that involves an entirely different way of handling material. In this category, a transforming and overriding viewpoint on the part of the author produces satirical or light and humorous verse.

SATIRE

In satirical poetry, which has had a long history in both Occident and Orient, the satirical attitude is adopted by the writer who wishes to expose the weakness and vice of society or of individuals through ridicule, usually in order to awaken the public conscience and bring about reform. A satire may deal with narrative, dramatic, descriptive, or expository material. Whatever its subject, it is treated in terms of wit, irony, farce, and sometimes bitter laughter. The satirical writer is, to a greater or less degree, angry, and he strives to express his critical vision in memorable terms that bite deeply.

Satire is likely to be dry and earth-bound rather than imaginative and soaring. Elizabeth Drew says, "Satire is in fact the most mundane form of poetry and comes closest to our common judgments as social beings."

Vigorous and angry, or witty and urbane, satire has the power to disillusion the reader or to influence him to take sides in political and social controversy. Dryden, Pope, Swift, and Byron in past centuries in England and John Betjeman and W. H. Auden in this century are satirical writers whose work will repay the student's attention. Aristophanes was the greatest Greek satirical dramatist, and the biting satires of Molière and other French dramatists are well known.

A brief example may be chosen from Swift's satirical "Verses on the Death of Dr. Swift, D.S.P.D.":

> My female Friends, whose tender Hearts
> Have better learned to act their Parts,
> Receive the News in *doleful Dumps*,
> "The Dean is dead, (*and what is Trumps?*)...."

LIGHT AND HUMOROUS VERSE

The light and humorous attitude toward life is exemplified in verse by many writers who are at bottom serious, who seem to say, like the eternal clown, that one might as well laugh as cry before the spectacle of life's tragedy.

Light and humorous verse may take up any kind of subject, narrative, descriptive, lyric, or mock didactic, but instead of the bitterness and anger of satire, it treats its material with gentle or raucous fun. It interprets life lightly, and aims to arouse a smile or a laugh in the reader. Its humor can be wry, and it can even deal with a horrendous mock bloodthirstiness, but it never smites to kill as satire often does.

ELEMENTS OF SUBJECT MATTER

THE IMAGE

It seems at first glance that everybody knows what an image is, but in actuality the image is not so simple in poetry. It is a graphic description or representation of an object so vividly rendered that its reality seems immediate. All the five senses may be called into play, or the one or two whose apprehension of the image in question are most vivid; in particular, of course, visual comprehension is recreated.

Ezra Pound, who was the main advocate of the imagist movement wrote: "An 'image' is that which presents an intellectual or emotional complex in an instant of time." The original "rules" of the imagist movement spoke of the "direct treatment of the 'thing,' whether subjective or objective."

The image, then, is like an instantaneous snapshot of an object, thing, or state of mind. It is vividly present. It is important in itself; if it has a premonitory or general significance it is implicit rather than explicit. The image is *presented;* though it often raises further thoughts or echoes in the mind, it is not weakened or watered down by discussion. For the imagist movement, the image was the whole point of poetry. The influence of that movement has done much to strip subsequent poetry of vagueness and generalities, and the image is of prime importance in the subject matter of contemporary poetry.

Usually, however, the image is a vehicle to build a mood or to convey feeling or thought, as in Amy Lowell's "Patterns." Only rarely, as in the Japanese haiku, is the image presented totally without context, and left to echo hauntingly in the mind. This was the imagist's theory of what the image ought to do, but the practice of the movement was usually somewhat closer to conventional usage.

Imagery can bring before us all kinds of intense impressions—heat, cold, sickness, health, and other states of being — in a combination of sensory stimuli. Of all images, visual ones are the most frequent. "The blue and yellow flowers stood up proudly in the sun" is a piece of visual imagery, while "the plopping of the waterdrops" in the same poem ("Patterns," by Amy Lowell, a leader of the imagist movement) is auditory, one can almost hear them plop, since the word is an onomatopoeic one. "The sliding of the water | Seems the stroking of a dear | Hand..." (from "Patterns") is definitely tactile in effect. Imagery that calls on the senses of taste and smell is rarer, but examples are not difficult to find. Keats' "whose strenuous tongue | Can burst Joy's grape against his palate fine" ("Ode on Melancholy") is a vivid gustatory image. Wallace Stevens, in writing "when the grapes | Made sharp air sharper by their smell" ("A Postcard from the Volcano"), is appealing to the olfactory faculty of his readers to make clear the particular sharpness of that autumn air.

THE SYMBOL

The symbol is an image used symbolically, which is to say that it means something more than itself. Its importance lies in the hidden meaning, rather than the surface significance.

The French symbolists wrote poetry which on the surface made no sense; its meaning was supposed to be conveyed " directly " to the subconscious mind by the symbolic meaning or effect of the words. The modern symbolist does not always go that far. His symbols are often meaningful on a logical level, and whether they are universal symbols, like certain well-established symbols in Christian iconography, or personal symbols, they are likely to be recognizable. Certain objects are laden with deep symbolical meaning for certain poets — for Yeats the tower, for Edith Sitwell the rose, for T. S. Eliot the city.

However, much obscurity in modern poetry is caused by obscure symbols. When T. S. Eliot, in " Ash Wednesday, " introduces three white leopards, it is unclear what these animals symbolize, if anything, and just what they are doing in the poem — except that they have apparently just finished eating the poet. The passage in which they appear is enormously effective, a change and contrast to what went before, but the symbols are mysterious. Perhaps that is all they are meant to be — part of the mystery about which he is writing.

NEW SUBJECTS

PSYCHOLOGY

The conscious exploration of the unconscious mind has become a major pre-occupation of lyric poetry since Freud revolutionized the concepts of psychology at the end of the last century and the beginning of this one. "The Love Song of J. Alfred Prufrock," by T. S. Eliot, is one of the first great poems on this theme, and many others have been written since.

The exploration of the human psyche has always been a favorite subject of literature, since human motives and dilemmas are major elements not only of plot, but of history. Freud used situations of mythology and classical drama to state his concepts, such as the "Oedipus complex," which refers to the tragic fate of Oedipus in the trilogy of Theban dramas by Sophocles. Oedipus was fated to kill his father and marry his mother, and efforts to avert this fate were in vain.

The emphasis placed by the concept of democracy on the rights of the individual human being perhaps readied people for profound probing into the psychological self; another age might have found such a preoccupation trifling. Is Prufrock an ineffectual, indecisive individual? A Napoleon might rejoin with an impatient "So what? Away with him!" The spotlight used to be on the Napoleonic heroes of this world, who were seen even larger than life, and from without. It is now on the Prufrocks, the antiheroes; it probes into the hidden recesses of their minds in an effort to explain the sources of their failures. Since more members of the population are antiheroes than heroes, this direction of interest ought to strike a popular chord. However, what is significant about Prufrock comes from Eliot; Prufrock in the hands of a lesser writer would be of little interest. Napoleon is more fascinating, in himself, than Mr. Milquetoast, and there is a limit to how far it is possible to develop the antihero in literature.

THE CHALLENGE OF SCIENCE

Poetry has not been able to do much with the staggering advances of physical science in the twentieth century, except in interpreting the climate of the age, which has been materially revolutionized and intellectually overwhelmed by science. This inability to cope with science is not confined to poetry — philosophy has not managed very well either. Our age seems tragically fragmented because nobody has succeeded in digesting the brute facts of our existence as they have evolved with terrifying rapidity.

The borderline between fact and fiction, scientific observation and fevered hallucinations, is sometimes now difficult to distinguish. Scientists as well as crackpots take the sightings of flying saucers seriously. The further penetration of science reveals ever-deeper realms of the unknown beyond. Meanwhile, the masses of people everywhere, like children who are astonished at nothing because everything is new and strange anyway, have absorbed the products and machines of science into their daily lives.

If it is true that our civilization is split into several cultures that are unable to communicate with one another — the world of science versus the world of humanism — a real need exists to bring the parts together again into a functioning whole. The poets, with their leaps of vision and intuitive understanding, are uniquely equipped to perform this function, for great poetry possesses the art of seeing the world whole to a greater extent than any other literary form. Because of the leaps of imagination that poetry wields, it is capable of a synthesizing vision, as in the works of Dante and Milton, and a profound and revelatory insight, as in Tennyson's "In Memoriam" or T. S. Eliot's "Four Quartets." The poets, however, have been retreating, in the main, into private worlds of analysis and description on a personal level. A few reflections concerning "the mushroom cloud," which has already become a stereotype, and many well-written reactions of fear and horror, beg the question rather than deal with it.

Science is without doubt the most challenging and difficult subject of our day. It would not be sensible to argue that it is the poet's duty to become a scientist in his pursuit of understanding. Yet, short of that, one wonders whether understanding is possible. Can a poet who is not a scientist learn enough about science so that it is a real part of his intellectual world? Until the present time this has been abnormally difficult; the atomic age, however, was ushered in only a few short years ago. Perhaps perspective may come with more time and further experience.

It is up to the poets of the latter decades of the twentieth century to try to reconcile the scientific and humanistic worlds of the intellect and to incorporate them both into the whole vision of poetry. Possibly it will require a new Milton to do the job.

HOW TO FIND A SUBJECT

The poet is, at least to a certain extent, a player with words, and he makes what Auden has referred to as a "verbal contraption." Words are to him what clay is to the sculptor, a tangible material. To what degree a poem is fashioned as a vehicle for an idea and to what degree as a verbal bauble created out of sheer exuberance varies with the poet and the occasion of the particular poem. Does the poet always begin by having a subject clear-cut in his mind, and is his poem simply a way of saying what he has to say? The testimony of the poets themselves indicates that this is not usually the case. A poem may begin with a line or with a phrase, and the poet may feel his way to the poem's final shape without having much idea how it is going to turn out. He knows the direction he is going in, but is not sure where he will end up. Poetry is different in this way from prose, which is primarily a vehicle for meaning; poetry "should not mean, but be," as Archibald MacLeish said in his "Ars Poetica." This is an extreme statement that could not be completely supported by logic, but there is some truth in it.

Because of the nature of poetry-writing, then, a poet does not necessarily start out with a full-blown idea — he may begin with a feeling in his bones or a tickle in the end of his right index finger. In that case, he must cast around for a point of departure, a word, an image, or a remembered moment of illumination, to use as a springboard to plunge into his poem.

THE POET'S WORKING NOTEBOOK

It is an excellent thing for a poet to keep a working notebook or a card catalogue of ideas, lines, and passages from poems that never came to anything, as well as clippings from newspapers — in fact, anything that may serve to start him off on his next poem. He should always be on the *qui vive* for anything he thinks he might use. Above all, he should jot down information and ideas as they come to him; a small pocket notebook for jottings is a prime necessity. Many a poem has been lost because the poet did not put down his idea on the wing, and a mere noted phrase would have kept it for him.

The habit of clipping articles and references from newspapers and magazines is a good one. Did someone say something particularly incisive about the preservation of wilderness lands? Have a billion tons of grain disappeared into thin air? Anything that seems interesting to the poet can be grist to his mill, and he should make sure that he stores up enough material so that there is something to grind when the wheels start turning.

However, not all poets are methodical in keeping notes and papers, and there may come a day when even the best kept notebook seems to have nothing more to offer. What is the poet to do in that case?

One of the main fears of any artist is that his well of creativity will run dry, that suddenly he may not have any more pictures to paint or poems to write, as the case may be. For the poet, there are various ways to prime the pump, and he should take action without delay to get things going again.

THE SUBJECT CHECK LIST

A device that the poet may use in thinking over future projects is a general but personal check list of common subjects of lyric poetry. Such a list need not be unduly extensive, and the poet will fill in whatever details are of special interest to him, as well as specific ideas jotted down for future verses. In general, the list should be suggestive rather than exhaustive. The main headings of the poet's list might eventually serve as the basis for the arrangement of his first book.

The poet must build up his own check list, and for every poet it will be somewhat different, according to his interests. All that will be attempted here is to suggest a few general headings which might serve as a beginning.

People, since poems about people are always interesting when the subject is presented in a vivid and particularized way. Five kinds of poems about people are frequently seen in print:

1. A glimpse that reveals the whole person, a portrait of a particular person engaged in some characteristic activity (an example is "Mr. Flood's Party," by Edwin Arlington Robinson);

2. A whole life or career summed up (examples are "Richard Cory" or "Miniver Cheevy," by Edwin Arlington Robinson, the poems in the *Spoon River Anthology,* by Edgar Lee Masters, or "The Ballad of William Sycamore," by Stephen Vincent Benét);

3. A poem to or about a beloved person (examples are "Upon a Dying Lady," by Yeats, and "To Helen," by Poe);

4. A historic personage (an example is "Abraham Lincoln Walks at Midnight," by Vachel Lindsay);

5. A group of people — a family, a school class, an athletic team, or neighbors, with all their ironical and revealing contrasts.

The *human predicament,* especially one's own predicament. Examples are "Let No Charitable Hope," by Elinor Wylie, and "Isolation," by Matthew Arnold.

Landscapes, with or without figures. Examples are "The Lake Isle of Innisfree," by Yeats; "Stopping by Woods," by Robert Frost; "The Sea," by Byron; and "The Tide Rises, the Tide Falls," by Longfellow.

Animals. Examples are "The Cow in Apple Time," by Robert Frost, "Ode on the Death of a Favorite Cat," by Thomas Gray, and "On the Naming of Cats" and "The Hippopotamus," by T. S. Eliot.

Philosophy and Religion. Examples are "Ash Wednesday," by T. S. Eliot, "Ode on the Morning of Christ's Nativity," by Milton, "Batter My Heart, Three-Person'd God," by Donne, and "Brahma," by Emerson.

Art and Poetry. Examples are "Musée des Beaux Arts," by W. H. Auden, "Ode," by Arthur O'Shaughnessy, and "Not Marble Nor the Gilded Monuments," by Shakespeare.

Science and Scientists. The poet must provide examples in this field — up to now there are practically none available.

The poet should continue his check list, adding general categories and specific instances as they occur to him.

VII

Style

WHAT IS STYLE?

What is style? One definition would be: "how the verbal contraption is held together." *Webster's Third New International Dictionary* puts it this way: "style — the aspects of literary composition that are concerned with mode and form of expression as distinguished from content or message." It is clear from these definitions that the devices of prosody are instruments of poetic style, and that this is what concerned us for the first four chapters. Now, however, we are to return to the subject of style in its widest sense, not as prosody, but as general use of language. Although the techniques of versewriting are indispensable to the poet, they would not get him far if he were unable to compose distinctive sentences or wield the primary tool of writing, vocabulary, in a fresh and exact way. Style in this sense is an intensely individual thing. It may not be the man, but it reveals the man. It is, in a way, the tone of his written voice and the visible sign of how his mind works.

Style in works of literature can be analyzed, and the sources of an author's characteristic rhythm of thought and language can be identified in such matters as his use of periodic and simple sentences, the richness of his vocabulary, and his use of figures of speech. Yet such analysis is an *ex post facto* procedure. How should an author go about forming a style? And if he is a poet, should he approach the search in a manner different from that of the writer of prose? Style is no less important to one than to the other; but although writers in both mediums share the search, the problems they face vary considerably.

ATTITUDE

It may seem strange to set out on the quest for style with a discussion of the writer's attitude, but this is so basic that it colors everything he writes. Fundamental to it is the sense of dedication that animates most serious writers, and poets perhaps more than any others. Indeed, it is a sense of being "called" that keeps poets going, for the material rewards of poetry have always been conspicuously few, and are now less than ever.

The lyric poet finds much of his material in general autobiographical incident and in his own ideas and emotions, yet he must be careful to place the emphasis in his poems more on the idea or the emotion he wishes to communicate than on himself. The "I" of a lyric poem must be someone with whom the reader can identify. Whenever possible, this "I" must stand aside. He is the experiencer and the relater, but it is the thing experienced that is the real point of the poem. When Yeats writes, "I shall arise and go now, and go to Innisfree, | And a small cabin build there, of clay and wattles made," the emphasis is upon Innisfree and the cabin, upon the vision of escape to a simpler world which is a universal longing and with which the reader can identify. The "I" is therefore read by the reader as himself, rather than as Yeats, and thus attains the stature of a universal entity.

One danger in lyric poetry, as in any autobiographical or confessional writing, is that the writer may reveal (or seem to reveal) himself as egotistical and self-engrossed. Thus the would-be poet must try to take an objective view of his poetry, to make sure that what he has to say is really of interest in itself, and not to inject his own presence any more than is absolutely necessary. Even though he is, in the last analysis, writing about himself, he must be careful not to use the first-person-singular pronoun any more than is absolutely necessary. It is a good idea to bring other characters into the poem when possible, and to prefer any other pronoun, if it makes sense, to the ubiquitous "I."

Objectivity, modesty, sincerity, and seriousness of purpose are the qualities of attitude with which the poet must start. Sometimes a well-known poet, like Dylan Thomas, leads the kind of flamboyant and notorious life which would seem to deny these qualities, but life should not be confused with art; if one examines this poet's work carefully it is apparent that modesty and sincerity animate his poetry. His life was his own business, but his poetry belongs to the world—and not the other way around.

FORM AND DESIGN

Form and design are necessary parts of style, both in the construction of a work and in that of a paragraph or sentence. The traditional forms of poetry provide a choice of designs; the sonnet form, for example, can help the poet achieve his poem and at the same time develop his sense of form and balance. It is important to choose a form appropriate to the subject; otherwise the poet may find himself like a woodcarver working against the grain of the wood. The form should also be appropriate to the size of the idea; extensive material will not fit into a sonnet, nor would a sonnet idea be sufficient for a sestina.

Within the form chosen for the poem the subject should be well defined and organized. In a set form, the shape and development of the subject work out in a kind of counterpoint with the form. Free verse is composed freely for the express purpose of fitting the contours of the subject. Since poetry, like music, is a temporal art and has extension in time, it must be conceived with a beginning, a middle, and an end. These parts usually correspond with an introduction, a development, and a climax (or climax-plus-resolution).

A simple lyric by William Blake may be used to illustrate such organization of material in a poem.

LONDON

I wander through each chartered street,
Near where the chartered Thames does flow,
And mark in every face I meet
Marks of weakness, marks of woe.

In every cry of every man,
In every infant's cry of fear,
In every voice, in every ban,
The mind-forged manacles I hear:

How the chimney-sweeper's cry
Every blackening church appalls,
And the hapless soldier's sigh
Runs in blood down palace walls.

But most, through midnight streets I hear
How the youthful harlot's curse
Blasts the new-born infant's tear,
And blights with plagues the marriage hearse.
—William Blake

Stanza 1 states the subject, a walk through the streets of London, and the theme of the human misery of the city. Stanzas 2 and 3 develop the theme further, each image becoming more powerful. Stanza 4 reaches the climax: the harlot's cry (human prostitution) blights both newborn infant and the marriage "hearse" (what is supposed to be good in life). It is easy to see the progression in this poem as it builds in intensity to the terrible curse of the last stanza and the ruin it brings down upon ordinary life.

Occasionally a poem may be developed in two or more parallel parts, rather than in the cumulative structure described in the previous paragraph. In parallel structure, the subject is essentially a comparison or contrast between two or more elements, and the poem need not rise to a climax at all. Such a poem is likely to be brief and pithy, and to appeal to the intellect rather than the emotions.

One example of a poem with such structure — and this one does appeal to sentiment — is the following.

MISCONCEPTIONS

This is a spray the Bird clung to,
　　Making it blossom with pleasure,
Ere the high tree-top she sprung to,
　　Fit for her nest and her treasure.
　　Oh, what a hope beyond measure
Was the poor spray's, which the flying feet hung to,—
So to be singled out, built in, and sung to!

This is a heart the Queen leant on,
　　Thrilled in a minute erratic,
Ere the true bosom she bent on,
　　Meet for love's regal dalmatic.*
　　Oh, what a fancy ecstatic
Was the poor heart's, ere the wanderer went on—
Love to be saved for it, proffered to, spent on!

　　　　　　　　　　—Robert Browning

DICTION

THREE CRITERIA FOR THE RIGHT WORD

In poetry, the individual word must be chosen for its exact meaning, invisible aura of connotations, and music. The choice of the right words is crucial in getting a poem off the ground and making it soar into poetry. There is something mysterious about the way one combination of words is memorable and another is not, and teachers often delight in rewriting famous passages to show how flat they would be in any other form. Yet certain qualities are usually present in the memorable phrase. It is likely to be particular rather than general, to be concise, and to have rhythm as well as a touch of alliteration or assonance or both.

THE WORDS SHOULD BE KEPT IN TONE

The words in a poem should be kept in tone, or in the same key, except when a writer intends to produce an effect of shock or discord. As in music, the writer can modulate from one key into another — but he must not strike false notes.

In general, the language of a poem can be literary (which includes the dignified vocabulary of more or less formal writing, the rhetorical flights of a Whitman, or the poetic flights of a Shelley), or it can be familiar, including the contractions, short cuts, familiar and dialect expressions, and even slang and colorful language of ordinary speech. At one end of the spectrum stands Milton's grand style; at

*A king's or prelate's robe, worn on state occasions.

the other, certain contemporary versewriters who try to reproduce the usages of the street.

As an example of tone in poetry, one might well think of the work of Robert Frost, written in so natural a vocabulary that it appears easy at first sight, although further reading reveals its depth. "My little horse must think it queer | To stop without a farmhouse near" is a very simple statement, couched in Frost's usual short words; yet the poem it comes from, "Stopping by Woods on a Snowy Evening," haunts the memory. The tone of Frost's poetry is the tone of a voice speaking, dry and matter-of-fact, yet soaring over all barriers. His vocabulary is literary, but close to the dividing line between the literary and the familiar.

T. S. Eliot uses contrasting words and concepts deliberately, and we have "One-night cheap hotels" and "sawdust restaurants" on streets "like a tedious argument | Of insidious intent." However, there is nothing shocking or out of key in mixing these words. Eliot does not call the hotels "fleabags," which would be out of tone; "one-night cheap hotel" is composed of acceptable literary words, while fleabag is a slang term. Eliot's use of contrast involves a mixture of the specific, often sordid image with an abstract concept expressed in complicated words; the image is usually expressed at least partially in words of Anglo-Saxon origin, while the concept is expressed in words of Latin origin, words further removed from the texture of everyday life than the former.

A "jazz" poet might write a verse in which the word "fleabag" would be quite at home, along with the argot of jazz music, the entertainment world, and perhaps dope addiction, drink, and prostitution. The ballades of François Villon, in another place and another time, dealt with this racy kind of world. Verse written on such subjects necessarily has its own tone.

Colloquial words are out of tone in a poem couched in formal literary words or written in a vein of high seriousness, but in a more familiarly pitched poem, such as a folk ballad, they may be just right.

Slang should always be handled with care in literature, for it has explosive qualities. It must either be kept in tone with the poem (a jazz poem, for example) or used for its shock value. The poet should bear in mind that slang becomes dated very quickly; although ten or fifty years hence may seem a long way in the future, he should consider what the use of slang will do to his poem then. Will it still be vivid, or will it be merely incomprehensible?

Nouns and active verbs are strong and direct agents in poetry as in prose, and are to be recommended for carrying the main burden of the meaning.

In spite of all that has been said against the excessive use of adjectives and adverbs, they are both full of magic properties when used with just the right force and music. The invariable epithet as used by Homer, whose ocean was always "wine-dark" and whose dawn was always "rosy-fingered," has fallen into disuse with a few mannered exceptions, but the single powerful adjective, as used in Yeat's phrase "the bee-loud glade," still has what it takes to make poetry.

The terse words of Anglo-Saxon origin are in general stronger and more familiar in English than those of Latin or Romance derivation, which impart a literary or learned flavor to writing in which they predominate. This fact can be enormously helpful to the ballad writer, for example, who should in general prefer the Anglo-Saxon word where he has a choice. However, no writer need be afraid of the Romance word, and most good writing has elements of both streams of English vocabulary in it. Whether one writes "come" or "approach," "eat" or "consume," not to mention "brittle" or "frangible," is often a matter of which best fits the metrical and sound patterns of a line. The writer in English is fortunate in having this double vocabulary at his disposal, for it furnishes him with twice as many words as the other major modern languages from which to choose.

Wordiness, of course, is to be avoided. The diction of modern poetry is in general simple and direct; floweriness has gone out, if, indeed, it was ever "in." A certain sparseness in style has become popular, but there is nothing wrong with the more fully rounded style of a Dylan Thomas or a Thomas Wolfe.

Although every word must tell in prose, in poetry every word counts double, both for meaning and music. Therefore extra words in poetry seem twice as extra, if such a thing is possible. The line should never be padded with an extra word for the sake of the meter or the rhyme — it will be painfully apparent. The poet who is willing to work long and hard enough on a recalcitrant line can usually work out the thorniest problem of prosody without verbal padding. Sometimes this requires the introduction of a new idea, but never of an extra word.

The vivid and particular word and concept should always be preferred to the vague and general one. If an individual example is substituted for a general whole, the lines will usually come alive.

Trite words and phrases should be avoided. Clichés have been debased, like bad coinage, by inflated use; they have thus lost the full force of their meaning and effectiveness. Lovely, pretty, fair, nice, sweet, and awful, for example, are trite words, as are many other general and overworked adjectives. In fact, it is these words and others like them that have been responsible to a large extent for discrediting all adjectives, a reaction that is illogical, but understandable.

The ever-ready little clichés spring into action whenever the writer's mind relaxes for an instant; thus words and figures of speech that come to mind with too much facility should be closely scrutinized. What one has read or heard is recalled all too easily, so that frequently one has to probe relentlessly for real meaning and real words of his own.

The "poetic" words and contractions were done to death in the last century and early in this one, but some of them linger on. Such contractions as e'er, ne'er, 'tis, 'twas, 'gainst, 'gan, and 'neath, as well as shortened forms of words such as morn, ope, oft, and yon, even though they are found throughout the poetry of earlier periods than our own, are now considered bad style. Archaic words, such as ere, affright, bark (for boat), wight, wroth, and ruth, and archaic verb and pronoun forms, such as hath, hast, doth, dost, singeth, singest, and thou, thee, thy, and ye, are also out of use.

Current jargon is also composed of clichés, even though it may sound deliciously up-to-date to the inexperienced writer. "Grass roots" and "a two-way street" have the merit of being figurative language, but, unfortunately, by being on everybody's tongue, they have lost the freshness they may once have possessed.

The advertising slogan can kill a phrase faster than any other weapon, and if a new kind of cosmetic is widely proclaimed to have "the velvet touch," that phrase has to be outlawed from serious writing from then on, probably for our lifetime. Clichés can be made overnight in the mass media of our day that spoil many perfectly good words for a generation.

Words that are a sort of touchstone for a famous poet — like "numinous" for W. H. Auden — are very tempting to the poetry lover, but they should be firmly eschewed. One sees the word "numinous" in verse and criticism wherever one looks these days. Such a word is in danger of becoming current jargon.

The writer should always remember that it is plagiarism to borrow another poet's phrases. Yeats wrote that "peace comes dropping slow" in a famous poem, and anybody else says that something "comes dropping slow" at his own peril.

There are other words or expressions that leap into fashion in some inexplicable way from time to time, and which everybody who wishes to appear to be in the know uses *ad nauseam*. A few years ago "permissive" was such a word, and a little more recently all conversation hissed with the word "this," which for a while replaced the pronouns "it" and "that" in all uses. Faddish words and expressions of this kind are also clichés, and should be avoided by the careful writer.

GRAMMAR AND SYNTAX

A handbook of English grammar is a useful item for the writer's bookself, and much can be learned from such a brief guide as Strunk and White's *Elements of Style*. One who is born to a language and enjoys writing it usually has the illusion that he knows it perfectly, and may be surprised when it comes to revising what he has written. It is amazing how a brief review of a text on grammar can clarify matters and firm up one's approach to his work.

The poet is not excused from the rules of grammar, and an E. E. Cummings must know exactly what he is doing when he occasionally takes liberties with them. Since most readers, in these hard days, have lost the habit of reading poetry or are easily discouraged, it is more than ever necessary that the poet should wield the tools of grammar effectively, and should have his words, phrases, and clauses in good syntactical order to be understood or to pose his riddle.

The simple sentences of a Hemingway, the extremely long and involved sentences of a Proust or a Faulkner, the stately periodic sentences of a Milton, all have the stamp of their author's individual style. Variation in the construction of sentences provides endless modulation of tempo, and every writer should devote careful attention to this element of composition. The artless innocence of a loose compound sentence is effective in a ballad, while the mounting elegance of the periodic sentence is at home in the formal ode or elegy. The varied music of several types of sentences can come to a stunning climax in the stark statement of a simple sentence at a peak of emotion or tension.

Parallelism is a rule for the construction of sentences containing coordinate elements; its music is familiar to all English readers because of its use in the Bible. Indeed, it is a strong element in all Hebrew literature. Listen to the Beatitudes:

> Blessed are the poor in spirit: for theirs is the kingdom of heaven.
> Blessed are they that mourn: for they shall be comforted.
> Blessed are the meek: for they shall inherit the earth.
> Blessed are they which do hunger and thirst after righteousness: for they shall
> be filled.

Is not this kind of incantatory magic part of the very essence of poetry?

No style comes about automatically; style has to be endlessly worked at and improved, and no instrument of style requires more attention or repays it better than sentence structure.

FIGURES OF SPEECH AND FIGURATIVE LANGUAGE

Both imagination and intelligence come into play in the employment of figures of speech in composition. What is a figure of speech? It is the use of a word or a longer expression in an imaginative rather than a literal way. And what is the object of using figures of speech? Their use is at the same time practical, as a means of definition, and aesthetic, as the means of making the specific passage of a composition more lively and pleasing.

Whereas the modern prose writer is careful not to use too many figures of speech, the poet seeks ever more effective figurative language, for imagination is the breath of life to poetry.

METAPHOR AND SIMILE

Metaphor and simile are the two main figures of speech. They are found everywhere, in everyday speech as well as in prose and poetry.

A simile makes an explicit comparison between two things of a different kind or quality, usually introduced by "like" or "as." An example is "The voice returns *like the insistent out-of-tune | Of a broken violin on an August afternoon*," from Part II of "Preludes," by T. S. Eliot.

In metaphor the comparison is implied, and one thing is said actually to be another or to function as another. *Webster's Third New International Dictionary* calls it "a figure of speech in which a word or phrase literally denoting one kind of object or idea is used in place of another by way of suggesting a likeness between them (the ship *plows* the sea)." Many verbs are thus used metaphorically, as when the teakettle sings, the motorcar purrs or hums, and the wind whispers in the trees. A great fighter is said to be a lion in battle (metaphor) or to fight like a lion (simile).

In everyday life, people use metaphor and simile constantly. Many figurative expressions are so common that nobody is conscious of using imaginative language— hot as blazes, slow as molasses in January, dumb as a post, hard as pulling teeth. "To get on one's high horse" is a metaphorical expression, as is "to be knocked all of a heap," for neither phrase means what it says literally. The universal human need for colorful language is satisfied by such expressions, even though they soon become hackneyed.

Probably the main reason why comparisons are used in literature is to express exact shades of meaning, for the literal meanings of words often are not sufficiently differentiated to give the nuance that is desired. Though English has so many more words than the other major languages, the words are still insufficient to express all possible shades of meaning.

The perception of likenesses and relationships is a major function of intelligence, as any taker of intelligence tests will remember. To find new and unexpected relationships and likenesses is a property of the imaginative intelligence that is extremely useful in writing poetry. Metaphor and simile are more than mere stylistic devices, they are also an element of subject matter and of thought. Here are a few examples:

Metaphors

> "I too knitted the old knot of contrariety" — Walt Whitman.
>
> "And the waves, the waves were soldiers moving" — Wallace Stevens.
>
> "Then is my daily life a narrow room" — Edna St. Vincent Millay.

Similes

> "Thou, from whose presence the leaves dead
> Are driven, like ghosts from an enchanter fleeing"
> > —Percy Bysshe Shelley.
>
> "Now the chimney was all of the house that stood,
> Like a pistil after the petals go. "
> > —Robert Frost.

"He stood there in the middle of the road
Like Roland's ghost winding a silent horn"
    —Edwin Arlington Robinson.

Three Warnings

1. The writer should not try too hard for a fresh comparison, for it is possible to strain the bounds of likelihood to such a point that the simile or metaphor is unbelievable, grotesque, or distasteful.

2. He should not employ similes or metaphors too vague to be meaningful, as Shelley did when he wrote, "Like an unbodied joy whose race is just begun." What is an unbodied joy? What kind of race could possibly be meant?

3. He should not employ mixed metaphors, in which the poet begins by speaking of his subject in one set of terms and in the same breath ends with another set, creating an absurd jumble; he should take his metaphors one at a time, and should be consistent.

PERSONIFICATION

Personification is a figure of speech in which an institution, quality, natural object, or other nonhuman attribute is represented as a person. It was common in the poetry of past centuries, and although it has gone out of style to a considerable extent at present, it is still used more than one would expect. All pageants depend on it. The Mississippi is still called "the father of waters," and one's college or university is still called the "alma mater," or fostering mother.

Emerson used personification when he wrote, in "Days":

> Daughters of Time, the hypocritic Days
> Muffled and dumb, like barefoot dervishes,
> And marching single in an endless file,
> Bring diadems and faggots in their hands.

METONYMY

Metonymy is the substitution of the name of an object for that of something else, usually a larger concept, to which it is related. Examples are "scepter" for "sovereignty," "the ring" for "boxing," and so on.

SYNECHDOCHE

Synechdoche gives the part instead of the whole, as in "fifty head" for "fifty cattle." Shakespeare used it in Sonnet LXXI when he wrote:

> Nay, if you read this line, remember not
> The *hand* that writ it.

Both metonymy and synechdoche make writing more vivid by substituting the particular for the more general. "The ring" is more picturesque than " boxing," and "the hand that writ it" is more specific and more vivid than "him who writ it."

LITOTES

Litotes is the name of a whimsical kind of understatement which affirms something by denying its opposite, as in the statement "Shakespeare was not a bad poet."

HYPERBOLE

Hyperbole is a deliberate overstatement or exaggeration for effect, as in "I was fainting from hunger," or "The waves were mountainous, and the ship was constantly ascending or descending a new Mount Everest."

APOSTROPHE

Apostrophe is the direct address, usually exclamatory, of a person or thing, present or absent, for rhetorical effect. The envoi of the ballade form always begins with an apostrophe to the poet's patron or someone else who is connected with the subject of the poem. In apostrophe, the thing addressed is often personified, as in "Hence, loathed Melancholy!" which begins Milton's "L'Allegro." It is frequently a real person, living or dead, as in "Milton! thou shouldst be living at this hour," the beginning of Wordsworth's sonnet on Milton.

ONOMATOPOEIA

Onomatopoeia is the use of words or combinations of words that imitate or suggest the sound being described. This is a figure of speech that is particularly useful in poetry, which depends upon musical effects far more than ordinary writing or ordinary speech.

VISIONS AND REVISIONS

And time yet for a hundred indecisions
And for a hundred visions and revisions...
—T. S. Eliot

It is seldom indeed that a poem turns out to be exactly right in its first version, as Robert Frost tells us that "Stopping by Woods on a Snowy Evening" was when it came to him. Yet, even though the first version can be recognized as not quite final, it usually has qualities of naturalness, spontaneity, and unexpected music, in spite of its roughnesses and imperfections. Sometimes it almost seems as if the poem had been dictated to the poet by some outside power, and the fact that the poet's receptive antennae were not quite perfect accounts for the flaws in it. This is a strange feeling for a poet to have about his work, but almost all poets have it upon occasion; it seems that they cannot account for certains poems consciously at all.

However the first version was produced, in hypnotic trance or otherwise, a second look is likely to show that the poem needs some rewriting. In particular, the poet should scrutinize every word to make sure it is the best one in its particular place, for it is very easy in the heat of writing to put down an approximation of what one means in order to get on with the poem. Such hasty choices should be reconsidered, and the precise word substituted for them.

A second point to look at carefully is whether too much has been said. Is there a repetition? Is one part of the poem weaker than the rest, and could it be omitted without spoiling anything? Perhaps the poem will be strengthened by a little careful cutting.

Care must be taken, however, not to spoil the spontaneity — or impression of spontaneity — of the original version of the poem in revising it. Nothing is more difficult than to tell when the right point has come to stop revising, but the poet should bear in mind that overrevision is a very real danger. It is quite possible to revise all life out of what began as a delightful and spontaneous lyric. A good safeguard is to save the successive versions of the poem for a few days or a few weeks and then look at them again. With better perspective, the poet can doubtless tell if the last round of revision was too drastic, and in that case he can go back to one of his earlier versions.

Rhyming Dictionary

See p. xvii, "How to Use the Rhyming Dictionary"

Ā (ay)

Single (Masculine) Rhymes

Primary or Secondary Accent Falls on Last Syllable; Imperfect Rhymes Are in Italics.

A— 1. a, A, ay, aye, eh.
2. Coué, roué.
3. à pied [F.], mariée [F.]; dossier.
4. couturier [F.], habitué.
BA— 1. bay, bey.
2. abbé [F.], *ambay*, flambé [F.], embay, Bombay, *bomb bay*, obey.
3. dapple bay, disembay, Baffin Bay, Hudson Bay, disobey.
DA— 1. day, dey.
2. *heyday, playday, Mayday, payday, midday,* idée [F.], *Friday, weekday,* undé, *Monday, Sunday, noonday,* today, Lord's Day, *doomsday, Wednesday, Tuesday, Thursday, birthday.*
3. workaday, décédé [F.], wedding day, working day, holiday, everyday, démodé [F.], quarter day, Easter Day, yesterday, Labor Day, Saturday, market day, judgment day, Christmas Day.
4. alackaday.
FA— 1. fay, fey, fe [Sp.].
2. café, parfait, au fait [F.].
3. pousse café [F.], Santa Fe, coryphée, rechauffé [F.].
4. auto-da-fé.
GA— 1. gay, gai [F.].
2. *margay, morgay, nosegay.*
3. distingué, toujours gai [F.].
HA— 1. hay, hey.
2. ahey, *gahe.*
JA— 1. j, J, jay, Jay.
3. popinjay.
KA— 1. k, K, Kay, kay, cay, quai [F.].
2. decay, piqué, okay, bouquet, roquet, croquet, tokay, parquet, ¿por qué? [Sp.], *Biscay,* risqué.
3. appliqué, sobriquet.
4. communiqué.
LA— 1. lay, lai, lei, blé [F.], flay, clay, Clay, play, splay, slay, sley, sleigh.
2. allay, ailé, chalet, Calais, *Malay,* waylay, belay, delay, gelée [F.], melee, *melee,* relay, souffle, *morglay,* inlay, olé [Sp.], soleil [F.],

replay, fair play, *byplay,* display, misplay, *horseplay, parlay,* parler [F.], *bobsleigh,* mislay, *outlay,* coulé [F.].
3. Mandalay, accablé [F.], roundelay, rokelay, virelai [F.], virelay, De Molay, reveille, Chevrolet, underlay, interlay, overlay, rissolé [F.], photoplay, Passion Play etc., underplay, overplay, interplay, pourparler [F.].
4. cabriolet, café-au-lait [F.], au pis aller [F.], coup de soleil [F.], cantabile.
MA— 1. Mae, May.
2. lamé, semé [F.], *gourmet,* dismay.
3. entremets, consommé, resumé.
NA— 1. nay, nee, né, née [both F.], neigh.
2. ainé [F.], Chiné [F.], donnée [F.], tourné [F.].
3. Hogmanay, matinee, satiné, Ciboney, dragonné [F.], raisonné [F.], déjeuner [F.], âme damnée [F.], cloisonné.
4. estaminet [F.].
PA— 1. pay, spay.
2. frappé, epée [F.], repay, prepay, Gaspé, coupé, toupet, toupée.
3. canapé, overpay.
RA— 1. ray, re, rey [Sp.], bray, brae, dray, fray, gray, gré [F.], grey, scray, pray, pré [F.], prey, spray, tray, trey, stray.
2. array, bewray, *chambray,* padre, André, Deirdre, affray, defray, beret, Tigré, *stingray,* doré [F.], *foray, moray,* moiré, soiree, repray, bespray, respray, betray, entrée, portray, astray, estray, distrait, outré [F.], hurray, curé, purée.
3. disarray, liseré, emigree, émigré [F.], dapple gray, iron-gray, silver gray, autospray, Honoré, Monterrey.
4. bon gré mal gré [F.], jeunesse dorée [F.].
SA— 1. say, se.
2. assay, glacé [F.], *naysay,* passé, chassé, essay, essai [F.], blessé [F.], presay, missay, lycée [F.], plissé [F.], gainsay, pensée [F.], in se [L.], unsay, chaussée [F.], *hearsay,*

per se [L.], foresay, *soothsay*.
3. fiancé, fiancée, déclassé [F.], divorcé, divorcée, repoussé [F.], retroussé [F.].
4. ballon d'essai [F.], ex capite [L.].
SHA— 1. shay, chez [F.].
2. cachet, sachet, sashay, cliché, broché, crochet, cherchez [F.], bouchée [F.], touché [F.].
3. panaché, attaché, détaché [F.], ricochet, recherché.
4. papier mâché, à bon marché [F.].
TA— 1. tay, thé [F.], stay.
2. paté [F.], été [F.], astay, *bobstay, backstay, jackstay, mainstay, forestay*, outstay, santé [F.], bonté [F.].
3. comité [F.], exalté [F.], overstay, liberté [F.], déporté [F.], naïveté, velouté [F.].
4. légèreté, égalité, fraternité, éternité [all F.].
5. actualité [F.].
THA— 1. they.
2. Cathay.
VA— 2. pavé [F.], nevé [F.], inveigh, convey, corvée [F.], kurvey, purvey, survey.
3. reconvey, repurvey, resurvey, énervé [F.].
WA— 1. way, wey, Wei, weigh, qua, quey, sway, tway, whey.
2. away, aweigh, *subway, hatchway, archway, headway*, midway, *guideway, roadway, Broadway, leeway*, reweigh, *seaway*, halfway, *gangway, cogway, byway, highway, walkway, railway, hallway, tramway, someway, runway, slipway, fairway, stairway, doorway, crossway, straightway, outway*, outweigh, *pathway, causeway*.
3. breakaway, Rockaway, stowaway, wellaway, runaway, caraway, straightaway, getaway, castaway, cutaway, milky way, entryway, everyway, passageway, cableway, Galloway, underweigh, waterway, overweigh.
WHA— 1. juey, whey.
YA— 1. yea.
2. denier [F.], foyer, croupier [F.], dossier, métier, soigné [F.].
3. ennuyé, escalier, chevalier [all F.].
ZA— 2. blasé, visé.
3. exposé.
4. Champs Élysées.
ZHA— 2. congé [F.], Roget.
3. dégagé [F.], agrégé, protégé, protégée, négligée.

AB— 1. Abe, babe.
3. cosmolabe, astrolabe.
ACH— 1. h, H, aitch.
AD— 1. ade, aid, aide, bade, bayed, fade, hade, jade, cade, lade, laid, blade, flayed, glade, played, sleighed, slade, made, maid, neighed, paid, spade, spayed, raid, braid, brayed, grayed, grade, prayed, preyed, sprayed, trade, strayed, shade, staid, stayed, wade, weighed, suéde, wheyed.
2. gambade, obeyed, forbade, brigade, de-

cayed, alcaide, falcade, cockade, blockade, brocade, stockade, arcade, cascade, allayed, delayed, relayed, relade, relaid, inlaid, unlade, unlaid, parleyed, old-maid, handmade, *handmaid*, remade, self-made, *milkmaid*, homemade, pomade, unmade, *mermaid, bridesmaid*, dismayed, *nursemaid, housemaid*, grenade, apaid, repaid, prepaid, unpaid, postpaid, respade, croupade, arrayed, parade, charade, abrade, unbraid, upbraid, afraid, defrayed, aggrade, degrade, regrade, tirade, besprayed, resprayed, unsprayed, betrayed, retrade, portrayed, estrade, glacéed, passade, chasséd, glissade, torsade, crusade, *sunshade*, crocheted, *nightshade*, sautéed, unstaid, evade, invade, pervade, conveyed, purveyed, surveyed, reweighed, persuade.
3. renegade, orangeade, appliquéd, barricade, cavalcade, ambuscade, escalade, defilade, enfilade, fusillade, accolade, everglade, readymade, dairymaid, undismayed, esplanade, promenade, serenade, marinade, pasquinade, dragonnade, gasconade, colonnade, lemonade, cannonade, carronade, citronade, escapade, gallopade, overpaid, disarrayed, gingerade, masquerade, unafraid, centigrade, retrograde, balustrade, palisade, overweighed.
4. harlequinade, fanfaronade, rodomontade.
AF— 1. chafe, kef, strafe, safe, waif.
2. enchafe, vouchsafe, unsafe.
AFD— 1. chafed, strafed.
2. vouchsafed.
AG— 1. Hague, plague, Prague, vague.
2. fainaigue.
AJ— 1. age, gage, gauge, cage, mage, page, rage, sage, stage, wage, swage.
2. engage, encage, *nonage*, repage, rampage, enrage, outrage, presage, Osage, backstage, *downstage, forestage*, upstage, assuage.
3. overage, disengage.
AJD— 1. aged, gauged, caged, paged, raged, staged, waged.
2. engaged, encaged, repaged, rampaged, enraged, outraged, upstaged, assuaged.
3. disengaged.
AK— 1. ache, bake, fake, hake, haik, jake, cake, lake, flake, slake, make, snake, spake, rake, brake, break, drake, frake, crake, traik, strake, sake, take, stake, steak, wake, quake.
2. *headache, backache, earache, heartache, toothache, clambake, friedcake, hoecake, nocake, shortcake, nutcake, fruitcake*, remake, opaque, *daybreak, windbreak, heartbreak, outbreak, sheldrake, mandrake, muckrake, namesake, keepsake*, forsake, betake, retake, *intake, uptake*, partake, *grubstake, beefsteak*, mistake, *sweepstake*, awake, rewake, *earthquake*.
3. johnnycake, griddlecake, havercake, rattlesnake, undertake, overtake.
AKS— *see* **ĀK**, plus " s " or " 's "; **1.** Aix.
AKT— 1. ached, baked, faked, caked, flaked, slaked, snaked, raked, braked, traiked, staked, quaked.

2. *grubstaked*, bewegt [G.], rewaked.

AL–ĀL– 1. ail, ale, bale, bail, Bel, dale, fail, gale, Gael, hale, hail, gaol, jail, kale, scale, flail, mail, male, nail, snail, pail, pale, spale, rail, brail, Braille, frail, grail, Graal, trail, sale, sail, shale, tale, tail, tael, stale, vale, vail, veil, wail, wale, quail, squail, whale, Yale.

2. *Clydesdale*, regale, inhale, exhale, percale, hallel, remail, *blackmail*, *agnail*, *hangnail*, canaille, *hobnail*, tenaille, *thumbnail*, empale, impale, *handrail*, *landrail*, *pedrail*, *guardrail*, derail, *taffrail*, *cograil*, engrail, assail, asale, *wholesale*, grisaille, *staysail*, *headsail*, resail, *resale*, *lugsail*, *skysail*, *trysail*, *mainsail*, *topsail*, *foresail*, *spritsail*, outsail, *telltale*, *bobtail*, broadtail, detail, retail, entail, *pigtail*, *bangtail*, *cocktail*, *forktail*, *bucktail* *fantail*, *pintail*, *horntail*, *thorntail*, *sheartail*, curtail, *foxtail*, *cattail*, *sprittail*, *boattail*, *coattail*, *shavetail*, *dovetail*, avail, travail, prevail, enveil, bewail, *narwhale*.

3. Abigail, farthingale, nightingale, martingale, fingernail, monorail, tattletale, fairy tale, draggletail, disentail, swallowtail, scissortail, paravail, intervale.

ALD– 1. ailed, aled, baled, bailed, failed, galed, haled, gaoled, jailed, scaled, flailed, mailed, nailed, snailed, paled, railed, trailed, sailed, tailed, veiled, wailed, waled, quailed, whaled.

2. regaled, inhaled, exhaled, remailed, *blackmailed*, *hobmailed*, empaled, impaled, derailed, assailed, resailed, outsailed, *bobtailed*, *broadtailed*, detailed, retailed, retailed, entailed, *pigtailed*, *bangtailed*, *cocktailed*, curtailed, availed, travailed, prevailed, enveiled, unveiled, bewailed.

3. unregaled, farthingaled, draggletailed, disentailed, swallowtailed.

ALZ– see **ĀL**, plus " s " or " 's "; **1.** Wales. **2.** Marseilles, Versailles.

AM– 1. aim, dame, fame, game, hame, came, lame, blame, flame, claim, maim, name, frame, same, Sejm [Pol.], shame, tame.

2. defame, became, aflame, inflame, acclaim, declaim, reclaim, proclaim, disclaim, exclaim, *quitclaim*, rename, *byname*, *nickname*, *forename*, *surname*, misname, *doorframe*, *selfsame*.

3. overcame, counterclaim.

AMD– 1. aimed, famed, gamed, lamed, blamed, flamed, claimed, maimed, named, framed, shamed, tamed.

2. defamed, inflamed, acclaimed, declaimed, reclaimed, proclaimed, disclaimed, exclaimed, renamed, *nicknamed*, misnamed, ashamed.

3. undefamed, unacclaimed, unreclaimed, counterclaimed, unashamed.

AMZ– see **ĀM**, plus " s " or " 's "; **1.** James. **2.** St. James.

AN– 1. bane, chain, Dane, deign, feign, fane, fain, gain, gaine, Jane, cane, Cain, skein, lane, lain, laine, blain, plane, plain, slain,

Maine, main, mane, pain, pane, Paine, Spain, rain, rein, reign, brain, drain, grain, crane, sprain, train, strain, sane, sain, tain, stain, thane, vane, vain, vein, wane, swain, twain, zain.

2. urbane, *herbbane*, *fleabane*, *wolfsbane*, rechain, enchain, unchain, *mundane*, ordain, disdain, profane, again, regain, chicane, cocaine, Cockaigne, Biscayne, Elaine, delaine, *chilblain*, *seaplane*, *biplane*, *triplane*, *volplane*, *airplane*, Champlain, explain, amain, demesne, remain, domain, romaine, ptomaine, germane, humane, chow mein, inane, campaign, champagne, champaign, arraign, darrein, terrane, terrain, *checkrein*, unrein, forane, moraine, *subdrain*, refrain, migraine, engrain, ingrain, *grosgrain*, *crossgrain*, detrain, entrain, restrain, distrain, constrain, *sixain*, insane, attain, obtain, detain, retain, maintain, contain, pertain, abstain, *bloodstain*, *tearstain*, distain, dustain, *cordwain*, *coxswain*, *boatswain*.

3. inurbane, reordain, preordain, foreordain, hurricane, sugar cane, aquaplane, multiplane, monoplane, aeroplane, hydroplane, gyroplane, Charlemagne, inhumane, windowpane, counterpane, scatterbrain, featherbrain, subterrane, suzerain, overstrain, chevrotain, appertain, ascertain, entertain, quatorzain.

4. demimondaine, legerdemain, elecampane, mediterrane.

AND– 1. chained, deigned, feigned, gained, caned, planed, pained, rained, reined, reigned, brained, drained, grained, craned, sprained, trained, strained, stained, veined, waned.

2. rechained, enchained, unchained, ordained, disdained, unfeigned, profaned, regained, explained, remained, campaigned, arraigned, unreined, engrained, ingrained, detrained, entrained, restrained, distrained, constrained, attained, detained, retained, maintained, contained, pertained, abstained, *bloodstained*.

3. preordained, foreordained, scatterbrained, featherbrained, overstrained, ascertained, entertained.

ANJ– 1. change, mange, range, grange, strange.

2. exchange, shortchange, arrange, derange, estrange.

3. interchange, rearrange, prearrange, disarrange.

ANT– 1. faint, feint, plaint, paint, saint, taint, quaint.

2. complaint, bepaint, repaint, Geraint, restraint, distraint, constraint, ensaint, attaint, acquaint.

AP– 1. ape, chape, gape, jape, cape, scape, nape, rape, drape, grape, crape, crepe, scrape, shape, tape, swape [dial. Eng.].

2. agape, *landscape*, escape, *seascape*, *skyscape*, bedrape, reshape, misshape, transhape, *shipshape*, red-tape.

APS– *see* **ĀP**, plus " s " or " 's "; **1.** traipse. **3.** jackanapes.

APT– 1. aped, gaped, raped, draped, scraped, shaped, taped. **2.** escaped, bedraped, reshaped, red-taped, untaped.

AR– 1. air, Eir, heir, eyre, e'er, bear, bare, chair, chare, dare, fair, fare, faire [F.], hair, hare, Herr [G.], gare, care, scare, lair, blare, flare, flair, glare, glair, Clare, mare, mer [F.], mère [F.], n'er, snare, pair, pare, pear, père [F.], spare, rare, frère [F.], prayer, share, cher, chère [both F.], tear, tare, terre [F.], stair, stare, there, their, vair, ware, wear, swear, square, where, yare. **2.** Pierre, coheir, whene'er, where'er, howe'er, *threadbare, cudbear, bugbear, forebear,* forbear, misbear, *armchair,* bedare, outdare, affair, affaire [F.], *Mayfair, fieldfare, welfare, fanfare, warfare,* mohair, *horsehair,* eclair, declare, *nightmare,* grand'mère [F.], belle-mère [F.], ensnare, repair, prepare, impair, compare, grand-père [F.], beau-père [F.], despair, *confrere, corsair,* ma chère [F.], mon cher [F.], *plowshare,* Voltaire, parterre, outstare, hiver [F.], couvert [F.], trou-vère [F.], aware, *hardware,* beware, resquare, unsquare, *tinware, glassware,* forswear, *foot-wear,* outwear, *somewhere, nowhere, elsewhere,* première [F.], portière [F.]. **3.** Camembert, overbear, rocking-chair, homme d'affaires [F.], laissez-faire, thor-oughfare, savoir-faire [F.], c'est la guerre [F.], maidenhair, mal de mer [F.], jardin-ière [F.], doctrinaire, debonair, billionaire, millionaire, questionnaire, wheresoe'er, dis-repair, au contraire [F.], proletaire, solitaire, Finistère, Finisterre, countervair, Delaware, unaware, earthenware, ironware, under-wear, silverware, otherwhere, anywhere, everywhere. **4.** vivandière, en arrière, fonctionnaire, pied-à-terre, propriétaire [all F.]. **5.** concessionnaire, commissionnaire [both F.].

ARD– 1. aired, bared, chaired, dared, fared, hared, cared, scared, laird, blared, flared, glared, snared, paired, spared, rared, shared, stared, squared. **2.** gray-haired, fair-haired etc., declared, ensnared, repaired, prepared, impaired, compared, outstared. **3.** curly-haired, golden-haired, Titian-haired, raven-haired, undeclared etc.

ARN– 1. bairn, cairn, tairn.

ARS– 1. scarce, Perse [F.]. **2.** commerce [F.].

AS– 1. ace, base, bass, chase, dace, dais, face, case, lace, place, plaice, mace, pace, space, race, res [L.], brace, grace, trace, Thrace, vase. **2.** abase, debase, surbase, enchase, efface, deface, reface, *boldface, frogface, blackface, paleface, catface,* outface, *cardcase, bookcase,*

encase, *showcase, staircase, notecase, suitcase,* ukase, belace, *bridelace,* enlace, unlace, *shoelace,* replace, *fireplace,* displace, misplace, *birthplace,* grimace, apace, *footpace,* outpace, erase, *tailrace, millrace,* embrace, *drag race, dog race, scapegrace,* disgrace, *horse race, rat race,* retrace, Alsace, *ambsace.* **3.** contrabass, octobass, steeplechase, Boni-face, baby face, angel face, platterface, interlace, populace, hiding place, resting place, commonplace, interspace, chariot race. **5.** in medias res [L.].

AST– 1. baste, based, chaste, chased, faced, ghaist [Scot.], haste, cased, laced, placed, paste, paced, spaced, raced, braced, graced, traced, taste, waste, waist. **2.** abased, debased, lambaste, unchaste, *bald-faced, bold-faced,* effaced, defaced, refaced, *shamefaced, two-faced* etc., posthaste, encased, enlaced, displaced, misplaced, grimaced, outpaced, erased, embraced, disgraced, retraced. **3.** baby-faced, dirty-faced, angel-faced, double-faced, freckle-faced, interlaced, interspaced, aftertaste.

AT– 1. eight, ate, ait, bate, bait, date, fate, fête, gate, gait, hate, Kate, skate, late, plate, plait, slate, mate, pate, rate, freight, grate, great, crate, prate, trait, strait, straight, sate, state, weight, wait. **2.** create, abate, debate, rebate, *crowbait, whitebait,* redate, predate, sedate, misdate, postdate, outdate, *floodgate, negate, seagate, Vulgate, placate, oblate,* sublate, elate, belate, relate, dilate, deflate, inflate, conflate, sufflate, collate, *breastplate,* translate, play-mate, cremate, *checkmate, stalemate, comate, shipmate, helpmate, classmate, messmate,* mismate, *tentmate,* enate, innate, ornate, berate, orate, prorate, cut-rate, estate, restate, instate, misstate, await, *lightweight.* **3.** recreate, procreate, discreate, celibate, approbate, reprobate, incubate, depredate, antedate, candidate, validate, lapidate, cuspidate, liquidate, inundate, afterdate, *decaudate, denudate,* nucleate, permeate, roseate, nauseate, propagate, divagate, ablegate, delegate, relegate, abnegate, segregate, aggre-gate, congregate, crash the gate, get the gate [both slang], obligate, profligate, fumigate, irrigate, litigate, mitigate, casti-gate, instigate, navigate, abrogate, subro-gate, subjugate, conjugate, corrugate, glad-iate, radiate, mediate, foliate, opiate, expiate, seriate, floriate, fasciate, satiate, vitiate, tertiate, aviate, obviate, deviate, deprecate, imprecate, abdicate, dedicate, mendicate, judicate, delicate, triplicate, implicate, complicate, supplicate, duplicate, explicate, formicate, tunicate, fabricate, imbricate, fimbricate, lubricate, rubricate, intricate, extricate, dessicate, exsiccate, vesi-cate, corticate, masticate, rusticate, relocate, allocate, collocate, dislocate, embrocate, advocate, demarcate, altercate, bifurcate, confiscate, expiscate, obfuscate, infuscate, coruscate, educate, correlate, sibilate, jubilate, depilate, pupilate, mutilate, ventilate, flagellate, lamellate, crenellate, cancellate, immolate, desolate, isolate, contemplate, copperplate, silver plate, legislate, mistranslate, ambulate, tubulate, adulate, pendulate, undulate, nodulate, regulate, angulate, ungulate, peculate, speculate, calculate, flocculate, circulate, osculate, stellulate, ululate, emulate, simulate, stimulate, formulate, cumulate, granulate, crenulate, lunulate, stipulate, copulate, populate, spherulate, insulate, consulate, decimate, animate, ultimate, intimate, optimate, estimate, consummate, dichromate, conformate, explanate, sultanate, hyphenate, alienate, arsenate, catenate, septenate, juvenate, *impregnate, obsignate,* designate, turbinate, ordinate, marginate, machinate, echinate, declinate, pollinate, geminate, fulminate, dominate, *bipinnate,* marinate, vaccinate, fascinate, patinate, pectinate, destinate, glutinate, carbonate, functionate, coronate, assonate, detonate, intonate, hibernate, quaternate, inornate, fortunate, adipate, dissipate, exculpate, syncopate, extirpate, saccharate, separate, disparate, celebrate, cerebrate, calibrate, dehydrate, liberate, federate, moderate, tolerate, numerate, generate, operate, asperate, desperate, lacerate, macerate, ulcerate, literate, integrate, emigrate, immigrate, transmigrate, aspirate, obscerate, desecrate, consecrate, execrate, perforate, biforate, camphorate, decorate, pignorate, corporate, perorate, doctorate, overrate, penetrate, impetrate, perpetrate, arbitrate, infiltrate, concentrate, orchestrate, fenestrate, *sequestrate,* magistrate, registrate, *capistrate,* demonstrate, *remonstrate,* illustrate, obdurate, figurate, fulgurate, sulphurate, accurate, tellurate, suppurate, purpurate, saturate, *inspissate,* tête-à-tête, vegetate, acetate, *delectate,* meditate, agitate, digitate, cogitate, gurgitate, militate, imitate, limitate, sanitate, capitate, crepitate, palpitate, irritate, hesitate, oscitate, nictitate, quantitate, gravitate, levitate, *eructate, occultate, edentate,* segmentate, potentate, annotate, connotate, *decurtate,* devastate, *intestate,* reinstate, *apostate,* understate, interstate, overstate, *degustate, acutate,* permutate, amputate, graduate, vacuate, valuate, tenuate, sinuate, actuate, punctuate, fluctuate, fructuate, situate, excavate, aggravate, depravate, elevate, salivate, derivate, titivate, cultivate, motivate, captivate, estivate, renovate, innovate, enervate, *recurvate,* hundredweight, pennyweight, heavyweight, adequate, antiquate, bantamweight, underweight, paperweight, welterweight, featherweight, overweight.

4. invalidate, consolidate, intimidate, elucidate, accommodate, enucleate, delineate,

extravagate, variegate, eradiate, irradiate, repudiate, collegiate, trifoliate, calumniate, pogoniate, ammoniate, marsupiate, inebriate, excoriate, depatriate, depreciate, appreciate, officiate, associate, dissociate, negotiate, exuviate, asphyxiate, hypothecate, syllabicate, irradicate, rededicate, revindicate, adjudicate, indelicate, multiplicate, authenticate, decorticate, domesticate, sophisticate, prognosticate, intoxicate, reciprocate, equivocate, annihilate, assimilate, salicylate, nucleolate, alveolate, inviolate, interpolate, disconsolate, apostolate, emasculate, capitulate, expostulate, amalgamate, legitimate, penultimate, permanganate, hydrogenate, concatenate, rejuvenate, decaffeinate, predesignate, vaticinate, hallucinate, inordinate, immarginate, ingeminate, inseminate, disseminate, peregrinate, indoctrinate, procrastinate, predestinate, conglutinate, exsanguinate, bicarbonate, impersonate, subalternate, emancipate, invertebrate, deliberate, reverberate, protuberate, confederate, preponderate, vociferate, exaggerate, refrigerate, accelerate, conglomerate, exonerate, remunerate, cooperate, exasperate, recuperate, commiserate, eviscerate, incarcerate, reiterate, adulterate, presbyterate, asseverate, imperforate, invigorate, ameliorate, redecorate, commemorate, evaporate, incorporate, recalcitrate, extravasate, improvisate, tergiversate, premeditate, tridigitate, capacitate, felicitate, resuscitate, effectuate, perpetuate, accentuate, eventuate, insalivate, recaptivate, inadequate.

5. baccalaureate, circumnavigate, supererogate, intermediate, unifoliate, circumstantiate, differentiate, renegotiate, quadrifoliate, excommunicate, recapitulate, insubordinate, incompassionate, unaffectionate, disproportionate, deteriorate, incommensurate, incapacitate, individuate, superannuate.

ATH— **1.** faith, wraith, staith.

2. unfaith, misfaith.

ATH— **1.** bathe, scathe, lathe, snathe, spathe, rathe, swathe.

2. unswathe.

ATHD— **1.** bathed, scathed, lathed, swathed.

ATS— *see* **ĀT**, plus "s" or "'s"; **1.** nates, Yeats.

2. wie geht's [G.].

AV— **1.** Dave, gave, cave, lave, glaive, slave, nave, knave, pave, rave, brave, grave, crave, trave, save, shave, tave [dial.], stave, wave, waive, suave.

2. forgave, behave, *portglaive,* enslave, repave, engrave, ingrave, deprave.

3. misbehave, autoclave, antenave, architrave.

AVD— **1.** caved, laved, slaved, paved, raved, braved, craved, saved, shaved, staved, waved, waived.

2. behaved, enslaved, repaved, unpaved, engraved, depraved.

3. misbehaved, unenslaved, unengraved.

AZ– *see* **Ā** through **ZHĀ**, plus " s " or " 's "
(except for French plurals, where the " s "
is not pronounced); **1.** baize, daze, faze,
phase, gaze, haze, Hayes, laze, blaze, glaze,
maze, maize, raze, raise, braise, braze,
fraise, frase, phrase, graze, craze, praise,
chaise, vase.
2. bedaze, malaise, ablaze, emblaze, liaise,
amaze, bemaze, *mizmaze*, rephrase, upraise,
appraise, bepraise, *sideways*.
3. nowadays, hollandaise, Marseillaise, may-
onnaise, lyonnaise, polonaise, paraphrase,
metaphrase, reappraise, underpraise, over-
praise.

AZD– **1.** dazed, fazed, phased, gazed, hazed,
lazed, blazed, glazed, mazed, raised, razed,
braised, brazed, fraised, phrased, grazed,
crazed, praised.
2. bedazed, emblazed, unglazed, amazed,
bemazed, rephrased, unphrased, unraised,
upraised, appraised, unpraised, dispraised.
3. paraphrased, reappraised, underpraised,
overpraised.

AZH– **1.** beige, greige.

Ā (ay)

Double (Feminine) Rhymes

Primary or Secondary Accent Falls on Next to Last Syllable; Imperfect Rhymes Are in Italics.

A′a– 2. haya, Maia, Freya.
   3. Isaiah.
   4. Himalaya.
A′ad– 1. naiad, sayid.
A′al– 1. Baal.
   2. Ethbaal.
   3. defrayal, betrayal, portrayal, conveyal, purveyal, surveyal.
A′am– 2. faham, mayhem, graham, play 'em.
A′an– 3. Biscayan, Malayan.
   4. Paraguayan, Uruguayan.
A′ans– 3. abeyance, conveyance, purveyance, surveyance.
A′ant– 2. mayn't.
   3. abeyant.
AB′an– 2. Laban, Leben [G.], geben [G.].
AB′ee– 2. baby, gaby, maybe.
   3. *crybaby.*
AB′eez– 2. babies, gabies, Jabes, scabies, rabies, maybes.
   3. *crybabies.*
AB′er– 2. Gheber, Ghabre, caber, labor, neighbor, saber, sabre, tabor.
   3. belabor.
AB′erz– *see* ĀB′er; 2. jabers.
   3. bejabers.
AB′l– 2. Abel, able, Babel, fable, gable, cable, label, labile, Mabel, nabel [dial.], nable [dial.], sable, table, stable.
   3. enable, unable, disable, retable, *timetable, turntable,* unstable.
   4. fibblefable [dial.].
AB′ld– 2. fabled, gabled, cabled, labeled, sabled, tabled, stabled.
   3. enabled, disabled, besabled, retabled.
AB′ler– 2. abler, fabler, cabler, labeler, sabler, tabler, stabler.
   3. enabler, disabler, retabler, unstabler.
AB′lest– 2. ablest, stablest.
   3. unstablest.
AB′ling– 2. cabling, labelling, tabling, stabling.
   3. enabling, disabling, retabling.

AB′rum– 2. Abram, labrum, flabrum.
   4. candelabrum.
AD′a– 2. Ada, Veda.
   3. cicada, armada, Pinctada.
   5. Digitigrada.
A′da– 2. heyday, Mayday, payday, playday.
AD′ans– 2. aidance, cadence.
   3. decadence.
AD′ant– 2. aidant, cadent.
   3. decadent, abradent.
AD′ed– 2. aided, faded, jaded, bladed, gladed, spaded, raided, braided, graded, traded, shaded, waded.
   3. unaided, unfaded, cockaded, blockaded, brocaded, cascaded, paraded, unbraided, upbraided, degraded, crusaded, evaded, invaded, pervaded, dissuaded, persuaded.
   4. barricaded, ambuscaded, enfiladed, double-bladed, accoladed, promenaded, serenaded, colonnaded, cannonaded, carronaded, masqueraded, retrograded, balustraded, palisaded, unpersuaded.
AD′ee– 2. fady, shady, jady, cadi, lady, glady, maidy, Brady, 'fraidy, Grady, Sadie, vade.
   3. O'Grady, milady, *forelady.*
AD′eez– 2. Hades, ladies, Brady's, Grady's, Sadie's.
AD′en– 2. Aden, Haydn, laden, maiden.
   3. menhaden, snow maiden.
   4. overladen, heavy-laden.
AD′ens– 2. cadence.
   3. decadence.
AD′er– 2. aider, fader, nadir, spader, raider, braider, grader, trader, Seder, staider, wader.
   3. blockader, parader, unbraider, upbraider, crusader, evader, invader, dissuader, persuader.
   4. barricader, promenader, serenader, masquerader.
AD′ing– 2. aiding, fading, lading, spading, raiding, braiding, grading, trading, shading, wading.
   3. blockading, cascading, unfading, parading,

unbraiding, upbraiding, degrading, crusading, evading, invading, pervading, dissuading, persuading.
4. barricading, ambuscading, serenading, cannonading, masquerading.
AD′ish– 2. jadish, staidish.
3. oldmaidish, *mermaidish*.
AD′l– 2. ladle, dreidel, gradal, cradle, tradal.
3. encradle.
AD′lee– 2. staidly.
3. dismayedly.
AD′less– 2. aidless, fadeless, bladeless, spadeless, braidless, gradeless, tradeless, shadeless.
3. paradeless, cockadeless, crusadeless.
AD′ling– 2. ladling, maidling, cradling.
3. encradling.
AD′ness– 2. frayedness, staidness.
3. afraidness, unstaidness.
AD′o– 2. dado, credo.
3. gambado, fumado, tornado, strappado.
4. bastinado, carbonado, desperado, camisado.
AD′os– 3. Barbados, intrados, extrados.
AD′us– 2. cladus, gradus.
A′ee– 2. Dei [L.], clayey, Mayey, wheyey.
4. Agnus Dei [L.].
A′er– 2. feyer, gayer, layer, flayer, player, slayer, mayor, payer, brayer, grayer, prayer, preyer, sprayer, strayer, stayer, weigher.
3. obeyer, waylayer, delayer, *bricklayer*, parleyer, *outlayer*, displayer, mormaor, *taxpayer*, *forayer*, hoorayer, defrayer, betrayer, portrayer, assayer, essayer, gainsayer, *soothsayer*, inveigher, conveyer, purveyor, surveyor.
A′est– 2. feyest, gayest, grayest, greyest.
3. assayist, *essayist*; *see also* Ā′ist.
AF′er– 2. chafer, safer, strafer, wafer.
3. cockchafer, vouchsafer.
AF′ing– 2. chafing, strafing.
3. enchafing, vouchsafing.
AG′a– 2. saga.
3. omega.
4. rutabaga, Onondaga.
AG′er– 2. plaguer, vaguer, jager, jaeger.
AG′in– 2. Fagin, regen [G.].
4. Copenhagen.
AG′l– 2. plagal, paigle, vagal.
3. finagle.
AG′o– 2. Dago, sago.
3. Sebago, lumbago, plumbago, Diego, galago, imago, farrago, suffrago.
4. Solidago, San Diego, Archimago, galapago.
5. hasta luego [Sp.].
6. Tierra del Fuego.
AG′rans– 2. flagrance, fragrance, vagrance.
AG′rant– 2. flagrant, fragrant, vagrant.
3. infragrant, unfragrant.
AG′us– 2. Magus, pagus, plague us, tragus, vagus.
3. choragus.
4. archimagus.

A′ij– 2. drayage, weighage.
A′ik– 2. laic.
3. Chaldaic, Judaic, trochaic, archaic, Romaic, Spondaic, Hebraic, Passaic, mosaic, prosaic, altaic, deltaic, voltaic, stanzaic.
4. Aramaic, Ptolemaic, stenopaic, algebraic, tesseraic, Pharisaic.
A′ing– 2. baying, laying, slaying, sleighing, Maying, neighing, fraying, graying, preying, praying, straying, saying, weighing.
3. obeying, decaying, croqueting, waylaying, parleying, displaying, a-Maying, dismaying, foraying, defraying, portraying, assaying, essaying, gainsaying, crocheting, conveying, surveying, reweighing.
4. disobeying, appliquéing, overpaying, disarraying, overstaying.
A′is– 2. dais, Lais, nais.
A′ish– 2. bayish, gayish, clayish, grayish, wheyish.
A′ist– 4. Ptolemaist, algebraist, Pharisaist; *see also* Ā′est.
AJ′ee– 2. cagey, Meiji, sagy, stagy.
AJ′er– 2. ager, gager, gauger, major, pager, sager, stager, wager, swager.
3. drum major, presager, assuager.
4. trumpet major.
AJ′ez– 2. ages, gages, gauges, cages, pages, rages, sages, stages, wages, swages.
3. engages, encages, impages, compages, outrages, presages.
4. disengages.
AJ′ing– 2. aging, gauging, caging, paging, raging, staging, waging.
3. engaging, enraging, presaging, assuaging.
4. disengaging.
AJ′less– 2. ageless, gageless, gaugeless, cageless, pageless, stageless, wageless.
AJ′ment– 3. engagement, enragement, presagement, assuagement.
4. pre-engagement, disengagement.
AJ′us– 2. age us etc.
3. ambagious, rampageous, outrageous, courageous, umbrageous, contagious, enrage us etc.
4. advantageous, noncontagious.
5. disadvantageous.
AK′a– 2. Cheka, raca, weka, cueca.
3. Macaca, Jamaica, Kapeika, bareca.
4. abhiseka.
AK′ate– 2. placate, pacate, vacate.
AK′ee– 2. acky, faky, caky, laky, slaky, snaky, braiky, traiky, shaky, guaky.
3. headachy.
AK′en– 2. Aiken, bacon, Macon, shaken, taken, waken.
3. Jamaican, forsaken, unshaken, *windshaken*, untaken, mistaken, awaken, rewaken.
4. Godforsaken, unforsaken, undertaken, overtaken, reawaken.
AK′er– 2. acher, acre, baker, faker, fakir, laker, maker, nacre, raker, breaker, shaker, Shaker, taker, staker, waker, Quaker.

3. *wiseacre, matchmaker, watchmaker, bookmaker, peacemaker, dressmaker, lawmaker, shoemaker, strikebreaker, heartbreaker, lawbreaker,* forsaker, *salt-shaker,* partaker, mistaker, *painstaker.*
4. simulacre, mischief-maker, Sabbathbreaker, pepper-shaker, undertaker.

AK′erd– **2.** acred, nacred.
3. *wiseacred.*

AK′ij– **2.** flakage, brakeage, breakage.

AK′ing– **2.** aching, baking, faking, caking, slaking, raking, braking, breaking, shaking, waking, quaking.
3. *watchmaking, bookmaking, dressmaking, heartbreaking,* forsaking, partaking, mistaking, *painstaking.*
4. merrymaking, unforsaking, unpartaking, undertaking.

AK′ish– **2.** achish, snakish, rakish.

AK′less– **2.** acheless, fakeless, cakeless, lakeless, slakeless, snakeless, rakeless, breakless, shakeless, takeless, stakeless, steakless, wakeless, quakeless.
3. mistakeless.

AK′man– **2.** cakeman, brakeman, steakman.

AK′o– **2.** Draco, Waco.
3. macaco.

AK′on– *see* **ĀK′en.**

AK′rum– **2.** sacrum.
3. synsacrum.
4. simulacrum.

AL′a– **2.** ala, chela, gala, mala.
3. kamala, canela [Sp.], panela, osela.

AL′aks– **2.** Galax, malax, Spalax.

AL′anks– **2.** phalanx, Caranx.

AL′ee– **2.** aly, bailie, Bailey, daily, gaily, scaly, snaily, grayly, traily, taily, waily.
3. shillalah.
4. apercaillie, ukelele, counterpaly; *see also* **ĀL′lee.**

AL′ens– **2.** valence.
3. trivalence, covalence.
4. univalence, equivalence.

AL′ent– **2.** valent.
3. inhalant, exhalant, transcalant, assailant, bivalent, trivalent, surveillant.
4. polyvalent.

AL′er– **2.** alar, baler, bailer, bailor, haler, jailer, jailor, gaoler, scalar, scaler, malar, mailer, nailer, paler, frailer, trailer, sailer, sailor, talar, tailer, tailor, Taylor, staler, wailer, squalor, whaler.
3.′ regaler, inhaler, exhaler, assailer, *wholesaler, retailer.*

A′less– **2.** dayless, payless, playless, rayless, prayless, preyless, wayless, swayless.

AL′est– **2.** halest, palest, frailest, stalest.

AL′ful– **2.** baleful, pailful, wailful.

AL′if– **2.** aleph, alef, bailiff, calif, caliph.
3. bumbailiff.

AL′ij– **2.** bailage, scalage, sailage.
3. *retailage,* curtailage.

AL′ik– **2.** Gaelic, malic, Salic.

AL′iks– **2.** calix, calyx, Salix.
4. epicalyx.

AL′ing– **2.** ailing, bailing, failing, hailing, jailing, scaling, mailing, paling, railing, grayling, trailing, sailing, tailing, veiling, wailing, whaling.
3. unfailing, regaling, inhaling, exhaling, *blackmailing,* impaling, *wholesaling,* detailing, retailing, entailing, curtailing, *dovetailing,* availing, prevailing, bewailing.
4. countervailing.

AL′ish– **2.** palish, frailish, stalish.

AL′lee– **2.** halely, palely, frailly, stately; *see also* **ĀL′ee.**

AL′less– **2.** aleless, bailless, failless, jailless, scaleless, maleless, mailless, nailless, trailless, sailless, tailless, veilless, whaleless.

AL′ment– **2.** ailment, bailment.
3. regalement, impalement, derailment, assailment, retailment, entailment, curtailment, availment, bewailment.

AL′o– **2.** halo.
3. Canelo, canelo.

AL′ya– **5.** regalia, cacalia, Centralia, Australia, azalea.
6. paraphernalia; *see also* **ĀL′i–a.**

AL′yun– **3.** alien.
4. regalian, Centralian, Australian, Pygmalion.
5. bacchanalian, saturnalian.
6. sesquipedalian, tatterdemalion; *see also* **ĀL′i–an.**

AM′a– **2.** Fama, lama, Brahma, drama, krama, squama.
3. kalema, salema, Bahama.

A′man– **2.** dayman, cayman, layman, drayman.
3. *highwayman; see also* **ĀM′en.**

AM′ant– **2.** claimant, clamant.
3. adhamant, reclaimant.

AM′ate– **2.** hamate, squamate.
3. desquamate.

AMB′er– **2.** chamber.
3. *bedchamber.*
4. antechamber.

AM′ee– **2.** Amy, gamy, Jamie, flamy, Mamie, rami, zemi.

AM′en– **2.** amen, Haman, daimen, flamen, Bremen, stamen.
3. velamen, clinamen, foramen, duramen, examen, putamen, gravamen; *see also* **Ā′man.**

AM′ent– **2.** ament, pament, payment, raiment.
3. allayment, repayment, defrayment, betrayment.

AM′er– **2.** aimer, gamer, lamer, blamer, claimer, maimer, namer, framer, shamer, tamer.
3. acclaimer, declaimer, reclaimer, proclaimer, disclaimer, exclaimer, *nicknamer,* testamur.

AM′est– **2.** gamest, lamest, tamest.

AM′ful– **2.** aimful, gameful, blameful, shameful.

AM′ing– **2.** aiming, gaming, laming, blaming,

flaming, claiming, maiming, naming, framing, shaming, taming.

3. acclaiming, declaiming, reclaiming, proclaiming, disclaiming, exclaiming, inflaming, *nicknaming*, misnaming.

AM′ish– **2.** Amish, lamish, samish, Samish, tamish.

AM′lee– **2.** gamely, lamely, namely, samely, tamely.

AM′less– **2.** aimless, fameless, gameless, blameless, claimless, flameless, nameless, frameless, shameless, tameless.

3. *nicknameless.*

AM′ness– **2.** gameness, lameness, sameness, tameness.

AM′us– **2.** Amos, famous, hamus, hamous, ramus, ramous, samos, Seamas, squamous.

3. mandamus, biramous.

4. ignoramus.

AN′a– **2.** ana, Dana, Rana, rena, scena.

3. arcana, campana.

4. Cartagena, omniana, Geoplana.

5. Americana.

AN′al– **2.** banal, manal, veinal.

3. bimanal.

4. septimanal, interveinal.

AND′er– **3.** remainder, attainder, detainder.

AN′ee– **2.** cany, Janey, rainy, brainy, grainy, veiny, zany.

4. Allegheny, miscellany, castellany.

AN′er– **2.** chainer, feigner, caner, gainer, plainer, drainer, trainer, strainer, saner, seiner, stainer, vainer.

3. urbaner, ordainer, profaner, chicaner, Biscayner, complainer, humaner, inaner, retainer, abstainer.

A′ness– **2.** gayness, grayness, greyness; *see also* **ĀN′ness.**

AN′est– **2.** plainest, sanest, vainest.

3. urbanest, profanest, humanest, inanest.

AN′ful– **2.** baneful, gainful, painful.

3. disdainful, ungainful, complainful.

AN′ij– **2.** chainage, drainage, cranage, trainage.

AN′ing– **2.** deigning, feigning, caning, planing, paining, reigning, reining, raining, draining, craning, training, straining, seining, waning.

3. ordaining, disdaining, complaining, *airplaning*, campaigning, arraigning, unreining, detraining, entraining, restraining, retaining.

4. uncomplaining, aquaplaning, ascertaining, entertaining.

AN′ish– **2.** Danish, sanish, vainish.

3. urbanish.

ANJ′ee– **2.** mangy, rangy.

ANJ′el– **2.** angel.

3. archangel.

ANJ′er– **2.** changer, danger, manger, ranger, stranger.

3. exchanger, endanger, arranger, deranger, *bushranger*, estranger.

4. money-changer, interchanger, rearranger, disarranger.

ANJ′ez– **2.** changes, ranges, granges.

3. exchanges, shortchanges, arranges, deranges, estranges.

4. rearranges, prearranges, interchanges, disarranges.

ANJ′ing– **2.** changing, ranging.

3. unchanging, exchanging, shortchanging, estranging.

4. interchanging, rearranging, prearranging, disarranging.

ANJ′less– **2.** changeless, mangeless, rangeless, grangeless.

3. exchangeless.

ANJ′ling– **2.** changeling, strangeling.

ANJ′ment– **2.** changement.

3. arrangement, derangement, estrangement.

4. rearrangement, prearrangement, disarrangement.

AN′lee– **2.** fainly, plainly, mainly, sanely, vainly.

3. urbanely, profanely, ungainly, humanely, inanely, insanely.

4. inhumanely.

AN′less– **2.** chainless, gainless, maneless, painless, rainless, brainless, grainless, strainless, stainless, vaneless, veinless, waneless, swainless.

AN′ment– **3.** enchainment, ordainment, regainment, arraignment, attainment, detainment, retainment.

4. reordainment, ascertainment, entertainment.

AN′ness– **2.** plainness, saneness, vainness.

3. urbaneness, profaneness, humaneness, inaneness, insaneness; *see also* **Ā′ness.**

AN′o– **2.** Drano.

3. volcano, sereno [Sp.].

ANT′ed– **2.** fainted, feinted, painted, sainted, tainted.

3. ensainted, attainted, acquainted.

4. unacquainted.

ANT′ee– **2.** dainty, fainty.

ANT′er– **2.** fainter, feinter, painter, quainter.

ANT′est– **2.** faintest, quaintest.

ANT′if– **2.** plaintiff.

3. coplaintiff.

ANT′ing– **2.** fainting, feinting, painting, sainting, tainting.

3. repainting, attainting, acquainting.

ANT′ish– **2.** faintish, saintish.

ANT′iv– **2.** plaintive.

3. complaintive, constraintive.

ANT′lee– **2.** faintly, saintly, quaintly.

3. unfaintly, unsaintly.

ANT′ness– **2.** faintness, quaintness.

AN′um– **3.** Arcanum, Solanum.

AN′us– **2.** heinous, Janus, manus, veinous, pain us.

3. ananas, Silvanus.

4. decumanus.

A′o– **2.** kayo, bleo, Mayo.

3. cacao.

6. Jubitate Deo.

A′on– **2.** rayon, crayon.

3. Lycaon.
A'or– 2. mayor.
3. mormaor, conveyor, purveyor, surveyor; *see also* **Ā'er.**
A'os– 2. chaos, naos, Naos, Taos.
3. pronaos.
4. epinaos.
AP'ee– 2. gapy, grapy, crapy, crepy, scrapy.
3. red-tapey.
AP'en– 2. shapen, tapen.
3. unshapen, misshapen.
AP'er– 2. aper, gaper, caper, paper, draper, scraper, sapor, shaper, taper, tapir, vapor.
3. *nordcaper, landscaper,* escaper, *wallpaper, gunpaper, newspaper, skyscraper,* red-taper.
AP'ing– 2. aping, gaping, Peiping, draping, scraping, shaping, taping.
3. escaping, *landscaping, skyscraping,* reshaping, misshaping, retaping.
AP'is– 2. apis, tapis.
3. sinapis, Serapis.
AP'ish– 2. apish, gapish, papish.
3. red-tapish.
AP'ist– 2. papist, tapist.
3. *landscapist,* escapist, red-tapist.
AP'l– 2. capel, maple, papal, staple.
3. nonpapal.
4. antipapal.
AP'lee– 2. shapely.
3. unshapely, *shipshapely.*
AP'less– 2. capeless, grapeless, shapeless, tapeless.
AP'let– 2. apelet, capelet, grapelet.
AP'lz– 2. maples, Naples, staples.
AP'ron– 2. apron, napron.
AR'a– 2. Eire, Sara, Sarah, tera.
3. Madeira, caldera, Sahara, cascara, gallera.
AR'ans– 3. forbearance, appearance.
4. unforbearance.
AR'ee– 2. airy, aerie, chary, dairy, fairy, faerie, Gary, hairy, Carey, scary, lairy, blary, flary, glary, glairy, clary, Mary, nary, snary, prairie, seri, stary, vary, wary.
3. *quandary,* vagary, *rosemary,* canary, contrary, unwary.
4. syllabary, columbary, dromedary, lapidary, prebendary, legendary, secondary, airy-fairy, nucleary, tertiary, formicary, persicary, tutelary, mammilary, capillary, ancillary, axillary, maxillary, corollary, medullary, formulary, scapulary, titulary, calamary, lachrymary, customary, millenary, parcenary, mercenary, centenary, ordinary, culinary, seminary, luminary, doctrinary, sanguinary, legionary, regionary, pulmonary, coronary, sublunary, stationary, cautionary, missionary, dictionary, functionary, pensionary, passionary, questionary, visionary, cinerary, numerary, vulnerary, Tipperary, literary, honorary, temporary, arbitrary, *accessary,* necessary, emissary, commissary, janissary, adversary, dietary, proletary, planetary, monetary, secretary, military, solitary, sanitary, dignitary, sedentary, frag-

mentary, commentary, momentary, voluntary, tributary, salutary, reliquary, antiquary, January, February, statuary, actuary, sanctuary, sumptuary, mortuary, estuary, salivary, cassowary.
5. subsidiary, stipendiary, incendiary, pecuniary, fiduciary, apothecary, hypothecary, epistolary, vocabulary, constabulary, accustomary, bicentenary, tercentenary, imaginary, disciplinary, preliminary, veterinary, ganglionary, probationary, precautionary, discretionary, processionary, additionary, traditionary, seditionary, petitionary, tuitionary, reactionary, confectionary, ablutionary, revisionary, divisionary, provisionary, itinerary, contemporary, extemporary, unnecessary, proprietary, depositary, prothonotary, contributary, residuary, obituary, tumultuary, voluptuary.
6. beneficiary, intermediary, accidentiary, adminiculary, prolegomenary, valetudinary, latitudinary, multitudinary, eleemosynary, abolitionary, insurrectionary, elocutionary, evolutionary, revolutionary, supernumerary.
7. consuetudinary, vicissitudinary; *see also* **ĂR'ee, ĔR'ee.**
AR'eed– 2. varied.
3. unvaried; *see also* **ĂR'eed, ĔR'eed.**
AR'eez– 2. Ares, Aries, aeries, dairies, Dares, fairies, Gary's, caries, Carey's, lares, Mary's, nares, prairies, varies.
3. *quandaries,* vagaries, canaries, Canaries, Benares, contraries.
4. syllabaries, columbaries, dromedaries, lapidaries, prebendaries, tertiaries, capillaries, corollaries, mercenaries, centenaries, seminaries, luminaries, legionaries, coronaries, missionaries, dictionaries, functionaries, pensionaries, visionaries, Tipperary's, temporaries, necessaries, emissaries, commissaries, janissaries, adversaries, secretaries, solitaries, dignitaries, commentaries, Buenos Aires, voluntaries, tributaries, reliquaries, antiquaries, Januaries, Februaries, actuaries, sanctuaries, mortuaries, estuaries, cassowaries.
5. subsidiaries, stipendiaries, incendiaries, apothecaries, vocabularies, constabularies, bicentenaries, tercentenaries, preliminaries, veterinaries, reactionaries, confectionaries, itineraries, contemporaries, depositaries, prothonotaries, obituaries, voluptuaries.
6. beneficiaries, intermediaries, insurrectionaries, revolutionaries, supernumeraries.
AR'er– 2. airer, error, bearer, barer, darer, fairer, farer, carer, scarer, blarer, flarer, glarer, snarer, pairer, parer, sparer, rarer, sharer, tearer, terror, starer, wearer, swearer, squarer.
3. *sword-bearer, talebearer, pallbearer, cupbearer, mace-bearer,* outdarer, *wayfarer, seafarer,* declarer, ensnarer, repairer, preparer, impairer, comparer, despairer, awarer, forswearer.
4. standard-bearer, armor-bearer.

AR′ess– 2. heiress, bearess.
3. coheiress.
AR′est– 2. barest, fairest, rarest, squarest.
3. unfairest.
AR′ful– 2. dareful, careful, prayerful.
3. uncareful, despairful.
AR′go– 2. ergo, fair-go.
3. albergo [It.].
AR′ing– 2. airing, bearing, daring, faring, haring, herring, caring, chairing, scaring, blaring, flaring, glaring, pairing, paring, sparing, sharing, tearing, staring, wearing, Waring, swearing, squaring.
3. *talebearing*, *seafaring*, declaring, repairing, impairing, despairing, outstaring, outwearing, outswearing, forswearing.
4. overbearing, undeclaring; *see also* ĂR′ing.
AR′is– 2. naris.
3. Polaris.
4. cucullaris.
AR′ish– 2. bearish, fairish, cherish, rarish, squarish.
3. nightmarish.
4. debonairish.
AR′lee– 2. fairly.
3. unfairly.
4. debonairly; *see also* ĂR′lee.
AR′less– 2. airless, heirless, hairless, chairless, pairless, prayerless, tearless, stairless; *see also* AR′less.
AR′line– 2. airline, hairline.
AR′man– 2. airman, chairman.
AR′ness– 2. fairness.
3. unfairness.
4. debonairness; *see also* ĂR′ness.
AR′o– 2. aero, Pharaoh.
3. ranchero, cochero, vaquero, bolero, llanero, dinero, sombrero, torero [all Sp.].
4. sudadero, matadero, hacendero, caballero, bandolero, campanero, zapatero [all Sp.]; *see also* ĂR′o.
AR′u– 2. Meru, Nehru.
AR′um– 2. arum, garum, harem, carrom.
4. harumscarum.
9. scientia scientiarum.
AS′a– 2. Asa, mesa, presa [It.], vasa [L.].
3. cabeza [Sp.].
AS′al– 2. basal, casal, vasal.
3. oasal.
AS′ee– 2. lacy, Macy, racy, Gracie, précis, Tracy.
4. contumacy.
AS′eez– 2. bases.
3. oases.
AS′en– 2. basin, hasten, Jason, chasten, mason, sasin.
3. *washbasin*, enchasten, freemason, *stonemason; see also* ĀS′on.
AS′ens– 3. abaisance, obeisance, adjacence, complaisance, complacence, renascence, connascence.
4. interjacence, uncomplaisance.
AS′ent– 2. jacent, nascent, naissant.
3. obeisant, subjacent, adjacent, complacent,

renascent, renaissant, connascent.
4. circumjacent, interjacent, uncomplacent.
AS′er– 2. Acer, baser, chaser, facer, caser, lacer, placer, macer, pacer, spacer, racer, bracer, tracer.
3. abaser, debaser, defacer, effacer, eraser, horse racer, embracer, begracer, disgracer, retracer, encaser, belacer, enlacer, unlacer, grimacer, outpacer, replacer, misplacer, displacer.
4. steeplechaser, interlacer.
AS′ez– 2. aces, bases, basses, chases, daces, daises, faces, cases, laces, places, maces, paces, spaces, races, braces, graces, traces, vases.
3. abases, debases, surbases, enchases, effaces, defaces, refaces, *frog faces*, *blackfaces*, *palefaces*, *catfaces*, outfaces, *cardcases*, *bookcases*, encases, *showcases*, *staircases*, *notecases*, *suitcases*, ukases, belaces, *bridelaces*, enlaces, unlaces, *shoelaces*, replaces, *fireplaces*, displaces, misplaces, *birthplaces*, grimaces, outpaces, erases, *tailraces*, *millraces*, embraces, *drag races*, *dog races*, *scapegraces*, disgraces, *horse races*, *rat races*, retraces, Alsace's.
4. contrabasses, octobasses, steeplechases, Boniface's, platterfaces, baby faces, angel faces, interlaces, populaces, hiding places, resting places, commonplaces, interspaces, chariot races.
AS′ful– 2. spaceful, graceful.
3. ungraceful, disgraceful.
ASH′a– 2. Asia, geisha.
3. Acacia, Dalmatia, Eurasia.
ASH′al– 2. facial, glacial, spatial, racial.
3. abbatial, palatial, prelatial, primatial.
4. unifacial, interspatial, interracial.
ASH′an– 2. Asian.
3. predacean, phocacean, cetacean, testacean, crustacean; *see also* ĀSH′un.
ASH′ens– 2. facients, patience, patients.
3. impatience, outpatients.
ASH′ent– 2. facient, patient.
3. impatient, outpatient.
4. sorbefacient, rubefacient, calefacient, tumefacient, stupefacient, somnifacient, liquefacient.
ASH′un– 2. nation, ration, station.
3. cibation, libation, limbation, jobation, probation, gradation, foundation, laudation, sudation, creation, legation, ligation, rogation, purgation, jugation, striation, placation, vacation, peccation, plication, sulcation, truncation, location, vocation, furcation, piscation, alation, halation, ablation, oblation, sublation, elation, delation, gelation, relation, velation, deflation, sufflation, inflation, conflation, dilation, vallation, illation, collation, prolation, cremation, sigmation, himation, gemmation, commation, summation, formation, planation, adnation, enation, agnation, signation, cognation, damnation, conation, donation, phonation, pronation, lunation, libration, vibration, hydration,

ceration, spheration, migration, liration, oration, moration, nitration, titration, filtration, curation, duration, neuration, gyration, cessation, pulsation, causation, pausation, natation, jactation, lactation, tractation, dictation, nictation, citation, saltation, peltation, cantation, plantation, dentation, mentation, tentation, floatation, notation, potation, rotation, quotation, votation, captation, septation, flirtation, hortation, curtation, substation, laxation, taxation, vexation, fixation, luxation, fluxation, gestation, testation, crustation, gustation, guttation, lutation, mutation, nutation, putation, lavation, ovation, novation, starvation, nervation, servation, curvation, equation.
4. reprobation, approbation, perturbation, accubation, incubation, titubation, intubation, degradation, aggradation, depredation, validation, lapidation, trepidation, liquidation, emendation, commendation, inundation, retardation, denudation, desudation, transudation, trabeation, ideation, nucleation, permeation, lineation, recreation, procreation, propagation, divagation, delegation, relegation, allegation, abnegation, segregation, aggregation, congregation, obligation, ‚ fumigation, irrigation, litigation, mitigation, castigation, instigation, fustigation, elongation, prolongation, abrogation, derogation, objurgation, expurgation, subjugation, conjugation, corrugation, radiation, mediation, ciliation, filiation, palliation, foliation, spoliation, expiation, variation, seriation, fasciation, satiation, vitiation, aviation, obviation, deviation, dessiccation, exiccation, deprecation, imprecation, comprecation, albication, radication, abdication, dedication, medication, predication, indication, vindication, syndication, replication, triplication, implication, complication, application, supplication, duplication, explication, varication, fabrication, imbrication, lubrication, rubrication, lorication, extrication, vesication, mastication, rustication, toxication, allocation, collocation, dislocation, embrocation, avocation, convocation, provocation, debarkation, embarkation, demarkation, demarcation, altercation, bifurcation, confiscation, obfuscation, coruscation, inhalation, exhalation, congelation, correlation, revelation, insufflation, sibilation, jubilation, strigilation, vigilation, depilation, compilation, ventilation, mutilation, installation, flabellation, cancellation, flagellation, lamellation, crenelation, compellation, appellation, tessellation, castellation, constellation, vacillation, oscillation, fibrillation, titillation, scintillation, distillation, instillation, decollation, percolation, violation, immolation, desolation, isolation, insolation, consolation, avolation, legislation, contemplation, tabulation, tribulation, ambulation, peculation, speculation, cal-

culation, circulation, osculation, adulation, undulation, stridulation, modulation, nodulation, regulation, angulation, ululation, emulation, simulation, stimulation, nummulation, formulation, cumulation, granulation, crenulation, annulation, population, stipulation, sporulation, insulation, postulation, ovulation, defamation, acclamation, declamation, reclamation, proclamation, exclamation, desquamation, racemation, decimation, sublimation, acclimation, collimation, animation, lachrymation, intimation, estimation, inflammation, consummation, affirmation, confirmation, deformation, reformation, malformation, information, conformation, transformation, inhumation, exhumation, profanation, explanation, emanation, impanation, hyphenation, alienation, catenation, impregnation, indignation, obsignation, designation, resignation, assignation, consignation, combination, turbination, vaccination, fascination, ordination, pagination, machination, declination, reclination, inclination, pollination, lamination, gemination, semination, culmination, fulmination, commination, domination, nomination, germination, termination, vermination, lumination, rumination, supination, fibrination, destination, glutination, ruination, divination, condemnation, carbonation, condonation, coronation, personation, detonation, intonation, incarnation, hibernation, alternation, consternation, subornation, eburnation, dissipation, inculpation, exculpation, syncopation, extirpation, usurpation, occupation, nuncupation, declaration, reparation, preparation, separation, celebration, palpebration, cerebration, terebration, vertebration, calibration, adumbration, lucubration, obsecration, desecration, consecration, execration, dehydration, liberation, verberation, laceration, maceration, ulceration, carceration, federation, ponderation, moderation, toleration, numeration, generation, veneration, cineration, operation, asperation, desperation, iteration, literation, alteration, severation, integration, emigration, remigration, immigration, transmigration, admiration, aspiration, respiration, transpiration, inspiration, perspiration, suspiration, expiration, adoration, perforation, decoration, coloration, imploration, exploration, pignoration, corporation, peroration, restoration, aberration, saburration, susurration, penetration, impetration, perpetration, arbitration, infiltration, concentration, orchestration, fenestration, sequestration, registration, ministration, demonstration, remonstration, illustration, procuration, obduration, induration, figuration, fulguration, objuration, conjuration, depuration, suppuration, mensuration, maturation, saturation, trituration, suturation, condensation, compensation, dispensation, conversation, endorsation, incrassation, inspissation, succussation, decussation, dilatation, delactation, affectation, delectation, humectation, expectation, reluctation, eructation, hebetation, vegetation, habitation, dubitation, recitation, incitation, oscitation, excitation, meditation, agitation, digitation, cogitation, gurgitation, militation, imitation, limitation,sanitation,exploitation,crepitation, palpitation, irritation, hesitation, visitation, nictitation, gravitation, levitation, invitation, exaltation, occultation, auscultation, consultation, exultation, decantation, recantation, incantation, implantation, transplantation, indentation, lamentation, segmentation, pigmentation, augmentation, commentation, fomentation, fermentation, frumentation, presentation, ostentation, sustentation, frequentation, confrontation, denotation, annotation, connotation, compotation, misquotation, adaptation, impartation, dissertation, dehortation, exhortation, deportation, importation, transportation, exportation, devastation, infestation, molestation, forestation, detestation, intestation, contestation, protestation, attestation, reinstation, degustation, incrustation, confutation, refutation, salutation, immutation, commutation, permutation, transmutation, deputation, reputation, amputation, imputation, computation, disputation, graduation, valuation, adequation, actuation, punctuation, fluctuation, fructuation, situation, excavation, aggravation, depravation, elevation, salivation, derivation, deprivation, cultivation, motivation, captivation, estivation, renovation, innovation, enervation, innervation, observation, reservation, preservation, conservation, decurvation, incurvation, relaxation, annexation, prefixation, affixation, suffixation, solmization.

5. disapprobation, exacerbation, retrogradation, invalidation, consolidation, intimidation, delapidation, recommendation, accommodation, enucleation, delineation, allineation, variegation, investigation, interrogation, emaciation, depreciation, appreciation, officiation, enunciation, denunciation, renunciation, annunciation, pronunciation, excruciation, eradiation, irradiation, remediation, repudiation, retaliation, conciliation, affiliation, humiliation, defoliation, exfoliation, despoliation, calumniation, columniation, inebriation, excoriation, appropriation, expropriation, repatriation, expatriation, infuriation, luxuriation, expatiation, ingratiation, initiation, propitiation, novitation, substantiation, negotiation, alleviation, abbreviation, lixiviation, exuviation, asphyxiation, hypothecation, syllabication, eradication, revindication, adjudication, albification, pacification, specification, calcification, dulcification, edifi-

cation, nidification, codification, modification, deification, salification, qualification, vilification, mellification, jollification, mollification, nullification, prolification, amplification, simplification, magnification, dignification, signification, damnification, unification, aerification, clarification, verification, nigrification, glorification, petrification, thurification, purification, falsification, versification, classification, ossification, ratification, gratification, lactification, rectification, sanctification, notification, certification, fortification, mortification, testification, justification, mystification, vivification, republication, multiplication, misapplication, reduplication, quadruplication, communication, prevarication, authentication, domestication, sophistication, prognostication, intoxication, reciprocation, equivocation, disembarkation, intercalation, interrelation, invigilation, annihilation, assimilation, horripilation, circumvallation, interpellation, vitriolation, etiolation, interpolation, disconsolation, confabulation, somnambulation, perambulation, noctambulation, ejaculation, fasciculation, vermiculation, matriculation, reticulation, denticulation, articulation, gesticulation, miscalculation, turbeculation, emasculation, triangulation, dissimulation, accumulation, manipulation, depopulation, repopulation, congratulation, capitulation, expostulation, amalgamation, reanimation, approximation, reaffirmation, misinformation, malconformation, hydrogenation, alienation, concatenation, rejuvenation, hallucination, subordination, preordination, coordination, imagination, origination, disinclination, contamination, insemination, dissemination, elimination, recrimination, incrimination, discrimination, abomination, predomination, denomination, renomination, prenomination, determination, extermination, acumination, illumination, peregrination, indoctrination, assassination, procrastination, predestination, agglutination, conglutination, impersonation, anticipation, participation, emancipation, preoccupation, exhilaration, deliberation, reverberation, incarceration, evisceration, confederation, desideration, consideration, preponderation, immoderation, vociferation, proliferation, exaggeration, refrigeration, acceleration, deceleration, intoleration, concameration, agglomeration, conglomeration, enumeration, renumeration, degeneration, regeneration, incineration, itineration, exoneration, remuneration, co-operation, exasperation, depauperation, recuperation, vituperation, commiseration, reiteration, obliteration, alliteration, transliteration, adulteration, asseveration, redintegration, elaboration, collaboration, corroboration, imperforation, invigoration, amelioration, deterioration, discoloration commemoration, incorporation, expectoration, recalcitration, administration, prefiguration, transfiguration, inauguration, commensuration, circumgyration, intravasation, extravasation, improvisation, tergiversation, interpretation, inhabitation, premeditation, exagitation, recogitation, precogitation, ·regurgitation, habilitation, debilitation, facilitation, delimitation, relimitation, decapitation, decrepitation, precipitation, capacitation, felicitation, solicitation, resuscitation, revisitation, necessitation, ornamentation, supplementation, sedimentation, regimentation, alimentation, documentation, argumentation, instrumentation, representation, inadaptation, coadaptation, manifestation, deforestation, reforestation, circumnutation, evaluation, revaluation, attenuation, extenuation, insinuation, continuation, effectuation, perpetuation, habituation, accentuation, insalivation, recaptivation, ostracization, hybridization, iridization, oxidization, aggrandization, standardization, syllogization, eulogization, catechization, focalization, vocalization, feudalization, vandalization, scandalization, realization, legalization, racialization, socialization, alkalization, formalization, normalization, penalization, moralization, centralization, neutralization, vitalization, tantalization, totalization, equalization, chattelization,· stabilization, mobilization, sterilization, fertilization, utilization, tranquilization, civilization, crystallization, verbalization, symbolization, idolization, formulization, minimization, victimization, atomization, urbanization, vulcanization, organization, Christianization, humanization, galvanization, pollenization, scrutinization, solemnization, columnization, carbonization, ionization, colonization, mnemonization, harmonization, canonization, synchronization, patronization, modernization, fraternization, polarization, summarization, mercerization, mesmerization, pauperization, cauterization, pulverization, arborization, theorization, authorization, vaporization, temporization, proctorization, phosphorization, pasteurization, sulphurization, dramatization, stigmatization, magnetization, monetization, sensitization, amortization, analyzation, paralyzation.

6. interlineation, supererogation, mispronunciation, intermediation, domiciliation, reconciliation, misappropriation, transubstantiation, consubstantiation, circumstantiation, differentiation, contraindication, decalcification, solidification, disqualification, exemplification, indemnification, saponification, personification, transmogrification, electrification, emulsification, intensification, diversification, beatification, identification, excommunication, unsophistication, tintinnabulation, circumambulation, recapitulation, abalienation, ratiocination, insubordination,

inco-ordination, indiscrimination, predetermination, indetermination, reconsideration, inconsideration, maladministration, incapacitation, unpremeditation, prestidigitation, interdigitation, rehabilitation, experimentation, misrepresentation, individuation, discontinuation, superannuation, deoxidization, devocalization, commercialization, idealization, decimalization, nationalization, liberalization, generalization, demoralization, decentralization, naturalization, capitalization, devitalization, revitalization, immortalization, visualization, caramelization, demobilization, remobilization, monopolization, legitimization, economization, anatomization, epitomization, reorganization, inorganization, disorganization, antagonization, recolonization, familiarization, depolarization, formularization, popularization, militarization, polymerization, characterization, deodorization, categorization, systematization, acclimatization, aromatization, alphabetization, anesthetization, arithmetization, demonetization, desensitization.

7. intercommunication, intercolumniation, denationalization, denaturalization, universalization, spiritualization, Americanization.
8. internationalization, individualization, intellectualization.

ĀSH′und – **2.** rationed, stationed.
3. vacationed.

ĀSH′us – **2.** caseous, spacious, gracious.
3. sebaceous, bibacious, bulbaceous, herbaceous, edacious, predacious, mendacious, bodacious, smordacious, audacious, safacious, fugacious, salacious, fallacious, fumacious, tenacious, pugnacious, capacious, rapacious, rampacious, feracious, veracious, ungracious, disgracious, voracious, firtatious, setaceous, rutaceous, sequacious, loquacious, vivacious, vexatious.
4. efficacious, perspicacious, pervicacious, contumacious, pertinacious, incapacious, orchidaceous, corallaceous, liliaceous, scoriaceous, capillaceous, farinaceous, carbonaceous, saponaceous, camphoraceous, pulveraceous, frumentaceous, ostentatious, disputatious.
5. inefficacious.
ĀS′ik – **2.** basic, phasic, mässig [G.].
3. tribasic, aphasic.
4. diabasic, polybasic, monophasic, carapacic, diastasic.
ĀS′in – **2.** basin, sasin.
3. *washbasin; see also* ĀS′en *and* ĀS′on.
ĀS′ing – **2.** acing, basing, chasing, facing, casing, lacing, placing, pacing, spacing, racing, bracing, gracing, tracing.
3. abasing, debasing, effacing, defacing, refacing, outfacing, encasing, belacing, enlacing, unlacing, shoe lacing, replacing, displacing, misplacing, grimacing, outpacing, erasing, embracing, *drag racing, dog*

racing, disgracing, *horse racing*, retracing,
4. steeplechasing, interlacing.
AS′is– **2.** basis, phasis, glacis, crasis, stasis.
3. oasis.
AS′iv– **2.** suasive.
3. occasive, abrasive, assuasive, dissuasive, persuasive, evasive, invasive, pervasive.
AS′lee– **2.** basely.
4. commonplacely.
AS′less– **2.** aceless, baseless, faceless, caseless, laceless, placeless, maceless, paceless, spaceless, raceless, braceless, graceless, traceless, vaseless.
3. embraceless.
AS′let– **2.** lacelet, bracelet.
AS′ment– **2.** basement, casement, placement.
3. abasement, effacement, defacement, encasement, enlacement, replacement, emplacement, displacement, misplacement, embracement, retracement.
AS′o– **2.** peso, say-so.
3. Congreso.
AS′on– **2.** caisson, meson; *see also* **ĀS′en.**
AST′ed– **2.** basted, hasted, pasted, tasted, wasted, waisted.
3. unbasted, unpasted, untasted, unwasted, long-waisted, high-waisted, short-waisted.
AST′ee– **2.** hasty, pasty, tasty.
3. unhasty, untasty.
AST′er– **2.** baster, chaster, paster, taster, waster.
3. foretaster.
AST′ful– **2.** tasteful, wasteful.
3. distasteful, unwasteful.
AST′ing– **2.** basting, hasting, pasting, tasting, wasting.
3. unbasting, untasting, foretasting, unwasting.
AST′ingz– *see* **ĀST′ing–** plus "s" or "'s";
2. Hastings.
AST′less– **2.** basteless, hasteless, pasteless, tasteless, wasteless, waistless.
AS′um– **3.** omasum.
4. abomasum.
AT′a– **2.** Eta, Beta, data, rata, strata, Theta, Zeta.
3. albata, Caudata, relata, Squamata, pro rata.
4. Cingulata, Vertebrata, ultimata.
5. Invertebrata, desiderata.
AT′al– **2.** datal, fatal, natal, ratal, stratal, statal.
3. prenatal, postnatal, substratal.
AT′ed– **2.** bated, baited, dated, fated, fêted, gated, gaited, hated, skated, lated, plated, plaited, slated, mated, pated, rated, freighted, grated, crated, prated, sated, stated, waited, weighted.
3. abated, debated, rebated, predated, postdated, outdated, created, ill-fated, elated, belated, related, deflated, inflated, cremated, checkmated, stalemated, berated, orated, *frustrated*, instated, awaited.

4. antedated, validated, liquidated, inundated, ideated, permeated, recreated, re-created, procreated, propagated, delegated, relegated, abnegated, aggregated, segregated, obligated, fumigated, irrigated, litigated, mitigated, instigated, subjugated, corrugated, radiated, mediated, predicated, indicated, vindicated, syndicated, implicated, complicated, duplicated, supplicated, fabricated, lubricated, extricated, rusticated, advocated, altercated, confiscated, educated, unrelated, correlated, clavellated, ventilated, scintillated, mutilated, percolated, contemplated, tabulated, modulated, regulated, speculated, circulated, osculated, emulated, formulated, granulated, stipulated, acclimated, animated, intimated, estimated, consummated, emanated, hyphenated, designated, terminated, ruminated, fascinated, carbonated, detonated, intonated, hibernated, addle-pated, dissipated, syncopated, separated, celebrated, desecrated, consecrated, federated, moderated, tolerated, generated, venerated, operated, emigrated, perforated, decorated, underrated, penetrated, arbitrated, concentrated, demonstrated, illustrated, saturated, compensated, meditated, agitated, cogitated, imitated, palpitated, irritated, hesitated, gravitated, reinstated, amputated, graduated, situated, actuated, punctuated, fluctuated, aggravated, elevated, cultivated, captivated, renovated, antiquated.
5. invalidated, consolidated, intimidated, dilapidated, elucidated, accommodated, repudiated, retaliated, affiliated, humiliated, appropriated, emaciated, ingratiated, appreciated, depreciated, initiated, enunciated, negotiated, associated, annihilated, assimilated, matriculated, articulated, gesticulated, inoculated, accumulated, manipulated, congratulated, capitulated, approximated, subordinated, coordinated, originated, contaminated, disseminated, illuminated, opinionated, impersonated, anticipated, participated, emancipated, exaggerated, accelerated, enumerated, exonerated, remunerated, cooperated, recuperated, commiserated, reiterated, obliterated, disintegrated, elaborated, collaborated, corroborated, commemorated, evaporated, incorporated, inaugurated, premeditated, debilitated, facilitated, precipitated, necessitated, felicitated, resuscitated, orientated, evaluated, devaluated, insinuated, infatuated, accentuated.
6. circumstantiated, differentiated, recapitulated, incapacitated.
AT′ee– **2.** Ate, eighty, Haiti, Katie, Leyte, slaty, slatey, maty, matey, weighty.
AT′eez– *see* **ĀT′ee–** plus "s" or "'s"; **2.** vates.
3. Primates, penates, Euphrates.
AT′en– **2.** Aten, straighten, straiten, Satan.
AT′ent– **2.** latent, blatant, natant, patent.
3. inflatant, dilatant.

AT′er– 2. bater, baiter, dater, gaiter, hater, cater, skater, later, plater, slater, mater, pater, rater, crater, cratur, frater, freighter, greater, grater, prater, traitor, satyr, sater, 'tater, stater, waiter.
3. abater, debater, rebater, *placater*, vacatur, Decatur, elater, delator, relater, Dis pater, confrater, *barrator*.
4. allocatur, deleatur [L.], imprimatur, annotater, exequatur; *see also* ĀT′or.
AT′est– 2. latest, greatest.
AT′ful– 2. fateful, hateful, plateful, grateful.
3. ungrateful.
ATH′er– 2. bather, lather, swather.
ATH′ing– 2. bathing, scathing, lathing, swathing.
ATH′os– 2. bathos, pathos.
AT′im– 3. verbatim, gradatim [L.].
4. seriatim, literatim [both L.].
AT′ime– 2. daytime, Maytime, playtime, pay time.
AT′ing– 2. baiting, bating, dating, fêting, gating, gaiting, hating, skating, plating, plaiting, slating, mating, rating, freighting, grating, crating, prating, sating, waiting, weighting.
3. abating, debating, rebating, predating, outdating, creating, elating, belating, relating, deflating, inflating, *cremating, checkmating, stalemating,* berating, orating, *frustrating,* instating, awaiting.
4. antedating, validating, liquidating, inundating, ideating, permeating, re-creating, recreating, procreating, propogating, delegating, relegating, abnegating, aggregating, segregating, obligating, fumigating, irrigating, litigating, mitigating, instigating, subjugating, corrugating, radiating, mediating, predicating, indicating, vindicating, syndicating, implicating, complicating, duplicating, supplicating, fabricating, lubricating, extricating, rusticating, advocating, altercating, confiscating, educating, correlating, ventilating, scintillating, mutilating, percolating, comtemplating, tabulating, modulating, regulating, speculating, circulating, osculating, emulating, formulating, granulating, stipulating, acclimating, animating, intimating, estimating, consummating, emanating, hyphenating, designating, terminating, ruminating, fascinating, carbonating, detonating, intonating, hibernating, dissipating, syncopating, separating, celebrating, venerating, operating, integrating, emigrating, desecrating, consecrating, perforating, decorating, underrating, penetrating, arbitrating, concentrating, demonstrating, illustrating, saturating, compensating, meditating, agitating, cogitating, imitating, palpitating, irritating, hesitating, gravitating, reinstating, amputating, graduating, situating, actuating, punctuating, fluctuating, aggravating, elevating, cultivating, captivating, renovating.

5. invalidating, consolidating, intimidating, dilapidating, elucidating, accommodating, repudiating, retaliating, affiliating, humiliating, appropriating, emaciating, ingratiating, appreciating, depreciating, initiating, enunciating, negotiating, associating, annihilating, assimilating, matriculating, articulating, gesticulating, inoculating, accumulating, manipulating, congratulating, capitulating, approximating, subordinating, coordinating, originating, contaminating, disseminating, illuminating, impersonating, anticipating, participating, emancipating, exaggerating, accelerating, enumerating, exonerating, remunerating, cooperating, recuperating, commiserating, reiterating, obliterating, disintegrating, elaborating, collaborating, corroborating, commemorating, evaporating, incorporating, inaugurating, premeditating, debilitating, facilitating, precipitating, necessitating, felicitating, resuscitating, orientating, evaluating, devaluating, insinuating, accentuating.
6. circumstantiating, differentiating, recapitulating, incapacitating.
AT′ish– 2. latish, slatish, straightish.
AT′iv– 2. dative, native, stative.
3. creative, elative, prolative, dilative, *frustrative.*
4. approbative, reprobative, recreative, uncreative, procreative, propagative, abnegative, segregative, aggregative, irrigative, mitigative, abrogative, radiative mediative, palliative, variative, desiccative, exsiccative, deprecative, dedicative, medicative, vindicative, judicative, vellicative, replicative, implicative, complicative, duplicative, explicative, suffocative, invocative, educative, nomenclative, ventilative, oscillative, violative, contemplative, legislative, speculative, calculative, circulative, modulative, regulative, emulative, simulative, stimulative, cumulative, animative, estimative, emanative, designative, geminative, dominative, nominative, germinative, terminative, ruminative, lacerative, federative, generative, operative, decorative, pignorative, ministrative, illustrative, suppurative, compensative, dispensative, vegetative, meditative, cogitative, qualitative, imitative, limitative, irritative, hesitative, quantitative, gravitative, facultative, punctuative, innovative.
5. elucidative, consolidative, accommodative, investigative, depreciative, appreciative, enunciative, denunciative, renunciative, pronunciative, associative, dissociative, retaliative, conciliative, appropriative, initiative, alleviative, eradicative, adjudicative, significative, multiplicative, communicative, prognosticative, gesticulative, coagulative, accumulative, manipulative, congratulative, expostulative, approximative, subordinative, imaginative, originative, contaminative, dis-

seminative, recriminative, discriminative, denominative, determinative, illuminative, opinionative, anticipative, participative, exhilarative, deliberative, confederative, desiderative, exaggerative, accelerative, enumerative, exonerative, remunerative, inoperative, cooperative, recuperative, vituperative, reiterative, alliterative, corroborative, invigorative, ameliorative, commemorative, evaporative, administrative, interpretative, inhabitative, necessitative, resuscitative, premeditative, authoritative, insinuative, continuative.

6. insignificative, uncommunicative, excommunicative, unappreciative, recapitulative, unimaginative, unremunerative, deteriorative.

AT′lee– 2. lately, greatly, straitly, straightly, stately.

3. sedately, striately, oblately, *prolately*, *truncately*, *palmately*, innately, *pinnately*, *ternately*, ornately, irately, *dentately*, unstately.

4. delicately, intricately, mediately, desolately, ultimately, intimately, proximately, obstinately, passionately, *biternately*, *triternately*, alternately, fortunately, separately, moderately, temperately, desperately, corporately, accurately, obdurately, *insensately*, *decussately*, adequately.

5. indelicately, immediately, appropriately, inviolately, disconsolately, immaculately, legitimately, approximately, subordinately, inordinately, co-ordinately, effeminately, discriminately, determinately, impassionately, compassionately, dispassionately, affectionately, proportionately, unfortunately, importunately, deliberately, considerately, immoderately, degenerately, intemperately, illiterately, elaborately, inaccurately, commensurately, precipitately, inadequately,

6. intermediately, inappropriately, unappropriately, illegitimately, insubordinately, indiscriminately, indeterminately, unaffectionately, disproportionately, inconsiderately, incommensurately.

AT′less– 2. baitless, dateless, fateless, gateless, gaitless, hateless, mateless, pateless, freightless, grateless, traitless, sateless, stateless, weightless.

3. estateless.

AT′ness– 2. lateness, greatness, straightness, straitness.

3. sedateness, oblateness, innateness, ornateness, irateness.

AT′o– 2. Cato, Plato.

3. abeto [Sp.], pomato, tomato, potato.

AT′or– 2. gator [slang], traitor.

3. abator, probator, mandator, laudator, creator, legator, negator, ligator, viator, plicator, locator, piscator, elator, delator, relator, dilator, collator, translator, cremator, signator, spinator, donator, *vibrator*, *migrator*, orator, *barrator*, narrator, curator, gyrator, pulsator *natator*, tractator, spec-

tator, dictator, punctator, potator, rotator, portator, testator, equator, levator.

4. incubator, depredator, liquidator, emendator, commendator, recreator, procreator, caveator, propagator, abnegator, obligator, alligator, fumigator, irrigator, litigator, mitigator, castigator, instigator, navigator, promulgator, compurgator, expurgator, subjugator, corrugator, gladiator, radiator, mediator, palliator, spoliator, expiator, vitiator, aviator, deviator, desiccator, exsiccator, deprecator, imprecator, abdicator, dedicator, predicator, indicator, vindicator, judicator, duplicator, explicator, fabricator, lubricator, rubricator, extricator, masticator, rusticator, inculcator, advocator, evocator, invocator, convocator, demarcator, confiscator, educator, escalator, inhalator, nomenclator, revelator, depilator, ventilator, scintillator, mutilator, flagellator, vacillator, oscillator, desolator, percolator, violator, immolator, isolator, contemplator, tabulator, ambulator, speculator, calculator, circulator, adulator, modulator, regulator, emulator, simulator, stimulator, granulator, stipulator, insulator, decimator, estimator, consummator, emanator, designator, propugnator, vaccinator, buccinator, fascinator, machinator, comminator, dominator, nominator, terminator, ruminator, divinator, cachinnator, personator, detonator, intonator, alternator, extirpator, separator, celebrator, lucubrator, desecrator, consecrator, execrator, Pantocrator, liberator, moderator, numerator, generator, venerator, operator, integrator, emigrator, immigrator, transmigrator, aspirator, respirator, inspirator, cospirator, decorator, perforator, perpetrator, arbitrator, concentrator, demonstrator, remonstrator, illustrator, instaurator, procurator, depurator, obturator, condensator, compensator, dispensator, meditator, agitator, cogitator, imitator, commentator, annotator, devastator, reinstator, commutator, amputator, valuator, elevator, cultivator, captivator, innovator, enervator, conservator, renovator, malaxator.

5. elucidator, invalidator, consolidator, intimidator, delineator, investigator, variegator, interrogator, repudiator, conciliator, calumniator, depreciator, appreciator, officiator, enunciator, annunciator, pronunciator, initiator, propitiator, negotiator, alleviator, abbreviator, asphyxiator, hypothecator, adjudicator, pacificator, edificator, modificator, qualificator, significator, purificator, classificator, multiplicator, communicator, prevaricator, sophisticator, prognosticator, reciprocator, equivocator, annihilator, assimilator, interpellator, interpolator, perambulator, coagulator, gesticulator, inoculator, emasculator, accumulator, pedipulator, manipulator, congratulator, expostulator, amalgamator, rejuvenator, originator, contaminator, disseminator, eliminator, denominator, exterminator, illuminator, peregrinator, assassinator, procrastinator, predestinator, impersonator, anticipator, participator, emancipator, deliberator, vociferator, exaggerator, refrigerator, decelerator, accelerator, enumerator, regenerator, incinerator, remunerator, vituperator, commiserator, disintegrator, elaborator, collaborator, corroborator, invigorator, incorporator, administrator, inaugurator, improvisator, tergiversator, resuscitator, habilitator, facilitator, decapitator, evacuator, extenuator, insinuator, continuator, totalizator, catalyzator.

6. circumnavigator, supererogator, excommunicator, prestidigitator; *see also* ĀT′er.

AT′ress– 2. traitress, waitress.
3. oratress, dictatress.
4. imitatress.

AT′rik– 2. matric, phratric.

AT′riks– 2. matrix, patrix.
3. fundatrix, cicatrix, quadratrix, dictatrix, testatrix,
4. mediatrix, aviatrix, indicatrix, legislatrix, osculatrix, gubernatrix, nominatrix.
5. administratrix.

AT′ron– 2. matron, natron, patron.
3. salnatron.

AT′um– 2. datum, stratum.
3. relatum, pomatum, quadratum, erratum, substratum, testatum.
4 seriatim, petrolatum, postulatum, ultimatum, Ageratum, capitatum.
5. desideratum.

AT′ure– 2. nature.
3. denature.
4. nomenclature, legislature.

AT′us– 2. latus, flatus, stratus, stratous, status.
3. beatus, hiatus, afflatus, inflatus, senatus [L.], conatus, postnatus, quadratus.
4. apparatus, saleratus, literatus, comitatus.

AV′a– 2. Ava, deva.

AV′al– 2. naval, navel.
3. precaval, octaval.

AV′ee– 2. ave, Davy, Devi, cavy, cavie, slavey, navy, pavy, gravy, wavy.
3. agave, peccavi.
4. Mahadevi.

AV′en– 2. haven, raven, graven, craven, shaven.
3. engraven, unshaven.

AV′er– 2. laver, flavor, claver, slaver, paver, raver, braver, graver, craver, savor, shaver, waver, waiver, quaver, suaver.
3. cadaver, disfavor, enslaver, Papaver, engraver, depraver, *livesaver, time saver.*
4. demiquaver, semiquaver.

AV′erd– 2. favored, flavored, wavered, quavered.
3. ill-favored, disfavored, unflavored.

AV′est– 2. bravest, gravest, suavest.

AV′id– 2. David, flavid.

AV′ing– 2. caving, laving, paving, raving, braving, craving, saving, shaving, staving, waving, waiving.
3. behaving, enclaving, enslaving, engraving, depraving, *lifesaving, timesaving.*
4. misbehaving, unenslaving.

AV′is– 2. Avis, Davis, clavis, mavis, pavis.
4. rara avis [L.].

AV′ish– 2. slavish, knavish, bravish.

AV′it– 2. davit.
3. cessavit.
4. affidavit, indicavit [L.], devastavit.

AV′lee– 2. knavely, bravely, gravely, suavely.

AV′less– 2. caveless, slaveless, graveless, waveless.

AV′ment– 2. lavement, pavement.
3. enslavement, engravement, depravement.

AV′ness– 2. braveness, graveness, suaveness.

AV′o– 2. Pavo, bravo.
3. octavo, centavo.

AV′or– 2. favor, flavor, savor.
3. disfavor; *see also* ĀV′er.

AV′yer– 2. clavier, pavior, savior, saviour, Xavier.
3. behavior.
4. misbehavior.

AZ′ee– 2. daisy, gazy, hazy, jasey, lazy, glazy, sleazy, mazy, phrasy, crazy.
3. patesi.
4. lackadaisy, ups-a-daisy, upsy-daisy.

AZ′el– 2. basil, gazel, Hazel, nasal.
3. witch-hazel, appraisal, Azazel.
4. reppraisal.

AZ′en– 2. raisin, glazen, brazen.

AZ′er– 2. gazer, hazer, lazar, blazer, mazer, raser, raiser, razor, phraser, grazer, praiser.
3. *stargazer,* upraiser, appraiser, self-praiser, dispraiser.
4. paraphraser.

AZ′ez– 2. dazes, fazes, phases, gazes, hazes, lazes, blazes, glazes, mazes, razes, raises, braises, brazes, phrases, fraises, frases, grazes, crazes, praises, chaises, vases.
3. bedazes, malaises, emblazes, liaises, amazes, bemazes, rephrases, upraises, appraises, bepraises.
4. polonaises, paraphrases, metaphrases, reappraises, underpraises, overpraises.

AZH′a– 2. Asia.
3. abasia, aphasia, ergasia, aplasia, gymnasia, Eurasia, acrasia, Acrasia, fantasia, astasia.
4. paraphrasia, Australasia, Anastasia, hemostasia.

AZH′al– 2. basial.
3. gymnasial.

AZH′an– 2. Asian.
3. Caucasian, Eurasian, equation.
4. Australasian; *see also* ĀZH′un.

AZH′er– 2. azure, glazier, rasure, frasier, brazier, grazier.
3. embrasure, erasure.

AZH′un– 2. rasion, suasion.

3. occasion, abrasion, corrasion, equation, persuasion, dissuasion, evasion, invasion, pervasion; *see also* **ĀZH'an.**

AZ'ing– **2.** dazing, fazing, phasing, gazing, hazing, lazing, blazing, glazing, mazing, razing, raising, braising, brazing, phrasing, fraising, frasing, grazing, crazing, praising. **3.** bedazing, emblazing, amazing, bemazing, rephrasing, upraising, appraising, bepraising. **4.** paraphrasing, reappraising, underpraising, overpraising.

AZ'less– **2.** dazeless, fazeless, phaseless, gazeless, hazeless, blazeless, glazeless, mazeless, raiseless, phraseless, fraiseless, crazeless, praiseless.

AZ'ment– **3.** amazement, appraisement. **4.** reappraisement.

AZ'o– **2.** Mazo. **4.** Valparaiso.

AZ'on– **2.** scazon, blazon. **3.** emblazon, Malmaison. **4.** diapason.

Ā (ay)

Triple Rhymes

Primary or Secondary Accent Falls on Second from Last Syllable; Imperfect Rhymes Are in Italics.

A′a–bl– **3.** playable, payable, sayable, weighable, swayable.
4. repayable, prepayable, impayable, unpayable, defrayable, portrayable, unsayable, unswayable, conveyable, surveyable.
5. unportrayable, unconveyable.
AB′i–a– **3.** labia, trabea, Swabia.
4. Arabia.
AB′i–an– **3.** Fabian, Sabian, Swabian.
4. Arabian.
AB′l–ness– **3.** ableness, stableness.
4. unableness, unstableness.
AB′or–er– **3.** laborer, taborer.
AB′or–ing– **3.** laboring, neighboring, taboring.
4. belaboring, unlaboring.
AD′a–bl– **3.** gradable, tradable, shadabel, wadable.
4. retradable, persuadable, evadable.
5. unpersuadable, undissuadable.
AD′ed–lee– **3.** fadedly, jadedly.
4. degradedly.
AD′ed–ness– **3.** fadedness, jadedness, shadedness.
4. degradedness.
AD′i–a– **3.** stadia.
4. Acadia, Arcadia, Palladia.
AD′i–al– **3.** radial.
5. uniradial, multiradial, interstadial.
AD′i–an– **3.** radian.
4. Barbadian, Acadian, Akkadian, Arcadian, Palladian, nomadian, Canadian.
AD′i–ans– **3.** radiance.
4. irradiance.
AD′i–ant– **3.** radiant, gradient.
4. irradiant.
AD′i–ate– **3.** radiate.
4. eradiate, irradiate.
AD′ing–lee– **3.** fadingly.
4. degradingly, pervadingly.
AD′i–um– **3.** radium, stadium, vadium.
4. Palladium, vanadium.
AD′i–us– **3.** gladius, radius.

4. adradius.
5. hyporadius.
AG′rans–ee– **3.** flagrancy, fragrancy, vagrancy.
A′ik–al– **3.** laical.
4. archaical, Hebraical.
5. algebraical, pharisaical.
6. paradisaical.
A′it–ee– **3.** gaiety, laity.
AJ′a–bl– **3.** gaugeable, stageable.
4. assuageable, dissuageable.
AJ′i–a– **3.** Hagia.
4. aphagia, dysphagia, Panagia.
5. polyphagia.
AJ′i–an– **3.** Magian.
4. pelagian, contagion.
5. Brobdignagian.
6. archipelagian.
AJ′i–lee– **3.** cagily, stagily.
AJ′us–lee– **4.** rampageously, outrageously, courageously, contagiously.
5. advantageously.
6. disadvantageously.
AJ′us–ness– **4.** rampageousness, outrageousness, courageousness, contagiousness.
5. advantageousness.
6. disadvantageousness.
AK′a–bl– **3.** acheable, placable, slakalbe, breakable, shakable, takable.
4. implacable, unslakable, unbreakable, unshakable, mistakable, awakable.
5. undertakable, unmistakable.
AK′at–ed– **3.** placated, vacated.
4. unplacated, revacated.
AK′er–ee– **3.** bakery, fakery, snakery, rakery, Quakery.
AK′er–izm– **4.** fakirism, Lakerism, Shakerism, Quakerism.
AK′i–a– **3.** trachea.
4. Batrachia.
AK′i–al– **3.** rachial, brachial, tracheal.
AK′i–an– **3.** trachean.
4. Noachian, batrachian, Eustachian.

AK′i-ness– **3.** fakiness, shakiness, flakiness, snakiness, quakiness.

AK′we-us– **3.** aqueous.
4. subaqueous, terraqueous.

AL′a-bl– **3.** bailable, mailable, salable, sailable.
4. inhalable, exhalable, unmailable, wholesalable, unsalable, assailable, unsailable, available, retailable.
5. unassailable, unavailable.

AL′i-a– **3.** galea, palea, Thalia.
4. Sedalia, idalia, Westphalia, regalia, Eulalia, Mammalia, Massalia, azalea, sponsalia, Psoralea, Arctalia.
5. Lupercalia, paralalia, pseudolalia, echolalia, Bacchanalia, marginalia, Terminalia, Saturnalia, Antarctalia.
6. Marsupialia, paraphernalia; *see also* **ĀL′ya.**

AL′i-an– **3.** alien.
4. Daedalian, Idalian, regalian, mammalian, Castalian.
5. phantasmalian, bacchanalian, saturnalian.
6. sesquipedalian, Episcopalian; *see also* **ĀL′yun.**

AL′i-as– **3.** alias.
4. Sibelius, Ortelius.

AL′i-ness– **3.** dailiness, scaliness, wailiness.
4. tridailiness.

AL′i-um– **3.** Galium, kalium.
4. Idalium.

AM′a-bl– **3.** blamable, claimable, namable, framable, tamable.
4. unblamable, reclaimable, unnamable, unframable, untamable.

AM′ful-ness– **3.** gamefulness, blamefulness, shamefulness.
4. unshamefulness.

AM′i-a– **3.** lamia.
5. academia, Macadamia, adynamia.
6. Mesopotamia.

AM′less-ness– **3.** aimlessness, famelessness, blamelessness, namelessness, shamelessness, tamelessness.

AN′a-bl– **3.** chainable, gainable, planable, drainable, sprainable, trainable, strainable.
4. ordainable, profanable, explainable, untrainable, restrainable, constrainable, attainable, obtainable, maintainable, sustainable.
5. inexplainable, unexplainable, unobtainable, unattainable, ascertainable.

AN′a-blee– **4.** explainably.
5. unexplainably, unrestrainably, unattainably, unobtainably.

AN′e-a– **4.** Castanea.
5. succedanea, miscellanea, collectanea; *see also* **ĀN′i -a.**

AN′e-an– **4.** terranean, castanean.
5. subterranean.
6. Mediterranean, circumforanean, contemporanean, extemporanean; *see also* **ĀN′i- an.**

AN′e-us– **4.** siccaneous, araneous, terraneous, spontaneous, castaneous, cutaneous.
5. succedaneous, miscellaneous, temporaneous, subterraneous, coetaneous, simultaneous, instantaneous, consentaneous, dissentaneous, subcutaneous.
6. antecedaneous, contemporaneous, extemporaneous.

AN′ful-ee– **3.** banefully, gainfully, painfully.
4. disdainfully, ungainfully.

AN′ful-ness– **3.** gainfulness, painfulness.
4. disdainfulness, ungainfulness.

AN′i-a– **3.** mania.
4. Albania, amania, Tasmania, Rumania, Ukrainia, Urania, Titania, Castenea.
5. succedanea, miscellanea, florimania, theomania, Gallomania, melomania, Anglomania, monomania, hydromania, pyromania, nosomania, dipsomania, potomania, kleptomania, Pomerania, Aquitania, collectanea, Lithuania, Transylvania, Pennsylvania.
6. bibliomania, decalcomania, megalomania, demonomania, Tripolitania.

AN′i-ak– **3.** maniac.
5. egomaniac, ergomaniac, Gallomaniac, Anglomaniac, monomaniac, pyromaniac, dipsomaniac, kleptomaniac.
6. bibliomaniac, curiomaniac, megalomaniac.

AN′i-al– **3.** cranial.
4. domanial, acranial, cutaneal.
5. subterraneal.

AN′i-an– **4.** Albanian, volcanian, Vulcanian, Tasmanian, Rumanian, Iranian, Ukrainian, Uranian.
5. Pomeranian, Lithuanian, Transylvanian, Pennsylvanian; *see also* **ĀN′e-an.**

AN′i-ness– **3.** raininess, braininess, graininess, veininess.

AN′ing-lee– **4.** complainingly.
5. uncomplainingly, entertainingly.

AN′i-um– **3.** cranium.
4. germanium, geranium, uranium, titanium.
5. succedaneum.

ANJ′a-bl– **3.** changeable.
4. unchangeable, exchangeable, arrangeable, derangeable.
5. interchangeable, rearrangeable.

ANJ′a-blee– **3.** changeably.
4. unchangeably, exchangeably.
5. interchangeably.

ANJ′i-ness– **3.** manginess, ranginess.

ANT′a-bl– **3.** paintable, taintable.
4. acquaintable.

AP′a-bl– **3.** capable, papable, drapable, shapable.
4. incapable, escapable, reshapable, unshapable.
5. inescapable.

AP′a-blee– **3.** capably.
4. incapably.
5. inescapably, unescapably.

AP′er-ee– **3.** apery, capery, japery, napery,

papery, drapery, grapery, vapory.
AP′er–er–   3. caperer, naperer, paperer, taperer, vaporer.
AP′er–ing–   3. capering, papering, tapering, vaporing.
AP′i–an– 3. Apian.
   5. Aesculapian.
AR′a–bl–   3. airable, bearable, pairable, tearable, wearable, swearable.
   4. unbearable, repairable, unwearable,
   5. unrepairable; *see also* **ĂR′a –bl.**
AR′ful–ee–   3. carefully, sparefully, prayerfully.
   4. uncarefully.
AR′ful–ness–   3. carefulness, sparefulness, prayerfulness.
   4. uncarefulness.
AR′i–a– 3. aria, area, feria, pariah.
   4. herbaria, Bulgaria, Icaria, cercaria, malaria, talaria, solaria, ranaria, dataria, cataria, wistaria, aquaria, Bavaria.
   5. topiaria, Berengaria, urticaria, cineraria, honoraria, adversaria, planetaria.
AR′i–al– 3. aerial, areal, Ariel, narial.
   4. diarial, vicarial, malarial, riparial, glossarial, bursarial, nectarial, sectarial, notarial, ovarial.
   5. calendarial, commissarial, secretarial, actuarial.
AR′i–an– 3. Arian, Aryan, Marian, Parian.
   4. barbarian, gregarian, Bulgarian, vulgarian, Hungarian, Icarian, grammarian, lunarian, riparian, librarian, agrarian, Caesarian, rosarian, nectarean, sectarian, Bavarian, ovarian.
   5. millenarian, centenarian, septenarian, Sabbatarian, vegetarian, proletarian, Trinitarian, Unitarian, nonsectarian, libertarian, antiquarian.
   6. abecedarian, quinquagenarian, septuagenarian, nonegenarian, octogenarian, disciplinarian, predestinarian, totalitarian, utilitarian, humanitarian, necessitarian, ubiquitarian, parliamentarian, sacramentarian, veterinarian, alphabetarian.
   7. valetudinarian, latitudinarian, platitudinarian, antitrinitarian.
AR′i–ant– 3. variant.
   4. contrariant, bivariant, invariant, covariant.
AR′i–eez– 3. Aries, caries, paries.
AR′i–er– 3. airier, charier, hairier, glarier, varier, warier.
AR′i–est– 3. airiest, chariest, hairiest, glariest, wariest.
AR′i–form– 3. aeriform, nariform, variform.
   4. scalariform.
AR′i–lee– 3. airily, charily, hairily, warily.
AR′i–ness– 3. airiness, chariness, hairiness, glariness, wariness.
   4. contrariness,
   5. sanguinariness, temporariness, arbitrariness, solitariness, sedentariness, momentar-

iness, voluntariness.
AR′ing–lee– 3. daringly, blaringly, flaringly, glaringly, sparingly.
   4. forbearingly.
AR′I–um– 3. barium.
   4. herbarium, verbarium, solarium, fumarium, ranarium, terrarium, sacrarium, rosarium, lactarium, vivarium. aquarium.
   5. columbarium, cinerarium, honorarium, cometarium, planetarium, sanitarium.
AR′i–us– 3. carious, scarious, various.
   4. nefarious, vagarious, gregarious, precarious Icarius, vicarious, calcareous, hilarious, senarius, riparious, setarious, nectareous, octarius, Aquarius.
   5. multifarious, septenarius, quaternarius, confessarius, Sagittarius, Januarius, Februarius, Stradivarius.
AS′a–bl– 3. faceable, laceable, placeable, traceable.
   4. effaceable, defaceable, replaceable, unplaceable, erasable.
   5. irreplaceable, unerasable; *see also* **ĀS′i –bl.**
AS′ed–lee– 4. shamefacedly, barefacedly.
AS′en–see– 4. adjacency, complacency.
ASH′al–ee– 3. facially, glacially, racially.
   5. interracially.
ASH′i–a– 3. Asia.
   4. Sabbatia, acacia, solatia, Dalmatia, Alsatia, Cetacea, Crustacea.
ASH′i–al– 3. basial, spatial.
   4. abbatial, palatial, primatial.
   5. interspatial.
ASH′i–an– 3. Asian, Haitian, Thracian.
   4. Sabbatian, Dalmatian, Horatian, Alsatian, Eustachian.
ASH′i–ate– 3. glaciate, satiate.
   4. sagaciate, emaciate, expatiate, ingratiate, insatiate.
ASH′i–ent– *see* **ĀSH′ent.**
ASH′i–o– 3. ratio.
   4. Horatio.
   7. Nova Constellatio.
ASH′un–al– 3. stational.
   4. probational, vocational, relational, translational, vibrational, gyrational, sensational, rotational, quotational, equational.
   5. incubational, congregational, recreational, conjugational, variational, convocational, educational, revelational, informational, combinational, inclinational, terminational, occupational, inspirational, condensational, compensational, gravitational, presentational, salutational, deputational, derivational, observational.
   6. interrogational, denominational, commemorational, representational.
ASH′un–er– 3. stationer.
   4. probationer, foundationer, oblationer.
   5. restorationer.
ASH′un–ist– 4. creationist, deflationist, inflationist, salvationist.
   5. convocationist, federationist, moderationist, tolerationist, emigrationist, inspira-

tionist, restorationist, conversationist, imitationist, annotationist, transmutationist, innovationist.

6. repudiationist, annihilationist, emancipationist, colonizationist.

ASH'un–less– 3. nationless, rationless, stationless.

4. foundationless, vibrationless, temptationless.

3. educationless, inspirationless, conversationless, imitationless; *see also* **ASH'un.**

ASH'us–lee– 3. spaciously, graciously.

4. predaciously, audaciously, mendaciously, sagaciously, fallaciously, salaciously, tenaciously, pugnaciously, capaciously, rapaciously, veraciously, ungraciously, voraciously, vexatiously, vivaciously, loquaciously.

5. efficaciously, perspicaciously, contumaciously, pertinaciously, ostentatiously, disputatiously.

ASH'us–ness– 3. spaciousness, graciousness.

4. edaciousness, predaciousness, audaciousness, mendaciousness, sagaciousness, fugaciousness, fallaciousness, salaciousness, pugnaciousness, tenaciousness, capaciousness, rapaciousness, ungraciousness, veraciousness, voraciousness, vexatiousness, vivatiousness, sequaciousness, loquaciousness.

5. efficaciousness, contumaciousness, pertinaciousness, incapaciousness, perspicaciousness, ostentatiousness, disputatiousness.

AS'i–bl– 3. suasible.

4. evasible, persuasible.

5. unpersuasible; *see also* **ĀS'a–bl.**

AS'i–ness– 3. laciness, raciness.

AS'iv–ness– 4. abrasiveness, evasiveness, invasiveness, pervasiveness, assuasiveness, dissuasiveness, persuasiveness.

AST'ful–ee– 3. tastefully, wastefully.

4. distastefully.

AST'i–lee– 3. hastily, pastily, tastily.

AT'a–bl– 3. baitable, hatable, matable, ratable, gratable, satable, statable.

4. abatable, debatable, creatable, relatable, inflatable, dilatable, translatable, beratable. unsatable.

5. unrelatable, regulatable.

AT'a–blee– 3. ratably.

5. untranslatably.

AT'a–lee– 3. fatally.

4. prenatally.

AT'en–see– 3. latency, patency.

AT'ful–ee– 3. fatefully, hatefully, gratefully.

4. ungratefully.

AT'ful–ness– 3. fatefulness, hatefulness, gratefulness.

4. ungratefulness.

AT'i–ness– 3. slatiness, weightiness.

AT'ing–lee– 3. gratingly.

5. deprecatingly, nauseatingly, mediatingly, contemplatingly, calculatingly, fascinatingly, alternatingly, penetratingly, meditatingly, irritatingly, hesitatingly, aggravatingly, captivatingly.

6. accommodatingly, interrogatingly, excruciatingly, alleviatingly, discriminatingly, premeditatingly, insinuatingly.

AT'iv–lee– 3. natively.

4. creatively.

5. predicatively, implicatively, legislatively, speculatively, emulatively, simulatively, cumulatively, germinatively, terminatively, operatively, decoratively, dubitatively, meditatively, cogitatively, qualitatively, imitatively, hesitatively, quantitatively.

6. significatively, multiplicatively, gesticulatively, accumulatively, manipulatively, imaginatively, determinatively, opinionatively, anticipatively, participatively, co-operatively, vituperatively, commiseratively, reiteratively, alliteratively, corroboratively, invigoratively, commemoratively, administratively, interpretatively, authoritatively. insinuatively.

7. incommunicatively.

AT'iv–ness– 3. nativeness.

4. creativeness.

5. speculativeness, emulativeness, cumulativeness, decorativeness, penetrativeness, meditativeness, cogitativeness, imitativeness, hesitativeness.

6. communicativeness.

AT'ron–al– 3. matronal, patronal.

AT'ron–ij– 3. matronage, patronage.

AV'a–bl– 3. lavable, savable, shavable.

4. unsavable, unshavable.

AV'er–ee– 3. Avery, slavery, knavery, bravery, wavery, quavery, savory.

4. unsavory.

5. antislavery.

AV'er–er– 3. favorer, laverer, flavorer, waverer, quaverer.

AV'er–ing– 3. favoring, flavoring, savoring, wavering, quavering.

4. unwavering.

AV'er–us– 3. favorous, flavorous, quaverous, savorous.

4. papaverous.

AV'i–a– 3. Pavia.

4. Moravia, Belgravia, Batavia, Octavia.

5. Scandinavia.

AV'i–al– 3. gavial, clavial.

AV'i–an– 3. avian, Shavian.

4. Moravian, Belgravian, Batavian, Octavian.

5. Scandinavian.

AV'i–er– 3. clavier, wavier.

AV'ish–ness– 3. slavishness, knavishness.

AZ'a–bl– 3. raisable, praisable.

4. appraisable, persuasible.

5. unpersuasible.

AZH'i–a– 3. Asia.

4. abasia, aphasia, ergasia, aplasia, gymnasia, Eurasia, acrasia, Acrasia, fantasia, astasia.

5. paraphasia, Australasia, Anastasia, hemostasia.

AZH'i–al– 3. basial.

4. gymnasial.
AZH′i–an– 3. Asian.
   4. Caucasian, Eurasian.
   5. Australasian.
AZ′i–lee– 3. hazily, lazily, crazily.

AZ′i–ness– 3. haziness, laziness, maziness, craziness.
AZ′ing–lee– 3. dazingly, gazingly, blazingly.
   4. amazingly.

Ä (ah)

[See also Ŏ (bob)]

Single (Masculine) Rhymes

Primary or Secondary Accent Falls on Last Syllable; Imperfect Rhymes Are in Italics.

A– 1. ah.
3. oh-and-ah.
BA– 1. baa, bah, bas [F.].
2. caba, à bas [F.], en bas [F.], Casbah, Kasbah.
CHA– 1. cha [Chin.].
2. cha-cha.
3. cha-cha-cha.
DA′ 1. da.
2. dada, *Dada, purdah, pardah, houdah, howdah, lowdah.*
3. Merida.
FA– 1. fa.
2. *buffa* [It.], *luffa, loofah.*
4. apocrypha.
GA– 1. ga.
2. *aga, agha.*
HA– 1. ha, hah.
2. aha, ahah, haha, *Maha, maha.*
KA– 1. ka.
2. *jaca, kaka.*
3. abacá, abaká, *Kabaka,* silica, replica, Monica, parica, Erica, avocat [F.].
4. basilica, majolica, sciatica.
LA– 1. la, blah, [slang].
2. lala, éclat [F.], holla, voilà [F.].
3. alala, tralala, oh là là [F.], oo-la-la [slang], Angela, gondola, cupola, nebula, formula, insula [L.], Ursula.
4. parabola, tarentola, peninsula, tarantula.
MA– 1. ma, maa.
2. amah, mama, sama, *grandma.*
3. Panama, elema, cinema.
4. grandmama, anathema.
NA– 1. na, nah.
2. ana, an'a [Scot.], *anna, ana, nana, bwana.*
3. Paraná, Elena, Helena.
4. phenomena.
PA– 1. pa, pah, pas [F.], spa.
2. papa, *grandpa, oompah,* faux pas [F.], n'est-ce pas? [F.].
3. grandpapa.

RA– 1. rah, Ra, bra, bras [F.], fra [It.], kra.
2. *para,* Seurat, hurrah.
3. ma'abara, acará, baccarat, algebra, vertebra, cholera, camera, opera, ça ira [F.]. plethora.
4. *candelabra,* et cetera, mandragora.
5. *abracadabra,* che sará, sará [It.], à bon chat, bon rat [F.].
SA– 1. sa, saa, saah.
2. comme ça [F.].
4. comme çi, comme ça [F.].
SHA– 1. shah, chat [F.].
2. Zaza, pasha.
TA– 1. ta, t'a, taa.
2. ta-ta, état [F.].
3. coup d'état, taffeta, tiers état [F.], Bogotá.
4. automata.
6. patati-patata [F.].
VA– 1. va [F.].
2. ava [Scot.], brava, ça va [F.].
3. baklava.
WA– 1. wa, wa' [Scot.], Wa, foi [F.], joie [F.], qua, quoi [F.], loi [F.], moi [F.], noix [F.], pois [F.], roi [F.], droit [F.), soie [F.], soi [F.], schwa, toi [F.], voie [F.], voix [F.].
2. ma foi [F.], bourgeois, François, en soi [F.], patois.
3. autrefois [F.], fille de joie [F.], feu de joie [F.], petits pois [F.], vive le roi [F.].
4. je ne sais quoi [F.], Dieu et mon droit [F.].
YA– 1. ya, yah, ja [G.].

AB– 1. ab [Heb.], wab [dial.], squab, swab.
2. kitab, *gabgab,* jawab, nawab.
ABD– 1. squabbed, swabbed.
AD– 1. ahed, baaed, had, wad, quad.
2. aubade, falcade, ballade, roulade, pomade, charade, estrade, hurrahed, façade, glissade, metad.
3. ohed-and-ahed, esplanade, promenade,

gallopade.

AF– 1. half, Kaf, calf, laugh, Graf [G.], strafe, quaff.
2. behalf, *moon calf, horse laugh.*
3. better half, half and half.

AFT– 1. aft, laughed, strafed, quaffed, waft.
2. abaft.

AG– 1. Dag, blague [F.], Prague.

AJH– 1. raj, saj, taj.
2. coupage, barrage, garage, mirage, massage, corsage, potage [F.], lavage.
3. entourage, vernissage, sabotage, esclavage [F.].

AK– 1. ach [G.], Bach, lac [F.], Mach, plaque.
2. tumbak, macaque, *gopak*, Irak, chittak.
3. Sarawak.

AL– 1. Baal, dal, mal, mâle [F.], malle [F.], râle [F.], kraal, salle [F.], Taal, Saal [G.], bual.
2. cabal, Yigdal, *Heimdall*, agal, mahal, jacal, locale, *Landsmaal*, choral, chorale, morale, bual, cheval [F.], Transvaal, étoile [F.], quetzal.
3. Taj Mahal, laical, farcical, radical, medical, codical, magical, tragical, nymphical, ethical, mythical, biblical, cyclical, helical, comical, technical, ethnical, finical, cynical, conical, apical, epical, topical, typical, centrical, vesical, whimsical, classical, musical, physical, optical, cryptical, vertical, cortical, vortical, mystical, nautical, silvical, cardial, cordial, genial, splenial, finial, hernial, aerial, ferial, serial, ambrosial, tertial, bestial, animal, minimal, lachrymal, petit mal, decanal, bacchanal, tympanal, turbinal, carcinal, marginal, virginal, machinal, echinal, staminal, matinal, pectinal, retinal, inguinal, regional, torsional, missional, synchronal, seasonal, cantonal, principal, cerebral, vertebral, visceral, general, mineral, funeral, vesperal, geyseral, several, integral, admiral, anchoral, doctoral, cantoral, pastoral, mayoral, magistral, scriptural, sculptural, pastural, gestural, postural, guttural, sutural, textural, Provençal, palatal, vegetal, skeletal, orbital, digital, capital, hospital, marital, nepotal, pivotal, pedestal, gradual, casual, visual, usual, punctual, virtual, sexual, a cheval [F.], carnival, interval.
4. sporadical, unethical, encyclical, dynamical, inimical, tyrannical, dominical, ironical, cylindrical, electrical, eccentrical, nonclassical, antarctical, despotical, erotical, synoptical, majestical, Apocryphal, microbial, connubial, commercial, fiducial, novendial, gerundial, primordial, collegial, vestigial, conjugial, congenial, marsupial, colloquial, indigenal, phenomenal, intestinal, matutinal, adhesional, convulsional, expansional, partitional, precautional, municipal, Episcopal, preceptoral, carnivoral, continual, ventriloqual, unusual, perpetual.

5. lackadaisical, participial, entente cordiale [F.]; *see also* **ÄL–**.

ALD– 1. kraaled.
2. caballed.

AM– 1. âme [F.], balm, dame [F.], caam, calm, malm, palm, drâme [F.], psalm, Guam, qualm.
2. embalm, madame, Baham, salaam, imam, hammam, impalm.
3. Amsterdam, Rotterdam.
4. ad nauseam [L.].

AMP– 1. swamp, whamp.

AN– 1. âne [F.], khan, crâne [F.], pan [sp.], wan, swan.
2. cabane [F.], Iban, liane, macan, pecan, Iran, Koran, Kashan, Bataan, sarwan.
3. balmacaan, Yucatan, capitan [Sp.], transmontane, Turkestan, Pakistan, Parmesan.
4. Beluchistan.

AND– 1. wand, swanned.
4. Chateaubriand.

ANS– 1. Frans, France.
2. seance, nuance.
3. nonchalance, Renaissance.
4. insouciance.

ANT– 1. aunt, want.
2. grandaunt, great-aunt, gallant, courant, courante.
3. confidant, confidante, nonchalant, revenant, dilettante, dilettant, debutant, debutante.

ANTS– *see* **ÄNT** plus "s" or "'s"; 1. Franz.
3. Liederkranz.

AR– 1. are, aar [D.], ar, r, R, bar, char, dar [slang], darr, far, gar, ghar [Hind.], haar [Scot.], jar, car, scar, mar, nar, gnar, gnarr, knar, par, spar, tsar, tar, star, guar, boire [F.], foire [F.], poire [F.], Loire, gloire [F.], voir [F.], yar, yarr.
2. debar, rebar, embar, unbar, disbar, *crossbar, crowbar*, sirdar, afar, Safar, segar, cigar, bahar, kahar, ajar, *evejar, nightjar, sidecar, tramcar*, sircar, *forecar*, Bakar, shicar, *Lascar, Kedar, streetcar*, simar, canard [F.], *feldspar*, hussar, catarrh, katar, guitar, sitar, kantar, *daystar, lodestar, polestar, earthstar, evestar, jaguar*, pourboire [F.], armoire, bête noire, espoir [F.], savoir [F.], devoir [F.], bazaar, bizarre.
3. gangliar, foliar, caviar, jaguar, Malabar, cinnabar, centibar, Zanzibar, saddle bar, axle bar, wunderbar [G.], deodar, calendar, objet d'art, insofar, vinegar, *Trafalgar*, railroad car, gyrocar, autocar, tutelar, flagellar, lamellar, tessellar, similar, tonsillar, axillar, tabular, nebular, globular, tubular, schedular, glandular, modular, Cagoulard [F.], regular, angular, singular, jugular, stellular, secular, ocular, jocular, circular, torcular, vascular, scapular, popular, spherular, insular, consular, capsular, spatular, titular, ovular, uvular, valvular, tintamarre, laminar, seminar, columnar,

registrar, commissar, avatar, scimitar, evening star, morning star, boulevard [F.], Bolivar, samovar, aide memoire, abattoir, escritoire, directoire, repertoire, au revoir, Wanderjahr [G.].

4. Excalibar, dissimilar, somnambular, irregular, triangular, quadrangular, spectacular, vernacular, molecular, vehicular, funicular, particular, binocular, crepuscular.

5. perpendicular.

ARB– **1.** barb, darb [slang], garb, carb [slang], marb [slang], yarb [dial.].

2. coarb, *rhubarb*.

ARBD– **1.** barbed, garbed.

ARCH– **1.** arch, larch, march, parch, starch.

2. inarche, remarch, outmarch, *cornstarch*.

3. overarch, countermarch, understarch, overstarch.

ARCHT– **1.** arched, marched, parched, starched.

2. unarched, remarched, unparched, unstarched.

3. overarched, countermarched, understarched, overstarched.

ARD– **1.** bard, barred, chard, charred, fard, hard, guard, garred [Scot & dial.], jarred, card, carred [coll.], scarred, lard, marred, nard, gnarred, pard, sparred, sard, shard, tarred, starred, yard.

2. debarred, bombard, *laggard, blackguard,* regard, *safeguard, lifeguard, vanguard,* en garde! [F.], unguard, *placard,* discard, unscarred, foulard, poulard, Reynard, canard, Girard, *spikenard,* Bernard, petard, retard, bestarred, *churchyard,* back yard, *dockyard, steelyard, barnyard, foreyard,* front yard, *courtyard, graveyard.*

3. disregard, bodyguard, avant-garde, Dieu vous garde [F.], interlard, boulevard.

4. camelopard.

ARF– **1.** scarf, tharf [dial.], zarf.

ARJ– **1.** barge, charge, large, marge, sparge, sarge, targe.

2. recharge, surcharge, discharge, LaFarge, enlarge.

3. undercharge, countercharge, overcharge, re-enlarge.

ARJD– **1.** barged, charged, sparged, targed. **2.** recharged, surcharged, discharged, enlarged.

3. undercharged, countercharged, overcharged, re-enlarged, unenlarged.

ARK– **1.** arc, ark, bark, barque, dark, hark, cark, lark, Clark, clerk, mark, marque, nark, snark, park, spark, sark, shark, stark, yark.

2. *shagbark, snakebark, shellbark,* embark, *tanbark, woodlark, skylark, titlark, landmark,* remark, *hallmark, thumbmark,* Denmark, *earmark, reichsmark, postmark, birthmark,* anarch, *monarch,* impark, dispark, *exarch, whitesark, aardvark,* Ozark.

3. Noah's ark, disembark, matriarch,

patriarch, oligarch, meadowlark, easy mark, watermark, countermark, hierarch.

4. ecclesiarch.

ARKS– *see* **ÄRK,** plus " s " or " 's "; **1.** Marx,

ARKT– **1.** arced, barked, darked, carked, larked, clerked, marked, narked, snarked [dial.], parked, sparked, sharked.

2. embarked, *skylarked,* remarked, *thumbmarked, earmarked, postmarked, birthmarked.*

3. disembarked, watermarked.

ARL– **1.** harl, jarl, carl, Carl, Karl, marl, gnarl, snarl, parle.

2. imparl.

3. Albemarle.

ARLD– **1.** gnarled, snarled.

ARLZ– *see* **ÄRL,** plus " s " or " 's "; **1.** Arles, Charles.

ARM– **1.** arm, barm, charm, farm, harm, larme [F.], marm, tharm.

2. yardarm, rearm, inarm, unarm, *firearm,* forearm, disarm, *crossarm,* gendarme, alarm, *schoolmarm,* aux armes [F.].

3. underarm, overarm.

ARMD– **1.** armed, charmed, farmed, harmed.

2. rearmed, inarmed, unarmed, forearmed, disarmed, alarmed.

3. overarmed, underarmed, unalarmed.

ARN– **1.** barn, charn [dial.], darn, larn [dial.], Marne, tarn, yarn.

2. lucarne [F.], goldarn [slang], consarn [slang].

ARND– **1.** barned, charned [dial.], darned, larned [dial.], yarned.

2. goldarned [slang], consarned [slang].

ARNZ– *see* **ÄRN,** plus "s" or "'s"; **1.** Barnes.

ARP– **1.** Arp, harp, carp, scarp, sharp, tarp, yarp [slang], zarp.

2. *Jew's harp,* syncarp, escarp, *cardsharp.*

3. clivaharp, Irish harp, epicarp, pericarp, endocarp, monocarp, counterscarp.

ARPT– **1.** harped, carped, scarped, sharped. **2.** escarped.

ARS– **1.** arse, farce, garce, parse, sparse, sarse [dial.].

ARSH– **1.** harsh, marsh, warsh [slang].

2. démarche.

ART– **1.** art, Bart, chart, dart, hart, heart, cart, carte, quarte [F.], blart [dial.], clart, mart, smart, part, Sart, tart, start.

2. *sweetheart, faintheart, dogcart, gocart, dumpcart,* apart, depart, repart, impart, *rampart,* dispart, *forepart,* assart, astart, *redstart,* restart, upstart.

3. à la carte, counterpart, apple tart, sugar tart.

ARTH– **1.** garth, hearth, swarth.

2. *fishgarth.*

ARTS– *see* **ÄRT,** plus " s " or " 's "; **1.** Hartz.

ARV– **1.** carve, larve, starve, varve.

ARVD– **1.** carved, starved, varved.

ARVZ– **1.** carves, scarves, larves, starves, varves.

ARZ– *see* **ÄR,** plus "s" or "'s"; **1.** Lars, Mars.

AS– **1.** blas, ras [Amh.], tasse [F.], vas.

2. fougasse, en masse, Madras, terrasse, *Honduras*.
3. coup de grâce [F.].

ASH– 1. lache [F.], tache [F.], vache [F.], quash, squash, wash, swash.
2. panache, apache, gouache, Chuvash.

ASHT– 1. quashed, squashed, washed, swashed.

AST– 1. faste [F.], wast.
2. néfaste [F.].

AT– 1. pâte [F.], what, squat, swat, watt, boite [F.], yacht.
2. salat, berat, Duat, *kumquat*.
3. Al Sirat, Bundesrat [G.].

ATH– 1. bath, path, rath, wrath, swath.
3. isobath.

ATS– *see* **ÄT**, plus " s " or " 's "; 1. batz.
2. ersatz.

AV– 1. gav, halve, calve, Slav, salve, suave.
2. Zouave.
3. Jugoslav, Yugoslav.

AVD– 1. halved, calved, salved.

AZ– *see* **Ä** through **YÄ**, plus " s " or " 's ";
1. vase, was, 'twas, yahzz [slang].
2. namaz, Shiraz, Françoise.
3. Vichyssoise.
4. à la chinoise [F.].

AZH– 2. chauffage [F.], menage, barrage, mirage.
3. bavardage [F.], fuselage, persiflage, camouflage, badinage, cabotage, sabotage.
4. espionage.

Ä (ah)

[See also Ŏ (bob)]

Double (Feminine) Rhymes

Primary or Secondary Accent Falls on Next to Last Syllable; Imperfect Rhymes Are in Italics.

AB′a— 2. aba, baba, haba [Sp.], Caaba, Kaaba, Kaba, Kabah, draba.
  3. casaba, aftaba.
  4. piassaba, Ali Baba.
  5. Addis Ababa, Cayubaba.
AB′ee— 2. rabi, drabi, tabi [Jap.], wabe, wabby, whabby, squabby.
  3. Wahabi, Panjabi, Punjabi, kohlrabi.
AB′l— 2. wabble, squabble.
AB′ra— 2. abra.
  4. candelabra.
  5. abracadabra.
AD′a— 2. dada, nada [Sp.], sraddha.
  3. Haggada, Haggadah, cicada, Colada, armada, Granada, panada, contrada [It.], posada [Sp.], Nevada, shahzada.
  6. Sierra Nevada.
AD′ed— 2. wadded.
  3. pomaded.
  4. promenaded.
AD′ee— 2. cadi, Mahdi, wadi, waddy, squaddy.
  3. abadi [Hind.], irade.
AD′ing— 2. wadding.
  3. pomading.
  4. promenading.
AD′l— 2. waddle, swaddle, twaddle.
AD′lee— 2. waddly, twaddly.
AD′ler— 2. waddler, swaddler, twaddler.
AD′ling— 2. waddling, swaddling, twaddling.
AD′o— 2. dado, Prado.
  3. soldado [Sp.], Mikado, sticcado, stoccado, strappado, dorado, passado, pintado, bravado.
  4. abogado [Sp.], avocado, bastinado, desperado, Eldorado, Colorado.
  5. amontillado.
  6. incommunicado.
A′ee— 2. kai, blahy [slang], tai, sai.
  4. kai-kai.
A′ek— 2. kaik, saic.
AF′a— 2. Daffa, Jaffa, Yafa.
AF′ing— 2. laughing, strafing, quaffing.
AF′l— 2. faffle, taffle, tafel [G.], waffle.

AF′ter— 2. after, laughter.
AG′a— 2. aga, gaga [F.], glaga, maga, Naga, saga.
AG′ar— 2. agar, laager, lager.
  4. agar-agar.
AG′o— 2. kago, lago [It.], drago.
  3. Iago, briago, Chicago, salago, farrago.
  4. Santiago.
AG′wa— 2. agua [Sp.], jagua, Yagua.
  3. mahagua, majagua, Managua, piragua.
A′ha— 2. kaha, Maha, maha, taha.
  3. *taiaha.*
A′hu— 2. kahu, Mahu, Rahu, sahu, wahoo, Yahoo.
  3. Oahu.
A′ing— 2. ahing, baaing, bahing, blahing [slang], maaing.
  3. hahaing, blah-blahing [slang].
  4. oh-and-ahing.
  5. ohing and ahing.
AJ′a— 2. rajah.
  4. maharajah.
AJ′ee— 2. haje, hagi, Bragi.
AJ′o— 2. agio.
  3. adagio, formaggio [It.].
AK′a— 2. Dacca, haka [Maori], Hakka, raca.
  3. Karaka, Osaka, pataca.
  4. Titicaca.
AK′ee— 2. kaki, khaki, sake, saki.
  3. tumbaki, Abnake.
  4. Abanake, Wabanake, Anunnaki, sukiyaki.
AK′en— 2. Aachen, Achen, baken [D.], kraken.
  4. Interlaken.
AK′er— 3. fiacre, polacre.
AK′o— 2. Chaco, hako, caco, mako, paco, guaco, huaco.
  3. cheechako, *fondako,* guanaco.
  4. makomako.
AK′wa— 2. aqua [L.], acqua [It.].
  3. namaqua, anaqua.
AL′a— 2. Allah, gala, hala, kala, wallah, Rwala.
  3. koala, gabbala, gabbalah, kabala, kabbala,

kabbalah, cabala, cabbala, cabbalah, Mahala, impala, Marsala, Patala, chuckwalla, owala, Ruwala.

4. Guatemala, Walla Walla.

AL'ee– **2.** Ali, Bali, dalli, Dali, gali, galee, Kali, pali, tali, Vali.

3. Bengali, tahali, tamale, Somali, finale.

4. Mexicali, pastorale.

AL'er– **2.** daler, haler, caller [Scot.], taler, thaler, swaller [dial.], squalor.

AL'et– **2.** wallet, swallet.

AL'o– **2.** calo, lalo, malo, palo, talo, wallow, swallow.

3. *cembalo*, hog wallow.

4. *a cembalo* [It.].

AL'u– **2.** baloo, balu.

AL'yo– **3.** caballo, seraglio, intaglio.

AM'a– **2.** ama, gama, jama, caama, Kama, kaama, lama, llama, mama, mamma, Rama, Brahma, drama, grama, shama, Tama.

3. Bahama, pajama, pyjama.

4. Alabama, Yokohama, ramarama, melodrama, monodrama, diorama, cyclorama, cosmorama, panorama, Fujiyama.

5. myriorama, polyorama.

AM'an– **2.** Brahman, saman, shaman, zaman.

4. Parabrahman.

AM'ba– **2.** samba.

3. caramba [Sp.].

AM'ee– **2.** balmy, jami, calmy, malmy, palmy, pahmi, qualmy, swami.

3. palame, salami.

AM'er– **2.** calmer, Kammer [D.], palmer.

3. embalmer.

AM'ing– **2.** calming, malming, palming, qualming.

3. embalming, becalming, salaaming, empalming.

AM'ish– **2.** Amish, calmish, qualmish.

AM'ist– **2.** palmist, psalmist.

3. embalmist.

AN'a– **2.** Bana, Ghana, kana, mana, manna [L.], rana, prana, tana, thana, bwana.

3. nagana, Guiana, liana, gymkhana, banana, mañana [Sp.], kerana, zenana, purana, Etana, gitana [Sp.], Sultana, lantana, Montana, Curtana, nirvana, iguana.

4. apadana, damiana, dulciana, tramontana, Tia Juana, marijuana.

5. Fata Morgana, Americana.

6. cassabanana, Shakespeariana.

AND'er– **2.** wander, squander.

AN'ee– **2.** ani, rani, ranee, Swanee, swanny.

3. Sekani, sherwani.

4. frangipani, Maharani, Maharanee, Hindustani.

AN'ish– **2.** wannish, swannish.

AN'o– **2.** ano, anno, mano, grano.

3. piano, solano, soprano, gitano [Sp.].

4. pudiano, castellano, altiplano, bonamano [It.], Montesano, capitano.

5. Americano.

9. mens sana in corpore sano [L.].

ANT'a– **2.** danta.

3. Vedanta, Infanta.

ANT'ay– **2.** Dante, santé [F.].

3. andante, volante.

4. diamanté.

5. procurante.

ANT'ee– **2.** aunty, Dante, Fantee, Fanti, tanti.

3. Chianti, andante, Kiranti.

ANT'o– **2.** tanto, quanto.

6. allegro non tanto.

AN'ya– **2.** Anya, Hanya.

4. do svidaniya [Russ.].

A'o– **2.** ao, dao, tao.

3. cacao, macao, talao, Karao [Hind.], parao.

4. carabao, Mindanao.

AP'a– **2.** apa, capa, kapa, papa, tapa.

5. anapanapa.

AP'ee– **2.** Hapi.

3. okapi, serape.

AP'er– **2.** swapper, whapper.

AP'ing– **2.** swapping, whapping.

AR'a– **2.** cara, Mara, narra, Tara, vara.

3. tiara, ziara, fugara, Sahara, vihara, Sakkara, kaikara, cascara, mascara, Damara, Gemara, apara, arara, chitarra.

4. caracara, sayonara [Jap.], tantarara, Demerara, solfatara.

5. Guadalajara, taratantara.

ARB'er– **2.** arbor, barber, Barbour, harbor.

3. enharbor.

ARB'l– **2.** barbel, barble, garble, garbill, marble.

3. enmarble.

ARB'on– **2.** charbon, carbon.

4. hydrocarbon.

ARB'ord– **2.** arbored, harbored, larboard, starboard.

ARCH'ee– **2.** Archie, archy, larchy, starchy.

ARCH'er– **2.** archer, marcher, parcher, starcher.

4. countermarcher.

ARCH'ez– *see* **ÄRCH**, plus " es " or " 's. "

ARCH'ing– **2.** arching, marching, parching, starching.

3. outmarching.

4. countermarching, overarching.

ARCH'ment– **2.** archment, parchment.

3. emparchment.

ARD'ant– **2.** ardent, gardant, guardant.

3. regardant, retardant.

ARD'ed– **2.** farded, guarded, carded, larded, sharded.

3. bombarded, *safeguarded*, regarded, placarded, discarded, retarded.

4. unbombarded, unregarded, unsafeguarded, disregarded, unplacarded, undiscarded, interlarded, unretarded.

ARD'ee– **2.** bardy, bardee, bardie [Scot.], hardy, lardy, mardy [dial.], Mardi, tardy.

3. *Lombardy*, foolhardy.

ARD'el– **2.** bardel, fardel, cardel, sardel, sardelle.

ARD′en– 2. Arden, garden, harden, cardan, Varden.
3. tea garden, enharden.
4. Dolly Varden [Dickens].
ARD′end– 2. gardened, hardened, pardoned.
3. unhardened, unpardoned.
ARD′er– 2. ardor, guarder, harder, carder.
3. discarder, retarder.
4. disregarder.
ARD′ik– 2. bardic.
3. Lombardic, Sephardic.
4. anacardic, pericardic.
ARD′ing– 2. farding, guarding, Harding, carding, larding.
3. bombarding, regarding, unguarding, discarding, retarding.
4. disregarding, interlarding.
ARD′less– 2. bardless, fardless, guardless, cardless, lardless, shardless.
3. regardless, retardless.
4. irregardless.
ARD′ment– 3. bombardment, retardment.
ARD′ship– 2. guard ship, hardship.
AR′ee – 2. bari, barry, charry, jarry, scarry, lari, Mahri, Mari, pari, sparry, sari, tarry, starry, quarry.
3. safari, shikari, canari, curare.
4. Karharbari, aracari, hari-kari, Carbonari.
AR′er– 2. barrer, charrer, jarrer, marrer, sparrer, tarrer.
3. debarrer, bizarrer.
AR′fish– 2. barfish, garfish, starfish.
3. cigarfish, guitarfish.
AR′gan– 2. bargain, Darghin.
ARG′l– 2. argal, argol, gargle.
4. argle-bargle.
ARG′o– 2. Argo, argot, Fargo, cargo, largo, Margo, Margot, pargo, sargo.
3. embargo, Wells Fargo, botargo.
4. supercargo.
ARG′on– 2. argon, jargon.
ARG′u– 2. argue.
3. reargue, redargue.
AR′ik– 3. Amharic, Gemaric, tartaric.
AR′ing– 2. barring, charring, garring [Scot. & dial.], jarring, carring [coll.], scarring, marring, parring, sparring, tarring, starring.
3. debarring, rebarring, embarring, unbarring, disbarring, bestarring.
ARJ′ent– 2. argent, margent, sergeant, Sargent.
3. minargent.
ARJ′er– 2. barger, charger, larger, sparger.
3. surcharger, discharger, enlarger.
ARJ′ez– 2. barges, charges, marges, targes.
3. recharges, surcharges, discharges, enlarges.
4. countercharges, overcharges.
ARJ′ik– 3. pelargic, lethargic.
ARJ′in– 2. bargin', chargin', margin.
ARJ′ing– 2. barging, charging.
3. discharging, enlarging.
4. overcharging.
ARK′a– 2. Charca, parka, markka.

3. bidarka.
ARK′al– 3. anarchal, monarchal.
4. oligarchal, matriarchal, patriarchal, hierarchal.
ARK′ee– 2. arky, barky, darky, carky, larky, Markey, sparky, sharky, Sharkey, starky.
3. malarkey [slang].
4. oligarchy, hagiarchy, chiliarchy, matriarchy, patriarchy, hierarchy.
ARK′en– 2. barken, darken, hearken, starken.
3. bedarken, endarken.
ARK′er– 2. barker, darker, harker, carker, larker, marker, markhor, parker, sharker, sparker, starker.
3. embarker, skylarker.
ARK′est– 2. darkest, starkest.
ARK′et– 2. market.
3. newmarket.
ARK′ik– 3. anarchic, monarchic.
4. oligarchic, matriarchic, patriarchic, hierarchic.
ARK′ing– 2. barking, darking, harking, carking, larking, marking, parking, sparking, sarking, starking.
3. embarking, disbarking, *skylarking, earmarking*.
4. disembarking.
ARK′ish– 2. barkish, darkish, carkish, larkish, parkish, sparkish, starkish.
3. skylarkish.
ARK′ist– 4. oligarchist, matriarchist, patriarchist, hierarchist.
ARK′l– 2. barkle, darkle, sparkle.
3. besparkle.
ARK′ld– 2. barkled, darkled, carkled, sparkled.
3. besparkled.
ARK′lee– 2. Barkley, Berkeley, darkly, clerkly, sparkly, starkly.
ARK′less– 2. arkless, barkless, darkless, carkless, larkless, markless, parkless, sparkless, sharkless.
ARK′let– 2. parklet, sparklet.
ARK′ling– 2. darkling, larkling, sparkling.
ARK′ner– 3. darkener, hearkener.
ARK′ness– 2. darkness, starkness.
ARK′o– 2. charco [Sp.], Marco.
ARK′tik– 2. Arctic.
3. subarctic, Nearctic, Holarctic, Antarctic.
4. Palearctic.
ARK′us– 2. Barkis [Dickens], carcass, Marcus.
ARL′and– 2. garland.
3. McFarland, engarland.
ARL′ee– 2. barley, Charlie, Farley, marly, marli, gnarly, snarly, parley.
3. bizarrely.
ARL′er– 2. gnarler, snarler, parlor.
3. sunparlor.
ARL′es– 2. barless, jarless, carless, scarless, marless, parlous, tarless, starless, czarless.
3. cigarless, catarrhless.
ARL′et– 2. carlet, scarlet, marlet, starlet, varlet; *see also* **ÄRL′ot.**
ARL′ik– 2. garlic, sarlyk.

3. pilgarlic.
ARL'ike– 2. barlike, carlike, scarlike, tarlike, starlike, czarlike.
3. cigarlike, catarrhlike.
ARL'in– 2. carlin, marlin, marline.
ARL'ing– 2. darling, harling, carling, marling, gnarling, snarling, parling, sparling, starling.
ARL'ot– 2. harlot, carlot, Charlotte; *see also* **ARL'et.**
ARL'us– 2. parlous; *see also* **ÄRL'es.**
ARM'a– 2. dharma, karma.
3. adharma.
ARM'ee– 2. army, barmy, farmy.
ARM'ent– 2. garment, sarment.
3. debarment, disbarment.
ARM'er– 2. armer, armor, charmer, farmer, harmer.
3. disarmer, snake charmer, dirt farmer, alarmer.
4. dairy farmer.
ARM'ful– 2. armful, charmful, harmful.
3. unharmful.
ARM'ik– 2. pharmic, ptarmic.
4. polypharmic.
5. alexipharmic.
ARM'in– 2. charmin', harmine, carmine.
3. encarmine.
ARM'ing– 2. arming, charming, farming, harming.
3. uncharming, forearming, dirt farming, alarming, disarming.
4. dairy farming, unalarming.
ARM'less– 2. armless, charmless, harmless.
3. alarmless.
ARM'let– 2. armlet, charmlet.
ARM'ot– 2. carmot, marmot.
ARN'a– 2. arna, sarna.
ARN'al– 2. charnel, darnel, carnal.
3. uncarnal.
ARN'at– 2. carnate.
3. incarnate, discarnate.
4. reincarnate.
ARN'ee– 2. barny, carney, blarney.
3. Killarney.
ARN'el– 2. charnel, darnel.
ARN'er– 2. darner, garner, Garner, yarner.
ARN'erd– 2. Barnard, garnered.
ARN'ess– 2. farness, harness, yarness.
3. reharness, unharness, bizarreness.
ARN'ing– 2. darning, yarning.
3. goldarning, consarning [both slang].
ARN'ish– 2. garnish, tarnish, varnish.
ARN'isht– 2. garnished, tarnished, varnished.
3. ungarnished, untarnished, unvarnished.
AR'o– 2. karo, claro, taro.
3. denaro, cantaro, saguaro.
4. carbonaro.
ARP'al– 2. carpal.
4. metacarpal, intercarpal.
ARP'ee– 2. harpy, carpy, sharpy, sharpie.
ARP'er– 2. harper, carper, sharper.
3. *cardsharper.*
ARP'ing– 2. harping, carping, sharping.

3. *cardsharping.*
ARS'al– 2. carcel, parcel, tarsal.
4. metatarsal.
ARS'er– 2. carcer [L.], parser, sparser, Sarsar.
ARS'ez– 2. farces, parses, sarses.
ARSH'al– 2. marshal, Marshall, martial, partial.
3. field marshal, impartial.
ARSH'an– 2. darshan, harshen, Martian.
ARS'lee– 2. parsley, sparsely.
ARS'on– 2. arson, Carson, Larson, parson, squarson.
ARS'us– 2. tarsus.
3. protarsus.
4. metatarsus.
ART'a– 2. charta [L.], Sparta, cuarta.
4. Magna Charta.
ART'an– 2. partan, Spartan, tartan, Tartan; *see also* **ÄRT'en.**
ART'ay– 3. ex parte, Astarte.
4. colla parte [It.].
ART'ed– 2. charted, darted, hearted, carted, smarted, parted, started.
3. uncharted, kindhearted, hardhearted, freehearted, weakhearted, warmhearted, downhearted, falsehearted, softhearted, lighthearted, fainthearted, stouthearted, truehearted, outsmarted, departed, imparted, upstarted.
4. stonyhearted, heavyhearted, simplehearted, singlehearted, gentlehearted, chickenhearted, brokenhearted, openhearted, lionhearted, ironhearted, tenderhearted.
ART'ee– 2. arty, charty, darty, hearty, smarty, party, tarty, starty.
3. tea party, ex parte, Astarte.
ART'en– 2. barton, Barton, hearten, carton, marten, smarten, tarten.
3. enhearten, dishearten.
4. *Tiergarten* [G.], kindergarten; *see also* **ÄRT'an.**
ART'er– 2. arter, barter, charter, darter, garter, carter, martyr, smarter, parter, tartar, tarter, starter.
3. departer, bemartyr, imparter, restarter, self-starter.
4. protomartyr, cream-of-tartar.
ART'erd– 2. bartered, chartered, gartered, martyred.
ART'ful– 2. artful, heartful, startful.
ART'ing– 2. charting, darting, carting, smarting, parting, starting.
3. *sweethearting,* departing, imparting, disparting, restarting, self-starting, upstarting.
ART'ist– 2. artist, chartist, Chartist.
4. Bonapartist.
ART'l– 2. dartle, spartle, startle.
4. Rosa Dartle [Dickens].
ART'lee– 2. smartly, partly, tartly.
ART'less– 2. artless, chartless, dartless, heartless, cartless, smartless, partless, startless.
ART'let– 2. artlet, Bartlett, heartlet, partlet,

martlet, tartlet.
ART'ling– 2. dartling, spartling, startling.
ART'ment– 3. apartment, department, impartment, compartment.
ART'ness– 2. smartness, tartness.
ART'o– 3. lagarto, esparto.
ART'on– 2. barton, Barton, carton.
  4. set one's heart on; *see also* **ÄRT'en.**
ART'rij– 2. cartridge, partridge.
AR'u– 2. baru, maru.
AR'um– 2. garum, larum.
  3. alarum.
ARV'a– 2. arva, larva.
ARV'al– 2. Arval, arval, barvel, carval, larval, marvel.
ARV'er– 2. carver, marver, starver.
AS'a– 2. bassa, Bassa, casa [Sp., It., Pg., L.], pasa [Sp.], guasa.
  3. Hadassah.
  4. Missa bassa [L.].
ASH'er– 2. washer, quasher, squasher, swasher.
  3. *dishwasher, whitewasher.*
ASH'ing– 2. washing, quashing, squashing, swashing.
  3. *dishwashing, whitewashing.*
AS'ta– 2. basta, hasta [dial.], pasta [It.].
AT'a– 2. bata [Tag.], data, gata, kata, plata, rata.
  3. reata [Sp.], regatta, riata, toccata, stoccata, ballata, volata, camata, Renata, sonata, pro rata, batata, patata, cantata.
  4. alpargata [Sp.], boniata, Punta Plata, matamata, carromata, serenata, Edentata.
  5. enamorata, inamorata.
AT'ee– 2. Sati, squatty, swatty, whatty, yachty, zati.
  3. piatti [It.], coati, Amati.
  4. Jubilate, Cincinnati.
  5. illuminati.
ATH'er– 2. bather, father, rather, swather.

AT'ing– 2. swatting, squatting, yachting.
AT'ish– 2. squattish, yachtish.
AT'l– 2. wattle, twattle.
AT'ling– 2. wattling, twattling.
AT'o– 2. dato, datto, gato [all Sp.], Kato.
  3. legato, fugato, staccato, spiccato, marcato [It.], pomato, tomato, annatto, barato [Sp.], Renato, vibrato, ritratto [It.].
  4. ben tornato [It.], moderato, obligato, pizzicato, ostinato [It.], passionato [It.], disperato [It.], allentato [It.], ben trovato [It.].
  5. demilegato, appassionato.
AT'ra– 2. matra.
  3. Sumatra.
  4. Cleopatra.
AT'um– 2. datum.
  3. pomatum.
AV'a– 2. Java, cava, kava, lava, brava, guava.
  3. cassava.
  4. kavakava, lava-lava, Costa Brava, piassava, Cayuvava.
AV'ee– 2. Ave, Kavi.
  3. Mohave, Mojave, peccavi.
  6. Rikki-tikki-tavi [Kipling].
AV'er– 2. halver, calver, salver, suaver.
  3. palaver.
AV'ing– 2. halving, calving, salving.
AV'o– 2. bravo.
  3. octavo, centavo.
A'wa– 2. awa, tawa.
  3. Tarawa, Chihuahua.
A'ya– 2. aya, Maya, raya, saya.
  3. kabaya, papaya, karaya, Hawaii.
  4. Surabaya.
AZ'a– 2. plaza, maza [Sp.].
  5. tabula rasa [L.].
AZ'ee– 2. ghazi.
  3. Benghazi.
AZH'ing– 3. barraging, garaging.
  4. persiflaging, camouflaging.

Ä (ah)

[See also Ŏ (bob)]

Triple Rhymes

Primary or Secondary Accent Falls on Second from Last Syllable; Imperfect Rhymes Are in Italics.

A'ing–lee– 3. ahingly, baaingly, bahingly, blahingly [slang].
  4. blah-blahingly [slang].
  5. oh-and-ahingly.
AB'i–lay– 4. cantabile.
  5. lamentabile [It.].
AB'u–la– 3. tabula.
  5. incunabula.
  6. acta est fabula [L.].
AJ'i–o– 3. agio.
  4. adagio, Di Maggio, formaggio [It.].
AK'i–a– 4. Slovakia.
  6. Czechoslovakia.
AL'o–er– 3. wallower, swallower.
AL'o–ing– 3. wallowing, swallowing.
AL'op–er– 3. dalloper, scalloper, walloper.
AL'op–ing– 3. dalloping, scalloping, walloping.
AM'i–lee– 3. balmily, palmily.
AM'ish–lee– 3. calmishly, qualmishly.
AM'ist–ree– 3. palmistry, psalmistry.
ARB'er–ing– 3. barbering, harboring.
ARD'en–ing– 3. gardening, hardening, pardoning.
ARD'i–lee– 3. hardily, tardily.
  4. foolhardily.
AR'i–ness– 3. barriness, tarriness, starriness.
AR'i–o– 4. scenario, Cesario.
  5. impresario.
ARK'i–kal– 3. archical.
  4. hylarchical, anarchical, monarchical, tetrarchical.
  5. hierarchical.
ARL'a–tan– 3. charlatan, tarlatan.
ARM'a–bl– 3. armable, farmable, harm-

able, charmable.
  4. disarmable, unfarmable, unharmable, uncharmable, alarmable.
ARM'ing–lee– 3. farmingly, harmingly, charmingly.
  4. disarmingly, alarmingly.
ARN'ish–er– 3. garnisher, tarnisher, varnisher.
ARN'ish–ing– 3. garnishing, tarnishing, varnishing.
  4. revarnishing.
ARS'en–ee– 3. larceny.
  4. coparceny.
ARS'en–er– 3. larcener, parcener.
  4. coparcener.
ART'ed–lee– 4. halfheartedly, lighheartedly, faintheartedly, stoutheartedly.
ART'ed–ness– 4. kindheartedness, hardheartedness, downheartedness, lightheartedness.
  5. simpleheartedness, openheartedness, lionheartedness.
ART'er–ee– 3. artery, bartery, martyry.
ART'er–er– 3. barterer, charterer.
ART'i–kl– 3. article, particle.
ART'i–zan– 3. artisan, bartizan, partisan.
ART'less–lee– 3. artlessly, heartlessly.
AT'i–er– 3. squattier, swattier, whattier, yachtier.
AT'i–est– 3. squattiest, swattiest, whattiest, yachtiest.
AT'i–lee– 3. squattily, swattily, whattily, yachtily.
AT'i–ness– 3. squattiness, swattiness, whattiness, yachtiness.

Ă (cab)

Single (Masculine) Rhymes

Primary or Secondary Accent Falls on Last Syllable; Imperfect Rhymes Are in Italics.

AB– 1. ab, abb, Bab, dab, gab [coll.], jab, cab, scab, lab, blab, slab, Mab, nab, snab [slang], rab, brab, drab, grab, crab, tab, stab.
2. *Joab, confab, lablab,* Queen Mab, *eartab.*
3. baobab, taxicab.
ACH– 1. batch, bach [slang], datch [dial.], hatch, catch, latch, slatch, match, natch, snatch, patch, ratch, brach, cratch, scratch, thatch.
2. crosshatch, *nuthatch, seecatch, potlatch,* mismatch, *tolpatch,* dispatch, *Wasatch,* attach, detach.
3. shooting match, undermatch, overmatch.
ACHT– 1. batched, bached [slang], datched [dial.], hatched, latched, matched, snatched, patched, scratched, thatched.
2. mismatched, dispatched, attached, detached.
3. undermatched, overmatched.
AD– 1. ad, add, bad, bade, Chad, Tchad, dad, fad, gad, had, cad, scad, lad, blad [Scot.], glad, clad, plaid, mad, pad, rad [dial.], brad, grad [slang], sad, shad, tad.
2. readd, *Sindbad,* forbade, egad, begad, *mailclad,* unclad, kneepad.
3. Iliad, chiliad, myriad, Trinidad, ironclad, winter clad, heavy clad, ivy clad, reculade [F.], Leningrad, undergrad, Olympiad, little tad.
ADZ– *see* **ĂD**, plus " s " or " 's "; **1.** adze.
3. Lusiads.
AF– 1. aff [Scot.], baff, chaff, daff, faff, gaff, half, calf, laugh, laff [slang], raff, Wraf, draff, graph, strafe, staff, quaff.
2. *chiffchaff,* behalf, *mooncalf, horselaugh,* carafe, *riffraff,* agraffe, giraffe, *gibstaff, half-staff, flagstaff, distaff,* Falstaff, *forestaff.*
3. shandygaff, anagraph, paragraph, telegraph, melograph, phonograph, monograph, dictograph, autograph, photograph, lithograph, epitaph, cenotaph, better half, understaff, quarter staff, overstaff.
4. mimeograph, stereograph, radiograph, cardiograph, heliograph.
AFT– 1. aft, baffed, chaffed, daft, daffed, gaffed, haft, laughed, raft, draft, graft, graphed, craft, shaft, strafed, Taft, staffed, waft, quaffed.
2. abaft, engraft, *witchcraft, woodcraft, seacraft, folkcraft, aircraft,* awaft.
3. overdraft, paragraphed, telegraphed, autographed, photographed, lithographed, handicraft, metalcraft, understaffed, overstaffed.
4. *antiaircraft.*
AG– 1. ag [slang], bag, dag, fag, gag, jag, cag [slang], scag, skag, lag, flag, slag, mag [coll. and slang], nag, knag, snag, rag, brag, drag, crag, scrag, sag, shag, tag, stag, vag [slang], wag, quag, swag, zag.
2. *handbag, gasbag, shagrag, ragtag, wigwag, zigzag.*
3. moneybag, saddlebag, demihag, scalawag, chew the rag [slang], Brobdingnag.
AGD– 1. bagged, fagged, gagged, cagged, lagged, flagged, nagged, snagged, dragged, sagged, tagged, wagged.
2. betagged, *wigwagged, zigzagged.*
AJ– 1. badge, fadge, hadj, cadge, Madge.
AK– 1. back, bac, hack, jack, kak [slang], kack [slang], cack [slang], lack, lac, black, flac, flack, clack, claque, plack, plaque, slack, mack, mac [both slang], smack, knack, snack, pack, pac, rack, crack, track, wrack, sack, sac, sacque, shack, tac, tack, stack, Wac, wasck [slang], quack, whack, thwack, yak, yack [slang].
2. *ack-ack,* aback, *wayback, pinchback, hunchback, humpback, switchback, holdback, halfback, puffback, crookback, quillback, fullback, comeback, drawback, throwback, horseback, outback, kodak, kiack, blackjack, flapjack, slapjack, skipjack, bootjack, muntjak,* macaque, alack, shellac, *flicflac, lampblack, bootblack, knickknack,* repack, unpack, *calpac, woolpack, gimcrack, wisecrack,*

162

retrack, *backtrack, racetrack,* tesack, *sicsac, rucksack, woolsack,* ransack, attack, *hardtack, ticktack, thumbtack, haystack, bullwhack, Anzac.*
3. zodiac, cardiac, umiac, comiak [both Esk.], maniac, Pontiac, piggyback, pickaback, huckaback, saddleback, turtleback, quarterback, leatherback, razorback, Union Jack, natterjack, almanac, tamarack, bric-abrac, cul-de-sac, haversack, bivouac, Sarawak, paddywhack, cattleyak.
4. tacamahac, yakkity-yak [slang].
ĂKS– *see* **ĂK,** plus " s " or " 's "; **1.** ax, lax, flax, max, Max, Thrax, sax, tax, wax, zax.
2. *addax, pickax, poleax,* relax, *toadflax,* unlax, *climax,* dewax, rewax, *chaffwax, beeswax, paxwax.*
3. battle-ax, Halifax, parallax, income tax, undertax, supertax, overtax.
ĂKST– **1.** axed, flaxed, taxed, waxed.
2. dewaxed, rewaxed.
3. undertaxed, supertaxed, overtaxed.
ĂKT– **1.** act, backed, fact, hacked, jacked, lacked, blacked, clacked, slacked, smacked, knacked, snacked, pact, packed, racked, wracked, bract, cracked, tract, tracked, sacked, shacked, tact, tacked, stacked, quacked, whacked, thwacked, yakked [slang], yacked [slang].
2. react, *triact,* coact, redact, *hunchbacked, humpbacked,* enact, epact, impact, compact, unpacked, defract, refract, diffract, infract, attract, subtract, *sidetracked,* retract, entr'acte, untracked, protract, abstract, ransacked, transact, intact, *contact,* exact.
3. saddle-backed, re-enact, retroact, cataract, underact, interact, counteract, overact, cataphract, inexact.
4. matter-of-fact.
ĂKTS– *see* **ĂKT,** plus " s " or " 's ".
ĂL– **1.** Al, dalle, gal [slang], Hal, Cal, mal, pal, sal [slang], salle, shall.
2. cabal, locale, canal, corral, morale, La Salle, *aval.*
3. musicale, chaparral, pastorale, entresalle [F.]; *see also* **ĂL.**
ĂLD– **1.** palled.
2. caballed, corralled.
3. emerald.
ĂLK– **1.** alk, calk, calc, talc.
3. catafalque.
ĂLKS– **1.** falx, calks, calx.
ĂLP– **1.** alp, scalp, palp.
3. auriscalp.
ĂLPS– *see* **ĂLP,** plus " s " or " 's "; **1.** Alps.
ĂLT– **1.** alt, shalt.
ĂLV– **1.** salve, valve.
2. bivalve.
ĂM– **1.** am, bam, Cham, cham [dial.], dam, damn, gam, gamb, ham, jam, jamb, cam, camm [slang], lam, lamb, flam, clam, slam, ma'am, pam, rhamn, ram, dram, drachm, dramme, gram, gramme, cram, pram, tram, Sam, sham, tam, swam, wham, yam, zam [slang].

2. madame, *beldam, grandam,* Siam, *jimjam,* enjamb, *flimflam,* Assam, *tamtam, whimwham,* Khayyam.
3. Alabam', cofferdam, Amsterdam, Rotterdam, Abraham, Birmingham, Nottingham, choriamb, demijambe, diaphragm, diagram, anagram, telegram, milligram, epigram, centigram, cablegram, kilogram, melogram, monogram, cryptogram, marjoram, dithyramb, petersham, Uncle Sam.
4. ad nauseam [L.].
5. parallelogram.
ĂMB– **1.** amb, gamb.
3. choriamb, dithyramb.
ĂMD– **1.** damned, dammed, gammed, hammed [slang], jammed, lambed, lammed [slang], flammed, clammed, slammed, rammed, crammed, shammed, whammed.
2. *flimflammed.*
3. diagrammed, monogrammed.
ĂMP– **1.** amp, champ, damp, gamp, guimpe, camp, scamp, lamp, clamp, ramp, cramp, tramp, samp, tamp, stamp, vamp, yamp.
2. *chokedamp, firedamp,* decamp, encamp, restamp, *backstamp,* revamp.
3. Davy lamp, safety lamp, signal lamp.
ĂMPT– **1.** champed, damped, camped, scamped, lamped, clamped, ramped, cramped, tramped, tamped, stamped, vamped.
2. decamped, encamped, restamped, revamped.
ĂN– **1.** Ann, Anne, ban, Chan, Dan, dan, fan, gan [slang], khan, can, scan, clan, plan, man, pan, Pan, panne, span, ran, bran, Fran, fran [slang], gran, cran, scran, san, tan, than, van.
2. cabane, redan, sedan, Sudan, began, bahan, pecan, *oilcan, cancan, ashcan,* Milan, replan, reman, *seaman, cabman, clubman, subman, tubman, headman, leadman, madman, odd man, bandman, sandman, bondman, hodman, woodman, rodman, wardman, birdman, iceman, freeman, cageman, bargeman, brakeman, lineman, tapeman, fireman, wireman, shoreman, horseman, Norseman, flagman, ragman, dragman, swagman, pegman, yeggman, hangman, songman, cogman, tugman, coachman, Welchman, ranchman, henchman, Frenchman, churchman, watchman, switchman, Scotchman, Dutchman, ploughman, freshman, Welshman, Bushman, Northman, packman, checkman, lockman, stockman, milkman, bankman, bookman, workman, oilman, bellman, billman, millman, tollman, Pullman, schoolman, penman, trainman, gunman, yeoman, capman, chapman, shipman, tipman, shopman, topman, barman, carman, spearman, merman, airman, floorman, beadsman, headsman, leadsman, oddsman, bandsman, landsman, bondsman, woodsman, guardsman, herdsman, swordsman, tribesman, tradesman, spokesman, salesman, talesman, dolesman, shoresman, statesman, dragsman, gangsman, marksman, bailsman, spoilsman, almsman, helmsman, groomsman, clansman, kinsman, townsman, oarsman, passman,*

*messman, pressman, batsman, craftsman, drafts-
man, yachtsman, huntsman, Scctsman, sportsman,
batman, meatman, boatman, pitman, footman,
postman, crewman, bowman, cowman, showman,
plowman, cayman, layman, playman, drayman,
wayman, flyman,* Japan, sapan, hardpan,
trepan, *sampan,* Chopin, *inspan, outspan,*
Iran, outran, Bataan, rattan, *fantan,* divan.
3. Marianne, Caliban, balmacaan, barbican,
rubican, indican, Anglican, Gallican, pem-
mican, African, Vatican, Mexican, Oppidan,
harridan, orlean, joulean, tinean, Marnean,
Etnean, Kordofan, suffragan, cardigan,
Michigan, mulligan, hooligan, ptarmigan,
wanigan, origan, larrigan, Jonathan, Ser-
bian, Lesbian, Nubian, Indian, guardian,
Gordian, Lydian, saffian, ruffian, Belgian,
Georgian, Pythian, Fijian, Anglian, Tul-
lian, Julian, simian, Marnian, Appian,
Caspian, Thespian, Marian, Austrian, Ser-
vian, Latvian, astrakhan, gamelan, China-
man, husbandman, Orangeman, noble-
man, middleman, rifleman, gentleman,
longshoreman, signalman, Mussulman, drag-
oman, midshipman, alderman, superman,
fisherman, waterman, peterman, slaugh-
terman, quarterman, overman, sailorman,
backwoodsman, policeman, Irishman, talisman,
frontiersman, aircraftsman, *selectman,* mer-
chantman, highwayman, clergyman, tally-
man, dollyman. liveryman, dairyman, ferry-
man, merryman, countryman, vestryman,
marzipan, tragopan, Lutheran, veteran, Al-
coran, Parmesan, courtesan, Powhatan,
Yucatan, Puritan, rheotan, Turkestan,
Pakistan, caravan, cordovan, Libyan,
Wesleyan.
4. militiaman, jinrikiman, artilleryman,
deliveryman, infantryman, Aldebaran, cata-
maran, Baluchistan, Afghanistan.

ANCH– 1. ganch, canch [slang], Blanche,
blanch, flanch, ranch, branch, stanch.
3. avalanche.

AND– 1. and, band, banned, dand [slang],
fanned, hand, canned, scànned, land,
bland, gland, clanned, planned, manned,
panned, spanned, rand, brand, grand,
strand, sand, tanned, stand, vanned.
2. *headband, neckband,* disband, *breastband,
wristband,* offhand, *backhand,* unhand, *short-
hand,* firsthand, *headland, midland, woodland,
eland, mainland, dreamland, Greenland, Rhineland, inland, lowland, Lapland, upland, moorland,
grassland, Queensland, wasteland, northland,*
demand, remand, command, expand, *fire-
brand, quicksand, greensand, lampstand,* with-
stand.
3. saraband, contraband, bellyband, four-in-
hand, behindhand, secondhand, evenhand,
underhand, upper hand, afterhand, over-
hand, Samarcand, Holy Land, fairyland,
wonderland, borderland, hinterland, father-
land, motherland, overland, reprimand,
confirmand, countermand, Rio Grande,

ampersand, understand.
4. multiplicand, misunderstand.

ANG– 1. bang, bhang, dang [dial.], fang,
gang, hang, lang [Scot. and dial.], clang,
slang, pang, spang [coll.], rang, sprang,
sang, tang, vang, swang, twang, whang.
2. shebang, *gambang,* gobang, *holmgang,
ingang, sirgang, outgang, oxgang, boomslang,*
Penang, trepang, harangue, meringue, serang,
mustang.
3. overhang, boomerang, burrawang.
4. orangoutang.

ANGD– 1. banged, danged [dial.], fanged,
ganged [coll.], hanged, clanged, slanged,
twanged, whanged.
2. bifanged, harangued.
3. boomeranged.

ANJ– 1. banj [slang], bange, gange, flange.
2. *phalange, orange, sporange.*

ANK– 1. ank [slang], bank, banc, dank,
hank, lank, blank, flank, clank, plank,
pank [dial.], spank, rank, frank, Frank,
franc, crank, prank, trank, sank, shank,
tank, thank, swank, yank, Yank.
2. embank, point-blank, outflank, *gangplank,*
disrank, outrank, *redshank, foreshank.*
3. mountebank, riverbank, savings bank,
hanky-pank, capintank, copertank.

ANKS– *see* **ĂNK,** plus " s " or " 's "; **1.** Manx,
thanx [slang].
2. *Fairbanks, phalanx, longshanks.*
3. bonyshanks.

ANKT– 1. banked, blanked, flanked, clanked,
planked, spanked, ranked, franked, cranked,
sanct, tanked, thanked, swanked, yanked.
2. outflanked, outranked.
3. sacrosanct, spindle-shanked.

ANS– 1. anse, chance, dance, hanse, lance,
glance, manse, nance [slang], France,
prance, trance, stance.
2. bechance, perchance, mischance, *barn
dance,* enhance, askance, romance, finance,
expanse, entrance, *brilliance,* advance.
3. *disturbance, impedance, misguidance, avoidance,
ascendance,* permeance, elegance, arrogance,
radiance, *allegiance, appliance,* variance, nonchalance, sibilance, jubilance, vigilance,
ambulance, simulance, petulance, main-
tenance, countenance, sustenance, préve-
nance [F.], provenance, convenance [F.],
repugnance, ordinance, high finance, dominance, resonance, consonance, assonance,
dissonance, governance, *remembrance, encum-
brance,* sufferance, furtherance, tolerance,
temperance, utterance, severance, ignorance,
aberrance, penetrance, *remonstrance, defeasance,
malfeasance, complaisance, obeisance, conversance,
expectance, inductance, conductance, reluctance,*
oscitance, hesitance, *repentance, acceptance,*
circumstance, *inconstance, pursuance,* issuance,
relevance, *clairvoyance.*
4. significance, extravagance, inelegance,
insouciance, irradiance, luxuriance, dis-
countenance, appurtenance, preordinance,

predominance, inconsonance, vociferance, intemperance, deliverance, recalcitrance, reconnoisance, reconnaissance, exorbitance, concomitance, precipitance, inheritance, continuance, perpetuance, irrelevance.

5. insignificance, disinheritance, discontinuance.

ĂNST– 1. chanced, danced, lanced, glanced, pranced, tranced.

2. enhanced, romanced, financed, entranced, advanced.

ĂNT– 1. ant, aunt, bant, chant, gant [dial.], hant [slang], cant, can't, scant, plant, slant, pant, rant, grant, shan't.

2. enchant, decant, recant, askant, descant, gallant, replant, *eggplant*, *pieplant*, implant, transplant, supplant, aslant, courant, courante, extant, levant, bezant.

3. Corybant, confidant, confidante, permeant, recreant, procreant, miscreant, elegant, congregant, obligant, irrigant, litigant, mitigant, arrogant, elephant, oliphant, *triumphant*, sycophant, resiant, otiant, desiccant, exsiccant, dodecant, imprecant, albicant, radicant, abdicant, dedicant, mendicant, indicant, applicant, formicant, fabricant, lubricant, vesicant, toxicant, coruscant, libelant, revelant, sibilant, jubilant, vigilant, tremolant, circulant, osculant, stridulant, undulant, ululant, stimulant, cumulant, petulant, postulant, *informant*, revenant, covenant, ordinant, culminant, dominant, consonant, assonant, dissonant, mancipant, Sacripant, celebrant, tolerant, alterant, cauterant, integrant, emigrant, immigrant, odorant, colorant, cormorant, ignorant, penetrant, registrant, ministrant, *obscurant*, figurant, fulgurant, hebetant, vegetant, dilettant, habitant, oscitant, militant, comitant, crepitant, irritant, hesitant, visitant, *important*, *inconstant*, issuant, fluctuant, *gallivant*, relevant, innovant, cognizant.

4. consolidant, extravagant, inelegant, depreciant, officiant, renunciant, insouciant, communicant, intoxicant, circumvolant, matriculant, coagulant, articulant, congratulant, impetulant, capitulant, appurtenant, discriminant, determinant, agglutinant, conglutinant, horrisonant, reverberant, protuberant, exuberant, preponderant, refrigerant, intolerant, agglomerant, itinerant, deodorant, ameliorant, decolorant, expectorant, recalcitrant, administrant, resuscitant, incogitant, regurgitant, concomitant, continuant, attenuant, irrelevant, incognizant.

ĂNTS– *see* ANT, plus " s " or " 's "; *also* **ĂNS**; 1. crants.

3. Liederkranz.

ĂNZ– *see* **ĂN**, plus " s " or " 's "; 1. banns.

ĂP– 1. chap, dap, gap, hap, Jap, cap, lap, Lapp, flap, clap, slap, map, nap, knap, snap, pap, rap, wrap, crap, scrap, trap, strap, sap, tap, yap, yapp.

2. *stopgap*, mayhap, *mishap*, *madcap*, *redcap*,

becap, *kneecap*, recap, *skullcap*, uncap, *icecap*, nightcap, *whitecap*, *foolscap*, bluecap, catlap, dewlap, flyflap, flip-flap, beclap, *backslap*, genapp, genappe, *surnap*, resnap, unsnap, catnap, enwrap, *mantrap*, entrap, *claptrap*, bestrap, *checkstrap*, *rattrap*, *winesap*, *heeltap*, lagniappe.

3. handicap, wishing cap, overlap, thunderclap, afterclap, photomap, rattletrap.

ĂPS– *see* **ĂP**, plus " s " or " 's "; 1. apse, lapse, schnapps.

2. perhaps, elapse, relapse, collapse, prolapse, synapse.

3. pettichaps.

ĂPST– 1. lapsed.

2. elapsed, relapsed, collapsed.

ĂPT– 1. apt, chapped, gapped, happed, capped, lapped, flapped, clapped, slapped, mapped, napped, snapped, rapt, rapped, wrapt, wrapped, scrapped, trapped, strapped, sapped, tapped, yapped.

2. unchapped, adapt, becapped, recapped, uncapped, *snow-capped*, beclapped, *backslapped*, unslapped, remapped, unmapped, resnapped, unsnapped, *catnapped*, enwrapped, unwrapped, entrapped.

3. handicapped, overlapped.

ĂR– through **ĂRZ**, *see* **Ā** (ay): **ĀR** through **ĀRZ**; *also* **Ä** (ah): **ÄR** through **ÄRZ**.

ĂS– 1. ass, bass, fas [L.], gas, lass, blas, glass, class, mass, pass, wrasse, brass, brasse, grass, crass, strass, sass [dial. and slang], tass, tasse, vas.

2. *jackass*, rubasse, *Midas*, *nefas* [L.], bagasse, fougasse, *fracas*, *Dorcas*, alas, *Hellas*, *eyeglass*, *hourglass*, declass, reclass, outclass, amass, remass, *Lammas*, en masse, *Thomas*, *Christmas*, repass, *pampas*, *compass*, impasse, surpass, *trespass*, upas, arras, harass, Madras, *Mithras*, terrass, cuirass, morass, *dronkgrass*, *eelgrass*, kavass, crevasse.

3. anabasse, contrabass, octobass, pancreas, Boreas, isinglass, looking glass, galloglass, weatherglass, middle class, working class, sonderclass, underclass, upper-class, superclass, bonny lass, Nicholas, Pythias, alias, Elias, Candlemas, Michaelmas, Martinmas, Hallowmas, underpass, overpass, Khyber Pass, *encompass*, Hudibras, sassafras, peppergrass, sparrowgrass, Alcatras, *Honduras*, demitasse, tarantass.

ĂSH– 1. ash, bash, dash, gash, hash, hache, cash, cache, lash, flash, clash, plash, splash, slash, mash, smash, gnash, pash [dial.], rash, brash, crash, thrash, tache, tash, sash, stash [dial. and slang].

2. abash, rondache, *slapdash*, rehash, encash, *eyelash*, *backlash*, *pearlash*, *mishmash*, panache, apache, pistache, moustache, soutache [F.].

3. calabash, balderdash, spatterdash, sabretache.

ĂSHT– 1. bashed, dashed, gashed, hashed, cashed, cached, lashed, flashed, clashed, plashed, splashed, slashed, mashed, smashed, gnashed, pashed, crashed, thrashed, sashed, tashed, tached, stashed.

2. abashed, panached, moustached.

ASK– **1.** ask, bask, Basque, casque, cask, flask, mask, task.

2. bemask, remask, unmask.

3. antimask, antimasque.

ASKT– **1.** asked, basked, casked, flasked, masked, tasked.

2. unasked, recasked, uncasked, bemasked, remasked, unmasked.

ASP– **1.** asp, gasp, hasp, clasp, rasp, grasp.

2. agasp, unhasp, enclasp, unclasp.

ASPT– **1.** gasped, hasped, clasped, rasped, grasped.

2. unhasped, enclasped, unclasped, regrasped.

AST– **1.** bast, dast [dial.], fast, gassed, gast [slang], hast, cast, caste, last, blast, classed, mast, massed, nast [dial.], past, passed, sassed, vast.

2. *bombast, steadfast, holdfast, handfast, breakfast,* aghast, *broadcast, molecast,* recast, forecast, *dicast, downcast,* upcast, miscast, outcast, *ballast, portlast,* outlast, outclassed, amassed, remast, *foremast, mainmast, durmast,* unmast, dismast, *gymnast, dynast,* repast, repassed, *mainpast, trispast,* surpassed, harassed, contrast, *peltast, phantast,* avast.

3. flabbergast, undercast, overcast, scholiast, counterblast, unsurpassed, antispast, pederast, paraphrast, metaphrast.

4. elegiast, bucoliast, ecclesiast, symposiast, enthusiast, iconoclast.

AT– **1.** at, bat, chat, fat, gat, hat, cat, scat, skat, lat, blat, flat, plat, plait, splat, slat, mat, matte, gnat, pat, patte, spat, rat, brat, drat, frat [slang], prat, sprat, sat, tat, that, vat.

2. hereat, thereat, whereat, *brickbat, hurlbat, woodchat, whinchat, stonechat, grasschat, chitchat,* begat, highhat, top hat, *bobcat, wildcat, hellcat, polecat, tipcat, bearcat,* plakat, *muscat,* surat, cravat.

3. caveat, acrobat, flitterbat, *waterchat,* tabby cat, kittycat, pussycat, Krazy Kat, lariat, diplomat, pitapat, tokopat, Ararat, democrat, monocrat, bureaucrat, autocrat, plutocrat, thermostat, Rubaiyat.

4. Magnificat, aristocrat, heliostat.

5. commissariat, proletariat, secretariat.

ATCH– *see* **ĂCH.**

ATH– **1.** bath, Gath, hath, lath, math, snath, path, rath, wrath, strath.

2. *bypath, towpath, warpath, footpath.*

3. demibath, isobath, polymath, misomath, aftermath, philomath, allopath.

4. homeopath, osteopath, physiopath.

ATS– *see* **ĂT,** plus " s " or " 's "; **1.** Katz.

AV– **1.** bave [F.], have, halve, calve, lav [slang], Slav, salve.

2. épave [F.].

3. Jugoslav.

AVZ– **1.** halves, calves, Slavs, salves.

3. Jugoslavs.

AX– *see* **ĂKS.**

AZ– **1.** as, chaz [slang], has, jazz, razz [slang], yazz [slang].

2. thereas, whereas.

3. razzmatazz.

AZM– *see* **ĂZ'm.**

Ă (cab)

Double (Feminine) Rhymes

Primary or Secondary Accent Falls on Next to Last Syllable: Imperfect Rhymes Are in Italics.

AB′ee— **2.** abbey, Abbie, babby [dial.], dabby, gabby, cabby, scabby, blabby, flabby, rabbi, Rabi, crabby, shabby, tabby, yabby, yabbi.
3. kohlrabi.

AB′er— **2.** dabber, gabber, jabber, blabber, clabber, slabber, nabber, grabber, stabber, yabber.

AB′erd— **2.** gabbard, jabbered, scabbard, blabbered, clabbered, tabard.

AB′id— **2.** rabid, tabid.

AB′ik— **2.** rabic.
3. syllabic, cannabic.
4. asyllabic, bisyllabic, trisyllabic.
5. polysyllabic, multisyllabic, monosyllabic.

AB′il— **2.** habile; *see also* **ĀB′l.**

AB′in— **2.** cabin, sabin.
3. log cabin.

AB′ing— **2.** dabbing, gabbing, jabbing, cabbing, scabbing, blabbing, slabbing, nabbing, drabbing, grabbing, crabbing, stabbing.
3. confabbing.
4. taxicabbing.

AB′it— **2.** Babbitt, habit, rabbet, rabbit, drabbet.
3. inhabit, cohabit.

AB′l— **2.** babble, dabble, gabble, habile, jabble, cabble, scabble, rabble, brabble, drabble, grabble, scrabble.
3. bedabble, bedrabble.
4. malleable, permeable, amiable, expiable, variable, leviable, valuable, issuable, formidable, propagable, segregable, obligable, irrigable, mitigable, navigable, gibble-gabble, marriageable, damageable, manageable, knowledgeable, challengeable, *dischargeable,* applicable, duplicable, explicable, amicable, despicable, extricable, practicable, masticable, educable, manducable, violable, calculable, regulable, estimable, fathomable, *reformable,* terminable, pardonable, fashionable, pensionable, actionable, sanctionable, mentionable, questionable, poisonable, personable, governable, exculpable, separable, renderable, ponderable, preferable, offerable, sufferable, tolerable, numerable, venerable, vulnerable, temperable, superable, alterable, utterable, conquerable, severable, answerable, miserable, admirable, execrable, ribblerabble, memorable, honorable, favorable, pleasurable, measurable, exorable, censurable, mensurable, purchasable, noticeable, serviceable, balanceable, publishable, perishable, marketable, covetable, habitable, dubitable, creditable, *forgettable,* profitable, limitable, hospitable, charitable, irritable, evitable, equitable, comfortable, *unlivable, inequable.*
5. impermeable, remediable, affiliable, inexpiable, invariable, renunciable, imperviable, unformidable, immitigable, interrogable, unmanageable, acknowledgeable, unchallengeable, eradicable, *multiplicable,* inapplicable, inexplicable, inextricable, impracticable, prognosticable, inviolable, incalculable, inoculable, coagulable, inestimable, unfathomable, inalienable, imaginable, *disciplinable,* contaminable, examinable, abominable, determinable, interminable, unpardonable, companionable, impassionable, impressionable, objectionable, exceptionable, proportionable, unquestionable, developable, inseparable, rememberable, considerable, imponderable, insufferable, decipherable, intolerable, innumerable, invulnerable, insuperable, unalterable, inseverable, deliverable, recoverable, discoverable, unanswerable, commemorable, dishonorable, unfavorable, immeasurable, impenetrable, incensurable, immensurable, commensurable, unnoticeable, disserviceable, distinguishable, extinguishable, interpretable, inhabitable, indubitable, discreditable, hereditable, unprofitable, illimitable, inimitable, indomitable, decapitable, precipitable, inhospitable, uncharitable, inequitable, inevitable, un-

comfortable, contributable, distributable, attributable, invaluable, perpetuable.

6. ineradicable, indistinguishable, inextinguishable, irremediable, inalienable, unimaginable, undevelopable, inconsiderable, undecipherable, irrecoverable, incommensurable, uninhabitable; *see also* **ĬB'l, ŬB'l.**

AB'ld– **2.** babbled, dabbled, gabbled, jabbled, cabbled, scabbled, brabbled, drabbled, grabbled, scrabbled.
3. bedabbled, bedrabbled.
4. scribble-scrabbled.

AB'lee– **2.** babbly, dabbly, gabbly, drably, drabbly, scrabbly.

AB'ler– **2.** babbler, dabbler, gabbler, jabbler, cabbler, scabbler, brabbler, grabbler, scrabbler.
3. bedabbler, bedrabbler.
4. scribble-scrabbler.

AB'let– **2.** crablet, tablet.

AB'ling– **2.** babbling, dabbling, gabbling, jabbling, cabbling, scabbling, brabbling, grabbling, scrabbling.
3. bedabbling, bedrabbling.
4. scribble-scrabbling.

AB'lish– **2.** babblish, dabblish, gabblish, drabblish, scrabblish.
3. establish.
4. re-establish, disestablish.

AB'o– **2.** jabot, sabot.

AB'ot– **2.** abbot, Abbot, Caboto.

ACH'ee– **2.** batchy, catchy, matchy, machi, snatchy, patchy, scratchy.
3. seecatchie.

ACH'el– **2.** hatchel, ratchel, satchel.

ACH'er– **2.** batcher, hatcher, catcher, latcher, matcher, snatcher, patcher, scratcher, thatcher.
3. *dogcatcher, flycatcher,* despatcher, dispatcher, *back-scratcher.*

ACH'et– **2.** hatchet, latchet, matchet, ratchet, brachet.

ACH'ez– **2.** batches, baches, hatches, catches, latches, Natchez, snatches, patches, scratches, thatches.
3. *crosshatches, nuthatches,* unlatches, rematches, mismatches, despatches, dispatches, *crosspatches, back-scratches,* attaches, detaches.
4. Kaffee-klatsches [G.].

ACH'ing– **2.** batching, baching, hatching, catching, latching, matching, snatching, patching, scratching, thatching.
3. *crosshatching,* unlatching, rematching, dispatching, attaching, detach-ing, backscratching.

ACH'less– **2.** batchless, hatchless, catchless, latchless, matchless, patchless, scratchless, thatchless.
3. dispatchless.

ACH'ment– **2.** hatchment, ratchment.
3. attachment, detachment, dispatchment.

AD'a– **2.** adda, dada, stadda.

AD'am– **2.** Adam, madam.
3. macadam.

AD'ed– **2.** added, dadded, gadded, plaided, padded, bradded.
3. readded, unadded, unpadded.

AD'ee– **2.** baddie [slang], baddy [slang], daddy, faddy, caddy, caddie, laddie, laddy, gladdy, plaidie, maddy, paddy.
4. finnan haddie.

AD'en– **2.** gladden, madden, sadden.
3. engladden, Macfadden.

AD'er– **2.** adder, badder, dadder, gadder, ladder, bladder, gladder, madder, sadder.
3. stepladder.

AD'est– **2.** baddest, gladdest, maddest, saddest.

AD'ik– **3.** decadic, haggadic, triadic, Helladic, nomadic, monadic, faradic, sporadic, octadic, Sotadic, dyadic, nexadic.

AD'ing– **2.** adding, dadding, gadding, padding, bradding.

AD'ish– **2.** faddish, caddish, gladdish, plaidish, maddish, radish, saddish.

AD'ist– **2.** faddist, sadist.

AD'l– **2.** addle, daddle [dial.], scaddle, skaddle, paddle, raddle, spraddle, straddle, saddle, staddle [dial.].
3. skedaddle, astraddle, bestraddle, unsaddle.
4. fiddle-faddle.

AD'ld– **2.** addled, daddled [dial.], scaddled, skaddled, paddled, raddled, spraddled, straddled, saddled, staddled [dial.].
3. skedaddled, bestraddled, unsaddled.
4. fiddle-faddled.

AD'lee– **2.** badly, Hadley, gladly, madly, Radley, Bradley, spraddly, sadly.

AD'ling– **2.** addling, daddling [dial.], scaddling, skaddling, paddling, spraddling, straddling, saddling, spraddling, staddling [dial.].
3. skedaddling, bestraddling, unsaddling.
4. fiddle-faddling.

AD'lz– *see* **ĂD'l,** plus " s " or " 's "; **4.** Thomas Traddles [Dickens].

AD'ness– **2.** badness, gladness, madness, sadness.

AD'o– **2.** shadow.
3. foreshadow.
4. Colorado, overshadow.

AD'ok– **2.** baddock, haddock, paddock, shaddock.

AF'ee– **2.** baffy, chaffy, daffy, faffy, draffy, taffy.

AF'er– **2.** chaffer, gaffer, ghaffir, Kaffir, laugher, quaffer, piaffer, zaffer.

AF'ik– **2.** maffick, graphic, traffic, Sapphic.
3. seraphic, engraphic.
4. diagraphic, paragraphic, telegraphic, choregraphic, calligraphic, geographic, melographic, zoographic, lithographic, orthographic, biographic, holographic, stylographic, demographic, homographic, seismographic, cosmographic, chromographic, stenographic, ethnographic, phonographic, chronographic, topographic, typographic, macrographic, micrographic, chirographic, chorographic,

'ij– 2. damage, ramage.
3. endamage.
ĬK– 2. amic, gamic.
3. Adamic, agamic, syngamic, cinnamic, dynamic, ceramic, engrammic, balsamic, potamic, Benthamic.
3. preadamic, polygamic, homogamic, monogamic, Abrahamic, dioramic, cycloramic, cosmoramic, panoramic, telegrammic, monogrammic, cryptogrammic.
Ĭ'in– 2. amine, famine, gamin, lamin, stamin.
3. prolamine, examine.
4. reexamine, cross-examine.
Ĭ'ing– 2. damming, damning, gamming, hamming [slang], jamming, lambing, lamming [slang], flamming, clamming, slamming, ramming, cramming, tramming, shamming, whamming.
Ĭ'is– 2. amice, chlamys, tamis.
3. dynamis.
Ĭ'ish– 2. Amish, famish, lambish, clammish, rammish.
3. enfamish.
Ĭ'let– 2. hamlet, Hamlet, camlet, samlet.
Ĭ'ok– 2. hammock, cammock mammock.
Ĭ'on– 2. ammon, Ammon, daman, gammon, mammon, salmon, shaman.
3. backgammon.
ĂMP'an– 2. jampan, sampan, tampan.
ĂMP'as– 2. lampas, pampas.
ĂMP'ee– 2. dampy, crampy, vampy.
ĂMP'er– 2. champer, damper, hamper, camper, scamper, clamper, pamper, pampre, ramper, tramper, tamper, stamper, vamper.
3. decamper, revamper.
ĂMP'ing– 2. champing, damping, camping, scamping, clamping, ramping, cramping, tramping, tamping, stamping, vamping.
3. decamping, encamping, revamping.
ĂMP'ish– 2. dampish, campish, scampish, crampish, trampish, vampish, wampish.
ĂMP'l– 2. ample, trample, sample.
3. ensample, example.
ĂMP'lee– 2. amply, damply.
ĂMP'ler– 2. ampler, trampler, sampler.
3. exampler.
ĂMP'ling– 2. sampling, trampling.
3. ensampling.
ĂMP'ment– 3. decampment, encampment.
ĂMP'us– 2. campus, grampus, wampus.
4. hippocampus.
ĂM'ut– 2. gamut, Mammut.
ĂMZ'el– 2. amsel, damsel.
ĂMZ'un– 2. damson, ramson.
ĂN'a– 2. ana, Ana, anna, Anna, Hannah, canna, Lana, manna.
3. Urbana, bandanna, Diana, Guiana, liana, banana, sultana, lantana, Montana, ruana, Havana, savanna, Savannah, hosanna, Susanna.
4. Indiana, Georgiana, Pollyanna, Marianna, dulciana, Gloriana, tertiana, Susquehanna, Poinciana, Texarkana.
5. Americana, Shakespeariana, Louisiana.
ĂN'al– 2. annal; see also ĂN'el.
ĂNCH'ee– 2. ranchy, branchy.
ĂNCH'er– 2. blancher, plancher, rancher, brancher, stancher.
ĂNCH'ez– 2. blanches, ranches, branches, stanches.
4. avalanches.
ĂNCH'ing– 2. blanching, planching, ranching, branching, stanching.
4. avalanching.
ĂNCH'less– 2. ranchless, branchless, stanchless.
4. avalanchless.
ĂND'a– 2. panda, vanda.
3. Uganda, Amanda, veranda, Miranda.
4. propaganda, jacaranda, memoranda, observanda.
ĂND'al– 2. scandal, pandal, sandal, Randall, crandall, vandal, Vandal; see also ĂND'l.
ĂND'ant– 2. mandant.
3. demandant, commandant.
ĂND'ed– 2. banded, handed, candid, landed, glanded, randed, branded, stranded, sanded.
3. disbanded, red-handed, freehanded, three-handed, highhanded, backhanded, black-handed, fullhanded, cleanhanded, unhanded, forehanded, four-handed, closehanded, neat-handed, left-handed, light-handed, right-handed, shorthanded, two-handed, un-landed, demanded, remanded, commanded, expanded, unbranded, unsanded.
4. contrabanded, empty-handed, heavy-handed, singlehanded, openhanded, even-handed, overhanded, underhanded, repri-manded, countermanded, unexpanded.
ĂND'ee– 2. Andy, bandy, dandy, handy, candy, Mandy, pandy, randy, brandy, sandy, shandy.
3. unhandy, Jim Dandy.
4. jack-a-dandy, sugar-candy, spick-and spandy, Rio Grande, jaborandi.
6. Yankee Doodle Dandy.
ĂND'eed– 2. bandied, candied, brandied.
ĂND'er– 2. bander, dander, gander, hander, candor, Landor, lander, blander, slander, pandar, pander, rander, brander, grander, strander, sander, stander, zander.
3. disbander, Leander, meander, backhander, left-hander, right-hander, philander, Ice-lander, inlander, outlander, demander, reman-der, commander, pomander, germander, Menander, expander, Isander, goosander, dittander, bystander, outstander, withstander.
4. oleander, coriander, Afrikander, New-foundlander, salamander, gerrymander, re-primander, Alexander, understander.
ĂND'erd– 2. slandered, pandered, standard.
3. meandered, philandered.
4. gerrymandered.
ĂND'erz– see ĂND'er– plus "s" or "'s"; 2. Flanders, glanders.

---

neurographic, pyrographic, isographic, pan-tographic, photographic, cryptographic, car-tographic, histographic, autographic, poly-graphic.
5. paleographic, oleographic, ethneographic, idiographic, bibliographic, heliographic, crystallographic, dactylographic.
6. autobiographic, cinematographic.
ĂF'ing– 2. chaffing, faffing [dial.], gaffing, laughing, graphing, strafing, staffing, quaffing.
4. telegraphing, autographing, paragraph-ing, multigraphing, photographing, litho-graphing.
ĂF'l– 2. baffle, daffle [dial.], gaffle, snaffle, raffle, scraffle, yaffle.
ĂF'ling– 2. baffling, haffling, calfling, snaffling, raffling, scraffling.
ĂFT'ed– 2. rafted, drafted, grafted, crafted, shafted, wafted.
3. undrafted, engrafted, ingrafted, ungrafted, handcrafted.
ĂFT'ee– 2. rafty, drafty, grafty, crafty, wafty.
ĂFT'er– 2. after, dafter, laughter, rafter, drafter, draughter, grafter, wafter.
3. hereafter, thereafter, whereafter.
4. hereinafter, thereinafter.
ĂFT'ij– 2. draftage, draughtage, graftage, waftage.
ĂFT'ing– 2. hafting, rafting, drafting, draught-ing, grafting, shafting, wafting.
3. engrafting, ingrafting.
ĂFT'less– 2. draftless, graftless, craftless, shaftless.
ĂG'a– 2. Agha, dagga, saga, quagga.
ĂG'ed– 2. jagged, knagged, ragged, crag-ged, scragged.
ĂG'ee– 2. Aggie, baggie, baggy, daggy, faggy, gaggy, haggy [Scot. and. dial. Eng.], jaggy, laggy, flaggy, slaggy, Maggie, naggy, knaggy, snaggy, raggy, raggee, braggy, draggy, craggy, scraggy, saggy, shaggy, taggy, staggy, quaggy, waggy, swaggy.
ĂG'er– 2. bagger, dagger, fagger, gagger, jagger, lagger, flagger, nagger, snagger, ragger, bragger, dragger, sagger, tagger, stagger, wagger, swagger.
3. two-bagger, wigwagger, zigzagger.
4. agar-agar, carpetbagger.
ĂG'erd– 2. haggard, laggard, blackguard, staggard, staggered, swaggered.
ĂG'ert– 2. braggart, staggart.
ĂG'et– 2. agate, baggit, fagot, faggot, maggot.
ĂG'ing– 2. bagging, fagging, gagging, jagging, lagging, flagging, nagging, snagging, rag-ging, bragging, dragging, sagging, shagging, tagging, stagging, wagging.
3. unflagging, wigwagging, zigzagging.
ĂG'ish– 2. haggish, flaggish, laggish, naggish, braggish, waggish.
ĂG'l– 2. daggle, gaggle, haggle, raggle, draggle, straggle, waggle, waggel.
3. bedraggle.
4. raggle-taggle.

ĂG'ld– 2. daggled, gaggled, haggled, raggled, draggled, straggled, waggled.
3. bedraggled.
ĂG'ler– 2. daggler, gaggler, haggler, raggler, draggler, straggler, waggler.
3. bedraggler.
ĂG'ling– 2. daggling, gaggling, haggling, raggling, draggling, straggling, waggling.
3. bedraggling.
ĂG'ma– 2. magma.
3. malagma.
ĂG'man– 2. bagman, flagman, ragman, dragman.
ĂG'nate– 2. agnate, magnate, stagnate.
ĂG'nes– 2. Agnes, Sphagnous, magnus.
ĂG'net– 2. magnet, dragnet.
ĂG'num– 2. Sphagnum, magnum.
ĂG'on– 2. agon, flagon, dragon, wagon.
3. pendragon, snapdragon.
ĂG'ot– see ĂG'et.
ĂJ'ee– 2. hadji, cadgy.
3. koradji.
ĂJ'er– 2. agger, badger, fadger, cadger.
ĂJ'ik– 2. magic, tragic.
3. pelagic, choragic.
4. theophagic, sarcophagic, theomagic, hemorrhagic, antitragic.
5. archipelagic.
ĂJ'il– 2. agile, fragile.
ĂK'a– 2. bacca, lacca.
3. sifaka, Malacca, alpaca.
ĂK'ate– 2. baccate, placate, saccate.
ĂK'ee– 2. hacky, Jacky, khaki, lackey, blackie, blacky, maki, knacky, raki, cracky, sake, tacky, quacky, wacky, whacky.
3. gimcracky.
4. Nagasaki.
ĂK'en– 2. blacken, slacken, bracken, kraken.
ĂK'er– 2. backer, hacker, lacquer, lacker, blacker, clacker, slacker, smacker, knacker, snacker, packer, racker, cracker, tracker, sacker. tacker, stacker, whacker, quacker, thwacker, yakker [slang], yacker [slang].
3. whinchacker, hijacker, shellacker, polacre, unpacker, clamcracker, corncracker, firecracker, nutcracker, ransacker, attacker, bushwhacker.
ĂK'est– 2. blackest, slackest.
ĂK'et– 2. jacket, flacket, placket, packet, racket, rackett, racquet, bracket, sacket, tacket.
3. redjacket, bluejacket.
4. smoking jacket, dinner jacket.
ĂK'ij– 2. backage, package, wrackage, track-age, sackage, stackage.
ĂK'ing– 2. backing, hacking, jacking, lacking, blacking, clacking, slacking, smacking, knacking, snacking, packing, racking, cracking, tracking, sacking, shack-ing, tacking, stacking, quacking, whacking, thwacking, yakking [slang], yacking [slang].
3. shellacking, repacking, unpacking, wise-cracking, ransacking, attacking, thumbtacking.
4. bivouacking, paddywhacking.
ĂK'ish– 2. blackish, slackish, knackish,

brackish, quackish.

AK′l– 2. hackle, cackle, mackle, macle, grackle, crackle, shackle, tackle, quackle,
3. debacle, *piacle, manacle, pinnacle, barnacle. miracle, oracle, coracle, ramshackle,* unshackle, *spectacle, obstacle.*
4. tabernacle, hibernacle.

AK′ld– 2. hackled, cackled, crackled, shackled, tackled, quackled.
3. *manacled,* unshackled.

AK′lee– 2. cackly, blackly, slackly, crackly.
3. *ramshackly.*

AK′ler– 2. hackler, cackler, crackler, shackler, tackler.
3. unshackler.

AK′less– 2. backless, hackless, lackless, clackless, slackless, knackless, snackless, packless, rackless, crackless, trackless, sackless, shackless, tackless, stachless, quackless, whackless, thwackless, yakless, yackless [slang].
3. shellacless, *wisecrackless, rucksackless,* attackless.

AK′ling– 2. cackling, crackling, shackling, tackling.

AK′ma– 2. chacma, drachma.
4. tetradrachma.

AK′nee– 2. acne, hackney.

AK′ness– 2. blackness, slackness.

AK′o– 2. jako, shako, squacco.
3. tobacco, icaco, goracco.

AK′see– 2. flaxy, Maxie, braxy, taxi, taxy, waxy.
4. biotaxy, zootaxy, hemotaxy.

AK′sen– 2. flaxen, waxen.

AK′ser– 2. taxer, waxer.
3. relaxer.

AK′sez– 2. axes, laxes, flaxes, taxes, waxes.
3. relaxes, unlaxes, retaxes, dewaxes, rewaxes.
4. battle-axes, income taxes.

AK′shum– 2. action, faction, paction, fraction, traction, taction.
3. abaction, subaction, reaction, enaction, inaction, coaction, compaction, refraction, diffraction, infraction, attraction, contraction, protraction, abstraction, distraction, extraction, transaction, contaction, exaction.
4. interaction, counteraction, rubefaction, calefaction, malefaction, benefaction, stupefaction, torrefaction, putrefaction, liquefaction, satisfaction.
5. dissatisfaction, counterattraction.

AK′shus– 2. factious, fractious.

AK′sing– 2. axing, flaxing, taxing, waxing.
3. relaxing, unlaxing, *pole-axing,* rewaxing.

AK′sis– 2. axis, praxis, taxis, staxis.
3. synaxis, syntaxis.
4. prophylaxis, parapraxis, chiropraxis, parataxis, hypotaxis, epistaxis.

AK′son– 2. axon, Jackson, klaxon, Saxon.
3. diaxon, dendraxon.
4. Anglo-Saxon.

AKT′a– 2. acta, facta.

AKT′ed– 2. acted, pacted, fracted.
3. enacted, coacted, redacted, reacted, impacted, defracted, diffracted, attracted, subtracted, detracted, retracted, contracted, protracted, abstracted, distracted, extracted, transacted, contacted, exacted.
4. retroacted, abreacted, arefacted.

AKT′er– 2. acter, actor, factor, tractor, tactor.
3. abactor, redactor, attracter, diffractor, subtracter, contracter, contractor, protracter, protractor, abstracter, extractor, exacter, exactor.
4. calefactor, malefactor, benefactor.

AKT′ful– 2. tactful.
3. distractful, untactful.

AKT′ik– 2. lactic, practic, tactic.
3. didactic, galactic, stalactic, malactic, phylactic, climactic, synactic, emphractic, syntactic, protactic.
4. parallactic, catallactic, prophylactic, chiropractic.

AKT′il– 2. dactyl, fractile, tractile, tactile.
3. adactyl, didactyl, syndactyl, retractile, contractile, protractile.
4. pterodactyl.

AKT′ing– 2. acting.
3. redacting, enacting, defracting, attracting, retracting, contracting, protracting, abstracting, distracting, transacting, exacting.
4. double-acting, retroacting, underacting, counteracting, overacting.

AKT′is– 2. practice, practise,
3. malpractice.

AKT′iv– 2. active, factive.
3. reactive, enactive, inactive, olfactive, refractive, diffractive, attractive, subtractive, detractive, retractive, contractive, protractive, abstractive, distractive, extractive.
4. radioactive, retroactive, counteractive, calefactive, benefactive, stupefactive, rarefactive, putrefactive, liquefactive, unattractive.

AKT′lee– 3. compactly, abstractly, intactly, exactly.
5. matter-of-factly.

AKT′less– 2. actless, factless, pactless, bractless, tractless, tactless.
3. *compactless, abstractless.*

AKT′ment– 3. enactment, impactment, extractment.
4. re-enactment.

AKT′ness– 3. compactness, intactness, exacness.
4. inexactness.
5. matter-of-factness.

AKT′o– 2. facto.
3. de facto.
4. ex post facto [L.].

AKT′or– 2. actor, acter, factor, tractor, tactor.
3. enacter, diffractor, extractor, exactor.
4. benefactor; *see also* **ĂK′ter.**

AKT′ress– 2. actress.
3. exactress.
4. malefactress, benefactress.

AKT′um– 2. factum, pactum [L.].

AKT′ure– 2. facture, fracture.
3. compacture, contracture.
4. manufacture.

AKT′us– 2. actus, cactus, tactus.
4. Ferocactus.

AL′a– 2. alla, Allah, galla, gala, calla, palla, pallah.
3. *cabala,* emagalla, Valhalla, mashallah, cavalla.

AL′ad– 2. balad, salad; *see also* **ĂL′id.**

AL′ans– 2. balance, valance.
3. unbalance.
4. counterbalance, overbalance.

AL′ant– 2. gallant, callant, talent.
3. ungallant.

AL′as– 2. balas, Dallas, Pallas.

ALB′a– 2. alba, galba.
3. xibalba.

ALB′ee– 2. albe, halbe.

ALB′ert– 2. Albert, halbert.

AL′ee– 2. alley, ally, bally, dally, galley, gally, pally, rally, sally, Sallie, challie, challis, tally, valley.
3. Bengali, tamale.
4. dilly-dally, Mexicali, shilly-shally, hot tamale.

AL′eed– 2. dallied, rallied, sallied, tallied,
4. dilly-dallied, shilly-shallied.

AL′ent– 2. talent; *see also* **ĂL′ant.**

AL′er– 2. pallor, valor.
3. caballer.

AL′et– 2. ballet, ballot, gallet, callet, mallet, palate, pallet, palette, sallet, tallet [dial.], valet.

ALF′a– 2. alfa, alpha.
3. alfalfa, pentalpha.

AL′id– 2. calid, pallid, valid.
3. impallid, invalid; *see also* **ĂL′ad.**

AL′ik– 2. Aleck, Gallic, phallic, malic, grallic, Salic, thallic.
3. cabalic, vocalic, vandalic, Uralic, medallic, metallic, italic, Tantalic, smart aleck [coll.], oxalic.
4. encephalic, misogallic, intervallic.

AL′is– 2. Alice, allice, chalice, malice, palace.
4. digitalis.

ALJ′ee– 2. algae, Algy.
3. neuralgy, nostalgy.

ALJ′ik– 2. algic.
3. gastralgic, neuralgic, antalgic, nostalgic.

ALM′a– 2. Alma, halma.
3. agalma.

ALM′ud– 2. almud, Talmud.

AL′o– 2. aloe, fallow, gallow, hallow, callow, mallow, sallow, shallow, tallow.
3. Allhallow, unhallow, dishallow, *marshmallow.*

AL′od– 2. hallowed, sallowed, tallowed.
3. unhallowed.

AL′on– 2. gallon, kalon, salon, talon.

AL′op– 2. galop, gallop,
3. escallop.

AL′or– 2. pallor, valor.
3. caballer.

AL′ot– 2. ballot; *see also* **Ă**

ALP′ine– 2. Alpine.
3. subalpine, Cisalpine, tr

ALP′ing– 2. scalping, palpir

ALT′o– 2. alto.
3. Rialto, contralto.

AL′um– 2. alum, vallum.
3. chloralum, catallum.

AL′us– 2. phallus, Gallus, thallus.
4. aryballus.

AL′ya– 2. Alya, dahlia.

AL′u– 2. value.
3. evalue, devalue, revalue.
4. undervalue.

AL′yun– 2. scallion, pallion,
3. medallion, rapscallion, bat

AM′a– 2. amma, chamma, Ga Shammah, Yama.
3. Digamma, pajama, pyjama
4. Alabama, Cinerama, pan drama, monodrama, duodram

AM′al– 2. Hamal, mammal; *se*

AMB′er– 2. amber, camber, c bar, tambour.
3. grisamber.
4. liquidamber.

AMB′ik– 3. iambic.
4. galliambic, choliambic, chori iambic, dithyrambic.

AMB′ist– 2. gambist, cambist.
3. iambist.

AMB′it– 2. ambit, gambit.

AMB′l– 2. amble, gamble, gamb bramble, scramble, shamble, w
3. *preamble,* unscramble.

AMB′ler– 2. ambler, gambler, scrambler, shambler, wambler.

AMB′ling– 2. ambling, gambling, brambling, scrambling, wamblin
3. unscrambling.

AMB′o– 2. ambo, jambeau, flambea sambo, Sambo, zambo.

AMB′ol– 2. gambol; *see also* **AM**

AMB′us– 3. iambus.
4. dithyrambus.

AM′el– 2. camel, Hamal, mamm mel.
3. enamel, entrammel, untrammel

AM′er– 2. ammer, dammer, damne mer, hammer, jammer, lamber, clamor, slammer, rammer, gramma mer, shammer, stammer, yammer.
3. *sledgehammer,* exhammer, *win* enamor.
4. yellowhammer.

AM′fer– 2. camphor, chamfer.

AM′i– 2. gammy, hammy, jammy, ch mammy, sammy, chamois, shammy, t
3. Miami.

AND'ij– 2. bandage, standage.
AND'ik– 3. Icelandic.
    4. propagandic.
AND'ing– 2. banding, handing, landing, randing, branding, stranding, sanding, standing.
    3. disbanding, unhanding, demanding, remanding, commanding, expanding, outstanding, withstanding.
    4. reprimanding, countermanding, understanding, notwithstanding.
    5. misunderstanding.
AND'ish– 2. blandish, brandish, grandish, standish.
    3. outlandish, Myles Standish.
AND'ist– 4. contrabandist, propagandist.
AND'it– 2. bandit, Pandit.
AND'l– 2. dandle, handle, candle, scandle, pandle, pandal, sandal, vandal.
    3. manhandle, mishandle; see also ĂND'al.
AND'lee– 2. blandly, grandly.
AND'ler– 2. chandler, dandler, handler, candler.
    3. panhandler.
AND'less– 2. bandless, handless, landless, glandless, brandless, strandless, sandless.
    3. demandless, commandless.
AND'ling– 2. bandling, candling, handling, brandling.
    3. manhandling, mishandling.
AND'ment– 3. disbandment, remandment, commandment.
AND'ness– 2. blandness, grandness.
AND'o– 2. bandeau, landau.
    3. Orlando, commando, Fernando, Hernando, lentando [It.].
    4. Ferdinando.
AND'on– 2. Landon, Brandon.
    3. abandon.
AND'ra– 2. mandra, Sandra.
    3. Cassandra.
    4. Alessandra, Alexandra.
AND'stand– 2. bandstand, handstand, grandstand.
AND'um– 2. mandom, random, tandem.
    3. notandum.
    4. memorandum, observandum, avizandum.
    10. de gustibus non est disputandum [L.].
ANDZ'man– 2. bandsman, landsman.
AN'ee– 2. Annie, Danny, Fanny, canny, Lannie, clanny, mannie, nanny, nannie, branny, Franny, granny, cranny.
    3. Aani, afghani, uncanny, tin-panny.
    4. frangipani.
AN'eed– 2. nannied, grannied, crannied.
    3. benannied, begrannied, becrannied.
AN'el– 2. annal, channel, cannel, flannel, panel, scrannel, stannel.
    3. empanel, impanel.
    4. outing flannel.
AN'er– 2. banner, fanner, canner, scanner, lanner, planner, manner, manor, panner, spanner, tanner, vanner.

    3. japanner, trepanner.
AN'erd– 2. bannered, mannered.
    3. unmannered, well-mannered, ill-mannered.
AN'et– 2. gannet, Janet, cannet, planet, vannet; see also ĂN'it.
ANG'ee– 2. bangy, fangy, clangy, slangy, tangy, tangy, twangy, whangy.
ANG'er– 2. banger, danger [dial.], ganger, hanger, hangar, clangor, Sanger, whanger.
    3. haranguer, strap-hanger.
    4. paper hanger.
ANG'ger– 2. anger, angor, Bangor, hangar, languor, clangor.
ANG'gl– 2. angle, bangle, dangle, fangle, jangle, mangle, spangle, wrangle, sprangle, strangle, tangle, wangle.
    3. fandangle, *quadrangle*, *leeangle*, *triangle*, *rectangle*, *pentangle*, *septangle*, *sexangle*, bespangle, entangle, untangle.
    4. jingle-jangle, interjangle, intertangle, disentangle.
ANG'gld– 2. angled, dangled, fangled [dial.], jangled, mangled, spangled, wrangled, sprangled, strangled, tangled, wangled.
    3. new-fangled, bespangled, star-spangled, entangled, untangled.
    4. jingle-jangled, intertangled, disentangled.
ANG'glee– 2. bangly, dangly, gangly, jangly, spangly, wrangly, sprangly, strangly, tangly.
ANG'gler– 2. angler, dangler, gangler, jangler, mangler, spangler, wrangler, strangler, tangler, wangler.
    3. entangler, untangler.
ANG'gling– 2. angling, dangling, fangling [dial.], gangling, jangling, mangling, spangling, wrangling, sprangling, strangling, tangling, wangling.
    3. entangling, untangling.
    4. jingle-jangling.
ANG'gwij– 2. language, slanguage.
ANG'ing– 2. banging, danging [dial.], hanging, clanging, slanging, twanging, whanging.
    3. strap-hanging, haranguing.
    4. paper hanging, overhanging.
ANG'less– 2. bangless, dangless, fangless, gangless, clangless, pangless, twangless, whangless.
    3. harangueless, meringueless.
ANG'man– 2. hangman, gangman.
ANG'o– 2. bango, mango, tango.
    3. fandango, Cipango, contango.
    4. Pago Pago, Pangopango.
ANG'ster– 2. bangster, gangster, slangster.
ANG'win– 2. anguine, sanguine.
    3. ensanguine, consanguine, exsanguine.
ANG'wish– 2. anguish, languish.
AN'ij– 2. manage, pannage, crannage, tannage.
    3. mismanage.
AN'ik– 2. phanic, panic, tannic, stannic,
    3. neanic, paganic, organic, cyanic, mechanic, volcanic, vulcanic, Brahmanic, Ger-

manic, tympanic, Hispanic, Iranic, tyrannic, Koranic, uranic, satanic, tetanic, Britannic, titanic, sultanic, botanic, Spartanic, galvanic.

4. oceanic, diaphanic, lexiphanic, theophanic, inorganic, exorganic, cosmorganic, opianic, Messianic, porcelanic, aldermanic.

5. hydrocyanic, transoceanic, Aristophanic.

AN'ing– 2. banning, fanning, canning, scanning, flanning, clanning, planning, manning, nanning, panning, spanning, tanning.

3. japanning, trepanning, replanning, remanning, unmanning, outspanning.

AN'ish– 2. banish, fannish, clannish, planish, mannish, Spanish, vanish.

3. evanish, revanish.

AN'ist– 2. tanist.

3. pianist, sopranist.

AN'it– 2. granite.

4. pomegranate; *see also* **ĂN'et.**

ANJ'ent– 2. plangent, frangent, tangent.

3. refrangent, bitangent, cotangent.

ANJ'ez– 2. banges, ganges, flanges.

3. *phalanges, oranges.*

ANK'a– 2. tanka.

3. Bianca, barranca.

4. Casablanca.

ANK'ee– 2. ankee, banky, hanky, hankie, lanky, clanky, planky, cranky, pranky, tranky, tanky, swanky, Yankee.

4. hanky-panky, hankey-pankey.

ANK'er– 2. anchor, banker, danker, hanker, canker, chancre, lanker, blanker, flanker, clanker, planker, spanker, ranker, rancor, franker, cranker, pranker, shanker, tanker, thanker, yanker.

3. unanchor, up-anchor, sheet anchor, embanker, encanker, outflanker, outranker.

ANK'erd– 2. anchored, cankered, brancard, tankard.

3. unanchored, uncankered.

ANK'est– 2. dankest, lankest, blankest, rankest, frankest.

ANK'et– 2. banket, blanket.

ANK'ful– 2. prankful, tankful, thankful.

3. unthankful.

ANK'ing– 2. banking, blanking, flanking, clanking, planking, panking [dial.], spanking, ranking, franking, cranking, tanking, thanking, swanking, yanking.

3. embanking, outflanking, unclanking, outranking.

ANK'ish– 2. dankish, lankish, blankish, sankish, frankish, prankish.

ANK'l– 2. ankle, hankle, rankle, crankle, tankle.

ANK'lee– 2. dankly, lankly, blankly, rankly, frankly.

ANK'less– 2. bankless, hankless, blankless, flankless, clankless, plankless, spankless, rankless, frankless, francless, crankless, prankless, shankless, tankless, thankless.

ANK'ment– 2. bankment.

3. embankment.

ANK'ness– 2. dankness, lankness, blankness, rankness, frankness.

ANK'or– 2. anchor, rancor; *see also* **ĂNK'er.**

AN'lee– 2. manly, tanly, Stanley.

3. unmanly, *statesmanly.*

4. gentlemanly, spick-and-spanly.

AN'less– 2. banless, fanless, canless, clanless, planless, manless, panless, spanless, branless, tanless.

3. pecanless, divanless.

AN'o– 2. piano, soprano.

5. melopiano, mezzo-soprano.

AN'ok– 2. bannock, Bannock, jannock.

AN'on– 2. fanon, canon, cannon, Shannon, tannin.

3. Rhiannon, colcannon.

ANS'a– 2. hansa, Hansa.

ANS'ee– 2. Ancy, antsy [slang], chancy, dancy, fancy, Nancy, prancy, Sancy.

3. unchancy, *verdancy, mordancy,* unfancy, *infancy, vacancy, peccancy, brilliancy, tenancy, stagnancy, pregnancy, vagrancy, errancy, blatancy, constancy, piquancy, truancy, buoyancy.*

4. mendicancy, *redundancy, accordancy, discordancy,* recreancy, termagancy, elegancy, arrogancy, sycophancy, sibilancy, petulancy, chalcomancy, sycomancy, pedomancy, podomancy, geomancy, theomancy, psychomancy, lithomancy, halomancy, belomancy, xylomancy, onomancy, capnomancy, oomancy, ceromancy, necromancy, hydromancy, aeromancy, chiromancy, aldermancy, gyromancy, pyromancy, cartomancy, lithomancy, *lieutenancy, discrepancy,* occupancy, *expectancy,* habitancy, oscitancy, *accountancy, inconstancy.*

5. ornithomancy, bibliomancy, theriomancy, cephalomancy, selenomancy, icthyomancy, aleuromancy, sideromancy, hieromancy, oneiromancy, diathermancy, significancy, extravagancy, predominancy, preponderancy, recalcitrancy, inhabitancy, exorbitancy, precipitancy, irrelevancy.

6. dactyliomancy, logarithmomancy, insignificancy.

ANS'el– 2. chancel, Handsel, handsel, cancel.

ANS'er– 2. Anser, answer, chancer, dancer, cancer, lancer, glancer, prancer.

3. fan dancer, tap dancer, merganser, enhancer, romancer, entrancer, advancer.

4. hula dancer, ballet dancer, geomancer, chiromancer, necromancer.

ANS'ez– *see* **ĂNS,** plus " s " or " 's ".

ANSH'al– 3. ganancial, financial, substantial.

4. transubstantial, insubstantial, unsubstantial, circumstantial.

ANSH'un– 2. scansion, mansion, panchion, stanchion.

3. expansion.

ANS'ing– 2. chancing, dancing, Lansing, glancing, pracing, trancing.

3. enhancing, affiancing, romancing, financing, entrancing, advancing.

4. necromancing, unentrancing.

ANS'iv– 3. enhancive, expansive, advancive.

4. inexpansive.
ANS'ment– 3. enhancement, entrancement, advancement.
4. nonadvancement.
ANS'um– 2. hansom, handsome, ransom, transom.
3. unhandsome.
ANT'a– 2. anta, danta, planta, manta, Santa,
3. Vedanta, infanta, Atlanta.
4. Atalanta.
ANT'al– 2. antal.
3. gigantal, atlantal, quadrantal, octantal.
4. consonantal; *see also* ĂNT'l.
ANT'ed– 2. banted, ganted [dial.], hanted, chanted, canted, scanted, planted, slanted, panted, ranted, granted.
3. enchanted, decanted, recanted, descanted, implanted, supplanted.
ANT'ee– 2. ante, anti, auntie, aunty, banty, chanty, Dante, scanty, slanty, panty, ranty, Santy, shanty, tanti.
3. andante, bacchante, Chianti, durante [L.].
4. Rosinante, Hypapante, dilettante.
5. pococurante, non obstante [L.].
ANT'eez– 2. Dantes, mantes.
3. atlantes.
4. Corybantes.
ANT'en– 2. canton, plaintain, santon.
ANT'er– 2. banter, hanter, chanter, canter, cantor, scanter, planter, slanter, panter, ranter, granter, grantor.
3. enchanter, decanter, recanter, descanter, supplanter, transplanter, *instanter*, levanter.
ANTH'er– 2. anther, panther.
ANTH'us– 2. canthus.
3. Dianthus, acanthous, ananthous, synanthous, monanthous, epanthous, chrysanthous.
4. polyanthus, amianthus.
ANT'ij– 2. chantage, plantage, vantage.
3. advantage.
4. disadvantage.
ANT'ik– 2. antic, antick, mantic, frantic.
3. pedantic, Vedantic, gigantic, Atlantic, semantic, romantic.
4. corybantic, elephantic, sycophantic, cisatlantic, transatlantic, geomantic, theomantic, chiromantic, pyromantic, necromantic, consonantic.
ANT'ing– 2. banting, ganting [dial.], hanting, chanting, canting, scanting, planting, slanting, panting, ranting, granting.
3. enchanting, decanting, recanting, descanting, implanting, supplanting.
ANT'ist– 2. Dantist, Kantist.
3. Vedantist.
4. Esperantist, noncurantist, ignorantist, dilettantist.
ANT'l– 2. cantle, mantle, mantel.
3. dismantle, immantle; *see also* ĂNT'al.
ANT'lee– 2. scantly, slantly.
3. *gallantly*, aslantly.
ANT'ler– 2. antler, mantler, pantler.
3. dismantler.
ANT'let– 2. gantlet, cantlet, plantlet, mantelet.

ANT'ling– 2. bantling, scantling, plantling, mantling.
3. dismantling.
ANT'ment– 2. chantment.
3. enchantment.
4. disenchantment.
ANT'o– 2. canto, manteau, panto.
3. portmanteau, Lepanto, pro tanto [L.].
4. Esperanto.
ANT'ree– 2. chantry, gantry, pantry.
ANT'rum– 2. antrum, tantrum.
3. hypantrum.
ANT'um– 2. Antum, bantam, phantom.
4. adiantum.
AN'yel– 2. Daniel, Haniel, spaniel.
3. Nathaniel, field spaniel, toy spaniel.
4. springer spaniel, water spaniel.
AN'yun– 2. banian, banyan, fanion, canyon.
3. companion.
ANZ'a– 2. stanza.
3. bonanza.
5. extravaganza.
ANZ'ee– 2. pansy, tansy.
3. chimpanzee.
AP'a– 2. Cappagh, Kappa, kappa, lappa.
AP'ee– 2. chappie, chappy, gappy, gapy, happy, flappy, mappy, nappy, snappy, pappy, crappie, crappy [slang], scrappy, trappy, sappy.
3. unhappy, serape.
AP'en– 2. happen, mappen [dial.].
AP'er– 2. chapper, dapper, gaper, capper, flapper, clapper, slapper, mapper, napper, knapper, rapper, wrapper, scrapper, trapper, sapper, tapper, yapper.
3. *didapper, kidnapper*, entrapper, unwrapper, *wiretapper*, backslapper.
4. handicapper, overlapper, snippersnapper, whippersnapper.
AP'et– 2. lappet, scrappet, tappet.
AP'id– 2. rapid, sapid, vapid.
AP'ij– 2. lappage, scrappage, wrappage.
AP'ing– 2. chapping, dapping, gapping, gaping, capping, lapping, clapping, flapping, slapping, mapping, napping, knapping, snapping, rapping, wrapping, scrapping, trapping, strapping, sapping, tapping, yapping.
3. entrapping, enwrapping, unwrapping.
4. handicapping, overlapping.
AP'is– 2. lapis, tapis.
AP'ish– 2. gappish, knappish, snappish, yappish.
AP'ist– 2. mappist, Trappist.
AP'l– 2. apple, chapel, dapple, capple, scapple, grapple, scrapple.
3. *Whitechapel, pineapple*, love apple.
4. antechapel.
AP'less– 2. hapless, gapless, capless, lapless, clapless, flapless, slapless, mapless, napless, snapless, papless, rapless, wrapless, crapless, scrapless, trapless, strapless, sapless, yapless.
4. handicapless.

AP'let– 2. chaplet, taplet.
AP'ling– 2. dappling, lapling, grappling, sapling.
AP'nel– 2. grapnel, shrapnel.
APSH'un– 2. caption.
3. recaption, elapsion, collapsion, contraption.
4. usucaption, manucaption.
APS'ing– 2. lapsing.
3. relapsing, collapsing.
APT'er– 2. apter, chapter, captor, rapter, raptor.
3. adapter, recaptor.
4. manucaptor.
APT'est– 2. aptest, raptest.
3. inaptest, unaptest.
APT'ist– 2. Baptist.
4. Anabaptist.
APT'iv– 2. captive.
3. adaptive.
4. unadaptive.
APT'ure– 2. capture, rapture.
3. recapture, enrapture.
4. manucapture.
AR'a– 2. Eire, Clara.
3. Sahara, tiara.
AR'ab– 2. Arab, scarab.
AR'ak– 2. arrack, barrack, carrack, carack, carac.
AR'ans– 2. bearance, Clarence.
3. forbearance, apparence, transparence.
AR'ant– 2. arrant, parent.
3. forbearant, declarant, apparent, stepparent, transparent.
4. unapparent, nontransparent.
AR'as– 2. arras, barras, harass, naras, terrace.
3. debarras, embarras, embarrass.
4. disembarrass.
AR'ee– 2. ary [dial.], Barrie, Barry, bury, harry, Harry, carry, Carrie, Larry, marry, nary [dial.], tarry.
3. Du Barry, shooldarry, Glengarry, miscarry, remarry.
4. hari-kari, intermarry, charivari; *see also* **ĀR'ee, ĂR'ee, ÉR'ee.**
AR'eed– 2. harried, carried, married, parried, tarried.
3. miscarried, unmarried.
4. intermarried.
AR'el– 2. barrel, carrel, carrell, carol, parrel, parral.
3. *pork-barrel*, apparel.
4. disapparel.
AR'eld– 2. barreled, parraled, parreled, caroled.
3. appareled.
4. disappareled.
AR'en– 2. barren, Karen; *see also* **ĂR'on.**
AR'ent– 2. parent.
3. apparent, stepparent, transparent.
4. unapparent; *see also* **ĂR'ant.**
AR'er– 2. barer, bearer, darer, farer, snarer, parer, sparer, sharer, tearer, starer, wearer, swearer, squarer.

3. *wayfarer, seafarer,* forswearer.
AR'est– 2. barest, rarest, sparest, squarest.
AR'et– 2. garret, carat, caret, claret; *see also* **ĂR'ot.**
AR'ij– 2. carriage, marriage.
3. miscarriage, disparage.
4. intermarriage.
AR'ik– 2. baric.
3. barbaric, Pindaric, agaric, Bulgaric, saccharic, polaric, tartaric.
4. centrobaric, isobaric, Balearic.
AR'ing– 2. baring, daring, faring, haring, caring, scaring, blaring, glaring, flaring, paring, pairing, sparing, sharing, tearing, staring, wearing, waring, swearing, squaring.
3. *tale bearing, seafaring,* declaring, repairing, impairing, despairing, outstaring, forswearing, outwearing.
4. overbearing, undeclaring; *see also* **ĀR'ing, ĔR'ing.**
AR'is– 2. arris, baris, Harris, Clarice, Paris.
3. Polaris.
AR'ish– 2. barish, garish, marish, parish, rarish, quarish, squarish.
3. *nightmarish; see also* **ĀR'ish.**
AR'lee– 2. barely, rarely, quarely, squarely, yarely.
3. awarely; *see also* **ĀR'lee.**
AR'less– 2. careless, glareless, snareless, spareless, shareless, tareless; *see also* **ĀR'less.**
AR'ness– 2. bareness, spareness, rareness, thereness, quareness, squareness, whereness, yareness.
3. *threadbareness,* awareness.
4. unawareness; *see also* **ĀR'ness.**
AR'o– 2. arrow, barrow, farrow, faro, harrow, marrow, narrow, sparrow, yarrow.
3. *wheelbarrow, restharrow; see also* **ĀR'o.**
AR'on– 2. Aaron, baron, barren, Charon, Karen, Sharon.
AR'ot– 2. garrot, carrot, parrot; *see also* **ĂR'et.**
AR'um– 2. arum, carom, harem, larum, 3. alarum.
4. harum-scarum.
AS'a– 2. massa.
3. Hadassah, Manasseh, madrasah, oquassa.
AS'ee– 2. dassie, gassy, Cassie, lassie, glassy, classy, massy, brassie, brassy, grassy, sassy, chassis, tassie [Scot.].
3. morassy.
4. Malagásy, Tallahassee.
AS'en– 2. fasten, casson.
3. assassin.
AS'er– 2. gasser, hassar, placer, masser, passer.
3. Macassar, amasser, surpasser, harasser.
5. antimacassar.
AS'et– 2. asset, basset, facet, fascet, placet, brasset, tacet, tasset, tacit.
AS'ez– 2. asses, gases, lasses, glasses, classes, masses, passes, brasses, grasses, sasses.
3. *eyeglasses, hourglasses,* declasses, reclasses, outclasses, molasses, amasses, surpasses, harrasses, cuirasses, morasses.

4. looking glasse, underclasses, superclasses, underpasses, overpasses.

ASH′ee– **2.** ashy, bashy, dashy, hashy, flashy, clashy, plashy, splashy, slashy, mashie, trashy.

ASH′en– *see* **ĂSH′un.**

ASH′er– **2.** Asher, basher, dasher, gasher, hasher, casher, lasher, clasher, flasher, splasher, slasher, masher, smasher, gnasher, pasher, rasher, brasher, crasher, thrasher, tacher, tasher, stasher. **3.** abasher, rehasher. **4.** haberdasher.

ASH′ez– **2.** ashes, bashes, dashes, gashes, hashes, cashes, caches, lashes, flashes, clashes plashes, splashes, slashes, mashes, smashes, nashes, gnashes, pashes, rashes, crashes, thrashes, sashes. **3.** abashes, rehashes, *eyelashes, backlashes, mishmashes,* mustaches. **4.** balderdashes, spatterdashes.

ASH′ing– **2.** bashing, dashing, hashing, cashing, caching, lashing, flashing, clashing, plashing, splashing, slashing, mashing, gnashing, crashing, sashing. **3.** *backlashing, mishmashing.* **4.** balderdashing, spatterdashing.

ASH′less– **2.** dashless, hashless, cashless, cacheless, lashless, flashless, clashless, plashless, splashless, slashless, mashless, rashless, crashless, sashless, tacheless.

ASH′un– **2.** ashen, fashion, passion, ration. **3.** refashion, prefashion, disfashion, Circassian, Parnassian, impassion, compassion, dispassion.

ASH′und– **2.** fashioned, passioned, rationed. **3.** old-fashioned, refashioned, prefashioned, unfashioned, impassioned, unrationed. **4.** unimpassioned.

AS′id– **2.** acid, placid. **3.** subacid, antacid.

AS′ij– **2.** passage, brassage.

AS′ik– **2.** classic. **3.** Liassic, Triassic, sebacic, thalassic, post-classic, boracic, thoracic, Jurassic, potassic. **4.** pseudoclassic, neoclassic.

AS′il– **2.** facile, gracile; *see also* **ĂS′l. AS′in–** **3.** assassin, *see also* **ĂS′en.**

AS′ing– **2.** gassing, classing, massing, passing, sassing. **3.** reclassing, outclassing, amassing, repassing, surpassing, harassing. **4.** underclassing, underpassing, overpassing.

AS′is– **2.** assis, fascis, chassis, Cassis.

AS′it– **2.** tacit; *see also* **ĂS′et.**

AS′iv– **2.** massive, passive. **3.** impassive.

ASK′a– **3.** Alaska, marasca, Nebraska. **4.** Athabasca, baked Alaska.

ASK′al– **2.** pashal, mascle, rascal, tascal.

ASK′er– **2.** asker, basker, lascar, flasker, masker, masquer, tasker. **3.** unmasker. **4.** Madagascar, antimasker, antimasquer.

ASK′et– **2.** basket, gasket, casket, casquet, lasket, flasket, taskit. **3.** breadbasket.

ASK′ing– **2.** asking, basking, casking, flasking, masking, tasking. **3.** bemasking, remasking, unmasking.

ASK′o– **2.** casco, tasco. **3.** Tabasco, verbasco, fiasco, Belasco.

AS′l– castle, tassel, wrastle, vassal. **3.** *forecastle,* Newcastle, envassal; *see also* **ĂS′il.**

AS′man– **2.** gasman, glassman, classman, passman, grassman, Tassman. **4.** underclassman, upperclassman.

AS′o– **2.** basso, lasso, Tasso. **3.** Sargasso.

AS′ok– **2.** hassock, cassock.

ASP′er– **2.** asper, gasper, jasper, Jasper, Casper, clasper, rasper, grasper.

ASP′ing– **2.** gasping, clasping, rasping, grasping. **3.** enclasping, unclasping, ungrasping.

AST′a– **2.** Shasta. **3.** shikasta, canasta, catasta.

AST′ed– **2.** fasted, lasted, blasted, masted, **3.** bombasted, broad-lasted, outlasted, three-masted, contrasted. **4.** flabbergasted, counterblasted.

AST′ee– **2.** blasty, masty, nasty, vasty. **3.** *dynasty.* **4.** anaplasty, cineplasty, dermoplasty, autoplasty, epinasty, hyponasty, pederasty.

AST′er– **2.** aster, Astor, faster, gaster, caster, castor, blaster, plaster, master, pastor, vaster. **3.** cadaster, piaster, *broadcaster, forecaster,* pilaster, Stylaster, beplaster, unplaster, court plaster, *paymaster, cubmaster, bandmaster, taskmaster, schoolmaster, choirmaster, bushmaster, postmaster,* pinaster, disaster. **4.** Zoroaster, alabaster, oleaster, flabbergaster, criticaster, sticking plaster, burgomaster, quartermaster, overmaster, concertmaster, poetaster.

AST′erd– **2.** bastard, dastard, plastered, mastered. **3.** pilastered, beplastered, unplastered, court-plastered, unmastered. **4.** overmastered.

AST′est– **2.** fastest, vastest.

AST′ik– **2.** clastic, plastic, mastic, spastic, rastic, drastic. **3.** bombastic, dichastic, sarcastic, elastic, gelastic, scholastic, gum mastic, dynastic, gymnastic, monastic, tetrastich, fantastic. **4.** orgiastic, scholiastic, inelastic, anaclastic, cataclastic, bioplastic, ceroplastic, protoplastic, Hudibrastic, pederastic, paraphrastic. **5.** ecclesiastic, iconoclastic, enthusiastic. **6.** unenthusiastic.

AST′ing– **2.** fasting, casting, lasting, blasting. **3.** bombasting, *broadcasting,* recasting, forecasting, outlasting, contrasting. **4.** flabbergasting, everlasting.

AST′lee– **2.** ghaslty, lastly, vastly.

3. steadfastly.

AST′ness– 2. fastness, vastness.

3. steadfastness.

AST′ral– 2. astral, castral.

3. subastral, cadastral.

AST′rik– 2. gastric.

3. digastric.

4. perigastric, hypogastric.

AST′rum– 2. castrum, plastrum.

4. alabastrum, periastrum.

AS′us– 2. bassus, passus.

3. Parnassus.

AT′a– 2. atta, batta, data, strata.

3. regatta, pro rata.

4. matamata, yerbamata, paramatta.

AT′ed– 2. batted, chatted, fatted, hatted, catted, scatted, blatted, flatted, platted, plaited, splatted, slatted, matted, patted, spatted, ratted, dratted, pratted, spratted, tatted, vatted.

3. unfatted, high-hatted, top-hatted, replaited, unplaited, rematted, unmatted, cravatted.

4. caryatid.

AT′ee– 2. batty, chatty, fatty, Hattie, catty, matty, Mattie, natty, gnatty, patty, ratty, yati.

3. chapatty.

4. Cincinnati.

AT′en– 2. Aten, batten, fatten, flatten, platan, platen, patten, paten, ratten, gratten.

3. Manhattan; *see also* **ĂT′in.**

AT′er– 2. attar, batter, chatter, fatter, hatter, quatre, catter, scatter, latter, blatter, flatter, clatter, platter, splatter, matter, smatter, patter, spatter, ratter, pratter, spratter, satyr, shatter, tatter, vatter.

3. Mad Hatter, bespatter.

AT′ern– 2. slattern, pattern, Saturn.

ATH′er– 2. gather, lather, blather, slather, rather.

3. upgather, foregather, forgather.

ATH′erd– 2. gathered, lathered, blathered, slathered.

3. upgathered, foregathered, forgathered, unlathered.

ATH′ik– 2. bathic, spathic.

3. agnathic, apathic, empathic.

4. philomathic, telepathic, antipathic, psychopathic, allopathic, cosmopathic, hydropathic, neuropathic.

5. homeopathic, osteopathic, idiopathic.

AT′ik– 2. attic, Attic, platic, static, vatic.

3. Sabbatic, ecbatic, creatic, phreatic, sulphatic, emphatic, lymphatic, phosphatic, sciatic, viatic, villatic, dramatic, hematic, schematic, rheumatic, thematic, sematic, pragmatic, judgmatic, phlegmatic, smegmatic, stigmatic, dogmatic, zeugmatic, asthmatic, climatic, dalmatic, pelmatic, grammatic, domatic, commatic, gromatic, chromatic, somatic, stomatic, termatic, plasmatic, osmatic, traumatic, unstatic, pneumatic, fanatic, enatic, agnatic, un-Attic, hepatic,

pancratic, Socratic, quadratic, geratic, piratic, erratic, astatic, ecstatic, aquatic, lavatic.

4. anabatic, catabatic, metabatic, acrobatic, enneatic, cuneatic, pancreatic, ischiatic, opiatic, Adriatic, mydriatic, psoriatic, muriatic, Asiatic, aviatic, fluviatic, unthematic, emblematic, problematic, kinematic, systematic, astigmatic, dilemmatic, zygomatic, diplomatic, monomatic, aromatic, achromatic, symptomatic, automatic, miasmatic, aseismatic, numismatic, porismatic, diprismatic, macrosmatic, microsmatic, onymatic, morganatic, aplanatic, Pherecratic, theocratic, ochlocratic, democratic, timocratic, gynocratic, androcratic, autocratic, plutocratic, bureaucratic, polycratic, hieratic, operatic, diastatic, anastatic, catastatic, metastatic, geostatic, hemostatic, thermostatic, apostatic, hydrostatic, aerostatic, gyrostatic, photostatic, caryatic.

5. melodramatic, anathematic, theorematic, episematic, anallagmatic, synallagmatic, diaphragmatic, apothegmatic, paradigmatic, diagrammatic, anagrammatic, chronogrammatic, cryptogrammatic, polygrammatic, idiomatic, axiomatic, undiplomatic, iconomatic, monochromatic, isochromatic, polychromatic, cataclysmatic, empyreumatic, physiocratic, arithmocratic, hierocratic, pantisocratic, aristocratic, idiostatic, heliostatic.

6. paleoclimatic, idiosyncratic.

7. parallelogrammatic.

AT′iks– 2. attics, statics.

3. dramatics, pneumatics, quadratics.

4. aerobatics, acrobatics, kinematics, mathematics, systematics, biostatics.

AT′in– 2. Latin, matin, Patine, gratin [F.], satin.

3. au gratin [F.]; *see also* **ĂT′en.**

AT′ing– 2. batting, chatting, fatting, hatting, catting, scatting, blatting, flatting, plaiting, platting, splatting, slatting, matting, patting, spatting, ratting, dratting, pratting, spratting, tatting, vatting.

3. high-hatting, replaiting, unplaiting, rematting, unmatting, cravatting.

4. cotton batting.

AT′is– 2. lattice, brattice, gratis.

AT′ish– 2. battish, fattish, cattish, scattish, flattish, rattish, brattish.

AT′l– 2. battle, battel, chattel, cattle, rattle, brattle, prattle, tattle.

3. Seattle, embattle, death rattle.

AT′lee– 2. Attlee, fatly, flatly, patly, rattly.

AT′ler– 2. battler, rattler, prattler, tattler, Statler.

AT′less– 2. atlas, Atlas, batless, chatless, fatless, hatless, catless, flatless, plaitless, splatless, slatless, matless, gnatless, patless, ratless, bratless, pratless, spratless, vatless.

3. cravatless.

AT′ling– 2. battling, batling, fatling, Gatling, catling, rattling, prattling, tattling.

AT′ness– 2. fatness, flatness, patness.

AT′o– **2.** *chateau, gateau, plateau.*
  3. mulatto, tomato.
AT′rik– **2.** Patrick.
  3. theatric, iatric.
  4. pediatric, psychiatric, hippiatric, physiatric.
AT′riks– **3.** theatrics.
  4. pediatrics ,cyniatrics, phoniatrics, physiatrics.
AT′um– **2.** atom, datum, stratum.
AV′a– **2.** Java, lava.
AV′ee– **2.** slavey, navvy, savvy.
AV′el– **2.** gavel, cavil, ravel, gravel, travel, tavell.
  3. unravel.
AV′eld– **2.** gaveled, gavelled, caviled, cavilled, raveled, ravelled, graveled, gravelled, traveled, travelled.
  3. unraveled, unravelled.
AV′er– **2.** haver, claver.
  3. cadaver, palaver.
AV′ern– **2.** cavern, tavern.
AV′id– **2.** avid, pavid, gravid.
  3. impavid.
AV′ij– **2.** scavage, ravage, savage.
AV′ik– **2.** Slavic.
  3. atavic, octavic.
  4. Yugoslavic.

AV′ing– **2.** having, halving, calving, salving.
AV′ish– **2.** lavish, ravish.
  3. enravish.
AZ′a– **2.** Gaza, plaza.
  3. piazza.
AZ′ard– **2.** hazard, mazzard.
  3. haphazard.
AZ′l– **2.** Basil, basil, dazzle, razzle, frazzle.
  3. bedazzle.
  4. razzle-dazzle.
AZ′ling– **2.** dazzling, jazzling, frazzling.
  3. bedazzling.
  4. razzle-dazzling.
AZ′m– **1.** phasm, chasm, plasm, spasm.
  2. *sarcasm, orgasm, miasm, empasm, phantasm.*
  3. idiasm, schediasm, chiliasm, cataclasm, metaplasm, pseudoplasm, neoplasm, protoplasm, pleonasm.
  4. enthusiasm, demoniasm, iconoclasm.
AZ′ma– **2.** asthma, phasma, plasma.
  3. chiasma, miasma, empasma, phantasma.
  4. bioplasma, protoplasma.
AZ′mal– **2.** chasmal.
  3. miasmal, phantasmal.
  4. protoplasmal.
AZ′mik– **2.** chasmic, plasmic, spasmic.
  3. miasmic, marasmic, phantasmic.
  4. bioplasmic, protoplasmic.

Ă (cab)

Triple Rhymes

Primary or Secondary Accent Falls on Second from Last Syllable; Imperfect Rhymes Are in Italics.

AB′a–bl– **3.** nabbable, grabbable, tabbabble.
AB′a–sis– **4.** anabasis, parabasis, catabasis, metabasis.
AB′id–ness– **3.** rabidness, tabidness.
AB′i–er– **3.** gabbier, scabbier, blabbier, flabbier, crabbier, shabbier.
AB′i–est– **3.** gabbiest, scabbiest, blabbiest, flabbiest, crabbiest, shabbiest.
AB′i–fi– **3.** labefy, tabefy.
4. syllabify.
5. dissyllabify.
AB′i–kal– **3.** syllabical, Arabical.
6. polysyllabical, monosyllabical, multisyllabical.
AB′i–lee– **3.** gabbily, blabbily, scabbily, flabbily, crabbily, shabbily.
AB′i–ness– **3.** gabbiness, scabbiness, blabbiness, flabbiness, slabbiness, crabbiness, shabbiness.
AB′i–net– **3.** cabinet, tabinet.
AB′it–ee– **3.** Babbitty, rabbity.
AB′it–ing– **3.** Babbitting, rabbiting.
4. inhabiting, cohabiting.
AB′la–tiv– **3.** ablative, babblative.
AB′l–ment– **3.** babblement, dabblement, gabblement, rabblement, brabblement, scrabblement.
AB′o–la– **4.** parabola, Metabola.
AB′o–rate– **4.** elaborate, collaborate.
AB′u–la– **3.** fabula, tabula.
4. cunabula.
5. incunabula.
AB′u–lar– **3.** fabular, pabular, tabular.
4. confabular, vocabular, conabular.
5. acetabular, tintinnabular.
AB′u–late– **3.** fabulate, tabulate.
4. confabulate.
5. tintinnabulate.
AB′u–list– **3.** fabulist.
4. vocabulist.
5. incunabulist, tintinnabulist.
AB′u–lum– **3.** pabulum.
5. incunabulum, acetabulum, tintinnabulum.

AB′u–lus– **3.** fabulous, pabulous, sabulous.
5. tintinnabulous.
ACH′a–bl– **3.** batchable, hatchable, catchable, latchable, matchable, snatchable, patchable, scratchable, thatchable.
4. unhatchable, uncatchable, unlatchable, rematchable, immatchable, unmatchable, repatchable, unpatchable, dispatchable, unscratchable, attachable, detachable.
ACH′er–ee– **3.** hatchery, patchery.
ACH′i–ness– **3.** catchiness, snatchiness, patchiness, scratchiness.
AD′a–bl– **3.** addable, daddable.
4. unaddable.
AD′i–kal– **3.** radical.
4. sporadical.
AD′ish–ness– **3.** faddishness, caddishness.
AD′i–tiv– **3.** additive, traditive.
4. readditive.
AD′o–ing– **3.** shadowing.
4. foreshadowing.
5. overshadowing.
AF′a–bl– **3.** affable.
4. inaffable, unaffable.
AF′i–a– **3.** maffia, mafia, raffia, tafia.
4. agraphia, asaphia.
AF′i–kal– **3.** graphical.
4. seraphical.
5. diagraphical, paragraphical, calligraphical, lexigraphical, geographical, biographical, orthographical, cosmographical, ethnographical, telegraphical, pornographical, glossographical, topographical, typographical, photographical, cartographical, phytographical, epitaphical.
6. bibliographical, physiographical, anthropographical, lexicographical.
7. autobiographical, paleontographical.
AF′l–ment– **3.** bafflement, snafflement, rafflement, scrafflement.
AFT′i–lee– **3.** draftily, craftily.
AFT′less–lee– **3.** draftlessly, graftlessly, craftlessly, shaftlessly.

AG′a–bl– **3.** faggable, gaggable, flaggable, naggable, snaggable, draggable, saggable, taggable, waggable.
AG′ed–lee– **3.** jaggedly, raggedly, scraggedly.
AG′ed–ness– **3.** jaggedness, raggedness, craggedness, scraggedness.
AG′er–ee– **3.** faggery, jaggery, raggery, staggery, waggery.
4. zigzaggery.
AG′er–er– **3.** staggerer, swaggerer.
AG′er–ing– **3.** staggering, swaggering.
AG′i–lee– **3.** baggily, raggily, craggily, scraggily, shaggily.
AG′i–ness– **3.** bagginess, flagginess, knagginess, bragginess, cragginess, scragginess, shagginess.
AG′ish–lee– **3.** haggishly, braggishly, waggishly.
AG′on–ist– **3.** agonist.
4. antagonist, protagonist.
5. deuteragonist.
AG′on–ize– **3.** agonize.
4. antagonize.
AG′on–izm– **4.** antagonism, protagonism.
AG′ot–ee– **3.** fagoty, faggoty, maggoty.
AJ′er–ee– **4.** menagerie, potagerie.
AJ′ik–al– **3.** magical, tragical.
5. theomagical.
AJ′il–ness– **3.** agileness, fragileness.
AJ′in–al– **3.** paginal.
4. imaginal.
AJ′in–us– **4.** farraginous, voraginous.
5. oleaginous, mucilaginous, cartilaginous.
AJ′u–tant– **3.** adjutant.
4. coadjutant.
AK′en–ing– **3.** blackening, slackening.
AK′er–ee– **3.** hackery, knackery, Thackeray, quackery, Zachary.
4. hijackery, knickknackery, gimcrackery.
AK′er–el– **3.** cackerel, mackerel.
AK′et–ed– **3.** jacketed, placketed, packeted, racketed, bracketed.
AK′et–ing– **3.** jacketing, packeting, racketing, bracketing.
AK′i–ness– **3.** hackiness, tackiness, wackiness, whackiness.
4. gimcrackiness.
AK′ish–ness– **3.** blackishness, slackishness, knackishness, brackishness, quackishness.
AK′rit–ee– **3.** acrity.
4. alacrity.
AK′ron–ism– **4.** anachronism, metachronism.
AKS′a–bl– **3.** taxable.
4. relaxable, nontaxable, untaxable.
AKSH′un–al– **3.** actional, factional, pactional, fractional, tractional.
4. reactional, redactional.
5. interactional, rarefactional.
AKSH′us–ness– **3.** factiousness, fractiousness.
AKS′i–al– **3.** axial.
4. abaxial, biaxial, coaxial.
AKT′a–bl– **3.** actable, tractable, tactable.
4. olfactable, refractable, attractable, re-

tractable, intractable, extractable, intactable; *see also* ĂKT′i–bl.
AKT′e–al– **3.** lacteal, bracteal.
AKT′ed–ness– **4.** impactedness, contractedness, protractedness, abstractedness, distractedness.
AKT′er–ee– **3.** factory, lactary, tractory.
4. olfactory, phylactery, enactory, refractory, detractory.
5. calefactory, malefactory, benefactory, manufactory, satisfactory.
6. dissatisfactory.
AKT′i–bl– **4.** olfactible, compactible, detractible, contractible, distractible; *see also* ĂKT′a–bl.
AKT′i–kal– **3.** practical, tactical.
4. didactical, stalactical, impractical, unpractical, syntactical.
AKT′iv–ness– **3.** activeness.
4. defractiveness, attractiveness, detractiveness, contractiveness, protractiveness, abstractiveness, distractiveness.
AKT′or–ee– *see* ĂKT′er–ee.
AKT′or–ship– **3.** actorship, factorship.
4. contractorship.
AKT′u–al– **3.** actual, factual, tactual.
4. impactual, contractual, contactual.
AKT′ur–ing– **3.** fracturing.
4. refracturing.
5. manufacturing.
AK′u–ate– **3.** acuate.
4. evacuate.
AK′u–la– **3.** bacula, facula, macula, Dracula.
4. tentacula.
AK′u–lar– **4.** piacular, vernacular, oracular, spectacular, jentacular, tentacular.
5. tabernacular, supernacular.
AK′u–late– **3.** jaculate, maculate.
4. ejaculate, bimaculate, immaculate.
5. interjaculate.
AK′u–lum– **4.** piaculum, tentaculum.
AK′u–lus– **3.** baculus, sacculus.
4. abaculus, vernaculous, miraculous, oraculous.
AL′ans–ing– **3.** balancing.
4. unbalancing.
5. counterbalancing, overbalancing.
AL′ant–ed– **3.** talented.
4. begallanted.
AL′a–ree– **3.** alary, gallery, salary, vallary.
4. subalary.
5. intercalary.
AL′er–jee– **3.** allergy.
4. *metallurgy.*
AL′et–ed– **3.** balloted, valeted.
4. unvaleted.
AL′i–ans– **3.** dalliance, ralliance, valiance.
AL′i–ate– **3.** malleate, palliate, talliate.
4. retaliate.
AL′ib–er– **3.** caliber, calibre, calabur.
4. Excalibur.
AL′id–lee– **3.** pallidly, validly.
4. invalidly.
AL′id–ness– **3.** callidness, pallidness, validness.

4. impallidness, invalidness.
AL'i–er– 3. dallier, rallier, sallier, tallier.
AL'i–fi– 3. calefy, salify.
4. alkalify.
AL'i–ing– 3. dallying, rallying, sallying, tallying.
AL'ik–lee– 3. Gallicly.
4. vocaliclly, metalliclly, smart-aleckly [coll.].
AL'i–ped– 3. aliped, taliped.
AL'i–sis– 4. dialysis, analysis, paralysis, catalysis.
6. psychoanalysis.
AL'i–son– 3. alison, Alison, malison.
AL'i–tee– 4. verbality, pedality, modality, sodality, feudality, reality, egality, legality, regality, frugality, locality, vocality, rascality, formality, normality, banality, venality, signality, finality, tonality, zonality, carnality, spirality, morality, spectrality, dextrality, plurality, rurality, nasality, fatality, natality, vitality, mentality, totality, mortality, brutality, lethality, duality, rivality.
5. bipedality, ideality, lineality, unreality, illegality, prodigality, conjugality, speciality, sociality, cordiality, filiality, geniality, seriality, spatiality, partiality, bestiality, triviality, joviality, farcicality, laicality, radicality, Biblicality, comicality, technicality, finicality, clericality, whimsicality, classicality, practicality, verticality, informality, abnormality, feminality, criminality, nationality, rationality, personality, internality, externality, principality, liberality, generality, laterality, literality, severality, integrality, immorality, temporality, corporality, pastorality, naturality, gutturality, commensality, vegetality, hospitality, immortality, visuality, sensuality, actuality, punctuality, virtuality, mutuality, sexuality, coevality.
6. sesquipedality, ethereality, corporeality, proverbiality, connubiality, provinciality, primordiality, parochiality, congeniality, perenniality, imperiality, materiality, substantiality, prudentiality, essentiality, potentiality, sequentiality, impartiality, colloquiality, conviviality, inimicality, theatricality, nonsensicality, pragmaticality, impracticality, fantasticality, reciprocality, originality, irrationality, conditionality, conventionality, devotionality, exceptionality, proportionality, tripersonality, impersonality, municipality, illiberality, ephemerality, collaterality, conjecturality, universality, orientality, fundamentality, elementality, sentimentality, instrumentality, horizontality, effectuality, unpunctuality, conceptuality, asexuality.
7. immateriality, territoriality, artificiality, superficiality, confidentiality, insubstantiality, consubstantiality, unsubstantiality, circumstantiality, consequentiality, septentrionality, unconditionality, unconventionality, constitutionality, preternaturality, individuality, ineffectuality, intellectuality.
8. exterritoriality, inconsequentiality, un-

constitutionality.
9. extraterritoriality.
ALJ'i–a– 4. myalgia, gastralgia, neuralgia, dentalgia, nostalgia.
AL'o–er– 3. fallower, hallower, callower, sallower, shallower, tallower.
AL'o–est– 3. fallowest, callowest, sallowest, shallowest.
AL'o–ish– 3. callowish, sallowish, shallowish, tallowish.
AL'o–jee– 4. mammalogy, analogy, paralogy, oralogy, petralogy, tetralogy, crustalogy.
5. genealogy, mineralogy, pyroballogy.
6. genethlialogy.
AL'o–jist– 4. dialogist, Decalogist, mammalogist, analogist, penalogist.
5. genealogist, mineralogist.
AL'o–jize– 4. dialogize, analogize, penalogize, paralogize.
5. genealogize, mineralogize.
AL'o–jizm– 3. alogism.
4. dialogism, analogism, paralogism.
AL'o–ness– 3. fallowness, callowness, sallowness, shallowness.
AL'op–er– 3. galoper, galloper, scalloper.
4. escalloper.
AL'op–ing– 3. galoping, galloping, scalloping.
4. escalloping.
AL'u–ate– 3. valuate.
4. devaluate, revaluate.
5. re-evaluate.
AL'us–ez– 3. phalluses, galluses, calluses.
AL'yun–ish– 3. scallionish, stallionish.
4. medallionish, rapscallionish.
AM'a–bl– 3. Amabel, flammable.
4. inflammable.
AM'a–tist– 3. dramatist, grammatist.
5. melodramatist, anagrammatist, epigrammatist, lipogrammatist.
6. hierogrammatist.
AM'a–tiv– 3. amative.
4. exclamative.
AM'a–tize– 3. dramatize.
5. diagrammatize, anagrammatize, epigrammatize.
AMB'u–lans– 3. ambulance.
4. somnambulance.
AMB'u–lant– 3. ambulant.
4. somnambulant, noctambulant.
AMB'u–late– 3. ambulate.
4. deambulate, somnambulate, funambulate, perambulate.
5. circumambulate.
AMB'u–list– 4. somnambulist, funambulist, noctambulist.
AM'er–a– 3. camera.
4. in camera [L.], Pentamera.
AM'er–al– 3. cameral.
4. decameral, bicameral, hexameral, tetrameral, pentameral.
AM'er–er– 3. hammerer, clamorer, stammerer, yammerer.
AM'er–ing– 3. hammering, clamoring, stammering, yammering.

4. enamoring, beglamouring.
AM'er–on– 4. Decameron, hexameron, Heptameron.
AM'er–us– 3. amorous, glamorous, clamorous.
   4. unglamorous, hexamerous, heptamerous.
AM'et–er– 4. diameter, decameter, dynameter, parameter, tetrameter, octameter, pentameter, hexameter, heptameter, voltameter.
AM'ik–al– 3. amical.
   4. dynamical, balsamical.
AM'in–a– 3. lamina, stamina.
   4. foramina.
AM'in–ate– 3. laminate, staminate.
   4. foraminate, contaminate.
AM'i–ness– 3. hamminess, jamminess, clamminess.
AM'it–ee– 3. amity.
   4. calamity.
AM'on–ite– 3. Ammonite, mammonite, Shamanite.
AM'on–izm– 3. mammonism, Shamanism.
AM'or–ing– *see* ĂM'er–ing.
AM'or–us– *see* ĂM'er–us.
AMP'er–er– 3. hamperer, scamperer, pamperer, tamperer.
AMP'er–ing– 3. hampering, scampering, pampering, tampering.
AMP'i–lee– 3. crampily, vampily.
AMP'i–on– 3. champion, Campion, lampion, tampion.
AM'u–la– 3. ammula, mammula.
AM'u–lus– 3. famulus, hamulus, ramulus, ramulous.
AN'a–ble– 3. Annabel, bannable, cannable, cannibal, mannable, pannable, sanable, tannable.
   4. insanable, untannable; *see also* ĂN'i–bal.
AN'ar–ee– 3. panary, granary; *see also* ĂN'er–ee.
AND'a–ble– 3. bandable, handable, mandible, sandable, standable.
   4. demandable, commandable, unstandable.
   5. reprimandable, countermandable, understandable.
   6. misunderstandable.
AND'al–ize 3. scandalize, vandalize.
AND'ed–lee– 3. candidly.
   4. highhandedly, backhandedly.
   5. openhandedly, underhandedly.
AND'ed–ness– 3. candidness.
   4. highhandedness, backhandedness, lefthandedness.
   5. openhandedness, underhandedness.
AND'er–er– 3. slanderer, panderer.
   4. meanderer, philanderer.
AND'er–ing– 3. slandering, pandering.
   4. meandering, philandering.
AND'er–us– 3. slanderous, panderous.
AND'i–al– 3. prandial.
   4. postprandial.
   5. anteprandial.
ADN'i–an– 3. Andean, Scandian.

AND'i–er– 3. bandier, dandier, handier, randier, sandier.
   4. unhandier.
AND'i–fi– 3. dandify, candify.
AND'i–ing– 3. bandying, candying, randying.
AND'i–lee– 3. bandily, dandily, handily, randily, sandily.
   4. unhandily.
AND'i–ness– 3. bandiness, dandiness, handiness, randiness, sandiness.
   4. unhandiness.
AND'ing–lee– 4. demandingly, commandingly, outstandingly.
   5. understandingly.
AND'ing–ness– 4. demandingness, commandingness, outstandingness.
   5. understandingness.
AND'ish–ing– 3. blandishing, brandishing.
AND'ish–ment– 3. blandishment, brandishment.
AN'el–ing– 3. channelling, flannelling, panelling.
AN'er–ee– 3. cannery, panary, granary, tannery.
AN'er–et– 3. banneret, lanneret.
ANG'gling–lee– 3. anglingly, danglingly, ganglingly, janglingly, manglingly, spanglingly, stranglingly, tanglingly, wranglingly, wanglingly.
ANG'gl–som– 3. anglesome, danglesome, janglesome, wranglesome, tanglesome.
ANG'gu–lar– 3. angular, slangular.
   4. triangular, quadrangular, rectangular, octangular, pentangular.
ANG'gu–late– 3. angulate, strangulate.
   4. triangulate.
ANG'i–lee– 3. bangily, clangily, slangily, tangily, twangily.
ANG'ing–lee– 3. bangingly, hangingly, clangingly, slangingly, twangingly, whangingly.
   4. haranguingly.
AN'i–bal– 3. Hannibal, cannibal; *see also* ĂN'a–bl.
AN'i–el– 3. Daniel, Haniel, spaniel, Saniel.
   4. Nathaniel.
AN'i–est– 3. canniest, clanniest.
   4. uncanniest.
AN'i–fi– 3. sanify.
   4. humanify.
AN'i–form– 3. Janiform, raniform, graniform.
   4. campaniform.
AN'i–kal– 4. organical, mechanical, Brahmanical, tyrannical, botanical, galvanical.
   5. charlatanical, puritanical; *see also* ĂN'i–kl.
AN'i–kin– 3. Anniekin, cannikin, manikin, pannikin.
AN'i–kl– 3. manacle, panicle, sanicle; *see also* ĂN'i–kal.
AN'i–mate– 3. animate.
   4. reanimate, inanimate, exanimate.
AN'i–mus– 3. animous, animus.
   4. magnanimous, unanimous, multanimous.
   5. pusillanimous.
AN'i–ness– 3. canniness, clanniness.

AN′ish–ing– 3. banishing, planishing, vanishing.
AN′ish–ment– 3. banishment, vanishment.
4. evanishment.
AN′ist–er– 3. banister, ganister, canister.
AN′it–ee– 3. sanity, vanity.
4. inanity, urbanity, mundanity, profanity, paganity, organity, volcanity, gigmanity, immanity, humanity, insanity.
5. inurbanity, inorganity, Christianity, inhumanity, subterranity.
ANJ′en–see– 3. plangency, tangency.
ANJ′er–ee– 3. lingerie, singerie [F.].
ANJ′i–a– 3. cangia.
4. hydrangea, sporangia.
ANJ′i–bl– 3. frangible, tangible.
4. refrangible, infrangible, intangible.
ANK′er–er– 3. anchorer, hankerer.
ANK′er–ing– 3. anchoring, hankering, cankering.
4. reanchoring, encankering.
ANK′er–us– 3. cankerous.
4. cantankerbus.
ANS′i–lee– 3. chancily, fancily, prancily.
ANS′ing–lee– 3. dancingly, glancingly, prancingly, trancingly.
4. entrancingly.
ANS′it–iv– 3. transitive.
4. intransitive.
ANS′iv–ness– 4. expansiveness, advanciveness.
5. inexpansiveness, unexpansiveness.
ANS′om–er– 3. handsomer, ransomer.
ANT′a–bl– 3. plantable, grantable.
4. transplantable, ungrantable.
ANT′el–ope– 3. antelope, cantaloupe.
ANT′er–er– 3. banterer, canterer.
ANT′er–ing– 3. bantering, cantering.
ANTH′ro–pee– 4. theanthropy, lycanthropy, philanthropy, psilanthropy, misanthropy, zoanthropy.
5. aphilanthropy.
6. theophilanthropy.
ANTH′ro–pist– 4. theanthropist, philanthropist, psilanthropist, misanthropist.
6. theophilanthropist.
ANTH′ro–pizm– 4. theanthropism, philanthropism, psilanthropism.
6. theophilanthropism.
ANT′ik–lee– 3. anticly, franticly.
4. pedanticly, giganticly, romanticly.
ANT′ik–ness– 3. anticness, franticness.
4. pedanticness, giganticness, romanticness.
ANT′i–lee– 3. bantily, scantily, slantily, rantily.
ANT′i–ness– 3. bantiness, scantiness, slantiness, rantiness.
ANT′ing–lee– 3. cantingly, slantingly, pantingly, rantingly.
4. enchantingly.
ANT′u–a– 3. mantua.
4. Gargantua.
AN′u–al– 3. annual, manual, Manuel.
4. biannual, bimanual, Immanuel.

5. semiannual.
AN′u–la– 3. cannula, ranula, granula.
4. Campanula.
AN′u–lar– 3. annular, cannular, ranular, granular.
4. penannular, campanular.
AN′u–late– 3. annulate, granulate.
4. campanulate.
AN′u–let– 3. annulet, granulet.
AP′a–bl– 3. mappable, snappable, strappable, tappable.
4. unmappable.
AP′id–lee– 3. rapidly, sapidly, vapidly.
AP′id–ness– 3. rapidness, sapidness, vapidness.
AP′i–er– 3. happier, gappier, lappier, nappier, snappier, scrappier, sappier.
4. unhappier.
AP′i–est– 3. happiest, gappiest, lappiest, nappiest, snappiest, scrappiest, sappiest.
4. unhappiest.
AP′i–lee– 3. happily, gappily, snappily, scrappily, sappily.
4. unhappily.
AP′o–lis– 4. Annapolis, tetrapolis, pentapolis.
5. Minneapolis.
6. Indianapolis.
AP′tur–ing– 3. capturing, rapturing.
4. recapturing, enrapturing.
AR′a–bl– 3. arable, bearable, dareable, parable, sparable, tearable, wearable, squarable.
4. unbearable, declarable, unsparable, unwearable, unsquarable.
5. undeclarable, see also ĀR′a–bl.
AR′a–blz– 3. parables, wearables.
AR′a–gon– 3. paragon, tarragon.
AR′ant–lee– 3. arrantly.
4. apparently, transparently.
AR′as–ing– 3. harassing, terracing.
4. embarrassing.
5. disembarrassing.
AR′as–ment– 3. harassment.
4. embarrassment.
AR′at–iv– 3. narrative.
4. declarative, reparative, preparative, comparative.
AR′el–ing– 3. barreling, caroling.
4. pork-barreling, appareling.
AR′i–at– 3. lariat.
4. salariat.
5. commissariat, proletariat, secretariat.
AR′i–er– 3. barrier, charier, farrier, harrier, carrier, marrier, parrier, tarrier, warier.
AR′i–fi– 3. scarify, clarify.
4. saccharify.
AR′i–form– 3. nariform, variform.
4. scalariform.
AR′i–ing– 3. harrying, carrying, marrying, parrying, tarrying.
5. intermarrying.
AR′in–ate– 3. carinate, marinate.
AR′i–ness– 3. chariness, wariness.

4. contrariness; *see also* **ĀR′i–ness.**

AR′ing–lee– 3. daringly, blaringly, flaringly, glaringly, sparingly, tearingly, wearingly.

AR′i–o– 4. Philario, scenario, Lothario.

5. impresario.

AR′i–on– 3. carrion, clarion, Marion, Marian.

4. Maid Marian.

AR′i–ot– 3. chariot.

4. Iscariot.

AR′ish–lee– 3. bearishly, garishly.

AR′ish–ness– 3. bearishness, garishness.

AR′is–on– 3. garrison, Harrison, parison.

4. caparison, comparison.

AR′it–ee– 3. charity, clarity, parity, rarity.

4. barbarity, vagarity, vulgarity, uncharity, hilarity, molarity, polarity, imparity, disparity.

5. solidarity, similarity, capillarity, bipolarity, exemplarity, globularity, secularity, jocularity, circularity, vascularity, muscularity, regularity, angularity, singularity, granularity, popularity, insularity, gemmiparity, omniparity, fissiparity, multiparity, oviparity.

6. familiarity, peculiarity, dissimilarity, piacularity, vernacularity, orbicularity, molecularity, particularity, irregularity, triangularity, rectangularity, unpopularity, peninsularity, ovoviparity.

7. rectilinearity, curvilinearity, perpendicularity.

AR′o–ee– 3. arrowy, marrowy, sparrowy.

AR′o–er– 3. harrower, narrower.

4. *wheelbarrower.*

AR′o–ing– 3. arrowing, farrowing, harrowing, narrowing.

4. *wheelbarrowing.*

AR′o–like– 3. arrowlike, barrowlike, farrowlike, farolike, harrowlike, marrowlike, sparrowlike.

AR′ot–ing– 3. garroting, parroting.

AS′a–bl– 3. classable, massable, passable, sassable.

4. amassable, impassable, surpassable, unsassable; *see also* **ĂS′i–bl.**

AS′a–blee– 3. classably, passably.

4. unclassably, unpassably, surpassably.

5. unsurpassably; *see also* **ĂS′i–blee.**

AS′er–ate– 3. lacerate, macerate.

4. emacerate.

ASH′er–ee– 3. ashery, fasherie or fashery [dial.], hashery [slang], trashery, sashery.

5. haberdashery.

ASH′i–a– 3. fascia, cassia, quassia.

4. Circassia, parnassia.

ASH′i–an– 4. Circassian, Parnassian; *see also* **ĂSH′un.**

ASH′i–er– 3. ashier, dashier, hashier, flashier, plashier, splashier, trashier.

ASH′i–est– 3. ashiest, dashiest, hashiest, flashiest, plashiest, splashiest, trashiest.

ASH′i–ness– 3. ashiness, flashiness, splashiness, trashiness.

ASH′un–al– 3. national, passional, rational.

4. irrational.

5. supranational, international.

ASH′un–at– see ĂSH′un–it.

ASH′un–ing– 3. fashioning, rationing.

4. refashioning, disfashioning.

ASH′un–it– 3. passionate.

4. impassionate, compassionate, unpassionate, dispassionate.

AS′i–bl– 3. passible.

4. impassible, renascible, irascible; *see also* **ĂS′a–bl.**

AS′i–blee– 3. passibly.

4. impassibly, irascibly; *see also* **ĂS′a–blee.**

AS′i–fi– 3. classify, pacify.

4. reclassify.

AS′i–kl– 3. fascicle, classical.

4. nonclassical.

5. neoclassical.

AS′i–nate– 3. fascinate.

4. abacinate, deracinate, assassinate.

AS′i–ness– 3. gassiness, glassiness, classiness, massiness, brassiness, grassiness, sassiness.

AS′it–ee– 4. bibacity, edacity, mendacity, mordacity, audacity, sagacity, fugacity, dicacity, procacity, salacity, tenacity, pugnacity, minacity, capacity, rapacity, opacity, feracity, veracity, voracity, vivacity, sequacity, loquacity.

5. perspicacity, pervicacity, contumacity, pertinacity, saponacity, incapacity.

AS′iv–lee– 3. massively, passively.

4. impassively.

AS′iv–ness– 3. massiveness, passiveness.

4. impassiveness.

ASP′er–ate– 3. asperate, aspirate.

4. exasperate.

ASP′ing–lee– 3. gaspingly, raspingly, graspingly.

AST′er–ee– 3. plastery, mastery.

4. dicastery, self-mastery.

AST′er–ing– 3. plastering, mastering, pastoring.

4. beplastering.

5. overmastering, poetastering.

AST′ik–al– 4. elastical, gymnastical, monastical, fantastical.

6. ecclesiastical, enthusiastical.

AST′ik–lee– 3. plasticly, drasticly.

4. bombasticly, sarcasticly, elasticly, scholasticly, gymnasticly, monasticly, fantasticly.

AST′i–lee– 3. ghastily, nastily.

AST′i–sizm– 4. plasticism.

5. scholasticism, monasticism, fanaticism.

AST′ri–an– 4. Lancastrian.

5. Zoroastrian, alabastrian.

AST′ro–fee– 4. diastrophe, anastrophe, catastrophe.

5. epanastrophe.

AT′a–bl– 3. atabal, battable, hattable, mattable, pattable, rattable, vattable.

4. combatable, come-at-able, get-at-able; *see also* **ĂT′i–bl.**

AT′en–ing– 3. battening, fattening, flattening.

AT′er–al– 3. lateral.

4. collateral.

5. unilateral, quadrilateral, plurilateral.

AT′er–ee– 3. battery, hattery, scattery, flattery, slattery, shattery, tattery.

AT′er–er– 3. batterer, chatterer, scatterer, flatterer, clatterer, splatterer, smatterer, patterer, shatterer.

4. bespatterer.

AT′er–ing– 3. battering, chattering, scattering, flattering, clattering, splattering, smattering, pattering, spattering, shattering.

4. besplattering, bespattering, unflattering.

ATH′er–er– 3. gatherer, latherer, blatherer, slatherer.

4. *woolgatherer*, ingatherer, foregatherer.

ATH′er–ing– 3. gathering, lathering, blathering, slathering.

4. *woolgathering*, ingathering, upgathering, foregathering.

ATH′e–sis– 4. diathesis, parathesis, metathesis.

ATH′ik–al– 5. philomathical.

6. idiopathical.

AT′i–bl– 3. patible.

4. combatable, impatible, compatible.

5. incompatible, uncompatible; *see also* **ĂT′a–bl.**

AT′i–fi– 3. ratify, gratify, stratify.

4. beatify.

AT′ik–a– 3. Attica.

4. sciatica, hepatica.

AT′ik–al– 3. statical, vatical.

4. abbatical, sabbatical, emphatical, dramatical, pragmatical, dogmatical, grammatical, climatical, somatical, asthmatical, schismatical, prismatical, fanatical, erratical, piratical, Socratical, ecstatical, aquatical.

5. acrobatical, mathematical, emblematical, problematical, systematical, enigmatical, ungrammatical, diplomatical, automatical, symptomatical, numismatical, democratical, bureaucratical, autocratical, apostatical, hypostatical, hydrostatical.

6. anagrammatical, idiomatical, axiomatical, unsystematical, anagrammatical, epigrammatical, aristocratical, aerostatical.

7. anidiomatical, idiosyncratical.

AT′in–ate– 3. patinate.

4. Palatinate, gelatinate.

AT′i–ness– 3. battiness, chattiness, fattiness, cattiness, nattiness, rattiness.

AT′in–ize– 3. Latinize, platinize.

4. gelatinize.

AT′in–us– 3. Latinus, platinous.

4. gelatinous.

AT′is–ing– 3. latticing, bratticing.

AT′i–sizm– 4. pragmaticism, grammaticism, fanaticism.

5. Asiaticism.

AT′i–tude– 3. attitude, latitude, platitude, gratitude.

4. beatitude, ingratitude.

AT′l–ment– 3. battlement, prattlement, tattlement.

4. embattlement.

AT′o–mee– 3. atomy.

4. anatomy.

5. tesseratomy.

AT′o–mist– 3. atomist.

4. anatomist.

AT′rik–al– 3. matrical.

4. theatrical, iatrical.

5. psychiatrical, idolatrical.

AT′ri–side– 3. matricide, patricide, fratricide.

AT′ron–ij– 3. matronage, patronage.

AT′ron–ize– 3. matronize, patronize.

AT′ul–a– 3. scatula, spatula.

4. comatula.

AT′ul–ate– 3. spatulate, gratulate.

4. congratulate.

AT′ur–al– 3. natural.

4. unnatural.

5. supernatural, preternatural.

AT′ur–ate– 3. maturate, saturate.

5. supersaturate.

AV′aj–er– 3. scavager, ravager, savager.

AV′aj–ing– 3. scavaging, ravaging.

AV′an–eez– 3. Havanese, Javanese.

AV′el–er– 3. caviler, raveler, traveler.

4. unraveler.

AV′el–in– 3. javelin, ravelin.

AV′el–ing– 3. caviling, raveling, graveling, traveling.

4. unraveling.

AV′end–er– 3. chavender, lavender.

AV′er–ing– 3. havering, clavering.

4. palavering.

AV′er–us– 4. cadaverous, papaverous.

AV′ish–er– 3. lavisher, ravisher.

AV′ish–ing– 3. lavishing, ravishing.

4. enravishing.

AV′ish–ment– 3. lavishment, ravishment.

4. enravishment.

AV′i–tee– 3. cavity, gravity, pravity, suavity.

4. concavity, depravity.

AX′a–bl– *see* **ĂKS′a–bl.**

AZ′l–ment– 3. dazzlement, frazzlement.

4. bedazzlement.

$\bar{\text{E}}$ (bee)

Single (Masculine) Rhymes

Primary or Secondary Accent Falls on Last Syllable; Imperfect Rhymes Are in Italics.

E– 1. e, E, ee, 'ee, ea [dial.].

BE– 1. b, B, be, bee.

2. A.B., bawbee, Bebe, brebis [F.], bribee, *Seabee*, queen bee.

3. Araby, honeybee, bumblebee, humblebee, scarabee, Niobe, wallaby, Barnaby, sassaby, jacoby, cenoby.

CHE– 1. chee, Chi.

2. *chee-chee, Geechee, leechee, litchi,* vouchee.

3. debauchee.

DE– 1. d, D, dee, Dee, dit [F.].

2. D.D., M.D., dédit [F.], Didi, deedee, Midi [F.], Chaldee, killdee, grandee, on-dit [F.], spondee, vendee.

3. C.O.D., Ph.D., chickadee, malady, tragedy, remedy, comedy, Kennedy, perfidy, subsidy, tweedledee, organdy, Ormandy, Normandy, dispondee, arrondi [F.], Burgundy, theody, melody, psalmody, threnody, hymnody, monody, dipody, tripody, parody, prosody, rhapsody, custodee, custody, Lombardy, Picardy, jeopardy, bastardy.

4. fiddlededee.

FE– 1. fee, phi.

2. feoffee, Fifi, *strophe*.

3. atrophy, dystrophy.

4. telegraphy, calligraphy, geography, biography, biographee, pornography, ethnography, topography, anaglyphy, xylography, photography, cryptography, catastrophe, antistrophe, apostrophe, theosophy, philosophy.

5. hagiography, paleography, dactylography, dolichomorphy.

6. dactyliography.

GE– 1. ghee.

2. McGee, whangee, *thuggee*.

3. Portugee.

HE– 1. he.

2. hehee, tehee, bohea.

JE– 1. g, G, gee.

2. agee [dial.], *geegee* [coll.], Gigi, *squeegee*, pledgee, N.G., pongee, ogee, bargee, *burgee*.

3. mortgagee, salvagee, elegy, strategy, prodigy, effigy, obligee, perigee, exchangee, elogy, apogee, dilogy, trilogy, dyslogy, eulogy, sylloge, lethargy, energy, synergy, theurgy, telurgy, zymurgy, liturgy, refugee, syzygy.

4. analogy, geology, theology, morphology, biology, ecology, psychology, demology, chronology, ethnology, zoology, typology, astrology, neurology, misology, doxology, cytology, dactology, proctology, otology, cryptology, pathology, mythology, telenergy.

5. cardiology, teleology, geneology, embryology, sociology, physiology, laryngology, ophthalmology, criminology, demonology, anthropology, dermatology.

6. microbiology, bacteriology, epistomology, endocrinology.

KE– 1. key, cay, quay, chi, ski, skee.

2. maquis, raki, *kiki*, croquis [F.], marquee, marquis [F.], Torquay.

3. collicky, garlicky, Manichee, panicky, finicky, hillocky, hummocky, Cherokee, anarchy, monarchy, master key.

4. synecdoche.

LE– 1. lee, Lee, lea, li, Leigh, flea, flee, glee, clee, plea, slee [dial.].

2. alee, bailee, belee, peelee, pili, folie [F.].

3. Thessaly, Italy, Castaly, Rosalie, libelee, fleur-de-lis, appellee, Cybele, jubilee, simile, enrollee, panoply, Kinberly, Waverley, Beverley.

4. anomaly, Robert E. Lee, facsimile, Annabel Lee, hyperbole.

5. lapis lazuli.

6. dolicocephaly; *also adverbs composed of adjective plus suffix "-ly"* (e. g. toothsomely, longingly); *also adjectives composed of noun plus suffix "-ly"* (e. g. brotherly, sisterly).

ME– 1. me, smee, mi.

2. ami, Mimi, Maumee.

3. infamy, bigamy, balsamy, jessamy, dittamy, blasphemy, alchemy, Ptolemy, enemy,

sodomy, bonhomie, atomy, confirmee.

4. polygamy, endogamy, monogamy, academy, economy, taxonomy, autonomy, anatomy, epitome, phlebotomy, lobotomy, dichotomy, Philotome, zootomy.

5. physiognomy, anthroponomy, Deuteronomy.

NE– 1. nee, knee, snee.

2. trainee, Beni, Chinee, donee, pawnee, Pawnee, Shawnee.

3. bargainee, distrainee, designee, assignee, consignee, alienee, domine, nominee, internee, optionee, snickersnee, tiffany, Tuscany, Romany, Germany, tyranny, botany, progeny, eugeny, Eugenie, kitcheny, villainy, larcony, scrutiny, ebony, symphony, disphony, euphony, agony, felony, colony, simony, harmony, barony, Saxony, cushiony, Antony, cottony, gluttony, muttony, Anthony, oniony, crimsony.

4. Epiphany, mahogany, Gethsemane, accompany, Melpomene, misogyny, examinee, illuminee, Mnemosyne, Euphrosyne, abandonee, Persephone, cacophony, telegony, Antigone, petitionee, monotony.

5. aborigine, laryngophony, physiogony.

PE– 1. p, P, pe, pee, pea.

2. rapee, rappee, *earthpea*, *cowpea*, wampee, topee, toupee, rupee.

3. agape, escapee, cap-a-pie, therapy, calipee, recipe, canopy, epopee, entropy.

4. R. S. V. P., de mal en pis [F.], sur le tapis [F.], Calliope, microscopy, Penelope, philanthropy, misanthropy.

5. hydrotherapy.

6. physiotherapy.

7. electromicroscopy.

RE– 1. re, ree, bree [dial.], Brie, dree [dial.], free, gris [F.], Cree, scree, pre [slang], spree, tree, three.

2. farree, Marie, Paree, in re [L.], abri [F.], debris, enfree, unfree, *carefree, germ-free, heart-free, dust-free*, agree, degree, puggree, Machree, doree, choree, épris [F.], esprit [F.], patrie [F.], oak tree, hall tree, elm tree, pine tree, hat tree, shoe tree, clothes tree.

3. Barbary, quandary, boundary, vagary, beggary, sangaree, stingaree, dungaree, pugaree, sugary, diary, chickaree, salary, burglary, bain-marie [F.], summary, Rose Marie, senary, rapparee, library, contrary, notary, rotary, votary, Tartary, shivaree, Calvary, rosary, ribaldry, heraldry, husbandry, bribery, robbery, treachery, archery, witchery, thundery, broderie [F.], prudery, referee, transferee, lingerie, waggery, roguery, snuggery, drudgery, forgery, bakery, quackery, trickery, mockery, rockery, rookery, raillery, gallery, flummery, mummery, scenery, finery, fernery, drapery, peppery, slippery, trumpery, foppery, popery, tracery, chancery, sorcery, nursery, battery, flattery, watery, lottery, wintery, artery, mastery,

mystery, cautery, feathery, heathery, slavery, knavery, bravery, reverie, thievery, livery, shivery, silvery, equerry, misery, fancy-free, duty-free, imagery, savagery, mimicry, dernier cri [F.], disagree, cavalry, chivalry, rivalry, jugglery, hostelry, revelry, jewelry, devilry, bottomry, yeomanry, demonry, masonry, jamboree, theory, priory, chicory, hickory, calory, pillory, memory, armory, honoree, vapory, sensory, factory, rectory, victory, history, savory, signiory, homme d'esprit [F.], jeu d'esprit [F.], salad tree, poetry, apple tree, doubletree, whiffletree, deviltry, bigotry, harlotry, Christmas tree, forestry, ancestry, sequestree, chemistry, augury, injury, perjury, mercury, penury, potpourri, treasury, luxury, usury, century.

4. infirmary, Sault Sainte Marie, debauchery, embroidery, commandery, sculduddery, skulduggery, diablerie, artillery, tomfoolery, gendarmerie [F.], gendarmery, perfumery, chicanery, machinery, rotisserie, phylactery, adultery, effrontery, upholstery, delivery, recovery, discovery, Mother Machree, corroboree, Terpsichore, extempore, compulsory, precursory, allusory, elusory, illusory, refractory, directory, perfunctory, unsavory, psychiatry, telemetry, geometry, psychometry.

5. anniversary, parliamentary, testamentary, elementary, rudimentary, alimentary, complementary, complimentary, passementerie, extrasensory, satisfactory, contradictory, valedictory, craniometry, sociometry, trigonometry.

SE– 1. c, C, see, sea, cee, si.

2. asea, assis, voici [F.], besee, lessee, précis, ici [F.], sycee, Parsee, foresee, North Sea, South Sea, souci [F.].

3. abbacy, embassy, surfacy, legacy, fricassee, fallacy, releasee, prelacy, primacy, pharmacy, Christmasy, China Sea, lunacy, papacy, piracy, euphrasy, curacy, fantasy, ecstasy, privacy, prophecy, Tennessee, poesy, addressee, heresy, assessee, courtesy, Odyssey, Holy See, policy, promisee, Pharisee, par ici [F.], pleurisy, galaxy, Baltic Sea, normalcy, Marshalsea, colonelcy, minstrelcy, mordancy, infancy, pliancy, surgeoncy, vacancy, peccancy, romancy, nomancy, stagnancy, regnancy, pregnancy, sonancy, flippancy, flagrancy, fragrancy, blatancy, captaincy, constancy, frequency, piquancy, truancy, brilliancy, poignancy, buoyancy, lambency, cadency, pendency, ardency, regency, tangency, pungency, cogency, cliency, valency, licensee, latency, potency, fluency, fervency, frequency, saliency, leniency, idiocy, Argosy, leprosy, autopsy, unforesee, undersea, sans merci [F.], oversea, oversee, endorsee, divorcee, bankruptcy, Debussy, Sadducee, seducee, jealousy, sans souci [F.].

4. celibacy, candidacy, delegacy, delicacy, intricacy, advocacy, supremacy, intimacy, obstinacy, federacy, literacy, conspiracy, democracy, magistracy, accuracy, obduracy, intestacy, apostasy, adequacy, discourtesy, hypocrisy, ascendancy, discordancy, compliancy, sibilancy, petulancy, malignancy, consonancy, descrepancy, oscitancy, irritancy, hesitancy, expectancy, accountancy, acceptancy, inconstancy, relevancy, conservancy, recumbency, resplendency, impudency, negligency, emergency, insurgency, saliency, leniency, repellency, excellency, succulency, truculency, corpulency, flatulency, inclemency, permanency, prominency, pertinency, abstinency, renascency, indecency, complacency, efficiency, proficiency, sufficiency, competency, penitency, consistency, delinquency, idiocy.

5. immediacy, inebriacy, inefficacy, prolificacy, indelicacy, immaculacy, legitimacy, effeminacy, episcopacy, confederacy, regeneracy, illiteracy, aristocracy, inaccuracy, inadequacy, irradiancy, preponderancy, recalcitrancy, irrelevancy, independency, expediency, incipiency, equivalency, impermanency, impertinency, belligerency, insufficiency, incompetency, impenitency, omnipotency, inconsistency, constituency.

6. idiosyncrasy.

SHE— **1.** she, shee, shea, ski.

2. hachis [F.], Vichy, *banshee, banshie.*

3. garnishee, rubbishy, flourishy, debauchee.

TE— **1.** t, T, tee, tea.

2. settee, titi, draftee, high tea, grantee, goatee, coatee, giftee, mestee, mustee, trustee, bootee, suttee, Q. T.

3. legatee, hatchety, witchety, crotchety, fidgety, trinkety, trumpety, snippety, nicety, russety, velvety, laity, crudity, deity, jollity, amity, remittee, dimity, enmity, comity, *committee,* permittee, sanity, dignity, trinity, unity, charity, purity, laxity, scarcity, falsity, density, tensity, sparsity, sanctity, entity, chastity, cavity, gravity, levity, brevity, electee, inductee, spiralty, subtlety, cruelty, faculty, occulty, guaranty, guarantee, warranty, warrantee, sovereignty, absentee, presentee, patentee, certainty, seventy, appointee, maggoty, picottee, allottee, carroty, devotee, repartee, liberty, puberty, property, poverty, deportee, dynasty, contrasty, majesty, amnesty, honesty, sacristy, deputy, amputee.

4. anxiety, acerbity, cupidity, aridity, acridity, acidity, avidity, commodity, absurdity, dedicatee, morality, dextrality, fatality, syntality, totality, mortality, brutality, equality, ability, debility, agility, facility, docility, servility, credulity, utility, futility, civility, servility, credulity, calamity, deformity, conformity, amenity, benignity, affinity, infinity, divinity, eternity, community, barbarity, polarity, disparity, celebrity,

celerity, asperity, sincerity, austerity, dexterity, alacrity, authority, security, audacity, capacity, felicity, duplicity, complicity, complexity, convexity, propensity, attensity, intensity, ferocity, atrocity, adversity, diversity, annuity, fatuity, depravity, acclivity, declivity, passivity, activity, captivity, festivity, iniquity, antiquity, casualty, dishonesty.

5. spontaneity, personality, actuality, probability, affability, changeability, capability, sensibility, anonymity, Christianity, consanguinity, similarity, electricity, authenticity, elasticity, domesticity, curiosity, animosity, assiduity, ambiguity, contiguity, creativity, relativity, absorbtivity, sensitivity, collectivity, receptivity.

6. reliability, amiability, amicability, amenability, advisability, adaptability, inferiority, superiority.

THE— **1.** the, thee.

2. prithee.

3. apathy, empathy, sympathy, dyspathy, eupathy, timothy, Timothy.

4. telepathy.

VE— **1.** v, V, vee, vie [F.].

2. T. V., teevee.

3. vis-à-vis, joie de vie [F.], eau de vie [F.], anchovy, Muscovy.

WE— **1.** wee, we, oui [F.], whee, puy [F.], Twe, twee.

2. ennui, pui [F.], etui, etwee, drawee.

3. mildewy, meadowy, shadowy, sallowy, yellowy, billowy, pillowy, willowy, arrowy, furrowy, point d'appui [F.].

YE— **1.** ye.

2. payee, bouilli [F.].

3. employee.

ZE— **1.** z, Z, zee.

2. razee, fusee.

3. bourgeoisie [F.], frénésie [F.], cognizee, advisee, devisee, chimpanzee, Tappan Zee, Zuyder Zee, jalousie [F.].

4. recognizee.

EB— **1.** dieb, feeb [slang], glebe, plebe, reeb [slang], grebe.

2. ephebe, tanjib.

3. caraibe.

EBZ— *see* **ĒB,** plus " s " or " 's "; **1.** Thebes.

ECH— **1.** each, beach, beech, keach, keech, leach, leech, bleach, fleech, pleach, sleech, meech, peach, speech, reach, breach, breech, screech, preach, teach, queach [dial.].

2. appeach, impeach, outreach, beseech.

3. overreach.

ECHT—1. beached, leeched, bleached, pleached, meeched, peached, reached, breached, breeched, screeched, preached, queached [dial.].

2. unbleached, impeached, unbreached, unbreeched, unreached, outreached, beseeched.

3. unimpeached, overreached, unbeseeched.

ED— **1.** Ede, bead, Bede, deed, feed, gied

[dial.], heed, he'd, geed, keyed, lead, bleed, flead, gleed, glede [Scot.], plead, mead, meed, Mede, need, knead, kneed, snead, peed, speed, read, reed, rede, Reid, breed, brede, dreed [dial.], freed, greed, creed, screed, treed, threed, seed, cede, teed, teaed, steed, weed, Swede, tweed, yede.

2. Candide, indeed, misdeed, unfeed, *Lockheed*, unkeyed, *nosebleed*, implead, mislead, *knock-kneed*, stampede, impede, Godspeed, jereed, reread, misread, outread, inbreed, *crossbreed*, enfreed, agreed, degreed, decreed, *hayseed*, reseed, *linseed*, *flaxseed*, recede, precede, secede, accede, succeed, concede, *seaweed*, *chickweed*, *milkweed*, *pokeweed*, ennuied.

3. underfeed, overfeed, interplead, millepede, centipede, interbreed, refereed, disagreed, pedigreed, filigreed, epicede, antecede, aniseed, cottonseed, retrocede, supersede, intercede, guaranteed, tumbleweed, locoweed.

4. velocipede, unpedigreed, unguaranteed.

EF– 1. beef, chief, deef [dial.], feoff, fief, Lif, leaf, lief, neif, reef, reif, brief, grief, sheaf, thief.

2. naif, redif, enfeoff, belief, relief, *flyleaf*, *broadleaf*, hanif, shereef, tashrif, motif.

3. handkerchief, neckerchief, unbelief, disbelief, misbelief, bas-relief, interleaf, overleaf, velvetleaf, Teneriffe.

4. apéritif [F.].

EG– 1. digue [F.], league, skeeg, kleig, peag, brigue, Grieg, Teague.

2. enleague, *colleague*, banig, renege, intrigue, fatigue, squeteague.

EGD– 1. leagued.

2. enleagued, unleagued, intrigued, fatigued.

EJ' 1. liege, siege.

2. besiege.

EK– 1. eke, beak, beek, cheek, Deke, deek, deak [both slang], feke [slang], geek, geke [both slang], keek [slang], leek, leak, bleak, gleek, clique, cleek, sleek, meek, sneak, pique, peak, peek, Peke, speak, reek, freak, Greek, creek, creak, shriek, streak, wreak, seek, Sikh, chic, sheik, teak, weak, week, squeak, tweak, Zeke.

2. saic, caique, *halfbeak*, *grosbeak*, aleak, *houseleek*, oblique, silique, comique [F.], clinique [F.], technique, unique, apeak, repique, *forepeak*, forspeak, areek, perique, cacique, reseek, batik, critique, antique, boutique, bezique, physique.

3. Mozambique, Martinique, demipique, fenugreek, politique, novantique, Holy Week, yesterweek.

5. Realpolitik [G.], Geopolitik.

EKT– 1. eked, beaked, cheeked, leaked, sneaked, peaked, peeked, piqued, cliqued, reeked, shrieked, streaked, wreaked, squeaked, tweaked.

2. pink-cheeked, unpiqued, antiqued.

3. eagle-beaked, apple-cheeked, rosycheeked.

EL– 1. eel, beal, deal, dele, feal, feel, heal, heel, jeel, jheel, jhil, keel, skeel, leal, leel, Lille, meal, mil, neele, kneel, peal, peel, speel, spiel, reel, creel, seal, seel, ceil, sheel [Scot.], teal, teil, til, steal, steel, veal, ville [F.], weal, weel, squeal, wheal, wheel, twille, zeal.

2. abele, cebil, Mobile, redeal, ideal, ordeal, misdeal, refeel, forefeel, congeal, *clownheal*, vakil, coquille, Camille, kameel, schlemiel [slang], *inchmeal*, *cornmeal*, *piecemeal*, *oatmeal*, landmil, *fistmele*, anneal, anele, chenille, appeal, repeal, *kriegspiel*, *Singspiel*, *Festspiel* [G.], *bonspiel*, baril [Tag.], surreal, Avril [F.], enseal, conceal, unseal, datil, manteel, genteel, Bastille, castile, pastille, De Stijl, reveal, aiguille, *cogwheel*.

3. dishabille, immobile, unideal, Guayaquil, havermeal, camomile, manchineel, cochineal, glockenspiel, difficile, goldenseal, endocoele, neurocoele, commonweal, paddle wheel, balance wheel, alguazil, cacozeal.

4. locomobile, automobile, poisson d'Avril [F.], hôtel de ville [F.].

ELD– 1. eeled, field, heeled, healed, keeled, kneeled, pealed, peeled, spieled, reeled, sealed, shield, steeled, squealed, weald, wield, wheeled, yield.

2. afield, *Sheffield*, *Springfield*, *Canfield*, *infield*, *cornfield*, *airfield*, *Garfield*, *Warfield*, *Mansfield*, *outfield*, congealed, unhealed, annealed, aneled, appealed, repealed, concealed, unsealed, *windshield*, revealed.

3. battlefield, *Copperfield*, *Chesterfield*, uncongealed, unannealed, unaneled, unappealed, unrepealed, unconcealed, unrevealed.

EM– 1. eme, beam, deme, deem, scheme, leam, gleam, neem, reem, ream, riem, rheme, bream, dream, fream, cream, scream, stream, seam, seem, teem, team, steam, theme, yeme.

2. abeam, *moonbeam*, *hornbeam*, *sunbeam*, *crossbeam*, adeem, addeem, redeem, misdeem, blaspheme, regime, hakeem, agleam, supreme, extreme, *daydream*, ice-cream, escrime [F.], *millstream*, downstream, upstream, raceme, Nashim, beseem, unseam, centime, esteem.

3. académe, hyporcheme, disesteem, self-esteem, anatheme.

EMD– 1. beamed, deemed, schemed, gleamed, reamed, dreamed, creamed, screamed, streamed, seamed, seemed, teemed, teamed, steamed.

2. redeemed, blasphemed, daydreamed, beseemed, meseemed, reseamed, unseamed, esteemed.

3. unredeemed, unesteemed.

EN– 1. ean [dial.], e'en, been, bean, dean, dene, gean, jean, Jean, Jeanne, gene, Keene, keen, skean, lean, lien, glean, clean, spleen, mean, mien, meen [Scot.], mesne, pean, peen, breen [slang], green, screen, preen, threne, seen, scene, sheen, teen, 'steen, visne, wean, ween, queen, quean, yean.

2. shebeen, gombeen, ich dien [G.], gardeen, sardine, dudeen, *caffeine, morphine, phosphene,* Beguine, sagene, Valjean, Eugene, sakeen, nankeen, buckeen, baleen, scalene, maline, *Hellene,* colleen, Pauline, moulleen, unclean, Kathleen, bemean, demean, demesne, Benin, treneen, shoneen, alpeen, scalpeen, spalpeen, careen, marine, serene, terrene, Irene, pyrene, Dorine, toureen, shagreen, *peagreen, sea-green, gangrene,* bescreen, rescreen, unscreen, Racine, obscene, Essene, Nicene, piscine, unseen, foreseen, dasheen, machine, eighteen, lateen, patine, ratteen, sateen, fifteen, canteen, nineteen, umpteen, tartine [F.], thirteen, fourteen, sixteen, costean, routine, ravine, subvene, prevene, convene, May queen, atween, between, cuisine, benzine.

3. Capuchin, Aberdeen, gabardine, en sourdine [F.], Josephine, carrageen, polygene, photogene, supergene, palanguin, palankeen, damaskeen, Magdalene, opaline, philhellene, mousseline, crinoline, gasolene, mezzanine, Philippine, atropine, submarine, bismarine, cismarine, transmarine, candareen, nectarine, mazarine, Nazarene, tangerine, pelerine, kittereen, smithereen, wolverine, tambourine, figurine, aquagreen, peregrine, mythogreen, wintergreen, evergreen, Hippocrene, damascene, Damascene, kerosene, overseen, unforeseen, velveteen, turbiteen, quarantine, Byzantine, Constantine, serpentine, seventeen, Argentine, Florentine, Celestine, guillotine, libertine, contravene, supervene, intervene, Halloween, harvest queen, go-between, therebetween, bombazine, magazine, louisine, limousine.

4. heterogene, ultramarine, aquamarine.

5. latin de cuisine [F.], *also feminine names ending in the suffix " -ine "* (e. g. Georgine, Albertine).

END— 1. eaned, beaned, fiend, keened, leaned, gleaned, cleaned, greened, screened, preened, weaned, weened, queened, teind, yeaned.

2. archfiend, uncleaned, demeaned, careened, unscreened, unweaned.

3. guillotined, contravened, intervened.

ENTH— 1. greenth, 'steenth.

2. eighteenth, fifteenth, nineteenth, umpteenth, thirteenth, fourteenth, sixteenth.

3. seventeenth.

EP— 1. beep, cheep, cheap, deep, heap, jeep, keep, leap, leep, clepe, sleep, neap, neep, sneap, peep, reap, creep, threap, threep, seep, sepe [slang], sheep, teap, steep, weep, sweep.

2. aheap, upkeep, asleep, bopeep, la grippe [F.], estrepe, upsweep.

3. overleap, unasleep, oversleep, chimney sweep.

EPT— 1. beeped, cheeped, heaped, jeeped,

leaped, neaped, peeped, reaped, seeped, steeped.

3. overleaped.

ER— 1. ear, beer, bier, cheer, dear, deer, fear, sphere, gear, here, hear, jeer, skeer [dial.], leer, lear, blear, fleer, clear, sclere, mere, mir, smear, near, neer, sneer, peer, pier, pear, pir, spear, rear, drear, seer, sear, sere, ser, cere, shear, sheer, tear, teer, tier, Tyr, stere, steer, vire, veer, weir, queer, year.

2. *wheatear, killdeer, reindeer,* endear, ensphere, *headgear, footgear,* adhere, inhere, cohere, Mynheer, fakir, King Lear, unclear, amir, emir, emeer, premier, besmear, anear, denier, veneer, appear, compeer, outpeer, arrear, career, uprear, plancier, sincere, cashier, frontier, austere, revere, brevier, severe, *midyear,* brassiere, plaisir [F.], vizier.

3. shillibeer, ginger beer, brigadier, grenadier, c'est à dire [F.], bombardier, commandeer, interfere, hemisphere, atmosphere, pedalier, cavalier, lavaliere, chevalier, chandelier, fusilier, chanticleer, gondolier, pistoleer, buccaneer, l'avenir [F.], souvenir, jardiniere, engineer, domineer, mountaineer, mutineer, scrutineer, chiffonier, cannoneer, pioneer, auctioneer, reappear, disappear, agricere, financier, insincere, caboceer, tabasheer, privateer, targeteer, racketeer, musketeer, muleteer, pamphleteer, sonneteer, profiteer, gazetteer, volunteer, à ravir [F.], persevere, yesteryear, au plaisir [F.].

4. il va sans dire [F.], avec plaisir [F.].

6. heute mir, morgen dir [G.].

ERD— 1. eared, beard, cheered, feared, sphered, geared, jeered, leered, bleared, fleered, cleared, smeared, neared, sneered, peered, speared, reared, seared, sheared, sheered, tiered, steered, veered, weird, queered.

2. uneared, *lop-eared, graybeard, treebeard, Bluebeard,* endeared, afeared, unfeared, ensphered, adhered, besmeared, veneered, appeared, outpeered, careered, upreared, cashiered, brassiered, revered.

3. commandeered, interfered, engineered, domineered, mountaineered, pioneered, reappeared, disappeared, racketeered, pamphleteered, privateered, profiteered, volunteered, persevered.

ERS— 1. Bierce, fierce, pierce, tierce.

2. transpierce.

ERZ— *see* ĒR, plus " s " or " 's "; 2. Algiers, Tangiers.

ES— 1. geese, lease, lis, lisse [F.], fleece, Nice, niece, peace, piece, grease, Greece, crease, creese, Kris, cease.

2. obese, esquisse [F.], sublease, release, valise, Felice, pelisse, police, coulisse, Bernice, apiece, *endpiece,* repiece, *neckpiece, timepiece, crosspiece, mouthpiece,* Clarice, cerise, decrease, recrease, increase, Lucrece, Maurice, caprice, cassis, decease, surcease, atis, métis.

3. prerelease, mantelpiece, cornerpiece, centerpiece, afterpiece, masterpiece, frontispiece, ambergris, predecease.
4. feu d'artifice [F.].
ESH– 1. biche [F.], fiche, leash, sneesh, riche [F.].
2. affiche [F.], unleash, Boule Miche [F.], potiche [F.], schottische, schottish, pastiche, postiche.
3. wawaskeesh, nouveau riche [F.].
EST– 1. east, beast, feast, geest, least, leased, fleeced, sneest, piste [F.], pieced, greased, creased, priest, triste [F.], ceased, teest, queest, yeast.
2. northeast, southeast, modiste, subleased, released, unleased, policed, decreased, recreased, increased, archpriest, deceased, batiste, artiste.
3. wildebeest, hartebeest, aubergiste.
4. à l'improviste [F.].
ET– 1. eat, beat, beet, cheat, cheet, feat, feet, Geat, heat, keet, skeet, scete, skete, leat, leet, Lied [G.], bleat, fleet, gleet, cleat, pleat, sleet, meat, meet, mete, neat, peat, Pete, reit, freit, greet, Crete, treat, street, cete, seat, sheet, teat, queet, vite [F.], weet, sweet, suite, tweet, wheat.
2. *deadbeat, offbeat, drumbeat, upbeat, heartbeat, browbeat,* escheat, effete, defeat, reheat, munjeet, mesquite, elite, delete, deplete, replete, complete, *athlete, helpmeet, mincemeat, forcemeat, sweetmeat,* repeat, compete, terete, afreet, congreet, accrete, secrete, concrete, discreet, excrete, retreat, maltreat, entreat, estreat, mistreat, downstreet, upstreet, reseat, receipt, disseat, conceit, unseat, *broadsheet, clipsheet,* petite, mansuete, ensuite [F.], unsweet, tout de suite [F.], *peetweet, buckwheat.*
3. overeat, parrakeet, lorikeet, incomplete, uncomplete, eau bénite [F.], marguerite, Marguerite, indiscreet, county seat, mercy seat, judgment seat, balance sheet, tout de suite [F.], bittersweet.
4. pour le mérite [F.], carte de visite [F.], pour faire visite [F.].
ETH– 1. heath, Keith, 'neath, sneath, sneeth, wreath, sheath, teeth.
2. beneath, eyeteeth, bequeath.
3. underneath.
ETHE– 1. sneathe, wreathe, breathe, seethe, sheathe, teethe, quethe.
2. enwreathe, imbreathe, inbreathe, outbreathe, ensheathe, bequeath.

ETS– *see* **ĒT**, plus " s " or " 's "; 1. Keats.
EV– 1. eve, Eve, eave, beeve, cheve, deave [dial.], gieve [slang], heave, keeve, leave, lieve, cleave, cleve, cleeve, sleave, sleeve, nieve, peeve, reave, reeve, reve, breve, greave, grieve, screeve, seave, sheave, steeve, Steve, thieve, weave, we've, queeve.
2. naïve, achieve, khedive, upheave, believe, relieve, bereave, aggrieve, reprieve, retrieve, *portreeve,* deceive, receive, conceive, perceive, qui vive [F.], reweave, inweave, unweave.
3. make-believe, unbelieve, disbelieve, interleave, semibreve, reconceive, preconceive, misconceive, apperceive, reperceive, preperceive, interweave.
4. recitative.
EVD– 1. eaved, cheved, deaved, heaved, keeved, leaved, cleaved, sleaved, sleeved, peeved, reaved, greaved, grieved, screeved, sheaved, steeved, thieved.
2. achieved, upheaved, believed, relieved, bereaved, aggrieved, reprieved, retrieved, deceived, received, conceived, perceived.
3. unbelieved, disbelieved, interleaved, reconceived, preconceived, unconceived, misconceived, apperceived, reperceived, preperceived, unperceived.
EVZ– *see* **ĒV**, plus " s " or " 's "; 1. Jeeves.
EZ– *see* **Ē** through **ZĒ**, plus " s " or " 's ";
1. ease, bise [F.], cheese, feaze, feeze, heeze, Geez [slang], Jeez [slang], please, mease, mise, neeze, neese, sneeze, pease, pes, Spes, reese, res [L.], breeze, freeze, frieze, grease, seize, tease, these, squeeze, weeze, tweeze, wheeze.
2. unease, *heartsease, nipcheese,* marquise, valise, Belize, displease, demise, chemise, remise, Burmese, Chinese, appease, trapeze, cerise, enfreeze, unfreeze, imprese, assise, reseize, disseize, bêtise [F.], D.T.'s, sottise [F.], Maltese, disease, Louise.
3. friandise [F.], Annamese, Portuguese, Singhalese, journalese, Nepalese, Pericles, Damocles, Androcles, Tyrolese, Hercules, Siamese, Assamese, manganese, Japanese, Havanese, Viennese, Pekinese, Cantonese, antifreeze, syntheses, indices, vortices, overseas, Genevese.
4. Atlantides, Hesperides, antipodes, parentheses, hypotheses, analyses, Xenocrates.
5. Mephistopheles.
EZH– 1. tige.
2. prestige.

$\overline{\text{E}}$ (bee)

Double (Feminine) Rhymes

Primary or Secondary Accent Falls on Next to Last Syllable; Imperfect Rhymes Are in Italics.

E′a– 2. chia, Dea, deah [slang], hia, Lea, Leah, rhea, Rea, Rhea, Sia, Thea, via, Zea.
3. Rabia, rebia, obeah, Lucia, badia [It.], Medea, idea, Chaldea, Judea, bahia [Sp.], Bahia, ohia, Hygeia, dulia, Mammea, Crimea, Carnea, Tarpeia, Maria, Sharia, Diria, Spiraea, spirea, Oriya, Korea, Nicaea, Althea, Hosea.
4. ratafia, Eogaea, Neogaea, Arctogaea, energeia, Latakia, dulcinea, melopoeia, pathopoeia, diarrhea, logorrhea, pyorrhea, panacea, fantasia, Galatea, Dorothea.
5. Antarctogea, Ave Maria, pharmacopoeia, peripeteia.
7. onomatopoeia; *see also* $\overline{\text{E}}$′ya.
E′ad– 2. Pleiad.
3. ideaed.
4. unideaed; *see also* $\overline{\text{E}}$′id.
E′al– 1. feal, pheal, real.
2. ideal, unreal, correal.
3. unideal, beau ideal, epigeal, perigeal, meningeal, laryngeal, Arctogaeal, hymeneal, empyreal.
E′an– 2. lien, paean.
3. Sabaean, plebeian, Chaldean, Andean, Pandean, Shandean, Judean, Orphean, Aegean, Hygeian, trachean, Achean, Crimean, pampean, Berean, Korean, petrean, lyncean, Dantean, protean, Lethean, Pantheian, pantheon.
4. Maccabean, amoebean, Carribean, Niobean, Jacobean, amphigean, perigean, phalangean, laryngean, apogean, Achillean, Galilean, Antillean, Sophoclean, Herculean, European, Eritrean, Tennessean, Pharisean, Sadducean, gigantean, Atlantean.
5. Archimedean, antipodean, terpsichorean, Epicurean.
6. Mephistophelean.
E′as– 3. Aeneas; *see also* $\overline{\text{E}}$′us.
EB′a– 2. iba, peba, Reba, Seba, Sheba.
3. amoeba, zareba, tiriba, Bath-sheba.
4. Jehosheba.

EB′an– 2. Sheban, Theban.
3. amoeban.
EB′ee– 2. Bebe, Phoebe, Hebe, Seabee.
4. heeby-jeeby [slang], heebee-jeebee [slang].
EB′er– 2. Eber, Heber, weber.
EB′o– 2. eboe, Ibo, Nebo.
3. placebo, gazebo.
EB′ra– 2. libra, zebra.
4. cuba libre.
EB′us– 2. Phoebus, glebous, rebus.
3. ephebus.
ECH′ee– 2. beachy, beechy, Geechee, leachy, leechy, litchi, bleachy, sleechy, meechy, peachy, speechy, reachy, reechy, breachy, screechy, preachy, teachy.
3. campeachy.
ECH′er– 2. beacher, Beecher, feature, leacher, leecher, bleacher, meecher, peacher, reacher, breacher, breecher, creature, screecher, preacher, teacher.
3. defeature, impeacher, beseecher.
ECH′ing– 2. beaching, leaching, leeching, bleaching, fleeching, pleaching, meeching, peaching, reaching, breeching, screeching, preaching, teaching.
3. impeaching, outreaching, farreaching, beseeching.
4. overreaching.
ECH′less– 2. beachless, beechless, leachless, leechless, bleachless, sleechless, peachless, speechless, reachless, breechless, breachless, screechless, preachless, teachless.
ECH′ment– 2. preachment.
3. appeachment, impeachment, beseechment.
ED′a– 2. Leda, Theda, Veda, Vida, Ouida.
3. Aïda, kasida, reseda.
4. alameda.
5. olla-podrida.
ED′al– 2. daedal, creedal.
ED′ay– 2. *bidet*, D-day, fee day.
ED′ed– 2. beaded, deeded, heeded, pleaded, needed, kneaded, reeded, dreeded [dial.], seeded, ceded, weeded, tweeded.

3. unheeded, stampeded, impeded, receded, preceded, seceded, acceded, exceeded, succeeded, conceded, proceeded, unweeded.

4. anteceded, retroceded, superseded, interceded.

ĒD'ee– 2. Edie, beady, deedy, heedy, gledy, Midi, needy, speedy, reedy, greedy, creedy, seedy, sidi, weedy, tweedy.

3. indeedy [coll.], unspeedy, *seaweedy*.

4. orthopaedy.

ĒD'en– 2. Eden, reeden, Sweden.

ĒD'ens– 2. credence.

3. recedence, precedence, concedence.

4. antecedence, antecedents, retrocedence, supersedence.

ĒD'ent– 2. needn't, credent, cedent, sedent.

3. decedent, recedent, precedent.

4. antecedent, retrocedent, intercedent.

ĒD'er– 2. beader, feeder, heeder, leader, bleeder, pleader, needer, kneader, speeder, reader, breeder, cedar, ceder, cedre, seeder, weeder.

3. bandleader, *ringleader*, misleader, impleader, stampeder, impeder, receder, preceder, seceder, acceder, exceeder, succeeder, conceder, proceeder.

4. interpleader, superseder, interceder.

ĒD'ez– 2. aedes [L.], greedies.

4. Palamedes, Archimedes, Dolomedes.

ĒD'ful– 2. deedful, heedful, needful, speedful, seedful.

3. unheedful, unneedful.

ĒD'ik– 2. Vedic.

3. comedic.

4. talipedic, cyclopedic, orthopedic.

5. encyclopedic.

ĒD'ing– 2. beading, deeding, feeding, heeding, leading, bleeding, pleading, kneading, needing, speeding, reeding, reading, breeding, dreeding [dial.], seeding, sheading, weeding.

3. unheeding, misleading, stampeding, impeding, outspeeding, rereading, misreading, inbreeding, *crossbreeding*, reseeding, receding, preceding, seceding, acceding, succeeding, conceding, proceeding, exceeding.

4. underfeeding, overfeeding, anteceding, retroceding, superceding, interceding.

ĒD'l– 2. beadle, daedal, needle, pedal, wheedle, tweedle.

3. bipedal, conquedle [dial.].

4. semipedal, centipedal.

ĒD'ler– 2. needler, wheedler.

ĒD'less– 2. beadless, Bedeless, deedless, feedless, heedless, leadless, needless, speedless, readless, breedless, dreedless [dial.], greedless, creedless, seedless, steedless, weedless, tweedless.

ĒD'ling– 2. needling, reedling, seedling, wheedling, tweedling.

ĒD'o– 2. Ido, Lido, credo.

3. albedo, libido, bandido [Sp.], Toledo, torpedo, Laredo, teredo, Bushido [Jap.].

ĒD'ra– 3. exedra, cathedra.

4. ex cathedra.

ĒD'ral– 3. dihedral, trihedral, cathedral.

4. decahedral, polyhedral, hemihedral.

ĒD'rik– 2. diedric.

4. polyhedric, holohedric.

ĒD'ron– 2. cedron.

3. dihedron, trihedron.

4. polyhedron.

ĒD'rus– 2. Cedrus.

4. polyhedrous.

ĒD'um– 2. Ledum, pedum, freedom, Sedum.

ĒD'ure– 3. procedure.

4. supersedure.

Ē'er– 2. fiar [Scot.], fleer, freer, seer.

3. agreer, decreer, foreseer, *sight-seer*.

4. disagreer, overseer.

Ē'est– 2. freest, weest.

EF'ee– 2. beefy, Fifi, leafy, reefy, sheafy.

3. Afifi, Rififi.

EF'er– 2. beefer, chiefer, deefer [dial.], liefer, leafer, reefer, briefer.

EF'lee– 2. chiefly, briefly.

EF'less– 2. beefless, chiefless, leafless, reefless, briefless, griefless, sheafless, thiefless.

3. beliefless, motifless.

EG'a– 2. Riga, Vega, ziega.

3. bodega, omega.

EG'al– 2. legal, regal, gregal.

3. illegal, unlegal, vice-regal; *see also* **EG'l.**

EG'er– 2. eager, eagre, leaguer, meager, meagre, zieger.

3. beleaguer, intriguer, fatiguer.

4. overeager, major leaguer, minor leaguer.

EG'ing– 2. leaguing.

3. enleaguing, intriguing, fatiguing.

EG'l– 2. eagle, beagle, kleagle, teagle, veigle [dial.].

3. bald eagle, sea eagle, porbeagle, espiègle [F.], inveigle.

4. double eagle, golden eagle; *see also* **ĒG'al.**

EG'ler– 2. beagler.

3. inveigler.

EG'o– 2. ego, grego.

3. amigo [Sp.], Otsego, Oswego.

EG'ress– 2. egress, Negress, regress.

EG'ro– 2. Negro.

4. Montenegro.

Ē'hi– 2. Lehigh, kneehigh.

Ē'hol– 2. keyhole, kneehole, frijol, frijole.

Ē'id– 3. Aeneid; *see also* **Ē'ad.**

Ē'ik– 2. rheic.

3. caffeic, Palaeic, oleic, tropeic, choreic, caseic, proteic.

4. mythopoeic.

5. xanthoproteic.

6. onomatopoeic.

Ē'ing– 2. being, feeing, geeing, keying, skiing, fleeing, gleeing, kneeing, dreeing [dial.], freeing, spreeing, treeing, seeing, teeing.

3. well-being, nonbeing, teheeing, agreeing, decreeing, unseeing, foreseeing, *sight-seeing*.

4. refereeing, disagreeing, overseeing, unforeseeing, guaranteeing.

Ē'ist– 2. deist, theist, zeist.

3. ideist.

4. Manicheist, polytheist, antitheist, monotheist.

E′it— 3. albeit, sobeit, howbeit.

E′izm— 2. deism, theism, weism.

3. Parseeism, sutteism.

4. Manicheism, Phariseeism, Sadduceeism, absenteeism, polytheism, philotheism, cosmotheism, misotheism.

EJ′an— 3. collegian, Norwegian, Glaswegian; *see also* **ĒJ′un.**

EJ′ee— 2. Fiji, Gigi, squeegee.

EJ′er— 2. aeger [L.], Aegir, leger, sieger.

3. besieger.

EJ′ik— 3. strategic.

4. paraplegic, hemiplegic, cycloplegic.

5. bibliopegic.

EJ′is— 2. aegis, egis.

3. St. Regis.

EJ′un— 2. legion, region.

3. collegian, Norwegian, Glaswegian.

EK′a— 2. chica, quica, sika, theca.

3. Topeka, Areca, paprika, eureka, zotheca.

4. Dominica, Salonika, Costa Rica, endotheca, Tanganyika.

5. bibliotheca.

EK′al— 2. fecal, faecal, caecal, thecal, treacle.

4. intrathecal.

5. bibliothecal; *see also* **ĒK′l.**

EK′ant— 2. piquant, precant, secant.

3. cosecant.

4. intersecant.

EK′ed— 2. peaked, streaked.

EK′ee— 2. beaky, cheeky, leaky, cliquey, sneaky, peaky, peeky, reeky, creaky, creeky, streaky, sheiky, Tiki, squeaky.

3. batiky.

4. tiki-tiki.

6. veni, vidi, vici [L.].

EK′en— 2. bleaken, sleeken, meeken, weaken.

3. Mahican, Mohican; *see also* **ĒK′on.**

EK′er— 2. beaker, leaker, bleaker, Bleecker, sleeker, meeker, sneaker, peaker, peeker, speaker, reeker, creaker, krieker, shrieker, weaker, squeaker, tweaker.

EK′est— 2. bleakest, sleekest, meekest, weakest.

EK′ing— 2. eking, beaking, cheeking, leaking, cliquing, sleeking, sneaking, peaking, peeking, piquing, speaking, reeking, wreaking, creaking, shrieking, streaking, seeking, squeaking, tweaking.

3. bespeaking, unspeaking, self-seeking, antiquing.

EK′ish— 2. bleakish, cliquish, meekish, sneakish, peakish, freakish, Greekish, weakish.

EK′l— 2. chicle, treecle.

3. Ezek'l; *see also* **ĒK′al.**

EK′lee— 2. bleakly, sleekly, meekly, treacly, weakly, weekly.

3. obliquely, uniquely, biweekly, triweekly.

4. semiweekly.

EK′ness— 2. bleakness, sleekness, meekness, weakness.

3. obliqueness, uniqueness, antiqueness.

EK′o— 2. fico, mico, Nico, pico [Sp], pekoe.

3. Tampico, matico.

4. orange pekoe.

EK′ok— 2. Leacock, meacock, peacock, sea cock.

EK′on— 2. beacon, deacon.

3. archdeacon; *see also* **ĒK′en.**

EK′wal— 2. equal, sequel.

3. subequal, inequal, unequal, coequal.

EK′wens— 2. frequence, sequence.

3. infrequence.

EK′went— 2. frequent, sequent.

3. infrequent.

EL′a— 2. Bela, belah, gila, Leila, Leilah, selah, Shelah, Sheila, Stela.

3. tequila, palila, sequela.

4. Philomela, Venezuela.

EL′and— 2. eland, Zeeland.

3. New Zealand.

ELD′ed— 2. fielded, shielded, wielded, yielded.

3. unfielded, unshielded, unwielded, unyielded.

ELD′ee— 2. wieldy, yieldy.

3. unwieldy.

ELD′er— 2. fielder, shielder, wielder, yielder.

3. infielder, outfielder, nonyielder.

ELD′ing— 2. fielding, shielding, wielding, yielding.

3. enshielding, unyielding.

EL′ee— 2. eely, Ealy, Ely, dele, feally, mealy, peele, pili, freely, Greeley, seely, steely, stele, squealy, wheely.

3. Belili, Point Pelee, genteely.

4. campanile, pili-pili, monostele, protostele.

EL′er— 2. eeler, dealer, feeler, healer, heeler, keeler, kneeler, pealer, peeler, spieler, reeler, sealer, seeler, stealer, stelar, velar, wheeler, squealer.

3. misdealer, New Dealer, congealer, annealer, appealer, repealer, concealer, revealer, two-wheeler.

4. double-dealer.

EL′est— 2. lealest.

3. genteelest.

EL′ij— 2. keelage, stealage, wheelage.

EL′ik— 2. velic.

3. parhelic.

EL′iks— 2. Felix, helix.

4. antihelix.

EL′ine— 2. beeline, feline, tree line, sea line.

EL′ing— 2. eeling, Ealing, dealing, feeling, healing, heeling, keeling, kneeling, pealing, peeling, reeling, ceiling, sealing, seeling, shealing, steeling, stealing, wheeling, squealing.

3. misdealing, unfeeling, congealing, Darjeeling, annealing, appealing, repealing, concealing, unsealing, revealing.

4. double-dealing.

5. automobiling.

EL′ment— 3. congealment, repealment, concealment, revealment.

EL'ness– 2. lealness.

3. genteelness.

EL'os– 2. Delos, melos, telos [Gr.].

EL'um– 2. Caelum, velum.

EL'ya– 2. Delia, Lelia, Celia.

3. lobelia, Bedelia, Cordelia, Ophelia, Amelia, Camellia, cimelia, Cornelia, Aurelia, Cecelia.

EL'yan– 2. Delian.

3. Mendelian, chameleon, carnelian, cornelian, aurelian.

EL'yus– 2. Delius.

3. Cornelius, Aurelius.

EM'a– 2. bema, schema, Lima, Pima, Rima, rhema, thema, Xema.

3. edema, emblema, sclerema, sorema, blastema, Fatima, enthema, eczema.

4. seriema, empyema, epiblema, hyporchema, terza rima [It.], emphysema.

EM'al– 2. demal, hemal, lemel.

3. blastemal.

4. pseudohemal.

EM'an– 2. beeman, freeman, G-man, he-man, seaman, T-man, Teman, teaman; *see also* **ĒM'on.**

EM'ee– 2. beamy, gleamy, Mime, Mimi, mneme, dreamy, creamy, screamy, streamy, seamy, teemy, steamy.

3. *daydreamy.*

EM'ent– 3. agreement, decreement.

4. disagreement.

EM'er– 2. beamer, deemer, femur, schemer, lemur, reamer, dreamer, creamer, screamer, streamer, seemer, seamer, teemer, steamer.

3. redeemer, blasphemer, *daydreamer,* supremer, extremer.

EM'est– 3. supremest, extremest.

EM'ful– 2. beamful, schemeful, dreamful, teemful.

EM'ik– 2. phemic, hemic, semic.

3. anemic, phonemic, eremic, racemic.

4. polyhemic, monoschemic, octasemic, septicemic, monosemic.

EM'ing– 2. beaming, deeming, scheming, gleaming, reaming, dreaming, creaming, screaming, streaming, seeming, seaming, teeming, steaming, theming.

3. redeeming, blaspheming, *daydreaming,* beseeming, esteeming.

4. unredeeming, unbeseeming.

EM'ish– 2. beamish, squeamish.

EM'ist– 2. schemist, Rhemist.

3. extremist.

EM'lee– 2. seemly.

3. unseemly, supremely, extremely.

EM'less– 2. beamless, schemeless, dreamless, gleamless, creamless, streamless, seamless, seemless, teemless, steamless, themeless.

EM'let– 2. beamlet, streamlet, themelet.

EM'o– 2. Nemo, primo [It.].

EM'on– 2. demon, daemon, leman, seaman.

3. eudemon.

4. cacodemon; *see also* **ĒM'an.**

EM'ster– 2. deemster, seamster, teamster.

EM'us– 2. Remus.

3. oremus [L.].

4. Academus, Nicodemus.

EN'a– 2. ina [Tag.], gena, Gina, keena, quina, lena, Lena, lina, Lina, Nina, crena, cena [L.], scena, scaena, Tina, vina.

3. pembina, verbena, adena, Medina, Modena, hyena, Georgina, galena, Salina, Paulina, guapena, subpoena, arena, farina, clarina, marina, Marina, tsarina, czarina, Andrena, Serena, Irena, cassena, Messina, piscina, encina, catena, patina, poltina, cantina, sestina, Christina, Faustina, flutina, Athena, Avena, novena, Rowena.

4. quintadena, contadina [It.], Cartagena, melongena, marikina, Magdalena, Catalina, cantilena, semolina, Wilhelmina, philopena, ocarina, ballerina, signorina [It], orchestrina, oficina [Sp.], officina [L.], sonatina, cavatina, Argentina, Clementina, Albertina, concertina, Celestina, aguavina.

EN'al– 2. plenal, penal, renal, venal.

3. marinal, adrenal, machinal.

4. duodenal.

EN'ate– 2. enate, crenate.

EN'ee– 2. eeny, beany, genie, lene, blini, pleny, spleeny, mene [Aram.], meeny, meanie [slang], sheeny, greeny, teeny, visne, weeny, Queenie, Sweeney, tweeny.

3. galeeny, clarini, Selene, Silene, Camenae, Irene, Rossini.

4. fantoccini, eeny-meeny, campanini, Hippocrene.

EN'er– 2. keener, leaner, gleaner, cleaner, meaner, greener, screener, preener, weaner, wiener.

3. demeanor, serener, obscener, machiner, convener.

4. misdemeanor, contravener, supervener, intervener, magaziner.

EN'est– 2. keenest, leanest, cleanest, meanest, greenest.

3. serenest, obscenest.

EN'id– 2. Enid, maenad.

EN'ij– 2. greenage, teenage.

3. careenage.

EN'ik– 2. phenic, splenic, Menic, scenic.

EN'ing– 2. eaning [dial.], beaning, deaning, keening, leaning, gleaning, cleaning, meaning, greening, screening, preening, weaning, weening, queening, yeaning.

3. bemeaning, demeaning, well-meaning, ill-meaning, unmeaning, careening, unscreening, machining, costeaning, subvening, advening, convening.

4. double meaning, quarantining, intervening, supervening, overweening.

EN'ish– 2. beanish, deanish, keenish, leanish, cleanish, spleenish, meanish, greenish, queenish.

EN'ist– 2. plenist.

3. machinist, routinist.

4. magazinist.
EN'lee– 2. keenly, leanly, cleanly, meanly, greenly, queenly.
3. serenely, obscenely.
EN'ling– 2. weanling, yeanling.
EN'ness– 2. keenness, leanness, cleanness, meanness, greenness.
3. uncleanness, sereneness, obsceneness.
EN'o– 2. beano, fino, keno, leno, mino, Nino, Reno.
3. wabeno, albino, bambino [It.], tondino, camino [Sp.], comino, clarino [It.], Merino, casino, batino.
4. palombino, baldachino, palomino, pianino, sopranino, Filipino, San Marino, peacherino, vetturino [It.], maraschino, andantino, Valentino.
EN'um– 2. plenum, frenum, fraenum.
4. duodenum.
EN'us– 2. Enos, genus, Venus, venous.
3. scalenus, Silenus.
EN'ya– 2. piña, Niña.
EN'yal– 2. genial, menial.
3. congenial.
4. uncongenial; see also ĒN'i–al.
EN'yens– 2. lenience.
3. prevenience, convenience.
4. inconvenience, intervenience.
EN'yent– 2. lenient.
3. convenient.
4. inconvenient, intervenient.
EN'yor– 2. senior, signor [It.], seignior.
3. monsignor.
EN'yus– 2. genius.
3. ingenious.
E'o– 2. Eo, Leo, Cleo, neo, Reo, Rio, trio, Theo.
3. sub Deo [L.], bohio [Sp.], con brio [It.].
E'ol– 2. Creole, Sheol.
E'on– 2. eon, aeon, pheon, Leon, pleon, neon, peon, paeon, Creon.
3. pantheon.
4. Ponce de Leon.
EP'a– 2. Nepa, nipa, niepa, pipa, cepa.
EP'al– 2. ipil, pipal, sepal; see also ĒP'l.
EP'ee– 2. cheepy, heapy, sleepy, creepy, seepy, sheepy, tepee, steepy, weepy, sweepy.
5. Fra Lippo Lippi.
EP'en– 2. cheapen, deepen, steepen.
3. alipin [Tag.].
EP'er– 2. beeper, deeper, cheeper, cheaper, heaper, keeper, leaper, sleeper, Dnieper, peeper, reeper, reaper, creeper, tepor, steeper, weeper, sweeper.
3. beekeeper, bookkeeper, timekeeper, innkeeper, shopkeeper, barkeeper, doorkeeper, horsekeeper, housekeeper, gatekeeper, mooncreeper.
EP'est– 2. deepest, cheapest, steepest.
EP'ij– 2. seepage, sweepage.
EP'ing– 2. beeping, cheeping, cheaping, deeping, heaping, jeeping, keeping, leaping, sleeping, neaping, peeping, reaping, creeping, threaping, seeping, steeping, weeping, sweeping.

3. beekeeping, safekeeping, shopkeeping, housekeeping.
4. overleaping, oversleeping, oversteeping.
EP'ish– 2. cheapish, deepish, sheepish, steepish.
EP'l– 2. people, steeple, wheeple.
3. repeople, empeople, unpeople, merpeople, dispeople, townspeople; see also ĒP'al.
EP'lee– 2. cheaply, deeply, steeply.
EP'less– 2. cheepless, deepless, jeepless, keepless, leapless, sleepless, peepless, seepless, sheepless, weepless.
EP'ness– 2. cheapness, deepness, steepness.
EP'oi– 2. sepoy, teapoy.
ER'a– 2. era, gerah, Hera, quira, lira, sclera, sera, Terah, Vera.
3. Madeira, galera, chimera, chimaera, lempira, Sarira, Sharira, asherah, hetaera.
4. rangatira.
ER'al– 2. eral, feral, spheral, scleral, ceral.
3. vicegeral.
4. hemispheral.
ER'ans-- 2. clearance.
3. adherence, inherence, coherence, appearance, arrearance.
4. interference, incoherence, reappearance, nonappearance, disappearance, perseverance.
ER'ant– 3. sederunt.
4. perseverant; see also ĒR'ent.
ER'ee– 2. aerie, eerie, Erie, beery, cheery, deary, sphery, jeery, keiri, kiri, leary, leery, bleary, smeary, sneery, peri, peery, speary, dreary, seri, teary, veery, weary, quaere [L.], query.
3. uncheery, hetaery, aweary, world-weary.
4. hara-kiri, overweary.
ER'eez– 2. dearies, heres [L.], Ceres, series, wearies, queries.
3. World Series.
ER'ens– 3. adherence, inherence, coherence.
4. interference, incoherence; see also ĒR'ans.
ER'ent– 2. gerent, querent.
3. adherent, inherent, coherent, vicegerent.
4. nonadherent, incoherent, perseverant.
ER'er– 2. cheerer, dearer, fearer, hearer, jeerer, leerer, clearer, smearer, nearer, sneerer, peerer, spearer, rearer, teerer, steerer, veerer, queerer.
3. endearer, adherer, coherer, besmearer, appearer, austerer, reverer, severer.
4. interferer, overhearer, disappearer, perseverer.
5. electioneerer.
ER'ess– 2. peeress, seeress.
ER'est– 2. dearest, merest, nearest, drearest, sheerest, queerest.
3. sincerest, austerest, severest.
ER'ful– 2. earful, cheerful, fearful, sneerful, tearful.
3. uncheerful, unfearful.
ER'id– 2. wearied, queried.
3. unwearied, world-wearied, unqueried.
ER'ij– 2. clearage, peerage, pierage, steerage.

3. arrearage.

ER'ing— 2. earing, earring, beering, Bering, cheering, dearing, fearing, gearing, hearing, jeering, leering, blearing, clearing, nearing, sneering, peering, spearing, rearing, searing, shearing, tiering, steering, veering, queering.
3. endearing, adhering, inhering, cohering, besmearing, veneering, appearing, careering, cashiering, revering.
4. interfering, overhearing, engineering, domineering, mountaineering, pioneering, cannoneering, auctioneering, reappearing, disappearing, privateering, profiteering, volunteering.
5. electioneering.

ER'lee— 2. dearly, clearly, merely, nearly, drearly, queerly, yearly.
3. sincerely, austerely, severely.
4. cavalierly, insincerely.

ER'less— 2. earless, beerless, cheerless, dearless, deerless, fearless, gearless, jeerless, leerless, Learless, mereless, peerless, spearless, tearless, yearless.

ER'ling— 2. shearling, steerling, yearling.

ER'ment— 2. cerement.
3. endearment.

ER'ness— 2. dearness, clearness, nearness, queerness.
3. sincereness, austereness, severeness.

ER'o— 2. hero, Nero, Piro, cero, sero, Ciro, zero.
5. lillibullero.

ERS'er— 2. fiercer, piercer.
3. ear piercer.

ERS'ing— 2. piercing.
3. transpiercing.

ER'us— 2. sclerous, serous, cirrus, cirrhous.

ERZ'man— 2. steersman.
3. frontiersman.
4. privateersman.

ES'a— 2. Lisa, Rise.
3. Elisa, Felica, camisa [Sp.], Theresa.

ES'ee— 2. fleecy, greasy, creasy.

ES'eez— 2. preces, praeses [L.], theses.

ES'ens— 2. decence.
3. obeisance, indecence.

ES'ent— 2. decent, recent.
3. obeisant, indecent, unrecent.

ES'er— 2. leaser, fleecer, piecer, greaser, creaser.
3. releaser, subleaser, decreaser, increaser.

ES'ez— 2. leases, fleeces, nieces, pieces, peaces, greases, creases, ceases.
3. subleases, releases, pelisses, valises, repieces, decreases, increases, caprices.
4. mantelpieces, centerpieces, masterpieces, frontispieces.

ES'ful— 2. peaceful.
3. unpeaceful, capriceful.

ESH'a— 3. silesia, magnesia.

ESH'an— 2. Decian, Grecian.
3. Silesian, Venetian, magnesian, Lutetian, Helvetian.
4. Polynesian; see also ĒSH'an.

ESH'ing— 2. leashing, sneeshing.
3. unleashing.

ESH'un— 3. deletion, depletion, repletion, impletion, completion, accretion, secretion, incretion, excretion.
4. incompletion, internecion; see also ĒSH'an.

ESH'us— 2. Decius, specious.
3. facetious.

ES'ik— 2. mnesic.
3. algesic, gynecic.
4. polynesic.

ES'ing— 2. leasing, fleecing, piecing, greasing, creasing, ceasing.
3. releasing, policing, decreasing, increasing, unceasing, surceasing.

ES'is— 2. schesis, tmesis, rhesis [Gr.], thesis.
3. Deësis, algesis, orchesis, ochlesis, mimesis, kinesis, phonesis, phronesis, noesis [Gr.], ascesis, ecesis, centesis, mathesis, anthesis, esthesis.
4. exegesis, catechesis, hyporchesis, anamnesis, Anamnesis, synteresis, hysteresis, catachresis, antichresis, erotesis, anesthesis.
5. diaphoresis, perichoresis, hyperesthesis; see also ĒS'us.

ES'iv— 3. adhesive, cohesive.
4. inadhesive, monadhesive, incohesive, noncohesive.

ES'less— 2. leaseless, fleeceless, nieceless, peaceless, pieceless, greaseless, creaseless, ceaseless.
3. valiseless, capriceless.

EST'a— 4. buena vista [Sp.].
5. hasta la vista [Sp.].

EST'ed— 2. easted, beasted, feasted, yeasted.

EST'ee— 2. beastie, bheesty, bheestie, sneesty, reasty, yeasty.

EST'er— 2. Easter, easter, feaster.
3. down-Easter, northeaster, southeaster.

EST'ern— 2. eastern.
3. northeastern, southeastern.

EST'ing— 2. easting, beasting, feasting, queesting, yeasting.

EST'li— 2. beastly, priestly.
3. nonpriestly, unpriestly.

ES'us— 2. Esus, rhesus, Rhesus, Croesus; see also ĒS'is.

ET'a— 2. eta, beta, cheetah, dita, keta, Fleta, meta, Meta, Nita, pita, Rita, Greta, creta, theta, seta, zeta.
3. pandita, Chiquita, Marquita, tablita [Sp.], bolita [Sp.], Lolita, mulita, Anita, planeta, Juanita, magneta, kareeta, amreeta, amrita, rasceta, partita [It.], sortita [It.].
4. manzanita, margarita, Señorita [Sp.], Carmencita, chirivita.
5. Isabelita.

ET'al— 2. fetal, foetal, ketal, setal.
3. decretal; see also ĒT'l.

ET'am— 2. retem, raetam.
3. Antietam.

ET'an— 2. Cretan, teetan; see also ĒT'en, ĒT'on.

ET'ed— 2. cheated, fetid, heated, bleated,

fleeted, gleeted, cleated, pleated, sleeted, meated, meted, neated, greeted, treated, seated, sheeted, teated.

3. escheated, defeated, reheated, preheated, unheated, deleted, depleted, repleted, completed, unmeted, repeated, competed, accreted, secreted, concreted, excreted, retreated, maltreated, entreated, mistreated, reseated, receipted, conceited, unseated.

4. undefeated, overheated, underheated, uncompleted, unreceipted, unconceited, self-conceited.

ĒT′ee– 2. beety, gleety, sleety, meaty, peaty, rete [L.], treaty, sweety, sweetie.

3. lanete, pariti, entreaty.

4. spermaceti.

ĒT′en– 2. eaten, beaten, keten, sweeten, wheaten.

3. uneaten, *worm-eaten*, *moth-eaten*, unbeaten, *browbeaten*.

4. weather-beaten; *see also* **ĒT′an, ĒT′on.**

ĒT′er– 2. eater, beater, cheater, heater, liter, litre, bleater, fleeter, pleater, meter, metre, meeter, neater, Peter, peter, rhetor, greeter, praetor, pretor, treater, seater, teeter, sweeter.

3. *beefeater*, *eggeater*, *fogeater*, *frogeater*, *cakeeater*, *anteater*, *fire-eater*, *drum beater*, *browbeater*, escheator, depleter, completer, Demeter, repeater, competer, saltpeter, propretor, retreater, entreater, reseater, receiptor, twoseater.

4. overeater, decaliter, hectoliter, centimeter, kilometer.

ĒT′est– 2. fleetest, meetest, neatest, sweetest.

3. effetest, elitest, repletest, completest, discreetest.

4. honey-sweetest.

ĒTH′al– 2. ethal, lethal.

3. bequeathal.

4. preterlethal.

ĒTH′an– 2. Ethan.

5. Elizabethan.

ĒTH′en– 2. heathen, wreathen.

ĒTH′er– 2. either, neither, wreather, breather, seether, sheather.

3. enwreather, inbreather, outbreather, bequeather.

ĒT′ij– 2. eatage, cheatage, cleatage, metage.

3. escheatage.

ĒT′ik– 2. cretic, Cretic, Rhaetic, cetic.

3. paretic, acetic.

ĒT′ing– 2. eating, beating, cheating, heating, Keating, bleating, fleeting, gleeting, cleating, pleating, sleeting, meting, meeting, neating, greeting, treating, seating, sheeting.

3. *beef-eating*, *man-eating*, *meat-eating*, *browbeating*, escheating, defeating, reheating, preheating, deleting, depleting, repleting, completing, repeating, competing, accreting, secreting, concreting, excreting, retreating, maltreating, ill-treating, entreating, mistreating, receipting, unseating.

4. undereating, overeating, nonrepeating,

overheating, underheating.

ĒT′is– 2. Metis, treatise, Thetis.

4. diabetes.

ĒT′ish– 2. beetish, fetish, fetich, sweetish.

ĒT′ist– 3. defeatist, decretist.

ĒT′iv– 3. depletive, repletive, completive, accretive, decretive, secretive, concretive, discretive, excretive.

ĒT′l– 2. beetle, betel, baetyl, fetal, wheetle.

3. decretal, acetyl.

4. chalchihuitl.

ĒT′lee– 2. featly, fleetly, meetly, neatly, sweetly.

3. completely, concretely, discreetly.

4. obsoletely, incompletely, indiscreetly.

ĒT′ment– 2. treatment.

3. defeatment, maltreatment, ill-treatment, entreatment, mistreatment.

ĒT′ness– 2. featness, fleetness, meetness, neatness, sweetness.

3. effeteness, repleteness, completeness, concreteness, discreetness, petiteness.

4. obsoleteness, incompleteness, indiscreetness.

ĒT′o– 2. keto, Leto, Tito, veto.

3. Chiquito, mosquito, bolito, magneto, Benito, bonito, Negrito.

4. angelito [Sp.], sanbenito.

ĒT′on– 2. Eton, Eaton, seton, Teton; *see also* **ĒT′an, ĒT′en.**

ĒT′um– 2. fretum.

3. zibetum, pinetum, decretum, floretum, rosetum, quercetum.

4. ad libitum [L.], arboretum, Tanacetum, salicetum, tilicetum, viticetum.

5. ad infinitum [L.].

ĒT′ure– 2. feature, creature.

3. defeature, refeature.

ĒT′us– 2. fetus, foetus, Cetus.

3. quietus, acetous.

Ē′um– 2. Chiam, meum [L.], Meum.

3. Te Deum [L.], odeum, trophaeum, nymphaeum, nympheum, Iseum, lyceum, bronteum, notaeum, museum.

4. amoebaeum, hypogeum, mausoleum, athenaeum, atheneum, gorgoneum, coliseum, Colosseum.

5. peritoneum.

Ē′us– 2. Deus [L.], deus [L.].

3. *plumbeous*, Zaccheus, Aeneas, choreus, gluteus.

4. scarabaeus, Amadeus, corypheus.

ĒV′a– 2. Eva, diva, jiva, kiva, Siva, viva.

3. khediva, Geneva, Yeshiva.

4. Mahadeva.

ĒV′al– 2. eval, sneevle [dial.], shrieval.

3. coeval, grandeval, upheaval, longeval, primeval, retrieval, equaeval.

4. medieval; *see also* **ĒV′il.**

ĒV′ans– 2. grievance.

3. achievance, aggrievance, retrievance, perceivance.

ĒV′ee– 2. Evie, levee, Levy, leavy, peevey, peevy, peavey, peavy, Stevie, Suevi.

EV′en– 2. even, Stephen, Steven.
  3. uneven, bereaven, good even.
  4. Hallow-even, yestereven.
EV′er– 2. beaver, deaver [dial.], fever, heaver, keever, leaver, lever, liever, livre, cleaver, reaver, reever, reiver, griever, sheaver, weaver, weever.
  3. naïver, achiever, enfever, hay fever, spring fever, coal heaver, believer, reliever, aggriever, repriever, retriever, deceiver, receiver, conceiver, perceiver.
  4. Danny Deever, jungle fever, yellow fever, cantilever, make-believer, nonbeliever, unbeliever, disbeliever, misbeliever, preconceiver, misconceiver, interweaver.
EV′ij– 2. leavage, cleavage.
EV′il– 2. evil, weevil; *see also* EV′al.
  3. boll weevil; *see also* EV′al.
EV′ing– 2. deaving [dial.], heaving, leaving, cleaving, grieving, sheaving, steeving, thieving, weaving.
  3. achieving, upheaving, believing, relieving, bereaving, aggrieving, reprieving, retrieving, deceiving, receiving, conceiving, perceiving, inweaving.
  4. disbelieving, misbelieving, unbelieving, preconceiving, interweaving.
EV′ish– 2. peevish, thievish.
EV′less– 2. Eveless, heaveless, leaveless, sleeveless, sheaveless, weaveless.
EV′ment– 3. achievement, relievement, bereavement, retrievement.
EV′us– 2. nevus, grievous.
  3. longevous, primevous.
  4. ambilevous.
E′wa– 2. leeway, seaway.
E′ward– 2. leeward, seaward.
E′ya– 3. Hygeia, Tarpeia.
  4. energeia, Barranquilla.
  6. onomatopoeia; *see also* E′a.

E′yan– 3. Hygeian, Tarpeian, Pantheian.
EZ′a– 2. pesa, Pisa, tiza, visa.
  3. Louisa.
EZ′ans– 3. defeasance, malfeasance, nonfeasance, misfeasance.
EZ′ee– 2. easy, cheesy, sleasy, sneezy, breezy, freezy, greasy, teasy, queasy.
  3. Zambesi, *speak-easy*, pachisi, parchesi, uneasy.
EZ′er– 2. easer, beezer, cheeser, geezer, pleaser, sneezer, freezer, friezer, greaser, Caesar, seizer, seizor, teaser, squeezer, tweezer, wheezer.
  3. misfeasor, appeaser, displeaser, Sharezer, disseizor.
  4. Ebenezer.
EZH′a– 2. Freesia.
  3. Zambesia, Rhodesia, ecclesia, magnesia, amnesia, trapezia, parrhesia, esthesia.
  4. anesthesia.
EZH′er– 2. leisure, seizure.
  3. reseizure.
EZH′un– 2. lesion.
  3. Ephesian, adhesion, inhesion, cohesion, Silesian, ecclesian, etesian, artesian.
  4. inadhesion, incohesion.
EZ′ing– 2. easing, feazing, feezing, pleasing, sneezing, breezing, freezing, friezing, greasing, seizing, teasing, squeezing, wheezing.
  3. unpleasing, displeasing, appeasing, reseizing.
EZ′l– 2. easel, mesel, measle, teasel, weasel, wheezle [dial.].
EZ′ment– 2. easement.
  3. appeasement.
EZ′on– 2. reason, treason, season, seisin, seizin.
  3. unreason, reseason, mid-season, unseason.
  4. demiseason.
EZ′ond– 2. reasoned, seasoned.
  3. unreasoned, reseasoned, unseasoned.

Ē (bee)

Triple Rhymes

E′a–bl– 3. feeable, fleeable, freeable, treeable, seeable, skiable.
  4. agreeable, decreeable, unseeable.
  5. disagreeable.
E′a–blee– 4. agreeably.
  5. disagreeably.
E′al–ee– 3. leally, really.
  4. ideally.
E′al–ist– 3. realist.
  4. idealist, surrealist.
E′al–iz– 3. realise.
  4. idealize.
E′al–izm– 3. realism.
  4. idealism, surrealism.
E′al–tee– 3. fealty, lealty, realty.
E′an–izm– 3. peanism.
  4. plebeianism, Sabaeanism.
  6. Epicureanism.
EB′ri–us– 3. ebrious.
  4. tenebrious, inebrious, funebrious.
ECH′a–bl– 3. bleachable, reachable, preachable, teachable.
  4. impeachable, unreachable, unteachable.
  5. unimpeachable.
ECH′i–ness– 3. peachiness, screechiness, preachiness.
ED′a–bl– 3. deedable, feedable, heedable, leadable, pleadable, kneadable, readable, seedable, weedable.
  4. impedible, unreadable, exceedable.
  5. unexceedable, supersedable.
ED′en–see– 4. precedency.
  5. antecedency.
ED′er–ship– 3. leadership, readership.
ED′ful–ee– 3. heedfully, needfully.
  4. unheedfully, unneedfully.
ED′ful–ness– 3. heedfulness, needfulness.
  4. unheedfulness, unneedfulness.
ED′i–a– 3. media.
  4. comedia, acedia.
  5. Fissipedia, cyclopedia, epicedia.
  6. pharmacopedia, encyclopedia.
ED′i–al– 3. medial, praedial.
  4. admedial, remedial, immedial, comedial.
  5. irremedial, intermedial, epicedial.
ED′i–an– 3. median.
  4. tragedian, symmedian, comedian.
  5. cosymmedian.
  6. encyclopedian.
ED′i–ate– 3. mediate.
  5. intermediate.
ED′i–ens– 4. obedience, expedience, expedients, ingredients.
  5. nonobedience, disobedience, inexpedience.
ED′i–ent– 4. obedient, impedient, expedient, digredient, ingredient.
  5. unobedient, disobedient, inexpedient.
ED′i–er– 3. beadier, needier, speedier, reedier, greedier, seedier, weedier.
ED′i–est– 3. beadiest, neediest, speediest, reediest, greediest, seediest, weediest.
ED′i–it– 4. immediate.
  5. intermediate.
ED′i–lee– 3. beadily, needily, speedily, reedily, greedily, weedily.
ED′i–ness– 3. beadiness, neediness, speediness, reediness, greediness, seediness, weediness.
ED′ing–lee– 3. heedingly, pleadingly.
  4. unheedingly, misleadingly, exceedingly.
ED′i–um– 3. medium, tedium.
  4. soredium.
  5. intermedium, epicedium.
ED′i–us– 3. medius, tedious.
  5. intermedius.
ED′less–lee– 3. heedlessly, needlessly.
EF′i–ness– 3. beefiness, leafiness, reefiness.
EG′al–ee– 3. legally, regally.
  4. illegally.
EG′al–ness– 3. legalness, regalness.
  4. illegalness.
EG′er–lee– 3. eagerly, meagerly.
  4. uneagerly.
EG′er–ness– 3. eagerness, meagerness.
  4. uneagerness.
  5. overeagerness.
E′it–ee– 3. deity, seity.

4. plebeity, tableity, velleity, omneity, aseity, gaseity, ipseity, multeity.
5. extraneity, spontaneity, femineity, personeity, corporeity.
6. simultaneity, instantaneity, momentaneity, incorporeity.
7. contemporaneity.
EJ'ens–ee– 3. regency.
4. vice-regency.
EJ'i–an– 4. collegian, Fuegian, Norwegian.
EJ'–ium– 4. collegium.
5. florilegium.
EJ'us–ness– 4. egregiousness.
5. sacrilegiousness.
EK'a–bl– 3. speakable.
4. unspeakable.
EK'i–lee– 3. beakily, cheekily, leakily, sleekily, sneakily, creakily, squeakily.
EK'i–ness– 3. beakiness, cheekiness, leakiness, sneakiness, creakiness, squeakiness.
EK'ish–ness– 3. cheekishness, cliquishness, sneakishness, freakishness.
EK'wen–see– 3. frequency, sequency.
4. infrequency.
EK'wi–al– 4. obsequial, exequial.
EL'a–bl– 3. dealable, feelable, healable, peelable, reelable, sealable, stealable.
4. unhealable, congealable, annealable, appealable, repealable, concealable, revealable.
5. unconcealable, unrevealable.
EL'i–a– 3. Elia, Delia, Lelia, Celia, Caelia, coelia.
4. lobelia, Bedelia, Cordelia, Ophelia, Amelia, Hamelia, cimelia, Cornelia, Karelia, Aurelia; *see also* **ĒL'ya.**
EL'i–an– 3. Elian, Delian, Caelian.
4. Hegelian, carnelian, Karelian, aurelian.
6. Mephistophelean, Aristotelian.
EL'i–on– 3. Pelion.
4. aphelion, parhelion, chameleon, anthelion.
5. perihelion.
EL'i–us– 3. Delius, Helios.
4. Cornelius, Aurelius.
5. contumelius.
EM'a–bl– 3. beamable, reamable, dreamable, creamable, seamable, steamable.
4. redeemable, esteemable.
EM'a–tist– 3. schematist, thematist.
EM'er–ee– 3. dreamery, creamery.
EM'i–a– 3. Nemea.
4. Euphemia, Bohemia, leukemia, anemia, paroemia, toxemia.
5. diarhemia, diarrhaemia.
EM'i–al– 3. cnemial, gremial.
4. endemial, vindemial, proemial, paroemial.
EM'i–an– 4. Bohemian.
5. academian.
EM'i–er– 3. beamier, gleamier, dreamier, creamier, premier, steamier.
EM'i–lee– 3. beamily, gleamily, dreamily, creamily, steamily.
EM'i–ness– 3. beaminess, gleaminess, dreaminess, creaminess, steaminess.
EM'ing–lee– 3. beamingly, gleamingly, dreamingly, seemingly.
4. beseemingly, unseemingly.
EM'i–um– 3. premium.
4. proemium, gelsemium.
EN'a–bl– 3. leanable, gleanable, meanable, weanable.
4. amenable, convenable, unweanable.
EN'er–ee– 3. deanery, plenary, greenery, scenery.
4. machinery.
EN'i–a– 3. taenia, xenia.
4. gardenia, Eugenia, Birkenia, Armenia.
5. neomenia, neurasthenia, schizophrenia.
EN'i–al– 3. genial, splenial, menial, taenial, venial, xenial.
4. congenial, demesnial.
5. uncongenial, primigenial, homogeneal.
EN'i–an– 3. Fenian.
4. Hellenian, Armenian, Cyrenian, sirenian, Athenian, parthenian, Ruthenian.
5. Esselenian, neomenian.
EN'i–ens– 3. lenience.
4. prevenience, convenience.
5. inconvenience, intervenience.
EN'i–ent– 3. lenient.
4. advenient, prevenient, convenient.
5. inconvenient, supervenient, intervenient.
EN'i–er– 3. beanier, spleenier, sheenier, teenier, weenier.
EN'i–um– 3. rhenium, xenium.
4. selenium, solenium, proscenium, postscenium.
5. calistheneum.
EN'i–us– 3. genius, splenius.
4. ingenious, arsenious.
5. homogeneous, pergameneous.
6. heterogeneous.
EN'yen–see– 3. leniency.
4. conveniency.
5. inconveniency.
EN'yent–lee– 3. leniently.
4. conveniently.
5. inconveniently.
E'o–krat– 3. rheocrat, theocrat.
E'o–la– 4. areola, roseola, alveola, foveola.
E'o–lus– 3. Aeolus.
4. malleolus, nucleolus, alveolus.
EP'i–ad– 4. asclepiad, Asclepiad.
EP'i–lee– 3. sleepily, creepily, weepily.
EP'i–ness– 3. sleepiness, creepiness, steepiness, weepiness.
ER'e–al– 3. cereal.
4. sidereal, funereal, ethereal; *see also* **ĒR'i–al.**
ER'en–see– 4. adherency, inherency, coherency.
5. incoherency.
ER'ful–ee– 3. cheerfully, fearfully, tearfully.
ER'ful–ness– 3. cheerfulness, fearfulness, tearfulness.
ER'i–a– 3. eria, feria, Scleria.
4. Iberia, Liberia, Siberia, Egeria, Nigeria, Algeria, Elyria, Hesperia, bacteria, criteria, asteria, hysteria, wisteria, diphtheria.

5. cafeteria, acroteria, Anthesteria, Eleutheria.

ER′i–ad– 3. myriad, nereid, period.
4. anteriad, posteriad.

ER′i–al– 3. ferial, serial, cereal.
4. aerial, sidereal, funereal, imperial, biserial, material, bacterial, arterial, asterial, ethereal, diphtherial.
5. managerial, immaterial, monasterial, magisterial, ministerial, presbyterial.

ER′i–an– 3. Erian.
4. aerian, Iberian, Liberian, Siberian, Algerian, Pierian, valerian, Cimmerian, Wagnerian, Shakespearean, Hesperian, vesperian, Spencerian, Spenserian, psalterian, trouserian.
5. Luciferian, Presbyterian, philotherian, Eleutherian; *see also* **ĒR′i–on.**

ER′i–er– 3. eerier, beerier, cheerier, blearier, drearier, tearier, wearier, *see also* **ĒR′i–or.**

ER′i–est– 3. eeriest, beeriest, cheeriest, bleariest, dreariest, teariest, weariest.

ER′i–form– 3. spheriform, Seriform.
4. viperiform.

ER′i–lee– 3. eerily, beerily, cheerily, blearily, drearily, tearily, wearily.

ER′i–ness– 3. eeriness, beeriness, cheeriness, bleariness, dreariness, teariness, weariness.

ER′ing–lee– 3. cheeringly, fearingly, jeeringly, peeringly.
4. endearingly.
5. domineeringly.

ER′i–o– 3. cheerio, serio.

ER′i–on– 3. allerion, Hyperion, criterion; *see also* **ĒR′i–an.**

ER′i–or– 4. inferior, superior, ulterior, anterior, interior, exterior, posterior; *see also* **ĒR′i–er.**

ER′i–um– 3. cerium.
4. imperium, bacterium, psalterium.
5. desiderium, elaterium, acroterium, magisterium.

ER′i–us– 3. Cereus, cereous, serious.
4. imperious, mysterious, ethereous.
5. jocoserious, deleterious.

ER′less–lee– 3. beerlessly, cheerlessly, fearlessly, peerlessly.

ER′less–ness– 3. beerlessness, cheerlessness, fearlessness, peerlessness.

ES′a–bl– 3. leasable, peaceable, creasable, ceasable.
4. releasable, increasable, unceasable.

ES′en–see– 3. decency, recency.
4. indecency.

ES′ent–lee– 3. decently, recently.
4. indecently.

ESH′i–a– 4. silesia, Silesia, telesia, Helvetia.
5. Polynesia, alopecia.

ESH′i–an– 3. Decian, Grecian.
4. Silesian, Venetian, Lutetian, Helvetian.

ESH′i–ate– 4. appreciate, depreciate.

ESH′un–al– 4. secretional, concretional.

ESH′us–ness– 3. speciousness.
4. facetiousness.

ES′i–er– 3. fleecier, greasier, creasier.

ES′ing–lee– 4. decreasingly, increasingly, unceasingly.

ES′iv–lee– 4. adhesively, inhesively, cohesively.

EST′i–ness– 3. reastiness, yeastiness.

EST′li–ness– 3. beastliness, priestliness.

ET′a–bl– 3. eatable, beatable, cheatable, heatable, treatable, seatable.
4. uneatable, unbeatable, escheatable, defeatable, deletable, repeatable, entreatable.
5. undefeatable, unrepeatable.

ET′ed–lee– 3. heatedly.
4. repeatedly.

ETH′e–an– 3. Lethean.
4. Promethean.

ET′i–ness– 3. meatiness, peatiness, sleetiness.

ET′or–ee– 4. depletory, repletory, completory, secretory.

EV′a–bl– 3. cleavable, grievable.
4. achievable, believable, relievable, retrievable, deceivable, receivable, conceivable, perceivable.
5. unbelievable, irretrievable, undeceivable, inconceivable, imperceivable.

EV′a–blee– 4. believably, retrievably, conceivably, perceivably.
5. unbelievably, irretrievably, inconceivably, imperceivably.

EV′i–ate– 3. deviate.
4. alleviate, abbreviate.

EV′ish–lee– 3. peevishly, thievishly.

EV′ish–ness– 3. peevishness, thievishness.

EV′i–us– 3. devious, previous.

EZ′a–bl– 3. feasible, freezable, seizable, squeezable.
4. defeasible, cohesible, appeasable.
5. indefeasible, inappeasable, unappeasable.

EZH′i–a– 3. Freesia.
4. Zambesia, Rhodesia, Silesia, ecclesia, magnesia, amnesia, trapezia, parrhesia, esthesia.
5. anesthesia.

EZH′i–an– 4. Ephesian, Silesian, trapezian, ecclesian, etesian, artesian.

EZ′i–a– 4. algesia, esthesia.

EZ′i–er– 3. easier, cheesier, sleazier, breezier, greasier, queasier, wheezier.
4. uneasier.

EZ′i–est– 3. easiest, cheesiest, sleaziest, breeziest, greasiest, queasiest, wheeziest.
4. uneasiest.

EZ′i–lee– 3. easily, cheesily, sleazily, sneezily, breezily, greasily, queasily, wheezily.
4. uneasily.

EZ′i–ness– 3. easiness, cheesiness, sleaziness, breeziness, greasiness, wheeziness, queasiness.
4. uneasiness.

EZ′ing–lee– 3. pleasingly, sneezingly, freezingly, teasingly, wheezingly.
4. displeasingly, appeasingly.

EZ′on–al– 3. seasonal.
4. unseasonal.

EZ′on–er– 3. reasoner, seasoner.

EZ′on–ing– 3. reasoning, seasoning.
4. unreasoning.

Ĕ (heh)

Single (Masculine) Rhymes

Primary or Secondary Accent Falls on Last Syllable; Imperfect Rhymes Are in Italics.

E– 1. heh, yeh [slang.].
2. effet [F.], briquet.
3. en effet [F.], à peu près [F.].
4. estaminet [F.].
EB– 1. ebb, deb, Geb, keb, Keb, bleb, pleb, Sleb, neb, reb, theb, web.
2. zibeb [obs.], cubeb, subdeb [coll.], *blackneb, cobweb.*
3. coulterneb.
EBD– 1. ebbed, kebbed, blebbed, nebbed, webbed.
2. *cobwebbed.*
EBZ– *see* **ĔB**, plus " s " or " 's "; 1. Debs.
ECH– 1. etch, fetch, ketch, sketch, letch, fletch, cletch, retch, wretch, stretch, tech [dial.], tetch [dial.], quetch [dial.], quetsch, vetch.
2. outstretch.
3. photoetch, bitter vetch.
ECHD– 1. etched, fetched, sketched, fletched, retched, stretched, teched [dial], quetched [dial.].
2. far-fetched, outstretched.
3. photoetched.
ED– 1. Ed, ed [slang], bed, dead, fed, ged, gedd, Ged, head, jed, ked, led, lead, bled, fled, gled [Scot.], plead, pled, sled, Ned, snead, t'nead [Scot.], ped, sped, red, redd, med [slang], read, bred, bread, dread, Fred, spread, shred, tread, thread, said, shed, ted, Ted, stead, wed, 'stead, zed.
2. co-ed, abed, embed, imbed, *hotbed*, wellfed, unfed, ahead, *deadhead, redhead, roundhead, godhead,* behead, *blackhead, blockhead, bulkhead, ramhead, drumhead, bonehead, towhead, drophead, spearhead, forehead, sorehead, hogshead, hothead,* bebled, *bobsled,* mislead, pre-med [slang], *biped,* reread, misread, outread, *highbred, homebred,* inbred, *lowbred, purebred, crossbred, sweetbread, shortbread, truebred, Alfred, Wilfred,* widespread, bespread, well-spread, outspread, retread, rethread, unthread, resaid, gainsaid, unsaid, *bloodshed,*

bedstead, roadstead, bestead, *homestead, farmstead,* instead, rewed, unwed.
3. truckle bed, trundle bed, feather bed, flower bed, underfed, marblehead, bufflehead, fountainhead, dragonhead, arrowhead, dunderhead, thunderhead, logger head, copperhead, overhead, figurehead, bullet-head, aliped, taliped, cheliped, milliped, soliped, remiped, semiped, palmiped, plumiped, pinniped, uniped, serriped, cirriped, fissiped, multiped, breviped, octoped, quadruped, thoroughbred, raisin bread, underbred, gingerbread, overbred, Winifred, Aethelred, underspread, overspread, *aforesaid,* watershed.
4. maxilliped, salt-rising bread.
6. parallelepiped; *also the past tense and past participle of regular verbs ending in " d " or " t "* (e.g. garlanded, coveted).
EDTH– 1. breadth.
2. *hairbreadth, hairsbreadth.*
EF– 1. f, F, ef, eff, deaf, def [slang], feoff, jeff, Jeff, clef, nef, ref [slang], bref [F.], chef.
2. enfeoff, en bref [F.].
EFT– 1. eft, deft, feoffed, heft, jeffed, left, cleft, klepht, reft, theft, weft, wheft.
2. enfeoffed, infeft, aleft, unleft, bereft.
3. unbereft.
EG– 1. egg, beg, keg, skeg, leg, cleg, gleg, Meg, sneg, peg, reg [slang], dreg, seg, teg, yegg [slang].
2. peg leg, *blackleg, bowleg, proleg, foreleg, nutmeg,* unpeg, *goose egg.*
3. philabeg, atabeg, filibeg, beglerbeg, Winnipeg, Silas Wegg [Dickens].
EGZ– *see* **ĔG**, plus " s " or " 's "; 1. Meggs.
2. sea legs.
4. *daddy longlegs.*
EJ– 1. edge, hedge, kedge, skedge, ledge, fledge, cledge, gledge [Scot.], pledge, sledge, dredge, sedge, tedge, wedge.
2. unedge, allege, impledge.
3. reallege, interpledge, sacrilege, privilege.

EJD– 1. edged, hedged, kedged, ledged, fledged, pledged, sledged, dredged, sedged, wedged.
2. two-edged, unfledged, alleged, impledged, unpledged.
3. double-edged, deckle-edged, privileged.
5. underprivileged.

EK– 1. ec [slang], beck, checque, check, Czech, deck, feck, geck, heck, haec, keck, lec, leck, lech, lek, fleck, cleck, smeck [slang], neck, sneck, peck, speck, spec [slang], reck, wreck, brek, trek, sec, tec, tech, teck.
2. home-ec [slang], *pinchbeck*, Quebec, re-check, bedeck, *foredeck, roughneck, wryneck, blackneck, breakneck, crookneck, swanneck*, sapek, *henpeck, flyspeck, shipwreck,* parsec.
3. Kennebec, countercheck, bottleneck, rubberneck, leatherneck, à la grecque [F.], discothèque [F.].
4. bibliothèque [F.].

EKS– *see* **ĔK,** plus " s " or " 's "; 1. x, X, ex, faex [L.], hex, kex, lex, flex, plex, spex, specs, rex, Rex, prex, sex, vex.
2. *index, codex,* deflex, *reflex, biflex,* inflex, *diplex, triplex,* complex, *simplex,* perplex, *duplex,* annex, connex, *apex,* unsex, *Essex, Sussex, vortex,* convex.
3. dorsiflex, circumflex, retroflex, genuflex, contraplex, nulliplex, veniplex, multiplex, disannex.

EKST– 1. hexed, flexed, next, sexed, sext, text, vexed.
2. annexed, perplexed, unsexed, pretext, *context.*
3. genuflexed.

EKT– 1. becked, checked, decked, flecked, flect, necked, pecked, specked, recked, wrecked, trekked, sect.
2. unchecked, bedecked, affect, effect, defect, refect, *prefect,* infect, perfect, traject, abject, subject, adject, eject, deject, reject, inject, conject, project, disject, elect, prelect, se-lect, deflect, reflect, inflect, neglect, col-lect, *crooknecked,* connect, respect, inspect, *prospect,* expect, suspect, arrect, erect, di-rect, correct, porrect, bisect, dissect, tran-sect, detect, contect, protect.
3. disaffect, misaffect, disinfect, retroject, interject, dialect, analect, re-elect, nonelect, intellect, circumflect, genuflect, recollect, reconnect, disconnect, self-respect, disre-spect, circumspect, retrospect, introspect, indirect, misdirect, incorrect, resurrect, in-surrect, intersect, architect.

EKTS– 1. sects.
2. affects, effects, *defects,* infects, perfects, trajects, subjects, adjects, ejects, dejects, rejects, injects, conjects, projects, disjects, elects, prelects, selects, deflects, reflects, inflects, neglects, collects, connects, respects, inspects, *prospects,* expects, suspects, arrects, erects, directs, corrects, porrects, bisects, dissects, transects, detects, contects, pro-tects.
3. disaffects, misaffects, disinfects, retrojects, interjects, dialects, analects, re-elects, intel-lects, circumflects, genuflects, recollects, reconnects, disconnects, disrespects, retro-spects, introspects, misdirects, resurrects, insurrects, intersects, architects.

EL– 1. l, L, el, El, ell, bel, Bel, bell, belle, Belle, dell, fell, hell, Hel, jell, gel, kell, mel, mell, smell, Nell, knell, snell, schnell [G.], pell, spell, rel, cell, sell, shell, tell, well, dwell, swell, quell, yell, zel.
2. gabelle, rebel, *dumbbell,* Nobel, *harebell, corbeil, bluebell, cowbell,* chandelle [F.], rondell, *sardelle,* cordelle, befell, refel, miel [F.], pall-mall, pell-mell, Carmel, quenelle, spinel, Cornell, prunelle, noel, Noel, appel [F.], lapel, rappel [F.], repel, *scalpel,* impel, com-pel, propel, dispel, expel, respell, misspell, morel, nacelle, resell, ficelle, pucelle, excel, encell, Moselle, marcel, échelle [F.], *bomb-shell, sea shell,* unshell, *nutshell,* retell, bre-telle, hotel, artel, cartel, foretell, cuartel [Sp.] *inkwell,* unwell, farewell, indwell, gazelle.
3. Annabel, Annabelle, mirabelle, Isabel, Jezebel, bonnibel, citadel, infidel, hirondelle, hydrogel, aguamiel [Sp.], parallel, caramel, bechamel, philomel, fontanel, fustanelle, sentinel, jargonelle, personnel, pimpernel, ritornel, mackerel, pickerel, nonpareil, aqua-relle, chanterelle [F.], pipistrel, unicell, undersell, oversell, carrousel, cockleshell, bagatelle, brocatel, muscatel, Neufchâtel, immortelle, caravel, demoiselle.
4. matériel, mademoiselle.
6. Canterbury bell, A.W.O.L.

ELB– 1. elb, skelb.

ELCH– 1. belch, keltch [slang], welsh, Welsh, quelch, squelch [both slang].

ELD– 1. eld, belled, felled, geld, held, helled, jelled, keld, meld, smelled, knelled, snelled, pelled, spelled, celled, shelled, welled, weld, dwelled, swelled, quelled, yeld, yelled, fjeld.
2. rebelled, beheld, upheld, withheld, repel-led, impelled, compelled, propelled, dispel-led, expelled, respelled, misspelled, excelled, marcelled, unquelled.
3. unicelled, parallelled.
4. unparallelled.

ELF– 1. elf, delf, pelf, self, shelf, Guelph.
2. *didelph,* myself, thyself, himself, oneself, herself, ourself, yourself, itself.

ELFT– 1. delft, Delft, pelfed, selfed.

ELK– 1. elk, whelk, yelk.

ELM– 1. elm, helm, realm, whelm.
2. unhelm, dishelm, Anselm.
3. overwhelm.

ELP– 1. help, kelp, skelp, whelp, swelp, yelp.
2. self-help.

ELT– 1. elt [dial.], belt, dealt, felt, gelt, kelt, Celt, Kelt, melt, smelt, knelt, pelt, spelt, celt, Celt, veld, veldt, svelte, welt, dwelt.
2. unbelt, misdealt, *homefelt,* unfelt, *heartfelt,* remelt, undwelt.

ELTH– 1. health, stealth, wealth.
3. commonwealth.
ELTS– 1. elts [dial.], belts, Celts, kelts, melts, smelts, pelts, welts.
2. unbelts, remelts.
ELV– 1. delve, helve, shelve, twelve.
ELVD– 1. delved, helved, shelved.
ELVZ– 1. elves, delves, helves, selves, shelves, twelves.
2. themselves, ourselves, yourselves.
ELZ– *see* **ĔL,** plus " s " or " 's "; 1. Welles, Wells.
2. Lascelles.
3. Dardanelles.
EM– 1. m, M, em, 'em, Em, Emm, Dem., fem, feme, hem, gem, kemb, chem [slang], Lem, phlegm, Flem, Clem, clem, mem, crème [F.], sem [slang], Shem, Tem, stem, them.
2. condemn, begem, ahem, quand même [F.], ad rem [L.], in rem [L.], *semsem*, contemn, protem, *pipestem*, ad quem [L.], *Zemzem*.
3. anadem, diadem, Bethlehem, requiem, stratagem, theorem, apothem, apothegm.
4. ad hominem [L.].
EMP– 1. hemp, kemp, Kemp, temp.
2. *kohemp*.
EMPT– 1. empt, kempt, dreamt, tempt.
2. pre-empt, coempt, adempt, unkempt, undreamt, perempt, attempt, retempt, contempt, exempt.
EMZ– *see* **ĔM,** plus " s " or " 's "; 1. Thames, temse.
EN– 1. n, N, en, ben, Ben, benn, Chen, den, fen, hen, gen [slang], Jen, ken, Ken, Len, glen, men, pen, wren, sen, Shen, ten, then, wen, when, yen, Zen.
2. Big Ben, *benben*, again, sans gène [F.], *peahen*, beken, amen, *seamen, horsemen, Norsemen, Bushmen, Northmen, pigpen*, impen, *cowpen*, marraine [F.], cayenne, Cheyenne.
3. oxygen, endogen, halogen, nitrogen, prairie hen, water hen, Magdalen, cyclamen, specimen, partimen, gentlemen, aldermen, Englishmen, Darien, julienne, brevipen, fountain pen, poison pen, Saracen, mise en scène [F.], denizen, citizen.
4. tragedienne, comedienne, sicilienne, éolienne [F.], Tyrolienne, equestrienne, Valenciennes, Parisienne [F.].
ENCH– 1. bench, kench, blench, flench, clench, drench, French, trench, wrench, tench, stench, wench, quench, squench.
2. unbench, disbench, unclench, bedrench, retrench, intrench.
3. monkey wrench.
END– 1. end, bend, fend, kenned, lend, blend, blende, mend, pend, penned, spend, rend, friend, trend, send, shend, tend, vend, wend, Zend.
2. upend, rebend, *prebend*, unbend, *addend*, defend, offend, forfend, *pitchblende, hornblende*, amend, emend, remend, commend, ap-

pend, depend, *stipend*, impend, *compend*, unpenned, perpend, misspend, expend, suspend, befriend, girl friend, boy friend, ascend, descend, *godsend*, transcend, attend, subtend, pretend, intend, contend, portend, extend, distend, ostend, Ostend, Land's End.
3. dividend, subtrahend, apprehend, reprehend, comprehend, recommend, discommend, vilipend, reverend, childhood friend, college friend, condescend, repetend, coextend minuend.
4. misapprehend, miscomprehend, superintend.
ENG– 1. dreng, drengh, kreng, sheng.
2. *thameng, ginseng, banteng*.
ENGTH– 1. length, strength.
2. full length, full strength.
ENJ– 2. *Stonehenge*, avenge, revenge.
ENJD– 2. avenged, revenged.
3. unavenged.
ENS– 1. ense [Scot.], dense, fence, hence, flense, mense [Scot. and N. of Eng.], pence, pense [obs.], Spence, cense, sense, tense, thence, vence [slang], whence.
2. condense, defense, defence, offense, herehence, immense, commence, prepense, *threepence*, propense, *sixpence, twopence*, dispense, expense, suspense, incense, *nonsense*, subtense, pretense, intense.
3. accidence, incidence, diffidence, confidence, subsidence, residence, dissidence, evidence, providence, impudence, recondense, self-defense, indigence, negligence, diligence, exigence, audience, prurience, excellence, prevalence, pestilence, redolence, indolence, condolence, violence, somnolence, insolence, turbulence, flocculence, succulence, truculence, fraudulence, opulence, corpulence, virulence, purulence, flatulence, lutulence, vehemence, recommence, immanence, permanence, eminence, imminence, prominence, continence, pertinence, abstinence, recompense, deference, reference, preference, difference, inference, conference, reverence, reticence, innocence, frankincense, commonsense, competence, appetence, penitence, impotence, refluence, affluence, effluence, influence, confluence, subsequence, consequence, eloquence, congruence.
4. self-confidence, coincidence, improvidence, nonresidence, malevolence, preeminence, obedience, expedience, ebulience, experience, subservience, intelligence, equivalence, insomnolence, benevolence, impermanence, incontinence, impertinence, indifference, circumference, belligerence, irreverence, beneficence, magnificence, munificence, incompetence, inappetence, impenitence, omnipotence, inconsequence, incongruence, grandiloquence, magniloquence.
ENST– 1. fenced, flensed, mensed, sensed, censed, tensed.

2. against, condensed, commenced, anenst, fornenst, dispensed, incensed, unsensed.

3. evidenced, recondensed, uncondensed, recommenced, recompensed, reverenced, influenced.

4. experienced, unrecompensed, cross-referenced, unreverenced, uninfluenced.

5. inexperienced.

ĔNT– 1. bent, dent, fent, Ghent, hent, gent, Kent, kent, lent, Lent, leant, blent, meant, pent, spent, rent, brent, Trent, sent, cent, scent, tent, stent, vent, went.

2. unbent, indent, relent, Ament, lament, dement, cement, augment, unmeant, foment, ferment, torment, anent, fornent, repent, forespent, misspent, unspent, resent, present, assent, ascent, descent, missent, dissent, unsent, concent, consent, docent, detent, intent, content, distent, extent, ostent, event, prevent, invent, frequent.

3. accident, occident, incident, diffident, confident, subsident, evident, provident, impudent, indigent, negligent, diligent, dirigent, corrigent, transigent, exigent, attrahent, contrahent, ambient, gradient, audient, salient, emollient, lenient, sapient, orient, prurient, prevalent, pestilent. excellent, violent, somnolent, insolent, turbulent, fraudulent, flocculent, succulent, esculent, luculent, muculent, truculent, opulent, corpulent, querulent, virulent, purulent, flatulent, lutulent, ligament, parliament, armament, firmament, ornament, tournament, sacrament, testament, management, vehement, element, implement, complement, supplement, tenement, increment, excrement, cerement, banishment, garnishment, punishment, nourishment, lavishment, ravishment, pediment, sediment, condiment, rudiment, regiment, aliment, compliment, liniment, merriment, worriment, flurriment, detriment, nutriment, sentiment, revelment, devilment, government, wonderment, document, tegument, argument, monument, instrument, remanent, immanent, permanent, thereanent, eminent, imminent, prominent, continent, pertinent, abstinent, underspent, overspent, deferent, preferent, afferent, efferent, different, reverent, Millicent, reticent, heaven-sent, innocent, competent, appetent, penitent, malcontent, affluent, effluent, refluent, confluent, congruent, subsequent, circumvent, underwent, represent.

4. coincident, improvident, intelligent, obedient, expedient, ingredient, convenient, recipient, accipient, incipient, percipient, aperient, parturient, subservient, equivalent, benevolent, malevolent, lineament, medicament, predicament, disarmament, temperament, disablement, ennoblement, bemuddlement, inveiglement, entanglement, disparagement, acknowledgment, abolishment, replenishment, diminishment, accomplishment, admonishment, relinquishment, presentiment, bedevilment, enlightenment, abandonment, apportionment, evironment, imprisonment, dismemberment, bewilderment, embitterment, accouterment, beleaguerment, encompassment, embarrassment, advertisement, aggrandizement, impermanent, incontinent, impertinent, indifferent, belligerent, irreverent, Privatdocent [G.], misrepresent, beneficent, magnificent, munificent, incompetent, impenitent, plenipotent, omnipotent, mellifluent, circumfluent, constituent, inconsequent, grandiloquent, magniloquent.

5. circumambient, disobedient, impoverishment, accompaniment, disillusionment.

ĔNTH– 1. tenth.

2. *seventh, dozenth.*

3. *eleventh.*

ĔNTS– *see* **ĔNT,** plus " s " or " 's "; 2. Coblentz.

ĔNZ– *see* **ĔN,** plus " s " or " 's "; 1. ense [Scot.], gens, lens, cleanse.

4. Valenciennes.

ĔNZD– 1. lensed, cleansed.

ĔP– 1. chep [slang], dep [slang], hep [slang], skep, clep, slep, nep, pep, rep, prep [slang], strep [slang], step, steppe, yep [slang], zep [slang].

2. *madnep, catnep, instep,* unstep, *stairstep,* misstep, *catstep, footstep.*

3. demirep, overstep.

ĔPT– 1. kept, slept, pepped, crept, sept, stepped, wept, swept.

2. adept, unkept, y-clept, inept, accept, *precept, concept, percept,* discept, except, suscept, unwept, unswept.

3. *preconcept,* intercept.

4. biblioklept, intussuscept.

ER– through **ĔRZ,** *see* **Ŭ** (tub); **ŬR** through **ŬRZ.**

ĔS– 1. s, S, es, ess, Bes, Bess, chess, dess, fess, fesse, 'fess, guess, Hess, jess, less, bless, mess, ness, pess [dial.], dress, cress, press, tress, stress, cess, sess, Tess, yes.

2. frondesce, confess, profess, quiesce, largesse, rejess, unjess, rebless, noblesse, unless, *kermess,* finesse, caress, address, *headdress,* redress, undress, egress, regress, digress, ingress, progress, transgress, accresce, depress, repress, impress, compress, oppress, suppress, express, distress, duress, assess, obsess, success, recess, precess, princesse, *princess,* possess, comtesse [F.], tristesse [F.].

3. SOS, incandesce, acquiesce, recalesce, coalesce, opalesce, convalesce, nonetheless, luminesce, baroness, readdress, maladdress, underdress, overdress, allegress [F.], retrogress, water cress, phosphoresce, effloresce, fluoresce, recompress, understress, overstress, reassess, repossess, prepossess, dispossess, politesse [F.], effervesce, deliquesce.

4. nevertheless, reconvalesce, rejuvenesce, ambassadress; *also all adjectives composed* of noun plus suffix "-less" (e. g. motionless, passionless); *all nouns composed of adjective plus suffix "-ness"* (e. g. tardiness, toothsomeness); *all nouns made feminine by the addition of the suffix "-ess"* (e. g. stewardess, poetess).

ESH– 1. hesh [slang], flesh, flèche, mesh, spesh [slang], fresh, crèche, thresh, sesh [slang].
2. calèche [F.], *horseflesh*, enmesh, afresh, unfresh, refresh, rethresh, secesh.

ESK– 1. esk [slang], desk.
2. burlesque, Moresque, grotesque.
3. arabesque, Romanesque, barbaresque, picaresque, chivalresque, humoresque, plateresque, picturesque, sculpturesque, statuesque.

EST– 1. est, best, chest, fessed, fest, guest, guessed, hest, gest, geste, jest, lest, blest, blessed, messed, nest, pest, rest, wrest, Brest, breast, dressed, crest, pressed, tressed, stressed, cest, cessed, test, vest, west, quest, yessed, zest.
2. Trieste, infest, behest, suggest, digest, ingest, congest, beau geste [F.], celeste, Celeste, molest, unblest, funest, impest, arrest, caressed, *headrest, bookrest,* unrest, *footrest,* abreast, *redbreast, blackbreast,* addressed, redressed, undressed, regressed, digressed, transgressed, progressed, *firecrest,* depressed, repressed, impressed, compressed, oppressed, suppressed, expressed, distressed, prestressed, assessed, Alceste, obsessed, recessed, possessed, attest, obtest, detest, retest, pretest, contest, protest, divest, invest, bequest, request, inquest, Midwest, Key West, northwest, southwest.
3. factum est [L.], S O S-ed, second best, incandesced, manifest, counterfessed, acquiesced, redigest, predigest, recalesced, coalesced, opalesced, convalesced, luminesced, Budapest, anapest, Bucharest, readdressed, unredressed, underdressed, overdressed, interest, Everest, retrogressed, phosphoresced, effloresced, fluoresced, recompressed, uncompressed, unimpressed, raven-tressed, overstressed, reassessed, unassessed, repossessed, prepossessed, self-possessed, unpossessed, dispossessed, palimpsest, effervesced, deliquesced.
4. disinterest, j'y suis, j'y reste [F.].
7. dulce et decorum est [L.]; *also the superlative degree of all one-and two-syllable adjectives takes the suffix "-est"* (e. g. fastest, sweetest,

shoddiest).

ET– 1. et, bet, bête [F.], Chet, debt, fet, fête [F.], get, het [dial.], jet, ket, khet, let, Lett, blet, flet, plet [Russ.], met, net, pet, ret, bret, fret, frette, pret, tret, threat, set, sett, shet [dial.], tête [F.], stet, vet, wet, quet, sweat, whet, yet, nyet [Russ.].
2. layette, abet, Tibet, barbette, cadet, vedette, bidet, indebt, Odette, Claudette, baguette, baguet, beget, forget, plaquette, coquette, coquet, croquette, casquette, ailette, alette, galette [F.], sublet, Gilette, toilette, roulette, plumette, Nanette, Jeannette, dinette, Ginette, cornet, lunette, brunette, pipette, aret, barrette, umbrette, soubrette, aigrette, egret, regret, curette, chevrette, beset, reset, thickset, *quickset,* dancette, inset, pincette [F.], *onset, moonset, sunset,* upset, farset, outset, flechette, clochette, brochette, plushette, octet, en tête [F.], quintet, motet, septet, sestet, sextet, duet, revet, brevet, crevette [F.], bewet, vignette, lorgnette, gazette, rosette, musette.
3. oubliette, Joliet, Juliette, Hariette, Harriette, Henriette, storiette, serviette, alphabet, misbeget, suffragette, etiquette, tourniquet, flannelette, novelette, landaulet, rigolette, *quadruplet, quintuplet,* epaulet, cassolette, allumette [F.], pianette, villanette, castanet, cravenette, bobbinet, stockinet, clarinet, bassinet, martinet, Antoinette, minionette, mignonette, maisonette, saxcornet, tabaret, cigarette, Margaret, collaret, minaret, lazaret, pierrette [F.], farmerette, banneret, leatherette, interfret, vinaigrette, taboret, anisette, marmoset, overset, tête-à-tête, epithet, alouette [F.], silhouette, minuet, pirouette, statuette.

ETH– 1. eth, Beth, death, breath, saith, Seth, teth, steth [slang].
2. Macbeth.
3. shibboleth, twentieth, thirtieth, fortieth, fiftieth, sixtieth, eightieth, ninetieth.
4. seventieth.

ETS– *see* ĔT, plus "s" or "'s"; **1.** Mets, Metz.
2. Steinmetz.

EV– 1. Bev, chev, fève [F.], rev [slang], rêve [F.], trêve [F.].

EX–*see* ĔKS.

EZ–1. Ez, fez, mezz [slang], knez, prez [slang], says, sez [slang], yez [slang].
2. Juarez, Cortes, Suez.
5. à la hollandaise [F.].

EZH– 2. manège, barège [F.], cortege.

Ĕ (heh)

Double (Feminine) Rhymes

Primary or Secondary Accent Falls on Next to Last Syllable; Imperfect Rhymes Are in Italics.

EB′ee– 2. debby [slang], Debby, kebbie, kebby [both Scot. & N. of Eng.], blebby, nebby, webby.
3. *cobwebby.*

EB′er– 2. ebber, blebber [dial.], nebber [dial.], webber, Weber.
3. Von Weber.

EB′ing– 2. ebbing, kebbing, blebbing [dial.], nebbing [dial.], webbing.
3. unebbing, *cobwebbing.*

EB′it– 2. debit.
3. redebit.

EB′l– 2. debile, djebel, pebble, rebel, treble.
3. archrebel.

EB′lee– 2. pebbly, trebly.

ECH′ee– 2. fetchy, sketchy, stretchy, techy, tetchy, vetchy.

ECH′er– 2. etcher, fetcher, sketcher, lecher, fletcher, retcher, stretcher, quetcher.

ECH′ing– 2. etching, fetching, sketching, fletching, retching, stretching, quetching.
3. outstretching.

ED′a– 2. Edda, khedda, Ledda, Nedda, Vedda.

ED′al– 2. medal, pedal.
3. bipedal, tripedal.
4. fissipedal, equipedal; *see also* **ĔD′l.**

ED′ed– 2. bedded, headed, leaded, sledded, redded, breaded, dreaded, shredded, threaded, tedded, wedded.
3. embedded, imbedded, hardheaded, round-headed, beheaded, pigheaded, longheaded, weakheaded, thickheaded, shockheaded, coolheaded, bullheaded, bareheaded, clearheaded, fatheaded, flat-headed, lightheaded, softheaded, hotheaded, unleaded, unredded, unbreaded, unshredded, unthreaded, unwedded.
4. puddingheaded, many-headed, hoary-headed, heavy-headed, addleheaded, double-headed, muddleheaded, chuckleheaded, rattleheaded, levelheaded, arrowheaded, Janus-headed, interthreaded.

ED′ee– 2. eddy, Eddie, beddy, heady, leady, neddy, ready, reddy, bready, Freddie, spready, shreddy, thready, Teddy, teddy, steady.
3. already, unready, unsteady.

ED′en– 2. deaden, leaden, redden, threaden.
4. Armageddon.

ED′er– 2. edder, bedder, Cheddar, deader, header, leader, sledder, nedder, redder, dreader, spreader, shredder, threader, treader, shedder, tedder.
3. embedder, beheader, unthreader, retreader, *homesteader.*
4. double-header, triple-header.

ED′est– 2. deadest, reddest, dreadest.

ED′ful– 2. headful, dreadful.

ED′head– 2. *deadhead, redhead.*

ED′ing– 2. bedding, heading, leading, sledding, redding, breading, dreading, spreading, shredding, treading, threading, shedding, tedding, steading, wedding.
3. embedding, imbedding, beheading, bespreading, outspreading, retreading, rethreading, unthreading, *homesteading,* rewedding.
4. overspreading, golden wedding.

ED′ish– 2. eddish, beddish, deadish, reddish, breadish.

ED′it– 2. edit, credit.
3. subedit, reedit, accredit, discredit, miscredit.

ED′l– 2. heddle, meddle, medal, peddle, pedal, reddle, treadle.
3. repeddle, repedal, *bipedal, tripedal.*
4. intermeddle.

ED′lee– 2. deadly, medley, redly.

ED′ler– 2. heddler, meddler, medlar, pedlar, peddler, treadler.
4. intermeddler.

ED′less– 2. bedless, headless, leadless, sledless, redless, breadless, dreadless, shredless, treadless, threadless, shedless, tedless.
3. co-edless, *bulkheadless, bedsteadless, home-*

209

steadless.
ED'line– 2. deadline, headline, red line, bread-line.
ED'ling– 2. heddling, meddling, peddling, reddling, treadling.
4. intermeddling.
ED'lok– 2. deadlock, headlock, kedlock, wedlock.
ED'na– 2. Edna, Sedna.
ED'ness– 2. deadness, redness.
ED'o– 2. eddo, meadow.
ED'on– 4. Armageddon; *see also* ĔD'en.
ED'rest– 2. headrest, bed rest.
ED'ward– 2. Edward, bedward.
ED'wood– 2. deadwood, redwood.
ED'zo– 2. mezzo.
4. intermezzo.
EF'en– 2. deafen, Strephon.
EF'er– 2. deafer, feoffor, Pfeffer [G.], heifer, kefir, zephyr.
4. Hasenpfeffer [G.].
EF'ik– 2. brephic.
3. malefic, benefic.
4. peristrephic, isopsephic.
EFT'ee– 2. hefty, Kefti, Lefty.
EFT'er– 2. defter, hefter, lefter, clefter.
3. berefter.
EFT'est– 2. deftest, leftist, cleftest.
3. bereftest.
EFT'lee– 2. deftly.
3. bereftly.
EFT'ness– 2. deftness, leftness, cleftness.
3. bereftness.
EG'ee– 2. eggy, keggy, leggy, Peggy, dreggy, seggy.
EG'er– 2. egger, beggar, skegger, legger, pegger.
3. *bootlegger.*
EG'ing– 2. egging, begging, kegging, legging, pegging, segging.
3. unkegging, bootlegging, unpegging.
EG'nant– 2. regnant, pregnant.
EJ'ee– 2. edgy, hedgy, ledgy, fledgy, cledgy, sedgy, wedgy.
EJ'er– 2. edger, hedger, kedger, ledger, pledger, sledger, dredger.
3. alleger, repledger.
EJ'ez– 2. edges, hedges, kedges, ledges, fledges, cledges, pledges, sledges, dredges, sedges, tedges, wedges.
3. alleges, repledges, unwedges.
4. interpledges, sacrileges, privileges.
EJ'ing– 2. edging, hedging, kedging, ledging, fledging, pledging, sledging, dredging, wedging.
3. enhedging, alleging, repledging, impledging.
EJ'less– 2. edgeless, hedgeless, kedgeless, ledgeless, pledgeless, sledgeless, dredgeless, sedgeless, tedgeless, wedgeless.
4. privilegeless.
EJ'o– 2. seggio [It.].
3. solfeggio, arpeggio.
EK'a– 2. Ecca, ekka, Mecca.

3. sabeca, Rebecca.
EK'ee– 2. Becky, checky, kecky, flecky, pecky, specky, wrecky.
3. *shipwrecky.*
EK'er– 2. becker, decker, checker, chequer, gecker, flecker, necker, snecker, pecker, trekker, wrecker.
3. rechecker, bedecker, exchequer, *woodpecker,* *henpecker.*
4. double-decker.
EK'erd– 2. checkered, record.
EK'et– 2. becket, fecket.
5. Thomas à Becket.
EK'ing– 2. becking, decking, checking, flecking, necking, snecking, pecking, specking, recking, wrecking, trekking.
3. bedecking, *henpecking,* bewrecking, *shipwrecking.*
EK'ish– 2. heckish, peckish, wreckish.
EK'l– 2. deckle, heckle, Jeckyll, keckle, speckle, brekkle, freckle, Seckel, shekel.
3. bespeckle, befreckle.
EK'ld– 2. deckled, heckled, keckled, speckled, freckled.
3. bespeckled, befreckled.
EK'lee– 2. speckly, freckly.
EK'ler– 2. heckler, speckler, freckler.
EK'less– 2. beckless, checkless, deckless, feckless, geckless, fleckless, necklace, neckless, peckless, speckless, reckless, wreckless.
EK'ling– 2. deckling, heckling, keckling, speckling, reckling, freckling.
EK'mate– 2. checkmate, deckmate.
EK'nee– 4. theotechny, agrotechny, pyrotechny.
EK'nik– 2. technic.
3. pantechnic.
4. polytechnic, theotechnic, philotechnic, pyrotechnic.
EK'niks– 3. eutechnics.
4. pyrotechnics.
EK'nist– 4. polytechnist, theotechnist, philotechnist, pyrotechnist.
EK'o– 2. echo, bekko, dekko, gecko, secco [It.].
3. re-echo.
EK'on– 2. beckon, Becken, flecken, reckon.
EK'ond– 2. beckoned, fleckened, reckoned, second.
EKS'a– 3. adnexa, annexa.
EKS'al– 2. plexal, nexal.
3. adnexal, annexal.
EKS'as– *see* ĔKS'us.
EKS'ee– 2. ecce [L.], kexy, prexy, sexy.
4. cataplexy, apoplexy.
EKS'er– 2. hexer, flexor, vexer.
3. *indexer,* annexer, perplexer.
4. dorsiflexor.
EKSH'un– 2. lection, flection, section, vection.
3. affection, defection, refection, effection, infection, confection, profection, perfection, abjection, adjection, trajection, ejection, dejection, rejection, injection, projection,

election, prelection, selection, deflection, reflection, inflection, dilection, collection, bolection, complexion, connection, inspection, prospection, erection, direction, correction, resection, bisection, trisection, dissection, insection, exsection, detection, protection, evection, invection, convection, provection.

4. disaffection, reinfection, disinfection, imperfection, insubjection, interjection, dorsiflexion, circumflexion, genuflection, predilection, intellection, recollection, reconnection, disconnection, circumspection, retrospection, introspection, redirection, indirection, misdirection, resurrection, insurrection, venesection, hemisection, vivisection, intersection, quarter section.

EKSH′ur– **2.** flexure, plexure.
3. deflexure, inflexure, complexure.
4. contraflexure.

EKSH′us– **3.** infectious, selectious.

EKS–ile– **2.** exile, flexile.

EKS′ing– **2.** X-ing, hexing, flexing, sexing, vexing.
3. inflexing, unflexing, complexing, perplexing, *duplexing*, annexing, unsexing, convexing.

EKS′is– **3.** Alexis, orexis, syntexis, cathexis.
4. catalexis, epiplexis.

EKS′lee– **3.** complexly, convexly.

EKS′tant– **2.** extant, sextant.

EKS′tile– **2.** sextile, textile.
3. bissextile.

EKS′us– **2.** plexus, nexus, Texas.
3. complexus, connexus.
4. solar plexus.

EKT′al– **2.** ectal, rectal, tectal.
4. dialectal.

EKT′ant– **3.** infectant, reflectent, amplectant, humectant, annectent, aspectant, respectant, expectant, suspectant.
4. disinfectant, unexpectant.

EKT′ed– **2.** sected.
3. affected, effected, defected, infected, confected, perfected, objected, subjected, ejected, dejected, rejected, injected, projected, elected, selected, collected, deflected, reflected, biflected, inflected, neglected, complected, connected, respected, expected, inspected, suspected, erected, directed, corrected, bisected, dissected, detected, protected, invected.
4. unaffected, disaffected, disinfected, unperfected, unsubjected, unejected, undejected, unrejected, uninjected, unprojected, interjected, re-elected, pre-elected, unelected, unselected, undeflected, unreflected, uninflected, retroflected, recollected, uncollected, dark-complected, light-complected, disconnected, unexpected, unsuspected, redirected, undirected, misdirected, uncorrected, resurrected, intersected, undetected, unprotected.

EKT′er– **2.** hector, Hector, lector, flector, nectar, specter, rector, sector, vector.

3. affecter, effecter, effector, infector, perfecter, objector, ejector, injector, projector, elector, prelector, selector, deflector, reflector, inflector, neglecter, collector, connector, respecter, expecter, inspector, prospector, erector, director, corrector, bisector, dissector, detector, protector, bivector.
4. disinfecter, interjecter, dialector, nonreflector, genuflector, disrespecter, ex-inspector, resurrecter, vivisector.

EKT′erd– **2.** hectored, nectared, spectered, sectored.

EKT′est– **3.** abjectest, selectest, directest.

EKT′ful– **3.** neglectful, respectful, suspectful.
4. unrespectful, disrespectful.

EKT′ik– **2.** hectic, pectic.
3. ephectic, eclectic, synectic, orectic, syntetic.
4. dialectic, analectic, catalectic, epiplectic, apoplectic, isopectic, orthotectic.
5. acatalectic.
6. hypercatalectic.

EKT′ile– **2.** sectile.
3. insectile, projectile.

EKT′ing– **3.** affecting, effecting, infecting, confecting, perfecting, objecting, subjecting, ejecting, dejecting, rejecting, injecting, conjecting, projecting, electing, selecting, deflecting, reflecting, inflecting, neglecting, collecting, connecting, respecting, expecting, inspecting, suspecting, erecting, directing, correcting, bisecting, trisecting, dissecting, detecting, protecting.
4. unaffecting, disinfecting, unreflecting, interjecting, re-electing, recollecting, disconnecting, self-respecting, unsuspecting, redirecting, misdirecting, resurrecting, intersecting, vivisecting.

EKT′iv– **3.** affective, effective, defective, refective, infective, perfective, objective, subjective, ejective, rejective, conjective, projective, elective, selective, deflective, reflective, inflective, collective, humective, connective, respective, inspective, prospective, perspective, erective, directive, corrective, detective, protective, invective.
4. ineffective, imperfective, unobjective, unselective, intellective, recollective, disconnective, irrespective, circumspective, retrospective, introspective.

EKT′lee– **3.** abjectly, selectly, suspectly, erectly, directly, correctly.
4. circumspectly, indirectly, incorrectly.

EKT′ment– **3.** ejectment, dejectment, rejectment, projectment.

EKT′ness– **3.** abjectness, subjectness, selectness, erectness, directness, correctness.
4. circumspectness, indirectness, incorrectness.

EKT′or– *see* ĔKT′er.

EKT′ress– **2.** lectress, rectress.
3. electress, inspectress, directress, protectress.

EKT′rik– **3.** electric.

4. dielectric, anelectric.
5. hydroelectric.
EKT′riks– 2. rectrix.
3. directrix, bisectrix, trisectrix.
EKT′rum– 2. plectrum, spectrum.
3. electrum.
EKT′ure– 2. lecture.
3. confecture, subjecture, conjecture, projecture, belecture.
4. architecture.
EKT′us– 2. pectous, rectus.
3. praefectus, delectus, conspectus, prospectus.
EL′a– 2. Ella, Bella, Della, fella, fellah, kella, kellah, cella, sella, Stella, yella [slang],
3. glabella, tabella, rubella, umbella, padella, predella, lamella, canella, prunella, Prunella, Capella, Kapelle [G.], umbrella, corella, doncella, osella, rosella, Marcella, patella.
4. Arabella, clarabella, Isabella, villanella, fustanella, a cappella, tiarella, Cinderella, agacella. varicella, navicella, panatela, tarantella, fenestella.
EL′an– 3. Magellan, Atellan; *see also* **ĔL′en, ĔL′on.**
EL′ant– 3. flagellant, appellant, repellent, impellent, propellent, propellant, expellent, expellant, revellent, divellent.
EL′ar– 2. cellar, sellar, stellar.
3. glabellar, lamellar, patellar.
4. interstellar; *see also* **ĔL′er.**
EL′as– 2. Hellas, pellas.
3. procellas; *see also* **ĔL′us.**
EL′ate– 2. pellate, prelate, cellate, stellate.
3. debellate, flabellate, appelate, ocellate, patellate, constellate, scutellate.
4. interpellate.
ELB′a– 2. Elba, Melba.
3. peach Melba.
ELCH′er– 2. belcher, welsher, squelcher.
ELCH′ing– 2. belching, welshing, squelching.
ELD′ed– 2. gelded, melded, welded.
ELD′er– 2. elder, gelder, skelder [old slang], melder, welder.
ELD′ing– 2. gelding, melding, welding.
EL′ee– 2. Elly, belly, delly, Delhi, .felly, jelly, kelly, Kelly, skelly, melee, smelly, Nelly, shelly, Shelley.
3. *shadbelly, redbelly, slowbelly, gorbelly, whitebelly, potbelly,* nice Nelly, cancelli.
4. checkerbelly, casus belli [L.], vermicelli, Botticelli.
EL′eed– 2. bellied, jellied.
3. *slowbellied, gorbellied, potbellied.*
EL′een– 2. Hellene, melene.
EL′en– 2. Ellen, Helen.
3. Llewellyn; *see also* **ĔL′an, ĔL′on.**
EL′ent– *see* **ĔL′ant.**
EL′er– 2. Eller, beller, feller, heller, Keller [G.], smeller, kneller, speller, seller, cellar, sheller, teller, stellar, weller, dweller, queller, sweller, yeller.
3. rebeller, lamellar, appellor, repeller,

impeller, compeller, propeller, dispeller, expeller, exceller, foreteller, nonstellar, cave dweller.
4. Rockefeller, underseller, storyteller, fortuneteller, interstellar.
ELF′ik– 2. Delphic, Guelphic.
3. didelphic.
4. diadelphic, monodelphic.
ELF′in– 2. elfin, Delphin, delphine.
ELF′ish– 2. elfish, pelfish, selfish, shellfish.
3. unselfish.
ELF′ree– 2. belfry, pelfry.
EL′ik– 2. bellic, fellic, skelic, melic, relic, telic.
3. angelic, scalpelic, Pentelic.
4. infidelic, evangelic, sapropelic, philatelic, autotelic.
EL′ing– 2. belling, Delling, felling, jelling, melling [dial.], smelling, knelling, spelling, selling, shelling, telling, welling, dwelling, swelling, quelling, yelling.
3. rebelling, repelling, impelling, compelling, propelling, dispelling, misspelling, expelling, outspelling, outselling, excelling, *taletelling,* foretelling, indwelling.
4. parallelling, uncompelling, underselling, overselling, storytelling, fortunetelling.
EL′is– 2. Ellis, trellis.
EL′ish– 2. hellish, relish, wellish, swellish.
3. embellish, disrelish.
EL′ist– 2. cellist, trellised.
EL′it– 2. prelate.
3. appellate.
ELM′a– 2. Elma, pelma, Selma, Thelma, Velma.
ELM′et– 2. helmet, pelmet.
ELM′ing– 2. helming, whelming.
3. unhelming, dishelming.
4. overwhelming.
EL′ness– 2. fellness, wellness, swellness.
3. unwellness.
4. caramelness.
EL′o– 2. bellow, cello, fellow, Jello, mellow, melo [slang], yellow.
3. *playfellow,* niello, prunello, morello, martello, Othello, duello, scrivello.
4. violoncello, punchinello, albarello, saltarello, Monticello, brocatello, Donatello.
EL′od– 2. bellowed, mellowed, yellowed.
3. unmellowed.
EL′on– 2. felon, melon.
3. *muskmelon, mushmelon.*
4. watermelon; *see also* **ĔL′an, ĔL′en.**
EL′op– 3. .develop, envelop.
EL′opt– 3. developed, enveloped.
4. undeveloped, unenveloped.
5. underdeveloped.
EL′ot– 2. helot, zealot.
ELP′er– 2. helper, yelper.
ELP′ful– 2. helpful.
3. self-helpful, unhelpful.
ELP′ing– 2. helping, whelping, yelping.
ELP′less– 2. helpless, kelpless, whelpless, yelpless.

ĔLT′a– 2. delta, pelta, shelta.
ĔLT′ed– 2. belted, felted, melted, smelted, pelted, spelted, welted.
3. unbelted, unmelted.
ĔLT′ee– 2. beltie, felty, kelty.
ĔLT′er– 2. belter, felter, kelter, melter, smelter, pelter, spelter, shelter, welter, swelter.
4. helter-skelter.
ĔLTH′ee– 2. healthy, stealthy, wealthy.
3. unhealthy, unwealthy.
ĔLT′ing– 2. belting, felting, melting, smelting, pelting, spelting, welting.
ĔLT′less– 2. beltless, feltless, peltless, weltless.
ĔLT′ree– 2. peltry, sweltry.
ĔL′um– 2. bellum [L.], vellum.
3. labellum, flabellum, prebellum, cribellum, flagellum, sacellum.
4. cerebellum, ante bellum.
ĔL′us– 2. Hellas, jealous, pellas, Tellus, zealous.
3. tassellus, ocellus, procellas, Marcellus, vitellus, entellus.
4. overzealous.
ĔLV′er– 2. delver, helver, shelver.
ĔLV′ing– 2. delving, helving, shelving.
ĔL′yun– 2. hellion, selion.
3. rebellion.
ĔM′a– 2. Emma, gemma, lemma, nema, stremma, stemma.
3. dilemma, trilemma, maremma.
4. analemma, tetralemma, neurilemma.
ĔMB′er– 2. ember, member.
3. remember, dismember, December, September, November.
4. disremember.
ĔMB′l– 2. tremble, semble.
3. atremble, assemble, dissemble, resemble.
4. reassemble.
ĔMB′lans– 2. semblance.
3. assemblance, dissemblance, resemblance.
ĔMB′lant– 2. semblant.
3. resemblant.
ĔMB′ld– 2. trembled, sembled.
3. assembled, dissembled, resembled.
4. reassembled, unassembled, undissembled.
ĔMB′lee– 2. trembly, Wembley.
3. assembly, dissembly.
ĔMB′ler– 2. trembler, tremblor.
3. assembler, dissembler, resembler.
ĔMB′ling– 2. trembling, sembling.
3. assembling, dissembling, resembling.
4. reassembling.
ĔMB′ral– 2. membral.
3. bimembral, trimembral, Septembral.
ĔMB′rans– 3. remembrance.
4. unremembrance.
ĔM′ee– 2. Emmy, gemmy, jemmy, phlegmy, tremie, stemmy.
ĔM′ent– 2. clement, Clement.
3. inclement.
ĔM′er– 2. emmer, hemmer, tremor, stemmer.
3. condemner, begemmer, contemner.

ĔM′ik– 2. chemic.
3. ecdemic, pandemic, endemic, alchemic, ischemic, polemic, totemic, systemic.
4. academic, epidemic, polydemic, stratagemic, theoremic.
ĔM′ing– 2. hemming, gemming, kembing, lemming, Fleming, clemming, stemming.
3. condemning, begemming, contemning.
ĔM′ish– 2. blemish, Flemish, flemish.
ĔM′ishd– 2. blemished, Flemished, flemished.
3. unblemished.
ĔM′ist– 2. chemist.
4. biochemist.
ĔM′lin– 2. gremlin, Kremlin.
ĔMP′er– 2. semper [L.], temper.
3. attemper, untemper, distemper.
ĔMP′erd– 2. tempered.
3. attempered, ill-tempered, distempered.
ĔMP′l– 2. Hempel, temple, stemple, stempel.
ĔMP′lar– 2. templar.
3. Knight Templar, exemplar.
ĔMPO– 2. tempo.
3. tiempo [Sp.], a tempo [It.].
ĔMP′shun– 2. emption.
3. ademption, redemption, pre-emption, co-emption, exemption.
ĔMP′ted– 2. empted, tempted.
3. adempted, pre-empted, attempted, untempted, exempted.
4. unattempted, unexempted.
ĔMP′ter– 2. emptor, tempter.
3. pre-emptor, coemptor, unkempter, attempter.
ĔMP′ting– 2. empting, tempting.
3. pre-empting, attempting, exempting.
ĔMP′tiv– 3. redemptive, pre-emptive.
ĔMP′tress– 2. temptress.
3. redemptress.
ĔN′a– 2. bena, henna, jenna, senna.
3. Gehenna, Alhenna, Siena, sienna, Vienna, antenna, duenna, Ravenna.
ĔN′ant– 2. pennant, tenant.
3. lieutenant.
ĔN′as– 2. menace, tenace; *see also* ĔN′is.
ĔN′ate– 2. pennate.
3. tripennate, impennate, antennate.
4. latipennate.
ĔNCH′ant– 2. penchant, trenchant.
3. intrenchant.
ĔNCH′er– 2. bencher, blencher, flencher, clencher, wrencher, drencher, trencher, censure, quencher.
3. retrencher, intrencher.
ĔNCH′ing– 2. benching, blenching, flenching, clenching, wrenching, drenching, trenching, quenching.
3. bedrenching, retrenching, unquenching.
ĔNCH′less– 2. benchless, trenchless, quenchless.
ĔNCH′man– 2. henchman, Frenchman.
ĔNCH′ment– 3. retrenchment, entrenchment, intrenchment.
ĔND′a– 2. benda, denda, Brenda, Zenda.
3. addenda, credenda, agenda, legenda,

delenda, commenda [L.].
4. referenda, hacienda, corrigenda.
ĔND′al– 2. trendle, sendal, sendle.
3. prebendal.
4. referendal.
ĔND′ans– 2. tendance.
3. ascendance, descendance, attendance;
see also **ĔND′ens.**
ĔND′ant– 2. pendant, tendant.
3. defendant, appendant, dependant, ascendant, descendant.
4. codefendant, codescendant; *see also*
ĔND′ent.
ĔND′ed– 2. ended, bended, fended, blended, mended, friended, trended, tended, vended, wended.
3. upended, defended, offended, unblended, amended, emended, commended, appended, depended, impended, expended, suspended, befriended, unfriended, ascended, descended, transcended, attended, pretended, intended, contended, portended, extended, distended.
4. undefended, apprehended, reprehended, comprehended, interblended, recommended, condescended, unattended, unintended, unextended.
5. misapprehended, miscomprehended, unrecommended, superintended.
ĔND′ee– 2. bendy, fendy, Mendi, Wendy.
3. effendi.
5. modus vivendi [L.].
ĔND′ens– 3. resplendence, dependence, impendence, transcendence, intendence.
4. independence, condescendence.
5. interdependence, superintendence; *see also*
ĔND′ans.
ĔND′ent– 2. splendent, pendent, tendent.
3. resplendent, transplendent, dependent, impendent, ascendent, descendent, transcendent.
4. independent, undependent, equipendent, condescendent.
5. interdependent, superintendent; *see also*
ĔND′ant.
ĔND′er– 2. ender, bender, fender, gender, lender, blender, splendor, slender, mender, spender, render, trender, sender, tender, vender, vendor, wender.
3. defender, offender, engender, amender, commender, depender, expender, suspender, befriender, surrender, ascender, descender, pretender, contender.
4. apprehender, reprehender, comprehender, moneylender, interblender, recommender.
ĔND′ing– 2. ending, bending, fending, lending, blending, mending, pending, spending, rending, trending, sending, tending, vending, wending.
3. unending, upending, unbending, defending, offending, amending, commending, depending, impending, perpending, expending, misspending, suspending, befriending, heart-rending, ascending, descending, transcending, attending, pretending, contend-

ing, portending, distending, extending.
4. unoffending, apprehending, reprehending, comprehending, interblending, moneylending, recommending, overspending, condescending, unpretending.
5. superintending.
ĔND′less– 2. endless, bendless, mendless, trendless, friendless.
ĔND′ment– 3. amendment, commendment, befriendment, intendment.
ĔND′o– 3. reddendo, morendo [It.], crescendo.
4. decrescendo, diluendo [It.], innuendo.
5. diminuendo.
ĔMD′or– *see* **ĔND′er.**
ĔND′um– 3. habendum, addendum, dedendum, reddendum, credendum, agendum, commendam, tenendum.
4. corrigendum, referendum.
ĔND′us– 3. tremendous, stupendous.
ĔN′ee– 2. any, benne, beni, benny, Benny, fenny, henny, jenny, Jennie, Lenny, blenny, many, penny, tenney, tenny, wenny.
3. Kilkenny, *catchpenny, pinchpenny, halfpenny, passpenny, sixpenny, twopenny, truepenny.*
4. Henny-Penny.
ĔN′el– 2. bennel, fennel, kennel, vennel.
ĔN′ent– tenent; *see also* **ĔN′ant.**
ĔN′er– 2. penner, tenner, tenor, Venner.
4. countertenor.
ĔN′et– 2. Bennett, bennet, dennet, jennet, genet, rennet, sennet, senate, tenet.
ĔNG′thee– 2. lengthy, strengthy.
ĔNG′then– 2. lengthen, strengthen.
ĔN′ik– 2. phenic, genic, splenic, phrenic, scenic, sthenic.
3. Edenic, hyphenic, dysgenic, eugenic, lichenic, Galenic, galenic, selenic, Hellenic, poimenic, irenic, *arsenic,* parthenic, asthenic.
4. metagenic, polygenic, oxygenic, authigenic, Diogenic, cacogenic, psychogenic, chromogenic, thermogenic, monogenic, nitrogenic, photogenic, pathogenic, philhellenic, Panhellenic, proselenic, paraphrenic, neurasthenic, calisthenic, Demosthenic.
ĔN′iks– 3. dysgenics, eugenics, poimenics, irenics.
ĔN′in– 2. Lenin, rennin, venin.
ĔN′ing– 2. denning, fenning, kenning, penning.
ĔN′is– 2. Dennis, menace, tenace, tennis, Venice; *see also* **ĔN′as.**
ĔN′ish– 2. hennish, plenish, Rhenish, wennish.
3. deplenish, replenish, displenish.
ĔN′it– 2. jennet, senate, sennit, sennet, sennight.
ĔNJ′er– 3. avenger, revenger.
ĔNJ′ing– 2. venging.
3. avenging, revenging.
ĔNJ′ment– 3. avengement, revengement.
ĔN′lee– 2. Henley, cleanly.
3. uncleanly.
ĔN′like– 2. denlike, fenlike, henlike, penlike, wrenlike.
ĔN′om– 2. venom, mennom.

3. envenom.
EN′on– 2. mennon, pennon, tenon.
ENS′al– 2. mensal.
   3. bimensal, commensal, forensal.
ENS′ate– 2. sensate.
   3. condensate, compensate, insensate, intensate.
ENS′eez– 2. menses.
   4. Albigenses.
   5. amanuenses.
ENS′en– 2. ensign, densen.
ENS′er– 2. denser, fencer, flenser, menser [Scot.], spencer, Spencer, Spenser, censer, censor, senser, sensor, tenser, tensor.
   3. condenser, prehensor, commencer, dispenser, extensor, intenser.
   4. recompenser.
ENS′est– 2. densest, tensest.
   3. intensest.
ENS′ez– 2. fences, flenses, menses [Scot.], censes, senses, tenses.
   3. condenses, commences, dispenses, incenses.
   4. recompenses, quartertenses, influences.
ENS′forth – 2. henceforth, thenceforth, whenceforth.
ENSH′al– 3. credential, rodential, prudential, agential, bigential, tangential, torrential, essential, sentential, potential, Provencial, sequential.
   4. precedential, confidential, residential, presidential, evidential, sapiential, pestilential, deferential, referential, preferential, differential, inferential, conferential, transferential, reverential, inessential, nonessential, penitential, influential, subsequential, consequential.
   5. jurisprudential, expediential, intelligential, circumferential, unreverential, irreverential, equipotential, inconsequential.
ENSH′ent– 2. sentient.
   3. assentient, presentient, dissentient, insentient, consentient.
ENSH′un– 2. gentian, mention, pension, tension.
   3. indention, prehension, declension, dimension, repension, propension, suspension, ascension, descension, recension, presention, dissension, accension, incension, consension, attention, obtention, detention, retention, pretension, intention, intension, contention, portention, abstention, extention, distention, ostension, obvention, subvention, prevention, invention, convention.
   4. apprehension, reprehension, comprehension, reascension, condescension, inattention, hypotension, hypertension, contravention, circumvention, supervention, intervention.
   5. inapprehension, misapprehension, incomprehension, uncondescension, nonintervention.
ENSH′und– 2. mentioned, pensioned.
   3. rementioned, unmentioned, repensioned, unpensioned.

   4. underpensioned, overpensioned.
ENSH′us– 3. tendentious, silentious, licentious, dissentious, pretentious, sententious, contentious.
   4. conscientious, unpretentious.
ENS′il– 2. bensel [Scot. & dial. Eng.], pencil, pencel, pensile, sensile, tensile, stencil.
   3. prehensile, depencil, blue-pencil, extensile, utensil.
   4. hyperpencil.
ENS′ild– 2. pencilled, tensiled, stencilled.
   3. blue-pencilled, utensilled.
ENS′ing– 2. fencing, flensing, censing, mensing [Scot. & N. of Eng.], tensing.
   3. condensing, commencing, dispensing, incensing, pretensing.
   4. recompensing, influencing.
ENS′iv– 2. pensive, tensive.
   3. defensive, offensive, prehensive, expensive, suspensive, intensive, extensive, distensive, ostensive.
   4. inoffensive, apprehensive, comprehensive, recompensive, inexpensive, condescensive, inextensive.
   5. inapprehensive, incomprehensive.
ENS′lee– 2. densely, tensely.
   3. immensely, propensely, intensely.
ENS′less– 2. fenceless, penceless, senseless.
   3. defenseless, offenseless, expenseless.
   4. recompenseless.
ENS′ment– 3. commencement, incensement.
ENS′ness– 2. denseness, tenseness.
   3. immenseness, propenseness, intenseness.
ENS′um– 2. pensum, sensum.
ENS′us– 2. census.
   3. consensus.
ENT′a– 2. nenta, Senta.
   3. magenta, polenta, Pimenta, pimienta, cuarenta, placenta.
   4. pedimenta.
   5. rejectamenta, impedimenta.
ENT′ad– 2. entad, pentad.
   4. ectoentad.
ENT′al– 2. ental, dental, gentle, mental, rental, trental, cental.
   3. edental, bidental, tridental, postdental, ungentle, amental, fragmental, segmental, tegmental, pigmental, momental, parental, percental.
   4. accidental, incidental, transcendental, interdental, oriental, fundamental, ligamental, firmamental, ornamental, tournamental, sacramental, atramental, testamental, elemental, complemental, supplemental, tenemental, recremental, incremental, pedimental, condimental, rudimental, regimental, alimental, complimental, detrimental, nutrimental, sentimental, governmental, apartmental, departmental, compartmental, documental, tegumental, argumental, monumental, instrumental, continental, componental, grandparental, biparental.
   5. antecedental, coincidental, medicamental, predicamental, temperamental, impedimen-

tal, experimental, developmental; *see also*
ĔNT′il; ĔNT′l.
ĔNT′ans– **2.** sentence.
3. repentance.
4. unrepentance.
ĔNT′ant– **3.** repentant.
4. unrepentant, representant.
ĔNT′ate– **2.** dentate.
3. edentate, bidentate, tridentate.
4. testamentate.
ĔNT′ay– **3.** niente, dolente [both It.].
4. presidente, tardamente [It.], lentamente
[It.], conoscente [It.].
5. aguardiente [Sp.].
6. dolce far niente [It.], furiosamente [It.].
ĔNT′ed– **2.** dented, rented, scented, tented,
vented.
3. indented, relented, lamented, demented,
cemented, augmented, fermented, tormented,
repented, unrented, assented, dissented,
consented, unscented, contented, prevented,
invented, frequented.
4. precedented, unindented, unlamented,
ornamented, supplemented, complemented,
complimented, battlemented, unrepented,
represented, discontented, circumvented,
unfrequented.
5. unprecedented, unornamented, misrepre-
sented, unrepresented.
ĔNT′ee– **2.** Henty, Lenty, plenty, twenty.
3. Amenti, aplenty.
4. diapente, conoscenti [It.].
ĔNT′eez– *see* **ĔNT′ee,** plus " s " or " 's ";
2. flentes [L.], twenties.
ĔNT′ens– **2.** sentence.
3. repentance.
4. unrepentance.
ĔNT′er– **2.** enter, denter, renter, center,
tenter, venter.
3. re-enter, indenter, lamenter, cementer,
augmenter, commenter, fomenter, fermenter,
tormenter, tormentor, repenter, assenter,
absenter, decenter, recenter, precentor,
dissenter, incenter, incentor, consenter,
retentor, preventer, inventor, frequenter,
resenter, presenter.
4. unrelentor, ornamenter, supplementer,
epicenter, barycenter, circumventor, repre-
senter.
5. experimenter, misrepresenter; *see also*
ĔNT′or.
ĔNT′erd– **2.** entered, centered, tentered.
3. re-entered, self-centered.
ĔNT′ful– **2.** scentful.
3. lamentful, contentful, resentful, eventful,
inventful.
4. unresentful, uneventful, uninventful.
ĔNT′ij– **2.** ventage.
3. percentage.
ĔNT′ik– **3.** identic, argentic, crescentic,
authentic.
ĔNT′il– **2.** dentil, dentile, lentil, centile,
ventil.
3. percentile; *see also* **ĔNT′al, ĔNT′l.**

ĔNT′ile– **2.** gentile, centile.
3. percentile.
ĔNT′in– **2.** dentin, dentine, Quentin.
3. Tridentine, San Quentin.
ĔNT′ing– **2.** denting, renting, scenting, tent-
ing, venting.
3. indenting, relenting, lamenting, cement-
ing, augmenting, fomenting, fermenting,
tormenting, repenting, accenting, assenting,
absenting, dissenting, consenting, contenting,
preventing, inventing, frequenting, resenting,
presenting.
4. unrelenting, ornamenting, supplementing,
complementing. complimenting, circumvent-
ing, representing.
5. experimenting, misrepresenting.
ĔNT′is– **2.** prentice.
3. apprentice.
5. non compos mentis [L.].
ĔNT′ist– **2.** dentist, prenticed.
3. apprenticed, trecentist, preventist, presentist.
ĔNT′iv– **3.** pedentive, lamentive, assentive,
incentive, attentive, detentive, retentive,
adventive, preventive, presentive.
4. inattentive, unretentive, circumventive,
interventive.
ĔNT′l– **2.** gentle.
3. ungentle; *see also* **ĔNT′al, ĔNT′il.**
ĔNT′lee– **2.** gently.
3. ungently, intently.
4. confidently, evidently, excellently, inso-
lently, eminently, innocently, impotently.
ĔNT′less– **2.** bentless, dentless, Lentless,
rentless, scentless, centless, tentless, ventless.
3. relentless, lamentless, cementless, ferment-
less, tormentless, repentless, descentless, con-
sentless, contentless, eventless, resentless.
ĔNT′ment– **3.** relentment, contentment,
resentment, presentment.
4. discontentment, representment.
ĔNT′ness– **2.** bentness, lentness, meantness,
pentness, spentness.
3. intentness.
4. confidentness, evidentness, excellentness,
insolentness.
ĔNT′o– **2.** lento, cento.
3. memento, pimento, pimiento, fomento
[Sp.], Sorrento, trecento [It.].
4. Sacramento, portamento, pentimento,
quattrocento [It.].
6. pronunciamento.
ĔNT′or– **2.** lentor, mentor, centaur, stentor.
3. fermentor, tormentor, precentor, suc-
centor, incentor, bucentaur, retentor.
4. unrelentor, circumventor; *see also* **ĔNT′er.**
ĔNT′ral– **2.** central, ventral.
3. subcentral, precentral, biventral.
4. paracentral, metacentral, dorsiventral.
ĔNT′rans– **2.** entrance, entrants.
3. re-entrance, re-entrants.
ĔNT′ree– **2.** entry, gentry, sentry.
ĔNT′rik– **2.** centric.
3. acentric, eccentric, concentric.

4. paracentric, metacentric, barycentric, geocentric, egocentric, homocentric.
5. Saturnicentric, heliocentric, anthropocentric.
ENT′rum— 2. centrum.
3. precentrum, epicentrum, pseudocentrum.
ENT′um— 2. mentum.
3. amentum, ramentum, cementum, tegmentum, momentum, sarmentum, fermentum, tormentum, frumentum [L.], percentum, unguentum.
4. fundamentum [L.], velamentum, sacramentum, testamentum.
5. paludamentum.
ENT′ur— 2. denture, tenture, venture.
3. debenture, indenture, rudenture, adventure, reventure.
4. maladventure, peradventure, misadventure.
ENT′us— 3. pigmentous, momentous, sarmentous, portentous, unguentous.
4. ligamentous, filamentous, immomentous, pedetentous.
EN′um— 2. venom, mennom.
3. envenom.
ENZ′a— 3. cadenza.
4. influenza.
ENZ′ee— 2. frenzy.
3. Rienzi.
ENZ′eez— 2. frenzies, Menzies.
ENZ′ez— 2. lenses, cleanses.
EP′ee— 2. kepi, peppy, tepee.
3. Apepi.
EP′er— 2. hepper, leper, pepper, strepor, tepor, stepper.
3. high-stepper.
EP′erd— 2. jeopard, leopard, peppered, shepherd.
EP′id— 2. lepid, trepid, tepid.
3. intrepid.
EP′ik— 2. epic.
3. monepic.
4. orthoëpic.
EP′ing— 2. pepping, stepping.
3. high-stepping.
4. overstepping.
EP′o— 2. Beppo, depot.
EP′ode— 2. epode, depoted.
EP′see— 3. apepsy, dyspepsy, eupepsy.
4. catalepsy, epilepsy.
EP′shun— 3. ereption, surreption, deception, reception, preception, exception, inception, conception, perception, susception.
4. beneception, antiseption, preconception, misconception, apperception, preperception, imperception, interception.
5. nociperception, introsusception, intussusception.
EP′sis— 2. pepsis, sepsis, scepsis.
3. syllepsis, prolepsis, asepsis.
4. analepsis, paralepsis, metalepsis, antisepsis.
EPT′al— 2. heptal, septal.
EPT′ans— 3. acceptance, exceptance.

EPT′ant— 2. reptant.
3. acceptant, exceptant.
EPT′ed— 3. accepted, excepted.
4. unaccepted, unexcepted, intercepted.
EPT′er— 2. scepter, sceptre.
3. adepter, receptor, preceptor, accepter, excepter, inceptor, susceptor.
4. intercepter; see also ĔPT′or.
EPT′ik— 2. skeptic, kleptic, peptic, threptic, septic, sceptic.
3. sylleptic, proleptic, apeptic, dyspeptic, eupeptic, aseptic.
4. analeptic, cataleptic, metaleptic, epileptic, nympholeptic, bradypeptic, antiseptic.
5. epanaleptic, acataleptic.
EPT′ile— 2. reptile, septile.
EPT′ing— 3. accepting, excepting, incepting.
4. intercepting.
EPT′iv— 3. acceptive, deceptive, receptive, preceptive, exceptive, inceptive, conceptive, perceptive, susceptive.
4. nociceptive, autoceptive, apperceptive, imperceptive, interceptive, insusceptive.
5. intussusceptive.
EPT′lee— 3. adeptly, ineptly.
EPT′ness— 3. adeptness, ineptness.
EPT′or— 3. receptor, preceptor, inceptor, susceptor.
4. beneceptor; see also ĔPT′er.
EPT′um— 2. septum.
3. perceptum.
ER′a— 2. serra, terra [It.].
3. sierra, acerra.
ER′af— 2. seraph, teraph; see also ĔR′if.
ER′ald— 2. Gerald, herald, Herrold, perilled.
3. imperilled.
ER′ant— 2. errant.
3. aberrant.
ER′ee— 2. berry, bury, cherry, derry, ferry, jerry, Kerry, skerry, flerry, merry, perry, serry, sherry, terry, very, wherry.
3. *bayberry, dayberry, burberry, redberry, breadberry, chokeberry, baneberry, wineberry, oneberry, Juneberry, youngberry, bogberry, dogberry, hackberry, blackberry, inkberry, pinkberry, bilberry, mulberry, cranberry, snowberry, crowberry, strawberry, squawberry, barberry, deerberry, mossberry, raspberry, catberry, dewberry, blueberry, gooseberry, chokecherry.*
4. chinaberry, guavaberry, coffeeberry, beriberi, partridgeberry, orangeberry, thimbleberry, bumbleberry, dangleberry, tangleberry, huckleberry, loganberry, rowanberry, checkerberry, winterberry, Christmasberry, lotusberry, locustberry, Pondicherry, millinery, stationery, Miserere, lamasery, cemetery, presbytery, mesentery, monastery; see also ĀR′ee, ĂR′ee.
ER′eed— 2. berried, buried, cherried, ferried, serried, wherried.
3. unburied, unserried.
ER′ens— 2. Terence.
3. aberrance.
ER′er— 2. error, terror.

ER′et– 2. ferret, lerret, terret, wherret; *see also* **ĔR′it.**

ER′if– 2. serif, sheriff.

4. undersheriff; *see also* **ĔR′af.**

ER′ik– 2. Eric, deric, derrick, ferric, spheric, Herrick, cleric, ceric, Seric, pteric, terek, steric, queric.

3. suberic, valeric, dimeric, chimeric, Homeric, mesmeric, generic, piperic, glyceric, icteric, enteric, hysteric.

4. peripheric, helispheric, hemispheric, perispheric, atmospheric, metameric, isomeric, polymeric, neoteric, esoteric, exoteric.

ER′iks– 2. derricks, clerics.

3. hysterics.

4. esoterics.

ER′il– 2. beryl, ferrule, peril, sterile.

3. imperil, unsterile.

4. chrysoberyl.

ER′in– 2. Erin, serin.

ER′ing– 2. erring, herring.

ER′is– 2. Eris, derris, ferris, terrace.

ER′ish– 2. cherish, perish.

ER′it– 2. merit.

3. inherit, demerit.

4. disinherit; *see also* **ĔR′et.**

ER′o– *see* **ĀR′o.**

ER′or– 2. error, terror.

ER′ul– 2. ferule, ferrule, spherule, perule.

ER′und– 2. errand, gerund.

ES′a– 2. dessa, sessa, Tessa.

3. Odessa, Marpessa, Duessa.

4. dogaressa.

ES′al– 2. quezal, vessel.

3. redressal, processal; *see also* **ĔS′il, ĔS′l.**

ES′ant– 2. jessant.

3. confessant, caressant, depressant, incessant.

ES′ay– 2. esse [L.], essay.

3. in esse [L.].

ESCH′al– 2. bestial.

3. celestial, agrestial.

ESCH′un– 2. question.

3. suggestion, digestion, ingestion, congestion, requestion.

4. indigestion.

ES′ed– 2. essed, blessed.

ES′ee– 2. esse [L.], Essie, Bessie, Jesse, Jessie, messy, dressy, tressy, Tessie.

3. in esse [L.].

ES′en– 2. Essen, lessen, lesson.

4. Mittagessen [G.], Abendessen [G.].

ES′ens– 2. essence, crescents.

3. albescence, rubescence, candescence, frondescence, turgescence, quiescence, glaucescence, calescence, mollescence, spumescence, tumescence, senescence, nigrescence, virescence, accrescence, increscence, concrescence, excrescence, florescence, vitrescence, putrescence, latescence, lactescence, quintessence, mutescence, fructescence, liquescence.

4. erubescence, iridescence, incandescence, recrudescence, acquiescence, requiescence, decalescence, incalescence, coalescence, opa-

lescence, convalescence, virilescence, adolescence, emollescence, obsolescence, detumescence, intumescence, evanescence, juvenescence, luminescence, supercrescence, arborescence, phosphorescence, calorescence, efflorescence, deflorescence, inflorescence, sonorescence, fluorescence, effervescence, deliquescence.

5. nonacquiescence, incoalescence, rejuvenescence, noneffervescence.

ES′ent– 2. crescent.

3. albescent, rubescent, candescent, frondescent, turgescent, quiescent, glaucescent, calescent, mollescent, spumescent, tumescent, senescent, nigrescent, virescent, accrescent, increscent, concrescent, excrescent, florescent, vitrescent, putrescent, latescent, lactescent, mutescent, fructescent, liquescent.

4. erubescent, iridescent, incandescent, recrudescent, acquiescent, requiescent, decalescent, incalescent, coalescent, opalescent, convalescent, virilescent, adolescent, emollescent, obsolescent, detumescent, intumescent, evanescent, juvenescent, luminescent, supercrescent, arborescent, phosphorescent, calorescent, efflorescent, deflorescent, inflorescent, sonorescent, fluorescent, effervescent, deliquescent.

5. nonacquiescent, incoalescent, rejuvenescent, noneffervescent, uneffervescent.

ES′er– 2. guesser, jessur, lesser, lessor, blesser, plessor, messer, dresser, presser, cesser.

3. confessor, professor, sublessor, addresser, addressor, redresser, redressor, aggressor, digressor, progressor, transgressor, depressor, represser, impresser, compressor, oppressor, suppressor, assessor, obsessor, successor, possessor.

4. acquiescer, second guesser, predecessor, antecessor, intercessor, dispossessor; *see also* **ĔS′or.**

ES′ez– 2. s's, S's, eses, esses, desses, fesses, 'fesses, guesses, jesses, blesses, messes, dresses, cresses, presses, tresses, stresses, sesses, cesses, yeses.

3. confesses, professes, turgesces, kermesses, finesses, caresses, addresses, redresses, undresses, regresses, digresses, progresses, transgresses, accresces, depresses, represses, impresses, compresses, oppresses, suppresses, expresses, distresses, assesses, obsesses, recesses, successes, possesses.

4. SOS's, incandesces, stewardesses, shepherdesses, second guesses, acquiesces, coalesces, convalesces, luminesces, baronesses, readdresses, retrogresses, water cresses, phosphoresces, effloresces, fluoresces, recompresses, overstresses, reassesses, repossesses, prepossesses, dispossesses, poetesses, effervesces, deliquesces.

5. rejuvenesces, ambassadresses.

ES′ful– 3. distressful, successful.

4. nonsuccessful, unsuccessful.

ESH′ee– 2. fleshy, meshy.

ESH'ens– 2. nescience, prescience.
ESH'er– 2. mesher, fresher, pressure, thresher, tressure.
  3. refresher, nonpressure.
ESH'ing– 2. meshing, threshing.
  3. refreshing.
ESH'l– 2. deasil, special.
  3. especial.
ESH'lee– 2. fleshly, freshly.
  3. unfleshly, unfreshly.
ESH'less– 2. fleshless, meshless.
ESH'ment– 3. enmeshment, refreshment.
ESH'un– 2. Hessian, freshen, cession, session.
  3. confession, profession, aggression, egression, regression, digression, ingression, congression, progression, transgression, discretion, depression, repression, impression, compression, oppression, expression, suppression, obsession, recession, precession, secession, accession, succession, concession, possession.
  4. nonaggression, retrogression, introgression, repossession, prepossession, self-possession, dispossession, retrocession, introcession, supersession, intercession, indiscretion, quarter session.
ESH'unz– see ĔSH'un, plus " s " or " 's ".
ES'ij– 2. message, presage.
  3. expressage.
ES'il– 2. decile, cresyl, sessile, Cecil; see also ĔS'l, ĔS'al.
ES'ing– 2. dessing [dial.], fessing [slang], 'fessing, guessing, jessing, blessing, messing, dressing, pressing, tressing, stressing, yessing.
  3. confessing, professing, rejessing, unjessing, reblessing, finessing, caressing, addressing, redressing, undressing, regressing, digressing, progressing, transgressing, depressing, repressing, impressing, compressing, oppressing, suppressing, expressing, retressing, restressing, distressing, assessing, recessing, possessing.
  4. acquiescing, incandescing, coalescing, convalescing, readdressing, salad dressing, underdressing, overdressing, retrogressing, phosphorescing, efflorescing, fluorescing, recompressing, understressing, overstressing, reassessing, repossessing, prepossessing, unpossessing, dispossessing, effervescing, deliquescing.
  5. unacquiescing, unincandescing, uncoalescing, reconvalescing, rejuvenescing, unphosphorescing, unefflorescing, unprepossessing, uneffervescing, undeliquescing.
ES'iv– 2. crescive.
  3. caressive, redressive, aggressive, regressive, digressive, ingressive, congressive, progressive, transgressive, depressive, repressive, impressive, compressive, oppressive, suppressive, expressive, obsessive, recessive, accessive, excessive, successive, concessive, possessive.
  4. unprogressive, retrogressive, unimpressive, unoppressive, inexpressive, unexcessive.

ESK'ee– 2. desky, pesky [coll.].
ESK'lee– 3. blottesquely, grotesquely.
  4. picturesquely, statuesquely.
ESK'ness– 3. grotesqueness.
  4. picturesqueness, statuesqueness.
ESK'o– 2. fresco.
  3. tedesco [It.], alfresco, grotesco [obs.].
ESK'u– 2. fescue, rescue.
ES'l– 2. deasil, chessel, nestle, pestle, wrestle, trestle, sessile, Cecil, vessel.
  3. unnestle; see also ĔS'al, ĔS'il.
ES'ler– 2. nestler, wrestler.
ES'ling– 2. nestling, wrestling.
ES'man– 2. pressman, yes man [slang].
ES'ment– 3. redressment, impressment, assessment.
ES'o– 2. Esso, gesso.
ES'on– 2. Essen, lesson, lessen.
ES'or– 2. lessor, plessor.
  3. confessor, professor, aggressor, possessor; see also ĔS'er.
EST'a– 2. festa [It.], testa, Vesta, cuesta.
  3. podesta, egesta, ingesta, fiesta [Sp.], siesta, Avesta.
EST'al– 2. festal, vestal.
  3. agrestal.
EST'ant– 2. gestant, restant.
  3. contestant.
EST'ed– 2. bested, chested, guested, jested, nested, rested, wrested, breasted, crested, tested, vested, wested, quested, zested.
  3. unbested, infested, suggested, digested, ingested, congested, molested, arrested, uncrested, unrested, attested, detested, retested, pretested, contested, untested, protested, divested, invested, unvested, requested.
  4. manifested, uninfested, unsuggested, redigested, predigested, undigested, uncongested, unmolested, rearrested, unarrested, doublebreasted, single-breasted, pigeon-breasted, interested, reattested, unattested, uncontested, reprotested, unprotested, undivested, uninvested.
  5. unmanifested, uninterested, disinterested.
EST'ee– 2. chesty, Feste, resty, cresty, teste, testy, westy, zesty.
EST'eez– 2. Estes, restes.
  3. Dermestes, Herpestes, Orestes.
EST'er– 2. ester, Esther, bester, Chester, fester, Hester, jester, Lester, Leicester, Nestor, nester, pester, rester, wrester, testar, tester, vester, wester, quester.
  3. infester, suggester, digester, molester, semester, trimester, arrester, attester, contester, protester, Sylvestor, requester, sequester, northwester, southwester.
  4. manifester, mid-semester.
EST'ern– 2. hestern [obs.], western, yestern [arch.].
  3. midwestern, northwestern, southwestern.
EST'ful– 2. jestful, restful, questful, zestful.
  3. unrestful.
EST'ik– 2. gestic.

3. asbestic, majestic, orchestic, telestic, telestich, domestic, amnestic, agrestic.
4. anapestic, catachrestic.
EST'in– 2. destine, sestine.
3. predestine, clandestine, intestine.
EST'ind– 2. destined.
3. predestined, undestined.
EST'ing– 2. besting, guesting, jesting, nesting, resting, wresting, breasting, cresting, testing, vesting, westing, questing.
3. infesting, suggesting, digesting, ingesting, congesting, molesting, arresting, unresting, attesting, detesting, retesting, pretesting, contesting, protesting, divesting, investing, requesting.
4. manifesting, redigesting, predigesting, uncongesting, rearresting, unarresting, interesting, reattesting, reprotesting, unprotesting.
5. uninteresting, disinteresting.
EST'is– 2. restis.
3. Alcestis; *see also* **ĔST'us.**
EST'iv– 2. estive, festive, restive.
3. infestive, suggestive, digestive, congestive, tempestive, attestive.
4. manifestive.
EST'less– 2. guestless, jestless, restless, breastless, crestless, questless.
EST'ling– 2. nestling, wrestling.
EST'ment– 2. vestment.
3. arrestment, divestment, investment.
EST'o– 2. presto.
4. manifesto.
EST'ral– 2. kestrel.
3. orchestral, palestral, semestral, trimestral, fenestral, campestral, ancestral.
EST'ure– 2. gesture, vesture.
3. revesture, divesture, investure.
EST'us– 2. Festus, restis, cestus.
3. asbestos, Alcestis.
ET'a– 2. eta, Eita, geta, meta, Greta, stretta.
3. vendetta, codetta [It.], Valetta, burletta, lametta, Minetta, Egretta, biretta, Rosetta, mozzetta.
4. arietta, Henrietta, animetta [It.], operetta.
5. comedietta.
ET'al– 2. metal, petal.
3. abettal, begettal; *see also* **ĔT'l.**
ET'ed– 2. betted, jetted, netted, petted, retted, fretted, stetted, vetted, wetted, whetted, sweated.
3. abetted, indebted, coquetted, unnetted, unpetted, unfretted, regretted, brevetted, unvetted, curvetted, rewetted, unwetted, unwhetted, gazetted.
4. unindebted, epauletted, coronetted, bayonetted, interfretted, unregretted, silhouetted, pirouetted.
ET'ee– 2. betty, Betty, chetty, Getty, Hetty, jetty, Letty, netty, Nettie, petty, petit, fretty, pretty, sweaty.
3. confetti, spaghetti, libretti, sunsetty, Rossetti.

4. spermaceti, Donizetti.
ET'en– 2. Breton, threaten, whetten.
3. rethreaten.
ET'er– 2. better, debtor, fetter, getter, letter, Blätter [G.], netter, petter, retter, fretter, setter, wetter, sweater, whetter.
3. abettor, enfetter, unfetter, begetter, gogetter, forgetter, dead letter, red-letter, blackletter, regretter, besetter, *typesetter*, upsetter.
4. Irish Setter.
ET'ful– 2. netful, fretful.
3. forgetful, regretful.
4. unforgetful, unregretful.
ETH'el– 2. Ethel, ethyl, Bethel.
ETH'er– 2. feather, heather, leather, blether, mether, nether, tether, weather, wether, whether.
3. tail feather, *pinfeather*, together, *whitleather*, comether [dial.], aweather, *bellwether*.
4. altogether, patent leather.
ETH'erd– 2. feathered, heathered, leathered, tethered, weathered.
3. *pinfeathered*, unfeathered, untethered, unweathered.
ET'ik– 2. Lettic, metic.
3. tabetic, syndetic, aphetic, Japhetic, prophetic, algetic, Gangetic, poietic, athletic, phyletic, gametic, emetic, mimetic, cometic, hermetic, seismetic, cosmetic, genetic, splenetic, frenetic, phrenetic, threnetic, magnetic, kinetic, phonetic, goetic, noetic, Noetic, poetic, zoetic, herpetic, paretic, syncretic, *heretic*, heuretic, pyretic, ascetic, auxetic, Ossetic, zetetic, bathetic, pathetic, synthetic, prothetic, aesthetic, Helvetic.
4. alphabetic, diabetic, asyndetic, geodetic, cynegetic, exegetic, analgetic, energetic, synergetic, syzygetic, rabietic, homiletic, arithmetic, Baphometic, hypnoetic, theoretic, anchoretic, diuretic, unascetic, apatetic, erotetic, synartetic, diathetic, apathetic, sympathetic, epithetic, antithetic, epenthetic, parenthetic, nomothetic, cosmothetic, hypothetic, anesthetic, unaesthetic.
5. apologetic, antipathetic, polysynthetic, polyprothetic, hyperesthetic, cosmopoietic, monophyletic, polyphyletic, metagenetic, psychogenetic, morphogenetic, pathogenetic, homogenetic, thermogenetic, monogenetic, oogenetic, pyrogenetic, polygenetic, diamagnetic, parakinetic, telekinetic, autokinetic, dianoetic, mythopoetic, chrysopoetic, diaphoretic, antipyretic, peripatetic.
6. heterophyletic, paleogenetic, parthenogenetic, heterogenetic.
7. onomatopoetic.
ET'iks– 2. metics.
3. athletics, emetics, Hermetics, cosmetics, magnetics, kinetics, phonetics, poetics, ascetics, synthetics, aesthetics.
4. diabetics, geodetics, cynegetics, exegetics, homiletics, theoretics, diuretics, dietetics.
ET'ing– 2. betting, getting, jetting, letting, bletting, netting, petting, retting, fretting,

setting, stetting, vetting, wetting, sweating, whetting.

3. abetting, begetting, forgetting, coquetting, unnetting, unfretting, regretting, besetting, upsetting, revetting, brevetting, curvetting, rewetting, gazetting.

4. unforgetting, bayonetting, somersetting, intersetting, oversetting, silhouetting, pirouetting, minuetting.

5. mosquito netting.

ET′ish– 2. fetish, fetich, Lettish, pettish, wettish.

3. coquettish.

ET′ist– 3. cornettist, librettist, motettist, duettist, vignettist.

4. clarinettist.

ET′l– 2. ettle [dial.], fettle, kettle, metal, mettle, nettle, petal, Gretel, settle, cetyl.

3. abettal, unmettle, resettle, unsettle.

4. centripetal.

6. Popocatepetl; *see also* **ĔT′al.**

ET′ld– 2. fettled, mettled, petalled, settled.

3. high mettled, unsettled.

4. double petalled.

ET′ler– 2. nettler, settler.

ET′less– 2. debtless, threatless.

ET′ling– 2. fettling, nettling, settling.

3. unsettling.

ET′ment– 3. abetment, indebtment, besetment, revetment.

ET′ness– 2. setness, wetness.

ET′o– 2. ghetto, stretto.

3. concetto [It.], zucchetto, stiletto, palmetto, in petto [L.], rispetto [It.], libretto, falsetto, terzetto.

4. lazaretto, allegretto, amoretto.

ET′rad– 2. retrad, tetrad.

ET′rik– 2. metric.

3. dimetric, symmetric.

4. diametric, dynametric, asymmetric, pedometric, geometric, logometric, ergometric, thermometric, chronometric, barometric, hydrometric, hygrometric, micrometric, isometric, photometric, autometric, tautometric.

5. trigonometric, magnetometric.

ET′sal– 2. quetzal, pretzel.

ET′so– 2. pezzo [It.].

4. intermezzo.

ET′work– 2. network, fretwork.

EV′an– 2. Evan, Bevan, Devon; *see also* **ĔV′en.**

EV′ee– 2. Evy, bevy, chevy, heavy, levee, levy, clevy, nevvy, Chevvy.

3. top-heavy, replevy.

EV′el– 2. bevel, kevel, level, nevel, revel.

3. sea level, dishevel.

4. water level, spirit level; *see also* **ĔV′il.**

EV′eld– 2. bevelled, deviled, levelled, nevelled, revelled.

3. bedevilled, dishevelled.

EV′en– 2. heaven, leaven, seven, chevon, steven, sweven.

3. eleven; *see also* **ĔV′an.**

EV′enth– 2. seventh.

3. eleventh.

EV′er– 2. ever, lever, levir, clever, never, sever.

3. whichever, whenever, wherever, forever, whatever, however, whoever, endeavor, unclever, asseyer, dissever.

4. whichsoever, whensoever, whencesoever, wheresoever, whatsoever, whosoever, whosesoever, howsoever, cantilever.

5. whithersoever.

EV′il– 2. devil, Neville.

3. bedevil, *daredevil*, she-devil, blue devil, red devil; *see also* **ĔV′el.**

EV′in– 2. levin.

3. replevin.

EV′is– 2. chevise, clevis, brevis [L.], crevice.

3. Ben Nevis.

7. ars longa, vita brevis [L.].

EZ′ans– 2. pleasance, peasants, presence, presents.

4. omnipresence.

EZ′ant– 2. pheasant, pleasant, peasant, bezant.

3. unpleasant.

4. omnipresent.

EZH′er– 2. leisure, pleasure, measure, treasure.

3. displeasure, admeasure, remeasure, commeasure, entreasure.

EZ′l– 2. bezel, bezzle.

3. embezzle.

Ĕ (heh)

Triple Rhymes

Primary or Secondary Accent Falls on Second from Last Syllable; Imperfect Rhymes Are in Italics.

EB′i–er– **3.** blebbier, nebbier, webbier.
  4. *cobwebbier.*
EB′i–est– **3.** blebbiest, nebbiest, webbiest.
  4. *cobwebbiest.*
EB′ri–tee– **4.** celebrity, tenebrity.
ECH′a–bl– **3.** etchable, fetchable, sketchable, stretchable.
ECH′er–ee– **3.** lechery, treachery.
ECH′er–us– **3.** lecherous, treacherous.
ECH′i–ness– **3.** sketchiness, stretchiness, tetchiness.
ED′a–bl– **3.** dreadable; *see also* ĔD′i–bl.
ED′en–ing– **3.** deadening, leadening, reddening.
ED′i–bl– **3.** edible, dreadable, credible.
  4. unedible, impedible, incredible; *see also* ĔD′a–bl.
ED′i–er– **3.** headier, readier, breadier, spreadier, shreddier, threadier, steadier.
  4. unreadier, unsteadier.
ED′i–est– **3.** headiest, readiest, breadiest, spreadiest, shreddiest, threadiest, steadiest.
  4. unreadiest, unsteadiest.
ED′i–ing– **3.** eddying, readying, steadying.
ED′i–kant– **3.** dedicant, medicant, predicant.
ED′i–kate– **3.** dedicate, medicate, predicate.
  4. rededicate, depredicate.
ED′i–kl– **3.** medical, pedicle.
  4. premedical.
ED′i–lee– **3.** readily, steadily.
  4. unreadily, unsteadily.
ED′i–ment– **3.** pediment, sediment.
  4. impediment.
ED′i–ness– **3.** headiness, readiness, breadiness, spreadiness, shreddiness, threadiness, steadiness.
  4. unreadiness, unsteadiness.
ED′it–ed– **3.** edited, credited.
  4. re-edited, unedited, accredited, discredited, miscredited.
  5. unaccredited, undiscredited.
ED′it–ee– **4.** rubedity, heredity.
ED′it–er– **3.** editor, creditor.

ED′it–ing– **3.** editing, crediting.
  4. accrediting, discrediting, miscrediting.
ED′it–iv– **3.** redditive, creditive, sedative.
  4. impeditive.
ED′it–or– **3.** editor, creditor.
  4. subeditor.
ED′u–lus– **3.** credulous, sedulous.
  4. incredulous, unsedulous.
EF′a–lus– **3.** Cephalus.
  4. acephalus, acephalous, encephalous, Bucephalus.
EF′er–ens– **3.** deference, reference, preference.
  4. cross-reference.
EF′er–ent– **3.** efferent, deferent, referent, preferent.
EF′in–it– **3.** definite.
  4. indefinite, undefinite.
EF′is–ens– **4.** maleficence, beneficence.
EF′is–ent– **4.** maleficent, beneficent.
EF′lu–ent– **3.** effluent, defluent, refluent.
EG′a–bl– **3.** beggable, peggable.
EG′ar–ee– **3.** beggary, Weggery.
EG′i–ness– **3.** egginess, legginess, dregginess.
EG′nan–see– **3.** regnancy, pregnancy.
EG′raf–ee– **4.** telegraphy, choregraphy.
EG′u–lar– **3.** regular, tegular.
  4. irregular, unregular.
EJ′a–bl– **3.** edgeable, hedgeable, legible, pledgeable, wedgeable.
  4. unedgeable, unhedgeable, allegeable, illegible, unpledgeable, unwedgeable.
EJ′i–blee– **3.** legibly.
  4. illegibly.
EJ′i–o– **4.** solfeggio, arpeggio.
EK′a–bl– **3.** checkable, peccable, secable.
  4. impeccable.
EK′ond–lee– **3.** fecundly, secondly.
EK′on–ing– **3.** beckoning, reckoning.
  4. dead reckoning.
EK′re–ment– **3.** decrement, recrement.
EKS′a–bl– **3.** vexable.
  4. annexable; *see also* ĔKS′i–bl.
EKS′ed–lee– **3.** vexedly.

4. perplexedly, convexedly.
EKSH′un–al– 3. flectional, sectional.
4. affectional, objectional, projectional, reflectional, inflectional, collectional, complexional, connectional, directional, correctional, resectional, bisectional, dissectional, protectional, convectional.
5. interjectional, resurrectional, insurrectional, vivisectional.
EKSH′un–er– 4. confectioner, perfectioner, correctioner.
EKSH′un–ist– 4. perfectionist, projectionist, protectionist.
5. resurrectionist, insurrectionist, vivisectionist.
6. antiprotectionist.
7. antivivisectionist.
EKS′i–bl– 3. flexible.
4. deflexible, reflexible, inflexible; *see also* **ĔKS′a–bl.**
EKS′i–kal– 3. lexical.
4. indexical, pyrexical.
EKS′i–tee– 4. complexity, perplexity, duplexity, convexity.
EKS′iv–ness– 4. reflexiveness, perplexiveness.
EKT′a–bl– 4. subjectable, objectable, rejectable, delectable, deflectable, respectable, expectable, suspectable, erectable, detectable.
5. indelectable, undetectable; *see also* **ĔKT′i–bl.**
EKT′a–blee– 4. delectably, respectably.
5. undelectably, unsuspectably.
EKT′a–kl– 3. spectacle.
4. bespectacle; *see also* **ĔKT′i–kl.**
EKT′a–ree– 3. nectary, sectary; *see also* **ĔKT′o–ree.**
EKT′ed–lee– 4. affectedly, subjectedly, dejectedly, reflectedly, neglectedly, collectedly, connectedly, respectedly, protectedly.
5. unaffectedly, disaffectedly, recollectedly, disconnectedly, unexpectedly, unsuspectedly.
EKT′ed–ness– 4. affectedness, infectedness, abjectedness, dejectedness, subjectedness, neglectedness, suspectedness.
5. unaffectedness, disaffectedness, disconnectedness, unexpectedness, unsuspectedness.
EKT′ful–ee– 4. neglectfully, respectfully.
5. unrespectfully, disrespectfully.
EKT′ful–ness– 4. neglectfulness, respectfulness, suspectfulness.
5. disrespectfulness.
EKT′i–bl– 4. affectible, effectible, defectible, infectible, perfectible, subjectible, reflectible, connectible, suspectible, dissectible.
5. unaffectible; *see also* **ĔKT′a–bl.**
EKT′i–fi– 3. rectify.
4. objectify, subjectify.
EKT′i–kl– 5. dialectical, apoplectical; *see also* **ĔKT′a–kl.**
EKT′ing–lee– 4. affectingly, objectingly, reflectingly.

EKT′i–tude– 3. rectitude.
4. senectitude.
EKT′i–vist– 4. objectivist, collectivist.
EKT′iv–lee– 4. affectively, effectively, defectively, infectively, perfectively, objectively, subjectively, projectively, electively, selectively, deflectively, reflectively, inflectively, neglectively, collectively, connectively, respectively, prospectively, perspectively, directively, correctively, protectively, invectively.
5. ineffectively, unreflectively, irreflectively, recollectively, irrespectively, retrospectively, introspectively.
EKT′iv–ness– 4. effectiveness, defectiveness, perfectiveness, objectiveness, subjectiveness, reflectiveness, collectiveness, prospectiveness, protectiveness.
5. unobjectiveness, irreflectiveness, unreflectiveness, recollectiveness.
EKT′or–al– 3. pectoral, rectoral, sectoral.
4. prefectoral, electoral, inspectoral, directoral, protectoral.
EKT′or–ate– 3. rectorate.
4. electorate, expectorate, directorate, protectorate.
EKT′or–ee– 3. rectory.
4. refectory, trajectory, directory, correctory, protectory.
5. interjectory; *see also* **ĔKT′ar–ee.**
EKT′u–al– 3. lectual.
4. effectual, prefectual.
5. ineffectual, intellectual.
EKT′ur–al– 4. prefectural, conjectural.
5. architectural.
EKT′ur–er– 3. lecturer.
4. conjecturer.
EK′u–lar– 3. specular, secular.
4. trabecular, vallecular, molecular.
EK′u–late– 3. peculate, speculate.
EK′und–lee– 3. fecundly, secondly.
EK′u–tiv– 4. executive, subsecutive, consecutive.
5. unconsecutive.
EL′a–bl– 3. bellable, delible, fellable, gelable, spellable, sellable, tellable, quellable.
4. indelible, compellable, expellable, unspellable, foretellable, unquellable; *see also* **ĔL′i–bl.**
EL′a–tin– 3. gelatin, gelatine, skeleton.
EL′a–tiv– 3. relative.
4. appellative, compellative, irrelative, correlative.
EL′e–gate– 3. delegate, relegate.
EL′er–ee– 3. celery, cellary, stellary.
EL′et–on– 3. skeleton, gelatin, gelatine.
ELF′i–a– 4. Didelphia.
5. Philadelphia, Monodelphia.
6. Polyadelphia.
ELF′i–an– 3. Delphian.
4. didelphian.
5. Philadelphian, Christadelphian.
ELF′ish–lee– 3. elfishly, selfishly.
4. unselfishly.

ĔLF'ish–ness– 3. elfishness, selfishness.
4. unselfishness.
EL'i–bl– 3. delible.
4. indelible; *see also* ĔL'a–bl.
EL'i–ing– 3. bellying, jellying.
EL'i–ka– 3. Melica.
4. Angelica.
EL'i–kl– 3. bellical, helical, pellicle.
4. angelical, vitellicle.
5. evangelical.
EL'ing–lee– 3. tellingly, quellingly, well-ingly.
4. compellingly.
EL'ish–ing– 3. relishing.
4. embellishing.
EL'ish–ment– 3. relishment.
4. ẹmbellishment.
EL'i–tee– 3. pellety.
4. fidelity.
5. infidelity.
EL'o–ee– 3. mellowy, yellowy.
EL'o–er– 3. bellower, mellower, yellower.
EL'o–est– 3. mellowest, celloist, yellowest.
EL'o–ing– 3. bellowing, mellowing, yellowing.
EL'on–ee– 3. felony, melony.
EL'op–ing– 4. developing, enveloping.
5. undeveloping.
EL'op–ment– 4. development, envelopment.
ELT'er–ee– 3. smeltery, sheltery, sweltery.
ELT'er–ing– 3. sheltering, weltering, swel-tering.
ELTH'i–er– 3. healthier, stealthier, wealth-ier.
ELTH'i–est– 3. healthiest, stealthiest, wealthiest.
ELTH'i–lee– 3. healthily, stealthily, wealthily.
EL'u–lar– 3. cellular, stellular.
4. bicellular.
5. unicellular, interstellular.
EL'us–lee– 3. jealously, zealously.
EL'us–ness– 3. jealousness, zealousness.
EM'an–ee– 4. anemone, Gethsemane.
5. pantanemone, Agapemone.
EM'a–tist– 4. emblematist.
5. theorematist.
EMB'er–ee– 3. embery.
4. Decembery, Septembery, Novembery.
EMB'er–ing– 3. membering.
4. remembering, dismembering.
EMB'er–ish– 3. emberish.
4. Decemberish, Septemberish, Novemberish.
EM'er–al– 3. femerell, femoral, nemoral.
4. ephemeral, trihemeral.
EM'er–ee– 3. emery, gemmary, memory.
EM'e–sis– 3. emesis, Nemesis.
EM'i–kal– 3. chemical.
4. endemical, alchemical, polemical.
5. academical, epidemical.
6. electrochemical.
EM'i–lee– 3. Emily, gemmily.
EM'in–al– 3. feminal, geminal, seminal.
4. bigeminal, tergeminal.
EM'in–ate– 3. feminate, geminate.
4. effeminate, ingeminate, tergeminate, dis-

seminate, inseminate.
EM'in–ent– 3. eminent.
4. pre-eminent.
5. supereminent.
EMN'i–tee– 4. indemnity, solemnity.
EM'o–nee– 4. anemone, Gethsemane.
5. pantanemone, Agapemone.
EM'o–ra– 3. femora, remora.
4. ephemera.
EM'o–ral– 3. femoral, nemoral; *see also* ĔM'er–al.
EM'o–ree– 3. emery, Emory, gemmary, memory.
EMP'er–ee– 3. empery, tempery, tempore [L.].
4. extempore.
EMP'er–er– 3. emperor, temperer.
EMP'or–al– 3. temporal.
4. atemporal, extemporal.
5. supertemporal.
EMP'to–ree– 4. redemptory, peremptory.
EM'u–lent– 3. emulant, tremulant, tem-ulent.
EM'u–lus– 3. emulous, tremulous.
EN'ar'ee– 3 denary, hennery, plenary, senary.
4. decennary, centenary, septennary.
EN'at–or– 3. senator; *see also* ĔN'i–tor.
END'a–bl– 3. endable, lendable, mendable.
4. defendable, amendable, emendable, commendable, dependable, ascendable, de-scendable.
5. recommendable, independable, undepend-able, unascendable; *see also* ĔND'i–bl.
END'an–see– 4. appendancy, ascendancy, attendancy, intendancy; *see also* ĔND' en–see.
END'en–see– 3. splendency, pendency, ten-dency.
4. transcendency, resplendency, transplen-dency, dependency, impendency, intend-ency.
5. independency, ambitendency, counter-tendency; *see also* ĔND'an–see.
END'er–er– 3. genderer, slenderer, ren-derer, tenderer.
4. engenderer, surrenderer.
END'er–est– 3. slenderest, tenderest.
END'er–ing– 3. gendering, rendering, ten-dering.
4. engendering, surrendering.
END'er–lee– 3. slenderly, tenderly.
END'er–ness– 3. slenderness, tenderness.
END'i–bl– 3. rendible, vendible.
4. ascendible, accendible, extendible, in-vendible.
5. comprehendible; *see also* ĔND'a–bl.
END'i–us– 4. compendious, dispendious.
END'less–lee– 3. endlessly, bendlessly, mend-lessly, friendlessly.
END'less–ness– 3. endlessness, bendlessness, mendlessness, friendlessness.
END'us–lee– 4. tremendously, stupendously, horrendously.

ĔND′us–ness– 4. tremendousness, stupendousness.
EN′er–ate– 3. generate, venerate.
4. degenerate, regenerate, ingenerate, progenerate, intenerate.
EN′es–is– 3. genesis.
4. regenesis, pangenesis, parenesis.
5. paragenesis, catagenesis, metagenesis, epigenesis, neogenesis, psychogenesis, morphogenesis, pathogenesis, biogenesis, homogenesis, monogenesis, oogenesis, zoogenesis, pyrogenesis, ectogenesis, ontogenesis, histogenesis, polygenesis.
6. osteogenesis, organogenesis, parthenogenesis, anthropogenesis, heterogenesis.
ENGTH′en–ing– 3. strengthening, lengthening.
EN′i–a– 4. millennia, quadrennia, decennia.
EN′i–al– 4. biennial, triennial, millennial, perennial, plurennial, decennial, tricennial, vicennial, sexennial, centennial, quotennial, septennial, novennial, quinquennial.
5. bicentennial, tricentennial, tercentennial.
6. duodecennial.
EN′i–form– 3. penniform.
4. bipenniform, antenniform.
EN′i–kal– 3. scenical.
4. Galenical, sirenical, arsenical.
5. hygienical, ecumenical.
6. catechumenical.
EN′i–tee– 3. lenity.
4. amenity, serenity, terrenity, obscenity.
EN′i–tiv– 3. genitive, lenitive, splenitive.
4. progenitive.
5. primogenitive.
EN′i–tor– 3. genitor, senator.
4. progenitor.
5. primogenitor: see also ĔN′at–or.
EN′i–tude– 3. lenitude, plenitude.
4. serenitude.
EN′i–ture– 3. geniture.
4. progeniture.
5. primogeniture.
6. ultimogeniture.
EN′i–um– 4. biennium, millenium, quadrennium, decennium, sexennium, septennium.
EN′i–zon– 3. benison, denizen, venison.
4. endenizen.
ENS′a–bl– 4. condensable, dispensable.
5. incondensable, indispensable; see also ĔNS′i–bl.
ENS′a–ree– dispensary; see also ĔNS′o–ree.
ENS′a–tiv– 3. pensative, sensitive.
4. condensative, compensative, dispensative, insensitive, intensive; see also ĔNS′i–tiv.
ENSH′a–ree– 4. sententiary.
5. residentiary, penitentiary.
ENSH′i–ate– 4. essentiate, licentiate, potentiate.
5. differentiate.
ENSH′i–ent– 3. sentient.
4. assentient, presentient, dissentient, insentient, consentient.

ENSH′u–al– 3. mensual, censual, sensual.
4. trimensual, consensual.
ENSH′un′al– 3. tensional.
4. dimensional, ascensional, descensional, attentional, intentional, contentional, extensional, preventional, conventional.
5. unintentional, unconventional.
ENSH′un–er– 3. mentioner, pensioner.
4. conventioner.
ENSH′un–ing– 3. mentioning, pensioning, tensioning.
ENSH′un–ist– 4. ascentionist, descentionist, recencionist, extensionist, preventionist, conventionist.
ENSH′us–ness– 4. licentiousness, pretentiousness, sententiousness, contentiousness.
5. conscientiousness, unpretentiousness.
ENS′i–bl– 3. sensible, tensible.
4. condensible, defensible, insensible, unsensible, distensible, ostensible.
5. indefensible, apprehensible, reprehensible, comprehensible, inostensible.
6. irreprehensible, incomprehensible; see also ĔNS′a–bl.
ENS′i–blee– 3. sensibly.
4. defensibly, insensibly, ostensibly.
5. reprehensibly, comprehensibly.
6. incomprehensibly.
ENS′i–fi– 3. densify, sensify.
4. intensify.
ENS′i–kal– 4. forensical, nonsensical.
ENS′i–tee– 3. density, tensity.
4. condensity, immensity, propensity, attensity, intensity.
ENS′i–tiv– 3. sensitive.
4. condensitive, insensative; see also ĔNS′a–tiv.
ENS′iv–lee– 3. pensively.
4. defensively, offensively, expensively, intensively, extensively.
5. inoffensively, apprehensively, reprehensively, comprehensively, inexpensively.
6. incomprehensively.
ENS′iv–ness– 3. pensiveness.
4. offensiveness, expensiveness, intensiveness, extensiveness.
5. comprehensiveness.
6. incomprehensiveness.
ENS′less–lee– 3. senselessly, tenselessly.
4. defenselessly, offenselessly.
ENS′less–ness– 3. senselessness, tenselessness.
4. defenselessness.
ENS′o–ree– 3. sensory.
4. condensery, defensory, prehensory, dispensary, suspensory, incensory, ostensory.
5. reprehensory; see also ĔNS′a–ree.
ENT′a–bl– 3. rentable, tentable.
4. lamentable, fermentable, repentable, contentable, preventable, inventable; see also ĔNT′i–bl; frequentable, presentable.
5. uncontentable, representable, unpresentable.
ENT′a–blee– 4. lamentably, preventably,

presentably.
5. unpreventably, unpresentably.
ENT′a–kl– 3. pentacle, tentacle.
ENT′a–lee– 3. mentally.
4. fragmentally, segmentally, pigmentally, momentally, parentally.
5. accidentally, occidentally, incidentally, orientally, fundamentally, ornamentally, elementally, supplementally, regimentally, alimentally, complimentally, detrimentally, sentimentally, governmentally, monumentally, instrumentally, continentally.
6. temperamentally, developmentally.
ENT′al–ist– 5. Occidentalist, transcendentalist, Orientalist, fundamentalist, sentimentalist, instrumentalist.
6. experimentalist.
ENT′al–izm– 5. Occidentalism, transcendentalism, Orientalism, elementalism, fundamentalism, sentimentalism.
ENT′a–ree– 3. dentary.
4. *fragmentary*, segmentary, pigmentary.
5. filamentary, sacramentary, testamentary, elementary, complementary, supplementary, sedimentary, rudimentary, alimentary, complimentary, documentary, tegumentary.
6. uncomplimentary, integumentary, emolumentary.
ENT′a–tiv– 3. tentative.
4. augmentative, fermentative, presentative, pretentative, sustentative, frequentative.
5. alimentative, complimentative, argumentative, representative.
6. experimentative, misrepresentative.
ENT′ed–lee– 4. dementedly, tormentedly, contentedly.
5. unlamentedly, discontentedly, unfrequentedly.
6. unprecedentedly.
ENT′ed–ness– 3. scentedness.
4. dementedness, fermentedness, tormentedness, contentedness, frequentedness, inventedness.
5. discontentedness, unfrequentedness.
6. unprecedentedness.
ENT′er–ing– 3. entering, centering.
4. re-entering, self-centering.
ENT′ful–lee– 4. resentfully, eventfully, inventfully.
5. unresentfully, uneventfully.
ENT′ful–ness– 4. resentfulness, eventfulness, inventfulness.
5. uneventfulness.
ENTH′e–sis– 4. epenthesis, parenthesis.
ENT′i–bl– 4. inventible; *see also* ĔNT′a–bl.
ENT′i–kal– 3. dentical, denticle.
4. identical, authentical, conventical, conventicle.
ENT′i–kule– 3. denticule, lenticule.
ENT′i–ment– 3. sentiment.
4. presentiment.
ENT′i–nel– 3. dentinal, sentinel.
ENT′ing–lee– 4. relentingly, lamentingly, augmentingly, tormentingly, repentingly,

assentingly, dissentingly, consentingly.
5. unrelentingly.
ENT′i–tee– 3. entity.
4. identity, nonentity.
ENT′iv–lee– 4. presentively, attentively, retentively, preventively, inventively.
ENT′iv–ness– 4. attentiveness, retentiveness, preventiveness, inventiveness, presentiveness.
5. inattentiveness, uninventiveness.
ENT′l–ness– 3. gentleness.
4. ungentleness.
5. Occidentalness, transcendentalness, Orientalness, elementalness, fundamentalness, sentimentalness.
ENT′ral–ee– 3. centrally, ventrally.
4. subcentrally, uncentrally.
5. dorsiventrally.
ENT′rik–al– 3. centrical, ventricle.
4. eccentrical, concentrical.
ENT′u–al– 4. accentual, percentual, adventual, eventual, conventual.
ENT′u–ate– 4. accentuate, eventuate.
ENT′us–lee– 4. momentously, portentously.
ENT′us–ness– 4. momentousness, portentousness.
EN′u–ate– 3. tenuate.
4. attenuate, extenuate.
EN′u–us– 3. tenuous, strenuous.
4. ingenuous.
5. disingenuous.
EP′a–rate– 3. reparate, separate.
EP′er–us– 3. leperous, streperous.
4. obstreperous.
EP′ik–al– 3. epical.
5. orthoëpical.
EP′it–ant– 3. crepitant, strepitant.
EPSH′un–al– 4. exceptional, conceptional.
5. unexceptional.
EPS′i–a– 4. apepsia, dyspepsia, eupepsia.
5. monoblepsia.
EPT′i–bl– 4. deceptible, receptible, acceptable, perceptible, susceptible.
5. imperceptible, insusceptible, unsusceptible.
EPT′i–blee– 4. perceptibly, susceptibly.
5. indeceptibly, imperceptibly, unsusceptibly.
EPT′ik–al– 3. skeptical, septical.
4. sylleptical, aseptical, receptacle, conceptacle.
5. antiseptical.
EPT′iv–ness– 4. deceptiveness, receptiveness, perceptiveness, susceptiveness.
5. imperceptiveness.
EPT′u–al– 4. preceptual, conceptual, perceptual.
5. preconceptual.
ER′a–fim– 3. seraphim, teraphim.
ER′an–see– 3. errancy.
4. aberrancy, inerrancy.
ER′a–pee– 3. therapy.
5. theotherapy, psychotherapy, hydrotherapy, autotherapy.
6. balneotherapy, radiotherapy.
ER′i–bl– 3. errable, terrible.

ĔR'i–deez– 4. Pierides, Hesperides.
ĔR'i–er– 3. berrier, burier, ferrier, merrier, terrier.
ĔR'i–fi– 3. spherify, terrify, verify.
ĔR'i–ing– 3. berrying, burying, ferrying, serrying, wherrying.
4. cranberrying, strawberrying, blueberrying.
5. huckleberrying.
ĔR'i–ka– 3. erica, erika.
4. America.
ĔR'i–kal– 3. spherical, sphericle, clerical.
4. chimerical, Homerical, mesmerical, numerical, generical, hysterical.
5. hemispherical, atmospherical, rhinocerical, climaterical, esoterical, exoterical.
ĔR'i–lee– 3. merrily, verily.
ĔR'i–ment– 3. merriment.
4. experiment.
ĔR'ish–ing– 3. cherishing, perishing.
4. uncherishing, unperishing.
ĔR'it–ans– 3. heritance.
4. inheritance.
5. disinheritance.
ĔR'it–ed– 3. ferreted, merited.
4. inherited, disherited, emerited, unmerited.
5. disinherited.
ĔR'it–ee– 3. verity.
4. legerity, celerity, temerity, asperity, prosperity, sincerity, alterity, dexterity, austerity, posterity, severity.
5. insincerity, indexterity.
6. ambidexterity.
ĔR'it–er– 3. ferreter, meriter.
4. inheritor, coheritor.
ĔR'it–ing– 3. ferreting, meriting.
4. inheriting, unmeriting.
5. disinheriting.
ĔR'it–iv– 4. aperitive, imperative, preteritive.
ERJ– through ERZ, see Ŭ (tub): ŬRJ'en–see through ŬRZH'un–ist.
ĔR'o–gate– 3. derogate.
4. interrogate.
5. supererogate.
ĔS'a–bl– 3. guessable, pressable.
4. unguessable, assessable, possessable.
5. unredressable, unassessable, unpossessable.
ĔS'a–ree– 4. confessary; see also ĔS'o–ree.
ĔS'en–see– 4. acescency, quiescency, turgescency, excrescency, liquescency.
5. erubescency, incandescency, acquiescency, convalescency, adolescency, efflorescency, delitescency, effervescency.
ĔS'ful–ee– 3. blessfully, stressfully.
4. successfully, distressfully.
ĔS'i–bl– 4. concrescible, redressible, transgressible, depressible, repressible, impressible, compressible, suppressible, expressible, vitrescible, putrescible, accessible, concessible.
5. irrepressible, insuppressible, unexpressible, inaccessible, unconcessible, fermentescible, effervescible.
6. ineffervescible.
ĔS'i–blee– 4. expressibly, accessibly.

5. irrepressibly, inexpressibly, inaccessibly.
ĔS'i–kate– 3. desiccate, vesicate, exsiccate.
ĔS'i–ma– 3. decima.
5. Quadragesima, Sexagesima, Quinquagesima.
6. Septuagesima.
ĔS'i–mal– 3. decimal.
4. trigesimal, vigesimal, millesimal, centesimal.
5. duodecimal, nonagesimal, quadragesimal, sexagesimal.
6. septuagesimal, infinitesimal.
ĔS'i–mo– 5. octodecimo, sextodecimo, duodecimo.
ĔS'ing–lee– 3. pressingly.
4. caressingly, depressingly, distressingly.
5. prepossessingly.
ĔS'i–tee– 4. obesity, necessity.
ĔS'iv–lee– 4. aggressively, regressively, digressively, progressively, transgressively, depressively, repressively, impressively, oppressively, expressively, excessively, successively, possessively.
ĔS'iv–ness– 4. aggressiveness, progressiveness, depressiveness, impressiveness, oppressiveness, expressiveness, excessiveness, successiveness, possessiveness.
ĔS'o–ree– 4. professory, confessary, accessory, successory, concessory, possessory.
5. intercessory.
ĔSH'i–ens– 3. nescience, prescience.
ĔSH'i–ness– 3. fleshiness, meshiness.
ĔSH'un–al– 3. sessional.
4. confessional, professional, digressional, congressional, progressional, transgressional, discretional, impressional, compressional, expressional, recessional, precessional, accessional, successional, possessional, processional.
5. retrocessional, intercessional.
ĔSH'un–er– 3. sessioner.
4. secessioner, possessioner, processioner.
ĔSH'un–ist– 4. confessionist, progressionist, impressionist, suppressionist, expressionist, secessionist, concessionist, successionist, processionist.
ĔST'a–bl– 3. testable.
4. detestable, intestable, contestable.
5. incontestable; see also ĔST'i–bl.
ĔST'a–blee– 3. testably.
4. detestably, contestably.
5. incontestably, uncontestably.
ĔST'a–ment– 3. testament, vestiment.
ĔST'er–ing– 3. festering, pestering, westering.
4. sequestering.
ĔST'ful–ee– 3. restfully, questfully, zestfully.
ĔST'i–al– 3. bestial.
4. celestial, agrestial.
5. uncelestial.
6. supercelestial.
ĔST'i–bl– 4. digestible, suggestible, comestible, divestible.
5. indigestible; see also ĔST'a–bl.

EST′i–kal– 4. majestical.
   5. anapaestical, catachrestical.
EST′in–al– 3. destinal.
   4. intestinal.
EST′i–ness– 3. restiness, testiness.
EST′ing–lee– 3. jestingly, testingly.
   4. protestingly.
   5. interestingly.
   6. uninterestingly.
EST′iv–lee– 3. festively, restively.
   4. suggestively.
EST′iv–ness– 3. festiveness, restiveness.
   4. suggestiveness.
EST′ri–al– 4. pedestrial, bimestrial, trimestrial, terrestrial.
   5. decimestrial.
   6. superterrestrial.
EST′ri–an– 4. pedestrian, palaestrian, campestrian, rupestrian, sylvestrian, equestrian.
EST′ri–us– 4. pedestrious, terrestrious.
EST′ur–al– 3. gestural, vestural.
EST′u–us– 4. tempestuous, incestuous.
ET′a–bl– 3. gettable, lettable, nettable, pettable, settable.
   4. forgettable, regrettable, upsettable.
   5. unforgettable, unregrettable.
ET′a–blee– 4. regrettably.
   5. unforgettably.
ET′a–lus– 3. petalous.
   4. apetalous.
   5. polypetalous.
ET′er–er– 3. betterer, fetterer, letterer.
ET′er–ing– 3. bettering, fettering, lettering.
ET′er–it– 3. preterit, preterite.
   4. inveterate.
ET′ful–ee– 3. fretfully.
   4. forgetfully, regretfully.
ET′ful–ness– 3. fretfulness.
   4. forgetfulness, regretfulness.
ETH′er–ee– 3. feathery, heathery, leathery, tethery, weathery.
ETH′er–ing– 3. feathering, leathering, tethering, weathering.
   4. untethering.
ETH′i–kal– 3. ethical.
   4. nonethical, unethical.
ETH′less–lee– 3. deathlessly, breathlessly.
ETH′less–ness– 3. deathlessness, breathlessness.
ET′i–kal– 4. prophetical, pathetical, synthetical, hermetical, cosmetical, planetical, genetical, threnetical, noetical, poetical, syncretical, heretical, ascetical.
   5. alphabetical, diabetical, exegetical, energetical, catechetical, homiletical, arithmetical, unpoetical, apathetical, metathetical, epithetical, antithetical, parenthetical, nomothetical, hyperthetical.
   6. apologetical, homogenetical, antipathetical.

ET′i–ness– 3. jettiness, pettiness, sweatiness.
ET′i–nu– 3. detinue, retinue.
ET′ish–lee– 3. pettishly.
   4. coquettishly.
ET′ish–ness– 3. pettishness.
   4. coquettishness.
ET′i–sizm– 4. athleticism, phoneticism, asceticism, aetheticism.
ET′i–tiv– 3. vetitive.
   4. repetitive, competitive.
   5. noncompetitive, uncompetitive.
ET′ri–fi– 3. metrify, petrify.
ET′ri–kal– 3. metrical.
   4. symmetrical, nonmetrical, unmetrical, obstetrical.
   5. diametrical, dynametrical, heptametrical, hexametrical, perimetrical, asymmetrical, pedometrical, geometrical, stichometrical, graphometrical, biometrical, thermometrical, clinometrical, chronometrical, barometrical, hydrometrical, horometrical, isometrical.
   6. craniometrical, trigonometrical, electrometrical.
   7. isoperimetrical.
EV′el–er– 3. beveler, deviler, leveler, reveler.
EV′el–ing– 3. beveling, deviling, leveling, reveling.
   4. bedeviling, disheveling.
EV′el–ment– 3. devilment, revelment.
   4. bedevilment, dishevelment.
EV′el–ree– 3. devilry, revelry.
EV′er–ans– 3. reverence, severance.
   4. irreverence, disseverance.
EV′er–er– 3. leverer, cleverer, severer.
   4. endeavorer.
EV′er–est– 3. Everest, cleverest.
EV′er–et– 3. Everett, leveret.
EV′er–ij– 3. beverage, leverage.
EV′er–ing– 3. levering, severing.
   4. endeavoring.
EV′i–tee– 3. levity, brevity.
   4. longevity.
EV′o–lens– 4. benevolence, malevolence.
   5. unbenevolence.
EV′o–lent– 4. benevolent, malevolent.
   5. unbenevolent.
EV′o–lus– 4. benevolous, malevolous.
EV′o–lute– 3. evolute, devolute, revolute.
EZ′ant–ree– 3. pheasantry, pleasantry, peasantry.
EZH′er–er– 3. pleasurer, measurer, treasurer.
EZH′er–ing– 3. pleasuring, measuring, treasuring.
EZ′i–dens– 3. residents, residence, presidents.
   4. vice-presidents.
EZ′i–dent– 3. resident, president.
   4. nonresident, vice-president.

Ī (eye)

Single (Masculine) Rhymes

Primary or Secondary Accent Falls on Last Syllable; Imperfect Rhymes Are in Italics.

I– 1. I, ay, aye, ai, eye.
2. *redeye, frogeye,* black eye, *black-eye, pinkeye, cockeye, buckeye, peepeye, fisheye, cat's-eye, oxeye, bull's-eye,* Bull's Eye.
3. naked eye, evil eye, weather eye.
6. amicus curiae [L.].
BI– 1. by, bye, buy.
2. good-bye, good-by, bye-bye, *go-by,* hereby, thereby, whereby, forby, foreby, pass by.
3. by-and-by, rockaby, lullaby, hushaby, by the by, by the bye. alibi, underbuy, passer-by, overbuy, incubi, succubi.
DI– 1. die, dye.
2. bedye, redye, undye.
3. sine die.
FI– 1. fie, phi.
2. defy, fie-fie [coll.].
3. labefy, tabefy, tumefy, tepefy, stupefy, arefy, rarefy, torrefy, putrefy, pinguefy, liquefy, verbify, rubify, preachify [coll.], speechify, Frenchify, churchify, ladify, edify, nidify, dandify, mundify, codify, modify, deify, qualify, steelify, vilify, jellify, mollify, nullify, amplify, simplify, duplify, ramify, mummify, humify, sanify, magnify, dignify, minify, damnify, bonify, carnify, unify, torpify, typify, scarify, clarify, lubrify, spherify, verify, terrify, nigrify micrify, horrify, glorify, petrify, nitrify, vitrify, aurify, purify, pacify, specify, calcify, classify, falsify, salsify, dulcify, ossify, versify, crucify, ratify, gratify, prettify, rectify, sanctify, fructify, stultify, quantify, daintify, notify, certify, fortify, mortify, testify, justify, mystify, beautify, mythify, sanguify, vivify, satisfy, argufy [coll. & dial.], ladyfy, monkeyfy.
4. syllabify, solidify, remodify, disqualify, exemplify, divinify, indemnify, personify, saccharify, transmogrify, electrify, complexify, decalcify, beatify, objectify, identify, revivify.
5. diabolify.
GI– 1. guy, Guy.

2. fall guy [slang], wise guy [slang].
HI– 1. hi [slang], hie, high, heigh.
2. knee-high, sky-high.
3. Bali-hi.
KI– 1. kai, chi, sky, Skye.
2. *haikai,* kai-kai, ensky, blue sky.
3. abacay, cloudy sky, sunny sky, starry sky.
4. mackerel sky.
LI– 1. lie, lye, fly, cly (cant), ply, sly.
2. ally, *Eli,* belie, rely, Philae, outlie, *dayfly, bobfly, gadfly, gallfly, jarfly, firefly, horsefly, housefly, botfly, shoofly,* apply, reply, imply, comply, supply, unsly, July.
3. re-ally, alkali, disally, misally, dragonfly, butterfly, reapply, misapply, multiply, reimply, underlie, overlie, lazuli.
4. undersupply, oversupply.
5. lapis lazuli.
MI– 1. my.
2. demi, demy.
3. animae [L.].
NI– 1. nigh, nye, sny.
2. deny, well-nigh.
3. redeny, termini, *alumnae, alumni.*
PI– 1. pi, pie, paille [F.], spy.
2. *magpie, nanpie, mincepie, potpie,* espy, bespy.
3. humble pie, apple pie, homme de paille [F.], philippi, Philippi, shoofly pie, occupy.
4. preoccupy.
RI– 1. rye, wry, dry, fry, gri [Gypsy], gry [Gypsy], cry, scry, pry, spry, try.
2. awry, adry, *roughdry, fish fry,* decry, descry, *outcry,* atry.
3. college try.
SI– 1. sigh, scye, psi.
2. *armscye,* Versailles.
3. prophesy.
SHI– 1. shy.
2. unshy.
TI– 1. tie, ty, tye, Tai, Thai, taille [F.], sty, stye.
2. retie, *hogtie, necktie,* untie, *pigsty.*

THI– 1. thigh, thy.
VI– 1. vie, Vi.
2. outvie.
WI– 1. y, Y, wye, Wye.

IB– 1. gibe, jibe, kibe, libe [slang], bribe, scribe, tribe, vibe.
2. imbibe, ascribe, subscribe, describe, prescribe, transcribe, inscribe, conscribe, proscribe, perscribe.
3. circumscribe, superscribe, diatribe.
IBD– 1. gibed, jibed, kibed, bribed.
2. imbibed, ascribed, subscribed, described, prescribed, transcribed, inscribed, conscribed, proscribed, perscribed.
3. circumscribed, superscribed.
ID– 1. ide, I'd, eyed, bide, chide, died, dyed, guide, guyed, hide, Hyde, lied, Clyde, glide, gleyd, gleyde, slide, nide, snide, pied, spied, ride, bride, dried, gride, cried, scried, pride, pried, tried, stride, side, sighed, tide, tied, vied, wide.
2. *red-eyed*, *calf-eyed*, *pie-eyed*, *black-eyde*, *snake-eyed*, *meek-eyed*, *pink-eyed*, *cock-eyed*, *hawk-eyed*, *pale-eyed*, *wall-eyed*, *owl-eyed*, *dull-eyed*, *green-eyed*, *pop-eyed*, *blear-eyed*, *clear-eyed*, *lynx-eyed*, *ox-eyed*, *cat-eyed*, *soft-eyed*, *squint-eyed*, *blue-eyed*, *dove-eyed*, abide, *carbide*, redyed, defied, *sulphide*, confide, misguide, *rawhide*, *cowhide*, allied, elide, collide, applied, *landslide*, *backslide*, *bromide*, denied, espied, unspied, arride, child bride, redried, undried, *hydride*, deride, descried, *boride*, *chloride*, self-pride, *nitride*, night ride, untried, astride, bestride, outstride, outride, aside, *wayside*, subside, *bedside*, *broadside*, beside, decide, *seaside*, offside, *lakeside*, *excide*, *brookside*, *hillside*, inside, onside, *topside*, *fireside*, *foreside*, *white-side*, outside, ebb tide, flood tide, high tide, low tide, neap tide, betide, retied, *Yuletide*, *springtide*, noon tide, *untied*, Shrove-tide, divide, provide, world-wide, reside, preside.
3. iodide, almond-eyed, bonafide, tumefied, tepefied, stupefied, rarefied, torrefied, putrefied, liquefied, edified, modified, deified, qualified, mollified, nullified, magnified, dignified, bonified, verified, glorified, terrified, petrified, vitrified, purified, pacified, specified, falsified, calcified, dulcified, versified, ossified, crucified, ratified, gratified, stratified, rectified, sanctified, fructified, stultified, notified, certified, fortified, mortified, testified, justified, mystified, beautified, vivified, satisfied, disulphide, eagle-eyed, goggle-eyed, evil-eyed, unallied, misallied, unbelied, reapplied, unapplied, misapplied, multiplied, cyanide, arsenide, occupied, saccharide, underdried, overdried, fluoride, override, telluride, prophesied, Barmecide, alongside, herbicide, verbicide, regicide, fungicide, homicide, germicide, vermicide, lapicide, herpicide, parricide, matricide, patricide, fratricide, countryside, vaticide, suicide, larvicide,

slickenside, oceanside, mountainside, coincide, glucoside, peroxide, put on side, genocide, underside, waterside, riverside, Argus-eyed, unbetide, eventide, Whitsuntide, Hallowtide, undertide, Eastertide, Lamnastide, Christmastide, subdivide, citywide, county-wide, country-wide, nationwide.
4. solidified, unqualified, saponified, unverified, electrified, decalcified, emulsified, intensified, diversified, beatified, unsanctified, identified, revivified, dissatisfied, formaldehyde, preoccupied, unoccupied, reprophesied, unprophesied, microbicide, tyrannicide, sororicide, uxoricide, insecticide, infanticide, giganticide, parenticide, liberticide, nematocide, Allhallowtide, Michealmastide.
5. underoccupied, overoccupied, parasiticide.
IDZ– *see* **ĪD**, plus " s " or " 's "; **3.** Ironsides, sobersides.
IF– 1. fife, kife [slang], life, knife, rife, strife, wife.
2. *jackknife*, *midwife*, *oldwife*, *goodwife*, *alewife*, *housewife*, *fishwife*.
3. afterlife, bowie knife, pocket knife, puddingwife.
IJ– 1. Lige, 'blige.
2. oblige.
3. reoblige, disoblige.
IK– 1. Ike, bike, dike, fike, fyke, hike, haik, Haikh, like, Mike, mike [slang], Smike, pike, pyke, spike, grike, shrike, trike [slang], strike, sike, tyke, tike, wike [obs.].
2. Vandyke, *hitchhike*, alike, *seedlike*, *childlike*, *godlike*, belike, *lifelike*, *wifelike*, *elflike*, *kinglike*, *winglike*, *flamelike*, *gemlike*, *homelike*, *manlike*, *swanlike*, *queenlike*, *hornlike*, unlike, *apelike*, *earlike*, *starlike*, *warlike*, *airlike*, dislike, *mislike*, *catlike*, *ghostlike*, *deathlike*, *toothlike*, *earthlike*, *dovelike*, *screwlike*, *rampike*, turnpike.
3. unalike, tunnellike, womanlike, tigerlike, Quakerlike, fatherlike, featherlike, motherlike, brotherlike, sisterlike, peasantlike, ladylike, fairylike, marlinspike.
IKS– *see* **ĪK**, plus " s " or " 's "; **1.** Sykes.
IL– 1. aisle, isle, I'll, bile, file, guile, gyle, Heil, chyle, lisle, Lyle, mile, smile. Nile, pile, spile, rile, tile, stile, style, vile, wile, weil, while.
2. Kabyle, defile, *profile*, beguile, enisle, *senile*, repile, compile, unpile, resile, *exile*, ensile, *centile*, *gentile*, *reptile*, *septile*, *fertile*, *turnstile*, *hostile*, *futile*, *rutile*, revile, awhile, meanwhile, therewhile, erstwhile, worthwhile.
3. atrabile, crocodile, photofile, rheophile, theophile, ergophile, Francophile, Turkophile, discophile, halophile, Anglophile, Gallophile, thermophile, Sinophile, hippophile, typophile, psychrophile. Negrophile, gastrophile, pyrophile, mesophile, Russophile, Slavophile, camomile, campa-

nile, juvenile, recompile, thermopile, puerile, domicile, reconcile, volatile, vibratile, versatile, infantile, mercantile, decastyle, pentastyle, peristyle, monostyle, polystyle, otherwhile.

4. bibliophile, Italophile, Germanophile, Japanophile, aelurophile, dodecastyle.

ĪLD– 1. aisled, child, filed, mild, smiled, piled, spiled, styled, wild, Wilde, whiled.

2. *grandchild, godchild,* defiled, beguiled, enisled, compiled, unpiled, self-styled, reviled.

3. great-grandchild, foster child, unbeguiled, recompiled, uncompiled, reconciled, Oscar Wilde.

4. unreconciled.

ĪM– 1. I'm, chime, dime, disme, chyme, lime, clime, climb, slime, mime, rhyme, grime, crime, prime, sime, cyme, time, thyme, zyme.

2. sublime, *birdlime, quicklime, brooklime,* beslime, berhyme, begrime, *daytime, playtime, bedtime,* betime, *lifetime, springtime,* meantime, *noontime,* sometime, mistime, enzyme.

3. paradigm, Hildesheim, Rudesheim, maritime, pantomime, underprime, overprime, undertime, summertime, aftertime, wintertime, overtime, harvest time.

ĪMD– 1. chimed, limed, climbed, mimed, rhymed, primed, timed.

2. unlimed, unclimbed, beslimed, berhymed, unrhymed, begrimed, well-timed, ill-timed.

3. pantomimed, underprimed, overprimed, undertimed, overtimed.

ĪMZ– *see* **ĪM,** plus " s " or " 's "; **2.** betimes, sometimes, ofttimes.

3. oftentimes.

ĪN– 1. eyn, eyne [both arch. & dial.], ein [G.], bine, chine, dine, dyne, fine, kine [arch. & dial.], line, spline, mine, nine, nein [G.], pine, spine, Rhine, brine, shrine, trine, sine, tsine, shine, tine, Tyne, stein, thine, vine, wine, swine, twine, whine.

2. *Sabine,* woodbine, combine, *carbine, turbine, Aldine,* indign, condign, *nundine,* define, refine, trephine, confine, aline, align, malign, *saline, headline, beeline, feline,* moline, *tapeline, carline, airline, hairline, crossline, fishline,* outline, *cauline,* Pauline, *bowline,* decline, recline, incline, *damine, gold mine, carmine, canine, ranine,* benign, *quinine,* repine, *Alpine, vulpine,* opine, *vespine, lupine, supine, cedrine, ferine, caprine,* enshrine, *Petrine, murrhine,* assign, design, resign, langsyne, *piscine,* calcine, *sinsyne,* consign, *phocine, cosine, hircine, porcine, ursine,* beshine, *shoeshine, moonshine, sunshine,* outshine, divine, *ovine, bovine, cervine, corvine,* May wine, *equine,* entwine.

3. cannabine, columbine, concubine, muscadine, anodyne, monodyne, hirundine, paludine, superfine, realign, alkaline, tourmaline, sepaline, opaline, disalign, petaline, hyaline, angeline, musteline, aniline, aqui-

line, inquiline, disincline, monocline, caballine, coralline, metalline, crystalline, sibylline, berylline, suilline, Caroline, underline, interline, figuline, Ursuline, vituline, sycamine, calamine, calcimine, undermine, countermine, asinine, leonine, pavonine, eburnine, saturnine, elapine, porcupine, catarrhine, saccharine, viberrine, viperine, anserine, passerine, riverine. Turnverein [G.], peregrine, sapphirine, platyrrhine, lemurine, azurine, soricine, reconsign, undersign, countersign, monkeyshine [slang], palatine, cisplatine, anatine, infantine, brigantine, Constantine, Byzantine, argentine, Argentine, valentine, serpentine, turpentine, Aventine, lacertine, Palestine, Celestine, Ernestine, Philistine, Frankenstein, Liechtenstein, brandywine, cherry wine, intertwine, Auld Lang Syne.

4. incarnadine, heterodyne, antalkaline, Evangeline, Capitoline, accipitrine, elephantine, hyacinthine, labyrinthine, aberdevine.

ĪND– 1. bind, dined, find, hind, kind, lined, blind, mind, mined, pined, rynd, rind, rined, grind, signed, tined, vined, wind, wined, twined, whined.

2. combined, unbind, *bearbind,* defined, refined, ahind, behind, mankind, unkind, aligned, maligned, *duckblind, purblind,* unlined, declined, reclined, inclined, outlined, repined, opined, *Gradgrind,* regrind, *millrynd,* resigned, unsigned, rewind, unwind, entwined, resigned.

3. uncombined, wined and dined, undefined, unrefined, unconfined, gavelkind, womankind, humankind, realigned, color-blind, disinclined, underlined, interlined undermined, mastermind, greasy grind, undersigned, countersigned, interwind, intertwined, undesigned, unresigned.

4. incarnadined.

ĪNDS– 1. binds, finds, hinds, kinds, blinds, minds, rinds, grinds, winds.

2. rebinds, unbinds, *duckblinds, Gradgrinds,* rewinds, unwinds.

3. masterminds, greasy grinds, interwinds.

ĪNT– 1. jint [dial.], pint.

2. ahint [Scot.], behint [Scot.], half pint.

ĪNTS– 1. Heintz, jints [dial.], pints.

2. half pints.

ĪP– 1. hipe, kipe, hyp [dial.], slipe [Scot. & dial.], slype, snipe, pipe, ripe, gripe, tripe, stripe, type, stipe, vipe [slang], wipe, wype, swipe.

2. *pitchpipe, windpipe, bagpipe, hornpipe, blowpipe, rareripe,* unripe, retype, *ectype, tintype, piewipe, sideswipe.*

3. guttersnipe, overripe, megatype, teletype, antitype, linotype, phototype.

4. stereotype.

5. daguerreotype.

ĪPS– *see* **ĪP,** plus " s " or " 's "; **1.** Cripes [slang], yipes [slang].

ĪPT– 1. hiped, sliped [Scot. & dial.], sniped,

piped, riped, griped, striped, typed, stiped, wiped, swiped.

2. unstriped, retyped, untyped, *sideswiped.*

4. stereotyped.

ĪR– 1. ire, byre, dire, fire, hire, gyre, lyre, mire, pyre, pyr, spire, sire, shire, tire, Tyre, wire, quire, choir, squire.

2. afire, *needfire, wildfire,* wood fire, *backfire, blackfire, hell-fire, shellfire,* coal fire, *bonfire,* misfire, peat fire, *spitfire,* rehire, admire, bemire, aspire., respire, expire, transpire, inspire, conspire, perspire, suspire, *grandsire, gudesire, belsire,* attire, retire, entire, envire, barbwire, rewire, unwire, acquire, require, enquire, inquire, esquire, desire.

3. signal fire, forest fire, overtire, heart's desire.

4. St. Elmo's fire.

ĪRD– 1. fired, hired, mired, spired, sired, tired, wired, squired.

2. *backfired,* misfired, admired, bemired, aspired, respired, expired, transpired, inspired, conspired, perspired, attired, retired, rewired, acquired, required, inquired, desired.

3. uninspired, overtired, unacquired, unrequired, reinquired, undesired.

ĪS– 1. ice, bice, dice, lice, splice, slice, mice, nice, gneiss, pice, spice, speiss, rice, rais, Brice, grice, price, trice, thrice, sice, syce, vice, vise, twice.

2. suffice, resplice, *titmice,* bespice, *allspice,* reprice, precise, concise, entice, advice, device.

3. paradise, sacrifice, overnice, camphor ice, edelweiss.

ĪST–1. iced, diced, feist [loc.], Geist [G.], spliced, riced, Christ, priced.

2. uniced, Zeitgeist [G.], Weltgeist [G.], bespiced, repriced, enticed.

3. poltergeist, antichrist.

4. emparadised, ein starke Geist [G.].

ĪT– 1. ite [slang], bite, bight, dite, dight, fight, fite, hight, height, kite, skite [dial.], light, lite [slang], blight, blite, flight, plight, slight, sleight, mite, might, smite, night, knight, snite [Scot. & dial.], spite, rite, right, write, wright, bright, fright, krait, sprite, trite, sight, site, cite, tight, tite [dial.], wight, Dwight, quite, white.

2. *Sadite,* bedight, *lyddite, endite,* indict, indite, condite, *podite, cordite,* sea fight, *graphite, cockfight, bullfight,* sulphite, *ophite, Ophite, turfite,* fist fight, *Shiite,* alight, *daylight, halite,* red light, *floodlight,* delight, relight, *skylight, stylite,* twilight, green light, *moonlight, sunlight,* go-light, polite, *lamplight, hoplite, stoplight, marlite, starlite, flashlight, footlight,* Hamite, Semite, bromite, *somite, termite, Danite, Tanite,* midnight, good night, benight, beknight, ignite, *lignite, finite, crinite, ichnite,* Stannite, *sennight,* unknight, *Sunnite,* tonight, *bornite, fortnight,* unite, despite, aright, barite, *playwright, bookwright, wheelwright,*

downright, *shipwright,* upright, *cartwright,* outright, birthright, forthright, *plowwright, pyrite,* eyebright, *dendrite,* affright, stage fright, contrite, attrite, eyesight, accite, *calcite, felsite, insight,* incite, *townsite, foresight,* excite, *latite, ratite, partite,* airtight, *Levite,* invite, *Servite,* bobwhite, snow-white, *lintwhite,* requite, *quartzite.*

3. Rechabite, Moabite, Jacobite, Niobite, trilobite, cenobite, extradite, expedite, recondite, incondite, troglodyte, erudite, *hanifite,* epiphyte, neophyte, sciophyte, dermophyte, zoophyte, microphyte, hydrophyte, aerophyte, mesophyte, ectophyte, entophyte, lithophyte, Fahrenheit, malachite, hyalite, corallite, crystallite, Ishmaelite, Israelite, proselyte, candlelight, nephelite, Carmelite, ampelite, satellite, menilite, acolyte, impolite, zoolite, chrysolite, Loyolite, kimberlite, spherulite, lazulite, Adamite, calamite, Elamite, Islamite, dynamite, wolframite, Hiramite, Gothamite, Moslemite, eremite, stalagmite, hellgrammite, Edomite, dolomite, widow's mite, manganite, vulcanite, melanite, Canaanite, sylvanite, day and night, reignite, ebonite, aconite, Mammonite, Maronite, overnight, reunite, disunite, Sybarite, Lazarite, siderite, dolerite, copyright, Laborite, anchorite, Minorite, underwrite, overwrite, azurite, lazurite, marcasite, pargasite, parasite, anthracite, boracite, second sight, plebiscite, phagocyte, leucocyte, oversight, hematite, magnetite, appetite, stalactite, tripartite, celestite, Ballistite, muscovite, Muscovite.

4. meropodite, Amalekite, Raphaelite, Ishmaelite, Israelite, monophylite, gastrophilite, toxophilite, theodolite, cosmopolite, siderolite, novaculite, ventriculite, Bethlehemite, labradorite, meteorite, Monophysite, Dyophysite.

ĪTH– 1. lithe, blithe, writhe, sithe, scythe, tithe, stythe, withe.

ĪTHD– 1. writhed, scythed, tithed, withed.

ĪV– 1. I've, chive, dive, five, hive, gyve, jive [slang], skive, live, clive, rive, drive, shrive, strive, thrive, shive, stive [Scot. & dial. Eng.], wive.

2. redive, *high dive, swan dive, nose dive,* ungyve, *ogive, beehive,* alive, connive, arrive, derive, deprive, contrive, revive, convive, survive.

3. unalive, rearrive, overdrive, rederive, redeprive, recontrive.

ĪVD– 1. dived, hived, gyved, skived, knived, rived, shrived, strived, thrived, shived, stived, wived.

2. long-lived, short-lived, connived, arrived, derived, deprived, contrived, revived, survived.

3. unarrived, underived, undeprived, recontrived, uncontrived, unrevived.

ĪVZ– *see* **ĪV,** plus " s " or " 's "; **1.** Ives.

2. St. Ives.

IZ– *see* **Ī** through **WĪ**, plus " s " or " 's ";

1. guise, rise, prize, prise, size, sice, vise, wise.

2. sheep's eyes, *brighteyes*, disguise, demise, remise, premise, *bromize*, surmise, despise, arise, *moonrise*, *sunrise*, apprise, reprise, emprise, comprise, uprise, misprize, surprise, assize, resize, excise, incise, capsize, baptize, chastise, advise, devise, revise, *sidewise*, *endwise*, *stagewise*, *edgewise*, *likewise*, *bookwise*, *clockwise*, unwise, *nowise*, *crosswise*.

3. Judaize, archaize, Hebraize, hybridize, iridize, chloridize, subsidize, oxidize, liquidize, merchandize, gormandize, aggrandize, iodize, melodize, psalmodize, rhapsodize, standardize, jeopardize, elegize, syllogize, eulogize, energize, catechize, verbalize, feudalize, realize, legalize, alkalize, localize, vocalize, formalize, penalize, signalize, finalize, journalize, papalize, opalize, moralize, centralize, neutralize, racialize, specialize, socialize, mortialize, vitalize, tantalize, dualize, equalize, royalize, obelize, angeleyes, novelize, stabilize, mobilize, sterilize, fossilize, fertilize, utilize, civilize, tranquilize, metallize, crystallize, symbolize, idolize, fabulize, formulize, euphemize, emblemize, itemize, minimize, pilgrimize, victimize, compromise, presurmise, urbanize, paganize, vulcanize, mechanize, Romanize, Germanize, humanize, Christianize, galvanize, Hellenize, heathenize, recognize, pollinize, feminize, Latinize, glutinize, scrutinize, solemnize, tyrannize, ebonize, carbonize, agonize, symphonize, euphonize, unionize, lionize, colonize, demonize, harmonize, sermonize, canonize, synchronize, patronize, fractionize, platonize, peptonize, modernize, fraternize, immunize, communize, syncopize, philippize, barbarize, vulgarize, plagiarize, burglarize, summarize, notarize, tenderize, mesmerize, pauperize, mercerize, cauterize, etherize, pulverize, satirize, theorize, memorize, vaporize, temporize, terrorize, proctorize, motorize, authorize, enterprise, pasteurize, sulphurize, martyrize, emphasize, ostracize, synthesize, laicize, Turkicize, publicize, Anglicize, Gallicize, Sinicize, classicize, criticize, ethicize, Gothicize, synopsize, exorcise, dramatize, pragmatize, dogmatize, magnetize, monetize, sensitize, narcotize, egotize, iotize, hypnotize, advertise, amortize, deputize, empathize, sympathize, improvise, supervise, colloquize, zigzagwise, anywise, penny-wise, moneywise, travelwise, copywise, cornerwise, weather-wise, otherwise.

4. italicize, catholicize, politicize, domesticize, deoxidize, apostrophize, theosophize, philosophize, radicalize, provincialize, commercialize, substantialize, potentialize, decimalize, nationalize, rationalize, sectionalize, personalize, liberalize, federalize, generalize, demoralize, decentralize, naturalize, capitalize, devitalize, revitalize, immortalize, visualize, sexualize, ritualize, actualize, mutualize, evangelize, caramelize, solubilize, diabolize, metabolize, monopolize, macadamize, legitimize, economize, epitomize, dehumanize, rejuvenize, antagonize, philanthropize, misanthropize, plagiarize, familiarize, regularize, singularize, circularize, formularize, popularize, militarize, characterize, deodorize, allegorize, categorize, extemporize, desulphurize, panegyrize, metastasize, hypostasize, parenthesize, emblematize, systematize, acclimatize, democratize, apostatize, alphabetize, demagnetize, demonetize, remonetize, anesthetize, desensitize, Protestantize, proselytize, contrariwise.

5. materialize, phenomenalize, professionalize, denationalize, irrationalize, conventionalize, impersonalize, denaturalize, sentimentalize, spiritualize, Americanize, deoxygenize, platitudinize, attitudinize, revolutionize, particularize, apotheosize, anathematize, legitimatize.

6. testimonialize, participialize, internationalize, institutionalize, constitutionalize, individualize, cosmopolitanize.

IZD– 1. prized, sized, wised [slang].

2. disguised, demised, surmised, despised, apprised, comprised, unprized, surprised, misprized, resized, incised, unsized, capsized, excised, baptized, chastised, advised, devised, revised.

3. redisguised, undisguised, reapprised, unapprised, uncomprised, unsurprised, unincised, unbaptized, unchastised, unadvised, undevised; *also past tense of all verbs ending in verbal suffix* " *-ize* "

Ī (eye)

Double (Feminine) Rhymes

Primary or Secondary Accent Falls on Next to Last Syllable; Imperfect Rhymes Are in Italics.

I′a– 2. ayah, dia, glia, pia, chria, praya, stria, via, Zia.
3. Tobiah, Sophia, Thalia, dulia, Maria, pariah, latria, Uriah, messiah, Josiah, Isaiah, Keziah.
4. Obadiah, Zebediah, asaphia, Hezekiah, Jeremiah, Black Maria, Zachariah, callisteia.
5. hyperdulia, Hippodamia, Iphigenia.
I′ad– 2. dyad, Pleiad, naiad, dryad, triad.
4. jeremiad, hamadryad.
I′adz– *see* **Ī′ad,** plus " s " or " 's "; 2. Hyads.
I′ak– 2. Dyak, kayak, guaiac.
4. elegiac.
I′al– 2. dial, phial, gayal, myall, pial, spial, ryal, trial, vial, viol.
3. *sundial,* defial, supplial, denial, genial, espial, decrial, retrial, mistrial, bass viol.
4. self-denial, intrapial, interstrial.
I′am– 2. I am, lyam, Priam, Siam.
I′amb– 2. iamb.
3. diiamb.
I′an– 2. Ian, Chian, Ryan, Bryan.
3. thalian, genian, Orion.
4. Jeremian; *see also* **Ī′on.**
I′ance– 2. fiance [obs.], science.
3. affiance, defiance, alliance, reliance, appliance, compliance, suppliance.
4. misalliance, selfreliance, incompliance, noncompliance; *see also* **Ī′ants.**
I′ant– 2. fiant, giant, client, pliant, riant, Bryant, scient.
3. affiant, defiant, reliant, appliant, repliant, compliant.
4. self-reliant, uncompliant.
I′ants– 2. fiants, giants, clients, Bryants.
3. affiants, repliants; *see also* **Ī′ans.**
I′ar– 2. liar, briar, friar; *see also* **Ī′er.**
I′as– 2. eyas, bias, Lias, drias, Trias.
3. unbias, Tobias, Elias, Messias, Josias.
4. Jeremias, Ananias; *see also* **Ī′us.**
I′at– 2. fiat; *see also* **Ī′et.**
IB′al– 2. Bible, libel, scribal, tribal.
4. intertribal.

IB′eks– 2. ibex, vibex.
IB′er– 2. fiber, giber, liber, Liber, briber, scriber, Tiber.
3. imbiber, subscriber, describer, prescriber, transcriber, inscriber, proscriber.
4. circumscriber.
IB′ing– 2. gibing, jibing, kibing, bribing, scribing.
3. imbibing, ascribing, subscribing, describing, prescribing, transcribing, inscribing, conscribing, proscribing, perscribing.
4. circumscribing, superscribing.
IB′l– 2. Bible, libel, scribal, tribal.
3. intertribal.
IB′ol– 2. eyeball, highball, fly ball.
IB′rate– 2. librate, vibrate.
4. equilibrate.
IB′rid– 2. hybrid, Librid.
4. polyhybrid.
I′brow– 2. eyebrow, highbrow.
ID′a– 2. Ida, Haida, Lida, cnida, Vida.
3. Oneida.
ID′al– 2. bridal, tidal.
3. cotidal.
4. regicidal, fungicidal, homicidal, germicidal, vermicidal, parricidal, matricidal, patricidal, fratricidal, septicidal, suicidal.
5. tyrannicidal, sororicidal, insecticidal, infanticidal; *see also* **ĪD′l.**
ID′ans– 2. guidance.
3. abidance, misguidance, subsidence.
ID′ed– 2. bided, chided, guided, glided, prided, sided, tided.
3. abided, confided, misguided, elided, collided, derided, subsided, decided, lopsided, one-sided, both-sided, two-sided, betided, divided, presided.
4. undecided, many-sided, coincided, subdivided, redivided, undivided, unprovided.
ID′ee– 2. didy, Friday, sidy, tidy, vide.
3. untidy.
4. bonafide.
ID′en– 2. Leyden, Dryden, widen.

234

3. rewiden; *see also* **ĪD′on.**

ĪD′ent– 2. bident, rident, trident, strident.

3. subsident.

ĪD′er– 2. eider, bider, chider, guider, hider, glider, slider, nidor, spider, rider, strider, stridor, sider, cider, wider.

3. abider, confider, misguider, backslider, derider, roughrider, outrider, decider, insider, East-sider, outsider, provider, resider, presider.

4. coincider, subdivider.

ĪD′est– 2. piedest, widest.

ĪD′ij– 2. guidage, hidage, sideage.

ĪD′ing– 2. biding, chiding, guiding, hiding, gliding, sliding, niding, riding, priding, striding, siding, tiding.

3. abiding, confiding, misguiding, eliding, colliding, *backsliding*, deriding, subsiding, betiding, dividing, providing, residing, presiding.

4. law-abiding, coinciding, redividing, subdividing.

ĪD′l– 2. idle, idol, idyl, idyll, bridle, bridal, sidle, tidal.

3. unbridle; *see also* **ĪD′al.**

ĪD′led– 2. idled, bridled, sidled.

3. unbridled.

ĪD′lee– 2. idly, bridely, widely.

ĪD′ler– 2. idler, bridler, sidler.

ĪD′less– 2. guideless, rideless, brideless, sideless, tideless.

4. suicideless.

ĪD′ling– 2. idling, bridling, sidling.

3. unbridling.

ĪD′ness– 2. piedness, wideness.

ĪD′o– 2. Dido, dido, Fido.

ĪD′on– 2. guidon, Sidon.

3. Poseidon; *see also* **ĪD′en.**

ĪD′or– 2. nidor, stridor; *see also* **ĪD′er.**

ĪD′rate– 2. hydrate.

3. dehydrate.

4. carbohydrate.

ĪD′us– 2. Didus, Midas, nidus.

Ī′ee– 2. eyey, skyey, criey.

Ī′ens– 2. clients, science; *see also* **Ī′ans.**

Ī′ent– 2. client, scient; *see also* **Ī′ant.**

Ī′er– 2. eyer, buyer, dyer, dier, higher, liar, lier, flier, flyer, plier, plyer, slyer, nigher, spyer, wrier, briar, brier, drier, friar, fryer, frier, crier, prier, pryer, prior, spryer, trier, trior, sigher, shier, tier, vier.

3. defier, applier, implier, complier, supplier, denier, greenbrier, sweetbrier, decrier, descrier.

4. stupefier, liquefier, speechifier, edifier, modifier, deifier, vilifier, qualifier, amplifier, simplifier, nullifier, ramifier, dignifier, signifier, unifier, typifier, clarifier, terrifier, verifier, glorifier, classifier, pacifier, falsifier, versifier, crucifier, ratifier, gratifier, rectifier, sanctifier, certifier, fortifier, testifier, justifier, beautifier, satisfier, multiplier, underlier, occupier, prophesier.

5. disqualifier, exemplifier, indemnifier,

personifier, calorifier, intensifier, diversifier, identifier; *see also* **ĪR′er.**

Ī′ern– 2. iron.

3. *sadiron, gridiron, andiron, flatiron.*

4. grappling iron, curling iron, waffle iron, gaufre iron.

Ī′est– 2. highest, slyest, nighest, wriest, driest, spryest, shyest, shiest.

Ī′et– 2. diet, fiat, piet, riot, quiet.

3. inquiet, unquiet, disquiet; *see also* **Ī′ot.**

IF′a– 2. Haifa, Typha.

IF′ee– 2. lifey, wifie, wifey.

IF′en– 2. hyphen, siphon, Typhon.

IF′er– 2. bifer, fifer, lifer, knifer, rifer, cipher, sypher.

3. decipher.

IF′id– 2. bifid, trifid.

IF′ing– 2. fifing, knifing, wifing.

IF′l– 2. Eiffel, rifle, trifle, stifle.

IF′lee– 2. rifely, wifely.

3. *housewifely.*

IF′ler– 2. rifler, trifler, stifler.

IF′less– 2. fifeless, lifeless, knifeless, strifeless, wifeless.

IF′like– 2. lifelike, knifelike, wifelike.

IF′ling– 2. rifling, trifling, stifling.

IG′a– 2. biga, striga, saiga.

3. quadriga.

IG′al– 2. pygal, zygal.

IG′ate– 2. ligate, strigate.

IG′er– 2. geiger, tiger.

Ī′glas– 2. eyeglass, spyglass.

Ī′glif– 2. diglyph, triglyph.

4. monotriglyph.

IG′o– 2. by-go, Sligo.

3. caligo, fuligo [L.], lentigo, vertigo.

4. impetigo.

IG′r– 1. nigre, tiger.

IG′rant– 2. migrant.

3. transmigrant.

Ī′ide– 2. sly-eyed, pie-eyed, dry-eyed.

Ī′ing– 2. eyeing, buying, bying, dying, dyeing, guying, hieing, skying, lying, flying, plying, pieing, piing, spying, drying, frying, crying, prying, trying, sighing, shying, tying, stying, vying.

3. undying, defying, allying, belying, relying, applying, replying, implying, complying, supplying, outlying, denying, espying, decrying, descrying, outcrying, outsighing, untying, outvying.

4. alibiing, underbuying, overbuying, labefying, tabefying, tumefying, tepefying, stupefying, torrefying, putrefying, liquefying, verbifying, rubifying, preachifying [coll.], speechifying, Frenchifying, churchifying, ladifying, edifying, dandifying, codifying, modifying, deifying, qualifying, vilifying, mollifying, nullifying, amplifying, simplifying, ramifying, magnifying, dignifying, signifying, unifying, torpifying, typifying, clarifying, terrifying, verifying, horrifying, glorifying, petrifying, purifying, classifying, pacifying, specifying, falsifying, ossifying, versifying, crucifying, ratifying, gratifying, prettifying, rectifying, sanctifying, fructifying, stultifying, quantifying, daintifying, notifying, certifying, fortifying, mortifying, testifying, mystifying, justifying, beautifying, mythifying, vivifying, satisfying, argufying [coll.], butterflying, multiplying, uncomplying, underlying, overlying, self-denying, occupying, prophesying.

5. syllabifying, solidifying, remodifying, disqualifying, exemplifying, divinifying, indemnifying, personifying, saccharifying, transmogrifying, electrifying, complexifying, decalcifying, emulsifying, beatifying, objectifying, identifying, revivifying, self-satisfying, unsatisfying, undersupplying, oversupplying, reoccupying, preoccupying.

Ī'ish–2. slyish, dryish, shyish.

IJ'a– 3. Abijah, Elijah.
 4. Jehudijah.

IJ'er– 2. Niger.
 3. obliger.

IK'a– 2. plica, mica, Micah, pica, pika, spica, Spika, styca.
 3. nagaika, lorica, vesica [L.].
 4. balalaika, hydromica.

IK'al– 2. plical, Michal, Michael, pical.
 4. interplical.

IK'ate– 2. plicate, spicate.

IK'ee– 2. ikey, piky, spiky, crikey, Psyche.
 3. by crikey.
 4. phytopsyche.

IK'en– 2. liken, lichen.
 3. unliken, disliken, misliken.

IK'er– 2. ichor, diker, hiker [coll.], liker, piker, spiker, striker.
 3. hitchhiker [slang], disliker.

IK'ik– 2. psychic.
 3. nonpsychic, unpsychic.
 4. metempsychic.

IK'ing– 2. diking, liking, piking, spiking, striking, viking.
 3. hitchhiking [slang], disliking, misliking.

IK'l– 2. plical, Michael, pical, cycle, psychal.
 3. recycle, *bicycle, tricycle.*
 4. interplical, hemicycle, epicycle, multicycle, monocycle, motorcycle.

IK'lik– 2. cyclic.
 3. acyclic, bicyclic, encyclic.
 4. polycyclic, epicyclic.

IK'ling– 2. cycling.
 3. bicycling.
 4. motorcycling.

IK'us– 2. Ficus, Picus, spicous.
 3. anticous, anticus [L.], posticous, posticus [L.].
 4. umbilicus, Andronicus.

IL'a– 2. Ila, Hyla, Lila, pyla.
 3. strobila, Delilah.

IL'aks– 2. lilacs, smilax.

IL'and– 2. island, highland, Thailand.
 3. Rhode Island, Long Island.

IL'ar– 2. filar, pilar, stylar.
 3. bifilar, trifilar; *see also* **ĪL'er.**

IL'ark– 2. phylarch, skylark.

ILD'er– 2. milder, wilder.

ILD'est– 2. mildest, wildest.

ILD'ish– 2. childish, mildish, wildish.

ILD'lee– 2. mildly, riledly [coll.], wildly.
 3. beguiledly.

ILD'like– 2. childlike, mild-like [dial.], riled-like [dial.], wild-like [dial.].
 3. beguiled-like [dial.].

ILD'ness– 2. mildness, riledness [coll.], wildness.
 3. beguiledness, unwildness.

IL'ee– 2. highly, hyle, slyly, smily, wryly, riley [coll.], Riley, dryly, shyly, wily.
 3. sedile, ancile.

IL'eks– 2. ilex, silex.

IL'er– 2. filer, filar, Schuyler, miler [slang], smiler, piler, pilar, Tyler, tiler, styler, stylar, viler.
 3. defiler, bifilar, trifilar, beguiler, compiler, reviler.
 4. reconciler.

IL'et– 2. eyelet, islet, smilet, stylet.

IL'ful– 2. guileful, smileful, wileful.

IL'ij– 2. mileage, smileage, silage.

IL'ing– 2. biling [dial.], filing, smiling, piling, spiling, riling, tiling, styling, wiling, whiling.
 3. ensiling, defiling, beguiling, repiling, compiling, unpiling, ensiling, exiling, restyling, reviling.
 4. domiciling, reconciling.

IL'is– 3. Aprilis, Quintilis, Sextilis.

IL'less– 2. guileless, smileless, styleless, wileless.

IL'ment– 3. defilement, beguilement, compilement, resilement, exilement.
 4. domicilement, reconcilement.
 5. irreconcilement.

IL'o– 2. bye-low, high-low, milo, silo, Shiloh, stilo [L.].

IL'oid– 2. styloid, xyloid.

IL'on– 2. phylon, nylon, pylon.

IL'ot– 2. Nilot, pilot.
 3. sky pilot.

IL'um– 2. filum [L.], phylum, hilum, pilum.
 3. asylum.

IL'us– 2. hilus, Nilous, Silas, stylus.

IM'a– 2. Phyma, Lima, mima, rima, tryma, sima, cyma.
 3. Tellima, Jemima.
 4. arapaima.

IM'aks– 2. Limax, climax.
 4. anticlimax.

IM'al– 2. rimal, primal, shtreimel.
 4. isocheimal, isocrymal.

IM'an– 2. highman, skyman, flyman, pieman, shy man, Wyman.

IM'ee– 2. limy, limey [slang], blimy, slimy, rimy, rhymy, primy, stymie, stimy, thymy.
 3. beslimy, old-timy.

IM'en– 2. daimon, Hymen, highmen, skymen, limen, flymen, piemen, crimen [L.], Simon, taimen, Timon, vimen.

IM'er– 2. chimer, limer, climber, mimer,

rimer, primer, timer, timor.
3. sublimer, begrimer, reprimer, old-timer,
4. Hildesheimer, Rudesheimer, Hergeshei-mer.
IM′est– 2. primest.
3. sublimest.
IM′ik– 2. rhymic, thymic, zymic.
3. enzymic.
4. isocheimic, catathymic.
IM′ing– 2. chiming, climbing, sliming, rhym-ing, griming, priming, timing.
3. begriming, berhyming, pump priming, two-timing [slang].
IM′ish– 2. chimish, rhymish, timish.
IM′ist– 2. rhymist, timist.
IM′it– 2. climate.
3. acclimate.
IM′lee– 2. primely, timely.
3. sublimely, untimely.
IM′less– 2. chimeless, dimeless, limeless, climbless, slimeless, mimeless, rhymeless, rimeless, grimeless, timeless.
IM′ness– 2. primeness.
3. sublimeness.
IM′us– 2. rimous, primus, simous, cymous, timeous [Scot. & Ir.], thymus.
IN′a– 2. Ina, China, Dinah, Heine, Jaina, mina, myna, vina [L.].
3. Sabina, Medina, Regina, Shekinah, trichina, Salina, salina, farina, Sabrina, piscina, Lucina, glucina.
4. Adelina, Angelina, Evelina, Carolina, Platyrrhina.
IN′aks– 2. pinax, Thrinax.
IN′al– 2. binal, final, spinal, rhinal, crinal, trinal, sinal, vinal.
3. acclinal, declinal, synclinal, caninal, prorhinal.
4. semifinal, isoclinal, periclinal, interspinal, endocrinal, matutinal.
5. cerebrospinal.
IN′an– 2. Hainan, Tainan.
3. Salinan.
IN′ate– 2. binate, spinate, quinate.
IND′ed– 2. blinded, minded, rinded, winded.
3. *snow-blinded*, reminded, free-minded, strong-minded, high-minded, weak-minded, like-minded, low-minded, fair-minded, light-minded.
4. unreminded, marriage-minded, public-minded, carnal-minded, feeble-minded, double-minded, travel-minded, evil-minded, simple-minded, bloody-minded, worldly-minded, lofty-minded, earthly-minded, even-minded, narrow-minded, sober-minded.
IND′er– 2. binder, finder, hinder, kinder, blinder, minder, grinder, winder.
3. *bookbinder, spellbinder, faultfinder, pathfinder*, reminder, *sidewinder*, stem-winder.
4. organ grinder.
IND′est– 2. hindest, kindest, blindest.
IND′ing– 2. binding, finding, blinding, minding, grinding, winding.
3. rebinding, *bookbinding*, unbinding, refind-

ing, reminding, regrinding, rewinding, unwinding.
IND′lee– 2. kindly, blindly.
3. unkindly, *purblindly*.
IND′less– 2. bindless, mindless, rindless, grindless, windless.
IND′–ness 2. kindness, blindness.
3. unkindness, snow blindness.
4. semiblindness, color blindness.
IN′ee– 2. Heinie, liny, miny, piny, spiny, briny, tiny, viny, winy, whiny.
3. *sunshiny, moonshiny.*
IN′er– 2. diner, finer, liner, miner, minor, piner, Shriner, signer, shiner, Steiner, winer, twiner, whiner.
3. combiner, definer, refiner, confiner, ma-ligner, *headliner*, recliner, incliner, *stream-liner*, outliner, benigner, repiner, supiner, assigner, resigner, consigner, diviner, entwiner, untwiner, designer, resigner.
4. underliner, underminer, intertwiner.
IN′ess– 2. highness, slyness, nighness, wryness, dryness, spryness, shyness.
IN′est– 2. finest.
3. benignest, supinest, divinest.
4. superfinest.
IN′ing– 2. dining, fining, lining, mining, pining, signing, shining, Vining, wining, twining, whining.
3. combining, defining, refining, confining, aligning, maligning, relining, declining, reclining, inclining, outlining, repining, opining, resigning, outshining, entwining, designing, resigning.
4. unconfining, underlining, interlining, undermining, countersigning, intertwining.
5. wining and dining.
IN′is– 2. finis.
3. Erinys.
IN′ite– 2. finite, crinite.
IN′land– 2. Rhineland, Vineland.
IN′lee– 2. finely.
3. codignly, malignly, benignly, supinely, divinely.
4. superfinely, unbenignly, saturninely, undivinely.
IN′less– 2. fineless, lineless, pineless, spineless, signless, tineless, vineless, wineless.
IN′like– 2. binelike, finelike, linelike, pinelike, spinelike, signlike, tinelike, vinelike, winelike.
IN′ment– 3. refinement, confinement, align-ment, malignment, enshrinement, assign-ment, entwinement, designment, resignment.
4. unrefinement, realignment, interlinement, intertwinement.
IN′ness– 2. fineness.
3. condignness, benignness, supineness, divineness.
4. superfineness.
IN′o– 2. Aino, rhino, Taino.
3. sabino, albino.
IN′um– 2. Linum, vinum [L.].
3. tablinum.
4. Antirrhinum.

IN′us– 2. dinus, Linus, minus, Minos, Pinus, spinous, sinus, vinous.
  3. echinus, Lupinus.
I′o– 2. io, Io, Clio, trio.
  3. Ohio.
I′ol– 2. viol.
  3. bass viol; *see also* **Ī′al.**
I′on– 2. ion, lion, scion, Zion.
  3. sea lion, Arion, Orion, Ixion.
  4. dandelion; *see also* **Ī′an.**
I′or– 2. prior, trior; *see also* **Ī′er.**
I′ot– 2. eyot, piot, riot, Sciot; *see also* **Ī′et.**
IP′a– 2. nipa, pipa, ripa, Stipa.
IP′al– 2. ripal, typal.
  4. archetypal; *see also* **ĪP′l.**
IP′ed– 2. biped, striped.
  6. parallelepiped.
IP′ee– 2. pipy, stripy, swipy.
  4. polytypy, antitypy, chromotypy, phonotypy.
  6. daguerreotypy.
IP′end– 2. ripened, stipend.
IP′er– 2. hyper, niper [obs.], sniper, piper, riper, griper, striper, typer, viper, wiper, swiper.
  3. *sandpiper, bagpiper, sideswiper.*
  4. linotyper, windshield wiper.
  5. stereotyper.
  6. daguerreotyper.
IP′est– ripest; *see also* **ĪP′ist.**
IP′ing– 2. piping, Peiping, riping, griping, striping, typing, wiping, swiping.
  3. restriping, retyping, sideswiping.
  4. linotyping.
  5. electrotyping.
  6. daguerreotyping.
IP′ist– 2. typist, ripest.
  4. linotypist, phonotypist.
  5. electrotypist.
  6. daguerreotypist.
IP′l– 2. stipel.
  3. disciple; *see also* **ĪP′al.**
IP′less– 2. pipeless, gripeless, stripeless, typeless, wipeless, swipeless.
IP′o– 2. hypo, typo.
IP′rus– 2. Cyprus, cypress, Cypris.
IR′a– 2. Ira, eyra, beira, daira, lira, Lyra, Mira, Myra.
  3. hegira, Almira, almirah, palmyra, Elmira, hetaira, Elvira.
IR′al– 2. gyral, chiral, pyral, spiral, styryl.
  3. papyral, retiral.
  4. polygyral, allochiral.
IR′ant– 2. gyrant, spirant, tyrant.
  3. aspirant, expirant, conspirant, archtyrant; *see also* **IR′ent.**
IR′ate– 2. irate, gyrate, lyrate, lirate.
  3. agyrate.
  4. circumgyrate, dextrogyrate.
  5. sinistrogyrate.
IR′ee– 2. eyrie, dairi, Dirae, fiery, kairi [Jap.]. miry, spiry, wiry, squiry.
  3. venire, expiry, perspiry, enquiry, inquiry.
  4. praemunire, Dies Irae [L.].

IR′een– 2. Irene, kyrine, kairine, pyrene, styrene, squireen.
IR′en– 2. kairine, siren.
  5. lepidosiren; *see also* **ĪR′on.**
IR′ent– 2. virent.
  3. inquirent.
  4. sempervirent; *see also* **ĪR′ant.**
IR′er– 2. direr, firer, hirer, mirer, tirer, wirer.
  3. admirer, bemirer, aspirer, respirer, expirer, inspirer, conspirer, perspirer, suspirer, attirer, retirer, *haywirer* [slang], rewirer, acquirer, requirer, enquirer, inquirer, desirer.
IR′est– 2. direst.
  3. *haywirest* [slang].
IR′ful– 2. ireful, direful.
  3. desireful.
IR′id– 2. irid, Lyrid, xyrid.
  3. mormyrid, Osiride.
  4. sempervirid.
IR′ik– 2. gyric.
  3. oneiric, epeiric.
  4. photogyric.
IR′ing– 2. firing, hiring, miring, spiring, tiring, wiring, squiring.
  3. admiring, bemiring, aspiring, respiring, expiring, inspiring, conspiring, perspiring, attiring, retiring, untiring, unwiring, acquiring, requiring, inquiring, desiring.
  4. unaspiring, uninspiring, reacquiring, reinquiring, uninquiring, undesiring.
IR′is– 2. iris, Iris, Siris.
  3. Osiris.
IR′ish– 2. Irish, squirish.
IR′ist– 2. irised, lyrist.
IR′lee– 2. direly, squirely.
  3. entirely.
IR′less– 2. tireless, wireless, squireless.
IR′like– 2. byrelike, firelike, lyrelike, mirelike, pyrelike, spirelike, tirelike, wirelike, choirlike, squirelike.
IR′ling– 2. hireling, squireling.
IR′ment– 3. bemirement, attirement, retirement, acquirement, requirement.
IR′ness– 2. direness.
  3. entireness.
IR′o– 2. gyro, Cairo, pyro, tyro.
  4. Autogiro.
IR′on– 2. Byron, gyron, Chiron, myron, Myron, siren.
  3. environ.
IR′one– 2. pyrone, Tyrone.
IR′ose– 2. gyrose, virose.
IR′sum– 2. iresome, tiresome.
  3. desiresome.
IR′us– 2. gyrus, Pyrus, spirous, Cyrus, virus.
  3. Epirus, apyrous, papyrus, desirous.
IS′a– 2. beisa, Meissa.
IS′al– 2. sisal.
  4. paradisal; *see also* **ĪZ′al.**
IS′ee– 2. icy, nisi [L.], spicy, ricey.
IS′ens– 2. license, licence.
  3. dog license.
  4. marriage license, driver's license.
  5. poetic license.

IS′er– 2. icer, dicer, geyser, splicer, slicer, nicer, spicer, ricer, pricer, cicer.
3. preciser, conciser, enticer.
4. sacrificer.
5. self-sacrificer.
IS′est– 2. nicest.
3. precisest, concisest.
IS′ez– 2. ices, dices, splices, slices, spices, rices, prices, vices.
3. suffices, entices, advices, devices.
4. sacrifices.
IS′ful– 3. enticeful, deviceful.
IS′ing– 2. icing, dicing, splicing, slicing, spicing, pricing.
3. sufficing, enticing.
4. sacrificing.
5. self-sacrificing.
IS′is– 2. Isis, physis [Gr.], lysis, crisis, phthisis; *see also* IS′us.
IS′iv– 3. collisive, derisive, decisive, precisive, incisive, divisive.
4. cicatrisive, indecisive, undivisive.
IS′lee– 2. nicely.
3. precisely, concisely.
4. overnicely.
IS′less– 2. iceless, diceless, spliceless, sliceless, spiceless, riceless, priceless, viceless.
3. adviceless.
4. sacrificeless.
IS′man– 2. iceman, diceman, viseman, viceman.
IS′ment– 3. sufficement, enticement.
IS′ness– 2. niceness.
3. preciseness, conciseness.
4. overniceness.
IS′on– 2. bison, hyson, grison, vison.
IST′er– 2. Meister [G.], shyster.
4. Kapellmeister [G.], Wilhelm Meister, Konzert-meister [G.].
IS′us– 2. nisus, Nisus, risus [L.].
4. Dionysus; *see also* IS′is.
IT′a– 2. vita.
3. baryta, Nerita.
4. amalaita.
IT′al– 2. dital, title, vital.
3. detrital, recital, entitle, mistitle, requital.
4. microphytal, parasital.
IT′ed– 2. bighted, dited, dighted, heighted, kited, lighted, blighted, plighted, slighted, knighted, nighted [rare], spited, righted, frighted, sighted, cited, sited, whited.
3. indited, indicted, alighted, delighted, relighted, unlighted, benighted, beknighted, unknighted, ignited, united, despited, affrighted, attrited, recited, excited, incited, long-sighted, farsighted, clear-sighted, near-sighted, shortsighted, invited, requited.
4. candlelighted, satellited, reunited, un-united, disunited, copyrighted, eagle-sighted, oversighted, uninvited, unrequited.
IT′ee– 2. blighty, flighty, mighty, mity, nighty, nightie, rite, whity, Whitey.
3. almighty, Venite.
4. Aphrodite, the Almighty, Amphitrite,

highty-tighty, lignum vitae, arbor vitae.
IT′eez– 2. nighties, Whitey's.
3. barytes, pyrites, sorites.
4. the Almighty's.
IT′en– 2. heighten, chitin, chiton, lighten, brighten, frighten, triton, Triton, tighten, Titan, whiten.
3. enlighten, retighten, untighten.
IT′er– 2. iter, biter, fighter, kiter, lighter, blighter, flighter, plighter, slighter, miter, mitre, smiter, niter, righter, writer, brighter, triter, sighter, citer, tighter, whiter.
3. *backbiter*, indicter, inditer, indictor, *bullfighter*, alighter, delighter, politer, *lamplighter*, unmiter, igniter, uniter, rewriter, *typewriter*, exciter, inviter, requiter.
4. candlelighter, impoliter, dynamiter, reuniter, copyrighter, copy writer, under-writer, und so weiter [G.].
IT′est– 2. lightest, slightest, rightest, brightest, tritest, tightest, whitest.
3. politest, *uprightest*.
4. impolitest.
IT′ful– 2. mightful, spiteful, rightful, frightful, sprightful.
3. delightful, despiteful, unrightful.
ITH′er– 2. either, blither, neither, writher, tither.
ITH′est– 2. lithest, blithest.
ITH′ful– 2. litheful, blitheful.
ITH′ing– 2. nithing, writhing, trithing, scything, tithing.
ITH′lee– 2. lithely, blithely.
ITH′nes– 2. litheness, blitheness.
ITH′sum– 2. lithesome, blithesome.
IT′ing– 2. biting, diting, fighting, kiting, skiting [dial.], lighting, blighting, plighting, slighting, smiting, knighting, spiting, writing, righting, frighting, citing, sighting, whiting.
3. *backbiting*, inditing, indicting, *cockfighting*, *bullfighting*, alighting, delighting, beknighting, uniting, affrighting, *handwriting*, reciting, inciting, exciting, inviting, requiting.
4. expediting, proselyting, dynamiting, reuniting, disuniting, copywriting, copyright-ing, underwriting, uninviting.
IT′is– 3. phlebitis, carditis, rachitis, nephritis, iritis, arthritis, neuritis.
4. meningitis, laryngitis, tonsillitis, dermatitis.
5. pericarditis, peritonitis, appendicitis.
IT′ish– 2. lightish, slightish, spitish, brightish, tritish, tightish, whitish.
4. eremitish, anchoritish.
IT′iv– 3. attritive, excitive.
4. expeditive, appetitive.
IT′l– 2. title, vital.
3. recital, betitle, entitle, mistitle, requital; *see also* IT′al.
IT′lee– 2. lightly, slightly, nightly, knightly, rightly, brightly, sprightly, tritely, sightly, tightly, whitely.
3. politely, *fortnightly*, *uprightly*, contritely, unsightly.
4. eruditely, impolitely.

IT′less– 2. bightless, fightless, heightless, kiteless, lightless, miteless, mightless, nightless, knightless, spiteless, riteless, rightless, frightless, frightless, sprightless, sightless.
3. delightless.
4. proselyteless, dynamiteless, copyrightless.
IT′ment– 3. indictment, affrightment, incitement, excitement, invitement.
IT′ness– 2. lightness, slightness, rightness, brightness, triteness, whiteness.
3. politeness, *uprightness*.
4. eruditeness, impoliteness.
IT′ning– 2. heightening, lightning, lightening, brightening, frightening, tightening, whitening.
3. streak lightning, chain lightning, heat lightning, sheet lightning.
IT′on– 2. chiton, Triton, cyton, Titan.
IT′um– 2. item, Blitum.
5. ad infinitum.
IT′us– 2. litus, ritus [L.], situs, Titus.
3. attritus, detritus, St. Vitus.
I′us– 2. pious, Pius, prius.
3. bacchius [L.], unpious, Darius.
4. nisi prius.
5. antibacchius; *see also* **I′as.**
IV′a– 2. iva, Iva, daiva, Siva, Saiva.
3. saliva.
4. conjunctiva.
IV′al– 2. nival, rival, thivel.
3. ogival, archival, salival, arrival, corrival, deprival, outrival, estival, revival, survival.
4. nonarrival, relatival, genitival, adjectival, conjunctival.
5. imperatival.
IV′an– 2. Ivan, divan; *see also* **ĪV′en.**
IV′ans– 3. connivance, arrivance, contrivance, survivance.
IV′ant– 2. trivant.
3. connivant, survivant.
IV′ee– 2. ivy, jivy [slang], skivie [Scot.], stivy.
4. poison ivy.
IV′en– 2. liven.
3. enliven; *see also* **ĪV′an.**
IV′er– 2. diver, fiver [slang], hiver, jiver [slang], skiver, liver, livor, sliver, river, driver, shriver, striver, thriver, stiver.
3. pearl diver, conniver, arriver, deriver, depriver, slave driver, contriver, survivor.
4. deep sea driver.
IV′ing– 2. diving, hiving, jiving [slang], skiving, riving, driving, striving, shriving, thriving, stiving [Scot. & dial. Eng.], wiving.
3. conniving, arriving, deriving, depriving, contriving, reviving, surviving.
IV′lee– 2. lively, Shively.
3. unlively.
IV′ment– 3. deprivement, revivement.
IV′us– 2. divus, clivus.
3. salivous, acclivous, declivous, proclivous.
I′way– 2. byway, highway, skyway.
IZ′a– 2. Isa, Liza.

3. Eliza, coryza.
IZ′al– 2. sizal.
3. surmisal, despisal, arrhizal, apprizal, reprisal, comprisal, surprisal, incisal, capsizal, advisal, revisal.
4. paradisal.
IZ′ee– 2. sizy.
3. capsizy.
IZ′en– 2. bison, dizen, greisen.
3. bedizen, horizon.
4. spiegeleisen, Blut und eisen [G.].
IZ′er– 2. geyser, Kaiser, miser, riser, prizer, sizer, sizar, visor, vizor, wiser.
3. disguiser, elisor, remiser, surmiser, appriser, surpriser, assizer, incisor, excisor, capsizer, baptizer, chastiser, deviser, devisor, reviser, divisor.
4. gormandizer, aggrandizer, eulogizer, catechizer, vocalizer, papalizer, analyzer, paralyzer, moralizer, neutralizer, vitalizer, tantalizer, totalizer, equalizer, sterilizer, fertilizer, civilizer, symbolizer, idolizer, itemizer, atomizer, organizer, humanizer, scrutinizer, solemnizer, lionizer, colonizer, harmonizer, sermonizer, canonizer, synchronizer, patronizer, modernizer, fraternizer, mesmerizer, cauterizer, pulverizer, theorizer, temporizer, terrorizer, authorizer, enterpriser, exerciser, exorciser, magnetizer, appetizer, sympathizer, improviser, supervisor.
5. apologizer, generalizer, demoralizer, monopolizer, economizer, epitomizer, deodorizer, extemporizer, nonsympathizer.
IZ′ing– 2. rising, prizing, sizing, wising.
3. disguising, surmising, despising, arising, apprising, comprising, uprising, surprising, misprizing, resizing, excising, incising, capsizing, baptizing, chastising, advising, devising, revising.
4. Judaizing, archaizing, Hebraizing, hybridizing, iridizing, chloridizing, subsidizing, oxidizing, liquidizing, merchandizing, gormandizing, aggrandizing, iodizing, melodizing, psalmodizing, rhapsodizing, standardizing, jeopardizing, redisguising, elegizing, syllogizing, eulogizing, energizing, catechizing, verbalizing, feudalizing, realizing, legalizing, alkalizing, localizing, vocalizing, formalizing, penalizing, signalizing, finalizing, journalizing, papalizing, moralizing, centralizing, neutralizing, specializing, socializing, vitalizing, tantalizing, dualizing, equalizing, stabilizing, mobilizing, sterilizing, fossilizing, fertilizing, utilizing, civilizing, tranquilizing, crystallizing, symbolizing, idolizing, formulizing, euphemizing, emblemizing, itemizing, minimizing, victimizing, compromising, urbanizing, paganizing, Christianizing, mechanizing, vulcanizing, Romanizing, Germanizing, humanizing, tyrranizing, galvanizing, Hellenizing, pollenizing, heathenizing, recognizing, feminizing, Latinizing, scrutinizing, solemnizing, carb-

onizing, agonizing, lionizing, unionizing, colonizing, harmonizing, sermonizing, canonizing, synchronizing, patronizing, modernizing, fraternizing, immunizing, communizing, vulgarizing, plagiarizing, burglarizing, summarizing, notarizing, tenderizing, mesmerizing, pauperizing, cauterizing, pulverizing, satirizing, theorizing, memorizing, vaporizing, temporizing, terrorizing, motorizing, authorizing, enterprising, pasteurizing, martyrizing, emphasizing, synthesizing, ostracizing, publicizing, Anglicizing, Gallicizing, criticizing, synopsizing, exorcising, dramatizing, dogmatizing, magnetizing, monetizing, sensitizing, hypnotizing, advertising, amortizing, deputizing, empathizing, sympathizing, improvising, supervising, colloquizing.

5. italicizing, apostrophizing, philosophizing, provincializing, commercializing, nationalizing, rationalizing, personalizing, liberalizing, federalizing, generalizing, demoralizing, decentralizing, naturalizing, capitalizing, devitalizing, revitalizing, immortalizing, visualizing, actualizing, evangelizing, caramelizing, metabolizing, monopolizing, legitimizing, economizing, epitomizing, dehumanizing, rejuvenizing, antagonizing, familiarizing, circularizing, regularizing, singularizing, popularizing, militarizing, characterizing, deodorizing, allegorizing, categorizing, extemporizing, parenthesizing, systematizing, acclimatizing, democratizing, apostatizing, alphabetizing, demagnetizing, anesthetizing, desensitizing; *and all other verbs ending in the verbal suffix " -ize " plus " -ing ": see* **ĪZ.**

ĪZ′ment– 3. franchisement, apprizement, assizement, baptizement, chastisement, advisement.

4. enfranchisement, disfranchisement, aggrandizement.

ĪZ′o– 3. aviso, proviso.

4. Valparaiso, improviso.

ĪZ′on– 2. bison.

3. horizon.

ĪZ′or– 2. visor, vizor.

3. elisor, incisor, devisor, divisor.

4. supervisor; *see also* **ĪZ′er.**

Ī (eye)

Triple Rhymes

Primary or Secondary Accent Falls on Second from Last Syllable; Imperfect Rhymes Are in Italics.

I′a–bl– **3.** eyeable, liable, pliable, friable, triable, viable.
4. reliable, appliable, impliable, compliable, deniable.
5. liquefiable, modifiable, qualifiable, verifiable, classifiable, pacifiable, falsifiable, rectifiable, sanctifiable, fortifiable, justifiable, satisfiable, unreliable, multipliable, undeniable.
6. solidifiable, exemplifiable, electrifiable, diversifiable, identifiable, unfortifiable, unjustifiable, unsatisfiable, unmultipliable.
7. unidentifiable.
I′a–blee– **3.** pliably.
4. reliably, appliably, compliably, deniably.
5. justifiably, unreliably, undeniably.
6. unjustifiably, unsatisfiably.
I′a–deez– **3.** Hyades, Pleiades, naiades, dryades.
5. hamadryades.
I′a–gram– **3.** diagram, skiagram, viagram.
I′a–kal– **3.** piacle.
4. dandiacal, zodiacal, heliacal, maniacal.
5. prosodiacal, elegiacal, demoniacal, simoniacal.
6. pyromaniacal, dipsomaniacal, kleptomaniacal, hypochondriacal, paradisiacal.
7. encyclopediacal, bibliomaniacal.
I′al–lik– **3.** dial-like, phial-like, trial-like, vial-like, viol-like.
4. *sundial-like.*
I′an–see– **3.** cliency, pliancy, riancy.
4. compliancy.
I′ant–lee– **3.** pliantly.
4. defiantly, reliantly, compliantly.
I′ar–ee– **3.** diary, briary, friary; *see also* Ī′er–ee.
I′ar–ist– **3.** diarist, Piarist.
I′ark–ee– **3.** diarchy, triarchy.
I′as–is– **4.** psychiasis, psoriasis.
5. odontiasis.
6. hypochondriasis, elephantiasis.
I′a–tree– **4.** podiatry, psychiatry, phoniatry, hippiatry.

I′a–trist– **4.** podiatrist, psychiatrist, hippiatrist.
IB′a–bl– **3.** bribable, scribable.
4. ascribable, subscribable, describable, prescribable, inscribable, proscribable.
5. indescribable, undescribable, circumscribable.
ID′a–bl– **3.** guidable, hidable, ridable.
4. unguidable, elidable, unridable, bestridable, decidable, dividable, providable.
5. undecidable, subdividable, undividable, unprovidable.
ID′ed–lee– **4.** unguidedly, misguidedly, decidedly, lopsidedly.
5. undecidedly, undividedly, unprovidedly.
ID′ing–lee– **3.** chidingly, guidingly, hidingly, glidingly, slidingly, stridingly, sidingly.
4. abidingly, unchidingly, confidingly, misguidingly, unhidingly.
I′en–see– **3.** cliency, pliancy, riancy.
4. compliancy.
I′er–ee– **3.** fiery, lyery, briery, priory; *see also* Ī′ar–ee.
I′et–al– **3.** dietal, hyetal.
4. parietal, varietal, societal.
5. isohyetal.
I′et–ed– **3.** dieted, rioted, quieted.
4. unquieted, disquieted.
I′et–ee– **3.** piety.
4. ubiety, dubiety, filiety, impiety, variety, ebriety, sobriety, propriety, society, satiety, anxiety.
5. contrariety, inebriety, insobriety, notoriety, impropriety.
I′et–er– **3.** dieter, rioter, quieter.
4. proprietor, disquieter.
I′et–est– **3.** quietest.
4. unquietest; *see also* Ī′et–ist.
I′et–ing– **3.** dieting, rioting, quieting.
4. unquieting, disquieting.
I′et–ist– **3.** dietist, pietist, quietist, quietest.
4. varietist, unquietest.
I′et–izm– **3.** pietism, quietism.

4. varietism.
IF′en–ate– 3. hyphenate, siphonate.
IF′er–ing– 3. ciphering, syphering.
4. deciphering.
IF′ling–lee– 3. triflingly, stiflingly.
I′ing–lee– 3. lyingly, flyingly, pryingly, sighingly, vyingly.
4. defyingly.
5. gratifyingly, mystifyingly, satisfyingly.
IK′a–bl– 3. likeable, spikeable.
4. unlikeable, dislikeable.
IK′lik–al– 3. cyclical.
4. bicyclical, encyclical.
IL′a–bl– 3. filable, smilable, rilable, stylable, wilable, whilable.
4. defilable, beguilable, unrilable.
5. undefilable, unbeguilable, reconcilable.
6. irreconcilable, unreconcilable.
IL′and–er– 3. islander, highlander, Thailander.
IL′er–ee– 3. guilery, pilary, tilery.
IL′ful–ee– 3. guilefully, wilefully.
4. beguilefully.
IL′ful–ness– 3. guilefulness, wilefulness.
4. beguilefulness.
IL′ing–lee– 3. smilingly.
4. beguilingly, unsmilingly.
IM′er–ee– 3. rhymery, primary.
IM′i–ness– 3. liminess, sliminess, riminess, griminess.
IN′a–bl– 3. finable, linable, signable.
4. combinable, definable, declinable, inclinable, opinable, assignable, designable, divinable.
5. undefinable, undeclinable, unassignable, undivinable.
IN′a–blee– 4. definably, assignably.
5. undefinably, undeclinably, unassignably.
IN′a–lee– 3. finally, spinally.
IND′er–ee– 3. bindery, grindery.
IN′er–ee– 3. binary, finery, finary, minery, pinery, vinery, winery, quinary, swinery.
4. refinery, alpinery.
IN′i–er– 3. spinier, brinier, shinier, tinier, winier.
IN′i–est– 3. spiniest, briniest, shiniest, tiniest, winiest.
IN′les–lee– 3. spinelessly, winelessly.
I′ol–a– 3. viola, Viola.
4. variola.
I′ol–et– 3. triolet, striolet, violet.
I′ol–ist– 3. sciolist, violist.
I′ol–us– 3. sciolous.
4. gladiolus, modiolus, variolous.
I′on–ize– 3. ionize, lionize.
I′op–ee– 3. myopy.
4. *presbyopy*, calliope, Calliope.
I′or–ee– 3. priory; *see also* **Ī′ar–ee, Ī′er–ee.**
I′os–een– 3. Pliocene, Miocene.
4. post-Pliocene, post-Miocene.
I′ot–er– 3. rioter, quieter.
IP′ing–lee– 3. pipingly, gripingly.
IP′les–lee– 3. pipelessly, gripelessly, stripelessly, typelessly.

IR′a–bl– 3. fireable, hirable.
4. respirable, expirable, transpirable, inspirable, perspirable, untirable, acquirable, requirable, inquirable, desirable.
5. uninspirable, undesirable.
IR′as–ee– 3. piracy.
4. retiracy.
IR′ful–ness– 3. irefulness, direfulness.
4. desirefulness.
IR′ing–lee– 4. admiringly, aspiringly, conspiringly, retiringly, inquiringly, desiringly.
IR′on–ee– 3. irony, sireny.
IS′a–bl– 3. sliceable, spiceable, riceable, priceable.
4. enticeable.
IS′er–ee– 3. spicery.
4. irrisory, derisory, incisory.
IS′i–er– 3. icier, spicier.
IS′i–est– 3. iciest, spiciest.
IS′i–kl– 3. icicle, bicycle, tricycle.
IS′i–lee– 3. icily, spicily.
IS′iv–lee– 4. derisively, decisively, incisively.
5. indecisively, undecisively.
IS′iv–ness– 4. derisiveness, decisiveness, incisiveness.
5. undecisiveness.
IS′or–ee– see IS′er–ee.
IT′a–bl– 3. lightable, writable, sightable, citable.
4. indictable, ignitable, unitable, recitable, excitable, incitable, requitable.
5. extraditable.
IT′a–blee– 4. indictably, unitably, excitably.
IT′al–ize– 3. vitalize.
4. devitalize, revitalize.
IT′at–iv– 3. writative.
4. recitative, excitative, incitative, requitative.
IT′en–er– 3. heightener, lightener, brightener, frightener, tightener, whitener.
4. enlightener.
IT′ful–ee– 3. spitefully, rightfully, frightfully, sprightfully.
4. delightfully.
ITH′som–lee– 3. lithesomely, blithesomely.
ITH′som–ness– 3. lithesomeness, blithesomeness.
IT′i–er– 3. flightier, mightier.
4. almightier.
IT′il–ee– 3. flightily, mightily, sprightily.
4. almightily.
IT′i–ness– 3. flightiness, mightiness.
4. almightiness.
IT′ing–lee– 3. bitingly, blightingly, slightingly.
4. excitingly, invitingly.
IT′less–ness– 3. nightlessness, sightlessness.
IT′li–ness– 3. knightliness, sprightliness, sightliness.
4. unsightliness.
IV′a–bl– 3. drivable.
4. undrivable, deprivable, derivable, contrivable, revivable.
5. unrevivable.

ĪV′an–see–ee– 4. connivancy, contrivancy, survivancy.

ĪV′ing–lee– 3. jivingly [slang], drivingly, strivingly, thrivingly.

ĪZ′a–bl– 3. prizable, sizable.
4. demisable, surmisable, despisable, comprisable, excisable, advisable, devisable.
5. subsidizable, oxidizable, realizable, analyzable, crystallizable, utilizable, civilizable, organizable, recognizable, incognizable, exercisable, inadvisable.

ĪZ′a–blee– 3. sizeably.
4. advisably.
5. inadvisably.

ĪZ′ed–lee– 4. surmisedly, advisedly.
5. unadvisedly, improvisedly, unprovisedly.

ĪZ′ing–lee– 4. despisingly, surprisingly.
5. enterprisingly, tantalizingly, scrutinizingly, agonizingly, appetizingly.

ĪZ′or–ee– 4. advisory, revisory, provisory.
5. supervisory.

Ĭ (bib)

Single (Masculine) Rhymes

Primary or Secondary Accent Falls on Last Syllable; Imperfect Rhymes Are in Italics.

IB– 1. bib, bibb, chib, dib, fib, gib, jib, Lib, lib [slang], glib, mib [dial.], nib, snib, rib, drib, crib, sib, Tib, tib [slang], quib, squib, zib [slang].
2. Adib, ad-lib, renib, *midrib.*
IBD– 1. bibbed, dibbed, fibbed, jibbed, ribbed, cribbed, squibbed.
2. unbibbed, ad-libbed, *rock-ribbed.*
IBZ– *see* **ĬB,** plus " s " or " 's ";.
2. his nibs.
ICH– 1. itch, bitch, ditch, dich, fitch, hitch, skitch [slang], lich, lych, flitch, miche, smitch [slang], niche, snitch, pitch, rich, britch [dial.], sich [dial.], stitch, witch, quitch, switch, twitch, which.
2. unhitch, enrich, restitch, *seamstitch, hemstitch, chainstitch, whipstitch, catstitch,* bewitch.
3. saddlestitch, featherstitch, czarevitch.
4. Ivanovitch.
ICHT– 1. itched, bitched [vulgar], ditched, hitched, flitched, miched, niched, snitched, pitched, britched, stitched, switched, twitched.
2 unhitched, enriched, restitched, bewitched.
3. unenriched, saddlestitched, feather-stitched, unbewitched.
ID– 1. id, bid, chid, did, fid, gid, hid, kid, Kidd, skid, lid, slid, mid, rid, grid, strid, Sid, Cid, quid, squid, whid.
2. rebid, forbid, outbid, undid, outdid, *aphid, bifid, trifid, eyelid,* amid, *Enid,* Madrid, *Muphrid, Astrid,* unthrid.
3. underbid, overbid, overdid, katydid, invalid, pyramid.
IF– 1. if, biff, diff [slang], pfiff, jiff [slang], skiff, glyph, cliff, miff [dial. & slang], sniff, piff, spiff [slang], riff, griffe, griph, Sif, tiff, stiff, wiff [slang], quiff, whiff.
2. *Saiph, midriff.*
3. handkerchief, neckerchief, logogriph, hippogriff, Teneriffe, bindle stiff [slang].
4. hieroglyph.

IFT– 1. biffed, gift, skiffed, skift, lift, cliffed, miffed [dial. & slang], sniffed, snift, spiffed [slang], rift, drift, shrift, thrift, sift, shift, tiffed, tift, squiffed [slang], swift, whiffed.
2. relift, uplift, adrift, *spindrift, spoondrift, snowdrift, spendthrift, muckthrift,* reshift, *makeshift, gearshift.*
3 chimney swift.
IG– 1. big, bigg, dig, fig, gig, jig, nig, snig, pig, spig [slang], rig, wrig, brig, brigg, Frigg, grig, crig, prig, sprig, trig, cig [slang], tyg, wig, swig, twig, Whig, zig.
2. *fishgig, fizgig,* renege, *bigwig,, whirlwig, earwig,* outrig.
3. Mr. Big, infra dig [coll.], caprifig, whirligig, Guinea pig, thimblerig, periwig.
4 thingumajig [coll.].
IGD– 1. figged, gigged, jigged, nigged, snigged, pigged, rigged, grigged, prigged, sprigged, trigged, wigged, swigged, twigged, zigged.
2. reneged, full-rigged, square-rigged, outrigged, bewigged.
IGZ– *see* **ĬG,** plus " s " or " 's ";.
1. Biggs, digs [slang], Jiggs, Riggs, Briggs.
3 Mrs. Wiggs.
IJ– 1. fidge [dial.], midge, smidge, nidge, ridge, bridge, whidge [slang], squidge.
2 enridge, abridge, *cabbage, cribbage, bondage, yardage, cordage, leafage, roofage, package, leakage, coinage, carnage, dumpage, stoppage, moorage, storage, dosage, message, sausage, usage, shortage, hostage, postage, language, selvage, drayage, voyage.*
3. brigandage, *appendage, impoundage,* lineage, verbiage, foliage, vassalage, *assemblage,* tutelage, mucilage, cartilage, pilgrimage, appanage, alienage, badinage, vicinage, peonage, siphonage, baronage, patronage, parsonage, personage, *equipage,* vicarage, plunderage, brokerage, cooperage, porterage, quarterage, fosterage, average, beverage, leverage, flowerage, saxifrage, harborage, anchorage, hemorrhage, tutorage, arbitrage, pasturage,

surplusage, armitage, hermitage, heritage, clientage, parentage.

4. espionage.

ĬJD– 1. fidged [dial.], nidged, ridged, bridged.

2. unridged, abridged, unbridged.

3. unabridged.

IK– 1. ich [G.], ick [slang], chic, chick, tchick, Dick, dick, hic, hick, kick, lick, flick, click, slick, mick, nick, snick, pick, pic [slang], spick, rick, wrick, brick, Frick, crick, cric, creek [coll.], scrick [slang], prick, trick, sick, sic, tick, tic, stick, stich, thick, Vic, vic [slang], wick, quick.

2. *dabchick, peachick, relic, cowlick, comic, hand-pick, nutpick, toothpick, hayrick, firebrick, landsick, seasick, homesick, brainsick, moonsick, heartsick, loversick, knobstick, yardstick, broomstick, drumstick, chopstick, metestick,* Old Vic, *lampwick Warwick, Brunswick.*

3. *trochaic, iambic,* Benedick, benedick, *dactylic,* Catholic, arsenic, chivalric, choleric, limerick, turmeric, tumeric, whitterick, maverick, plethoric, rhetoric, bishopric, lunatic, heretic, politic, walking stick, fiddlestick, candlestick, bailiwick, candlewick, double quick.

4. allocochick, ich liebe dich [G.], kinnikinnick, archbishopric, arithmetic, impolitic, anapestic.

5. *comic-iambic,* cosmopolitic.

IKS– *see* ĬK, plus " s " or " 's "; **1.** Bix, chix [slang], Dix, fix, mix, nix, Pnyx, pyx, pix, rix, Trix, six, Styx.

2. affix, adfix, refix, prefix, infix, confix, transfix, postfix, suffix, prolix, admix, immix, commix.

3. antefix, crucifix, intermix, undermix, overmix, acronyx, Beatrix, cicatrix, twenty-six etc., billywix.

4. aviatrix, inheritrix, executrix.

IKST– 1. fixed, mixed, nixed, [slang], sixte, 'twixt.

2. affixed, adfixed, refixed, prefixed, infixed, confixed, transfixed, postfixed, suffixed, admixed, immixed, commixed, betwixt.

3. antefixed, dorsifixed, intermixed, undermixed, overmixed.

IKT– 1. dict [arch.], chicked [dial.], tchicked, hicked, kicked, licked, flicked, clicked, slicked, nicked, snicked, picked, Pict, ricked, bricked, pricked, tricked, strict, sicked, sicced, ticked, sticked, thicked, wicked.

2. addict, *edict,* predict, delict, *relict,* afflict, inflict, conflict, relicked, unlicked, reslicked, unslicked, unnicked, depict, *hand-picked,* unpicked, unricked, rebricked, unbricked, astrict, restrict, constrict, evict, convict, two-wicked.

3. contradict, benedict, Benedict, interdict, derelict, overstrict, preconvict.

IL– 1. ill, bill, Bill, chill, chil, dill, fill, Phil, phil [slang], gill, hill, jill, kil, kill, kiln, skil, skill, lill, li'l [dial.], Lil. mill, mil, nil, pill, spill, rill, brill, drill, frill, grill,

grille, prill, shrill, trill thrill, sill, Shilh, shill, til, till, still, thill, vill, ville, will, Will, quill, squill, swill, twill.

2. *playbill, waybill, redbill, handbill, broadbill, ringbill, wrybill,* black bill, *cockbill, duckbill, hornbill, thornbill, spoonbill,* brown bill, *waxbill, crossbill, boatbill,* short bill, *bluebill, shoebill,* spadille, refill, fufill, *scrodgill, bluegill, molehill,* downhill, uphill, *anthill,* sijill [Ar.], *limekiln, treadmill, windmill,* quadrille, befrill, *footrill, headsill, groundsill,* retill, until, bestill, *standstill,* distill, instill, coutil, Seville, goodwill, ill will, *poorwill,* Brazil, frazil.

3 dishabille, yellowbill, dollar bill, razorbill, piccadill, daffodil, Francophil, Gallophil, Anglophil, demophil, Sinophil, Negrophil, chlorophyll, astrophil, chrysophyll, Celtophil, phytophil, underfill, overfill, cement mill, juvenile, puerile, imbecile, codicil, domicile, verticil, window sill, Mother Sill, volatile, vibratil, pulsatile, versatile, mercantile, infantile, thereuntil, intertill, undertill, overtill, reinstill, Faneuil, Louisville, Waterville, Evansville, whippoorwill.

ILCH– 1. filch. milch, pilch, zilch [slang].

ILD– 1. build, billed, chilled, filled, gilled, gild, guild, killed, skilled, milled, pilled, spilled, rilled, drilled, frilled, grilled, shrilled, trilled, thrilled, shilled, tilled. stilled, willed, quilled, squilled, swilled.

2. rebuild, rebilled, fulfilled, unfilled, begild, *wergild, Brunhild,* unskilled, unmilled unspilled, undrilled, ungrilled, unthrilled, untilled, distilled, instilled, unstilled, self-willed, strong-willed, weak-willed.

3. jerry-build, unfulfilled, octogild, undistilled.

ILK– 1. ilk, bilk, milk, silk, whilk.

2. sour milk, spilt milk, spun silk.

ILN– 1. kiln, Milne.

2. *limekiln.*

ILT– 1. built, gilt, guilt, hilt, jilt, kilt, lilt, milt, spilt, silt, tilt, stilt, wilt, quilt.

2. rebuilt, unbuilt, rejilt, respilt, unspilt, atilt, uptilt. requilt.

3. jerry-built, Vanderbilt, clipper built.

ILTS– 1. gilts, guilts, hilts, jilts, kilts, lilts, silts, tilts, stilts, wilts, quilts.

3. Vanderbilts.

IM– 1. Bim, bim [slang], dim, him, hymn, gym, Jim, jim [slang], Kim, skim, limn, limb, flim [slang], glim, Clim, Klim, slim, mim, nim, Nym, nimb, rim, brim, grim, grimme, scrim, prim, trim, Sim, shim, Tim, stim [slang], vim, swim, whim, zimb.

2. bedim, enlimn, *corymb,* betrim.

3. cherubim, paradigm, seraphim, pseudonym, synonym, antonym, undernim, Sanhedrim, interim, hexastigm, Tiny Tim.

IMD– 1. dimmed, hymned, skimmed, limned, limbed, slimmed, rimmed, brimmed, trimmed.

2. bedimmed, enlimned, untrimmed.

IMF– 1. lymph, nymph.

2. wood nymph, sea nymph.
3. endolymph, paranymph, water nymph.
IMP– 1. imp, gimp, jimp [dial.], skimp, limp, blimp, mimp [dial.], pimp, grimp, crimp, scrimp, primp, shrimp, simp [slang], tymp.
IMPS– *see* ĬMP, plus " s " or " 's "; 1. glimpse.
IMPT– 1. imped, gimped, jimped [dial.], skimped, limped, mimped [dial.], pimped, grimped, crimped, scrimped, primped, shrimped.
IN– 1. in, inn, bin, been. chin, tchin, din, fin, Finn, finn, [slang], gin, jinn, kin, skin, Lynn, lin, Glynn, Min, pin, spin, brin, grin, crin, sin, shin, tin, thin, win, twin, whin, Yin.
2. herein, therein, wherein, within, *nubbin, globin, robin, rubin,* has-been, *Cochin, urchin, Odin, Baffin,* Boffin [Dickens], *redfin, threadfin, blackfin, elfin, dolphin, dauphin, bowfin, Fagin,* begin, *piggin, noggin, pidgin, Elgin, engine, margin, virgin,* akin, Pekin, blood kin, *lambkin, bodkin, brodeguin, welkin, napkin, princekin, catkin,* reskin, *redskin, calfskin, pigskin, sharkskin, sealskin, moleskin, lambskin, doeskin, sheepskin, bearskin, deerskin, maudlin, mafflin, mufflin,* Franklin, *Kremlin, drumlin, dunlin, collin, colin, poplin, carline, marlin,* Berlin, *merlin,* Merlin, *muslin, villain, chaplain, stamin, vermin, tannin,* Lenin, *rennin, lignin, lapin,* repin, *inchpin, kingpin, pippin, sculpin,* unpin, *tenpin, ninepin, respin, Crispin, pushpin, hatpin, fibrin,* agrin, chagrin, *Corin,* corinne, *caprin, dextrin,* Turin, *tocsin, rosin, trypsin,* Tientsin, *Latin, pectin, glutin,* Swithin, *penguin, pinguin, sequin.*
3. carabin, jacobin, Jacobin, colobin, Capuchin, paladin, *Aladdin,* amidin, *morindin,* paraffin, Mickey Finn, origin, waringin, manakin, baldachin, ramekin, bodikin, birdikin, spilikin, billikin, manikin, cannikin, pannikin, bootikin, *grimalkin,* kilderkin, tigerkin, nipperkin, tigerskin, hyaline caballine, alkaline, tourmaline, coralline, crystalline, ptyalin, Gobelin, gobelin, capelin, capeline, Zeppelin, javelin, sibylline, aniline, aquiline, bandoline, mandolin, violin, lanoline, crinoline, Caroline, *tarpaulin,* globulin, masculine, insulin, Ursuline, discipline, Benjamin, jessamine, vitamin, *albumin, illumine,* mezzanine, Fescennine, feminine, pavonine, heroine, wankapin, chinquapin, terrapin, calepin, underpin, saccharine, whipper-in, margarin, tamarin, nectarine, Sanhedrin, viperine, aspirin, anserine, peregrine, glycerin, Catherine, Lohengrin, tambourin, moccasin, damassin, mortal sin, *Wisconsin,* agatine, bulletin, Byzantine, *asbestine, intestine, Rasputin,* thick, and thin. *absinthine,* genuine, Bedouin harlequin, mannequin, lambrequin, *Algonquin.*
4. *hemoglobin, ragamuffin digitalin,* Evangeline, tuberculin, elaterin, *alabastrine,* highfalutin.
5. nitroglycerin.
INCH– 1. inch, chinch, finch, kinch, linch, lynch, flinch, clinch, minch [slang], pinch, cinch, winch, squinch.
2. *redfinch, goldfinch, bullfinch, greenfinch, grass finch, hawfinch,* unclinch, bepinch, recinch, uncinch.
INCHT– 1. inched, lynched, flinched, clinched, minched [slang], pinched, cinched, winched, squinched [dial.].
2. unclinched, recinched, uncinched.
IND– 1. binned, chinned, dinned, finned, ginned, skinned, lind, lynde, pinned, grinned, sind, scind, sinned, tinned, thinned, wind, twinned.
2. thick-skinned, thin-skinned, unskinned, abscind, rescind, exscind, *whirlwind.*
3. disciplined, tamarind, Amerind.
4. undisciplined.
ING– 1. ing, Ing, Inge, bing, ching, ding, ging, hing, king, ling, fling, cling, Kling, pling [slang], Ming, ping, ring, wring, bring, dring, spring, string, sing, singh, ting, sting, thing, wing, swing, zing.
2. beking, Chungking, Nanking, *fledgeling, changeling, weakling, dukeling, stripling, Riesling, princeling,* Peiping, enring, aspring, *offspring, mainspring, latchstring, checkstring, hamstring, bowstring, shoestring,* Singsing, *Storting, something, nothing,* bewing, *redwing, pinwing, lapwing, waxwing, whitewing.*
3. scaffolding, horseshoeing, triumphing, pillaging, managing, foraging, à la king, mafficking, trafficking, dialing, rivaling, caviling, toweling, sanderling, underling, fingerling, easterling, maddening, widening, deafening, stiffening, roughening, toughening, slackening, thickening, sickening, opening, happening, lessening, threatening, sweetening, softening, fastening, hastening, moistening, fattening, strengthening, leavening, evening, rationing, pensioning, auctioning, questioning, echoing, larruping, sugaring, soldering, murdering, differing, suffering, angering, ushering, weathering, soldiering, hankering, hollering, summering, centering, sauntering, quartering, blistering, answering, doctoring, motoring, liquoring, conjuring, murmuring, featuring, fracturing, lecturing, picturing, culturing, posturing, purschasing, solacing, menacing, latticing, climaxing, financing, promising, witnessing, publishing, famishing, ravishing, fidgeting, blanketing, coveting, surfeiting, limiting, fagoting, balloting, adapting, ballasting, Odelsting, anything, everything, arguing, issuing, elbowing, swallowing, yellowing, billowing, merrywing, lobbying, fancyng, monkeying, volleying, journeying, moseying, curtseying, bullying, whinnying, copying, wearying, varying, querying, dairying, curtsying, emptying, partying, puttying, envying.
4. mismanaging, disparaging, encouraging, discouraging, awakening, imagining, determining, occasioning, envisioning, belea-

guering, continuing, mutinying.
5. administering, accompanying; *and present participle of all other verbs.*
ĬNGD– 1. dinged, pinged, ringed, stringed, tinged, winged, zinged.
2. beringed, *webwinged,* bewinged.
3. eagle-winged.
ĬNJ– 1. Inge, binge, dinge, hinge, fringe, cringe, scringe, springe, singe, tinge, swinge, twinge.
2. unhinge, impinge, befringe, infringe, syringe, astringe, obstringe, attinge.
ĬNJD– 1. binged [dial.], dinged, hinged, fringed, cringed, scringed, springed, singed, tinged, swinged, twinged.
2. unhinged, impinged, befringed, infringed, syringed, astringed, unsinged, attinged.
ĬNK– 1. ink, Inc., inc [slang], chink, dink, Fink, fink [slang], gink [slang], jink, kink, skink, link, blink, clink, slink, mink, smink [slang], pink, spink, rink, brink, drink, prink, shrink, trink, sink, cinque, stink, think, wink, quink [slang], twink, zinc.
2. perjink, *iceblink,* relink, enlink, unlink, *pincpinc, Sintsink,* bethink, forethink, *hoodwink.*
3. bobolink, interlink, countersink, tiddlywink, jinniwink.
ĬNKS– *see* **ĬNK,** plus " s " or " 's "; 1. sphinx jinx, lynx, minx.
2. high jinks, methinks.
3. criosphinx, Captain Jinks.
ĬNKT– 1. inked, chinked, kinked, linked, blinked, clinked, minked, pinked, rinked, prinked, tinct, winked.
2. beminked, succinct, discinct, instinct, distinct, extinct, *hoodwinked.*
3. indistinct.
ĬNS– 1. Ince, chinse, mince, rinse, prince, since, wince, quince.
2. evince; convince.
3. merchant prince; *see also* **ĬNTS.**
ĬNT– 1. bint, dint, hint, lint, blint [slang], flint, glint, splint, mint, print, sprint, tint, stint, vint, quint, squint.
2. *skinflint, gunflint, capmint, spearmint, catmint,* reprint, *hoofprint,* imprint, misprint, *footprint, blueprint.*
3. sodamint, calamint, peppermint, fingerprint, aquatint, monotint, mezzotint.
4. septuagint.
ĬNTH– 1. plinth.
2. *Corinth.*
3. terebinth, labyrinth, hyacinth, colocynth.
ĬNTS– *see* **ĬNT,** plus " s " or " 's "; 1. chintz, blintze, blintz; *see also* **ĬNS.**
ĬNZ– *see* **ĬN,** plus " s " or " 's "; 1. winze.
3. widdershins, withershins.
4. ods bodikins.
ĬP– 1. chip, dip, fip [slang], gip, hip, gyp, jip, jipp [both slang], kip, skip, lip, blip [slang], flip, glip [slang], clip, slip, nip, snip, pip, rip, drip, grip, grippe, scrip,

trip, strip, thrip, sip, ship, tip, quip, whip, yip, zip.
2. redip, inclip, unclip, *harelip, cowslip, catnip,* adrip, unrip, unstrip, outstrip, *sibship, headship, midship, friendship, hardship, lordship, wardship,* reship, *flagship, judgeship, clanship* transship, *queenship, kinship,* sonship, *township, troopship, airship, heirship, worship, warship, lightship, saintship, courtship,* equip, *coachwhip, horsewhip.*
3. pogonip, comradeship, *amidship,* stewardship, *trusteeship,* ladyship, battleship, seamanship, workmanship, penmanship, horsemanship, chairmanship, statesmanship, sportsmanship, fellowship, scholarship, membership, leadership, partnership, ownership, censorship, sponsorship, authorship.
4. guardianship, partisanship, citizenship, companionship, relationship, survivorship, acquaintanceship, apprenticeship.
ĬPS– *see* **ĬP,** plus " s " or " 's "; 1. Phipps.
2. ellipse, eclipse.
4. Apocalypse.
ĬPT– 1. chipped, dipped, hipped, gipped, gypped, kipped, skipped, lipped, flipped, clipped, clipt, slipped, nipped, snipped, pipped, ripped, dripped, gripped, crypt, script, tripped, stripped, sipped, shipped, tipped, tipt, quipped, whipped, yipped, zipped.
2. unchipped, redipped, undipped, *harelipped, thin-lipped, stiff-lipped, red-lipped, close-lipped, subscript, transcript,* conscript, proscript, *postscript,* unwhipped, *horsewhipped.*
3. eucalypt, antescript, superscript, manuscript.
4. apocalypt.
ĬR– through **ĬRZ–** *see* **Ŭ: ŬR** through **ŬRZ.**
ĬS– 1. bis, Dis, disc, hiss, kiss, lis, liss, bliss, gliss [slang], miss, Chris, priss [coll.], Tris, sis, siss, this, vis, wis [arch. or obs.], quis, cuisse, Swiss.
2. abyss, dehisce, amiss, remiss, dismiss, iwis, ywis [both arch.].
3. magadis, cowardice, prejudice, benefice, edifice, sacrifice, orefice, artifice, Judas kiss, chrysalis, fortalice, Salamis, Artemis, reminisce, precipice, avarice, dentifrice, verdigris, mistigris, ambergris, licorice, Beatrice, cockatrice, emphasis, emesis, Nemesis, genesis, synthesis, abatis, clematis, armistice, interstice.
4. Annapolis, Gallipolis, acropolis, necropolis, metropolis, anabasis, metabasis, psoriasis, diaeresis, periphrasis, metastasis, hypostasis, metathesis, antithesis, hypothesis, parenthesis, analysis, paralysis.
5. fideicommiss, sui generis [L.], biogenesis, metamorphosis.
6. elephantiasis, abiogenesis, adipogenesis.
ĬSH– 1. dish, fish, gish, lish, pish, wish, cuish, squish, swish, whish.
2. *mayfish, crayfish, redfish, goldfish, swordfish, kingfish, clingfish, stingfish, dogfish, hogfish,*

frogfish, *Backfisch* [G.], *blackfish*, *creekfish*, *weakfish*, *inkfish*, *sailfish*, *shellfish*, *filefish*, *tilefish*, *greenfish*, *queenfish*, *pinfish*, *jawfish*, *crawfish*, *sawfish*, *garfish*, *starfish*, *batfish*, *catfish*, *flatfish*, *ratfish*, *whitefish*, *jewfish*, *bluefish*, *cowfish*, *plowfish*, anguish.

3. jellyfish killifish, candlefish, devilfish, squirrelfish, tasselfish, cuttlefish, ribbonfish, surgeonfish, amberfish, barberfish, thunderfish, triggerfish, silverfish, babyish, dowdyish, devilish, womanish, heathenish, yellowish, willowish, ogreish, Quakerish, feverish, cleverish.

ĬSHT— **1.** dished, fished, wished, squished, swished, whisht, whished.

ĬSK— **1.** bisque, disc, disk, fisc, Fiske, lisk [dial.], pisk, risk, brisk, frisk, tisk! [coll.], whisk.

2. *lutfisk*, francisc.

3. odalisque, obelisk, basilisk, tamarisk, asterisk.

ĬSM— *see* **ĬZ′m.**

ĬSP— **1.** lisp, risp, crisp, wisp, whisp.

ĬSPT— **1.** lisped, risped, crisped, wisped, whisped.

ĬST— **1.** ist, fist, fyst, hissed, hist, gist, jist, kissed, list, missed, mist rist, frist [slang], wrist, grist, prissed [coll.], tryst, sist, sissed, cist, cyst, schist, wist, twist, whist.

2. *puckfist*, dehisced, agist, bekissed, unkissed, alist, enlist, bemist, unmissed, dismissed, assist, subsist, desist, resist, exist, encyst, insist, consist, persist, atwist, entwist, untwist.

3. Judaist, archaist, ultraist, prosaist, Arabist, psalmodist, threnodist, monodist, synodist, parodist, rhapsodist, methodist, *concordist*, Talmudist, atheist, tritheist, pacifist, specifist, elegist, strategist, eulogist, liturgist, monachist, catechist, anarchist, monarchist, cymbalist, pedalist, feudalist, racialist, specialist, socialist, martialist, formalist, annalist, analyst, journalist, choralist, moralist, pluralist, ruralist, fatalist, catalyst, vitalist, novelist, pugilist, nihilist, libellist, duellist, symbolist, Aeolist, sciolist, fabulist, querulist, dynamist, ceramist, alchemist, lachrymist, pessimist, optimist, *ophthalmist*, undismissed, urbanist, Urbanist, organist, mechanist, vulcanist, shamanist, Romanist, botanist, alienist, Hellenist, reminisced, terminist, Alpinist, Latinist, Calvinist, columnist, trombonist, hedonist, unionist, visionist, actionist, factionist, fictionist, notionist, Zionist, colonist, mammonist, mnemonist, harmonist, canonist, modernist, saturnist, communist, Taoist, egoist, jingoist, banjoist, soloist, Shintoist, landscapist, syncopist, Eucharist, diarist, solarist, summarist, glossarist, Lazarist, mesmerist, preterist, satirist, theorist, aphorist, colorist, amorist, armorist, humorist, terrorist, motorist, symmetrist, Scripturist, pharmacist, solecist, progressist, synthesist, biblicist, publicist, classicist, physicist, mythicist, pre-exist, co-exist, hydrocyst, col-

ipsist, exorcist, prelatist, schematist, stigmatist, dogmatist, pietist, quietist, magnetist, phonetist, syncretist, occultist, scientist, presentist, Adventist, egotist, narcotist, hypnotist, nepotist, despotist, apathist, amethyst, altruist, casuist, bolshevist, archivist, passivist, activist, intertwist, essayist, hobbyist, lobbyist, copyist.

4. mosaicist, polemicist, empiricist, romanticist, chiropodist, telegraphist, commercialist, nominalist, nationalist, liberalist, federalist, literalist, naturalist, Scripturalist, capitalist, ritualist, revivalist, evangelist, philatelist, parabolist, hyperbolist, monopolist, legitimist, epitomist, zootomist, accompanist, hygienist, alienist, determinist, protagonist, religionist, opinionist, communionist, revisionist, extensionist, delusionist, illusionist, reactionist, perfectionist, obstructionist, tobacconist eudaemonist, misogynist, emancipist, plagiarist, apiarist, secularist, ocularist, singularist, militarist, psychiatrist, hexametrist, pedometrist, problematist, systematist, enigmatist, diplomatist, automatist, numismatist, separatist, telepathist.

5. bibliopegist, industrialist, conventionalist, Universalist, transcendentalist, spiritualist, automobilist, indeterminist, revolutionist, particularist, caricaturist, experimentist, apocalyptist; *and other nouns ending in the suffix " -ist. ".*

ĬT— **1.** it, bit, bitt, chit, dit, ditt [both. dial.], fit, phit, git [dial.], hit, jit [slang], kit, skit, lit, flit, split, slit, mit, mitt, smit, nit, knit, pit, spit, writ, rit, brit, frit, grit, sprit, sit, cit, tit, wit, whit, quit, twit, zit [slang].

2. *tidbit*, *titbit*, *forebitt*, befit, unfit, misfit, *outfit*, alit, unlit, *twilit*, *moonlit*, *sunlit*, submit, admit, emit, demit, remit, commit, omit, permit, transmit, reknit, unknit, *cockpit*, *coalpit*, *armpit*, *ashpit*, *lickspit*, *turnspit*, *pitpit*, *daywrit*, outsit, tomtit, *godwit*, *chickwit*, outwit, acquit.

3. counterfeit, compromit, intromit, pretermit, intermit, manumit, Messerschmitt, definite, infinite, interknit, preterit, hypocrite, favorite, requisite, exquisite, perquisite, apposite, opposite, Jesuit.

4. lickety-split, indefinite, prerequisite, inapposite unopposite.

ĬTH— **1.** kith, lith, myth, smith, Smyth, pith, frith, crith, sith, with.

2. *trilith*, *goldsmith*, *locksmith*, *tinsmith*, *gunsmith*, herewith, therewith, wherewith, forthwith.

3. megalith, neolith, monolith, acrolith, coppersmith, silversmith, Arrowsmith.

4. paleolith, anthropolith.

ĬTHE— **1.** with, withe.

2. *bewith*, *hamewith*, herewith, therewith, wherewith, forthwith.

ĬTS— *see* **ĬT,** plus " s " or " 's "; **1.** Fitz, blitz, spitz, Ritz, Fritz, sitz.

3. slivovitz.

ĬV— **1.** chiv [slang], div [slang], give, live,

fliv [slang], spiv [slang], sieve, shiv [slang].

2. forgive, misgive, relive, outlive.

3. combative, sedative, quiddative, negative, purgative, talkative, ablative, amative, sanative, narrative, curative, causative, fixative, quietive, expletive, auditive, fugitive, primitive, dormitive, nutritive, tortitive, partitive, substantive .

4. figurative, intensative, consultative, impeditive.

5. conciliative; *and other adjectives ending in the suffix* " *-ive* "

IVD– **1.** lived, sieved.

2. relived, unlived, outlived, long-lived, short-lived.

3. negatived.

IX– *see* **ĬKS.**

IZ– **1.** is, biz [slang], Diz, fizz, phiz [slang], his, gizz [Scot. & N. of Eng.], Liz, riz [dial.], friz, sizz, 'tis, viz, wiz [slang], quiz, whiz, zizz.

2. Cadiz, gin fizz, befriz, requiz, gee whizz [coll.].

IZM– *see* **ĬZ′m.**

Ĭ (bib)

Double (Feminine) Rhymes

Primary or Secondary Accent Falls on Next to Last Syllable; Imperfect Rhymes Are in Italics.

IB–ald–a. 2. ribald; *see also* ĪB′ld.

IB′ee– 2. gibby, skibby [loc.], Libby, nibby [Scot. & N. of Eng.], ribby fribby, tibby. 4. nibby-jibby, nibby-gibby.

IB′er– 2. bibber, dibber, fibber, gibber, jibber, glibber, nibber, ribber, cribber, squibber. 3. *winebibber*, ad-libber.

IB′et– 2. gibbet, libbet, ribbet, Tibbett, zibet. 5. flibbertigibbet; *see also* ĪB′it.

IB′ing– 2. bibbing, fibbing, jibbing, ribbing, cribbing, squibbing. 3. *winebibbing*, ad-libbing.

IB′it– 3. adhibit, inhibit, prohibit, exhibit; *see also* ĪB′et.

IB′l– 2. bibble, dibble, gibel, kibble, nibble, ribble, dribble, fribble, gribble, cribble, scribble, tribble, thribble, sibyl, cibol, stibble, quibble. 3. transcribble. 4. ishkabibble [slang].

IB′ld– 2. bibbled, dibbled, ribald, dribbled, scribbled, quibbled.

IB′lee– 2. glibly, nibbly, dribbly, scribbly, quibbly.

IB′ler– 2. bibbler, dibbler, kibbler, nibbler, dribbler, fribbler, scribbler, quibbler. 3. transcribbler.

IB′let– 2. giblet, riblet, driblet, triblet.

IB′lik– Biblic, niblick. 4. philobiblic.

IB′ling– 2. bibbling, dibbling, kibbling, nibbling, dribbling, fribbling, cribbling, scribbling, sibling, quibbling. 3. transcribbling.

IB′on– 2. gibbon, ribbon. 3. blue ribbon.

IB′onz– *see* ĪB′on, plus "s" or "'s"; 2. bibbons, Gibbons.

IB′sen– 2. Ibsen, Gibson.

IB′ute– 2. tribute. 3. attribute, retribute, contribute, distribute.

ICH′ee– 2. itchy, bitchy, fitchy, hitchy, pitchy, stitchy, witchy, switchy, twitchy.

ICH′el– 2. Mitchell, switchel.

ICH′er– 2. itcher, bitcher, ditcher, hitcher, snitcher [slang], pitcher, richer, stitcher, switcher, twitcher. 3. enricher, bewitcher.

ICH′et– 2. fitchet, witchet, twitchet.

ICH′ez– 2. itches, bitches, ditches, hitches, flitches, niches, snitches [slang], pitches, riches, britches, breeches, stitches, witches, switches, twitches. 3. enriches, bewitches.

ICH′ing– 2. itching, bitching, ditching, hitching, pitching, stitching, witching, switching, twitching. 3. enriching, bewitching.

ICH′less– 2. itchless, ditchless, hitchless, pitchless, stitchless, witchless, switchless, twitchless.

ICH′ment– 3. enrichment, bewitchment.

ID′ans– 2. biddance, riddance. 3. forbiddance, good riddance.

ID′ed– 2. kidded, skidded, lidded, ridded. 4. invalided, pyramided.

ID′ee– 2. biddy, diddy [dial.], giddy, kiddy, skiddy, middy, tiddy, stiddy [dial.], widdy [Scot.]. 3. Dinwiddie. 4. chickabiddy.

ID′en– 2. bidden, hidden, slidden [arch.], midden, ridden, stridden. 3. unbidden, forbidden, beridden, bedridden, childridden, hagridden, plague-ridden, unthridden. 4. unforbidden, kitchen midden, feverridden, overridden.

ID′er– 2. bidder, kidder, Kidder, skidder, slidder, ridder, dridder, widder [dial.]. 3. rebidder, forbidder, outbidder, consider. 4. underbidder, overbidder, reconsider, disconsider.

ID′erd– 2. sliddered. 3. considered.

251

4. reconsidered, ill-considered, well-considered, unconsidered, disconsidered.

ID′ik– 3. rubidic, iridic, juridic, acidic, fatidic, druidic.

4. pyramidic.

ID′ing– 2. bidding, kidding, skidding, ridding.

3. forbidding, outbidding.

4. underbidding, overbidding, unforbidding, invaliding, pyramiding.

ID′ish– 2. kiddish, Yiddish.

ID′l– 2. diddle, fiddle, middle, niddle [Scot.], piddle, riddle, riddel, driddle [Scot.], griddle, widdle [dial.], twiddle, quiddle [dial.].

3. flumdiddle, condiddle, unriddle.

4. flummadiddle, taradiddle, tarradiddle.

ID′ld– 2. diddled, fiddled, middled, niddled [Scot.], piddled, riddled, driddled [Scot.], griddled, widdled [dial.], twiddled, quiddled [dial.].

3. condiddled, unriddled.

ID′ler– 2. diddler, fiddler, piddler, riddler, widdler, twiddler, quiddler.

4. tarradiddler.

ID′ling– 2. diddling, fiddling, kidling, middling, piddling, riddling, griddling, widdling, twiddling, quiddling.

ID′nee– 2. kidney, Sidney, Sydney.

ID′o– kiddo [slang], widow.

IF′ee– 2. iffy, biffy, jiffy, Liffey, cliffy, miffy, sniffy, spiffy [slang], squiffy [slang], whiffy.

4. River Liffey.

IF′en– 2. striffen, stiffen; *see also* ĬF′in.

IF′er– 2. differ, niffer, sniffer, stiffer, squiffer [slang], whiffer.

IF′ik– 2. glyphic.

3. tabific, morbific, rubific, deific, algific, triglyphic, prolific, magnific, somnific, cornific, terrific, aurific, horrific, classific, pacific, Pacific, specific, sensific, ossific, lucific, mucific, lactific, pontific, vivific.

4. lapidific, diaglyphic, anaglyphic, geoglyphic, logogriphic, calorific, dolorific, humorific, honorific, sonorific, saporific, soporific, beatific, scientific.

5. hieroglyphic.

6. dactylioglyphic.

IF′iks– 3. significs, specifics.

4. calorifics, colorifics, honorifics, soporifics.

5. hieroglyphics, dermatoglyphics.

IF′in– 2. biffin, griffin, striffen, tiffin, stiffen; *see also* ĬF′on.

IF′ing– 2. biffing, skiffing, cliffing, miffing [dial. & slang], sniffing, spiffing, tiffing, whiffing.

IF′ish– 2. sniffish, tiffish, stiffish.

IF′l– nifle [dial.], sniffle, piffle, riffle, whiffle.

IF′lee– 2. sniffly, stiffly.

IF′ler– 2. sniffler, piffler, riffler, whiffler.

IF′ling– 2. sniffling, piffling, riffling, whiffling.

IF′on– griffon, chiffon.

IFT′ed– 2. gifted, lifted, rifted, drifted, sifted, shifted.

3. ungifted, *shoplifted*, uplifted, resifted,

unsifted, reshifted, unshifted.

IFT′ee– 2. fifty, clifty, nifty [slang], snifty, rifty, drifty, thrifty, shifty.

4. fifty-fifty.

IFT′er– 2. lifter, drifter, sifter, shifter, swifter.

3. uplifter, *shoplifter*, *sceneshifter*.

IFT′ij– 2. driftage, siftage, shiftage.

IFT′ing– 2. gifting, lifting, snifting, rifting, drifting, sifting, shifting.

3. *shoplifting*, uplifting, resifting, *sceneshifting*, *earthshifting*.

IFT′less– 2. giftless, liftless, riftless, driftless, thriftless, shiftless.

IFT′ness– 2. miffedness, swiftness.

IG′an– 2. wigan.

3. balbriggan.

IG′ee– 2. biggy, piggy, spriggy, wiggy, twiggy.

4. piggy-wiggy.

IG′er– 2. bigger, chigger, digger, figger, gigger, jigger, ligger, nigger, snigger, rigger, rigor, prigger, sprigger, trigger, sigger, wigger, swigger, twigger, vigor.

3. gold digger, *gravedigger,* reneger, *outrigger.*

4. thimblerigger.

IG′erd– 2. jiggered, niggard, sniggered, triggered.

3. bejiggered, unniggard, *outriggered.*

IG′ers– *see* ĬG′er, plus " s " or " 's ".

IG′est 2. biggest, triggest.

IG′ing– 2. digging, figging, gigging, jigging, nigging, snigging, pigging, rigging, grigging, prigging, sprigging, trigging, wigging, swigging, twigging, jigging.

3. redigging, reneging, unrigging.

4. thimblerigging.

IG′ish– 2. giggish, jiggist, piggish, riggish, priggish, wiggish, Whiggish.

IG′it– 2. giggit, jigget, jiggit [both coll.], Brigit, frigate; *see also* ĬG′ot.

IG′izm– 2. priggism, wiggism, Whiggism.

IG′l– 2. giggle, higgle, jiggle, niggle, sniggle, wriggle, friggle [dial.], striggle [coll. Eng.], wiggle, swiggle [dial.], squiggle.

3. *porwigle.*

IG′lee– 2. bigly, giggly, jiggly, niggly, pigly, wriggly, wiggly, squiggly.

4. Uncle Wiggly.

IG′ler– 2. giggler, higgler, jiggler, niggler, sniggler, wriggler, squiggler [slang.]

IG′let– 2. giglet, piglet, wiglet, Whiglet.

IG′ling– 2. giggling, higgling, jiggling, niggling, pigling, wriggling, wiggling, swiggling [dial.], squiggling.

IG′ma– 2. sigma, stigma.

3. enigma, kerygma, sterigma.

4. hypostigma.

IG′mee– 2. pigmy, stigme.

IG′ment– 2. figment, pigment.

IG′nant– 3. indignant, malignant, benignant.

IG′net– 2. signet, cygnet.

IG′num– 2. lignum, rignum, signum, tignum.

IG′or– 2. rigor, vigor; *see also* ĬG′er.

IG′ot– 2. bigot, gigot, spigot, riggot, frigate;

see also **ĬG′it.**
IG′ure– 2. figure, ligure.
  3. refigure, prefigure, configure, disfigure, transfigure.
IJ′ee– 2. gidgee, midgy, ridgy, squidgy.
IJ′er– 2. ridger, bridger.
  3. abridger.
IJ′et– fidget, midget, nidget, Bridget, digit.
IJ′id– 2. rigid, frigid.
  3. unrigid, unfrigid.
IJ′il– 2. strigil, sigil, vigil.
IJ′ing– 2. fidging [dial.], nidging, ridging, bridging.
  3. abridging, enridging.
IJ′it– 2. digit; *see also* **ĬJ′et.**
IJ′on– 2. smidgen, pidgin, pigeon, widgeon, wigeon.
  3. religion.
  4. irreligion, gyropigeon.
IJ′us– 3. prodigious, religious, litigious.
  4. unreligious, irreligious, sacrilegious.
  5. overreligious, unsacrilegious.
IK′a– 2. licca, sicca, ticca, tikka.
  4. Missa sicca [L.].
IK′ee– 2. icky [slang], chicky, dicky, Dicky, dickey, hickey, kicky, blickey, Micky, Nicky, snickey, picky, rickey, Ricky, bricky, crickey [slang], pricky, tricky, ticky, tickey, sticky, Vicky, wicky.
  3. doohickey, jinriki, gin rickey.
IK′en– 2. chicken, Rikken, stricken, sicken, thicken, quicken.
  4. wonder-stricken, terror-stricken, horror-stricken.
IK′enz– *see* **ĬK′en,** plus " s " or " 's ".
  2. Dickens.
IK′er– 2. icker [Scot.], bicker, chicker, dicker, kicker, licker, liquor, flicker, clicker, slicker, smicker, nicker, knicker, snicker, picker, ricker, pricker, tricker, sicker, ticker, tikker, sticker, thicker, vicar, wicker, quicker, whicker.
  3. *bootlicker.*
  4. Dominicker, berry-picker, cherry-picker, apple-picker, cotton-picker.
IK′erd– 2. bickered, dickered, lickered [slang], liquored, flickered, nickered, snickered, whickered.
IK′erz– *see* **ĬK′er,** plus " s " or " 's "; 4. cami-knickers.
IK′est– 2. slickest, sickest, thickest, quickest.
IK′et– clicket, smicket, snicket, picket, spicket, cricket, pricket, siket [dial.], ticket, thicket, wicket.
  3. reticket, *mid-wicket.*
  4. walking ticket.
IK′ets– *see* **ĬK′et,** plus " s " or " 's "; 2. rickets.
IK′ing– 2. chicking [dial.], tchicking, hicking, kicking, licking, flicking, clicking, slicking, nicking, snicking, picking, ricking, bricking, cricking, pricking, tricking, ticking, sticking, thicking, wicking.
  3. *bootlicking, handpicking.*

  4. cotton-picking, pocket-picking.
IK′ish– 2. slickish, hickish [slang], pickish, prickish, trickish, sickish, stickish, thickish.
IK′l– 2. chickell, chicle, fickle, mickle [dial.], nickel, pickle, pikle, prickle, trickle, strickle, sickle, tickle, stickle.
  3. renickel, depickle.
  4. cupronickel, pumpernickel.
IK′lee– 2. fickly, slickly, prickly, trickly, sickly, tickly, stickly, thickly, quickly.
IK′ler– 2. fickler, pickler, prickler, strickler, tickler, stickler.
IK′let– 2. chiclet, tricklet.
IK′ling– 2. chickling, pickling, prickling, trickling, strickling, sickling, tickling, stickling.
IK′lish– 2. pricklish, ticklish.
IK′ness– 2. slickness, sickness, thickness, quickness.
  3. *homesickness, heartsickness, lovesickness.*
IK′nik– 2. picnic, pyknic, strychnic.
  4. isopycnic.
IK′ning– 3. sickening, thickening, quickening.
IKS′ee– 2. dixie, Dixie, dixy, jixie, mixy, nixie, nixy [cant.], pixy, pixie, rixy [loc. Eng.], tricksy, Trixie.
  4. water nixie.
IKS′en– 2. bixin, mixen, vixen.
IKS′er– 2. fixer, mixer, sixer.
  3. affixer, adfixer, refixer, prefixer, transfixer, elixir, admixer, commixer.
  4. undermixer, intermixer, overmixer.
IKSH′un– 2. diction, fiction, friction, striction.
  3. addiction, prediction, indiction, affixion, prefixion, transfixion, suffixion, reliction, affliction, infliction, confliction, depiction, obstriction, restriction, constriction, eviction, conviction.
  4. contradiction, malediction, valediction, benediction, interdiction, jurisdiction, crucifixion, dereliction, preconviction.
IKS′ing– 2. fixing, mixing.
  3. affixing, adfixing, refixing, prefixing, infixing, confixing, transfixing, postfixing, suffixing, admixing, commixing.
  4. undermixing, intermixing, overmixing.
IKS′it– 2. dixit.
  4. ipse dixit, Mr. Fix-it.
IKS′ture– 2. fixture, mixture.
  3. affixture, transfixture, immixture, commixture.
  4. intermixture.
IKT′al– 2. rictal.
  3. edictal.
IKT′ate– 2. dictate, nictate.
IKT′ed– 3. addicted, predicted, relicted, afflicted, inflicted, conflicted, depicted, restricted, constricted, evicted, convicted.
  4. contradicted, interdicted, self-inflicted, unrestricted, unconstricted.
IKT′er– 2. fictor, lictor, Pictor, stricter, victor.
  3. predictor, afflicter, inflicter, conflicter,

depicter, depictor, constrictor, evictor, convictor.

4. contradicter, contradictor, interdictor.

5. boa constrictor.

IKT′est– 2. lickedest, strictest.

IKT′ik– 2. ictic, dictic.

4. apodictic.

IKT′ing– 3. addicting, predicting, afflicting, inflicting, conflicting, depicting, restricting, constricting, evicting, convicting.

4. contradicting, unconflicting, interdicting, unrestricting, unconstricting.

IKT′iv– fictive.

3. addictive, predictive, indictive, afflictive, inflictive, conflictive, depictive, astrictive, restrictive, constrictive, convictive.

4. contradictive, maledictive, benedictive, apodictic, interdictive, jurisdictive, nonrestrictive.

IKT′or– see ĬKT′er.

IKT′um– 2. dictum.

3. delictum.

IKT′ure– 2. picture, stricture.

3. depicture, impicture, word picture.

IKT′us– 2. ictus, rictus.

3. Invictus.

4. Benedictus, acronyctous.

IK′up– 2. dikkop, hiccup, hiccough, kickup [slang], pickup, stick-up.

IL′a– Milla, Scylla, villa squilla. Squilla, Zilla.

3. chinchilla, cedilla, camilla, Camilla, armilla, manila, Manila, manilla, vanilla, papilla, guerrilla, spirilla, gorilla, Priscilla, axilla, maxilla, Drusilla, mantilla, scintilla, flotilla, favilla.

4. sabadilla, granadilla, cascarilla, camarilla.

5. sarsaparilla.

IL′an– 2. Dylan, Dillon, Villain, villein.

3. archvillain.

IL′ar– see ĬL′er.

ILB′ert– 2. filbert, Gilbert, Wilbert.

ILCH′er– 2. filcher, milcher, pilcher.

ILD′a– 2. Hilda, tilde.

3. Brünnhilde, Matilda, Mathilda.

ILD′ed– 2. builded, gilded.

3. begilded, ungilded.

ILD′er– 2. builder, gilder, guilder, wilder.

3. rebuilder, *shipbuilder*, *housebuilder*, begilder, bewilder.

ILD′ing– 2. building, gilding.

3. begilding, *shipbuilding*, *housebuilding*.

4. castle-building.

IL′ee– 2. billy, Billie, Billee, Billy, chilly, chili, Chile, dilly, dilli, filly, gillie, hilly, lily, Millie, rilly, frilly, grilly, shrilly, thrilly, silly, Scilly, tilly, tilley, Tillie, Willie, willy, willey, quilly, twilly.

4. Silly Billy, Piccadilly, daffodilly, piccalilli, tiger lily, water lily, willy-nilly.

5. daffydowndilly.

IL′eed 2. gillied, lilied.

IL′eez– 2. billies, Billie's, chilis, dillies, fillies,

gillies, lilies, Millie's, sillies, Scillies, Tillie's, Willie's, willies.

3. Achilles.

4. daffodillies, piccalillis, tiger lilies, water lilies.

IL′er– 2. iller, biller, chiller, filler, giller, hiller, killer, miller, pillar, spiller, driller, friller, griller, shriller, triller, thriller, siller, schiller, tiller, stiller, thiller, willer, quiller, swiller.

3. fulfiller, painkiller, man-killer, befriller, pralltriller, distiller instiller.

4. killer-diller [slang], giant-killer, lady-killer [slang], caterpillar.

IL′est– 2. illest, chillest, shrillest, stillest.

IL′et– 2. billet, fillet, skillet, millet, pillet, rillet, drillet, trillet, willet, quillet.

3. pilwillet.

IL′fer– 2. pilfer.

4. Bella Wilfer [Dickens].

IL′ful– 2. skillful, willful.

3. unskillful, unwillful.

IL′ij– pillage, grillage, tillage, stillage, village.

IL′ik– 3. idyllic, odylic, vanillic, Cyrillic, basilic, dactylic, exilic.

4. hemophilic, zoophilic, imbecilic, salicylic.

5. hōlodactylic.

IL′ing– 2. billing, chilling, filling, killing, milling, pilling, spilling, rilling, drilling, frilling, grilling, trilling, thrilling, shilling, schilling, tilling, stilling, willing, quilling, swilling.

3. refilling, fulfilling, unfilling, befrilling, distilling, instilling, unwilling.

4. unfulfilling, underfilling, overfilling, overwilling.

IL′is– 2. Phyllis, cilice, Willis.

4. amaryllis.

ILK′ee– 2. milky, silky, Willkie.

ILK′en– 2. milken, silken.

ILK′er– 2. bilker, milker, silker.

ILK′ing– 2. bilking, milking, silking.

IL′man– 2. billman, Gilman, hillman, Hillman, millman, pillman, grillman, Stillman.

IL′ment– 3. fulfillment, distillment, instillment.

IL′ness– 2. illness, chillness, shrillness, stillness.

IL′o– 2. billow, kilo, pillow, willow.

3. Camillo, lapillo, Negrillo.

4. peccadillo, armadillo, granadillo, tabardillo, weeping willow.

IL′ok– 2. fillock, hillock, sillock.

ILT′ed– 2. hilted, jilted, kilted, lilted, milted, silted, tilted, stilted, wilted, quilted.

3. *tiptilted*, unwilted.

4. crazy-quilted.

ILT′ee– 2. guilty, kilty, silty, tilty, stilty.

ILT′er– 2. filter, philter, jilter, kilter, milter, tilter, stilter, wilter, quilter.

3. refilter, infilter.

ILT′ing– 2. jilting, kilting, lilting, silting, tilting, stilting, wilting, quilting.

3. *tiptilting*, unwilting.

4. crazy-quilting.
IL′us– **2.** gryllus, villus, villous.
3. camillus, capillus [L.], lapillus, arillus, fibrillous, bacillus, favillous, pulvillus.
4. aspergillus.
ILV′er– **2.** silver.
3. resilver, *quicksilver.*
IL′yans– **2.** brilliance.
3. non-brillance, resilience, consilience; *see also* **ĬL′i–ens.**
IL′yant– **2.** brilliant.
3. unbrilliant, resilient.
4. overbrilliant; *see also* **ĬL′i–ent.**
IL′yar– **3.** familiar, auxiliar.
4. unfamiliar.
5. overfamiliar.
IL′yard– **2.** billiard, milliard.
IL′yun– **2.** billlion, million, pillion, prillion, trillion, stillion.
3. tourbillion, mandilion, modillion, vermillion, nonillion, carillon, quadrillion, decillion, octillion, centillion, quintillion, cotillion, septillion, sextillion, postilion, pavilion, civilian.
IL′yus– **2.** bilious.
4. atrabilious; *see also* **ĬL′i–us.**
IM′aj– **2.** image, scrimmage.
3. *archimage.*
IM′ba– **2.** simba.
3. marimba.
IMB′al– gimbol, cymbal, symbol, simball, timbal, timbale.
4. clavicymbal.
IMB′er– **2.** limber, timber, timbre.
3. unlimber, retimber.
IMB′l– **2.** bimbil, fimble, gimble [dial.], nimble, cymbal, simbil, symbol, simball, timbal, timbale, thimble, wimble.
IMB′o– **2.** kimbo, limbo.
3. akimbo.
IMB′us– **2.** limbus, limbous, nimbus.
IM′ee– **2.** gimme [slang], jimmy, Jimmy, limby, shimmy, swimmy, whimmy, zimmy.
IM′eed– **2.** jimmied, shimmied.
IM′el– **2.** Himmel [G.]; *see also* **ĬM′l.**
IM′er– **2.** dimmer, gimmer, hymmer, skimmer, limmer, limner, glimmer, slimmer, nimmer, brimmer, grimmer, krimmer, primer, primmer, trimmer, simmer, shimmer, swimmer.
3. aglimmer, asimmer, ashimmer.
4. trihemimer.
IM′est– **2.** dimmest, slimmest, grimmest, primmest, trimmest.
IM′ij– **2.** image, scrimmage.
3. *archimage,*
IM′ik– **2.** gimmick [slang], mimic, wimick, zymic.
3. alchimic, etymic.
4. cherubimic, zoomimic, pantomimic, pseudonymic, homonymic, synonymic, eponymic, patronymic, metronymic, metonymic.
IM′ing– **2.** dimming, skimming, lymning,

limbing, blimbing, slimming, brimming, trimming, swimming.
3. bedimming, retrimming.
IM′ish– **2.** dimmish, slimmish, grimmish, primmish, trimmish.
IM′l– **2.** gimmal, Himmel [G.], heml, kümmel, Friml.
IM′lee– **2.** dimly, slimly, grimly, primly, trimly.
IM′less– **2.** hymnless, limbless, rimless, brimless, vimless, swimless, whimless.
IM′ner– **2.** hymner, limner.
IM′ness– **2.** dimness, slimness, grimness, primness, trimness.
IMP′ee– **2.** impi, impy, skimpy, limpy, crimpy, scrimpy, shrimpy, shrimpi.
IMP′er– **2.** gimper, skimper, limper, crimper, scrimper, shrimper, simper, whimper.
IMP′ing– **2.** imping, gimping, skimping, limping, pimping, crimping, scrimping, primping, shrimping.
IMP′ish– **2.** impish, limpish, pimpish, shrimpish.
IMP′l– **2.** dimple, pimple, rimple, crimple, simple, wimple.
3. bewimple, unwimple.
IMP′lee– **2.** dimply, limply, pimply, simply.
IMP′ler– **2.** dimpler, rimpler, simpler, wimpler.
IMP′ling– **2.** impling, dimpling, pimpling, rimpling, crimpling.
IMZ′ee– **2.** flimsy, slimsy, mimsey, whimsey.
IN′a– **2.** binna [Scot.], Mina, pinna.
3. meminna, Corinna.
IN′as– inness, pinnace.
3. Erinys.
IN′ate– **2.** innate, pinnate.
3. bipinnate.
INCH′er– **2.** lyncher, flincher, clincher, pincher, cincher.
4. penny-pincher [slang].
INCH′ing– **2.** inching, lynching, flinching, clinching, pinching, cinching.
4. penny-pinching [slang].
IND′a– **2.** Linda, pinda.
3. Cabinda, Kabinda, Belinda, Melinda, Lucinda.
4. Ethelinda.
IND′ed– **2.** brinded, sinded, winded.
3. abscinded, rescinded, exscinded, longwinded.
IND′ee– **2.** Lindy, Mindy, pindy [dial.], Sindhi, Cindy, shindy [slang], windy.
3. Lucindy.
4. Rawalpindi.
IND′en– **2.** finden [G.], linden, Lyndon.
5. Unter den Linden [G.].
IND′er– **2.** dinder, hinder, linder, flinder, pinder, Pindar, cinder, tinder, winder.
3. unhinder, rescinder.
IND′ik– **2.** indic, Indic, syndic.
IND′l– **2.** dindle, kindle, Mindel, spindle, rindle, brindle, sindle, dwindle, swindle.

3. rekindle, enkindle.

ĬND′ler– 2. kindler, spindler, swindler.

3. enkindler.

ĬND′ling– 2. kindling, spindling, dwindling, swindling.

3. rekindling, enkindling.

ĬND′o– 2. lindo, window.

3. show window, shopwindow.

ĬN′ee– 2. Binnie, chinny, finny, guinea, hinny, ginny, jinni, jinny, Jinny, skinny, Pliny, Minnie, Minne, ninny, pinny, spinney, shinny, tinny, vinny, Winnie, squinny, whinny.

3. New Guinea.

4. ignominy, pickaninny, Ol′ Virginny.

ĬN′er– 2. inner, dinner, finner, ginner, skinner, pinner, spinner, grinner, sinner, shinner, tinner, thinner, winner, twinner.

3. beginner, *breadwinner*.

4. after-dinner.

ĬN′est– 2. innest, thinnest.

ĬN′et–,2. linnet, minute, pinnet, spinet.

ĬN′ful–· 2. skinful, sinful.

3. unsinful.

ĬNG′ee– 2. bingey, binghi, bingy, dingy, dinghy, flingy, clingy, pingy, ringy, springy, stringy, wingy, swingy.

ĬNG′er– 2. Inger, dinger, blinger [slang], flinger, clinger, slinger, ringer, wringer, bringer, springer, stringer, singer, stinger, winger, swinger, whinger.

3. humdinger, *mudslinger*, bell ringer, *klip-springer*, choir singer, jazz singer, left-winger, right-winger.

4. Minnesinger, ballad singer, Meistersinger, second-stringer.

ĬNG′ger– 2. finger, linger.

3. forefinger, malinger.

ĬNG′gl– 2. ingle, dingle, hingle, jingle, lingel, lingle, mingle, pingle, cringle, pringle, tringle, single, shingle, tingle, swingle.

3 *swingdingle*, immingle, commingle, Kriss Kringle, *surcingle*, reshingle.

4. intermingle.

ĬNG′lee– 2. dingly, jingly, singly, shingly, tingly.

ĬNG′gler– 2. dingler, jingler, mingler, pingler, shingler, tingler.

3. swing dingler, commingler.

4. intermingler.

ĬNG′gling– 2. dingling, jingling, mingling, pingling, singling, shingling, tingling.

3. remingling, immingling, commingling, unmingling, reshingling.

4. intermingling.

ĬNG′glish– 2. English, tinglish.

3. non-English, un-English.

ĬNG′go– 2. bingo, dingo, jingo, lingo, gringo, stingo.

3. flamingo, eryngo.

ĬNG′ing– 2. dinging, flinging, clinging, slinging, pinging, ringing, wringing, bringing, springing, stringing, singing, stinging, winging, swinging.

3. enringing, upbringing, unstringing, outwinging.

ĬNG′lee– 2. kingly.

4. bullyingly, whinnyingly, wearyingly, threateningly, strengtheningly, questioningly, sufferingly, saunteringly, blisteringly, murmuringly, posturingly, solacingly, menacingly, promisingly, billowingly; *also other present participles ending in the suffix " -ing ", plus the adverbial suffix " -ly "*.

ĬNG′less– 2. kingless, pingless, ringless, springless, stingless, wingless.

ĬNG′let– 2. kinglet, ringlet, springlet, winglet.

ĬNG′like– 2. kinglike, ringlike, springlike, winglike.

ĬNG′ling– 2. kingling, Ringling.

ĬN′ik– 2. dinic, finick, Finnic, clinic, pinic, Sinic, cynic, vinic, quinic.

3. Rabbinic, Odinic, delphinic, aclinic, triclinic, pollinic, Brahminic, encrinic, succinic, platinic.

4. Jacobinic, polyclinic, mandarinic, narcotinic.

ĬN′ing– 2. inning, binning, chinning, dinning, finning, ginning, skinning, linning [dial.], pinning, spinning, grinning, sinning, shinning, tinning, thinning, winning, twinning.

3. beginning, unpinning, *breadwinning*.

4. underpinning, overthinning.

ĬN′is– 2. Glynnis, pinnace.

3. Erinys.

ĬN′ish– 2. finish, Finnish, minish, tinnish, thinnish.

3. refinish, diminish.

ĬN′isht– 2. finished, minished.

3. refinished, unfinished, diminished.

4. undiminished.

ĬNJ′ee– 2. dingy, fringy, cringy, stingy, twingy.

ĬNJ′ens– 3. astringence, attingence, contingence.

ĬNJ′ent– 2. fingent, ringent, fringent, stringent, tingent.

3. impingent, refringent, astringent, restringent, constringent, attingent, contingent.

ĬNJ′er– 2. injure, hinger, ginger, fringer, cringer, singer, tinger, swinger.

3. impinger, infringer.

ĬNJ′ez– 2. binges, dinges, hinges, cringes, scringes [dial.], fringes, singes, tinges, swinges, twinges.

3. unhinges, impinges, befringes, infringes, constringes, perstringes, attinges.

ĬNJ′ing– 2. dingeing, hinging, cringing, fringing, singeing, tingeing, swingeing, twinging.

3. unhinging, impinging, refringing, infringing, constringing, perstringing.

ĬNJ′ment– 3. unhingement, impingement, infringement, perstringement.

ĬNK′a– 2. Inca, Dinka, Xinca, rinka.

3. Katinka, Katrinka, stotinka.

ĬNK′ee– 2. inky, chinky, dinky, dinkey, kinky, linky, blinky, pinky, sinky, stinky, zincky.

INK´er– 2. inker, skinker, linker, blinker, clinker, slinker, pinker, rinker, drinker, prinker, shrinker, sinker, tinker, stinker, thinker, winker, swinker.
3. enlinker, bethinker, freethinker, *hoodwinker*.
INK´ij– 2. linkage, shrinkage.
INK´ing– 2. inking, chinking, kinking, skinking, linking, blinking, clinking, slinking, pinking, rinking, drinking, prinking, shrinking, sinking, stinking, thinking, winking, swinking.
3. enlinking, unlinking, freethinking, unthinking, *hoodwinking*.
INK´l– 2. inkle, kinkle, wrinkle, crinkle, sprinkle, strinkle, tinkle, winkel [D.], winkle.
3. besprinkle, unwrinkle.
4. intersprinkle, periwinkle.
INK´lee– 2. pinkly, wrinkly, crinkly, tinkly, twinkly.
INK´ler– 2. inkler, wrinkler, sprinkler, tinkler, twinkler.
INK´ling– 2. inkling, wrinkling, crinkling, sprinkling, tinkling, twinkling.
INKT´iv– 3. distinctive, extinctive, instinctive.
4. indistinctive, undistinctive.
INKT´lee– 3. succinctly, distinctly.
4. indistinctly.
5. contradistinctly.
INKT´ness– 3. succinctness, distinctness.
4. indistinctness, undistinctness.
INKT´ure– 2. cincture, tincture.
3. pollincture, encincture.
INK´went– 3. delinquent, relinquent.
IN´land– 2. inland, Finland.
IN´lee– 2. inly, thinly, twinly.
3. McKinley.
IN´less– 2. innless, binless, dinless, finless, ginless, kinless, skinless, pinless, sinless, tinless, winless.
IN´let– 2. inlet, tinlet.
IN´ness– 2. inness, thinness.
IN´o– 2. minnow, winnow.
INS´ens– 2. incense.
3. St. Vincent's.
INS´er– 2. mincer, rinser, wincer.
3. convincer.
INS´ic– 3. intrinsic, extrinsic.
INS´ing– 2. mincing, rinsing, wincing.
3. evincing, convincing.
4. unconvincing.
INS´ment– 3. evincement, convincement.
INST´er– 2. minster, spinster.
3. Axminster, Westminster.
INT´ed– 2. dinted, hinted, linted, flinted, glinted, splinted, minted, printed, sprinted, tinted, stinted, squinted.
3. reprinted, imprinted, misprinted, *footprinted*, unstinted, rose-tinted.
4. fingerprinted, rosy tinted, mezzotinted.
INT´ee– 2. Dinty, linty, flinty, glinty, splinty, minty, shinty, tinty, squinty.
3. McGinty.

INT´er– 2. hinter, linter, splinter, minter, printer, sprinter, tinter, stinter, winter, squinter, twinter.
3. imprinter, midwinter.
4. mezzotinter.
INTH´in– 3. absinthin, absinthine.
4. terebinthine, labyrinthine, hyacinthine.
INT´ij– 2. splintage, mintage, tintage, vintage.
INT´ing– 2. dinting, hinting, linting, glinting, splinting, minting, printing, sprinting, tinting, stinting, squinting.
3. imprinting, misprinting.
4. mezzotinting.
INT´l– 2. lintel, pintle, scintle, quintal.
3. triginal.
INT´o– 2. pinto, Shinto.
4. mezzotinto.
INT´ree– 2. splintry, vintry, wintry.
IN´u– 2. sinew, continue.
3. unsinew, continue.
4. discontinue.
IN´yun– 2. minion, mignon, minyan, pinion, pignon.
3. Virginian, dominion, opinion.
IP´ant– 2. flippant, trippant.
3. unflippant.
4. countertrippant.
IP´ee– 2. chippy, dippy, hippy, lippy, klippe, slippy, nippy, snippy, pippy, drippy, grippy, shippy, tippy, zippy.
3. Xanthippe.
4. Aganippe, Mississippi.
IP´er– 2. chipper, dipper, kipper, skipper, lipper, flipper, clipper, slipper, nipper, snipper, ripper, dripper, gripper, tripper, stripper, sipper, shipper, tipper, whipper.
3. Big Dipper, Yom Kippur, outstripper, horsewhipper.
4. lady's-slipper, gallinipper.
IP´erd– 2. kippered, skippered, slippered.
IP´et– 2. skippet, snippet, pipit, rippet, rippit, trippet, sippet, tippet, whippet.
IP´ij– 2. chippage, kippage, slippage, scrippage, strippage.
IP´ik– 2. hippic, typic.
3. adipic, philhippic, Philippic, atypic.
4. polytypic, stenotypic.
5. electrotypic.
6. daguerreotypic.
IP´ing– 2. chipping, dipping, gipping, gypping, kipping, skipping, lipping, flipping, clipping, slipping, nipping, snipping, pipping, ripping, dripping, gripping, tripping, stripping, sipping, shipping, tipping, quipping, whipping, yipping, zipping.
3. outstripping, equipping, horse whipping.
IP´ish– 2. hippish, hyppish, snippish, grippish, quippish.
IP´it– 2. pipit, rippit; *see also* ĬP´et.
IP´l– 2. nipple, ripple, cripple, gripple, grippal, triple, sipple, tipple, tiple, stipple.
3. becripple.
4. participle.
IP´lee– 2. ripply, cripply, triply, stipply.

IP′ler– 2. rippler, crippler, strippler, tippler, stippler.

IP′let– 2. chiplet, liplet, ripplet, triplet, striplet, tiplet.

IP′ling– 2. chipling, Kipling, rippling, crippling, stripling, sipling, tippling, stippling.

IP′ment– 2. gripment, shipment.
   3. equipment, reshipment, transhipment.

IP′o– 2. hippo, gippo, *shippo.*
   3. filippo.

IP′on– 2. gipon, slip-on, Nippon, shippon.

IPS′ee– 3. ipse [L.], gypsy, tipsy.
   3. Poughkeepsie.

IPSH′un– 2. scription.
   3. Egyptian, conniption [coll.], ascription, subscription, description, prescription, transcription, inscription, proscription.
   4. circumscription, superscription.

IP′sis– 2. krypsis, tripsis, stypsis.
   3. ellipsis.

IPST′er– 2. tipster, quipster, whipster.

IPT′ik– 2. diptych, glyptic, cryptic, kryptic, triptych, styptic.
   3. ecliptic, elliptic, syncryptic.
   4. diaglyptic, anaglyptic, holocryptic, hypostyptic.
   5. apocalyptic.

IPT′iv– 3. descriptive, prescriptive, transcriptive, inscriptive, conscriptive, proscriptive.
   4. circumscriptive.

IP′us– 2. hippus.
   3. philippus.
   4. Epihippus, Protohippus.

IR– through **IRZ** *see also* **Ŭ: ŬR′a** through **ŬRZ′i.**

IR′a– 2. Irra, lira, sirrah.
   4. tirralirra.

IR′er– 2. dearer, clearer, mirror, nearer, sneerer, peerer.

IR′ik– 2. lyric, pyrrhic, Pyrrhic.
   3. argyric, vampiric, empiric, satiric, satyric, butyric.
   4. panegyric.

IR′il– 2. Cyril, squirrel, virile.
   3. unvirile.

IR′ist– 2. lyrist.
   4. panegyrist.

IRK– through **IRT–** *see* **Ŭ: ŬRK′a** through **ŬRT′um.**

IR′up– 2. chirrup, syrup, stirrup.

IR′us– 2. byrrus, cirrus, cirrous, cirrhous.

IS′a– 2. lyssa, Missa [L.].
   3. Melissa, Clarissa, vibrissa, Nerissa, abscissa, mantissa.
   4. paterissa.

IS′al– 2. missal, sisal.
   3. abyssal, dismissal.

ISCH′an– 2. Christian.
   3. non-Christian, unchristian.
   4. anti-Christian.

IS′ee– 2. hissy, missy, Chrissy, prissy [coll.], sissy [coll.].

IS′eez– 2. missies, Pisces, sissies.
   3. Ulysses.

IS′el– 2. missel, rissel, scissel, wissel [Scot.].
   3. dickcissel; *see also* **ĬS′l.**

IS′en– 2. listen, glisten, christen.
   3. relisten, rechristen.

IS′ens– 3. dehiscence.
   4. indehiscence, reminiscence, obliviscence, reviviscence.

IS′ent– 3. dehiscent.
   4. indehiscent, reminiscent, reviviscent.

IS′er– 2. hisser, kisser, misser, risser.
   3. remisser, dismisser.
   4. reminiscer.

IS′ez– 2. hisses, kisses, blisses, misses, Mrs., Chris's, prisses, Tris's, sis's.
   3. abysses, dismisses.
   4. prejudices, benefices, edifices, sacrifices, orifices, artifices, Judas kisses, reminisces, precipices, armistices, interstices.

IS′ful– 2. blissful.
   3. unblissful, remissful.

ISH′a– 3. Felicia, militia, Letitia.
   4. Aloysia.

ISH′al– 3. judicial, official, comitial, initial, solstitial.
   4. prejudicial, unjudicial, beneficial, edificial, sacrificial, artificial, unofficial, superficial, postcomitial, interstitial.
   5. extrajudicial, unbeneficial, unsuperficial.

ISH′an– 2. Priscian, Titian.
   3. magician, logician, technician, patrician, physician, musician, optician.
   4. rhetorician, politician, statistician.
   5. mathematician; *see also* **ĬSH′un.**

ISH′ee– 2. fishy, Vichy, swishy, squishy.

ISH′ens– 3. efficience, deficience, proficience, sufficience, omniscience.
   4. inefficience, self-sufficience, unsufficience.

ISH′ent– 3. efficient, deficient, proficient, sufficient, objicient, volitient, omniscient.
   4. inefficient, self-sufficient, insufficient, unproficient.

ISH′er– 2. disher, fisher, fissure, wisher, swisher.
   3. kingfisher, well-wisher, ill-wisher.

ISH′ez– 2. dishes, fishes, pishes, wishes, swishes, whishes, cuishes, squishes.

ISH′ful– 2. dishful, fishful, wishful.
   3. unwishful.

ISH′ing– 2. dishing, fishing, wishing, swishing, squishing.
   3. well-wishing, ill-wishing.

ISH′na– 2. Mishna, Krishna.

ISH′pan– 2. Ishpan, dishpan.

ISH′u– 2. issue, fichu, tissue.
   3. reissue.

ISH′un– 2. fission, mission, Priscian, Titian.
   3. ambition, addition, tradition, edition, dedition, reddition, sedition, rendition, vendition, condition, perdition, audition, magician, logician, volition, submission, admission, emission, demission, remission, omission, commission, permission, dismission, transmission, ignition, cognition, technician, munition, punition, suspicion, attrition,

patrician, detrition, metrician, contrition, nutrition, petition, tactician, optician, partition, sortition, fruition, tuition, physician, transition, position, musician.
4. inhibition, prohibition, exhibition, readdition, extradition, recondition, precondition, erudition, coalition, abolition, demolition, ebullition, insubmission, readmission, preadmission, intromission, intermission, manumission, mechanician, inanition, recognition, definition, admonition, premonition, ammunition, apparition, rhetorician, electrician, malnutrition, tralatition, repetition, competition, politician, statistician, superstition, intuition, acquisition, requisition, inquisition, perquisition, disquisition, apposition, deposition, preposition, imposition, supposition, disposition, exposition.
5. superaddition, preadmonition, mathematician, contraposition, juxtaposition, anteposition, decomposition, predisposition, indisposition.
ISH′us– 2. vicious.
3. ambitious, seditious, judicious, officious, flagitious, malicious, delicious, pernicious, puniceous, propitious, auspicious, suspicious, capricious, nutritious, factitious, fictitious.
4. expeditious, injudicious, unofficious, unpropitious, inauspicious, unsuspicious, avaricious, meretricious, tralatitious, repetitious, adventitious, surreptitious, supposititious.
5. supposititious.
IS′ik– 2. lyssic.
3. silicic, anisic, masticic.
IS′ing– 2. hissing, Gissing, kissing, missing, sissing [chiefly dial.].
3. dehiscing, dismissing.
4. prejudicing, reminiscing.
IS′it– 2. licit.
3. elicit, illicit, solicit, implicit, explicit.
4. inexplicit.
IS′iv– 2. fissive, missive.
3. submissive, admissive, emissive, remissive, omissive, commissive, promissive, permissive, dismissive, transmissive.
4. unsubmissive, intermissive.
ISK′a– 2. Kiska.
3. Mariska, francisca, Francisca.
ISK′al– 2. discal, fiscal, friscal.
4. obeliscal.
ISK′an– 2. priscan.
3. Franciscan.
4. San Franciscan.
ISK′ee– 2. pisky [dial.], risky, frisky, whisky, whiskey.
ISK′er– 2. risker, brisker, frisker, whisker.
3. bewhisker.
ISK′et– 2. biscuit, brisket, frisket, wisket.
3. Sea Biscuit.
ISK′in– 2. griskin, siskin, whiskin.
ISK′ing– 2. risking, brisking, frisking, whisking.
ISK′it– 2. biscuit, brisket.

3. Sea Biscuit; *see also* **ĬSK′et.**
ISK′o– 2. Frisco, cisco.
3. Nabisco, Morisco, Francisco.
4. non capisco [It.], San Francisco.
ISK′us– 2. discus, discous, fiscus [L.], viscous.
3. hibiscus, trochiscus, meniscus, lemniscus, lentiscus.
4. abaciscus, calathiscus.
IS′l– 2. fissile, missal, missel, missile, missle, rissel, rissle, bristle, gristle, sistle, scissel, scissile, thistle, wissel [Scot.], whistle.
3. abyssal, dismissal, epistle, dickcissel.
4. cacomistle.
IS′lee– 2. bristly, gristly, thistly.
IS′ler– 2. bristler, whistler.
3. epistler.
IS′ling– 2. bristling, brisling, whistling.
IS′mus– 2. isthmus, Christmas.
IS′n– 2. listen, glisten, christen.
3. relisten, rechristen.
IS′ness– 2. thisness.
3. remissness.
IS′ning– 3. listening, glistening, christening.
ISP′ee– 2. crispy, wispy.
ISP′er– 2. lisper, risper, crisper, whisper.
3. stage whisper.
ISP′ing– 2. lisping, crisping, wisping.
IST′a– 2. vista.
3. ballista, genista, Baptista.
IST′al– 2. distal, crystal, cystal, vistal; *see also* **ĬST′l.**
IST′ans– 2. distance.
3. outdistance, assistance, desistance, resistance.
4. equidistance, unresistance; *see also* **ĬST′ens.**
IST′ant– 2. distant.
3. assistant, resistant.
4. coassistant, equidistant, nonresistant, unresistant; *see also* **ĬST′ent.**
IST′ed– 2. fisted, listed, misted, wristed, trysted, cysted, twisted.
3. hardfisted, closefisted, tightfisted, two-fisted, enlisted, black-listed, white-listed, strong-wristed, thin-wristed, assisted, subsisted, desisted, resisted, existed, encysted, insisted, consisted, persisted, untwisted.
4. ironfisted, unassisted, unresisted, intertwisted.
IST′ene– 2. pristine, Sistine.
3. Philistine.
4. amethystine.
IST′ens– 3. subsistence, existence, insistence, consistence, persistence.
4. pre-existence, nonexistence, unexistence, coexistence, inconsistence; *see also* **ĬST′ans.**
IST′ent– 3. subsistent, existent, insistent, consistent, persistent.
4. pre-existent, nonexistent, coexistent, inconsistent; *see also* **ĬST′ant.**
IST′er– 2. bister, bistre, lister, blister, glister, mister, sister, twister, xyster.
3. agister, agistor, magister, enlister, assister, sob sister, subsister, resister, exister, insister,

stepsister, persister.

4. water blister, foster sister.

ĬST'ful– 2. listful, mistful, wistful.

ĬST'ik– 2. distich, fistic, mystic, pistic, cystic, schistic.

3. Buddhistic, deistic, theistic, sophistic, sphragistic, logistic, ballistic, stylistic, monistic, eristic, poristic, juristic, puristic, touristic, statistic, baptistic, artistic, linguistic.

4. Aphrodistic, atheistic, pantheistic, syllogistic, eulogistic, catechistic, anarchistic, cabalistic, feudalistic, realistic, formalistic, annalistic, journalistic, moralistic, socialistic, fatalistic, vitalistic, dualistic, royalistic, pugilistic, symbolistic, euphemistic, alchemistic, pessimistic, optimistic, Romanistic, humanistic, Calvanistic, Hellenistic, agonistic, canonistic, communistic, Taoistic, egoistic, eucharistic, egotistic, hypnotistic, inartistic, altruistic, casuistic, atavistic, Jehovistic.

5. polytheistic, antiphlogistic, cannibalistic, naturalistic, capitalistic, ritualistic, evangelistic, monopolistic, antagonistic, impressionistic, anachronistic, characteristic, allegoristic, romanticistic, Anabaptistic.

6. imperialistic, materialistic, phenomenalistic, universalistic.

7. supernaturalistic, individualistic.

ĬST'iks– 2. mystics.

3. sphragistics, logistics, ballistics, statistics, linguistics.

4. syllogistics, agonistics, solaristics.

ĬST'ing– 2. listing, misting, gristing, trysting, twisting.

3. enlisting, assisting, subsisting, desisting, resisting, existing, insisting, consisting, persisting, entwisting, untwisting.

4. pre-existing, nonexisting, intertwisting.

ĬST'iv– 3. assistive, desistive, resistive, persistive.

ĬST'l– 2. istle, distal, listel, pistil, pistol, Bristol, crystal, cystal, vistal.

ĬST'less– 2. listless, mistless, twistless.

3. resistless.

ĬST'ment– 3. agistment, enlistment.

ĬST'o– 3. Mephisto, Callisto.

ĬST'us– 2. cistus, schistous, xystus.

3. anhistous, rockcistus.

ĬS'um– 2. lissome.

3. Alyssum.

4. sweet alyssum.

6. fideicommissum.

ĬS'us– 2. Issus, byssus, missis, missus.

3. narcissus.

ĬT'a– 2. bitte [G.], Pitta, pitta, Sitta, shittah, vitta.

3. sagitta, Mylitta.

ĬT'al– 2. victual.

3. remittal, committal, transmittal, acquittal; *see also* **ĬT'l.**

ĬT'an– 2. Britain, Briton, witan.

3. Great Britain; *see also* **ĬT'en.**

ĬT'ans– 2. pittance, quittance.

3. admittance, remittance, omittance, permittance, transmittance, acquittance.

ĬT'ed– 2. bitted, fitted, flitted, slitted, knitted, pitted, spitted, ritted, gritted, witted, twitted, quitted.

3. unbitted, befitted, refitted, unfitted, submitted, admitted, emitted, demitted, remitted, omitted, committed, transmitted, unpitted, half-witted, quick-witted, sharp-witted, short-witted, outwitted, acquitted.

4. benefited, counterfeited, unremitted, recommitted, interknitted, ready-witted, nimble-witted.

ĬT'ee– 2. bitty, bittie, chitty, ditty, kitty, skitty, flitty, slitty, pity, gritty, grittie, pretty, city, witty, twitty.

3. ambitty, poditti, committee, self-pity.

4. itty-bitty.

ĬT'eed– 2. dittied, pitied, citied.

3. unpitied, uncitied.

ĬT'en– 2. bitten, kitten, litten, mitten, smitten, written, Britain, Briton.

3. *flea-bitten, fly-bitten, frost-bitten,* unsmitten, unwritten, Great Britain.

4. terror-smitten, conscience-smitten, underwritten.

ĬT'ent– 3. emittent, remittent.

4. unremittent, intromittent, intermittent.

ĬT'er– 2. bitter, fitter, hitter, jitter [slang], skitter, litter, flitter, glitter, splitter, slitter, knitter, pitter, spitter, Ritter, fritter, gritter, critter [dial. & coll.], sitter, titter, twitter, quitter.

3. embitter, befitter, refitter, outfitter, pinch hitter, rail splitter, submitter, admitter, emitter, remitter, omitter, committer, permitter, transmitter, outsitter, atwitter, outwitter, acquitter.

4. benefiter, counterfeiter, recommitter, manumitter, baby sitter.

ĬT'ern– 2. bittern, gittern, flittern, cittern.

ĬT'ful– 2. fitful, witful.

ĬTH'ee– 2. pithy, smithy, stithy, withy.

3. twigwithy.

ĬTH'er– 2. dither, hither, blither, slither, tither, thither, wither, swither, whither, zither.

ĬTH'ik– 2. lithic, mythic.

3. trilithic, ornithic.

4. megalithic, eolithic, neolithic, monolithic, polymythic, philornithic.

5. archaeolithic, palaeolithic.

ĬTH'm– 2. rhythm.

3. logarithm, algorithm.

ĬTH'mik– 2. rhythmic.

4. logarithmic, polyrhythmic, algorithmic.

ĬT'ik– 2. lytic, critic.

3. rachitic, graphitic, enclitic, proclitic, *politic,* Hamitic, Semitic, granitic, lignitic, nephritic, pyritic, arthritic, neuritic, Levitic.

4. Jacobitic, aphroditic, neophytic, zoophytic, dialytic, analytic, paralytic, granulitic, spherulitic, Adamitic, Islamitic, dynamitic, eremitic, stalagmitic, tympanitic, Sybaritic, Nazaritic, diacritic, hypercritic, parasitic, anthracitic, hematitic.

IT′ing– 2. bitting, chitting, fitting, hitting, skitting, flitting, splitting, slitting, knitting, pitting, spitting, gritting, sitting, witting, twitting, quitting.

3. befitting, *outfitting*, pinch-hitting, hard-hitting, *hairsplitting*, *earsplitting*, submitting, admitting, emitting, remitting, omitting, committing, permitting, transmitting, outsitting, unwitting, outwitting, acquitting.

4. unbefitting, benefiting.

IT′ish– 2. skittish, British.

IT′l– 2. kittle, kittel, skittle, little, spittle, brittle, grittle, tittle, victual, whittle.

3. belittle, remittal, committal, transmittal, *lickspittle*, acquittal.

4. noncommittal, nonacquittal.

IT′ler– 2. skittler, littler, brittler, tittler, victualer, whittler.

3. belittler.

IT′less– 2. bitless, fitless, hitless, pitless, spitless, gritless, witless.

IT′lest– 2. littlest, brittlest.

IT′ling– 2. kitling, brittling, titling, victualing, witling, whittling, whitling.

IT′lz– *see* **ĬT′l**, plus " s " or " 's ".

IT′ment– 2. fitment.

3. refitment, remitment, commitment, acquitment.

4. recommitment.

IT′ness– 2. fitness, witness.

3. unfitness, eyewitness.

IT′ni– 2. jitney, witney, Whitney.

3. Mt. Whitney.

IT′zee– 2. bitsy [dial.], Mitzy, ritzy, Fritzy.

4. itsy-bitsy.

IV′ee– 2. chivvy, divvy [slang], givey, Livy, privy.

3. tantivy.

IV′el– 2. snivel, drivel, swivel.

IV′en– 2. given, riven, driven, shriven, striven, thriven.

3. forgiven, wind-driven, rain-driven, undriven, unshriven.

4. unforgiven, overdriven.

IV′er– 2. giver, liver, flivver [slang], sliver, river, siever, shiver, stiver, quiver.

3. forgiver, *life-giver*, deliver, outliver, Spoon River.

5. Indian giver.

IV′erd– 2. livered, flivvered [slang], slivered, shivered, quivered.

3. delivered, pale-livered, white-livered.

4. undelivered, lily-livered, pigeon-livered, yellow-livered.

IV′et– 2. rivet, grivet, privet, trivet, civet.

IV′id– 2. livid, vivid.

IV′ing– 2. giving, living, sieving.

3. *lawgiving*, forgiving, misgiving, Thanksgiving, outliving.

4. unforgiving, everliving.

IV′l– 2. snivel, rivel, drivel, frivol, shrivel, civil, swivel.

3. uncivil.

IV′ling– 2. sniveling, driveling, shriveling, swiveling.

IV′ot– 2. divot, pivot.

IZ′ard– 2. izard, gizzard, blizzard, lizard, vizard, wizard.

3. lounge lizard [slang]; *see also* **ĬZ′erd.**

IZ′ee– 2. busy, dizzy, fizzy, Lizzie, mizzy, nizy, frizzy, tizzy, quizzy.

IZ′en– 2. dizen, mizzen, risen, ptisan, wizen.

3. bedizen, arisen.

IZ′er– 2. fizzer, rizzar, frizzer, scissor, whizzer, quizzer, visor, vizor.

3. befrizzer.

IZ′erd– 2. scissored, visored, vizored; *see also* **ĬZ′ard.**

IZH′un– 2. Frisian, scission, vision.

3. allision, elision, illision, collision, Parisian, derision, misprision, abscission, decision, recission, rescission, precision, incision, concision, excision, revision, prevision, division, envision, provision.

4. paradisian, aphrodisian, prodelision, television, subdivision, audivision, Eurovision, supervision.

IZ′ik– 2. physic, phthisic.

4. paradisic, metaphysic, biophysic.

IZ′iks– 2. physics.

4. cataphysics, metaphysics, geophysics, biophysics, psychophysics, zoophysics.

IZ′ing– 2. fizzing, frizzing, quizzing, whizzing.

3. befrizzing.

IZ′it– 2. visit.

3. revisit, exquisite.

IZ′l– 2. chisel, fizzle, mizzle, drizzle, frizzle, grizzle, sizzle, swizzle, twizzle.

3. enchisel, rumswizzle.

IZ′lee– 2. chiselly, mizzly, drizzly, frizzly, grisly, grizzly.

IZ′ler– 2. chiseler, frizzler, grizzler.

IZ′ling– 2. chiseling, fizzling, mizzling, drizzling, frizzling, grizzling, sizzling, swizzling.

IZ′m– 2. ism, schism, chrism, prism.

3. abysm.

4. Judaism, archaism, Lamaism, Hebraism, ultraism, Mosaism, prosaism, Methodism, Yankeeism, atheism, bitheism, dandyism, Toryism, rowdyism, pacifism, syllogism, eulogism, energism, synergism, liturgism, catechism, anarchism, monarchism, Baalism, cabalism, tribalism, verbalism, vandalism, feudalism, realism, legalism, regalism, frugalism, localism, vocalism, carnalism, journalism, papalism, moralism, centralism, pluralism, ruralism, racialism, socialism, fatalism, vitalism, dualism, loyalism, royalism, nihilism, pugilism, servilism, cataclysm, embolism, symbolism, idolism, botulism, euphemism, animism, pessimism, optimism, peanism, paganism, organism, Brahmanism, Romanism, Satanism, feminism, cretinism, destinism, Calvinism, Darwinism, lionism, Zionism, demonism, Mormonism, Platonism, modernism, communism, unionism,

Taoism, egoism, heroism, Shintoism, barbarism, plagiarism, solarism, Quakerism, mesmerism, mannerism, pauperism, theorism, aphorism, humorism, terrorism, historism, pasteurism, ostracism, solecism, Gallicism, Biblicism, publicism, Anglicism, synicism, Sinicism, stoicism, lyricism, classicism, criticism, witticism, skepticism, mysticism, paroxysm, Kukluxism, sabbatism, dogmatism, grammatism, pietism, quietism, magnetism, syncretism, Semitism, occultism, egotism, hypnotism, nepotism, despotism, Hinduism, altruism, *untruism*, atavism, Bolshevism, nativism, powwowism.

5. theosophism, philosophism, cannibalism, surrealism, radicalism, rationalism, liberalism, federalism, commercialism, capitalism, teetotalism, ritualism, evangelism, catabolism, metabolism, hyperbolism, alcoholism, monopolism, somnambulism, Confucianism, Puritanism, determinism, impressionism, infusionism, plagiarism, peculiarism, militarism, allegorism, Epicurism, amateurism, Italicism, Catholicism, empiricism, grammaticism, fanaticism, phoneticism, asceticism, romanticism, neuroticism, agnosticism, astigmatism, automatism, democratism, conservatism, favoritism, patriotism, absolutism, progressivism, subjectivism, collectiv-

ism, somniloquism, ventriloquism.

6. proverbialism, imperialism, materialism, colloquialism, phenomenalism, sensationalism, professionalism, conventionalism, municipalism, universalism, controversialism, sentimentalism, instrumentalism, spiritualism, republicanism, Americanism, Mohammedanism, microorganism, multitudinism, indeterminism, restorationism, prohibitionism, exhibitionism, evolutionism, revolutionism, incendiarism, peculiarism, particularism.

7. supernaturalism, individualism, cosmopolitanism.

8. humanitarianism, parliamentarianism.

9. valetudinarianism, establishmentarianism; *and other nouns ending in the suffix " -ism."*

IZ'mal— **2.** dismal, chrismal, prismal.

3. abysmal, strabismal, baptismal.

4. catechismal, cataclysmal, asterismal, paroxysmal.

IZ'mik— **2.** clysmic, trismic.

4. cataclysmic, embolismic, aphorismic, algorismic.

IZ'mus— **2.** trismus.

3. strabismus, accismus.

IZ'n— **2.** dizen, his'n [dial.], mizzen, risen, prison, wizen.

3. bedizen, arisen, imprison.

IZ'um— **2.** rizzom; *see also* **ĬZ'm.**

Ĭ (bib)

Triple Rhymes

Primary or Secondary Accent Falls on Second from Last Syllable; Imperfect Rhymes Are in Italics.

IB′i–a– **3.** Libya, tibia.
4. amphibia.
IB′i–al– **3.** tibial, stibial.
IB′i–an– **3.** Libyan.
4. amphibian, bathybian.
IB′ing–lee– **3.** bibbingly, fibbingly, jibbingly, ribbingly, cribbingly, squibbingly.
4. *wine bibblingly,* ad libbingly [slang].
IB′it–ed– **4.** inhibited, prohibited, exhibited.
5. uninhibited, unprohibited.
IB′it–er– **4.** inhibiter, inhibitor, prohibiter, prohibitor, exhibitor.
IB′it–ing– **4.** inhibiting, prohibiting, exhibiting.
IB′it–iv– **4.** inhibitive, prohibitive, exhibitive.
5. uninhibitive, unprohibitive.
IB′i–us– **3.** stibious.
4. amphibious, bathybius.
IB′on–like– **3.** gibbonlike, ribbonlike.
IB′u–lar– **3.** fibular.
4. mandibular, vestibular.
5. infundibular.
IB′ut–ed– **3.** tributed.
4. attributed, contributed, distributed.
IB′ut–er– **4.** attributer, contributor, distributer, distributor.
IB′ut–iv– **4.** attributive, retributive, contributive, distributive.
ICH′er–ee– **3.** bitchery, fitchery, michery, stitchery, witchery.
4. bewitchery.
ICH′et–ee– **3.** witchetty, twitchety.
ICH′i–ness– **3.** itchiness, hitchiness, pitchiness, switchiness, twitchiness.
ICH′ing–lee– **3.** itchingly, pitchingly, witchingly, switchingly, twitchingly.
4. enrichingly, bewitchingly.
ICH′ing–ness– **3.** itchingness, pitchingness, witchingness, switchingness, twitchingness.
4. enrichingness, bewitchingness.
ICH′less–lee– **3.** itchlessly, hitchlessly, pitchlessly, stitchlessly, switchlessly, twitchlessly.
ID′a–bl– **3.** biddable, kiddable.

4. rebiddable, unbiddable, forbiddable.
ID′en–ness– **3.** hiddenness.
4. forbiddenness.
5. unforbiddenness.
ID′i–a– **3.** Lydia, Nydia.
4. Ophidia, perfidia [Sp.], Numidia, Canidia.
6. absit invidia [L.].
ID′i–al– **4.** presidial, noctidial.
ID′i–an– **3.** Gideon, Lydian, Vidian.
4. ophidian, rachidian, Euclidean, Numidian, meridian, viridian, obsidian, quotidian, Ovidian.
5. nullifidian, taxaspidean, postmeridian.
6. antemeridian.
ID′if–i– **3.** nidify.
4. solidify, humidify, lapidify, acidify, rancidify, fluidify.
ID′ik–al– **4.** veridical, juridical, druidical, causidical.
5. pyramidical.
ID′it–ee– **3.** quiddity.
4. rabidity, morbidity, turbidity, rigidity, frigidity, algidity, turgidity, calidity, validity, squalidity, gelidity, solidity, stolidity, timidity, humidity, tumidity, rapidity, sapidity, vapidity, trepidity, tepidity, sipidity, limpidity, torpidity, cupidity, stupidity, aridity, hybridity, acridity, viridity, floridity, torridity, putridity, aqidity, flaccidity, placidity, rancidity, viscidity, lucidity, pinguidity, fluidity, avidity, pavidity, gravidity, lividity, liquidity.
5. invalidity, insolidity, intrepidity, insipidity, pellucidity, translucidity, impavidity.
ID′i–um– **3.** idiom, Psidium.
4. rubidium, iridium, presidium, cecidium.
ID′i–us– **3.** Phidias, hideous.
4. perfidious, lapideous, insidious, fastidious, avidious, invidious.
ID′u–al– **4.** residual, dividual.
5. individual.
ID′ul–ate– **3.** stridulate.

   4. acidulate.

ĬD′ul–us– 3. stridulous.

   4. acidulous.

ĬD′u–us– 3. biduous, viduous.

   4. assiduous, deciduous, residuous, dividuous.

   5. unassiduous, indeciduous.

IF′an–ee– 3. tiffany, Tiffany.

   4. Epiphany; *see also* ĬF′on–ee.

IF′er–us– 4. bulbiferous, limbiferous, herbiferous, morbiferous, nubiferous, splendiferous, frondiferous, tergiferous, branchiferous, conchiferous, aliferous, saliferous, melliferous, celliferous, stelliferous, veliferous, piliferous, foliferous, proliferous, cauliferous, comiferous, pomiferous, armiferous, laniferous, graniferous, igniferous, ligniferous, spiniferous, omniferous, somniferous, stanniferous, penniferous, coniferous, soniferous, Corniferous, pruniferous, umbriferous, ceriferous, floriferous, poriferous, cupriferous, ferriferous, cirriferous, rostriferous, auriferous, thuriferous, bacciferous, calciferous, vociferous, dorsiferous, ossiferous, furciferous, luciferous, muciferous, cruciferous, setiferous, lactiferous, fructiferous, multiferous, pestiferous, lethiferous, sanguiferous, valviferous, oviferous, aquiferous.

   5. oleiferous, umbiliferous, coralliferous, metalliferous, papilliferous, petroliferous, maculiferous, ramuliferous, granuliferous, atomiferous, luminiferous, resiniferous, antenniferous, carboniferous, nectariferous, tuberiferous, odoriferous, sudoriferous, saporiferous, boraciferous, corticiferous, calyciferous, argentiferous.

   6. diamondiferous, aluminiferous.

IF′ik–al– 4. magnifical, mirifical, pacifical, specifical, lactifical, pontifical, vivifical.

   5. saporifical, beatifical.

IF′ik–ant– 4. nidificant, mundificant, significant, sacrificant.

   5. insignificant.

IF′ik–ate– 4. nidificate, nostrificate, pacificate, pontificate, certificate.

IF′i–sens– 4. magnificence, munificence.

IF′i–sent– 4. magnificent, munificent.

IF′lu–us– 4. fellifluous, mellifluous, sanguifluous.

IF′on–ee– 3. triphony.

   4. polyphony, oxyphony, antiphony; *see also* ĬF′an–ee.

IFT′a–bl– 3. liftable, siftable, shiftable.

IFT′il–ee– 3. niftily [slang], shiftily, thriftily.

IFT′i–ness– 3. niftiness [slang], shiftiness, thriftiness.

IFT′less–lee– 3. thriftlessly, shiftlessly.

IFT′less–ness– 3. shiftlessness, thriftlessness.

IF′ug–al– 4. vermifugal, febrifugal, centrifugal.

IG′am–ee– 3. bigamy, digamy, trigamy.

   4. polygamy.

IG′am–ist– 3. bigamist, digamist, trigamist.

   4. polygamist.

IG′am–us– 3. bigamous, digamous, trigamous.

   4. polygamous.

IG′er–ee– 3. piggery, priggery, wiggery, Whiggery.

IG′ish–lee– 3. piggishly, priggishly, Whiggishly.

IG′mat–ist– 3. stigmatist.

   4. enigmatist.

IG′mat–ize– 3. stigmatize.

   4. enigmatize.

   5. paradigmatize.

IG′nan–see– 4. indignancy, malignancy, benignancy.

IG′nant–lee– 4. indignantly, malignantly, benignantly.

IG′ne–us– 3. igneous, ligneous, cygneous.

   5. pyroligneous.

IG′ni–fi– 3. ignify, dignify, lignify, signify.

   4. undignify.

IG′ni–tee– 3. dignity.

   4. indignity, condignity, malignity, benignity.

IG′on–al– 3. trigonal.

   4. polygonal, ditrigonal.

IG′or–us– 3. rigorous, vigorous.

IG′raf–ee– 4. tachygraphy, calligraphy, polygraphy, epigraphy, pasigraphy, stratigraphy, lexigraphy.

IG′u–us– 4. ambiguous, irriguous, exiguous, contiguous.

IJ′a–bl– 3. bridgeable.

   4. abridgable, unbridgeable.

   5. unabridgable.

IJ′en–us– 4. ambigenous, indigenous, cauligenous, terrigenous, rurigenous, oxygenous.

   5. alkaligenous, coralligenous, nepheligenous; *see also* ĬJ′in–us.

IJ′er–ent– 4. belligerent, refrigerant.

   5. hederigerent.

IJ′er–us– 4. pedigerous, armigerous, plumigerous, belligerous, piligerous, cirrigerous, discigerous, cornigerous, crucigerous, setigerous, navigerous, ovigerous.

IJ′et–ee– 3. fidgety, midgety.

IJ′i–a– 3. Phrygia.

   4. Ogygia, fastigia.

   5. Cantabrigia.

IJ′i–an– 3. Phrygian, Stygian.

   4. Ogygian, Vestigian.

   5. Cantabrigian.

IJ′id–lee– 3. rigidly, frigidly.

IJ′id–ness– 3. rigidness, frigidness.

IJ′in–al– 4. original.

   5. aboriginal, unoriginal.

IJ′in–us– 4. polygynous, uliginous, fuliginous, lentiginous, vertiginous, vortiginous; *see also* ĬJ′en–us.

IJ′i–um– 3. phrygium.

   4. pterygium, fastigium, syzygium.

IJ′us–lee– 4. prodigiously, religiously, litigiously.

   5. sacrilegiously.

IJ′us–ness– 4. prodigiousness, religiousness, litigiousness.

5. sacrilegiousness.
IK´a–ment– 4. medicament, predicament.
IK´ar–us– 3. Icarus, lickerous.
IK´at–iv– 3. fricative, siccative.
4. *abdicative*, predicative, indicative, vindicative, desiccative, exsiccative.
IK´en–er– 3. thickener, quickener.
IK´en–ing– 3. sickening, thickening, quickening.
IK´er–ee– 3. lickery, mickery, trickery; *see also* **ĬK´or–ee.**
IK´er–ing– 3. bickering, dickering, flickering, smickering, snickering.
IK´er–ish– 3. lickerish, liquorish, licorice.
IK´et–ee– 3. rickety, crickety, thickety.
4. pernickety, persnickety.
IK´et–er– 3. picketer, cricketer, ticketer.
IK´et–ing– 3. picketing, cricketing, ticketing.
IK´i–lee– 3. trickily, stickily.
IK´i–ness– 3. trickiness, stickiness.
IK´li–ness– 3. prickliness, sickliness.
IK´ol–us– 3. Nicholas.
4. urbicolous, sepicolous, terricolous, agricolous, silvicolous.
IK´or–ee– 3. chicory, hickory, liquory.
4. Halicore, Terpsichore; *see also* **ĬK´er–ee.**
IKS´a–bl– 3. fixable, mixable.
4. prefixable, unfixable, immixable, unmixable.
IKS´ed–lee– 3. fixedly, mixedly.
IKSH´un–al– 3. fictional, frictional.
4. convictional.
5. contradictional, benedictional, jurisdictional.
IKS´it–ee– 3. fixity, siccity.
4. prolixity.
IKT´a–bl– 4. predictable, convictable.
5. contradictable, unpredictable, unrestrictable.
6. uncontradictable.
IKT´iv–lee– 3. fictively.
4. predictively, vindictively, restrictively.
IKT´iv–ness– 3. fictiveness.
4. predictiveness, vindictiveness, restrictiveness.
IKT´or–ee– 3. victory.
4. serictery.
5. contradictory, maledictory, valedictory, benedictory, interdictory.
6. uncontradictory.
IK´ul–a– 4. fidicula, Canicula, reticula.
IK´ul–ant– 4. matriculant, articulant.
IK´ul–ar– 3. spicular.
4. orbicular, vehicular, follicular, canicular, funicular, apicular, matricular, ventricular, auricular, acicular, fascicular, vesicular, versicular, reticular, denticular, lenticular, articular, particular, clavicular.
5. appendicular, perpendicular, adminicular, quinquarticular.
IK´ul–ate– 3. spiculate.
4. orbiculate, pediculate, forficulate, folliculate, vermiculate, paniculate, geniculate, apiculate, turriculate, matriculate, auricu-

late, aciculate, fasciculate, straticulate, reticulate, denticulate, monticulate, articulate, particulate, gesticulate.
5. appendiculate, canaliculate, immatriculate, inarticulate, octarticulate, multarticulate.
IK´ul–um– 3. spiculum.
4. Janiculum, geniculum, periculum [L.], curriculum, reticulum.
IK´ul–us– 4. ridiculous, folliculous, cauliculus, cauliculous, vermiculous, panniculus, ventriculous, vesiculus, vesiculous, meticulous.
IK´u–us– 4. transpicuous, conspicuous, perspicuous.
5. inconspicuous.
IK´wit–ee– 4. ubiquity, obliquity, iniquity, antiquity.
IK´wit–us– 4. ubiquitous, obliquitous, iniquitous.
IL´a–bl– 3. billable, fillable, killable, millable, spillable, thrillable, syllable, tillable.
4. refillable, unfillable, unkillable, unspillable, unthrillable, untillable, distillable.
IL´aj–er– 3. pillager, villager.
IL´ar–ee– 3. phyllary, Hilary, pillary.
5. codicillary; *see also* **ĬL´er–ee.**
IL´er–ee– 3. pillery, pillory, frillery, cilery, Sillery.
4. artillery, distillery; *see also* **ĬL´ar–ee.**
IL´et–ed– 3. billeted, filleted.
4. unbilleted, unfilleted.
IL´et–ing– 3. billeting, filleting.
IL´ful–ee– 3. skillfully, willfully.
4. unskillfully, unwillfully.
IL´ful–ness– 3. skillfulness, willfulness.
4. unskillfulness.
IL´i–a– 3. ilia, cilia.
4. sedilia, familia, Emilia, similia [L.], Cecilia.
5. mirabilia [L.], notabilia, pedophilia, hemophilia, zoophilia, adactylia.
6. memorabilia.
IL´i–ad– 3. Iliad, Gilead, chiliad, milliad.
IL´i–ak– 3. iliac.
5. sacroiliac, hemophiliac.
IL´i–al– 3. ilial, filial.
4. grandfilial, familial.
IL´i–an– 3. Ilian, Ilion, Chilean, Gillian, Lillian.
4. Virgilian, Cecilian, Sicilian, reptilian, Castilian, civilian, Brazilian.
5. crocodilian, Maximilian.
IL´i–ar– 4. familiar, conciliar, auxiliar.
5. domiciliar.
IL´i–ate– 3. filiate, ciliate.
4. affiliate, humiliate, conciliate.
5. domiciliate, reconciliate.
IL´i–ens– 4. resilience, dissilience, transilience, consilience; *see also* **ĬL´yans.**
IL´i–ent– 4. resilient, dissilient, transilient, consilient; *see also* **ĬL´yant.**
IL´i–est– 3. chilliest, hilliest, silliest, stilliest.
IL´i–fi– 3. vilify.
4. stabilify, nihilify, fossilify.

IL'i–form– **3.** filiform, phylliform, liliform, stilliform.
4. papilliform.
IL'ij–er– **3.** pillager, villager.
IL'ik–a– **3.** silica.
4. basilica.
IL'ik–al– **3.** filical, silicle.
4. umbilical, basilical.
IL'ik–in– **3.** Billiken, billikin, spilikin, spillikin.
4. basilican.
IL'ik–um– **3.** tilikum, tillicum.
IL'i–ness– **3.** chilliness, dilliness, hilliness, silliness.
IL'ing–lee– **3.** chillingly, fillingly, killingly, trillingly, thrillingly, willingly.
4. unwillingly.
IL'it–ate– **3.** militate.
4. habilitate, stabilitate, debilitate, nobilitate, facilitate.
5. rehabilitate, imbecilitate.
IL'it–ee– **4.** ability, lability, debility, mobility, nobility, nubility, nihility, agility, fragility, humility, senility, febrility, sterility, virility, scurrility, neurility, facility, gracility, docility, exility, flexibility, tensility, tactility, ductility, gentility, motility, fertility, tortility, hostility, utility, futility, civility, servility.
5. bribability, probability, readability, laudability, affability, changeability, chargeability, liability, pliability, viability, placability, peccability, secability, vocability, workability, saleability, amability, flammability, namability, tenability, inability, capability, culpability, wearability, errability, curability, durability, traceability, taxability, disability, versability, ratability, tractability, notability, quotability, temptability, portability, instability, mutability, suitability, suability, solvability, movability, provability, knowability, edibility, credibility, vendibility, audibility, legibility, frangibility, tangibility, fallibility, gullibility, feasibility, risibility, visibility, flexibility, fluxibility, sensibility, tensibility, vincibility, docibility, miscibility, passibility, possibility, plausibility, fusibility, partibility, immobility, ignobility, solubility, volubility, juvenility, imbecility, indocility, prehensility, volatility, vibratility, versatility, retractility, contractility, inductility, infertility, inutility, incivility.
6. describability, improbability, absorbability, approachability, avoidability, manageability, exchangeability, malleability, permeability, ineffability, navigability, reliability, amiability, variability, insatiability, negotiability, implacability, impeccability, applicability, amicability, practicability, masticability, revocability, availability, violability, calculability, redeemability, inflammability, reformability, conformability, alienability, amenability, impregnability, attainability, mentionability, questionability, governability, incapability, impalpability, reparability, separability, comparability,

ponderability, preferability, transferability, venerability, vulnerability, utterability, integrability, answerability, desirability, acquirability, adorability, meliorability, deplorability, memorability, vaporability, exorability, inerrability, penetrability, demonstrability, endurability, incurability, measurability, censurability, insurability, advisability, condensability, dispensability, reversability, impassability, punishability, perishability, relatability, dilatability, translatability, retractability, attractability, delectability, respectability, predictability, marketability, habitability, creditability, imitability, irritability, excitability, unsuitability, presentability, accountability, adaptability, acceptability, attemptability, transportability, detestability, adjustability, immutability, commutability, transmutability, imputability, computability, disputability, inscrutability, retrievability, conceivability, resolvability, removability, immovability, improvability, cognizability, inedibility, incredibility, inaudibility, illegibility, dirigibility, infrangibility, intangibility, indelibility, infallibility, defeasibility, persuasibility, divisibility, invisibility, inflexibility, expansibility, defensibility, insensibility, distensibility, extensibility, invincibility, convincibility, responsibility, collapsibility, reversibility, impassibility, irascibility, impressibility, compressibility, expressibility, accessibility, admissibility, remissibility, immiscibility, transmissibility, cognoscibility, impossibility, reducibility, seducibility, inducibility, conducibility, producibility, diffusibility, infusibility, compatibility, defectibility, affectibility, effectibility, perfectibility, conductibility, destructibility, deceptibility, perceptibility, susceptibility, contemptibility, corruptibility, impartibility, convertibility, digestibility, resistibility, existibility, exhaustibility, combustibility, insolubility.
7. indescribability, imperturbability, irreproachability, interchangeability, impermeability, irrefragability, justifiability, invariability, influenciability, enunciability, communicability, impracticability, irrevocability, assimilability, reconcilability, inviolability, coagulability, incalculability, irredeemability, irreformability, determinability, impressionability, irreparability, inseparability, incomparability, imponderability, innumerability, invulnerability, unutterability, undesirability, inexorability, impenetrability, indemonstrability, immeasurability, commensurability, indispensability, inexcusability, imperishability, untranslatability, inhabitability, hereditability, incogitability, illimitability, inimitability, precipitability, inheritability, inevitability, insurmountability, incontestability, irrefutability, incommutability, indisputability, irretrievability, inconceivability, irresolvability, recognizability, incognizabil-

ity, incorrigibility, indefeasibility, indivisibility, indefensibility, comprehensibility, irresponsibility, incognoscibility, irreversibility, irredressibility, irrepressibility, incompressibility, inexpressibility, inaccessibility, inadmissibility, irremissibility, irreducibility, incompatibility, indefectibility, imperfectibility, indestructibility, imperceptibility, incorruptibility, inconvertibility, indigestibility, irresistibility, inexhaustibility, incombustibility.

8. incommunicability, indefatigability, irreconcilability, incommensurability, hyperirritability, incomprehensibility; *and other nouns ending in " -ility. "*

IL′i–um–   **3.** ilium, ileum, Ilium, illium, Lilium, Liliom, pileum, trillium.

  4. beryllium, auxilium, concilium.

  5. fuit Ilium [L.].

IL′i–us   **4.** punctilious.

  5. supercilious; *see also* **ĬL′yus.**

ILK′i–est–   **3.** milkiest, silkiest.

IL′o–ee–   **3.** billowy, pillowy, willowy.

IL′o–jee–   **3.** dilogy, trilogy, sylloge.

  4. palilogy, fossilogy, antilogy, festilogy.

IL′o–jize–   **3.** syllogize.

  4. epilogize.

IL′o–jizm–   **3.** syllogism.

  4. amphilogism, epilogism.

  5. pseudosyllogism.

IL′o–kwee–   **4.** soliloquy, somniloquy, ventriloquy, dulciloquy, pauciloquy, Centiloquy, dentiloquy, multiloquy, stultiloquy.

  5. pectoriloquy.

IL′o–kwens–   **4.** blandiloquence, grandiloquence, magniloquence, somniloquence, multiloquence, stultiloquence, breviloquence.

IL′o–kwent–   **4.** grandiloquent, melliloquent, magniloquent, somniloquent, veriloquent, flexiloquent, dulciloquent, pauciloquent, sanctiloquent, altiloquent, multiloquent, suaviloquent.

IL′o–kwist–   **4.** soliloquist, somniloquist, ventriloquist, gastriloquist, dentiloquist.

IL′o–kwize–   **4.** soliloquize, ventriloquize.

IL′o–kwizm–   **4.** somniloquism, ventriloquism, gastriloquism.

  5. pectoriloquism.

IL′o–kwus–   **4.** grandiloquous, tardiloquous, somniloquous, ventriloquous.

  5. pectoriloquous.

IL′yan–see–   **3.** brilliancy.

  4. resiliency, transiliency.

IL′yar–ee–   **3.** miliary.

  4. auxiliary.

IM′er–ee–   **3.** glimmery, simmery, shimmery.

IM′er–ing–   **3.** glimmering, simmering, shimmering.

IM′er–us–   **3.** dimerous, glimmerous, trimerous.

  4. polymerous.

IM′et–er–   **3.** dimeter, trimeter, scimiter.

  4. millimeter, polymeter, perimeter, altimeter, voltimeter, centimeter.

  5. alkalimeter, polarimeter, calorimeter.

IM′et–ree–   **3.** symmetry.

  4. perimetry, asymmetry, altimetry, bathymetry.

  5. alkalimetry, polarimetry, calorimetry.

IM′i–an–   **3.** simian, Simeon.

  4. Endymion.

IM′ik–al–   **3.** mimical.

  4. alchymical, inimical.

  5. homonymical, toponymical, patronymical, metonymical.

IM′ik–ree–   **3.** gimmickry, mimicry.

IM′il–ee–   **3.** simile.

  4. dissimile, facsimile.

IM′in–al–   **3.** biminal, liminal, criminal, Viminal.

  4. regiminal, subliminal.

IM′in–ate–   **3.** criminate.

  4. eliminate, recriminate, incriminate, discriminate.

IM′in–ee–   **3.** Bimini, jiminy, crimine, criminy [both slang].

  4. postliminy.

  6. niminy-piminy.

IM′it–ate–   **3.** imitate, limitate.

  4. delimitate.

IM′it–ee–   **3.** dimity, limity.

  4. sublimity, proximity.

  5. magnanimity, unanimity, sanctanimity, equanimity, pseudonymity, anonymity, synonymity.

  6. pusillanimity.

IM′it–er–   **3.** limiter, scimitar, scimiter.

IMP′er–er–   **3.** simperer, whimperer.

IMP′er–ing–   **3.** simpering, whimpering.

IM′u–lant–   **3.** simulant, stimulant.

IM′u–late–   **3.** simulate, stimulate.

  4. assimulate, dissimulate, restimulate.

IM′u–lus–   **3.** limulus, stimulus.

IN′a–kl–   **3.** binnacle, binocle, pinnacle; *see also* **ĬN′i–kal.**

INCH′ing–lee–   **3.** inchingly, flinchingly, clinchlingly, pinchingly, cinchingly.

  5. penny pinchingly [slang].

IND′er–ee–   **3.** cindery, tindery.

IND′i–kate–   **3.** indicate, syndicate, vindicate.

IN′e–a–   **3.** linea, tinea, vinea.

  4. dulcinea.

  5. Nemertinea; *see also* **ĬN′i–a.**

IN′e–al–   **3.** lineal, pineal, tineal, vineal.

  4. gramineal, stamineal, pectineal.

  5. interlineal, consanguineal; *see also* **ĬN′i–al.**

IN′e–ar–   **3.** linear.

  4. trilinear, collinear.

  5. rectilinear.

IN′e–ma–   **3.** kinema, cinema.

IN′e–us–   **4.** vimineous, fulmineous, sanguineous.

  5. testudineous, ignominious, consanguineous; *see also* **ĬN′i–us.**

ING′ger–er–   **3.** fingerer, lingerer.

  4. malingerer.

ING′ger–ing–   **3.** fingering, lingering.

  4. malingering.

ĬNG'gul–ar– **3.** cingular, singular.
ĬNG'gul–ate– **3.** lingulate, cingulate.
ĬNG'i–ness– **3.** ringiness, springiness, stringi-
ness.
ĬN'i–a– **3.** Inia, linea, tinea, vinea, zinnia.
4. Sardinia, Virginia, lacinia, dosinia,
Lavinia.
5. anodynia, pleurodynia, Abyssinia, Nem-
ertinea; *see also* ĬN'e–a.
ĬN'i–al– **3.** inial, finial, lineal, pineal, tineal,
vineal.
4. dominial; *see also* ĬN'e–al.
ĬN'i–an– **4.** Sardinian, Delphinian, Virginian,
Flaminian, Justinian, Darwinian.
5. Carthaginian, Carolinian, Abyssinian,
Serpentinean, Palestinian, Augustinian.
7. anthropophaginian.
ĬN'i–ate– **3.** lineate, miniate.
4. delineate, laciniate.
ĬN'i–er– **3.** finnier, skinnier, tinnier.
ĬN'i–kal– **3.** finical, clinical, cynical, binocle.
4. rabbinical, synclinical, Brahminical,
adminicle, dominical; *see also* ĬN'a–kl.
ĬN'i–kin– **3.** finikin, minikin.
ĬN'ish–er– **3.** finisher.
4. diminisher.
ĬN'ish–ing– **3.** finishing.
4. refinishing, diminishing.
5. undiminishing.
ĬN'ist–er– **3.** minister, sinister.
4. administer.
5. ambisinister.
ĬN'ist–ral– **3.** ministral, sinistral.
5. dextrosinistral.
ĬN'it–ee– **3.** finity, trinity.
4. affinity, diffinity, infinity, confinity,
virginity, salinity, felinity, caninity, vicinity,
Latinity, divinity.
5. masculinity, femininity, asininity, pere-
grinity, exsanguinity, consanguinity, pata-
vinity.
ĬN'i–um– **3.** minium.
4. delphinium, virginium, illinium, perinium,
actinium.
5. quadricinium, tirocinium, patrocinium.
ĬN'i–us– **5.** ignominious, consanguineous;
see also ĬN'e–us.
ĬNJ'ens–ee– **3.** stringency.
4. refringency, astringency, constringency,
contingency.
ĬNJ'il–ee– **3.** dingily, stingily.
ĬNJ'i–ness– **3.** dinginess, stinginess.
ĬNK'a–bl– **3.** drinkable, shrinkable, sinkable,
thinkable.
4. undrinkable, unshrinkable, unthinkable.
ĬNK'i–ness– **3.** inkiness, kinkiness, slinkiness,
pinkiness.
ĬNK'ing–lee– **3.** chinkingly, blinkingly,
clinkingly, slinkingly, prinkingly, shrinkingly,
sinkingly, stinkingly, thinkingly, winkingly.
4. unthinkingly.
ĬNK'wit–ee– **4.** longinquity, propinquity.
ĬN'land–er– **3.** inlander, Finlander.
ĬNS'i–bl– **4.** evincible, invincible, convincible.

ĬNS'ing–lee– **3.** mincingly.
4. convincingly.
ĬNT'er–ee– **3.** splintery, printery, wintery.
ĬNT'er–ing– **3.** splintering, wintering.
ĬNTH'i–a– **3.** Cynthia.
4. Carinthia.
ĬNTH'i–an– **3.** Cynthian.
4. Carinthian, Corinthian, absinthian.
5. hyacinthian, labyrinthian.
ĬN'u–ate– **3.** sinuate.
4. insinuate, continuate.
ĬN'u–us– **3.** sinuous.
4. continuous.
5. uncontinuous, discontinuous.
ĬP'a–bl– **3.** chippable, dippable, clippable,
nippable, rippable, shippable, tippable.
ĬP'ar–us– **3.** biparous.
4. ambiparous, deiparous, polyparous, pri-
miparous, gemmiparous, vermiparous, cri-
niparous, omniparous, uniparous, floripa-
rous, pluriparous, fissiparous, fructiparous,
multiparous, dentiparous, viviparous, ovi-
parous, larviparous.
6. ovoviviparous.
ĬP'ath–ee– **4.** somnipathy, antipathy.
ĬP'er–ee– **3.** flippery, slippery, pipery, frip-
pery.
ĬP'i–ent– **4.** desipient, incipient, insipient,
percipient.
5. appercipient.
ĬP'ik–al– **3.** typical.
4. atypical, etypical, nontypical, untypical.
ĬP'i–ness **3.** slippiness, nippiness, snippiness,
grippiness.
ĬP'it–al– **4.** centripetal, basipetal, bicipital,
occipital, ancipital, sincipital.
ĬP'ol–ee– **3.** Tripoli.
4. Gallipoli.
ĬP'ot–ens– **4.** armipotence, plenipotence,
ignipotence, omnipotence.
ĬP'ot–ent– **4.** deipotent, bellipotent, armipo-
tent, plenipotent, ignipotent, omnipotent,
noctipotent, multipotent.
ĬPSH'un–al– **4.** transcriptional inscriptional,
conscriptional.
ĬPT'er–al– **3.** dipteral.
4. hemipteral, peripteral.
ĬPT'er–us– **3.** dipterous, dipteros, Dipterus,
tripterous.
4. peripterous.
ĬPT'ik–al– **3.** cryptical.
4. elliptical.
6. apocalyptical.
ĬPT'iv–lee– **4.** descriptively, prescriptively.
5. circumscriptively.
ĬP'ul–ar– **3.** stipular.
4. manipular.
ĬP'ul–ate– **3.** stipulate.
4. pedipulate, manipulate, astipulate.
ĬR'a–see– through ĬR'i–us *see also* Ŭ:
ŬRB'a–bl through ŬRZH'un–ist.
ĬR'a–see– **4.** deliracy, conspiracy.
ĬR'i–a– **3.** Syria, Styria.
4. Valkyria, Elyria, Assyria; *see also* ĔR'i–a.

IR′i–an– 3. Syrian, Tyrian, Styrian.
  4. Valkyrian, Assyrian.
IR′ik–al– 3. lyrical, miracle.
  4. empirical, satirical, satyrical.
  5. panegyrical.
IR′is–ist– 3. lyricist.
  4. empiricist.
IR′is′izm– 3. lyricism.
  4. empiricism.
IR′i–um– 3. Miriam.
  4. delirium, imperium.
IR′i–us– 3. Sirius.
  4. delirious, imperious.
IS′a–bl– 3. kissable, missable.
  4. dismissable; see also ĬS′i–bl.
IS′en–ing– 3. listening, glistening, christening.
ISH′al–ee– 4. judicially, officially, initially.
  5. prejudicially, unjudicially, beneficially, sacrificially, artificially, unofficially, superficially, interstitially.
  6. extrajudicially, unbeneficially, unsuperficially.
ISH′ar–ee– 4. judiciary, justiciary.
  5. beneficiary.
ISH′ens–ee– 4. efficiency, deficiency, proficiency, sufficiency.
  5. beneficiency, inefficiency, unproficiency, self-sufficiency, insufficiency.
ISH′ent–lee– 4. efficiently, deficiently, proficiently, sufficiently.
  5. inefficiently, unproficiently, insufficiently.
ISH′i–a– 4. indicia, Alicia, Galicia, Felicia, comitia, Tunisia, asitia, Justitia.
  5. apositia.
ISH′i–ate– 3. vitiate.
  4. officiate, initiate, propitiate, patriciate, novitiate.
ISH′on–al– 3. missional.
  4. additional, traditional, conditional, volitional, commissional, nutritional, transitional, positional, petitional, tuitional.
  5. exhibitional, unconditional, recognitional, depositional, prepositional, impositional, compositional, propositional, expositional, suppositional, repetitional, intuitional,
ISH′on–er– 3. missioner.
  4. conditioner, commissioner, parishioner, petitioner, practitioner.
  5. exhibitioner, coalitioner, admonitioner.
ISH′on–ing– 4. conditioning, positioning, petitioning.
ISH′on–ist– 4. traditionist.
  5. prohibitionist, exhibitionist, expeditionist, coalitionist, abolitionist, requisitionist, oppositionist.
ISH′us–lee– 3. viciously.
  4. judiciously, officiously, maliciously, deliciously, perniciously, auspiciously, suspiciously, capriciously.
  5. injudiciously, inauspiciously, avariciously, meretriciously, adventitiously.
ISH′us–ness– 3. viciousness.
  4. ambitiousness, seditiousness, judiciousness, officiousness, flagitiousness, deliciousness, perniciousness, propitiousness, auspiciousness, suspiciousness, capriciousness, nutritiousness, fictitiousness.
  5. injudiciosness, inauspiciousness, avariciousness, meretriciousness, adventitiousness, superstitiousness. suppositiousness.
IS′i–bl– 3. missible, miscible, scissible.
  4. admissible, remissible, immiscible, omissible, permissible, transmissible.
  5. unremissible, unpermissible, obliviscible; see also ĬS′a–bl.
IS′i–blee– 4. admissibly, permissibly.
IS′i–lee– 3. prissily [coll.], sissily, Sicily.
IS′im–o– 4. dolcissimo [It.], altissimo, fortissimo, prestissimo, bravissimo [It.].
  5. pianissimo.
  6. generalissimo.
IS′in–al– 3. piscinal, vicinal.
  4. medicinal, fidicinal, officinal, vaticinal.
IS′i–pate– 3. dissipate.
  4. anticipate, participate.
IS′it–ee– 4. cubicity, mendicity, pudicity, publicity, felicity, triplicity, simplicity, complicity, duplicity, conicity, tonicity, unicity, stoicity, lubricity, rubricity, sphericity, centricity, toxicity, pepticity, septicity, stypticity, verticity, vorticity, plasticity, spasticity, causticity, mysticity, rusticity.
  5. benedicite, immundicity, spheroidicity, impudicity, infelicity, catholicity, multiplicity, accomplicity, quadruplicity, endemicity, atomicity, atonicity, canonicity, caloricity, electricity, eccentricity, concentricity, authenticity, eupepticity, ellipticity, autopticity, elasticity, domesticity.
  6. periodicity, egocentricity, inelasticity.
IS′it–ing– 4. eliciting, soliciting.
IS′it–lee– 3. licitly.
  4. illicitly, implicitly, explicitly.
IS′it–ness– 3. licitness.
  4. illicitness, implicitness, explicitness.
IS′it–or– 4. elicitor, solicitor.
IS′it–ude– 3. spissitude.
  4. solicitude, vicissitude.
IS′it–us– 4. felicitous, solicitous.
ISK′i–er– 3. riskier, friskier.
ISK′i–est– 3. riskiest, friskiest.
ISK′i–lee– 3. riskily, friskily.
ISK′i–ness– 3. riskiness, friskiness.
IS′or–ee– 4. admissory, remissory, dimissory, dismissory, rescissory.
IST′en–see– 3. distancy.
  4. subsistency, existency, insistency, consistency, persistency.
  5. pre-existency, inconsistency.
IST′ent–lee– 3. distantly.
  4. existently, insistently, persistently.
  5. inconsistently.
IST′er–ee– 3. blistery, mystery.
  4. baptistery; see also ĬST′or–ee.
IST′er–like– 3. blisterlike, sisterlike.
IST′ful–ee– 3. listfully, wistfully.
IST′i–bl– 4. resistible, existible.

5. irresistible, unresistible.

ĬST′ik–al– 3. mystical.

  4. deistical, theistical, sophistical, logistical, hemistichal, papistical, eristical, patristical, juristical, puristical, statistical, artistical, linguistical.

  5. atheistical, pantheistical, eulogistical, synergistical, catechistical, anarchistical, cabalistical, alchemistical, Calvinistical, canonistical, synchronistical, egoistical, eucharistical, syncretistical.

  6. theosophistical, antagonistical, characteristical, hypocoristical.

ĬST′ik–ate– 4. sophisticate, phlogisticate.

  5. unsophisticate, dephlogisticate.

ĬST′or–ee– 3. history.

  4. faldistory, consistory; *see also* ĬST′er–ee.

ĬT′a–bl– 3. fittable, hittable, knittable, pittable, quittable.

  4. Mehitable, admittable, remittable, omittable, committable, permittable, transmittable.

  5. unremittable, unacquittable.

ĬT′an–ee– 3. dittany, kitteny, litany, Brittany.

ĬT′er–al– 3. literal.

  4. presbyteral, alliteral, biliteral, triliteral.

ĬT′er–ate– 3. iterate.

  4. reiterate, presbyterate, alliterate, obliterate, transliterate.

ĬT′er–ee– 3. jittery [slang], littery, glittery, tittery, twittery.

ĬT′er–er– 3. bitterer, jitterer [slang], litterer, glitterer, fritterer, titterer, twitterer.

  4. embitterer.

ĬT′er–ing– 3. jittering [slang], littering, glittering, frittering, tittering, twittering.

  4. embittering.

ĬTH′er–ee– 3. dithery, smithery, withery.

ĬTH′er–ing– 3. dithering, blithering, withering.

ĬTH′es–is– 4. epithesis, antithesis.

ĬTH′i–a–3. lithia, Pythia.

  4. forsythia.

ĬT′i–er– 3. flittier, grittier, prettier, wittier, Whittier.

ĬT′i–est– 3. grittiest, prettiest, wittiest.

ĬT′ik–al– 3. critical.

  4. political, hermitical, acritical, soritical, Levitical.

  5. eremitical, stalagmitical, diacritical, hypocritical, hypercritical, parasitical, Jesuitical.

  6. cosmopolitical, metropolitical, oneirocritical.

ĬT′il–ee– 3. grittily, prettily, wittily.

ĬT′i–ness 3. fittiness, flittiness, grittiness, prettiness, wittiness.

ĬT′ing–lee– 3. fittingly, flittingly, wittingly, twittingly.

  4. befittingly, unwittingly.

  5. unbefittingly, unremittingly.

ĬT′is–izm– 3. Briticism, criticism, witticism.

ĬT′l–ness– 3. littleness, brittleness.

ĬT′u–al– 3. ritual, situal.

4. habitual, obitual.

  5. unhabitual.

ĬT′ul–ar– 3. titular.

  4. capitular.

ĬV′a–bl– 3. givable, livable.

  4. forgivable, unlivable.

  5. unforgivable.

ĬV′al–ent– 3. bivalent, divalent, trivalent.

  4. polyvalent, omnivalent, univalent, multivalent, multivolent, equivalent.

ĬV′at–iv– 3. privative.

  4. derivative, deprivative.

ĬV′el–er– 3. sniveller, driveller, civiller.

ĬV′er–ee– 3. livery, slivery, rivery, shivery, quivery.

  4. delivery.

ĬV′er′er′ 3. sliverer, shiverer, quiverer.

  4. deliverer.

ĬV′er–ing– 3. slivering, shivering, quivering.

  4. delivering.

ĬV′i–a– 3. trivia.

  4. Olivia, Bolivia.

ĬV′i–al– 3. trivial.

  4. oblivial, quadrivial. lixivial, convivial.

ĬV′i–an– 3. Vivian.

  4. Olivean, Bolivian.

ĬV′id–lee– 3. lividly, vividly.

ĬV′id–ness– 3. lividness, vividness.

ĬV′il–ee– 3. snivelly, civilly.

  4. uncivilly.

ĬV′ing–lee– 3. givingly, livingly.

  4. forgivingly, outgivingly.

ĬV′it–ee– 3. privity.

  4. acclivity, declivity, proclivity, passivity, nativity, activity, motivity, captivity, festivity.

  5. impassivity, compassivity, emissivity, negativity, relativity, sensitivity, positivity, inactivity, objectivity, subjectivity, electivity, collectivity, connectivity, inductivity, conductivity, productivity, receptivity, perceptivity, susceptivity.

  6. correlativity, alternativity, retroactivity, reproductivity.

ĬV′it–us– 4. acclivitous, declivitous, proclivitous.

ĬV′i–um– 3. trivium.

  4. quadrivium, lixivium.

ĬV′i–us– 3. bivious.

  4. oblivious, lascivious, lixivious, multivious.

ĬV′ok–al– 4. univocal, equivocal.

  5. unequivocal.

ĬV′ol–ee– 3. Rivoli, Tivoli.

ĬV′or–us– 4. herbivorous, frondiverous, amphivorous, frugivorous, mellivorous, pomivorous, vermivorous, panivorous, ranivorous, granivorous, lignivorous, omnivorous, baccivorous, piscivorous, fucivorous, mucivorous, nucivoruos, ossivorous, fructivorous, sanguivorous, equivorous.

  5. graminivorous, vegetivorous, insectivorous, sanguinivorous.

ĬX′a–bl– *see* ĬKS′a–bl.

IZ'er–ee– **3.** misery, quizzery.
IZH'on–al– **3.** visional.
    4. precisional, revisional, previsional, divisional, provisional.
IZ'i–an– **3.** Frisian.
    4. Elysian, Tunisian, Parisian, precisian.
    5. paradisian.
IZ'i–bl– **3.** risible, visible, quizzable.
    4. derisible, divisible, invisible, acquisible.
    5. indivisible, undivisible.
IZ'i–er– **3.** busier, dizzier, fizzier, frizzier.

IZ'i–est– **3.** busiest, dizziest, fizziest, frizziest.
IZ'ik–al– **3.** physical, phthisical, quizzical.
    5. paradisical, cataphysical, metaphysical, geophysical, biophysical, psychophysical, zoophysical.
IZ'il–ee– **3.** busily, dizzily, frizzily.
IZ'ing–lee– **3.** whizzingly, quizzingly.
IZ'it–iv– **4.** acquisitive, inquisitive, disquisitive.
IZ'it–or– **3.** visitor.
    4. acquisitor, requisitor, inquisitor, disquisitor.

Ō (oh)

Single (Masculine) Rhymes

Primary or Secondary Accent Falls on Last Syllable; Imperfect Rhymes Are in Italics.

O– 1. o, O, oh, oe, owe, eau, eaux [both F.].
2. K. O. [coll.], kayo [slang].
3. video, rodeo, studio, Indio [Sp.], Tokyo, oleo, folio, cameo, Romeo, Borneo, Scipio, Scorpio, embryo, cheerio, vireo, histrio, nuncio.
4. borachio, presidio, adagio, Borachio, religio [L.], pistachio, punctilio, portfolio.
5. Montevideo, impresario, oratorio, ex officio, braggadocio.

BO– 1. bo, boh, 'bo, 'boe [both slang], bow, beau.
2. jabot, sabot, embow, *rainbow*, oboe, *hobo, crossbow.*
3. saddlebow.

DO– 1. do, doe, doh, dough.
2. *Dido*, rideau, *rondo*, rondeau, Bordeau.
3. Rinaldo, *cabildo* [Sp.].

FO– 1. foe, Fo, faux [F.].
2. *Sappho, Morpho, bufo, buffo* [It.].
3. comme il faut [F.].

GO– 1. go.
2. ago, Van Gogh, *Argo*, argot, *Fargo, Margot*, forego, *sorgo, outgo.*
3. touch-and-go, long ago, indigo, vertigo, undergo.
5. archipelago.

HO– 1. ho, hoe, Hoh.
2. mahoe, heigh-ho, oho, *moho, mojo, rojo* [Sp.], soho, *Soho*, yo-ho, *brujo* [Sp.].
3. Idaho, Navaho, Westward Ho, tallyho.
4. Arapaho.

JO– 1. Jo, Joe, joe [slang].
2. *banjo.*
3. *adagio.*

KO– 1. ko, Ko, Co., Coe, coe [loc. Eng.].
2. *unco* [Scot. & N. of Eng.], *coco, cocoa*, koko, Ko-ko, *moko.*
3. medico [coll.], calico, Sinico, haricot, cantico, portico, Mexico, rococo, *albarco.*
4. magnifico, energico [It.], angelico, simpatico, patetico [both It.], *moko-moko.*

LO– 1. lo, Lo, low, Lowe, blow, flow, floe,

glow, slow, sloe.
2. alow, tableau, *flyblow, deathblow, pueblo*, below, hello, *inflow*, ice floe, *outflow*, aglow, *moonglow, sunglow*, pilau, kolo rouleau, hullo.
3. sabalo, buffalo, bungalow, counterblow, matelot [F.], bibelot [F.], overflow, alpenglow, counterglow, furbelow, pomelo, gigolo, tremolo.

MO– 1. mo, mho, Moe, mot, mow.
2. *haymow*, bon mot, *twelvemo.*
3. alamo, dynamo, jeu de mots [F.], Eskimo, centimo, ultimo, proximo, chalumeau.
4. dolcissimo [It.], altissimo, fortissimo, prestissimo, bravissimo [It.].
5. pianissimo.
6. generalissimo.

NO– 1. no, know, snow.
2. tonneau. foreknow, besnow, Gounod.
3. domino.

PO– 1. po, Po, Poe, peau [F.], poh, pow.
2. chapeau, drapeau [F.], *depot*, shippo, propos [F.], cachepot [F.].
3. entrepôt [F.], apropos.
4. malapropos, à tout propos [F.].

RO– 1. ro, Ro, roe, row, Rowe, rho, bro [slang], cro, fro, grow, crow, scrow, pro, trow, strow, throe, throw.
2. arow, Caro, carrow, carreau [F.], tarot, *windrow*, ingrow, outgrow, *hedgerow, cockcrow, pilcrow, scarecrow*, escrow, genro, de trop [F.], bestrow, rethrow, *downthrow*, upthrow, *bureau.*
3. to-and-fro, Pierrot, intergrow, Chatellerault, Rotten Row, overthrow.

SO– 1. so, So, soh, sow, sew.
2. resow, resew, *soso, so-so*, morceau [F.], *torso*, Rousseau, trousseau, how so.
3. curassow, curacao, so-and-so.

SHO– 1. show, shew, sho.
2. cachot [F.], *sideshow, style show*, no-show, foreshow, *horse show.*
3. picture show.

TO– 1. toe, tow, tôt [F.], stow.
2. bateau, gateau [F.], plateau, chateau,

272

molto [It.], manteau, coteau [F.], *tiptoe*, *torteau*, bestow, *sexto*, couteau [F.].
3. manito, mistletoe, portmanteau, timber toe [slang], undertow.
4. incognito.
THO– 1. though.
2. *litho*, although.
VO– 1. Vaux, voe, veau [F.].
3. *centavo*, côte de veau [F.], Marivaux.
4. blanquette de veau [F.].
WO– 1. wo, woa, woe, whoa, quo.
3. quid pro quo [L.], status quo [L.].
4. status in quo [L.], in statu quo [L.].
YO– 1. yo, yo' [dial.].
2. *bagnio*, noyau, *yo-yo*.
3. *seraglio*, *intaglio*, *imbroglio*.
4. *latticinio*.
ZO– 1. zo, zoh.
2. réseau [F.].

OB– 1. obe, aube, Job, lobe, globe, robe, probe.
2. conglobe, enrobe, unrobe, disrobe.
OCH– 1. coach, loach, poach, roach, broach, brooch, croche.
2. encoach, abroach, encroach, *cockroach*, approach, reproach.
3. self-reproach.
OCHT– 1. coached, poached, broached.
2. uncoached, unbroached, encroached, approached, reproached.
OD– 1. ode, ohed, owed, bode, goad, hoed, code, lode, load, blowed [slang & dial.], Claud [F.], Claude [F.], slowed, mode, mowed, node, spode, road, rode, rowed, crowed, strode, sowed, sewed, shoad, shode, showed, towed, toed, toad, stowed, woad, yod.
2. unowed, abode, *elbowed*, embowed, un-bowed, forebode, reine claude [F.], un-load, explode, commode, unmowed, *epode*, erode, corrode, bestrode, intoed, bestowed.
3. overload, à la mode, incommode, dis-commode, antipode, episode, pigeon-toed, timber-toed [slang].
ODZ– *see* **ŌD**, plus " s " or " 's "; **1.** Rhodes.
OF– 1. oaf, goaf, koph, loaf, toph.
2. *breadloaf*, *witloof*.
3. half a loaf, sugar loaf, monostrophe.
OG– 1. log, rogue, brogue, drogue, drogh, trogue, togue, vogue.
2. embogue, collogue, pirogue, prorogue.
3. disembogue.
OJ– 1. doge, loge.
2. gamboge, éloge.
3. horologe.
OK– 1. oak, oke [slang], boke [slang], choke, doke [dial.], folk, hoke [slang], joke, coak, coke, bloak, bloke [both slang], cloak, sloke, moke, moch, smoke, poke, spoke, broke, croak, stroke, soak, toque, stoke, woke, yoke, yolk.
2. *seafolk*, *kinfolk*, *townsfolk*, ad hoc, uncloak, besmoke, bespoke, forespoke, forspoke, baroque, *sunstroke*, asoak, evoke, revoke,

invoke, convoke, provoke, awoke.
3. polychoke, artichoke, okeydoke [slang], gentlefolk, womenfolk, Nanticoke, counter-stroke, equivoque.
OKS– *see* **ŌK,** plus " s " or " 's "; **1.** hoax, coax.
OKT– 1. choked, hoked [slang], joked, coaked, coked, cloaked, smoked, poked, spoked, croaked, stroked, soaked, stoked, yoked.
2. uncloaked, besmoked, evoked, revoked, invoked, convoked, provoked.
3. counterstroked, double yolked.
OL– 1. 'ole, ole [dial.], ol', bole, boll, bowl, dhole, dole, foal, goal, hole, whole, jowl [dial.], coal, cole, kohl, skoal, mole, knoll, poll, pole, roll, role, droll, drole [F.], scroll, troll, stroll, soul, sole, shoal, shole, toll, stole thole, vole, wohl [G.].
2. *Creole*, embowl, *obole*, condole, segol, *bunghole*, *manhole*, *pinhole*, *kilnhole*, *peephole*, *loophole*, *tophole*, *borehole*, *porthole*, *heart-whole*, cajole, bricole, *charcoal*, *Maypole*, *tadpole*, *redpole*, *flagpole*, *payroll*, parole, *logroll*, virole, enscroll, inscroll, enroll, unroll, patrol, control, furole, resole, *half-sole*, *rissole* [F.], ensoul, insoul, console, citole, *sestole*, pistole, extoll, jawohl [G.].
3. ariole, dariole, aureole, foliole, apiole, variole, cabriole, oriole, gloriole, capriole, petiole, ostiole, vacuole, amphibole, racam-bole, carambole, farandole, girandole, pigeonhole, buttonhole, cubbyhole, glory hole, caracole, arvicole, septimole, carma-gnole, Seminole, rantipole, metropole, barcarole, escarole, rigmarole, fumarole, fusarole, squatarole, azarole, banderole, casserole, self-control, girasole, camisole.
4. bibliopole, remote control.
OLD– 1. old, bold, bowled, bolled, fold, foaled, gold, hold, cold, coaled, scold, skoaled, mold, mould, polled, rolled, scld, soled, shoaled, told, tolled, stoled, wold.
2. *blindfold*, *twofold*, *threefold*, etc., *bifold*, enfold, infold, unfold, *sheepfold*, spun gold, fool's gold, behold, *freehold*, *stronghold*, uphold, *leasehold*, *household*, *threshold*, *foothold*, with-hold, cajoled, remold, *leagmold*, paroled, controlled, half-soled, unsold, retold, un-told, foretold, twice-told.
3. overbold, hundredfold, thousandfold, ma-nifold, multifold, interfold, marigold, copy-hold, pigeonholed, pudding mold, bullet mold, Leopold, self-controlled, uncon-trolled, undersold, oversold, sable-stoled.
OLK– 1. polk, Polk, yolk, Volk [G.].
OLT– 1. bolt, dolt, holt, jolt, colt, molt, smolt, poult, volt.
2. rebolt, *eyebolt*, *kingbolt*, *wringbolt*, unbolt, lavolt, revolt.
3. shackle bolt, thunderbolt, millivolt, demi-volt.
OLZ– *see* **ŌL** plus " s " or " 's "; **1.** Bowles, Rolls.
OM– 1. ohm, oam, dom, dome, foam, home,

holm, haulm, heaume, comb, loam, gloam, glome, mome, Nome, gnome, pome, roam, rom, Rome, drome, chrome, tome.

2. endome, afoam, befoam, *megohm, coxcomb,* aplomb, Jerome.

3. semidome, catacomb, honeycomb, currycomb, evenglome, metronome, gastronome, palindrome, hippodrome, aerodrome, Ethan Frome, polychrome, monochrome, chromosome, microsome.

ŌMZ– *see* **ŌM,** plus " s " or " 's "; **1.** Holmes, Soames.

ŌN– 1. own, bone, Beaune, phone, hone, Joan, cone, scone, lone, loan, blown, flown, mown, moan, known, None, pone, roan, rone, Rhone, drone, groan, grown, crone, prone, throne, thrown, sewn, sown, shown, shone, tone, stone, zone.

2. disown, *aitchbone, backbone, whalebone, trombone, jawbone, icebone, fishbone, wishbone, breastbone,* condone, euphon, euphone, alone, cologne, Cologne, *wind-blown, fly-blown,* fullblown, unblown, high-flown, unflown, bemoan, *hormone,* unknown, foreknown, depone, repone, *corn pone,* propone, dispone, postpone, ladrone, begroan, half-grown, fullgrown, ungrown, moss-grown, bestrown, dethrone, unthrown, unsewn, unsown, unshown, foreshown, atone, intone, fronton [Sp.], *curbstone, headstone, sandstone, end stone, grindstone, lodestone, bloodstone, keystone, freestone, flagstone, clingstone, hailstone, millstone, milestone, tilestone, limestone, brimstone, tombstone, rhinestone, moonstone, soapstone, whetstone, hearthstone,* enzone, *ozone.*

3. anklebone, knucklebone, cuttlebone, megaphone, vitaphone, dictaphone, telephone, graphophone, gramophone, xylophone, microphone, saxophone, unbeknown, unforeknown, interpone, chaperone, cicerone, undergrown, overgrown, semitone, baritone, dulcitone, monotone, undertone, overtone, cornestone, overthrown.

4. radiophone, electrophone, Eau de Cologne, sine qua non [L.], foundation stone.

ŌND–1. owned, onde [F.], boned, phoned, honed, conęd, loaned, moaned, monde, droned, groaned, throned, toned, stoned, zoned.

2. disowned, fine-boned, seconde [F.], bemoaned, beau monde [F.], haut monde [F.], postponed, dethroned, atoned, high-toned, intoned, *flagstoned,* enzoned, unzoned.

3. telephoned, demimonde, chaperoned.

ŌNT– 1. don't, conte, won't.

ŌNZ–*see* **ŌN,** plus " s " or " ' s "; **1.** Jones, nones, Nones.

3. Lazybones, Davy Jones.

ŌO– *see* **ŌO.**

ŌP– 1. ope [dial. or poetic], dope, hope, cope, scope, lope, slope, mope, nope [slang or loc.], pope, rope, grope, trope, soap, sope, tope, taupe, stope.

2. elope, aslope, agrope, *dragrope, towrope,* soft-soap.

3. telescope, periscope, seismoscope, gyroscope, microscope, horoscope, spectroscope, stethoscope, cantaloupe, antelope, envelope, interlope, protopope, philanthrope, misanthrope, isotope.

4. kaleidoscope, dipleidoscope, stereoscope, polemoscope, heliotrope.

ŌPS– *see* **Ōp,** plus " s " or " ' s "; **1.** Scopes, Stopes.

ŌPT– 1. oped [poetic], doped, hoped, coped, loped, sloped, moped, roped, groped, soaped. **2.** eloped.

OR– through **ORZ–** *see also* **Ŏ: ŎR** through **ŎRZ; Ō: ÔR, ÔRD.**

OR– 1. ore, oar, o'er, bore, boar, Boer, chore, door, fore, four, gore, hoar, whore, core, corps, score, lore, floor, more, mohr, snore, pour, pore, spore, roar, soar, sore, shore, tore, store, wore, swore, yore.

2. forebore, adore, Indore, indoor, outdoor, before, therefore, wherefore, Lahore, Johore, décor [F.], encore, threescore, fourscore etc., galore [coll.], *folklore, booklore,* deplore, implore, explore, amor [L. & Sp.], ignore, *downpour,* outpour, *uproar, eyesore, heartsore, footsore,* ashore, *seashore,* inshore, foreshore, restore, *drugstore,* forswore.

3. troubadour, mogadore, picador, matador, Isadore, stevedore, Polydore, battledore, open door, toison d'or [F.], louis d'or [F.], Theodore, commodore, two-by-four, semaphore, pinafore, heretofore, albacore, terpsichore, underscore, Sagamore, sycamore, paramour, Barrymore, Baltimore, sophomore, furthermore, evermore, nevermore, Singapore, por favor [Sp.], carnivore.

4. hereinbefore, l'étoile du nord [F.].

ORCH– 1. scorch, porch, torch.

2. front porch.

ORD– 1. oared, bored, board, doored, ford, Ford, gored, gourd, hoard, hoared, horde, whored, cored, scored, floored, snored, poured, pored, toward, stored, sword.

2. aboard, *clapboard, cupboard, switchboard, headboard, breadboard, sideboard, cardboard, seaboard, surfboard, springboard, blackboard, buckboard, wallboard, inboard, clapboard, outboard,* adored, *two-doored, four-doored,* afford, ungored, encored, uncored, deplored, implored, explored, restored.

3. shuffleboard, beaverboard, overboard, ironing board, open-doored, unexplored, unrestored.

ORJ– 1. forge, gorge, porge.

2. engorge, disgorge.

ORK– 1. pork.

2. morepork, salt pork.

ORN– 1. borne, bourn, Doorn, scorn, mourn, morn, shorn, worn, sworn.

2. forborne, bemourn, unshorn, betorn, *toilworn,* outworn, unsworn, forsworn.

3. unforsworn.

ŌRND– 1. scorned, mourned.
2. unscorned, bemourned, unmourned.
ORS– 1. force, hoarse, coarse, course, source.
2. enforce, inforce, perforce, recourse, discourse, resource, divorce.
3. tour de force, reinforce, watercourse, intercourse.
ORT– 1. fort, forte, court, mort, port, sport.
2. aport, apport, rapport, deport, report, *seaport*, import, comport, *airport*, *carport*, purport, *passport*, disport, export, transport, support, resort.
3. sally port, davenport, nonsupport.
4. pianoforte.
ORTH– 1. forth, fourth.
2. henceforth, thenceforth.
ORZ– *see* **ŌR,** plus " s " or " 's "; **2.** indoors, outdoors, all fours, plus fours, Azores.
OS– 1. boce, dose, kos, close, gross, soce, sauce [F.].
2. globose, verbose, nodose, jocose, *glucose*, alos, engross, morose.
3. overdose, adios [Sp.], grandiose, otiose, bellicose, allulose, cellulose, annulose, albumose, diagnose, adipose, comatose.
OSH– 1. Boche, gauche, cloche, sosh [slang].
2. à gauche [F.].
OST– 1. oast, boast, dosed, ghost, host, coast, most, post, roast, grossed, toast.
2. *seacoast*, Gold Coast, *headmost*, *endmost*, *hindmost*, almost, *inmost*, *topmost*, *upmost*, *foremost*, *utmost*, reposte, *milepost*, *signpost*, *outpost*, engrossed.
3. bottommost, easternmost, northernmost, hindermost, undermost, innermost, lowermost, uppermost, centermost, outermost, uttermost, nethermost, hithermost, furthermost, diagnosed, whipping post, hitching post, letter post.
4. Ivory Coast.
OT– 1. oat, boat, dote, faute [F.], goat, coat, cote, côte [F.], scote, bloat, float, gloat, moat, mote, smote, note, rote, wrote, groat, throat, shoat, shote, tote [coll. & slang], stoat, vote, quote.
2. *lifeboat*, *sailboat*, showboat, *houseboat*,, en faute [F.], *scapegoat*, *redcoat*, turncoat, *topcoat*, *waistcoat*, afloat, refloat, emote, demote, remote, promote, denote, *keynote*, connote, *gracenote*, *footnote*, capote, garrote, rewrote, *starthroat*, *whitethroat*, *cutthroat*, *aptote*, *diptote*, *triptote*, devote, outvote, bequote, misquote.
3. ferryboat, river boat, antidote, anecdote, table d'hote, billy goat, nanny goat, mountain goat, redingote, petticoat, overcoat, underwrote, creosote, asymptote.
OTH– 1. oath, both, loath, sloth, wroth, growth, troth, Thoth, quoth.
2. *outgrowth*, betroth.

3. behemoth, undergrowth, aftergrowth, overgrowth.
OTHE– 1. loathe, clothe.
2. reclothe, unclothe, betroth.
OTS– *see* **ŌT,** plus " s " or " 's "; **1.** Oates, Coates.
OV– 1. dove, hove, Jove, cove, loave, clove, mauve, rove, drove, grove, Shrove, trove, strove, throve, tove [Scot.], stove, wove.
2. behove, gemauve, *mangrove*, rewove, inwove.
3. perijove, apojove, treasure-trove, interwove.
OVZ– 1. Jove's, coves, loaves, cloves, mauves, roves, droves, groves, troves, toves [Scot.], stoves.
2. *mangroves*.
3. treasure-troves.
OZ– 1. owes, ohs, bows, beaux, Boz, chose, dos, do's, dohs, doze, doughs, does, foes, goes, hose, coze, lows, blows, flows, floes, glows, glose, gloze, close, clothes, slows, sloes, Mose, nose, knows, snows, pose, spose [slang], rows, rose, brose, froze, grows, croze, crows, prose, pros, strows, throes, throws, sows, sews, shows, toes, tows, toze, stows, those, thoughs, squoze [dial.].
2. jabots, sabots, *elbows*, embows, *rainbows*, rideaux, *bulldoze*, tableaux, hellos, ice floes, enclose, unclose, foreclose, disclose, foreknows, chapeaux, depose, repose, impose, compose, oppose, propose, dispose, cachepots [F.], expose, transpose, suppose, arose, tarots, *tuberose*, *tea rose*, *wild rose*, *dog rose*, *rockrose*, *primrose*, *moss rose*, refroze, unfroze, outgrows, rethrows, *bureaus*, trousseaux, *style shows*, foreshows, *tiptoes*, bestows.
3. rodeos, studios, folios, cameos, embryos, vireos, nuncios, saddlebows, medicos, calicos, porticos, buffalos, bungalows, counterblows, bibelots [F.], overflows, furbelows, gigolos, tremolos, dynamos, Eskimos, dominoes, decompose, recompose, discompose, superpose, interpose, predispose, indispose, presuppose, damask rose, bramble rose, Pierrots, overthrows, so-and-sos, picture shows, pettitoes, portmanteaus, undertows.
OZD– 1. dozed, hosed, glozed, closed, nosed, posed, prosed.
2. *bulldozed*, enclosed, unclosed, foreclosed, disclosed, deposed, reposed, imposed, composed, opposed, proposed, disposed, exposed, transposed, supposed.
3. decomposed, recomposed, discomposed, interposed, superposed, predisposed, welldisposed, ill-disposed, indisposed, presupposed.
OZH– 1. loge.
2. gamboge, éloge.

Ō (oh)

Double (Feminine) Rhymes

Primary or Secondary Accent Falls on Next to Last Syllable; Imperfect Rhymes Are in Italics.

O'a– 2. boa, koa, loa, Loa, moa, Noah, noa, proa, Shoa.
3. Gilboa, jerboa, aloha, Samoa, anoa, leipoa.
3. Kanaloa, Metazoa, Hydrozoa, microzoa, Sporozoa, entozoa, Protozoa, Anthozoa.
O'ab– 2. doab, Joab, Moab.
O'al– 3. bestowal, restowal.
O'an– 2. Goan, cowan, rowan.
3. eoan, Samoan, Minoan.
OB'a– 2. koba.
3. cohoba, arroba.
4. algarroba, bona roba [arch.], Manitoba.
OB'al– 2. lobal, global, probal.
3. microbal, Cristobal.
OB'ate– 2. lobate, globate, probate.
OB'ee– 2. obi, dobe, gobi, Gobi, goby, Kobe, globy, toby [slang], Toby.
3. adobe.
OB'eel– 2. mobile, Mobile.
3. immobile, *bookmobile.*
4. locomobile, automobile.
OB'er– 2. rober, robur, prober, sober.
3. amobyr, enrober, disrober, October.
OB'ik– 2. phobic, strobic.
3. niobic, microbic.
4. phobophobic, hydrophobic, claustrophobic, photophobic.
OB'ing– 2. globing, robing, probing.
3. englobing, enrobing, unrobing, disrobing.
OB'it– 2. obit, Tobit.
3. post-obit.
OB'l– 2. coble, noble.
3. ennoble, ignoble, unnoble.
OB'o– 2. oboe, bobo, hobo, lobo, zobo.
OB'ra– 2. dobra, cobra.
OB'ule– 2. lobule, globule.
OB'us– 2. obus [F.], Kobus, lobus, globus, globous.
3. jacobus.
OCH'er– 2. coacher, poacher, broacher.
3. encroacher, approacher, reproacher.
OCH'ez– 2. coaches, loaches, poaches, roaches,

broaches, brooches.
3. *stagecoaches*, encoaches *cockroaches*, encroaches, approaches, reproaches.
4. railroad coaches, self-reproaches.
OCH'ful– 3. reproachful.
4. self-reproachful, unreproachful.
OCH'ing– 2. coaching, poaching, roaching, broaching.
3. *stagecoaching*, encoaching, encroaching, approaching, reproaching.
4. self-reproaching.
OCH'ment– 3. encroachment, approachment.
OD'a– 2. oda, coda, Rhoda, soda, Toda.
3. pagoda, salsoda.
4. baking soda, ice-cream soda, Scotch and soda.
5. Chinese pagoda, whisky and soda.
OD'al– 2. odal, modal, nodal, yodel.
3. trinodal.
4. internodal.
OD'ed– 2. boded, goaded, coded, loaded, noded, woaded.
3. foreboded, decoded, unloaded, exploded, outmoded, corroded.
4. overloaded, incommoded, discommoded, uncorroded.
OD'ee– 2. bodhi, Dody, Godey, Cody, mody, Brody, sody, toady, tody, woady.
OD'en– 2. Odin, boden, Woden.
OD'ent– 2. rodent.
3. explodent, erodent, corrodent.
OD'er– 2. Oder, odor, boder, goader, loader, roader, woader.
3. foreboder, malodor, reloader, unloader, exploder, corroder.
4. muzzle-loader.
OD'ik– 2. odic.
4. palinodic.
OD'ing– 2. boding, goading, coding, loading.
3. foreboding, decoding, unloading, exploding, outmoding, eroding, corroding.
4. overloading, discommoding.

OD′ist– odist, codist, modist.
4. palinodist.
OD′o– 2. dodo, Jodo.
3. quomodo [L.],
4. Quasimodo.
OD′ster– 2. goadster, lodestar, roadster.
OD′us– 2. modus [L.], nodus, nodous.
O′ee– 2. bowie, Bowie, doughy, Joey, blowy, glowy, Chloë, snowy, poë, poi, rowy, showy, towy, Zoë.
3. evoe!
O′el– 2. Joel, koel, Lowell, Noel, nowel, Crowell.
O′em– 2. phloem, poem, proem.
4. mythopoem, jeroboam.
O′en– 2. Owen, Cohen, rowan.
O′er– 2. o'er, ower, Boer, goer, hoer, lower, blower, glower, slower, mower, knower, rower, grower, crower, thrower, sewer, sower, shower, tower, stower.
3. foregoer, outgoer, foreknower, *cockcrower*, foreshower, bestower.
4. overthrower.
O′erd– 2. lowered, froward, toward.
3. untoward.
O′est– 2. lowest, slowest.
OF′ee– 2. trophy, strophe, Sophie.
OF′er– 2. Ophir, gopher, gaufre, loafer, chauffeur.
OG′a– 2. snoga, toga, yoga.
3. daroga.
4. Saratoga, Conestoga.
5. Ticonderoga.
OG′an– 2. hogan, logan, slogan, rogan, brogan.
OG′ee– 2. bogy, bogie, dogie, fogy, fogey, fogy, pogy, stogy, stogie, voguey, yogi.
3. old-fogy, old-fogey.
6. cedant arma togae [L.].
OG′er– 2. ogre, drogher.
OG′ish– 2. roguish, voguish.
OG′l– 2. ogle, bogle, fogle, Vogel [G.], Vogul.
3. aasvogel [D.].
OG′o– 2. gogo, mogo, Pogo, zogo.
O′ha– 2. poha.
3. aloha, aloja [Sp.].
O′ho– 2. coho, moho, mojo, Mojo, Moxo, rojo [Sp.], Soho.
3. corojo.
O′ij– flowage, towage, stowage.
O′ik– 2. Troic, Stoic, stoic, zoic.
3. echoic, diploic, heroic, dichroic, azoic, benzoic.
4. authochroic, epizoic, Eozoic, Neozoic, hylozoic, protozoic.
5. Archaeozoic, Paleozoic.
O′iks– 2. Coix, stoics.
3. heroics.
O′ing– 2. owing, ohing, bowing, Boeing, going, hoeing, lowing, blowing, flowing, glowing, slowing, mowing, knowing, snowing, rowing, growing, crowing, strowing, throwing, sowing, sewing, showing, towing, toeing, stowing.

3. *elbowing*, *seagoing*, *ingoing*, foregoing, outgoing, helloing, inflowing, outflowing, foreknowing, unknowing, *ingrowing*, outgrowing, *cockcrowing*, foreshowing, *tiptoeing*.
4. easygoing, thoroughgoing, undergoing, overthrowing.
OJ′an– 2. Trojan, yojan.
OJ′ee– 2. shoji.
3. agoge.
4. anagoge, apagoge, epagoge, paragoge, isogoge.
OK′a– 2. oka, oca [Sp.], boca [Sp.], choca, phoca, coca, loka, loca, sloka, mocha, polka, troca, stocah.
3. jocoque.
4. tapioca, curiboca.
OK′al– 2. bocal, focal, phocal, local, trochal, socle, vocal, yokel.
3. bifocal, collocal, bivocal.
4. hyperfocal, patrilocal, multivocal, equivocal.
OK′ee– 2. oaky, Okie, choky, hokey, jokey, coky, Loki, moki, smoky, poky, roky, croaky, troche, trochee, soaky, yoky, yolky.
3. jocoqui, ditrochee.
4. okey-dokey [slang], hokeypokey [coll.].
OK′en– 2. oaken, spoken, broken, soaken, token.
3. bespoken, freespoken, well-spoken, plainspoken, unspoken, soft-spoken, short-spoken, outspoken, smooth-spoken, true-spoken, unbroken, *heartbroken*, betoken, foretoken.
OK′er– 2. ochre, choker, joker, coker, cloaker, smoker, poker, spoker, roker, broker, croaker, stroker, soaker, stoker, yoker.
3. *stockbroker*, *pawnbroker*, evoker, revoker, invoker, convoker, provoker.
4. mediocre.
OK′ij– 2. chokage, cloakage, rokeage [loc.], brokage, soakage.
OK′ing– 2. choking, joking, coking, cloaking, smoking, poking, spoking, croaking, troching, stroking, soaking, stoking, yoking.
3. uncloaking, evoking, revoking, invoking, convoking, provoking, unyoking.
OK′less– 2. oakless, jokeless, cokeless, blokeless [slang], cloakless, smokeless, pokeless, spokeless, croakless, yokeless, yolkless.
OK′ment– 3. revokement, invokement, provokement.
OK′o– 2. choco, coco, cocoa, koko, Koko, Ko-Ko, loco, moko, poco [It.], poco [slang], troco, soco, toco.
3. Kioko, rococo, al loco [It.], in loco [L.].
4. locofoco, moko-moko, Orinoco.
OKS′er– 2. hoaxer, coaxer.
OKS′ing– 2. hoaxing, coaxing.
OK′um– 2. oakum, kokum.
OK′us– 2. focus, hocus, locus, crocus.
4. hocus-pocus.
OK′ust– 2. focussed, hocussed, locust.
3. unfocussed, sweet locust.
OL′a– 2. ola, bola, bowla, gola, cola, kola,

schola, Lola, mola, Mola, Nola, sola, stola, vola [L.], Zola.

3. crayola, Viola, mandola, Angola, pimola, victrola.

4. carambola, Pensacola, pianola, Gorgonzola.

5. Savonarola.

OL'an 2. O-lan, Dolan, Nolan, tolan; *see also* **ŌL'en, ŌL'on.**

OL'ar– 2. bolar, molar, polar, solar, volar.

4. unipolar, circumpolar, lunisolar, circumsolar; *see also* **ŌL'er.**

OLD'ed– 2. folded, scolded, molded.

3. blindfolded, enfolded, unfolded.

4. manifolded.

OLD'ee– 2. oldy, foldy, goldy, Goldie, coldy, moldy, mouldy.

3. unmouldy.

OLD'en– 2. olden, holden, golden.

3. embolden, beholden.

4. misbeholden.

OLD'er– 2. older, bolder, boulder, folder, holder, colder, scolder, molder, smolder, polder, shoulder.

3. enfolder, unfolder, *landholder*, beholder, *freeholder*, upholder, *shareholder*, *leaseholder*, *householder*, withholder, *slaveholder*, coldshoulder.

4. manifolder, copyholder, candleholder, bottleholder.

OLD'erd– 2. bouldered, shouldered.

3. broad-shouldered, round-shouldered, stoop-shouldered, square-shouldered.

4. narrow-shouldered.

OLD'est– 2. oldest, boldest, coldest.

OLD'ing– 2. folding, holding, molding, scolding.

3. enfolding, *landholding*, beholding, *freeholding*, upholding, *leaseholding*, withholding, *slaveholding*, non-molding, unmolding.

4. interfolding, overfolding.

OLD'ish– oldish, boldish, coldish.

OLD'lee– 2. oldly, boldly, coldly.

4. manifoldly.

OLD'ment– 3. enfoldment, infoldment, withholdment.

OLD'ness– 2. oldness, boldness, goldness, coldness.

3. controlledness.

4. overboldness, uncontrolledness.

OL'ee– 2. bowly, bolly, foaly, goalie, holy, wholly, coaly, lowly, slowly, moly, knolly, rolly, drolly, scrolly, soli, solely, sholy [dial.], shoaly.

3. maholi, unholy, anole, pinole, posole.

4. roly-poly, caracoli.

OL'en– 2. solen, stolen, Stollen, swollen; *see also* **ŌL'an, Ōl'on.**

OL'ent– 2. olent, dolent, volant.

3. condolent.

OL'er– 2. Olor, bowler, bolar, dolor, coaler, koller, molar, knoller, poler, polar, poller, roller, droller, scroller, troller, stroller, soler, solar, shoaler, toller, volar.

3. condoler, cajoler, enroller, patroller, controller, comptroller, consoler, extoller.

4. piegonholer, unipolar, circumpolar, Holy Roller, lunisolar.

OL'ful– 2. bowlful, doleful, soulful.

OL'ing– 2. bolling, bowling, doling, foaling, goaling, holing, coaling, poling, polling, rolling, drolling, trolling, strolling, soling, tolling.

3. condoling, cajoling, paroling, enrolling, unrolling, patrolling, controlling, half-soling, consoling, extolling.

4. caracoling.

OL'ish– 2. Polish, drollish, soulish.

OL'ment– 3. condolement, cajolement, enrollment, contr015ment.

OL'ness– 2. wholeness, drollness, soleness.

OL'o– 2. bolo, Bolo, Cholo, Golo, Lolo, polo, solo, stolo [L.],.

3. barolo.

4. bolo-bolo.

OL'on– 2. colon, Solon, stolon.

3. eidolon.

4. semicolon; *see also* **ŌL'an, ŌL'en.**

OL'or– 2. Olor, dolor; *see also* **ŌL'er.**

OL'som– 2. dolesome, wholesome.

3. unwholesome.

OLST'er– 2. bolster, holster.

3. upholster.

OLT'ed– 2. bolted, jolted, colted, molted.

3. unbolted, revolted.

OLT'er– 2. bolter, jolter, colter, molter.

3. unbolter, revolter.

OLT'ij– 2. boltage, voltage.

OLT'ing– 2. bolting, jolting, colting, molting.

3. unbolting, revolting.

OLT'ish– 2. doltish, coltish.

OL'um– 2. solum [L.].

3. idolum.

OL'us– 2. bolus, dolose, dolous, dolus [L.], solus [L.].

4. holus-bolus, gladiolus.

OM'a– 2. coma, loma, noma, Roma, stroma, soma, stoma.

3. aboma, zygoma, Tacoma, sarcoma, aloma, diploma, aroma, prosoma, phytoma, rhizoma.

OM'al– 2. domal, bromal, somal, stromal.

OM'an– 2. bowman, foeman, gnomon, Roman, showman, yeoman.

OM'ee– 2. domy, foamy, homy, homey [both coll.], Kome, Komi, loamy.

3. Naomi.

4. lomi-lomi.

OM'en– 2. omen, bowmen, foemen, nomen [L.], gnomon, showmen, yeomen.

3. abdomen, praenomen, agnomen, cognomen.

4. absit omen [L.].

OM'end– 2. omened.

3. ill-omened, bad-omened.

4. happy-omened.

OM'ent– 2. foment, loment, moment.

3. bestowment, last moment.

OM'er– 2. omer, gomer, Gomer, homer, Homer, comber, roamer, vomer.
3. *beachcomber, wool comber,* misnomer.
OM'ij– 2. ohmage, homage.
OM'ik– 2. ohmic, domic, gnomic, bromic, chromic.
3. achromic, dichromic.
4. hydrobromic, polychromic.
OM'ing– 2. doming, foaming, homing, coaming, combing, gloaming, roaming.
3. befoaming, Wyoming, *beachcombing, woolcombing.*
OM'is– 3. Nokomis, exomis.
OM'ish– 2. domish, foamish, gnomish, Romish, tomish.
OM'less– 2. domeless, foamless, homeless, combless, loamless, gnomeless.
OM'o– 2. homo, Como, momo, chromo, duomo [It.].
3. Pokomo.
4. major-domo.
OM'us– 2. domus [L.], Comus, Momus, chromous.
3. *prodromus,* disomus.
4. Major Domus.
ON'a– 2. ona, bona [L.], Bona, dona, Dona [both Pg.], Gona, Jonah, kona, Mona, drona, krona, trona, zona [L.].
3. annona, Annona, ancona [It.], Ancona, cinchona, Bellona, Bologna, Ramona, Cremona, kimono.
4. Barcelona, Desdemona, Toromona, Arizona.
ON'al– 2. phonal, chronal, thronal, tonal, zonal.
3. coronal, atonal, azonal.
4. polytonal, polyzonal, interzonal.
ON'ant- 2. sonant, tonant.
4. supersonant, intersonant; *see also* ŌN'ent.
ON'ate– 2. donate, phonate, pronate, zonate.
ON'ee– 2. bony, phony [slang], gony, goney, cony, pony, drony, crony, tony [vulgar], stony.
3. bologna, Dione, polony, Shoshone.
4. chalcedony, abalone, ceremony, alimony, agrimony, acrimony, matrimony, patrimony, parsimony, sanctimony, antimony, testimony, macaroni, lazzaroni, cicerone.
ON'ent– 3. opponent, deponent, component, proponent, disponent, exponent.
4. interponent; *see also* ŌN'ant.
ON'er– 2. owner, boner, donor, phoner, loaner, moaner, droner, toner, stoner.
3. condoner, bemoaner, postponer, atoner, entoner, intoner.
O'ness– 2. lowness, slowness.
ON'ij– 2. dronage, tronage.
4. chaperonage.
ON'ing– 2. owning, boning, phoning, honing, loaning, moaning, droning, groaning, throning, toning, stoning, zoning.
3. disowning, condoning, bemoaning, postponing, dethroning, unthroning, atoning, intoning, enzoning.

4. telephoning, chaperoning.
ON'is 3. Adonis, Coronis.
ON'lee– 2. only, lonely, pronely.
3. alonely, unlonely.
4. one and only.
ON'less– 2. boneless, phoneless, loanless, moanless, groanless, throneless, toneless, stoneless, zoneless.
4. telephoneless, chaperoneless.
ON'ment– 3. disownment, condonement, postponement, dethronement, enthronement, atonement, intonement.
ON'ness– 2. ownness, loneness, proneness.
3. unknownness.
ON'o– 2. fono, phono, Nono.
3. kimono.
4. kakemono [Jap.]. makimono.
ON'us– 2. onus, bonus, conus, Cronus, tonus.
3. colonus.
4. dolus bonus [L.].
OO'– *see* ŌŌ.
OP'a– 2. opah, chopa, copa, scopa.
3. Bacopa, Europa.
OP'al– 2. opal. copal, nopal.
3. *sinople.*
4. periople.
5. Adrianople, Costantinople.
OP'ee– 2. dopey, Hopi, slopy, mopy, ropy, soapy, topee, topi.
OP'er– 2. doper, hoper, coper, loper, sloper, moper, roper, groper, soaper, toper, stoper.
3. eloper, soft-soaper.
4. interloper.
OP'ing– 2. doping, hoping, coping, loping, sloping, moping, roping, groping, soaping, toping, stoping.
3. eloping, soft-soaping.
4. interloping.
OP'l– 3. *sinople.*
4. periople.
5. Adrianople, Constantinople.
OP'less– 2. hopeless, popeless, soapless.
OP'us– 2. opus, Propus.
3. lagopous, Lagopus, Canopus, pyropus.
OR'a– through OR'us– *see also* Ō: ŌR'a through ǑR'ward; Ô: ÔR'a through ÔR'us.
OR'a– 2. ora, Ora, bora, Dora, goura, hora, Cora, kora, Korah, Lora, flora, Flora, Nora, tora, torah, Torah.
3. Eldora, Pandora, rhodora, angora, ancora [It.], señora [Sp.], signora [It.], aurora, Masora, totora.
4. Floradora, Theodora, passiflora, Passiflora.
OR'aks– 2. borax, Dorax, storax, thorax.
OR'al– 2. oral, horal, choral, loral, floral, chloral, poral, roral, thoral.
3. trifloral, auroral, sororal.
OR'an– 2. Koran, toran.
3. Sonoran.
OR'ate– 2. orate, borate, florate, chlorate, prorate.
3. deflorate, biflorate.

OR'ay– 2. foray, moire.
3. signore [It.], con amore [It.], con dolore [It.].
6. improvvisatore [It.].
ORD'ed– 2. boarded, forded, hoarded, sworded.
3. afforded, unhoarded.
ORD'er– 2. boarder, forder, hoarder.
ORD'ing– 2. boarding, fording, hoarding, swording.
3. affording, unhoarding.
4. beaverboarding.
OR'ee– 2. oary, ory, dory, gory, hoary, kori, Kore, lory, flory, glory, more, snory, pory, shory, Tory, story.
3. Old Glory, vainglory, maggiore [It.], pilori, signore [It.].
4. a priori, hunky-dory [coll.], allegory, category, tautegory, amphigory, counterflory, promissory, probatory, gradatory, predatory, mandatory, mundatory, laudatory, feudatory, sudatory, prefatory, negatory, rogatory, purgatory, nugatory, piscatory, oblatory, grallatory, parlatory, amatory, crematory, chrismatory, fumatory, sanatory, signatory, crinatory, donatory, phonatory, culpatory, vibratory, migratory, oratory, juratory, curatory, gyratory, pulsatory, natatory, citatory, dictatory, saltatory, potatory, rotatory, hortatory, gestatory, gustatory, mutatory, lavoratory, salvatory, deletory, suppletory, expletory, feretory, decretory, excretory, bibitory, auditory, plauditory, pellitory, olitory, dormitory, fumitory, crinitory, monitory, punitory, territory, transitory, petitory, desultory, inventory, promontory, offertory, repertory, statutory.
5. a fortiori, phantasmagory, memento mori [L.], approbatory, reverbatory, depredatory, commandatory, amendatory, emendatory, commendatory, transudatory, obligatory, fumigatory, derogatory, objurgatory, expurgatory, depreciatory, gladiatory, radiatory, mediatory, palliatory, expiatory, applicatory, explicatory, vesicatory, masticatory, advocatory, revocatory, invocatory, confiscatory, episcatory, manducatory, revelatory, habilatory, depilatory, flagellatory, constellatory, distillatory, condolatory, consolatory, ambulatory, adulatory, stridulatory, undulatory, regulatory, speculatory, circulatory, osculatory, emulatory, simulatory, postulatory, defamatory, acclamatory, declamatory, proclamatory, exclamatory, desquamatory, sublimatory, inflammatory, affirmatory, confirmatory, reformatory, informatory, lachrymatory, explanatory, designatory, criminatory, fulminatory, comminatory, terminatory, divinatory, condemnatory, cachinnatory, inculpatory, declaratory, preparatory, lucubratory, emigratory, immigratory, transmigratory, aspiratory, transpiratory, inspiratory, perspiratory, expiratory, consecratory, execratory, labo-

ratory, exploratory, demonstratory, remonstratory, procuratory, abjuratory, adjuratory, compulsatory, compensatory, dispensatory, accusatory, excusatory, excitatory, invitatory, auscultatory, consultatory, sussultatory, incantatory, dehortatory, exhortatory, refutatory, salutatory, Il Trovatore, observatory, preservatory, conservatory, inhibitory, prohibitory, exhibitory, recognitory, admonitory, premonitory, depository, repository, suppository, expository, competitory, retributory, contributory, executory, involutory.
6. a posteriori, pro patria mori [L.], disapprobatory, elucidatory, recommendatory, delineatory, investigatory, interrogatory, enunciatory, denunciatory, pronunciatory, retaliatory, conciliatory, initiatory, propitiatory, negotiatory, alleviatory, abbreviatory, significatory, purificatory, certificatory, communicatory, reciprocatory, equivocatory, preambulatory, funambulatory, perambulatory, ejaculatory, articulatory, gesticulatory, emasculatory, manipulatory, congratulatory, expostulatory, recriminatory, incriminatory, discriminatory, exterminatory, procrastinatory, anticipatory, emancipatory, reverberatory, exaggeratory, refrigeratory, acceleratory, remuneratory, corroboratory, circumgyratory, circumrotatory, extenuatory, improvisatory, improvvisatore [It.], circumlocutory, interlocutory.
7. supererogatory, reconciliatory.
OR'eez– 2. glories, mores, Tories, stories.
OR'er– 2. borer, gorer, corer, scorer, floorer, snorer, porer, pourer, roarer, soarer, sorer, shorer, storer.
3. adorer, encorer, deplorer, implorer, explorer, ignorer, *outpourer*, restorer.
OR'ij– 2. oarage, shorage, storage.
OR'ik– 2. boric, choric, chloric, roric, psoric.
3. perchloric.
4. hydrochloric.
OR'ing– 2. oaring, boring, choring, goring, coring, scoring, snoring, poring, pouring, roaring, soaring, shoring, storing.
3. adoring, encoring, deploring, imploring, exploring, ignoring, *outpouring*, restoring.
OR'is– 2. Boris, Doris, loris.
3. cantoris.
OR'ist– 2. chorist, florist.
ORJ'er– 2. forger, gorger.
3. disgorger.
ORJ'ing– 2. forging, gorging.
3. engorging, disgorging.
ORJ'ment– 3. engorgement, disgorgement.
OR'less– 2. oarless, oreless, boreless, doorless, goreless, whoreless, coreless, scoreless, loreless, poreless, pourless, sporeless, roarless, soreless, shoreless.
OR'man– 2. doorman, foreman, corpsman, floorman, shoreman, storeman.
3. longshoreman.
OR'ment– 3. adorement, deplorement, im-

plorement, explorement, ignorement, resto-
rement.
ŌRN'ful– 2. scornful, mournful.
ŌRN'ing– 2. scorning, mourning, morning.
   3. a-borning, unscorning, deep mourning.
OR'o– 2. oro [Sp.], Oro, boro, Boro, loro,
moro, Moro, Poro, toro.
   4. aposoro, torotoro.
OR'on– 2. boron, moron,
ŌRS'er– 2. forcer, hoarser, coarser, courser.
   3. enforcer, discourser, divorcer.
ŌRS'est– 2. hoarsest, coarsest.
ŌRS'ful– 2. forceful.
   3. unforceful, resourceful.
   4. unresourceful.
ŌRSH'un– 2. portion.
   3. apportion, proportion.
   4. disproportion; see also ŎRSH'un.
ŌRSH'und– 2. portioned.
   3. apportioned, unportioned, proportioned.
   4. reapportioned, unproportioned, dis-
proportioned.
ŌRS'ing– 2. forcing, coursing.
   3. enforcing, discoursing, divorcing.
   4. reinforcing.
ŌRS'iv– 3. enforcive, discoursive, divorcive.
ŌRS'lee– 2. hoarsely, coarsely.
ŌRS'less– 2. forceless, sourceless.
   3. discourseless, resourceless, divorceless.
ŌRS'ment– 2. forcement.
   3. deforcement, enforcement, divorcement.
   4. reinforcement.
ŌRS'ness– 2. hoarseness, coarseness.
ŌRS'o– 2. dorso, corso [It.], Corso, torso.
ŌRT'ans– 3. comportance, transportance,
supportance.
ŌRT'ed– 2. courted, ported, sported.
   3. deported, reported, imported, disported,
exported, transported, supported.
ŌRT'ee– 2. forty, porty, sporty.
ŌRT'er– 2. courter, porter, sporter.
   3. reporter, importer, exporter, transporter,
supporter.
ŌRT'ing– 2. courting, sporting, Storting.
   3. deporting, reporting, importing, export-
ing, transporting, supporting.
ŌRT'iv– 2. sportive.
   3. disportive, transportive.
ŌRT'lee– 2. courtly, portly.
   3. uncourtly, unportly.
ŌRT'ment– 3. deportment, comportment,
disportment, transportment.
OR'um– 2. forum, jorum [coll.], quorum.
   3. decorum.
   4. indecorum, variorum, cockalorum, pitto-
sporum.
   5. schola cantorum [L.].
OR'us– 2. Horus, chorus, porus, porous,
sorous, torus, torose, torous.
   3. decorous, pelorus, pylorus, canorous,
sonorous, imporous.
   4. indecorous.
OS'a– 2. dosa.
   3. Mendoza, mimosa, Formosa.

4. Mariposa, amorosa [It.].
OS'er– 2. doser, closer, grocer, grosser.
   3. jocoser, engrosser, greengrocer, moroser.
OS'est– 2. closest, grossest.
   3. morosest.
OSH'a– 2. Scotia.
   3. macrotia.
   4. Nova Scotia; see also ŌSH'i–a.
OSH'al– 2. social.
   3. precocial, asocial, dissocial.
   4. antisocial, intersocial.
OSH'er– 2. kosher, clocher.
OSH'un– 2. ocean, Goshen, lotion, motion,
notion, potion, groschen.
   3. Boeotian, nicotian, emotion, demotion,
commotion, promotion, devotion.
   4. braggadocian, locomotion, self-devotion.
OSH'us– 3. precocious, nepotious, ferocious,
atrocious.
OS'ing– 2. dosing, grossing.
   3. engrossing.
OS'is– 2. gnosis, ptosis.
   3. thrombosis, lordosis, morphosis, zygosis,
psychosis, zymosis, osmosis, prognosis, hyp-
nosis, necrosis, morosis, sorosis, neurosis.
   4. psittacosis, ankylosis, cyanosis, diagnosis,
adiposis, hematosis.
   5. pediculosis, tuberculosis.
OS'iv– 3. explosive, erosive, corrosive.
   4. inexplosive, unexplosive.
OS'lee– 2. closely, grossly.
   3. verbosely, jocosely, morosely.
   4. bellicosely.
OS'ness– 2. closeness, grossness.
   3. verboseness, jocoseness, moroseness.
   4. bellicoseness.
OS'o– 2. soso, so-so, mosso [It.].
   3. pomposo [It.], corozo.
   4. arioso, furioso [It.], curioso [It.], gra-
cioso, tremoloso [It.], animoso [It.], lagri-
moso [It.], pensieroso [It.], doloroso [It.],
amoroso, strepitoso [It.], maestoso [It.],
virtuoso.
OST'al– 2. coastal, postal.
   4. intracoastal, intercoastal.
OST'ed– 2. boasted, ghosted, hosted, posted,
roasted, toasted.
   3. enghosted, riposted.
OST'er– 2. boaster, coaster, poster, roaster,
toaster.
   3. four-poster.
   4. roller coaster.
OST'ing– 2. boasting, ghosting, hosting,
coasting, posting, roasting, toasting.
   3. riposting, imposting, retoasting.
OST'lee– 2. ghostly, mostly.
OT'a– 2. cota [Tag.], lota, lotah, Lota, flota,
nota, rota, tota [Amharic], vota, quota.
   3. iota, Dakota, pelota, nonquota.
   4. Minnesota.
OT'al– 2. dotal, notal, rotal, total, votal.
   3. teetotal, sum total, sum-total.
   4. extradotal, antidotal, anecdotal, sacerdotal.
OT'ate– 2. notate, rotate.

3. *annotate.*

OT′ed– 2. boated, doted, coated, bloated, floated, gloated, moated, moted, noted, throated, toted [coll.], voted, quoted.

3. refloated, demoted, promoted, denoted, connoted, unnoted, red-throated, dry-throated, full-throated, deep-throated, devoted, misquoted.

4. petticoated, parti-coated, sugar-coated, unpromoted, ruby-throated, yellow-throated, undevoted.

OT′ee– 2. doty, dhoti, goaty, bloaty, floaty, throaty.

3. coyote.

OT′en– 2. oaten, crotin, croton.

3. verboten [G.].

OT′ent– 2. flotant, potent.

3. prepotent.

4. counterpotent.

OT′er– 2. boater, doter, coater, scoter, bloater, floater, gloater, motor, noter, poter, roter, Soter, toter, voter, quoter.

3. demoter, remoter, promoter, bimotor, trimotor, denoter, devoter, misquoter.

4. locomotor, rotomotor.

OT′est– 2. protest.

3. remotest.

OTH′ful– 2. loathful, slothful, trothful.

OTH′ing– 2. loathing, clothing, trothing.

3. betrothing.

OT′ij– 2. boatage, dotage, floatage, flotage.

4. anecdotage, sacerdotage.

OT′ik– 2. otic, photic, lotic.

3. aphotic, dysphotic, parotic.

OT′ing– 2. boating, doting, coating, bloating, floating, gloating, noting, toting [coll.], voting, quoting.

3. demoting, promoting, denoting, connoting, devoting, misquoting.

4. sugar-coating.

OT′ish– 2. oatish, boatish, dotish, goatish.

OT′ist– 2. scotist, noticed, votist.

3. unnoticed.

4. anecdotist.

OT′iv– 2. floative, motive, votive.

3. emotive, promotive, denotive.

4. locomotive.

5. electromotive.

OT′o– 2. Oto, Otoe, photo, moto [It.], roto, toto.

3. Kioto, De Soto, in toto [L.], divoto, ex voto [L.], ex-voto.

4. Mr. Moto.

OT′um– 2. notum, totum, quotum.

3. pronotum, teetotum, factotum.

OT′us– 2. Otus, lotus, Notus.

3. amotus, macrotous.

OV′a– 2. ova, Ova, nova.

3. Jehovah, korova.

4. Villanova, Casanova.

OV′ee– 2. grovy.

3. anchovy.

OV′en– 2. cloven, woven.

3. uncloven, rewoven, inwoven, unwoven.

4. interwoven.

OV′er– 2. over, Dover, clover, plover, rover, drover, shrover, stover, trover.

3. *walkover*, walk over, *turnover*, sea rover, *pushover*, *leftover*, left over.

OV′ing– 2. coving, roving, shroving, stoving.

OV′o– 2. provo.

3. ab ovo [L.], in ovo [L.].

OV′um– 2. ovum, novum.

3. protovum.

O′yo– 2. coyo, yo-yo.

3. arroyo.

OZ′a– 2. boza, rosa [L.], Rosa.

3. Mendoza, flindosa, Spinoza, sub rosa [L.].

OZ′al– 2. rosal.

3. deposal, reposal, opposal, proposal, disposal, transposal, supposal.

4. interposal, presupposal, predisposal.

OZ′ee– 2. dozy, fozy, Josie, cozy, cosy, mosey, nosy, posy, rosy, prosy, tosy, tozie.

3. tea cozy, egg cozy.

OZ′en– 2. chosen, frozen.

3. unchosen, forechosen, unfrozen.

OZ′er– 2. dozer, hoser, cozer, glozer, closer, noser, poser, roser, proser.

3. *bulldozer*, encloser, incloser, forecloser, discloser, apposer, deposer, reposer, imposer, composer, opposer, proposer, disposer, exposer, transposer, supposer.

4. juxtaposer, decomposer, recomposer, interposer, predisposer, presupposer.

5. superimposer.

OZ′ez– 2. dozes, hoses, cozes, glozes, closes, Moses, noses, poses, roses, proses.

3. *bulldozes*, encloses, incloses, forecloses, discloses, apposes, deposes, reposes, imposes, composes, opposes, proposes, disposes, exposes, transposes, supposes.

4. juxtaposes, decomposes, recomposes, discomposes, interposes, predisposes, indisposes, presupposes.

5. superimposes.

OZH′er– 2. osier, hosier, closure, crosier.

3. enclosure, foreclosure, disclosure, reposure, composure, disposure, exposure.

4. decomposure, discomposure.

5. superimposure.

OZH′un– 3. icosian, applosion, implosion, explosion, ambrosian, erosion, corrosion.

OZ′ing– 2. dozing, hosing, cozing, glozing, closing, nosing, posing, rosing, prosing.

3. *bulldozing*, enclosing, inclosing, foreclosing, disclosing, apposing, deposing, reposing, imposing, composing, opposing, proposing, disposing, exposing, transposing, supposing.

4. juxtaposing, unimposing, decomposing, recomposing, discomposing, interposing, predisposing, indisposing, presupposing.

5. superimposing.

OZ′o– 2. bozo [slang], kozo.

OZ′ure– 2. closure.

3. enclosure, inclosure, foreclosure, disclosure, reposure, composure, disposure, exposure.

4. discomposure.

Ō (oh)

Triple Rhymes

Primary or Secondary Accent Falls on Second from Last Syllable; Imperfect Rhymes Are in Italics.

O'a–bl– **3.** blowable, slowable, mowable, knowable, rowable, throwable, showable, stowable.
4. unknowable, bestowable.
5. overthrowable.
OB'i–a– **3.** obeah, phobia.
4. Zenobia.
5. brontephobia, stasiphobia, toxiphobia, cibophobia, phobophobia, neophobia, theophobia, algophobia, ergophobia, Anglophobia, ochlophobia, Gallophobia, dromophobia, cremnophobia, phonophobia, hypnophobia, cynophobia, zoophobia, topophobia, acrophobia, androphobia, hydrophobia, negrophobia, claustrophobia, pyrophobia, nosophobia, lyssophobia, batophobia, nyctophobia, sitophobia, brontophobia, scotophobia, photophobia.
6. agoraphobia, batrachophobia, cardiophobia, bibliophobia, hagiophobia, Germanophobia, astrapophobia, anthropophobia, aelurophobia, thalassophobia, thanatophobia.
OB'i–an– **4.** Jacobian, cenobian, macrobian, microbian.
OCH'a–bl– **3.** poachable.
4. approachable, reproachable.
5. unapproachable, irreproachable.
OD'al–er– **3.** odaler, yodeler.
OD'i–ak– **3.** Kodiak, nodiak, zodiac.
OD'i–al– **3.** podial.
4. allodial, threnodial, prosodial, custodial.
5. palinodial, episodial.
OD'i–an– **3.** Rhodian.
4. Cambodian, Herodian, prosodian, custodian.
OD'i–on– **4.** Triodion, melodion, melodeon, collodion.
5. nickelodeon.
OD'i–um– **3.** odium, podium, rhodium, sodium.
4. allodium, taxodium.
OD'i–us– **3.** odious.
4. melodious, commodious.

5. unmelodious, incommodious, discommodious.
OG'i–zm– **3.** bogyism, fogyism.
O'ik–al– **3.** stoical.
4. heroical, unstoical.
5. unheroical.
O'il–ee– **3.** snowily, showily.
O'ing–lee– **3.** flowingly, glowingly, knowingly, crowingly.
4. unknowingly.
OJ'i–a– **3.** loggia.
4. alogia, dyslogia.
5. apologia.
OJ'i–an– **4.** gambogian.
5. geologian, neologian, theologian, philologian, astrologian, mythologian.
6. archaeologian.
OK'a–bl– **3.** smokable, vocable.
4. unsmokable, invocable.
5. uninvocable.
OK'al–ee– **3.** focally, locally, vocally.
OK'al–ist– **3.** localist, vocalist.
OK'al–ize– **3.** focalize, localize, vocalize.
OK'al–izm– **3.** localism, vocalism.
OK'en–lee– **3.** brokenly.
4. outspokenly.
OK'i–er– **3.** oakier, chokier, smokier, pokier, croakier, soakier, yolkier.
OK'i–ness– **3.** oakiness, chokiness, smokiness, pokiness, croakiness, soakiness, yolkiness.
OK'ing–lee– **3.** chokingly, jokingly, croakingly, strokingly, soakingly.
4. provokingly.
OK'less–lee– **3.** jokelessly, smokelessly.
OKS'ing–lee– **3.** hoaxingly, coaxingly.
OK'us–ing– **3.** focusing, hocusing.
OK'us–less– **3.** focusless, hocusless, locusless, crocusless.
OL'a–bl– **3.** bowlable, goalable, holable, pollable, rollable, tollable.
4. unbowlable, ungoalable, unholable, controllable, consolable.
5. uncontrollable, unconsolable, inconsolable.

283

OL'a–blee– 4. controllably, consolably.
5. uncontrollably, unconsolably, inconsolably.

OL'ar–ize– 3. polarize, solarize.
4. depolarize.

OLD'a–bl– 3. foldable, scoldable, moldable.
4. unfoldable, unscoldable.

OL'er–ee– 3. drollery, bolary, molary, polary, solary.
4. cajolery.
5. rigmarolery.

OL'e–um– 3. oleum.
4. linoleum, petroleum, crystoleum; *see also* **ŌL'i–um.**

OL'ful–ness– 3. dolefulness, soulfulness.

OL'i–a– 4. Mongolia, magnolia, Aetolia.
5. melancholia.

OL'i–an– 4. Aeolian, Mongolian, simoleon [slang], Napoleon, Aetolian, Pactolian.
5. metabolian, Anatolian, Capitolian.

OL'i–ate– 3. foliate, spoliate.
4. defoliate, infoliate.

OL'i–er– 3. holier, lowlier, Grolier.
4. unholier.

OL'i–est– 3. holiest, lowliest.
4. unholiest.

OL'i–ness– 3. holiness, lowliness, shoaliness.
4. unholiness.

OL'ing–lee– 4. condolingly, cajolingly, consolingly, extollingly.

OL'i–o– 3. oleo, olio, folio, roleo.
4. portfolio.

OL'i–um– 3. oleum, folium, scholium.
4. trifolium, linoleum, arolium, petroleum, crystoleum.
5. Capitolium.

OL'o–ist– 3. poloist, soloist.

OLST'er–er– 3. bolsterer.
4. upholsterer.

OM'at–izm– 3. chromatism.
4. achromatism, diplomatism.

OM'i–al– 3. nomial, tomial.
4. binomial, monomial.

OM'i–er– 3. domier, foamier, homier, loamier.

OM'i–est– 3. domiest, foamiest, homiest, loamiest.

OM'i–ness– 3. dominess, foaminess, hominess, loaminess.

OM'ing–lee– 3. foamingly, homingly, gloamingly, roamingly.

OM'i–o– 3. Romeo, Dromio.

OM'i–um– 3. chromium, tomium.
4. encomium.
5. nosocomium.

OM'luv–ing– 3. homeloving, chromeloving.

ON'a–bl– 3. ownable, bonable, phonable, honable, loanable, thronable, tonable, zonable.
4. condonable, atonable.
5. unatonable.

ON'i–a– 4. Adonia, aphonia, begonia, Ionia, bryonia, Laconia, Franconia, Slavonia, valonia, ammonia, Harmonia, pneumonia, asonia, Ausonia, Antonia.
5. Caledonia, Macedonia, Patagonia.

ON'i–al– 3. monial.
4. colonial, demonial, harmonial, baronial.
5. ceremonial, matrimonial, patrimonial, sanctimonial, testimonial.
6. intercolonial.

ON'i–an– 4. aeonian, Gorgonian, Ionian, Baconian, Lincolnian, chelonian, demonian, Simonian, Byronian, Oxonian, Wilsonian, Johnsonian, Smithsonian, Ausonian, Shoshonean, Platonian, Etonian, Miltonian, Estonian, Bostonian, Plutonian, favonian, pavonian, bezonian.
5. Caledonian, Macedonian, halcyonian, Patagonian, Thessalonian, Babylonian, Ciceronian, Jeffersonian, Washingtonian, Amazonian.

ON'i–er– 3. bonier, phonier [slang], dronier, tonier [vulgar], stonier.

ON'i–est– 3. boniest, phoniest [slang], toniest [vulgar], stoniest.

ON'i–um– 4. euphonium, agonium, polonium, stramonium, ammonium, harmonium, Plutonium.
5. sporogonium, pelargonium, pandemonium, testimonium.

ON'i–us– 4. euphonious, symphonious, felonious, Polonius, harmonious, erroneous, ultroneous, Antonius.
5. ceremonious, querimonious, acrimonious, matrimonious, parsimonious, sanctimonious, inharmonious.
6. unceremonious, unsanctimonious.

O'o–lite– 3. oolite, zoolite.

OP'i–a– 3. topia.
4. myopia, Utopia.
5. Ethiopia, presbyopia, cornucopia, nyctalopia.

OP'i–an– 4. Aesopian, Utopian.
5. Ethiopian, cornucopian.

OP'i–ness– 3. dopiness, ropiness, soapiness.

OP'ish–ness– 3. mopishness, popishness.

OR'a–bl– through **OR'us–lee–** *see also* **Ŏ: ŎR'ak–l** through **ŎRT'un–it; Ô: ÔR'e– ate, ÔR'i–an.**

OR'a–bl– 3. soarable, storable.
4. adorable, deplorable, explorable, restorable.

OR'a–blee– 4. adorably, deplorably.

OR'al–ee– 3. orally, florally.

OR'at–iv– 4. explorative, restorative.

OR'e–al– 3. boreal.
4. arboreal, phosphoreal, marmoreal, corporeal, aequoreal.
5. bicorporeal, incorporeal; *see also* **ŌR'i–al.**

OR'e–an– 4. roborean, marmorean, aurorean, Hectorean; *see also* **ŌR'i–an.**

OR'i–a– 3. doria, scoria, Gloria, noria.
4. Peoria, theoria, euphoria, dysphoria, memoria, emporia, Pretoria, Victoria, Astoria.
5. Infusoria.
6. phantasmagoria, Waldorf Astoria.

OR'i–al– 3. boreal.
4. arboreal, phosphoreal, marmoreal, corporeal, aequoreal, enchorial, Escorial, memo-

rial, armorial, manorial, rasorial, risorial, uxorial, scansorial, censorial, sensorial, sponsorial, tonsorial, rosorial, cursorial, gressorial, fossorial, praetorial, factorial, rectorial, sectorial, tectorial, vectorial, pictorial, tinctorial, doctorial, proctorial, auctorial, cantorial, raptorial, scriptorial, sartorial, quaestorial, haustorial, sutorial, tutorial, textorial, authorial.

5. bicorporeal, incorporeal, immemorial, responsorial, insessorial, dismissorial, purgatorial, piscatorial, grallatorial, amatorial, senatorial, oratorial, curatorial, natatorial, spectatorial, dictatorial, saltatorial, reptatorial, gestatorial, equatorial, prefectorial, electorial, inspectorial, directorial, editorial, territorial, sussultorial, inventorial, preceptorial, repertorial, assertorial, consistorial.

6. ambassadorial, phantasmagorial, expurgatorial, gladiatorial, mediatorial, legislatorial, gubernatorial, conspiratorial, visitatorial, observatorial, proprietorial, exterritorial, inquisitorial, executorial.

7. extraterritorial.

OR′i–an– 3. Dorian.
4. roborean, Gregorian, marmorean, aurorean, praetorian, Hectorean, Victorian, stentorian, Nestorian, historian.
5. hyperborean, purgatorian, amatorian, senatorian, oratorian, mid-Victorian.
6. salutatorian, valedictorian.

OR′i–ate– 3. floriate, storiate.
4. excoriate.
5. professoriate.

OR′i–fi– 3. scorify, glorify, storify.

OR′i–ness– 3. goriness, hoariness, poriness.
5. dilatoriness, desultoriness, peremptoriness.

OR′i–ole– 3. oriole, gloriole.

OR′i–um– 3. corium, thorium.
4. ciborium, triforium, emporium, sensorium, praetorium, scriptorium, pastorium, haustorium.
5. sudatorium, crematorium, fumatorium, sanatorium, moratorium, natatorium, auditorium, digitorium.

OR′i–us– 3. scorious, Lorius, glorious.
4. laborious, arboreous, inglorious, vainglorious, unglorious, uproarious, uxorious, censorious, victorious, stentorious, notorious, sartorius.
5. accessorius, amatorious, saltatorious, meritorious.

ORS′a–bl– 3. forceable, forcible.
4. enforceable, divorceable.
5. unenforceable, undivorceable.

ORT′a–bl– 3. courtable, portable.
4. deportable, reportable, importable, exportable, transportable, supportable.
5. insupportable.

ORT′li–ness– 3. courtliness, portliness.
4. uncourtliness.

OR′us–lee– 3. porously.
4. decorously, sonorously.

OSH′a–bl– 3. sociable.

4. negotiable, dissociable, unsociable.

OSH′i–a– 4. nicotia, anotia, macrotia, microtia; *see also* **ŌSH′a.**

OSH′i–an– 4. Boeotian, nicotian.
5. braggadocian.

OSH′i–ant– 3. otiant.
4. negotiant, dissociant.

OSH′i–ate– 4. negotiate, associate, dissociate, consociate.

OSH′un–al– 3. motional, notional.
4. emotional, commotional, promotional, devotional.
5. unemotional, nondevotional, undevotional.

OSH′us–lee– 4. precociously, ferociously, atrociously.

OSH′us–ness– 4. precociousness, ferociousness, atrociousness.

OS′iv–lee– 4. explosively, erosively, corrosively.
5. inexplosively.

OS′iv–ness– 4. explosiveness, erosiveness, corrosiveness.

OST′ful–ee– 3. boastfully, ghostfully.

OST′ing–lee– 3. boastingly, coastingly, roastingly, toastingly.

OST′li–ness– 3. ghostliness, hostliness.

OT′a–bl– 3. floatable, notable, potable, votable, quotable.
4. unfloatable, denotable, unquotable.

OT′ab–lee– 3. notably, quotably.

OT′al–er– 3. totaler.
4. teetotaler.

OT′al–izm– 4. teetotalism.
5. sacerdotalism.

OT′ar–ee– 3. coterie, notary, rotary, votary.

OT′at–iv– 3. flotative, rotative.
4. denotative, connotative.

OT′ed–lee– 3. bloatedly, notedly.
4. sweet-throatedly, devotedly.

OT′er–ee– 3. coterie, notary, rotary, votary.

OT′ing–lee– 3. dotingly, bloatingly, gloatingly, quotingly.

OT′iv–lee– 3. votively.
4. emotively.

OV′en–lee– 3. clovenly, wovenly.
5. interwovenly.

OV′i–a– 3. fovea.
4. synovia, Monrovia.

OV′i–al– 3. foveal, jovial.
4. unjovial, synovial.

OZ′a–bl– 4. deposable, imposable, opposable, disposable, transposable, supposable.
5. decomposable, indisposable, untransposable.

OZH′er–ee– 3. osiery, hosiery.

OZH′i–a– 4. symposia, ambrosia.

OZ′i–er– 3. dozier, cozier, moseyer, nosier, rosier, prosier.

OZ′i–est– 3. doziest, coziest, nosiest, rosiest, prosiest.

OZ′il–ee– 3. dozily, cozily, nosily, rosily, prosily.

OZ′i–ness– 3. doziness, foziness, coziness, nosiness, rosiness, prosiness.

Ŏ (bob)

[See also Ä, Ô.]

Single (Masculine) Rhymes

Primary or Secondary Accent Falls on Last Syllable; Imperfect Rhymes Are in Italics.

OB– **1.** ob, bob, fob, gob, hob, job, kob, cob, Cobb, scob [Scot., N. Eng. & Ir.], lob, blob, glob [slang], slob, mob, nob, knob, snob, rob, brob, throb, sob, stob, thob [slang], wob [slang].
2. cabob, kabob, kebob, *nabob, earbob, corncob, hoblob, hobnob, carob,* athrob.
3. thingabob, thingumbob.
4. thingamabob, thingumabob.
OBZ– see **ŎB**, plus " s " or " 's "; **1.** Dobbs, Hobbs.
OCH– **1.** botch, gotch, hotch [slang], cotch, scotch, Scotch, blotch, splotch, notch, rotch, crotch.
2. *hopscotch, hotchpotch.*
OCHT– **1.** botched, gotched, scotched, blotched, splotched, notched, crotched.
OD– **1.** odd, God, hod, cod, clod, plod, nod, pod, rod, scrod, prod, trod, sod, shod, tod, Todd, wod, quod [slang].
2. *tomcod, Nimrod, Penrod,* roughshod, unshod, *slipshod,* per quod [L.].
3. Ichabod, demigod, goldenrod.
ODZ– see **ŎD**, plus " s " or " 's "; **1.** Dodds.
OF– **1.** off, doff, goff, coff [slang], cough, koff, scoff, prof [slang], shroff, trough, soph [slang], toff [slang].
2. *play-off, kickoff, runoff, throwoff, setoff, castoff, chincough, Kharkov, Orloff,* Krushchev, Azov.
3. whooping cough, philosoph, Molotov.
4. bibliosoph.
OFT– **1.** oft, doffed, coughed, scoffed, loft, croft, soft, toft, woft [Scot.].
2. aloft, *hayloft.*
OG– **1.** Og, bog, dog, fog, gog, Gog, hog, jog, cog, log, blog [slang], flog, glogg, clog, slog, mog [slang], smog, nog, brog, frog, grog, sogg [slang], tog, wog.
2. embog, *watchdog, bird-dog, bulldog, firedog,* befog, agog, *Magog, sand hog, seahog, hedgehog, quahog, shearhog, backlog, putlog,* eggnog, *crannog, bullfrog, leapfrog,* tautog

3. underdog, prairie dog, megafog, pettifog, pedagogue, demagogue, Gogmagog, xenagogue, synagogue, hydragogue, mystagogue, logogogue, Tagalog, Decalogue, dialogue, trialogue, grammalogue, analogue, catalogue, theologue, melologue, homologue, Sinologue, monologue, apologue, necrologue, horologue, duologue, Dannebrog, golliwog, polliwog.
OGD– **1.** bogged, dogged, hogged, jogged, cogged, logged, flogged, clogged, slogged, sogged [slang], togged.
2. embogged, *bird-dogged,* befogged, *leapfrogged.*
3. pettifogged, catalogued, waterlogged.
OJ– **1.** bodge, dodge, lodge, podge, stodge, wodge.
2. unlodge, horloge, dislodge, *hodgepodge.*
3. horologe.
OJD– **1.** bodged, dodged, lodged, stodged.
2. unlodged, dislodged.
OK– **1.** bock, choc [slang], chock, doc [slang], dock, hock, Jock, jock [slang], cock, lock, loch, block, flock, clock, mock, smock, knock, pock, rock, roc, frock, crock, sock, shock, tock, stock, yock [slang], yok [slang].
2. *rhebok, klipbok, blesbok,* ad hoc [L.], acock, *woodcock, peacock, Hancock,* Bangkok, *padlock, deadlock, wedlock, Shylock, picklock, hemlock,* unlock, *gunlock, rowlock, oarlock, forelock, Sherlock, fetlock, flintlock, wristlock,* unblock, *bedrock,* unfrock, *traprock, ticktock,* restock, unstock, *livestock.*
3. bontebok, hollyhock, Antioch, poppycock, shuttlecock, weathercock, chockablock, stumbling block, fetterlock, interlock, Little Rock, laughingstock, alpenstock, understock, overstock.
4. tickety-tock, Vladivostok.
OKS– see **ŎK**, plus " s " or " 's "; **1.** ox, box, fox, cox, phlox, Nox, Knox, pox, vox.
2. abox, *bandbox, sandbox, snuffbox, strongbox, workbox, jukebox, mailbox, pillbox, hatbox,*

saltbox, *princox*, Coxcox, *smallpox*.
3. chatterbox, paradox, philodox, homodox, orthodox, Goldilocks, equinox, chicken pox.
4. heterodox, unorthodox.
ŎKT– 1. docked, hocked, cocked, locked, blocked, flocked, clocked, smocked, knocked, pocked, rocked, frocked, crocked, socked, shocked, stocked, yocked [slang], yokked [slang].
2. decoct, concoct, uncocked, unlocked, unblocked, unfrocked, unstocked.
OL– 1. doll, gol [slang], col, coll, loll, moll, pol, poll, Poll, Sol.
2. *atoll*, extol.
3. alcohol, protocol, folderol, parasol, girasol, entresol.
OLD– 1. dolled, lolled, polled.
OLF– 1. golf.
2. Adolphe, *Rudolph*.
OLV– 1. solve.
2. absolve, resolve, dissolve, evolve, devolve, revolve, involve.
3. circumvolve, disinvolve, intervolve.
OLVD– 1. solved.
2. absolved, resolved, dissolved, evolved, devolved, revolved, involved.
3. circumvolved, disinvolved, intervolved.
OM– 1. bomb, chom [slang], dom, domn, glom [slang], mom, pom, rhomb, from, prom [slang], Tom.
2. geom [slang], aplomb, coulomb, Bonhomme, *pompom*, therefrom, wherefrom, *pogrom*.
3. axiom, hecatomb.
OMB– 1. rhomb, stromb.
OMD– 1. bombed, glommed [slang], pommed.
OMP– 1. comp [slang], pomp, romp, tromp [dial], trompe, stomp, womp, whomp.
OMPT– 1. compt, romped, prompt, tromped [dial.], stomped, whomped.
ON– 1. on, bon, bonne [F.], don, Don, gone, John, john [slang], con, mon [Scot.], non [L.], shone, yon.
2. hereon, thereon, whereon, *bonbon*, chiffon, begone, *bygone*, *foregone*, *Yukon*, salon, Ceylon, anon, upon, Tucson, baton, cretonne, Yvonne, chignon, Luzon.
3. hanger-on, hangers-on, Audubon, Celadon, chelidon, myrmidon, Corydon, mastodon, galleon, pantheon, halcyon, colophon, Xenophon, nonagon, tarragon, tetragon, hexagon, octagon, pentagon, protagon, heptagon, martagon, woebegone, Oregon, polygon, perigon, oxygon, isogon, undergone, gabion, Albion, demijohn, Little John, Prester John, Rubicon, Helicon, silicon, lexicon, opticon, gonfalon, petalon, Avalon, echelon, Babylon, Pergamon, gonfanon, organon, xoanon, tympanon, noumenon, Parthenon, abipón, hereupon, thereupon, whereupon, fanfaron, megaron, Oberon, pentacron, Omicron, orison, Alençon, cabochon, phaeton, trilithon, ornithon, Amazon, cabezon, liaison, Barbizon.

4. melodeon, melodion, Napoleon, Anacreon, amphibion, Endymion, Hyperion, oblivion, alluvion, harmoniphon, melodicon, catholicon, eirenicon, irenicon, harmonicon, panopticon, Laocoon, hyperbaton, automaton.
5. synonymicon, stereopticon.
6. etymologicon.
OND– 1. bond, donned, fond, conned, blond, blonde, mond, pond, ronde, frond, sond [dial.], yond.
2. abscond, despond, respond, beyond.
3. vagabond, overfond, correspond.
ONG– 1. bong, dong, gong, long, flong, pong, rong [dial.], wrong, prong, strong, throng, song, tong, thong, wong.
2. Souchong, *dingdong*, mah-jongg, Hong Kong, along, *daylong*, *headlong*, belong, *lifelong*, prolong, erelong, *nightlong*, *pingpong*, sarong, *headstrong*, *singsong*, paktong, *quantong*, *diphthong*, *triphthong*, payong.
3. billabong, underfong, kurrajong, overlong, scuppernong, morningsong, evensong, undersong, aftersong.
ONK– 1. honk, conk, konk, conch, Lonk, bronc [slang], cronk, tonk, wonk, quonk, squonk [all slang].
2. triconch.
3. honky-tonk.
ONKS– *see* **ŎNK**, plus " s " or " 's "; **1.** Bronx.
ONKT– 1. honked, conked, cronked, tonked.
ONS– 1. bonce, sconce, nonce.
2. ensconce, response, patonce.
ONT– 1. font, pont, wont.
2. Vermont, Dupont.
3. Hellespont.
ONZ– 1. bonze, dons, Dons, fons, Johns, johns [slang], cons, mon's [Scot.], pons [L.], bronze.
2. *bonbons*, *bygones*, salons, batons, cretonnes, chignons.
3. myrmidons, mastodons, galleons, pantheons, colophons, nonagons, tetragons, octagons, pentagons, protagons, heptagons, martagons, hexagons, polygons, perigons, oxygons, isogons, gabions, demijohns, lexicons, opticons, gonfalons, echelons, gonfanons, organons, tympanons, fanfarons, orisons, cabochons, phaetons, ornithons, cabezons, liaisons.
4. melodeons, melodions, Napoleons, amphibions, alluvions, harmoniphons, melodicons, catholicons, eirenicons, irenicons, panopticons, hyperbatons, automatons.
5. synonymicons, stereopticons.
6. etymologicons.
OP– 1. op [slang], bop [slang], chop, dop, fop, hop, cop, lop, flop, plop, slop, mop, knop, pop, drop, crop, prop, strop, sop, shop, top, stop, wop, swap, quop, whop.
2. alop, *flip-flop*, *clip-clop*, aslop, *slipslop*, raindrop, *snowdrop*, teardrop, eavesdrop, *dewdrop*, outcrop, unprop, asop, *milksop*, *soursop*, *sweetsop*, *workshop*, *pawnshop*, *redtop*, *tiptop*, *foretop*, estop, *backstop*, nonstop, *shortstop*.

3. soda pop, lollipop, underprop, overtop.
4. flippety-flop, clippety-clop.
OPS– *see* **ŎP**, plus " s " or " 's "; **1.** copse.
OPT– 1. opt, bopped [slang], chopped, dopped, hopped, copped, lopped, flopped, plopped, slopped, mopped, popped, dropped, cropped, propped, stropped, sopped, shopped, topped, stopped, swapped, quopped, whopped.
2. adopt, *flip-flopped, clip-clopped, slipslopped, eaversdropped*, outcropped, unpropped, estopped, *backstopped*.
3. underpropped, overtopped.
4. flippety-flopped, clippety-clopped.
OPTS– 1. opts.
2. adopts.
OR– through **ORZ–** *see also* **Ō: ŌR** through **ŌRZ; Ô: ÔR, ÔRD.**
OR– 1. or, dor, for, cor, nor, tor, Thor, war.
2. Côte d'Or, *whyfor, wherefor*, abhor, décor [F.], Alcor, señor [Sp.], rapport [F.].
3. picador, Labrador, mirador, comprador, matador, cantador [Sp.], Ecuador, meteor, biophor, pastophor, mortgagor, chancellor, counselor, councillor, Eleanor, alienor, bargainor, en rapport [F.], conqueror, emperor, promisor, senator, tug of war, man of war.
4. capeador [Sp.], toreador, conquistador, Corregidor, heliodor, excelsior, recoveror, ichthyosaur, megalosaur.
ORB– 1. orb, sorb.
2. inorb, absorb, resorb, disorb.
ORCH– 1. scorch, porch, torch.
ORD– 1. board, bored, bord, cord, chord, lord, warred, ward, sward, fiord.
2. afford, abhorred, accord, *whipcord, discord, landlord*, belord, milord, award, reward, *greensward*.
3. unaccord, disaccord, octachord, polychord, lyrichord, harpsichord, clavichord, overlord.
4. harmonichord, misericord.
ORF– 1. corf, morph [slang], dwarf, swarf, wharf.
3. Dusseldorf.
ORG– 1. orgue, org [slang], borg, morgue.
3. Swedenborg.
ORJ– 1. forge, gorge, George, corge.
2. regorge, engorge, disgorge.
3. disengorge, overgorge.
ORK– 1. orc, fork, cork, Cork, corke, torque, stork, York.
2. *pitchfork*, New York.
ORKT– 1. forked, corked, torqued.
ORL– 1. orle, shorl, schorl, whorl.
ORM– 1. dorm, form, norm, storm, warm, swarm.
2. deform, reform, inform, conform, perform, misform, transform, bestorm, *barnstorm*, rewarm, lukewarm.
3. stelliform, uniform, aeriform, floriform, cruciform, multiform, misinform, chloroform, thunderstorm.
4. trapeziform.

ORMD– 1. formed, stormed, warmed, swarmed.
2. deformed, reformed, well-formed, ill-formed, informed, conformed, performed, misformed, transformed, bestormed, *barnstormed*, rewarmed, unwarmed.
3. unreformed, well-informed, uninformed, misinformed, chloroformed.
ORN– 1. born, dorn, horn, corn, scorn, lorn, morn, Norn, shorn, torn, thorn, worn, sworn.
2. suborn, reborn, *freeborn, highborn*, inborn, unborn, *lowborn, first-born, newborn, trueborn*, adorn, French horn, dehorn, *staghorn, bighorn, Longhorn, pronghorn, foghorn, greenhorn, shorthorn, shoehorn, popcorn*, forlorn, lovelorn, midmorn, untorn, *buckthorn, hawthorn*, rewarn, forewarn.
3. readorn, unadorn, Matterhorn, barleycorn, peppercorn, yestermorn.
ORND– 1. borned [dial.], horned, corned, scorned.
2. suborned, adorned, dehorned, rewarned, unwarned, forewarned.
ORP– 1. dorp, gorp [slang], torp [slang], thorp, warp.
2. moldwarp.
3. Oglethorpe.
ORPS– 1. corpse, warps.
2. moldwarps.
3. Oglethorpes.
ORS– 1. gorse, horse, corse, Morse, Norse, torse.
2. endorse, sea horse, unhorse, remorse, retrorse, introrse, extrorse, dextrorse.
3. rocking horse, hobbyhorse, Charley horse, sinistrorse.
ORT– 1. ort, bort, fort, mort, snort, sort, short, tort, wart, quart, swart, thwart.
2. abort, dehort, exhort, escort, amort, assort, resort, consort, retort, intort, contort, distort, extort, cavort, athwart.
ORTH– 1. morth, north, swarth, Jorth.
2. *commorth*.
ORTS– *see* **ŌRT**, plus " s " or " 's "; **1.** quartz.
2. biquartz, rose quartz.
ORZ– *see* **ŌR**, plus " s " or " 's "; **2.** quatorze.
4. Louis Quatorze.
OS– 1. os, Boss, boss, doss, fosse, joss, loss, floss, gloss, moss, ross, Ross, dross, cross, sauce, soss, toss, stoss.
2. emboss, *vanfoss*, kaross, across, lacrosse, recross, incross, *crisscross, christcross, ringtoss*.
3. double-cross, albatross, applesauce.
4. rhinoceros.
OSH– 1. bosh, bosch, Boche, gosh, josh, losh, slosh, posh [slang], sposh [slang], frosh [slang], sosh, tosh, wash, swash, quash, squash.
2. *kibosh*, galosh, awash, bewash, rewash, *hogwash, eyewash, siwash, backwash, wishwash, whitewash, musquash*.
3. mackintosh.
OSK– 1. bosk, Bosc, mosque.

2. kiosk, imbosk.
3. abelmosk.
OSP– 1. hosp [slang], knosp, wasp.
3. galliwasp.
OST– 1. bossed, dossed, fossed, cost, lost, glossed, mossed, frost, crossed, tossed.
2. cabossed, embossed, imbost, accost, enmossed, defrost, *hoarfrost*, recrossed, uncrossed, *crisscrossed*, betossed.
3. Pentecost, double-crossed, anagnost, geognost.
4. bibliognost.
OT– 1. bot [slang], bott, dot, got, ghat, hot, jot, cot, Scot, Scott, lot, Lot, blot, clot, plot, slot, mot, knot, not, snot [slang], pot, pott, spot, rot, trot, sot, shot, shott, tot, stot, watt, wot, swat, squat, what, yacht.
2. *abbot, Cabot, robot*, begot, forgot, *spigot, ingot, argot, Margot, ergot, eyot, ryot, riot, Sciot*, cocotte, *plumcot, mascot, wainscot, dovecot*, allot, shallot, *Helot, zealot, pilot, simblot, diglot, billot, tillot*, complot, culotte, *motmot*, cannot, unknot, *topknot, slipknot, love knot, whatnot*, repot, *teapot, crackpot, skilpot, trampot, despot*,

tosspot, fleshpot, sunspot, garrot, garrote, *parrot, hilltrot*, besot, *bloodshot, foreshot, slingshot, buckshot, gunshot, snapshot, hipshot, upshot, earshot, grapeshot, bowshot, potshot, forethought*, gavotte, *kumquat*, loquat, asquat.
3. larigot, unforgot, peridot, idiot, galiot, chariot, heriot, patriot, cheviot, haricot, apricot, persicot, cachalot, Lancelot, ocelot, hexaglot, pentaglot, heptaglot, polyglot, matalotte, counterplot, sans-culotte, bergamot, guillemot, Huguenot, flowerpot, coffeepot, galipot, talipot, tommyrot, overshot, Hottentot, aliquot.
4. forget-me-not, Iscariot.
5. witenagemot.
OTH– 1. Goth, cloth, moth, broth, froth, troth, swath.
2. *breecheloth, broadcloth, sackcloth, oilcloth, loincloth*, betroth.
3. Visigoth, Ostrogoth, saddlecloth, behemoth.
OX– *see* **ŎKS.**
OZ– 1. oz [slang], Oz, Boz.
OZM– *see* **ŎZ′m.**

Ŏ (bob)

[See also Ä, Ô.]

Double (Feminine) Rhymes

Primary or Secondary Accent Falls on Next to Last Syllable; Imperfect Rhymes Are in Italics.

OB′ee– 2. bobby, dobby, gobby, hobby, cobby, scobby, lobby, mobby, nobby, knobby, snobby.

OB′er– 2. jobber, cobber, lobber, blobber, slobber, knobber, snobber, robber, throbber, sobber.
3. beslobber.

OB′in– 2. bobbin, dobbin, robbin, robin, Robin.
3. round robin.

OB′ing– 2. bobbing, jobbing, cobbing, lobbing, mobbing, snobbing, robbing, throbbing, sobbing.
3. hobnobbing.

OB′ish– 2. bobbish, lobbish, mobbish, snobbish, squabbish.

OB′l– 2. gobble, hobble, cobble, nobble, wobble, squabble.

OB′lee– 2. obley, hobbly, cobbly, knobbly, wobbly.

OB′ler– 2. gobbler, hobbler, cobbler, nobbler, wobbler, squabbler.
4. turkey gobbler, cherry cobbler.

OB′lin– 2. goblin.
3. hobgoblin.

OB′ling– 2. gobbling, hobbling, cobbling, knobbling, snobling, wobbling, squabbling.

OB′ule– 2. lobule, globule.

OCH′ee– 2. botchy, Scotchy, blotchy, splotchy, notchy, crotchy.

OCH′er– 2. botcher, scotcher, notcher, splotcher.
3. topnotcher, *hopscotcher*.

OCH′ing– 2. botching, cotching, scotching, blotching, splotching, notching, crotching.
3. *hopscotching*.

OD′ed– 2. plodded, nodded, podded, prodded, sodded.

OD′ee– 2. body, hoddy, cloddy, noddy, poddy, soddy, shoddy, toddy, wadi, waddy, squaddy.
3. embody, *somebody*, *nobody*, dog's body.
4. anybody, everybody, busybody, antibody, disembody, hoddy-doddy [dial.],

coddy-moddy [loc. Eng.].

OD′eed– 2. bodied, toddied.
3. embodied, unbodied.
4. ablebodied, unembodied.

OD′en– 2. hodden, trodden, sodden.
3. introdden, downtrodden, untrodden.

OD′er– 2. odder, dodder, fodder, nodder, plodder, prodder, solder.
3. Cape Codder.

OD′ess– 2. bodice, goddess.
4. demigoddess.

OD′est– 2. oddest, modest.
3. immodest, unmodest.
4. supermodest.

OD′ik– 2. odic.
3. geodic, iodic, melodic, spasmodic, anodic, threnodic, synodic, epodic, rhapsodic, methodic.
4. periodic, unmelodic, hellanodic, episodic, kinesodic.

OD′ing– 2. codding, plodding, nodding, podding, prodding, sodding.

OD′is– 2. bodice, goddess.

OD′ish– 2. oddish, coddish, cloddish, noddish, poddish.

OD′l– 2. coddle, model, noddle, toddle.
3. remodel.
4. mollycoddle.

OD′ld– 2. coddled, modeled, toddled.
3. remodeled.
4. mollycoddled.

OD′lee– 2. oddly, Bodley, godly, coddly, toddly.

OD′ler– 2. coddler, toddler.
4. mollycoddler.

OD′ling– 2. godling, codling, coddling, modeling, toddling.
4. mollycoddling.

OF′ee– 2. coffee, toffee, toffy.

OF′er– 2. offer, doffer, goffer, coffer, scoffer, proffer.

OF′et– 2. prophet, profit, soffit.
3. archprophet.

290

4. weather prophet.
OF'ik– 2. ophic, trophic, strophic.
3. atrophic, jatrophic.
4. hypertrophic, catastrophic, antistrophic, apostrophic, theosophic, philosophic.
5. unphilosophic.
OF'in– 2. Boffin [Dickens], coffin.
3. encoffin.
OF'ing– 2. offing, doffing, scoffing.
OF'ish– 2. offish, spoffish.
3. standoffish.
OF'it– 2. prophet, profit, soffit.
OF'l– 2. offal, coffle.
OF'n– 2. often, soften.
OF'ner– 2. oftener, softener.
OFT'ee– 2. lofty, softy.
3. toplofty.
OFT'er– 2. lofter, crofter, softer.
OG'an– 2. goggan, moggan.
3. toboggan.
4. pogamoggan.
OG'ee– 2. boggy, doggy, foggy, joggy, loggy, cloggy, moggy, smoggy, poggy, froggy, groggy.
OG'er– 2. dogger, hogger, jogger, cogger, logger, flogger, clogger, slogger, togger.
3. befogger, whole-hogger.
4. pettifogger.
OG'in– 2. loggin, noggin.
OG'ing– 2. bogging, dogging, fogging, hogging, jogging, cogging, logging, flogging, clogging, slogging, frogging.
3. befogging, prologuing.
4. cataloguing, epiloguing.
OG'ish– 2. doggish, hoggish, froggish.
OG'l– 2. boggle, goggle, joggle, coggle, toggle.
3. *boondoggle* [slang].
OG'ler– 2. boggler, goggler, joggler.
OG'let– 2. boglet, loglet, froglet.
OG'ling– 2. boggling, goggling, joggling.
3. *boondoggling* [slang].
OJ'ee– 2. dodgy, podgy, stodgy.
4. pedagogy, demagogy.
OJ'er– 2. bodger, dodger, codger, lodger, podger, Roger, stodger.
3. corndodger, dislodger.
OJ'ez– *see* ŎJ, plus " s " or " 's ".
OJ'ik– 2. logic.
3. agogic, choplogic, eulogic.
4. pedagogic, psychagogic, demagogic, anagogic, hypnagogic, epagogic, paragogic, isagogic, mystagogic, dialogic, catalogic, metalogic, geologic, neologic, biologic, psychologic, philologic, homologic, cosmologic, penologic, chronologic, hypnologic, ethnologic, zoologic, hydrologic, agrologic, acrologic, necrologic, micrologic, astrologic, ontologic, tautologic, phytologic, cytologic, histologic, pathologic, ethologic, mythologic.
5. mineralogic, archaeologic, hagiologic, physiologic, sociologic, lexicologic, toxicologic, etymologic, entomologic, anthropologic.
6. meteorologic.

OJ'iks– 4. pedagogics, anagogics, theologics.
OJ'ing– 2. dodging, lodging.
3. unlodging, dislodging.
OK'a– 2. bocca, rocca [It.].
OK'ee– 2. hockey, jockey, cocky, locky, lochy, blocky, flocky, pocky, rocky, crocky, stocky.
3. field hockey, ice hockey, disk jockey [slang], horse jockey.
OK'er– 2. docker, cocker, locker, blocker, clocker, mocker, smocker, knocker, rocker, socker, soccer, shocker, stocker.
4. Knickerbocker.
OK'et– 2. docket, cocket, locket, pocket, rocket, brocket, crocket, krocket, sprocket, socket.
3. watch pocket, *pickpocket*, impocket, unpocket, hip pocket, air pocket, vest pocket, *skyrocket*.
OK'ij– 2. dockage, lockage, soccage.
OK'ing– 2. docking, hocking, cocking, locking, blocking, flocking, clocking, mocking, smocking, knocking, rocking, crocking, socking, shocking, stocking.
3. unlocking, unblocking, *bluestocking*.
OK'ish– 2. cockish, mockish, stockish.
3. peacockish.
OK'l– 2. cockle, strockle, socle.
OK'let– 2. cocklet, rocklet, stocklet.
OK'ling– 2. cockling, flockling, rockling.
OK'nee– 2. cockney, Procne.
OK'o– 2. jocko, socko [slang], yocco.
3. sirocco, Morocco.
OKS'a– 2. coxa, moxa, noxa, toxa.
OKS'al– 2. coxal, noxal.
4. paradoxal.
OKS'ee– 2. boxy, doxy, foxy, poxy, roxy, proxy.
3. Biloxi.
4. paradoxy, cacodoxy, orthodoxy.
5. heterodoxy.
OKS'en– 2. oxen, cockswain.
OKS'er– 2. oxer, boxer.
4. paradoxer, philodoxer.
OKSH'al– 3. trinoctial.
4. equinoctial.
OKS'ik– 2. toxic.
4. streptococcic, antitoxic.
OKS'in– 2. toxin, tocsin.
4. antitoxin.
OKS'ing– 2. boxing, foxing.
4. shadowboxing.
OKT'iv– 2. octave.
3. decoctive, concoctive.
OKT'or– 2. doctor, proctor.
3. concocter.
OK'us– 2. lochus, floccus.
4. pneumococcus, streptococcus.
5. staphylococcus.
OL'a– 2. olla, holla.
3. corolla.
OL'ard– 2. bollard, collard, collared, Lollard, pollard, scholard, scholared.
OL'ee– 2. dolly, folly, golly, holly, jolly, collie, Molly, molle, Polly, poly [slang], rolley,

trolley, volley.
3. *loblolly*.
4. melancholy.
OL′eed– 2. dollied, jollied, collied, trolleyed, volleyed.
OL′ej– 2. college, knowledge.
3. acknowledge, foreknowledge.
OL′en– 2. pollen, Stollen [G.].
OL′er– 2. dollar, holler, collar, choller, choler, scholar, loller, sollar.
3. extoller.
4. dorsicollar.
OL′erd– 2. hollered; *see also* ŎL′ard.
OL′et– 2. collet.
3. La Follette.
OL′id– 2. olid, solid, stolid, squalid.
4. semisolid.
OL′ik– 2. rollick, frolic.
3. embolic, symbolic, carbolic, bucolic, petrolic, systolic.
4. diabolic, metabolic, hyperbolic, alcoholic, vitriolic, melancholic, diastolic, epistolic, apostolic.
5. bibliopolic.
OL′in– 2. colin, Colin, collin, colline.
4. hemicollin.
OL′ing– 2. colling, lolling.
3. extolling.
OL′is– 2. follis, solace.
4. torticollis.
OL′ish– 2. dollish, lollish, mollish, polish.
3. abolish, demolish.
OL′iv– 2. olive.
3. stuffed olive, green olive, ripe olive.
OL′o– 2. follow, hollo, hollow, Rollo.
3. Apollo.
OL′op– 2. dollop, jollop, collop, scallop, scollop, lollop, trollop.
3. escallop.
OL′um– 2. column, solemn.
OLV′ent– 2. solvent.
3. absolvent, resolvent, dissolvent, insolvent, evolvent.
OLV′er– 2. solver.
3. absolver, resolver, dissolver, evolver, revolver, involver.
OLV′ing– 2. solving.
3. absolving, resolving, dissolving, evolving, devolving, revolving, involving.
4. undissolving, unrevolving.
OLV′ment– 3. evolvement, devolvement, involvement.
OM′a– 2. comma, momma.
OM′as– 2. Thomas, promise.
4. doubting Thomas.
OMB′a– 2. domba, pombe, tromba.
3. zambomba [Sp.], calomba.
OMB′at– 2. combat, wombat.
OMB′ee– 2. Dombey, zombie.
4. Abercrombie.
OMB′er– 2. omber, ombre, Scomber, somber.
OM′ee– 2. mommy, pommy, tommy, Tommy.
OM′et– 2. comet, domett, grommet.
3. Mahomet.

OM′ij– 2. homage, pommage.
OM′ik– 2. comic, nomic, dromic, promic.
3. encomic, dinomic, syndromic, achromic, dichromic, atomic, entomic, phantomic, dystomic, Suomic.
4. tragicomic, quasicomic, pathognomic, pyrognomic, economic, agronomic, chironomic, metronomic, astronomic, gastronomic, isonomic, taxonomic, autonomic, plutonomic, theobromic, hydrobromic, paradromic, palindromic, exodromic, loxodromic, orthodromic, polychromic, monochromic, bathochromic, xanthochromic, diatomic, triatomic, dermatomic, anatomic, monatomic, pentatomic, heptatomic, hexatomic, epitomic, microtomic, orthotomic.
5. heroicomic, seriocomic, physiognomic, Deuteronomic, tesseratomic.
OM′iks– 2. comics.
4. bionomics, economics, agronomics.
OM′ing– 2. bombing, glomming [slang].
OM′is– 2. promise, Thomas.
4. doubting Thomas.
OMP′ee– 2. Pompey, rompy.
OMP′us– 2. pompous.
3. unpompous.
4. catawampus.
ON′a– 2. donna, Donna.
3. madonna.
4. belladonna, prima donna.
ON′ald– 2. Donald, Ronald.
OND′a– 2. honda, nonda.
3. Golconda.
4. anaconda.
OND′ed– 2. bonded.
3. unbonded, absconded, responded.
4. corresponded.
OND′ens– 3. abscondence, despondence, respondence.
4. correspondence.
OND′ent– 2. frondent.
3. despondent, respondent.
4. co-respondent, correspondent.
OND′er– 2. bonder, fonder, condor, blonder, ponder, yonder.
3. absconder, responder.
4. corresponder.
OND′est– 2. fondest, blondest.
OND′ij– 2. bondage, frondage.
4. vagabondage.
OND′ing– 2. bonding.
3. absconding, responding.
4. vagabonding, corresponding.
OND′l– 2. fondle, rondle, rondel.
OND′lee– 2. fondly, blondly.
4. overfondly, overblondly.
OND′ness– 2. fondness, blondness.
OND′o– 2. hondo, rondo, tondo [It.].
ON′ee– 2. bonny, Bonny, Johnny, Connie, Lonnie, Ronnie.
3. gyronny.
ON′er– 2. honor, conner.
3. dishonor, *aleconner*.
ON′est– 2. honest, non est [L.].

3. dishonest.
ON'et– bonnet, sonnet.
  3. *sunbonnet, bluebonnet.*
ONG'er– 2. longer, wronger.
  3. prolonger.
ONG'ful– 2. wrongful, songful.
ONG'ga– 2. bonga [Tag.], donga, conga, tonga, Tonga, wonga.
  3. Batonga.
  4. wonga-wonga.
  5. Madame La Zonga.
ONG'ger– 2. conger, longer, stronger.
ONG'gest– 2. longest, strongest.
ONG'ing– 2. longing, wronging, thronging.
  3. ding-donging, belonging, prolonging.
ONG'ish– 2. longish, wrongish, prongish, strongish.
ONG'lee– 2. wrongly, strongly.
ON'ik– 2. phonic, conic, clonic, nonic, chronic, tonic.
  3. carbonic, bubonic, Adonic, hedonic, sardonic, paeonic, agonic, trigonic, jargonic, aphonic, siphonic, symphonic, euphonic, typhonic, Ionic, aconic, laconic, draconic, iconic, zirconic, cyclonic, colonic, demonic, mnemonic, pulmonic, gnomonic, harmonic, sermonic, pneumonic, canonic, zoonic, Japonic, Aaronic, Neronic, Pyrrhonic, ironic, Byronic, acronyc, masonic, parsonic, atonic, Platonic, subtonic, pretonic, Metonic, tectonic, Miltonic, syntonic, protonic, Teutonic, plutonic, benthonic, pythonic, Brythonic, Slavonic, ozonic.
  4. Pharaonic, polyconic, chalcedonic, algedonic, chelidonic, pantheonic, megaphonic, diaphonic, telephonic, antiphonic, cacophonic, xylophonic, microphonic, polyphonic, baryphonic, geogonic, theogonic, cosmogonic, polygonic, histrionic, polyconic, cinnamonic, eudaemonic, hegemonic, Solomonic, philharmonic, anharmonic, enharmonic, etymonic, geoponic, electronic, supersonic, diatonic, hematonic, Housatonic, pentatonic, heptatonic, monotonic, neurotonic, isotonic, orthotonic, hypertonic, intertonic, polytonic, embryonic.
  5. chameleonic, Napoleonic, Neoplatonic, architectonic, geotectonic, electrotonic.
ON'iks– 2. onyx.
  3. hedonics, sardonyx, mnemonics, harmonics.
  4. chalcedonyx, histrionics, geoponics.
ON'ing– 2. donning, conning.
ON'ish– 2. donnish, monish, tonnish.
  3. admonish, premonish, astonish.
ONK'ee– 2. donkey, conky.
ONK'er– 2. honker, conquer, conker.
  3. reconquer.
ONK'ing– 2. honking, conking [slang].
ONK'us– 2. rhonchus, bronchus.
ONS'al– 2. consul, sponsal, tonsil.
  3. proconsul, responsal.
ONS'er– 2. sponsor, tonsor.
  4. chirontonsor.
ONSH'us– 2. conscious, Pontius.

  3. subconscious, self-conscious, unconscious.
ONS'trant– 3. demonstrant, remonstrant, Premonstrant.
ONS'ul– 2. consul, sponsal, tonsil.
  3. proconsul, vice-consul, responsal.
ONT'al– 2. ontal, fontal, pontal.
  3. gerontal.
  4. horizontal.
ONT'ane– 2. montane.
  3. tramontane, submontane, cismontane, transmontane.
  4. ultramontane.
ONT'ed– 2. fonted, wonted.
  3. unwonted.
ONT'ik– 2. pontic.
  3. odontic, gerontic.
  4. mastodontic.
ONT'ine– 2. pontine, Pontine.
  3. dracontine, cispontine, transpontine.
  4. Hellespontine.
ONT'less– 2. fontless, pontless, wontless.
ONT'o– 2. conto, pronto, Tonto.
  3. Toronto.
ONZ'er– 2. bonzer, bronzer.
ONZ'o– 3. Alphonso, Alonzo.
OP'ee– 2. choppy, hoppy, copy, coppy, loppy, floppy, cloppy, ploppy, sloppy, moppy, poppy, droppy, croppy, soppy, shoppy.
  3. recopy, jalopy, *jollopy, clip-cloppy.*
OP'er– 2. chopper, hopper, copper, lopper, flopper, clopper, plopper, slopper, mopper, popper, dropper, cropper, proper, propper, stropper, sopper, shopper, topper, stopper, whopper [coll.].
  3. *clodhopper, grasshopper, flip-flopper, clip-clopper, eavesdropper, corn popper, sharecropper,* improper, tiptopper.
  4. table hopper, window shopper, Christmas shopper.
OP'et– 2. noppet [dial.], moppet, poppet.
OP'ij– 2. proppage, stoppage.
OP'ik– 2. scopic, tropic, topic.
  3. acopic, syncopic, Cyclopic, diplopic, canopic, Sinopic, hydropic, anthropic, atropic, Aesopic, prosopic, atopic, metopic, ectopic, entopic, syntopic, myopic.
  4. Ethiopic, telescopic, periscopic, geoscopic, rheoscopic, orthoscopic, thermoscopic, lychnoscopic, aposcopic, acroscopic, macroscopic, microscopic, hydroscopic, aeroscopic, hygroscopic, poroscopic, spectroscopic, gyroscopic, pantoscopic, photoscopic, autoscopic, polyscopic, nyctalopic, lycanthropic, theanthropic, philanthropic, misanthropic, diatropic, ametropic, nyctitropic, isentropic, geotropic, rheotropic, orthotropic, allotropic, monotropic, apotropic, hydrotropic, aerotropic, neurotropic, isotropic, autotropic, exotropic, polytropic, isotopic, polytopic, presbyopic, polyopic.
  5. kaleidoscopic, hagioscopic, helioscopic, deuteroscopic, fluoroscopic, electroscopic, hemeralopic, paleanthropic, heliotropic, dex-

iotropic, heterotopic.

OP´ing– 2. chopping, hopping, copping, lopping, flopping, clopping, plopping, slopping, mopping, popping, dropping, cropping, propping, stropping, sopping, shopping, topping, stopping, whopping [coll.].

3. *clodhopping, flip-flopping, clip-clopping, eavesdropping, sharecropping* estopping.

4. table hopping, window shopping, Christmas shopping, overtopping.

5. flippety-flopping, clippety-clopping.

OP´ish– 2. foppish, shoppish.

OP´l– 2. hopple, copple, popple, thropple, topple, stopple.

3. estoppel.

OP´ling– 2. fopling, hoppling, toppling, stoppling.

OP´see– 2. copsy, lopsy, Flopsy, Mopsy, popsy, dropsy, Topsy.

OP´shun– 2. option.

3. adoption.

4. readoption.

OP´sis– 3. synopsis.

4. thanatopsis.

OPT´ed– 2. opted.

3. co-opted, adopted.

4. unadopted.

OPT´er– 2. opter.

3. adopter, diopter, orthopter.

4. helicopter, phenicopter.

OPT´ik– 2. optic, Coptic.

3. synoptic, autoptic, orthoptic.

OPT´ing– 2. opting.

3. adopting.

OPT´iv– 2. optive.

3. co-optive, adoptive.

OR´a– through **OR´ward–** *see also* **Ō: ŌR´a** through **ŌR´us; Ô: ÔR´a** through **ÔR´us.**

OR´a– 2. orra, gora, gorah, sorra.

3. Andorra, begorra [dial. Ir.], Camorra, Gomorrah.

OR´al– 2. oral, horral, coral, moral, sorrel.

3. amoral, Balmoral, immoral, unmoral.

ORB´el– 2. orbell, corbeil, corbel, warble.

ORB´ing– 2. orbing.

3. absorbing, resorbing.

ORCH´er– 2. scorcher, torcher, torture.

ORCH´erd– 2. orchard, tortured.

ORCH´ing– 2. scorching, torching.

ORD´al– 2. chordal.

3. concordal.

ORD´ant– 2. mordant.

3. accordant, concordant, discordant.

4. disaccordant.

ORD´ed– 2. corded, chorded, lorded, sordid.

3. accorded, recorded, belorded, unlorded.

4. unrecorded.

ORD´en– 2. Borden, Gordon, Jorden, cordon, Norden.

4. auf den Norden [G.].

ORD´er– 2. order, border, corder, sworder.

3. reorder, disorder, emborder, accorder, recorder.

4. money order.

ORD´erd– 2. ordered, bordered.

3. reordered, well-ordered, unordered, disordered, embordered, unbordered.

ORD´ing– 2. cording, chording, lording, swording.

3. according, recording, belording, unswording.

ORD´on– 2. Gordon, cordon; *see also* **ŌRD´en.**

OR´ee– 2. corrie, lorry, sorry.

OR´el– 2. sorrel; *see also* **ŌR´al.**

OR´en– 2. foreign, sporran, warren, Warren.

OR´ens– 2. Lawrence, Florence.

3. abhorrence, St. Lawrence.

OR´ent– 2. horrent, torrent, warrant.

3. abhorrent, death warrant, search warrant.

OR´er– 2. horror, warrer.

3. abhorrer.

ORF´ee– 4. metamorphy, geomorphy, zoomorphy.

ORF´ik– 2. Orphic, morphic.

3. amorphic, dimorphic, trimorphic.

4. metamorphic, endomorphic, pseudomorphic, geomorphic, theomorphic, monomorphic, zoomorphic, theromorphic, tauromorphic, isomorphic, pantomorphic, automorphic, exomorphic, polymorphic.

5. ophiomorphic, theriomorphic, heteromorphic, deuteromorphic.

6. ephemeromorphic.

ORF´izm– 2. Orphism, morphism.

4. metamorphism, monomorphism, zoomorphism.

ORF´us– 3. amorphous, dimorphous, trimorphous.

4. paramorphous, metamorphous, polymorphous.

5. ophiomorphous, anthropomorphous.

ORG´an– 2. organ, Gorgon, Morgan, morgan, morgen.

3. *idorgan, biorgan.*

4. Demogorgon, Guten Morgen [G.].

OR´id– 2. horrid, florid, torrid.

OR´ij– 2. borage, forage, porridge.

OR´ik– 2. goric, choric, cloric, toric, Yorick.

3. sudoric, theoric, phosphoric, enchoric, caloric, pyloric, rhetoric, historic, plethoric.

4. meteoric, semaphoric, cataphoric, metaphoric, allegoric, paregoric, oratoric, prehistoric.

5. phantasmagoric; *see also* **ŌR´ik.**

OR´ing– 2. warring.

3. abhorring.

OR´is– 2. orris, Doris, Horace, morris.

OR´ist– 2. chorist, florist.

ORJ´ee– 2. orgy, Georgie, porgy, storge.

4. Georgy Porgy.

ORJ´er– 2. forger, gorger.

ORK´a– 2. Orca.

3. Majorca, Minorca.

ORK´ee– 2. forky, corky.

ORK´er– 2. forker, corker, porker, Yorker.

3. New Yorker.

ORK´ing– 2. forking, Dorking, corking.

3. uncorking.

ORK′us– 2. Orcus, Dorcas, orchis.
ORM′al– formal, cormel, normal.
  3. informal, unformal, abnormal, unnormal, transnormal.
  4. uniformal, supernormal.
ORM′an– 2. Mormon, Norman.
ORM′ans– 2. dormance.
  3. conformance, performance.
ORM′ant– 2. dormant, formant.
  3. undormant, informant, conformant, performant.
ORM′ee– 2. dormy, forme, horme, stormy, swarmy.
ORM′er– 2. ormer, dormer, former, stormer, warmer, swarmer.
  3. deformer, reformer, informer, conformer, performer, transformer, *barnstormer*, chair warmer.
  4. misinformer, nonconformer.
ORM′ing– 2. forming, storming, warming, swarming.
  3. deforming, reforming, informing, conforming, performing, transforming, bestorming, *barnstorming, housewarming.*
  4. misinforming, unconforming, nonconforming.
ORM′ist– 3. reformist, conformist.
  4. nonconformist, unconformist.
ORM′lee– 2. warmly.
  4. uniformly.
ORM′less– 2. formless, stormless.
ORM′us– 2. Ormus, cormus, cormous.
  3. abnormous, enormous.
ORN′a– 2. Lorna.
  3. cromorna.
ORN′ee– 2. horny, corny, scorny, thorny.
ORN′er– 2. horner, corner, scorner, warner.
  3. suborner, adorner, forewarner.
  4. chimney corner, catercorner, cattycorner, kittycorner.
  5. Little Jack Horner, puss in the corner.
ORN′ing– 2. horning, corning, scorning, morning, warning.
  3. suborning, a-borning, adorning, dehorning, good morning, forewarning.
ORN′is– 2. ornis, cornice.
  3. Dinornis, Notornis.
  4. Ichthyornis.
ORN′ish– 2. hornish, Cornish, Plornish [Dickens], warnish [Scot.].
ORN′less– 2. hornless, cornless, scornless, mornless, thornless,
OR′o– 2. borrow, morrow, sorrow.
  3. tomorrow, good morrow.
ORP′er– 2. scorper, torpor, warper.
ORS′al– 2. dorsal, morsal.
  3. dextrorsal.
  4. sinistrorsal.
ORS′el– 2. dorsel, morsel, norsel, torsel, torcel.
  3. ensorcell.
ORS′er– 2. dorser, horser.
  3. endorser.
ORS′ful– 2. forceful.

  3. remorseful, resourceful.
ORSH′un– 2. torsion.
  3. abortion, consortion, detorsion, retortion, intorsion, contortion, extortion; *see also* **ŌRSH′un.**
ORS′iv– 2. torsive.
  3. contorsive, extorsive.
ORS′o– 2. dorso, corso [It.], torso.
ORT′a– 2. torta, Torte [G.].
  3. aorta.
  4. sesquiquarta.
ORT′al– 2. mortal, sortal, chortle.
  3. aortal, immortal.
ORT′ans– 2. portance, sortance.
  3. importance.
  4. unimportance.
ORT′ed– 2. snorted, sorted, warted, thwarted.
  3. aborted, exhorted, escorted, assorted, resorted, consorted, unsorted, detorted, retorted, contorted, distorted, extorted, cavorted, resorted.
ORT′ee– 2. forty, forte, snorty, sortie, Shorty, warty, swarty.
ORT′eks– 2. cortex, vortex.
ORT′en– 2. chorten, shorten.
  3. foreshorten.
ORT′er– 2. mortar, snorter, sorter, shorter, quarter, swarter, thwarter.
  3. dehorter, exhorter, escorter, *hindquarter, forequarter,* assorter, resorter, consorter, retorter, contorter, distorter, extorter.
ORT′est– 2. shortest, swartest.
ORT′ing– 2. snorting, sorting, Storting, thwarting.
  3. aborting, exhorting, escorting, consorting, retorting, contorting, distorting, extorting, cavorting, resorting.
ORT′is– 2. fortis, mortise, tortoise.
ORT′iv– 2. ortive, tortive.
  3. abortive, retortive, contortive, distortive, extortive.
ORT′l– 2. chortle; *see also* **ŎRT′al.**
ORT′ment– 2. sortment.
  3. escortment, assortment, consortment.
ORT′shune– 2. fortune.
  3. misfortune, importune.
OR′ward– 2. forward, norward.
  3. henceforward, thenceforward, straightforward.
OS′a– 2. Ossa, ossa [L.], fossa, glossa.
OS′al– 2. ossal, dossal, glossal.
  3. colossal.
  4. hypoglossal; *see also* **ŎS′il, ŎS′l.**
OS′ee– 2. bossy, dossy, Flossie, glossy, mossy, posse, drossy, tossy.
OS′er– 2. bosser, dosser, josser, glosser, rosser, crosser, tosser.
  3. embosser.
OS′et– 2. bosset, cosset, posset.
OSH′ee– 2. boshy, joshy, sloshy, toshy.
OSH′er– 2. bosher, josher, cosher, slosher, posher, tosher.
OSH′ing– 2. joshing, coshing, sloshing.
OS′ij– 2. bossage, fossage.

OS'ik– 2. fossick, glossic.
3. molossic.
OS'il– 2. docile, dossil, fossil.
3. indocile; *see also* ŎS'l, ŎS'al.
OS'ing– 2. bossing, dossing, glossing, mossing, crossing, tossing.
3. embossing, grade crossing.
4. railroad crossing.
OS'l– 2. dossel, jostle, throstle, tossel, wassail.
3. apostle; *see also* ŎS'al, ŎS'il.
OS'ler– 2. ostler, hostler, jostler.
OS'om– 2. blossom, possum.
3. reblossom, emblossom, opossum.
4. orange blossom, apple blossom.
OST'a– 2. costa, Hosta.
3. subcosta.
OST'al– 2. costal.
4. Pentecostal, infracostal, supracostal, intercostal.
OST'ed– 2. frosted.
3. accosted, defrosted.
OST'el– 2. hostel, rostel.
OST'er– 2. foster, coster, Gloucester, roster, froster, zoster.
3. accoster, impostor.
4. pentecoster, paternoster, Pater Noster.
OST'ik– 2. gnostic.
3. agnostic, prognostic, acrostic.
4. diagnostic, geognostic, paracrostic, pentacrostic.
OST'il– 2. hostile, postil.
OST'ing– 2. costing, frosting.
3. accosting.
OST'ral– 2. costrel, nostril, rostral.
4. longirostral.
OST'rat– 2. rostrate, prostrate.
OST'rum– 2. nostrum, rostrum.
OS'um– 2. possum.
4. Geoglossum, *see also* ŎS'om.
OS'us– 3. colossus, molossus.
OT'a– 2. cotta, pottah, chrotta.
3. Carlotta.
4. terra cotta.
OT'al– 2. glottal.
4. epiglottal; *see also* ŎT'l.
OT'ed– 2. dotted, jotted, cotted, scotted, lotted, blotted, clotted, plotted, slotted, knotted, potted, spotted, rotted, trotted, sotted, shotted, totted.
3. undotted, uncotted, *wainscotted*, unscotted, allotted, unblotted, unclotted, unplotted, unknotted, repotted, unpotted, bespotted, *blood-spotted*, unspotted, *sunspotted*, garrotted, *globe-trotted*, *prom-trotted*, besotted.
OT'ee– 2. dotty, cotty, Scotty, Scottie, Lottie, blotty, clotty, plotty, knotty, potty, spotty, shotty, totty.
OT'en– 2. gotten, rotten, shotten.
3. hard-gotten, begotten, ill-gotten, ungotten, forgotten, misgotten.
4. misbegotten, unforgotten; *see also* ŎT'on.
OT'er– 2. otter, dotter, hotter, jotter, cotter, blotter, clotter, plotter, knotter, potter, spotter, rotter, trotter, shotter.

3. complotter, unknotter, garrotter, *globe-trotter*, *prom-trotter*, bogtrotter, breakwater, *limewater*, *firewater*.
OT'ful– 2. plotful, potful.
OTH'am– 2. Gotham, Jotham.
OTH'ee– 2. bothy, mothy, frothy.
OTH'er– 2. bother, fother, pother.
OTH'ik– 2. Gothic, Sothic.
4. Visigothic, Suigothic, Ostrogothic.
OTH'ing– 2. frothing, trothing.
3. betrothing.
OT'id– 3. carotid, parotid.
OT'ij– 2. cottage, clottage, plottage, pottage.
OT'ik– 2. otic, glottic.
3. chaotic, sybotic, thrombotic, morphotic, zygotic, argotic, biotic, meiotic, myotic, dichotic, psychotic, helcotic, narcotic, diglottic, Nilotic, psilotic, culottic, demotic, zymotic, thermotic, seismotic, osmotic, henotic, kenotic, binotic, pyknotic, monotic, hypnotic, zootic, nepotic, despotic, parotic, hydrotic, erotic, sclerotic, cerotic, xerotic, pyrotic, acrotic, necrotic, dicrotic, porotic, neurotic, exotic, quixotic, loxotic, entotic, aptotic, orthotic, xanthotic, rhizotic.
4. anecdotic, alloeotic, indigotic, abiotic, symbiotic, idiotic, semeiotic, periotic, patriotic, ichthyotic, epiglottic, polyglottic, enzymotic, endosmotic, exosmotic, cyanotic, melanotic, agrypnotic, escharotic, oneirotic, anacrotic, catacrotic, polycrotic, monocrotic.
5. catabiotic, amphibiotic, antibiotic, halobiotic, macrobiotic, Iscariotic, neurohypnotic, epizootic, rhinocerotic.
OT'iks– 3. biotics, demotics, thermotics.
5. antibiotics.
OT'ing– 2. dotting, hotting, jotting, cotting, scotting, blotting, clotting, plotting, knotting, potting, spotting, rotting, trotting, totting.
3. allotting, unclotting, reknotting, unknotting, garroting, repotting, unpotting, *globe-trotting*, *prom-trotting*, besotting.
OT'ish– 2. hottish, Scottish, sottish, schottische.
OT'l– 2. bottle, dottle, glottal, mottle, pottle, rotl, crottle, throttle, tottle.
3. *bluebottle*.
4. acocotl, epiglottal, axolotl.
OT'lee– 2. hotly, motley.
OT'ler– 2. bottler, mottler, throttler.
OT'less– 2. dotless, cotless, blotless, plotless, knotless, potless, spotless, rotless, totless.
OT'ling– 2. bottling, mottling, throttling.
OT'ment– 3. allotment, besotment.
OT'o– 2. Otto, lotto, blotto [slang], motto, potto, grotto, sotto [It.].
3. ridotto, fagotto [It.], risotto [It.].
OT'on– 2. cotton, frotton, Groton.
3. *guncotton*; *see also* ŎT'en.
OV'el– 2. hovel, novel, grovel.
OX'a– through OX'er; *see* ŎKS'a through ŎKS'er.
OZ'it– 2. closet, posit.

3. deposit, reposit, composite.
4. juxtaposit, oviposit, decomposite, incomposite, interposit.
OZ′l– **2.** nozzle, snozzle, schnozzle, sozzle.

OZ′m– **3.** macrocosm, microcosm, loxocosm.
OZ′mik– **2.** osmic, cosmic.
    3. aosmic.
    4. neocosmic, macrocosmic, microcosmic.

Ŏ (bob)

[See also Ä, Ô.]

Triple Rhymes

Primary or Secondary Accent Falls on Second from Last Syllable; Imperfect Rhymes Are in Italics.

OB′a–bl– 3. robbable, probable.
4. improbable.
OB′er–ee– 3. bobbery, jobbery, clobbery, slobbery, snobbery, robbery.
OB′er–ing– 3. clobbering, slobbering.
OB′ul–ar– 3. lobular, globular.
OD′er–er– 3. dodderer, fodderer, solderer.
OD′er–ing– 3. doddering, foddering, soldering.
OD′i–fi– 3. codify, modify.
OD′ik–al– 3. codical, nodical.
4. spasmodical, synodical, monodical, prosodical, rhapsodical, methodical.
5. periodical, episodical.
OD′it–ee– 3. oddity, quoddity.
4. commodity.
5. incommodity, discommodity.
OD′ul–ar– 3. modular, nodular.
OF′ag–a– 4. Sarcophaga, Zoophaga.
OF′ag–al– 4. sarcophagal, esophagal.
OF′ag–an– 4. zoophagan, saprophagan.
OF′ag–us– 4. geophagous, theophagous, sarcophagus, sarcophagous, zoophagous, hippophagous, androphagous, necrophagous, saprophagous, esophagus.
5. ichthyophagous.
OF′aj–ee– 4. theophagy, sarcophagy, hippophagy, phytophagy, pantophagy.
5. ichthyophagy, anthropophagy.
OF′aj–ist– 4. geophagist, omophagist, hippophagist, pantophagist.
5. ichthyophagist, galactophagist.
OF′er–er– 3. offerer, gofferer, cofferer, profferer.
OF′er–ing– 3. offering, goffering, coffering, proffering.
4. thank offering, peace offering.
5. freewill offering.
OF′ik–al– 3. trophical, sophical.
5. theosophical, philosophical.
OF′il–us– 4. Theophilus, sarcophilous, Sarcophilus, xylophilous, zoophilous, saprophilous.
5. acidophilus, heliophilous.

OF′on–ee– 4. theophany, cacophony, homophony, photophony, Cristophany, tautophony, orthophony.
OF′or–us– 4. phyllophorous, zoophorus, pyrophorous, pyrophorus.
5. galactophorous.
OG′am–ee– 4. endogamy, monogamy, misogamy, exogamy, cryptogamy.
5. deuterogamy.
OG′am–ist– 4. monogamist, misogamist, cryptogamist.
5. deuterogamist.
OG′am–us– 4. idogamous, endogamous, homogamous, monogamous, exogamous, cryptogamous.
5. heterogamous.
OG′at–iv– 4. derogative, prerogative.
5. interrogative.
OG′er–ee– 3. hoggery, froggery, groggery, toggery.
5. pettifoggery.
OG′er–el 3. doggerel, hoggerel.
OG′nom–ee– 4. pathognomy.
5. craniognomy, physiognomy.
OG′on–ee– 4. geogony, theogony, mahogany, homogony, cosmogony, monogony, zoogony, mythogony.
5. bibliogony, physiogony, heroogony, heterogony.
OG′raf–ee– 4. geography, morphography, logography, psychography, biography, micrography, cacography, phycography, chalcography, zincography, haplography, stylography, xylography, demography, psalmography, mimography, homography, nomography, cosmography, planography, scenography, sphenography, stenography, zenography, technography, ichnography, hymnography, phonography, chronography, pornography, ethnography, zoography, lipography, topography, typography, hydrography, cerography, pterography, *chirography*, macrography, micrography, orography,

horography, chorography, petrography, neurography, pyrography, isography, nosography, hypsography, glossography, ontography, photography, scotography, glyptography, cryptography, cartography, histography, autography, phytography, ethography, lithography, mythography, anthography, orthography.

5. celidography, archaeography, palaeography, ideography, stereography, osteography, radiography, cardiography, semeiography, ophiography, hagiography, heliography, bibliography, physiography, pharmacography, lexicography, hyalography, metallography, crystallography, sigillography, selenography, iconography, anthropography, siderography, hierography, heterography, papyrography, thalassography, sematography, pneumatography, thanatography, skeletography, cometography, hyetography, odontography, ichthyography.

6. zoogeography, pythogeography, autobiography, dactyliography, historiography, ecclesiography, oceanography, Christianography, cinematography, phantasmatography, numismatography, chromophotography, chromolithography.

ŎG′raf–er– 4. biographer, logographer, demographer, mimographer, nomographer, cosmographer, sphenographer, stenographer, hymnographer, chronographer, zoographer, topographer, typographer, chirographer, choreographer, doxographer, glossographer, photographer, cryptographer, cartographer, lithographer, mythographer, orthographer.
5. celidographer, choreographer, bibliographer, lexicographer, selenographer.
6. autobiographer.

ŎG′raf–ist– 4. biographist, stenographist, phonographist, monographist, zoographist, topographist, chirographist, photographist, orthographist.
5. metallographist, selenographist, siderographist.

OJ′en–ee– 3. progeny.
4. biogeny, homogeny, nomogeny, monogeny, ethnogeny, oögeny, zoogeny, misogyny, autogeny, pathogeny.
5. embryogeny, anthropogeny.

OJ′en–eez– 3. progenies.
4. Diogenes, protogenes.

OJ′en–ist– 4. biogenist, philogynist, monogenist, misogynist.
5. abiogenist, heterogenist.

OJ′en–us– 4. endogenous, biogenous, primogenous, homogenous, thermogenous, hypogenous, hydrogenous, pyrogenous, nitrogenous, exogenous, lithogenous.

OJ′ik–al– 3. logical.
4. alogical, illogical, unlogical.
5. anagogical, synagogical, apagogical, dialogical, analogical, symbological, geological, neological, theological, biological, psycho-

logica' lo͜ ɓ ty̟ mici rologi ical, h͜ pathologı
6. genealog ideological, physiological, entomological, logical, climatolo͜
7. bacteriological, logical, palaeontologi

OJ′in–ee– 4. philogyny, ͺ see also ŎJ′en–ee.

OJ′in–ist– 4. biogenist, p͜ genist, misogynist.

OK′at–iv– 3. locative, talka͜ 4. untalkative, invocative, pro͜

OK′er–ee– 3. mockery, rockery, c

OK′il–ee– 3. chalkily, gawkily, pawkily, stalkily, stockily.

OK′i–ness– 3. chalkiness, gawkiness, ness, rockiness, talkiness, stalkiness, s͜ ness.

OK′ing–lee– 3. mockingly, shockingly, stal͜ ingly, squawkingly.

OK′ras–ee– 4. landocracy, neocrasy, theocrasy, ptochocracy, ochlocracy, doulocracy, democracy, timocracy, nomocracy, cosmocracy, technocracy, ethnocracy, monocracy, androcracy, isocracy, chrysocracy, stratocracy, plantocracy, autocracy, plutocracy, bureaucracy.
5. idiocrasy, hagiocracy, physiocracy, gynaecocracy, arithmocracy, millionocracy, hierocracy, pantisocracy, thalassocracy, ergatocracy, gerontocracy, despotocracy, aristocracy.

OK′rat–ist– 3. Socratist.
4. theocratist, democratist, bureaucratist.

OK′rat–izm– 3. Socratism.
4. democratism, bureaucratism.

OKS′ik–al– 3. toxical.
5. paradoxical, orthodoxical.

OK′ul–ar– 3. ocular, jocular, locular, vocular.
4. binocular, monocular.

OK′ul–ate– 3. oculate, flocculate.
4. inoculate, binoculate.

OK′ul–us– 3. oculus, loculus, flocculus.
4. monoculus.

OK′ut–or– 4. oblocutor, collocutor, prolocutor.
5. interlocutor.

OL′a–bl– 3. callable.
4. recallable, enthrallable.

OL′at–er– 4. idolater, pyrolater, artolater.
5. bibliolater, heliolater, Mariolater, iconolater.

OL′a–tree– 4. symbolatry, mobolatry, idolatry, lordolatry, theolatry, cosmolatry, onolatry, monolatry, zoolatry, topolatry, ne-

ŎL′ at–rus
crolatry, py͜
litholatry.
5. archae͜
orphiolatr͜
latry, g͜
physiola͜
nolatry,͜
matol͜
olatry,͜
6. ec͜
ŎL′ at͜
5. k͜
OL′ i͜
OL′ :͜
4͜
Ol͜
O͜
C͜

olatry, Christolatry, plutolatry,

latry, hygeiolatry, gynaeolatry,
, hagiolatry, bibliolatry, helio-
iolatry, Mariolatry, patriolatry,
ry, angelolatry, symbololatry, ura-
Parthenolatry, iconolatry, demon-
anthropolatry, arborolatry, gram-
try, thaumatolatry, ichthyolatry.
lesiolatry.
–rus– 4. idolatrous, zoolatrous.
bliolatrous, heliolatrous.
–lee– 3. solidly, stolidly, squalidly.
f–i– 3. jollify, mollify, qualify.
idolify, disqualify.
i–form– 3. colliform, cauliform.
emboliform.
L'i–ing– 3. dollying, follying, jollying.
L'ik–al– 4. symbolical, catholical.
5. diabolical, parabolical, hyperbolical,
apostolical.
6. bibliopolical.
OL'ik–som– 3. rollicksome, frolicsome.
OL'ing–lee– 3. drawlingly, crawlingly.
4. appallingly, enthrallingly.
OL'ish–er– 3. polisher.
4. abolisher, demolisher.
OL'ish–ing– 3. polishing.
4. abolishing, demolishing, repolishing.
OL'is–is– 4. biolysis, hemolysis, hydrolysis,
neurolysis, autolysis, histolysis.
OL'it–ee– 3. jollity, polity, quality.
4. frivolity, equality.
5. isopolity, interpolity, inequality, co-
equality.
OL'it–iks– 3. politics.
5. geopolitics, cosmopolitics.
OL'o–er– 3. follower, hollower, wallower,
swallower.
OL'og–us– 4. homologous, isologous, tau-
tologous.
5. heterologous.
OL'o–ing– 3. following, hollowing, wallowing,
swallowing.
OL'oj–ee– 3. ology.
4. naology, symbology, pedology, tidology,
odology, podology, pseudology, geology,
rheology, theology, neology, graphology,
nephology, trophology, morphology, algol-
ogy, ergology, biology, myology, bryology,
cacology, ecology, oncology, tocology, sar-
cology, muscology, phycology, mycology,
trichology, conchology, ptochology, archol-
ogy, euchology, psychology, philology,
typhlology, haplology, hylology, xylology
sphygmology, gemmology, homology, no-
mology, gnomology, pomology, thermology,
desmology, chresmology, seismology, cosmology, pneumology, zymology, phenology,
menology, penology, phrenology, aphnology,
kinology, Sinology, technology, ichnology,
limnology, hymnology, phonology, monol-
ogy, chronology, tonology, hypnology, ethnology, runology, cynology, oology, noology,

zoology, apology, tropology, topology, hip-
pology, carpology, typology, barology, pha-
rology, ambrology, timbrology, ombrology,
dendrology, hydrology, therology, pterology,
agrology, hygrology, arthrology, chirology,
macrology, necrology, micrology, orology,
horology, chorology, latrology, patrology,
metrology, petrology, astrology, gastrology,
neurology, pyrology, misology, taxology,
sexology, doxology, auxology, dosology,
nosology, posology, threpsology, gypsology,
glossology, chrysology, battology, cetology,
ctetology, dittology, cytology, phytology, sitol-
ogy, planktology, pantology, ontology, otology,
photology, glottology, cryptology, typtology,
cartology, pestology, histology, Christology,
tautology, plutology, pathology, ethology,
lithology, mythology, anthology, orthology.
5. amphibology, monadology, acidology,
pteridology, dicaeology, archaeology, pa-
laeology, ideology, pantheology, speleology,
teleology, areology, thereology, phraseology,
osteology, atheology, edaphology, agathol-
ogy, ornithology, abiology, radiology, cardiology, semeiology, ophiology, sophiol-
ogy, hagiology, caliology, bibliology, heliol-
ogy, mommiology, craniology, koniology,
agriology, gnosiology, physiology, sociology,
axiology, praxiology, etiology, malacology,
pharmacology, gynecology, lexicology, toxic-
ology, angelology, dactylology, potamology,
anemology, docimology, ophthalmology,
paromology, atomology, entomology, oris-
mology, etymology, mechanology, volcan-
ology, organology, campanology, uranol-
ogy, lichenology, selenology, asthenology,
carcinology, criminology, terminology, ec-
crinology, actinology, arachnology, pogon-
ology, iconology, demonology, gnomon-
ology, synchronology, Hibernology, mater-
nology 'mmunology, heroology, antapology,
anthropology, hierology, ponerology, heter-
ology, enterology, oneirology, iatrology,
electrology, acyrology, papyrology, marty-
rology, parisology, psicatology, eschatology,
haematology, rhematology, sematology, ag-
matology, climatology, thremmatology, sto-
matology, dermatology, thermatology, thau-
matology, pneumatology, kymatology, than-
atology, geratology, teratology, olfactology,
esthetology, hyetology, melittology, seman-
tology, odontology, deontology, neontology,
erotology, Egyptology, heortology, aristol-
ogy, agrostology, ichthyology, embryology.
6. metamorphology, geomorphology, am-
phibiology, microbiology, stoichiology, dac-
tyliology, paroemiology, bacteriology, sote-
riology, heresiology, hamartiology, diabolol-
ogy, epistemology, phenomenology, paleeth-
nology, meteorology, universology, emblema-
tology, philematology, systematology, ono-
matology, numismatology, toreumatology,
dialectology, paleontology, psychopathol-
ogy, neuropathology, theomythology.

7. paleopsychology, idiopsychology.

OL'oj–er– 4. geologer, theologer, philologer, phrenologer, acknowledger, phonologer, chronologer, horologer, astrologer, mythologer.

5. physiologer, etymologer.

OL'oj'ist– 4. geologist, neologist, theologist, morphologist, biologist, bryologist, myologist, echologist, conchologist, psychologist, philologist, mimologist, palmologisst, homologist, pomologist, seismologist, cosmologist, zymologist, phrenologist, Sinologist, technologist, hymnologist, phonologist, monologist, chronologist, hypnologist, ethnologist, oologist, noologist, zoologist, apologist, dendrologist, hydrologist, chirologist, necrologist, horologist, petrologist, astrologist, neurologist, glossologist, nosologist, gypsologist, battologist, ontologist, otologist, photologist, histologist, tautologist, phytologist, pathologist, lithologist, anthologist, mythologist.

5. ideologist, archaeologist, teleologist, phraseologist, hagiologist, craniologist, physiologist, sociologist, pharmacologist, anthocologist, lexicologist, toxicologist, etymologist, ophthalmologist, arachnologist, monologist, anthropologist, hierologist, oneirologist, dermatologist, herpetologist, neontologist, Egyptologist, melittologist, ornithologist, ichthyologist, embryologist.

6. paroemiologist, bacteriologist, ecclesiologist, meteorologist, numismatologist, dialectologist, paleontologist.

OL'oj–ize– 4. geologize, neologize, theologize, philologize, homologize, monologize, apologize, astrologize, doxologize, battologize, mythologize.

5. sociologize, entomologize, etymologize.

OL'ub–lee– 3. solubly, volubly.

4. insolubly.

5. indissolubly.

OLV'a–bl– 3. solvable.

4. absolvable, resolvable, insolvable, unsolvable, dissolvable.

5. unresolvable, indissolvable.

OLV'en–see– 3. solvency.

4. insolvency, revolvency.

OM ak–ee– 4. theomachy, logomachy, sciomachy, psychomachy, monomachy. tauromachy, pyromachy, duomachy.

5. iconomachy, centauromachy, gigantomachy.

6. alectryomachy.

OM'ath–ee– 4. philomathy, chrestomathy.

OM'en–a– 4. phenomena.

5. prolegomena.

6. antilegomena, paralipomena.

OM'et–er– 4. tribometer, pedometer, speedometer, ondometer, undometer, geometer, rehometer, graphometer, ergometer, tachometer, oncometer, kilometer, sillometer, cyclometer, bolometer, stylometer, pulmometer, chromometer, tromometer, thermometer, seismometer, osmometer, atmometer,

cymometer, zymometer, planometer, manometer, clinometer, vinometer, pycnometer, phonometer, monometer, chronometer, sonometer, tonometer, oometer, tropometer, hippometer, barometer, vibrometer, ombrometer, dendrometer, hydrometer, spherometer, hygrometer, chirometer, spirometer, macrometer, micrometer, psychrometer, orometer, horometer, nitrometer, spectrometer, astrometer, pyrometer, gasometer, pulsometer, drosometer, hypsometer, passometer, lactometer, stactometer, hectometer, altometer, pantometer, photometer, haptometer, leptometer, comptometer, optometer, cyrtometer, bathometer, stethometer, cryometer.

5. tacheometer, oleometer, areometer, stereometer, heliometer, craniometer, variometer, fluviometer, pluviometer, oscillometer, scintillometer, dynamometer, anemometer, arithmometer, galvanometer, salinometer, declinometer, inclinometer, actinometer, harmonometer, respirometer, micronometer, electrometer, thalassometer, opisometer, climatometer, chromatometer, pneumatometer, thanatometer, magnetometer, olfactometer, refractometer, piezometer, horizometer.

6. diaphanometer, sphygmomanometer.

OM'et–ree– 4. geometry, rheometry, Mahometry, morphometry, biometry, psychometry, stichometry, cyclometry, colometry, thermometry, pneumometry, planometry, phonometry, chronometry, tonometry, tyopometry, barometry, hydrometry, gygrometry, micrometry, horometry, chorometry, astrometry, pyrometry, gasometry, isometry, hypsometry, photometry, autometry, orthometry.

5. areometry, stereometry, osteometry, cardiometry, stoichiometry, craniometry, anemometry uranometry, galvanometry, trigonometry, ozonometry, anthropometry, electrometry, piezometry.

6. historiometry.

OM'ik–al– 3. domical, comical.

4. atomical, phantomical.

5. tragicomical, economical, agronomical, metronomical, astronomical, anatomical, zootomical.

6. uneconomical.

OM'in–al– 3. nominal.

4. abdominal, adnominal, preanominal, cognominal, pronominal, surnominal.

OM'in–ans– 3. dominance, prominence.

4. predominance.

OM'in–ant– 3. dominant, prominent.

4. subdominant, predominant.

5. superdominant.

OM'in–ate– 3. dominate, comminate, nominate.

4. abominate, predominate, denominate, renominate, prenominate, innominate.

OM'in–ee– 3. dominie, hominy, Romany.

5. Chickahominy.

OM'in–us– 3. ominous, dominus.

4. abdominous, binominous.

OND'en–see– 4. despondency.

5. correspondency.

OND'er–er– 3. ponderer, wanderer, squanderer.

OND'er–ing– 3. pondering, wandering, squandering.

ON'if–i– 3. bonify.

4. saponify, personify, ozonify.

ON'ik–a– 3. Monica.

4. harmonica, japonica, Veronica.

ON'ik–al– 3. conical, chronicle, tonical.

4. euphonical, iconical, mnemonical, harmonical, canonical, ironical, synchronical, thrasonical.

5. diaphonical, tautophonical, cosmogonical, histrionical, geoponical.

ON'im–ee– 3. onymy.

4. homonymy, synonymy, eponymy, toponymy, patronymy, metronymy, metonymy; *see also* **ŎN'om–i.**

ON'im–ist– 4. synonymist, eponymist; *see also* **ŎN'om–ist.**

ON'im–us– 3. onymous.

4. anonymous, pseudonymous, eponymous, homonymous, synonymous, paronymous, autonymous.

5. heteronymous.

ON'ish–ing– 3. monishing.

4. admonishing, premonishing, astonishing.

ON'ish–ment– 4. admonishment, premonishment, astonishment.

ON'is–izm– 4. sardonicism, laconicism, teutonicism.

5. histrionicism.

ON'o–graf– 3. phonograph, monograph, chronograph, tonograph.

ON'o–gram– 3. monogram, chronogram, tonogram.

ON'om–ee– 4. morphonomy, economy, agronomy, astronomy, gastronomy, isonomy, taxonomy, nosonomy, autonomy.

5. dactylonomy, anthroponomy, Deuteronomy; *see also* **ŎN'im–ee.**

ON'om–er– 4. astronomer, gastronomer.

ON'om–ist– 4. economist, synonymist, eponymist, agronomist, gastronomist, autonomist, plutonomist.

ON'om–ize– 4. economize, astronomize, gastronomize, autonomize.

ONS'ul–ar– 3. consular.

4. nonconsular. proconsular, vice-consular.

ONT'ing–lee– 3. dauntingly, hauntingly, tauntingly, vauntingly, wantingly.

OP'ath–ee– 4. theopathy, psychopathy, allopathy, somnopathy, hydropathy, neuropathy, autopathy.

5. homoeopathy, osteopathy, deuteropathy.

OP'ath–ist– 4. psychopathist, allopathist, hylopathist, somnopathist, hydropathist, neuropathist.

5. homoeopathist, osteopathist.

OP'er–ee– 3. opery [dial.], foppery, coppery.

4. zoopery.

OP'i–er– 3. choppier, hoppier, copier, floppier, sloppier, soppier.

OP'i–est– 3. choppiest, hoppiest, floppiest, sloppiest, soppiest.

OP'ik–al– 3. tropical, topical.

4. subtropical.

5. microscopical, philanthropical, misanthropical.

OP'i–ness– 3. choppiness, floppiness, sloppiness, soppiness.

OP'ol–is– 3. propolis.

4. cosmopolis, acropolis, necropolis, metropolis.

5. Heliopolis.

OP'ol–ist– 4. monopolist.

5. bibliopolist, pharmacopolist.

OP'ol–ite– 4. cosmopolite, metropolite.

OPT'ik–al– 3. optical.

4. autoptical.

OP'ul–us– 3. opulus, populous.

4. unpopulous.

OR'ak–l– through ORT'un–it– *see also* **Ō: ŌR'a–bl through ŌR'us–lee; Ô: ŎR'e–ate, ŎR'i–an.**

OR'ak–l– 3. oracle, coracle; *see also* **ŎR'ik–al.**

OR'al–ist– 3. coralist, moralist.

ORD'er–ing– 3. ordering, bordering.

4. reordering, embordering.

ORD'i–al– 3. cordial.

4. primordial, exordial.

ORD'i–an– 3. Gordian.

4. accordion, Edwardian.

ORD'in–ate– 3. ordinate.

4. subordinate, inordinate, coordinate, foreordinate.

5. insubordinate, incoordinate, uncoordinate.

ORF'iz–m– 3. Orphism, morphism.

4. metamorphism, monomorphism, zoomorphism.

OR'gan–ize– 3. organize, gorgonize.

4. reorganize, disorganize.

OR'id–lee– 3. horridly, floridly, torridly.

OR'i–er– 3. sorrier, warrior, quarrier.

OR'if–i– 3. horrify, torrefy.

4. calorify, historify.

OR'i–form– 3. floriform, moriform, poriform.

4. arboriform, vaporiform.

OR'ik–al– 3. oracle, coracle.

4. rhetorical, historical.

5. meteorical, anaphorical, metaphorical, allegorical, categorical, tautegorical, oratorical.

OR'it–ee– 4. priority, majority, minority, sonority, sorority, authority.

5. meliority, seniority, juniority.

6. inferiority, superiority, deteriority, anteriority, interiority, exteriority, posteriority.

ORM'a–bl– 3. formable, warmable, stormable.

4. informable, conformable, performable, transformable, unwarmable.

ŎRM'al–ize– **3.** formalize, normalize.
4. informalize.
ŎRM'at–iv– **3.** dormitive, formative.
4. afformative, deformative, reformative, informative, transformative.
ŎRM'it–ee– **4.** deformity, conformity, abnormity, enormity.
5. uniformity, multiformity, inconformity, nonconformity, unconformity.
OR'o–er– **3.** borrower, sorrower.
OR'o–ing– **3.** borrowing, morrowing, sorrowing.
ORS'a–bl– **3.** forcible.
4. endorsable, enforceable, divorceable.
ORSH'un–al– **3.** torsional.
4. abortional, contortional, distortional.
ORSH'un–ist– **4.** contortionist, extortionist.
ORT'a–bl– **3.** sortable.
4. unsortable, distortable; *see also* ŌRT'a–bl.
ORT'if–i– **3.** fortify, mortify.
4. defortify, refortify.
ORT'ik–al– **3.** cortical, vortical.
ORT'un–it– **3.** fortunate.
4. unfortunate, misfortunate, importunate.
OS'for–us– **3.** Bosphorus, phosphorus, phosphorous.
OS'i–er– **3.** bossier, flossier, glossier, mossier, saucier.
OS'i–est– **3.** bossiest, flossiest, glossiest, mossiest, sauciest.
OS'i–ness– **3.** bossiness, glossiness, mossiness, sauciness.
OS'it–ee– **3.** docity.
4. gibbosity, globosity, verbosity, nodosity, fungosity, regosity, precocity, jocosity, hircosity, viscosity, muscosity, mucosity, velocity, pilosity, callosity, villosity, gulosity, rimosity, fumosity, venosity, spinosity, vinosity, pomposity, ferocity, serosity, porosity, atrocity, neurocity, nivosity, aquosity.
5. vitreosity, dubiosity, grandiosity, seriosity, curiosity, furiosity, graciosity, speciosity, preciosity, vitiosity, otiosity, bellicosity, varicosity, fabulosity, sabulosity, nebulosity, rugulosity, scrupulosity, animosity, arenosity, luminosity, glutinosity, tenebrosity, tuberosity, ponderosity, generosity, vaporosity, reciprocity, flexuosity, unctuosity, fructuosity, virtuosity, tortuosity.
6. religiosity, ridiculosity, meticulosity, fuliginosity, voluminosity, vociferosity, impetuosity, anfractuosity, infructuosity.
7. impecuniosity.
OSK'op–ee– **4.** necroscopy, microscopy, horoscopy, spectroscopy, gastroscopy, brontoscopy, autoscopy, stethoscopy, cryoscopy.

5. stereoscopy, radioscopy, cranioscopy, dactyloscopy, ophthalmoscopy, organoscopy, lecanoscopy, uranoscopy, retinoscopy, ceraunoscopy, metoposcopy, hieroscopy, deuteroscopy, fluoroscopy, ornithoscopy.
6. meteoroscopy.
OSK'op–ist– **4.** microscopist, misoscopist, stethoscopist.
5. stereoscopist, metoposcopist, oneiroscopist, ornithoscopist.
OS'of–ee– **4.** theosophy, philosophy, psilosophy, gymnosophy, misosophy.
OS'of–er– **4.** theosopher, philosopher, psilosopher, misosopher.
OS'of–ist– **4.** theosophist, philosophist, gymnosophist, chirosophist, misosophist.
OS'of–ize– **4.** theosophize, philosophize.
OST'ik–al– **4.** agnostical, acrostical.
OST'is–izm– **3.** Gnosticism.
4. agnosticism, acrosticism.
OST'rof–ee– **4.** monostrophe, apostrophe.
OT'an–ee– **3.** botany, cottony.
4. monotony.
OT'er–ee– **3.** lottery, pottery, tottery, watery.
OT'er–er– **3.** potterer, totterer, waterer.
OT'er–ing– **3.** pottering, tottering, watering.
OTH'es–is– **3.** prothesis.
4. apothesis, hypothesis.
OT'ik–al– **4.** biotical, despotical, erotical, exotical.
5. anecdotical, idiotical.
OT'il–ee– **3.** dottily, spottily.
OT'i–ness– **3.** dottiness, knottiness, spottiness.
OT'is–izm– **4.** eroticism, neuroticism, exoticism.
OT'om–ee– **3.** scotomy.
4. strabotomy, phlebotomy, lobotomy, dichotomy, trichotomy, cyclotomy, helotomy, aplotomy, tenotomy, zootomy, apotome, microtomy, nephrotomy, neurotomy, loxotomy, autotomy, phytotomy.
5. tracheotomy, stereotomy, osteotomy, cardiotomy, herniotomy, pogonotomy, anthropotomy, laparotomy, Caesarotomy, enterotomy, ichthyotomy, Ichthyotomi.
OT'on–ee– **4.** homotony, monotony, chirotony.
OV'el–er– **3.** hoveler, groveler.
OV'el–ing– **3.** hoveling, groveling.
OZ'it–iv– **3.** positive.
4. appositive, depositive, prepositive, compositive, expositive, transpositive, suppositive.
OZ'it–or– **4.** depositor, repositor, compositor, expositor, transpositor.
OZ'it–um– **4.** depositum, suppositum.

Ô (awe)

[See also Ŏ.]

Single (Masculine) Rhymes

Primary or Secondary Accent Falls on Last Syllable; Imperfect Rhymes Are in Italics.

O– 1. awe, aw [slang], chaw [dial.], daw, gaw, haw, jaw, caw, scaw, law, flaw, claw, slaw, maw, naw [slang], gnaw, paw, raw, braw, draw, craw, straw, saw, pshaw, taw, tau, thaw, squaw, yaw.

2. *jackdaw*, guffaw, *heehaw*, macaw, pilau, pilaw, *coleslaw*, begnaw, papaw, pawpaw, withdraw, hurrah, *seesaw*, foresaw.

3. overawe, overdraw, oversaw.

4. sister-in-law, father-in-law, mother-in-law, brother-in-law.

OB– 1. daub, gaub.

2. bedaub.

OCH– 1. nautch.

2. debauch.

OD– 1. awed, bawd, hawed, jawed, cawed, laud, lawed, flawed, clawed, Claud, Claude, maud, Maude, gnawed, pawed, broad, fraud, sawed, tawed, thawed, vaude [slang], yawed.

2. unawed, belaud, applaud, maraud, abroad, defraud, hurrahed.

3. overawed, underjawed.

ODZ– 1. bawds, lauds, broads, frauds.

2. belauds, applauds, marauds, defrauds.

OF– 1. cough, lof, trough.

2. *chincough*.

3. whooping cough.

OFT– 1. coughed, troughed.

OK– 1. auk, awk, balk, chalk, gawk, hawk, caulk, calk, cawk, lawk [dial.], mawk [slang], talk, stalk, walk, squawk.

2. *Mohawk*, *sparhawk*, *sorehawk*, *goshawk*, *sidewalk*.

3. tomahawk, tommyhawk, baby talk.

OKT– 1. balked, chalked, gawked, hawked, caulked, calked, cawked, talked, stalked, walked, squawked.

3. tomahawked, tommyhawked, baby talked.

OL– 1. all, awl, ball, bawl, fall, gall, Gaul, hall, haul, call, caul, mall, maul, small, pall, Paul, spall, spawl, brawl, drawl, crawl, scrawl, sprawl, trawl, thrall, Saul, shawl,

tall, stall, wall, squall, yawl.

2. *catchall*, *oddball*, *eyeball*, *highball*, *blackball*, *pinball*, *snowball*, *fireball*, *baseball*, *football*, *windfall*, befall, *rainfall*, *downfall*, *snowfall*, *nightfall*, *pitfall*, Bengal, *spurgall*, dance hall, *birdcall*, recall, miscall, *catcall*, bemaul, appall, epaule, Nepal, bethrall, enthrall, *boxstall*, *thumbstall*, install, forestall, withal, devall, sea wall, *stonewall*, *Cornwall*.

3. all in all, free-for-all, basketball, Montreal, evenfall, waterfall, overhaul, falderal, disenthrall, reinstall, fingerstall, therewithal, caterwaul.

OLD– 1. auld, bald, bawled, balled, galled, hauled, called, scald, mauled, palled, spalled, spawled, brawled, drawled, crawled, scrawled, sprawled, trawled, shawled, stalled, walled, squalled, yawled.

2. *blackballed*, *snowballed*, recalled, uncalled, so-called, miscalled, *catcalled*, bemauled, appalled, enthralled, installed, forestalled, *stonewalled*.

3. Archibald, overhauled, unappalled, unenthralled, disenthralled, reinstalled, uninstalled, unforestalled, caterwauled.

OLS– 1. false, halse, valse, waltz.

OLT– 1. halt, fault, gault, malt, smalt, salt, vault.

2. *cobalt*, default, assault, *basalt*, envault, exalt.

3. pseudosalt, somersault.

OM– 1. aum, chawm [slang], gaum, haulm, shawm.

2. imaum.

ON– 1. awn, bawn, dawn, fawn, faun, lawn, pawn, spawn, raun, brawn, drawn, prawn, yawn.

2. impawn, supawn [loc.], indrawn, undrawn withdrawn.

3. leprechaun, underdrawn, overdrawn.

ONCH– 1. haunch, launch, paunch, craunch, staunch.

OND– 1. awned, dawned, fawned, pawned, spawned, prawned, yawned.

2. undawned, unpawned, unspawned.

ONT– 1. daunt, gaunt, haunt, jaunt, flaunt, taunt, vaunt.

2. aflaunt, romaunt, avaunt.

OR–, ORD– *see also* **Ō: ŌR** through **ŌRZ; Ŏ: ŎR** through **ŎRZ.**

OR– 1. gaur, war.

3. balisaur, dinosaur, Minotaur.

4. megalosaur, ichthyosaur.

ORD– 1. ward, sward.

OS– 1. fause [dial.], gausse, hawse, sauce.

3. applesauce.

OST– 2. exhaust.

3. holocaust.

OT– 1. ought, aught, bought, fought, caught, naught, wrought, brought, fraught, sought, taught, taut, thought.

2. *onslaught, dreadnought,* inwrought, unwrought, unfraught, distraut, besought, resought, unsought, untaught, methought, unthought.

3. Argonaut, juggernaut, underwrought, overwrought, afterthought, aforethought.

OTH– 1. auth [slang], cloth, moth, broth, froth, troth.

2. *breechcloth, broadcloth, sackcloth, oilcloth, loincloth,* betroth.

3. saddlecloth.

OZ– *see* **O,** plus " s " or " 's "; **1.** gauze, hawse, cause, clause, pause.

2. because, applause.

3. Santa Claus.

Ô (awe)

[See also Ŏ.]

Double (Feminine) Rhymes

Primary or Secondary Accent Falls on Next to Last Syllable; Imperfect Rhymes are in Italics.

OB′ee– 2. dauby, gauby.
OB′er– 2. dauber.
  3. bedauber.
  5. Mr. Micawber [Dickens].
OCH′er– 2. watcher, swatcher.
  3. debaucher.
OCH′ing– 2. watching, swatching.
  3. debauching.
OD′al– *see* **ÔD′l.**
OD′ed– 2. lauded.
  3. belauded, applauded, marauded, defrauded.
OD′ee– 2. bawdy, dawdy, gaudy.
  3. cum laude.
  5. magna cum laude, summa cum laude.
OD′en– Auden, broaden.
OD′er– 2. lauder, broader, sawder, solder.
  3. belauder, applauder, marauder, defrauder.
OD′ing– 2. lauding.
  3. belauding, applauding, marauding, defrauding.
OD′it– 2. audit, plaudit.
OD′l– 2. dawdle, caudal, caudle.
  3. acaudal, subcaudal, bicaudal.
OD′ri– 2. Audrey, bawdry, tawdry.
O′ee– 2. jawy, flawy, strawy, thawy, yawy.
O′er– 2. jawer, clawer, gnawer, pawer, rawer, drawer, sawer, tawer.
  3. begnawer.
  4. overdrawer.
OF′ish– 2. *crawfish, sawfish, squawfish.*
O′ful– 2. awful, lawful.
  3. unlawful.
OG′er– 2. auger, augur.
O′ing– 2. awing, chawing, hawing, jawing, cawing, lawing, flawing, gnawing, pawing, drawing, sawing, pshawing, tawing, thawing, yawing.
  3. guffawing, heehawing, *outlawing*, withdrawing, hurrahing, *seesawing.*
  4. overawing, overdrawing.
OK′ee– 2. balky, chalky, gawky, hawky, cawky, pawky, talky, talkie, stalky, squawky.

  3. Milwaukee.
  4. walkie-talkie.
OK′er– 2. balker, chalker, gawker, hawker, calker, cawker, talker, stalker, walker, squawker.
  3. *jayhawker, jaywalker, sleepwalker, streetwalker, nightwalker.*
  4. tomahawker, tommyhawker.
OK′ing– 2. balking, chalking, gawking, hawking, calking, cawking, talking, stalking, walking, squawking.
  3. *jayhawking, jaywalking, sleepwalking, streetwalking, nightwalking.*
OK′ish– 2. balkish, chalkish, gawkish, hawkish, mawkish.
OK′us– 2. Daucus, caucus, Glaucus, glaucous, raucous.
OL′a– 2. aula, Paula.
  3. chuckwalla.
OL′boy– 2. ball boy, hallboy, callboy, tallboy.
OLD′er– 2. alder, balder, Balder, scalder.
OLD′ing– 2. balding, scalding, Spaulding.
OL′ee– 2. mauley, rawly, drawly, crawly, scrawly, sprawly, squally.
OL′en– 2. fallen.
  3. *downfallen, crestfallen.*
OL′er– 2. bawler, faller, hauler, caller, mauler, smaller, brawler, drawler, crawler, scrawler, sprawler, trawler, taller, staller.
  3. hog caller, enthraller, forestaller, *potwaller.*
  4. overhauler, caterwauler.
O′less– 2. awless, aweless, jawless, cawless, lawless, flawless, clawless, pawless, strawless.
OL′est– 2. smallest, tallest.
OL′ij– 2. haulage, stallage.
OL′ik– 2. aulic, Gaulic.
  3. hydraulic.
OL′in– 2. all-in, fall-in [slang], cauline, prawlin.
  3. tarpaulin.
OL′ing– 2. balling, bawling, falling, galling,

hauling, calling, mauling, palling, Pawling, brawling, drawling, crawling, scrawling, sprawling, trawling, thralling, shawling, stalling, walling, squalling.

3. *blackballing, snowballing,* befalling, recalling, miscalling, appalling, enthralling, installing, forestalling.

4. overhauling, unenthralling, caterwauling.

OL'is– **2.** caulis, Wallace.

3. Cornwallis.

OL'ish– **2.** Gaulish, smallish, tallish, squallish.

OL'ment– **2.** appallment, enthrallment, installment.

OL'ness– **2.** allness, smallness, tallness.

OLS'er– **2.** falser, waltzer.

OLT'ed– **2.** faulted, halted, malted, salted, vaulted.

3. defaulted, assaulted, exalted.

OLT'ee– **2.** faulty, malty, salty, vaulty.

OLT'er– **2.** alter, altar, falter, halter, malter, smalter, palter, salter, psalter, vaulter, Walter.

3. defaulter, unhalter, Gibraltar, assaulter, exalter.

OLT'ern– **2.** altern, saltern.

3. subaltern.

OLT'ij– faultage, maltage, vaultage.

OLT'ik– **2.** Baltic.

3. basaltic.

4. peristaltic.

OLT'ing– **2.** faulting, halting, malting, salting, vaulting.

3. defaulting, assaulting, exalting.

OLT'less– **2.** faultless, haltless, maltless, saltless.

3. defaultless, assaultless.

OM'a– **2.** cauma, trauma.

ON'a– **2.** fauna, sauna.

3. piscifauna, avifauna.

OND'er– **2.** launder, maunder.

OND'erd– **2.** laundered, maundered.

ON'ee– **2.** awny, dawny, fawny, lawny, Pawnee, pawny, brawny, scrawny, prawny, *Shawnee,* tawny, yawny.

5. mulligatawny.

ON'ing– **2.** awning, dawning, fawning, pawning, spawning, yawning.

ONT'ed– **2.** daunted, haunted, jaunted, flaunted, taunted, vaunted.

3. undaunted, unflaunted, untaunted, unvaunted.

ONT'ee– **2.** haunty, jaunty, flaunty, vaunty.

ONT'er– **2.** daunter, gaunter, haunter, jaunter, flaunter, saunter, taunter, vaunter.

ONT'ing– **2.** daunting, haunting, jaunting, flaunting, taunting, vaunting.

ONT'less– **2.** dauntless, hauntless, vauntless.

OP'er– **2.** scauper, pauper, yawper.

OR'a– through **OR'us–** *see also* **Ô: ÔR'a** through **ÔR'us; Ŏ: ŎR'a** through **ŎR'ward.**

OR'a– **2.** aura, gaura, Laura.

ORD'ed– **2.** warded, swarded.

3. awarded, rewarded.

4. unrewarded.

ORD'er– **2.** warder.

3. awarder, rewarder.

ORD'ing– **2.** warding, swarding.

3. awarding, rewarding.

OR'ee– **2.** scaurie, Laurie, saury.

4. Annie Laurie.

OR'el– **2.** aural, laurel, saurel, quarrel.

3. binaural.

OR'fing– **2.** dwarfing, wharfing.

OR'id– **2.** Taurid.

3. Centaurid.

OR'ik– **2.** auric, tauric, Tauric.

4. androtauric.

OR'us– **2.** Caurus, Laurus, Taurus.

3. thesaurus.

4. Labrosaurus, Hadrosaurus, Mixosaurus, Brontosaurus.

5. Ichthyosaurus, Megalosaurus, Ceratosaurus, Atlantosaurus.

OS'ee– saucy; *see also* **ŎS'ee.**

OS'er– Chaucer, hawser, saucer.

4. cup and saucer.

OS'et– **2.** faucet, Nauset.

OSH'ee– **2.** washy, squashy, swashy.

4. wishy-washy.

OSH'ing– **2.** washing, squashing, swashing.

3. *dishwashing, whitewashing.*

OS'ij– **2.** gaussage, sausage.

OST'ed– **3.** exhausted; *see also* **ŎST'ed.**

OST'er– **2.** Auster, Gloucester.

3. exhauster.

OST'ik– **2.** caustic.

3. encaustic.

4. diacaustic, catacaustic.

OST'ral– **2.** austral, claustral, plaustral.

OT'ee– **2.** haughty, naughty.

OT'en– **2.** boughten, Lawton.

OT'er– **2.** daughter, cauter, slaughter, water.

3. *granddaughter, breakwater, limewater, firewater.*

OTH'er– **2.** author, frother.

OT'ik– nautic.

4. Argonautic, aeronautic.

O'yer– **2.** lawyer, sawyer.

3. top sawyer, pit sawyer.

OZ'al– **2.** causal, clausal, pausal.

OZ'ee– **2.** gauzy, causey, lawzy [dial.].

OZ'er– **2.** hawser, causer, pauser.

OZ'ez– **2.** gauzes, causes, clauses, pauses.

3. becauses.

OZ'ing– **2.** causing, clausing, pausing.

Ô (awe)

[See also Ŏ.]

———————————◆———————————

Triple Rhymes

Primary or Secondary Accent Falls on Second from Last Syllable; Imperfect Rhymes Are in Italics.

OD′a–bl– 3. laudable, plaudable.
  4. applaudable.
OD′i–ness– 3. bawdiness, gaudiness.
OD′it–er– 3. auditor, plauditor.
OF′ul–ee– 3. awfully, lawfully.
  4. unlawfully.
OF′ul–ness– 3. awfulness, lawfulness.
  4. unlawfulness.
OLT′er–ee– 3. saltery, psaltery.
OLT′er–er– 3. alterer, falterer, palterer, psalterer.
OLT′er–ing– 3. altering, faltering, paltering.
  4. unaltering, unfaltering.
OLT′i–est– 3. faultiest, maltiest, saltiest.
OLT′i–ness– 3. faultiness, maltiness, saltiness.
ON′i–er– 3. brawnier, scrawnier, tawnier.
ON′i–est– 3. brawniest, scrawniest, tawniest.
ON′ing–lee– 3. fawningly, yawningly.

OR′e–ate–, OR′i–an– *see also* Ō: ŌR′a–bl
  through ŌR′us–lee; Ŏ: ŎRak–1 through
  ŎRT′un–it.
OR′e–ate– 3. aureate, laureate.
  5. baccalaureate, poet laureate.
OR′i–an– 3. saurian, taurian.
  4. centaurian.
  5. dinosaurian, morosaurian.
OS′it–ee– 3. paucity, raucity.
OT′er–ee– 3. cautery, slaughtery, watery.
OT′er–er– 3. slaughterer, waterer.
OT′er–ing– 3. slaughtering, watering.
OT′i–er– 3. haughtier, naughtier.
OT′i–lee– 3. haughtily, naughtily.
OT′i–ness– 3. haughtiness, naughtiness.
OZ′a–bl– 3. causable, plausible.
  4. uncausable, implausible, unplausible.

ŎŎ (good)

Single (Masculine) Rhymes

Primary or Secondary Accent Falls on Last Syllable; Imperfect Rhymes Are in Italics.

OOD– 1. good, hood, could, should, stood, wood, would.
2. *selfhood,* manhood, unhood, *monkshood,* knighthood, withstood, *scrubwood, beechwood, deadwood, wildwood, hardwood, cordwood, dogwood, plywood, teakwood, milkwood, wormwood, gumwood, greenwood, firewood, rosewood, driftwood, softwood.*
3. babyhood, hardihood, likelihood, livelihood, womanhood, maidenhood, widowhood, sisterhood, spinsterhood, fatherhood, motherhood, brotherhood, parenthood, understood, sandalwood, applewood, satinwood, cottonwood, underwood.
4. misunderstood.
OOF– 1. oof, hoof, poof, woof.
OOK– 1. book, hook, cook, cuck [dial.], look, Lug, Lugh, snook, rook, brook, crook, shook, took, stook, zook [slang].
2. *cookbook, hymnbook, songbook, sambuk, fonduk,* rehook, unhook, *fishhook,* French cook, *outlook,* Chinook, forsook, *ursuk,* betook, partook, mistook.
3. paperbook, prayerbook, pocketbook, account book, minute book, tenterhook, pastry cook, fancy cook, undercook, overcook, overlook, inglenook, undertook, overtook.
4. appointment book.
OOKS– *see* **ŎŎK,** plus " s " or " 's "; **2.** odzooks!
3. Baby Snooks, Richard Crooks.
OOKT– 1. booked, hooked, cooked, looked, rooked, brooked, crooked, stooked [dial.].
2. rebooked, unbooked, rehooked, unhooked, recooked, precooked, uncooked, unrooked, uncrooked.
3. undercooked, overcooked, overlooked.
OOL– 1. Ull, bull, full, pull, Pul, rull, shul, wool.
2. *bulbul, watchful, dreadful, handful, bodeful, gleeful,* half-full, *wrongful, eyeful, sackful, bookful, forkful, giuleful, soulful, brimful,* *roomful, baneful, manful, sinful, tuneful, helpful, cupful, carful, chanceful, glassful, useful, houseful, bashful, wishful, hatful, boatful, doubtful, tactful, artful, hurtful, boastful, loathful, wrathful, healthful, slothful, mirthful, mouthful, rueful, joyful, wirepull* [coll.], *lamb's wool.*
3. semibull, papal bull, chrysobull, meaningful, fanciful, merciful, pitiful, plentiful, bountiful, stomachful, tableful, thimbleful, barrelful, shovelful, teaspoonful, worshipful, teacupful, wonderful, tumblerful, masterful, platterful, colorful, overfull, powerful, prayerful, purposeful, pocketful, bucketful, sorrowful, bellyful [vulgar].
OOLD– 1. bulled, pulled, rulled, wooled.
2. *wirepulled.*
OOLF– 1. wolf.
2. *aardwolf, werewolf.*
3. demiwolf, timber wolf.
OOLZ– 1. bulls, pulls, rulls, shuls, wools.
2. *bulbuls, wirepulls.*
3. semibulls, papal bulls, chrysobulls.
OOM– 1. room, broom, groom, whom.
2. *bedroom, tearoom, cookroom cloakroom, ballroom, greenroom, gunroom, spare room, wareroom, barroom, storeroom, classroom, mushroom, stateroom, coatroom, courtroom, bathroom,* whisk broom, *bridegroom.*
3. coffeeroom, anteroom, sitting room, elbowroom; *see also* **ŪM.**
OOS– 1. puss.
2. *couscous,* sour puss [slang].
OOSH– 1. bush, cush, push.
2. *maybush, shadbush, peabush, dogbush, smokebush, buckbush, gallbush, pearlbush, ambush, pinbush, twinebush, sloebush snowbush, hempbush, forebush, spicebush kinksbush, horsebush, goatbush, saltbush, lotebush, squawbush, jewbush, rosebush, kiddush.*
3. coffeebush, bramblebush, hobblebush, needlebush, flannelbush, brittlebush, buttonbush, sugarbush, soldierbush, pepperbush, fetterbush.

OOT– 1. foot, put, soot.

2. afoot, *webfoot, lobefoot, clubfoot, padfoot, spadefoot, three-foot, Blackfoot, foalfoot, fan- foot, two-foot, crowfoot, barefoot, forefoot, four- foot, six-foot, crossfoot, coltsfoot, plotfoot, shotput.*

3. pussyfoot, tenderfoot, underfoot.

OŎ (good)

Double (Feminine) Rhymes

Primary or Secondary Accent Falls on Next to Last Syllable; Imperfect Rhymes Are in Italics.

OOD'ed– 2. hooded, wooded.
   3. rehooded, unhooded, rewooded, unwood-
ed, red-wooded, thick-wooded, well-wooded,
dense-wooded, soft-wooded, copsewooded.
OOD'ee– 2. hoodie, goody, woody.
   4. goody-goody.
OOD'ing– 2. gooding, hooding, pudding.
OOG'ar– 2. booger [dial.], sugar.
   3. loaf sugar, cane sugar, spun sugar, brown
sugar, beet sugar.
   4. maple sugar.
OOG'ee– 2. boogey, luggie.
   4. boogey-woogey [slang].
OOK'ee– 2. booky, bookie, hooky, cooky,
cookie, looky, snooky, rooky, brooky, crooky,
stookie.
OOK'er– 2. booker, hooker, cooker, looker,
snooker, rooker, stooker.
   3. onlooker.
   4. overlooker.
OOKi'ng– 2. booking, hooking, cooking,
looking, rooking, brooking, crooking, stook-
ing [dial.].
   3. rebooking, rehooking, unhooking, recook-
ing, precooking, good-looking, ill-looking,
onlooking, uncrooking.
   4. undercooking, overcooking, overlooking.
OOK'ish– 2. bookish, hookish, cookish, nook-
ish, rookish, crookish.
OOK'let– 2. booklet, nooklet, brooklet.

OOL'ee– 2. bully, fully, mulley, pulley woolly.
OOL'en– 2. pullen [dial.], woolen.
   3. Anne Boleyn.
OOL'er– 2. buller, fuller, puller,
   3. *wirepuller* [coll.].
OOL'et– 2. bullet, pullet.
OOL'ing– 2. bulling, pulling.
   3. *wirepulling* [coll.].
OOL'ish– 2. bullish, fullish, woollish.
OOM'an– 2. woman.
   3. horsewoman, washwoman.
   4. gentlewoman.
OOSH'er– 2. busher, pusher.
   3. *pen-pusher.*
   4. pedal-pusher.
OOT'ed– 2. footed, sooted.
   3. *splayfooted, web-footed, clubfooted, big-
footed, wing-footed, dog-footed, duck-footed, lame-
footed, one-footed, barefooted, four-footed,* sure-
footed, *catfooted, flat-footed, left-footed, swift-
footed, light-footed, right-footed, claw-footed,
two-footed.*
   4. nimble-footed, cloven-footed, slender-
footed, feather-footed, pussyfooted.
OOT'ee– 2. footy, sooty.
OOT'er– 2. footer, putter.
   3. *webfooter,* four-footer, six-footer.
   4. pussyfooter.
OOT'ing– 2. footing, putting, sooting.
   4. pussyfooting.

ŎŎ (good)

Triple Rhymes

Primary or Secondary Accent Falls on Second from Last Syllable; Imperfect Rhymes Are in Italics.

OOD′i–ness 3. goodiness, woodiness.

OOK′er–ee– 3. bookery, cookery, nookery, rookery.

OOK′ish–lee– 3. bookishly, cookishly, crookishy.

OOK′ish–ness– 3. bookishness, crookishness.

OOL′i–ness– 3. bulliness, pulliness. wooliness,

OOL′ish–ness– 3. bullishness, fullishness, woolishness.

OOM′an–lee– 3. womanly.

4. unwomanly.

5. gentlewomanly.

OOT′ed–ness– 4. splayfootedness, club-footedness, big-footedness, wing-footedness, duck-footedness, lame-footedness, one-footedness, barefootedness, sure-footedness, cat-footedness, flat-footedness, left-footedness, swift-footedness, light-footedness, right-footedness, two-footedness.

OOT′i–ness– 3. footiness, sootiness.

QI (boy)

Single (Masculine) Rhymes

Primary or Secondary Accent Falls on Last Syllable; Imperfect Rhymes Are in Italics.

OI– 1. oy, oye [both Scot.], boy, buoy, foy, goy, goi, joy, coy, koi, loy, cloy, moy, Roy, troy, Troy, soy, toy.

2. *playboy, highboy, ballboy, hallboy, callboy, tallboy, schoolboy, tomboy, doughboy, lowboy, messboy, bat boy, postboy, cowboy,* pakchoi, ahoy, *kill-joy,* enjoy, montjoy, decoy, alloy, deploy, employ, annoy, *viceroy,* destroy, travois, travoy, savoy, Savoy, convoy.

3. stableboy, altar boy, overjoy, hoi polloi [Gr.], Illinois, corduroy, Iroquois.

4. hobbledehoy, avoirdupois, paduasoy.

OID– 1. buoyed, joyed, Lloyd, Floyd, cloyed, sloyd, Freud, toyed, void.

2. rebuoyed, unbuoyed, *rhomboid, stromboid, globoid, cuboid,* enjoyed, decoyed, *sarcoid, discoid, muscoid, mycoid, gadoid, lambdoid, algoid, tringoid, spongoid, fungoid, conchoid, tronchoid, scaphoid, xiphoid, lymphoid, typhoid,* alloyed, *haloid,* deployed, employed, *maskoid, squaloid, tabloid, cycloid, veloid, styloid, diploid, sigmoid, comoid, prismoid,* annoyed, *nanoid, sphenoid, glenoid, ctenoid, spinoid, crinoid, conoid, lunoid, cynoid, ooid, zooid, trappoid, vespoid, laroid, fibroid, android, dendroid, chondroid, spheroid, theroid, pteroid, Negroid, congroid, ochroid, nephroid, toroid, cuproid, astroid,* destroyed, avoid, devoid, *neuroid, thyroid, ursoid, deltoid, lentoid, mastoid, lithoid,* convoyed, *ovoid, equoid, coroid, hyoid, myoid, rhizoid.*

3. scaraboid, overjoyed, pinacoid, coracoid, helicoid, toxicoid, *didelphoid,* ornithoid, ophioid, cardioid, histioid, cephaloid, omphaloid, alkaloid, unalloyed, sepaloid, opaloid, petaloid, hyaloid, hypsiloid, reptiloid, coralloid, metalloid, crystalloid, mongoloid, redeployed, undeployed, reëmployed, unemployed, misemployed, cuculoid, celluloid, condyloid, dactyloid, entomoid, balanoid, melanoid, drepanoid, tetanoid, adenoid, solenoid, catenoid, *arachnoid,* echinoid, cyprinoid, platinoid, belonoid, salamonoid, coronoid, anthropoid, saccharoid, xanthocroid,

cylindroid, amberoid, diphtheroid, antheroid, aneroid, bacteroid, asteroid, hysteroid, redestroyed, undestroyed, lemuroid, ankyroid, ellipsoid, prismatoid, rheumatoid, thanatoid, teratoid, planetoid, herpetoid, granitoid, *odontoid,* lacertoid, obovoid, ichthyoid, trapezoid.

4. pyramidoid, encephaloid, *epicycloid, varicelloid,* marioloid, tentaculoid, tuberculoid, albumenoid, gelatinoid, *tetrahedroid, octahedroid, polyhedroid, salamandroid,* rhinoceroid, *hemispheroid, Melanochroid,* meteoroid, *parathyroid.*

5. pachydermatoid.

OIK– 1. hoick, yoick.

OIKS– 1. hoicks, yoicks.

OIL– 1. oil, boil, Boyle, Doyle, foil, goyle, goil [slang], Hoyle, coil, Coyle, moil, moyle, noil, poil, spoil, roil, broil, stroil, soil, toil, voile.

2. enoil, aboil, *gumboil, parboil, trefoil, tinfoil, gargoyle,* accoil, recoil, uncoil, *turmoil,* despoil, embroil, assoil, *subsoil, topsoil,* etoile, entoil, estoile.

3. multifoil, quaterfoil, counterfoil, disembroil, overtoil.

OILD– 1. oiled, boiled, foiled, coiled, moiled, spoiled, roiled, broiled, soiled, toiled.

2. unoiled, hard-boiled, unboiled, parboiled, soft-boiled, recoiled, uncoiled, despoiled, embroiled, assoiled, entoiled.

3. multifoiled, undespoiled, disembroiled, unembroiled, overtoiled.

OIN– 1. foin, join, coin, coign, quoin, loin, groin.

2. sainfoin, sagoin, Burgoyne, subjoin, adjoin, rejoin, sejoin, enjoin, conjoin, disjoin, misjoin, recoin, eloign, purloin, sirloin, Des Moines, almoign, essoin.

3. surrejoin, interjoin, tenderloin, frankalmoign.

OIND– 1. foined, joined, coined, loined, poind.

2. subjoined, adjoined, rejoined, sejoined, enjoined, conjoined, disjoined, misjoined,

recoined, uncoined, eloigned, purloined, strong-loined.

OINT– 1. oint, joint, point,.

2. adjoint, unjoint, disjoint, *bluejoint*, anoint, appoint, *standpoint*, repoint, pour point, *pourpoint*, West Point, blue point, *viewpoint*, dry point.

3. reappoint, disappoint, needlepoint, counterpoint, cover-point.

OINZ– *see* **QIN,** plus " s " or " 's "; **1.** Poins.

OIS– 1. choice, Joyce, Royce, voice.

2. rejoice, Rolls-Royce, *invoice*.

3. second choice.

OIST– 1. foist, hoist, joist, moist, voiced.

2. rejoiced, revoiced, *invoiced*, unvoiced,

loud-voiced, weak-voiced, low-voiced, clear-voiced, harsh-voiced, sweet-voiced, soft-voiced, faint-voiced.

3. dreamy-voiced, empty-voiced, feeble-voiced, hollow-voiced, silver-voiced, trumpet-voiced.

4. clarion-voiced.

OIT– 1. doit, skoit [slang], moit, droit, toit, quoit.

2. dacoit, exploit, adroit, Detroit.

3. maladroit.

OIZ– *see* **QI,** plus " s " or " 's "; **1.** noise, poise, froise [dial.],.

3. Illinois, erminois, centipoise, equipoise, counterpoise, Iroquois.

4. avoirdupois.

OI (boy)

Double (Feminine) Rhymes

Primary or Secondary Accent Falls on Next to Last Syllable; Imperfect Rhymes Are in Italics.

OI′al– 2. loyal, royal.
   3. unloyal, disloyal, viceroyal, unroyal, sur-royal.
   4. pennyroyal, chapel royal.
OI′ans– 2. buoyance, joyance.
   3. flamboyance, annoyance, chatoyance, prevoyance, clairvoyance.
OI′ant– 2. buoyant.
   3. flamboyant, unbuoyant, chatoyant, prevoyant, clairvoyant.
OID′al– 3. ooidal, zooidal, rhomboidal, cuboidal, typhoidal, discoidal, colloidal, cycloidal, sigmoidal, spheroidal, ovoidal.
   4. anthropoidal, saccharoidal, asteroidal.
   5. paraboloidal, hemispheroidal, meteroidal, elephantoidal.
OID′ans– 2. voidance.
   3. avoidance.
   4. reavoidance.
OID′er– 2. moider [dial.], broider, voider.
   3. embroider, avoider.
OID′ik– 3. diploidic, spheroidic.
OI′er– 2. oyer, Boyer, foyer, coyer, toyer.
   3. enjoyer, decoyer, deployer, employer, annoyer, destroyer.
   4. self-employer, self-destroyer.
OI′ij– 2. buoyage, voyage.
   3. alloyage.
OI′ing– 2. buoying, joying, coying, cloying, ploying, toying.
   3. enjoying, decoying, alloying, deploying, employing, annoying, destroying, envoying, convoying.
OI′ish– 2. boyish, coyish, toyish.
OIL′ee– 2. oily, doily, coyly, noily, roily.
OIL′er– 2. oiler, boiler, foiler, coiler, moiler, spoiler, roiler, broiler, soiler, toiler.
   3. recoiler, uncoiler, despoiler, embroiler.
OIL′ing– 2. oiling, boiling, foiling, coiling, moiling, spoiling, roiling, broiling, soiling, toiling.
   3. recoiling, uncoiling, despoiling, embroiling.
OIL′ment– 3. despoilment, embroilment, entoilment.

OIL′som– 2. roilsome, toilsome.
OIM′ent– 2. cloyment, ployment.
   3. enjoyment, deployment, employment.
   4. unemployment.
OIND′er– 2. joinder, poinder.
   3. rejoinder, misjoinder.
   4. surrejoinder.
OIN′er– 2. joiner, coiner.
   3. rejoiner, enjoiner, conjoiner, purloiner.
OIN′ing– 2. foining, joining, coining, groining, quoining.
   3. subjoining, adjoining, rejoining, enjoining, disjoining, purloining.
OINT′ed– 2. jointed, pointed.
   3. unjointed, conjointed, disjointed, anointed, appointed, unpointed.
   4. unanointed, unappointed, disappointed.
OINT′er– 2. jointer, pointer.
   3. unjointer, disjointer, anointer, appointer, appointor.
   4. disappointer.
OINT′ing– 2. jointing, pointing.
   3. disjointing, anointing, appointing.
   4. disappointing.
OINT′less– 2. jointless, pointless.
OINT′ment– 2. ointment.
   3. disjointment, anointment, appointment.
   4. reappointment, disappointment.
OIS′er– 2. choicer, voicer.
   3. rejoicer.
OIS′ing– 2. voicing.
   3. rejoicing, *invoicing*.
   4. unrejoicing.
OIS′less– 2. choiceless, voiceless.
   3. rejoiceless, *invoiceless*.
OI′som– 2. noisome, cloysome, toysome.
OIST′er– 2. oyster, foister, hoister, cloister, moister, roister.
   3. encloister.
OIST′ing– 2. foisting, hoisting, joisting.
OIT′ed– 2. doited, quoited.
   3. exploited.
   4. unexploited.

OIT'ee– **3.** dacoity.
   4. hoity-toity.
OIT'er– **2.** goiter, loiter, quoiter.
   3. exploiter, adroiter.
   4. reconnoiter.

OI'us– **2.** joyous.
   3. annoyous.
OIZ'ez– **2.** noises, poises.
OIZ'on– **2.** foison, poison.
   3. empoison.

OI (boy)

Triple Rhymes

Primary or Secondary Accent Falls on Second from Last Syllable; Imperfect Rhymes Are in Italics.

OI′a–bl– 3. buoyable.
  4. enjoyable, employable.
  5. unenjoyable.
OI′al–ee– 3. loyally, royally.
  4. disloyally, unroyally.
OI′al–ist– 3. loyalist, royalist.
OI′al–tee– 3. loyalty, royalty.
  4. unloyalty, disloyalty, viceroyalty.
OI′an–see– 3. buoyancy.
  4. flamboyancy, chatoyancy, clairvoyancy.
OI′ant–lee– 3. buoyantly.
  4. flamboyantly, clairvoyantly.
OID′a–bl– 3. voidable.
  4. avoidable.
  5. unavoidable.
OI′ing–lee– 3. cloyingly, toyingly.
  4. annoyingly.
OI′ing–ness– 3. cloyingness, toyingness.
  4. annoyingness.

OI′ish–ness– 3. boyishness, toyishness.
OIL′ing–lee– 3. boilingly, coilingly, moilingly, spoilingly, roilingly, broilingly, soilingly, toilingly.
  4. recoilingly.
OIN′a–bl– 3. joinable, coinable.
  4. unjoinable, disjoinable.
OINT′ed–lee– 3. jointedly, pointedly.
  4. disjointedly.
OI′som–lee– 3. noisomely, cloysomely, toysomely.
OIST′er–er– 3. cloisterer, roisterer.
OIST′er–ing– 3. cloistering, roistering.
  4. uncloistering.
OIST′er–us– 3. boisterous, roisterous.
OIT′er–er– 3. loiterer.
  5. reconnoiterer.
OIT′er–ing– 3. loitering.
  5. reconnoitering.

OU (how)

Single (Masculine) Rhymes

Primary or Secondary Accent Falls on Last Syllable; Imperfect Rhymes Are in Italics.

OU– 1. ow, bow, bough, chow, dhow, fow, how, Howe, jhow, cow, scow, plow, plough, slough, mow, now, pow [slang], row, brow, frau, prow, sow, sough, tau, thou, vow, wow.

2. miaow, luaw, Foochow, Soochow, *chowchow*, endow, *hoosegow* [slang], somehow, allow, lau-lau, *snowplow, haymow*, Mau Mau, enow, erenow, *eyebrow, highbrow, kowtow*, avow, bowwow, *powwow*.

3. golden bough, disendow, anyhow, reallow, disallow, reavow, disavow.

OUCH– 1. ouch, couch, slouch, pouch, grouch, crouch, vouch.

2. avouch.

3. Scaramouch.

OUCHT– 1. oucht [Scot.], couched, slouched, pouched, grouched, crouched, vouched.

2. avouched.

OUD– 1. bowed, boughed, foud, cowed, dowd, loud, cloud, plowed, mowed, rowed, crowd, scrowd [slang], proud, shroud, stroud, vowed, wowed.

2. unbowed, endowed, aloud, allowed, becloud, encloud, replowed, unplowed, beshroud, enshroud, unshroud, avowed, bowwowed.

3. overcloud, overcrowd, unavowed, disavowed.

OUF– 1. ouf, ouphe, auf [G.], kauf [G.].

2. hinauf [G.], herauf [G.].

OUJ– 1. gouge, scrouge.

OUL– 1. owl, bowel, dowl, fowl, foul, howl, jowl, cowl, cowle, scowl, growl, prowl, yowl.

2. screech owl, night owl, afoul, befoul, *peafowl, seafowl*, encowl.

3. guinea fowl, waterfowl.

OULD– 1. owled, dowled, fouled, howled, jowled, cowled, scowled, growled, prowled, yowled.

2. befouled, uncowled.

3. disemboweled, heavy-jowled.

OUN– 1. down, gown, clown, noun, brown, drown, frown, crown, town.

2. adown, *rubdown, touchdown, shakedown, comedown, moondown, sundown*, godown, *lowdown, showdown, nightgown*, renown, *pronoun*, embrown, nut brown, uncrown, discrown, downtown, uptown, *Charlestown*.

3. upside-down, hand-me-down, tumbledown, eider-down, town and gown.

OUND– 1. bound, downed, found, gowned, hound, clowned, mound, pound, round, browned, drowned, frowned, ground, crowned, sound, wound.

2. abound, *hidebound*, rebound, *spellbound*, inbound, unbound, *icebound, eastbound, westbound*, outbound, *northbound, southbound*, redound, undowned, refound, dumbfound, confound, unfound, profound, ungowned, *greyhound, bloodhound, wolfhound, horehound, foxhound*, renowned, impound, compound, propound, expound, around, aground, reground, hard ground, *background*, fineground, unground, *fairground*, coarse-ground, sports ground, lift ground, soft ground, uncrowned, surround, resound, unsound, astound, resound.

3. unrenowned, triple-crowned, vantage ground, holy ground, middle ground, pleasure ground, underground.

4. superabound, merry-go-round, burying ground, burial ground.

OUNDZ– 1. bounds, hounds, pounds, rounds, grounds, sounds, wounds, zounds.

2. abounds, rebounds, dumbfounds, confounds, *greyhounds, bloodhounds, wolfhounds, foxhounds*, impounds, compounds, propounds, expounds, hard grounds, *backgrounds, fairgrounds*, sports grounds, lift grounds, soft grounds, surrounds, resounds, astounds.

3. pleasure grounds.

4. superabounds, merry-go-rounds, burying grounds, burial grounds.

OUNJ– 1. lounge, scrounge.

OUNS– 1. ounce, bounce, jounce, flounce, pounce, rounce, trounce.
2. announce, enounce, denounce, renounce, pronounce.
3. mispronounce.
OUNT– 1. fount, count, mount.
2. account, recount, discount, miscount, *viscount*, amount, remount, surmount, dismount.
3. paramount, catamount, tantamount.
OUR– 1. our, dour, hour, gaur, scour, lour, flour, sour.
2. bescour, besour, devour; *see also* **QU′er.**
OUS– 1. bouse, chouse, douse, gauss, house, louse, blouse, mouse, nous, 'raus [G.], grouse, souse.
2. *clubhouse, madhouse, guardhouse, birdhouse, doghouse, workhouse, warehouse, storehouse, poorhouse, lighthouse, penthouse, outhouse, hothouse, dormouse, titmouse,* hinaus [G.], heraus [G.].
3. countinghouse, public house, customhouse, summerhouse, slaughterhouse, chapter house, porterhouse, Mickey Mouse, fittermouse.
OUST– 1. oust, doused, bloused, roust, groused, soused.
OUT– 1. out, bout, doubt, gout, scout, lout, flout, clout, snout, pout, spout, rout, kraut, drought, grout, Prout, sprout, trout, shout, tout, stout.
2. hold out, *hangout* [slang], *dugout, tryout, blackout, knockout, walkout, lockout, lookout, hereout, thereout, whereout, shutout,* without, throughout, about, redoubt, misdoubt, mahout, boy scout, eelpout, bespout, *downspout,* derout, devout.
3. in-and-out, out-and-out, gadabout, roundabout, hereabout, thereabout, whereabout, knockabout, whirlabout, runabout, stirabout, rightabout, roustabout, waterspout, sauerkraut, undevout.
OUTH– 1. mouth, drouth, south.
2. *loudmouth, hardmouth, bigmouth, frogmouth, snakemouth, flutemouth.*
3. chiselmouth, cottonmouth.
OUTHD– 1. mouthed, southed.
2. *loudmouthed, bigmouthed,* closemouthed.
OUZ– see **QU,** plus " s " or " 's "; **1.** bouse, dowse, house, blouse, mouse, spouse, rouse, browse, drowse, touse, towse.
2. rehouse, espouse, arouse, carouse.
OUZD– 1. housed, bloused, browsed, drowsed, toused, towsed.
2. rehoused, espoused, aroused, caroused.

QU (how)

Double (Feminine) Rhymes

Primary or Secondary Accent Falls on Next to Last Syllable; Imperfect Rhymes Are in Italics.

OU′al– 2. cowal.
3. avowal.
4. disavowal; *see also* QU′el.
OU′an– 2. gowan, rowan, rowen.
OU′ans– 3. allowance, avowance.
4. disallowance, disavowance.
OU′ard– 2. Howard, coward.
OUCH′ee– 2. slouchy, pouchy, grouchy.
OUCH′er– 2. Goucher, coucher, sloucher, poucher, groucher, croucher, voucher.
3. avoucher.
OUCH′ing– 2. couching, slouching, pouching, grouching, crouching, vouching.
3. avouching.
OUD′ed– 2. clouded, crowded, shrouded.
3. beclouded, reclouded, unclouded, enshrouded, unshrouded.
4. unbeclouded, overclouded, overcrowded.
OUD′ee– 2. dowdy, Goudy, howdie, howdy, cloudy, rowdy, shroudy.
3. pandowdy, cum laude.
5. magna cum laude, summa cum laude.
OUD′er– 2. chowder, louder, powder, crowder, prouder.
3. clam chowder, *gunpowder*, face powder.
4. baking powder.
OUD′est– 2. loudest, proudest.
OUD′ing– 2. clouding, crowding, shrouding.
3. beclouding, reclouding, unclouding, enshrouding, unshrouding.
4. overclouding, overcrowding.
OUD′ish– 2. loudish, proudish.
OUD′li– 2. loudly, proudly.
OU′ee– 2. dowie, cowy, yowie [slang], zowie [slang].
OU′el– 2. bowel, dowel, howel, Howell, nowel, Powell, rowel, trowel, towel, vowel.
3. embowel, avowal.
4. disembowel, disavowal, semivowel; *see also* QUL.
OU′en– 2. gowan, rowen, rowan.
OU′er– 2. bower, dower, cower, lower, flower, glower, plower, plougher, power,

rower, shower, tower, vower.
3. embower, endower, allower, *dayflower*, *Mayflower*, *globeflower*, *lidflower*, *windflower*, *bloodflower*, beflower, deflower, *safflower*, *tongueflower*, *blackflower*, *snailflower*, *gallflower*, *wallflower*, *fameflower*, *fanflower*, *swanflower*, enflower, *twinflower*, *coneflower*, *moonflower*, *cornflower*, unflower, *sunflower*, *shoeflower*, *grapeflower*, *lampflower*, *horseflower*, *mistflower*, empower, *manpower*, horse power, *watchtower*, church tower, avower.
4. cauliflower, coralflower, passionflower, cuckooflower, tulipflower, honeyflower, gillyflower, *Julyflower*, candlepower, underpower, overpower, water power, overtower, disavower; *see also* QUR.
OU′ing– 2. bowing, cowing, ploughing, plowing, mowing, rowing, vowing.
3. allowing, avowing.
4. disallowing, disavowing.
OUL′ee– 2. owly, Rowley, growly.
OUL′er– 2. fouler, fowler, howler, scowler, growler, prowler, yowler.
OUL′et– 2. owlet, howlet, rowlet.
OUL′ing– 2. fouling, fowling, howling, cowling, scowling, growling, prowling.
OUL′ish– 2. owlish, foulish, growlish.
OU′ment– 3. endowment, allowment, avowment.
4. disavowment.
OUND′ed– 2. bounded, founded, hounded, mounded, pounded, rounded, drownded [substand.], grounded, sounded, wounded.
3. abounded, rebounded, unbounded, redounded, dumbfounded, confounded, wellfounded, ill-founded, unfounded, impounded, compounded, propounded, expounded, surrounded, regrounded, ungrounded, unsounded, astounded, resounded.
5. superabounded.
OUND′ee– 2. houndy, woundy.
OUND′er– 2. bounder, founder, hounder, flounder, pounder, rounder, sounder.

3. rebounder, dumbfounder, confounder, profounder, impounder, compounder, propounder, expounder, surrounder, resounder.
4. forty-pounder.

OUND′est– **2.** roundest, soundest.
3. profoundest.

OUND′ij– **2.** poundage, groundage, soundage.
3. impoundage.

OUND′ing– **2.** bounding, founding, hounding, mounding, pounding, rounding, grounding, sounding, wounding.
3. abounding, rebounding, unbounding, redounding, dumbfounding, confounding, impounding, compounding, propounding, expounding, surrounding, regrounding, resounding, loud-sounding, well-sounding, unsounding, deep-sounding, clear-sounding, high-sounding, astounding, resounding.
4. evil-sounding.
5. superabounding.

OUND′lee– **2.** roundly, soundly.
3. profoundly, unsoundly.

OUND′less– **2.** boundless, groundless, soundless.

OUND′ling– **2.** foundling, groundling.

OUND′ness– **2.** roundness, soundness.
3. profoundness, unsoundness.

OUN′ee– **2.** downy, brownie, browny, frowny, towny.

OUN′er– **2.** browner, drowner, frowner, crowner.
3. uptowner.

OUN′ing– **2.** downing, gowning, clowning, browning, Browning, drowning, frowning, crowning.
3. ungowning, encrowning, uncrowning, discrowning.

OUN′ish– **2.** clownish, brownish, frownish, townish.

OUNJ′er– **2.** lounger, scrounger.

OUNJ′ing– **2.** lounging, scrounging.

OUN′less– **2.** downless, gownless, frownless, crownless.

OUNS′er– **2.** bouncer, flouncer, pouncer, trouncer.
3. announcer, denouncer, renouncer, pronouncer.

OUNS′ez– **2.** ounces, bounces, flounces, pounces, trounces.
3. announces, denounces, pronounces.

OUNS′il– **2.** council, counsel.
3. recounsel.

OUNS′ing– **2.** bouncing, flouncing, pouncing, trouncing.
3. announcing, denouncing, renouncing, pronouncing.
4. mispronouncing.

OUNS′ment– **3.** announcement, enouncement, denouncement, renouncement, pronouncement.
4. mispronouncement.

OUNT′ed– **2.** counted, mounted.
3. accounted, recounted, uncounted, discounted, miscounted, amounted, remounted,

surmounted, dismounted.

OUNT′ee– **2.** bounty, county, mounty.
3. viscounty.

OUNT′er– **2.** counter, mounter.
3. accounter, encounter, discounter, remounter, surmounter.
4. re-encounter.

OUNT′in– **2.** fountain, mountain.
4. catamountain.

OUNT′ing– **2.** counting, mounting.
3. accounting, recounting, uncounting, discounting, miscounting, amounting, remounting, surmounting, dismounting.

OUN′ward– **2.** downward, townward.

OUR′ee– **2.** houri, dowry, cowrie, floury, flowery.
3. avowry.

OUR′er– **2.** scourer, sourer.
3. deflowerer, devourer.

OUR′est– **2.** dourest, sourest.

OUR′ing– **2.** bowering, cowering, scouring, louring, flouring, souring.
3. embowering, beflouring, devouring.

OUR′lee– **2.** hourly, dourly, sourly.
3. half-hourly.

OUR′ness– **2.** dourness, sourness.

OUS′ee– **2.** blousy, mousey, spousy.

OUS′er– **2.** douser, mouser, souser.

OUS′ez– **2.** douses, louses, blouses, spouses, souses.

OUS′ing– **2.** dousing, blousing, mousing, sousing.

OUST′er– **2.** ouster, jouster, rouster.

OUST′ing– **2.** ousting, jousting, rousting.

OUT′ed– **2.** doubted, gouted, scouted, flouted, clouted, pouted, spouted, routed, grouted, sprouted, shouted, touted.
3. undoubted, misdoubted, derouted, rerouted, unsprouted.

OUT′ee– **2.** doughty, gouty, louty, snouty, pouty, spouty, droughty, grouty, trouty.

OUT′er– **2.** outer, doubter, douter [dial.], jowter [dial.], scouter, louter, flouter, clouter, pouter, spouter, router, grouter, sprouter, trouter, shouter, touter, stouter, Wouter.
3. devouter.
4. in-and-outer, down-and-outer.

OUT′est– **2.** stoutest.
3. devoutest.

OUTH′ee– **2.** mouthy, drouthy.

OUTH′ing– **2.** mouthing, southing.
3. bemouthing.

OUT′ing– **2.** outing, doubting, scouting, flouting, clouting, knouting, pouting, spouting, routing, grouting, sprouting, shouting, touting.
3. undoubting, misdoubting, bespouting, derouting, rerouting, resprouting, unsprouting.

OUT′ish– **2.** outish, loutish, stoutish.

OUT′lee– **2.** stoutly.
3. devoutly.
4. undevoutly.

OUT′let– **2.** outlet, troutlet.

OUT′ness– 2. outness, stoutness.
3. devoutness.
OU′wou– 2. bowwow, powwow, wou-wou.
OUZ′al– 2. housal, spousal.
3. espousal, arousal, carousal; *see also* OUZ′l.
OUZ′ee– 2. bousy, housy, lousy, blowsy, mousy, drowzy, frowzy, grousy.
OUZ′er– 2. dowser, mouser, Mauser, schnauzer, rouser, browser, trouser, Towser.
3. espouser, arouser, carouser.
OUZ′ez– 2. houses, blouses, spouses, rouses, browses.

3. rehouses, unhouses, espouses, arouses, carouses.
4. public houses.
OUZ′ij– 2. housage, spousage.
3. espousage.
OUZ′ing– 2. dowzing, housing, blowzing, mousing, rousing, browsing, drowsing.
3. rehousing, unhousing, espousing, arousing, carousing.
4. public housing.
OUZ′l– 2. ouzel, housal, housel, mousle, spousal, tousle.
3. espousal, carousal.

QU (how)

Triple Rhymes

OU′a–bl– 3. plowable, ploughable.
4. endowable, allowable, avowable.
5. unallowable, disallowable, unavowable, disavowable.
OU′a–blee– 4. allowably, avowably.
5. unallowably, unavowably.
OUD′ed–ness– 3. cloudedness, crowdedness.
4. becloudedness, uncloudedness.
5. overcrowdedness.
OUD′il–ee– 3. dowdily, cloudily, rowdily.
OUD′i–ness– 3. dowdiness, cloudiness, rowdiness.
OU′er–ee– 3. bowery, Bowery, dowery, lowery, flowery, glowery, showery, towery.
OU′er–er– 3. lowerer, flowerer, glowerer, showerer.
4. deflowerer.
OU′er–ing– 3. dowering, cowering, lowering, flowering, glowering, showering, towering.
4. deflowering, empowering.
5. overpowering, overtowering.
OU′er–less– 3. dowerless, flowerless, powerless.
OUL′er–ee– 3. owlery, fowlery.
OUND′a–bl– 3. groundable, soundable.
4. confoundable, impoundable, compoundable, astoundable.
OUND′ed–lee– 3. roundedly.

4. unboundedly, dumbfoundedly, confoundedly.
5. unconfoundedly.
OUND′ed–ness– 3. roundedness.
4. unboundedness, dumbfoundedness, confoundedness, unfoundedness, ungroundedness.
OUND′ing–lee– 3. boundingly, poundingly, soundingly, woundingly.
4. aboundingly, confoundingly, resoundingly, astoundingly.
OUND′less–lee– 3. boundlessly, groundlessly, soundlessly.
OUND′less–ness– 3. boundlessness, groundlessness, soundlessness.
OUNT′a–bl– 3. countable, mountable.
4. accountable, uncountable, discountable, surmountable.
5. unaccountable, insurmountable, unsurmountable.
OUNT′a–blee– 4. accountably.
5. unaccountably, insurmountably, unsurmountably.
OUT′i–ness– 3. doughtiness, goutiness, spoutiness, droughtiness.
OUZ′il–ee– 3. drowsily, frowsily.
OUZ′i–ness– 3. lousiness, drowziness, frowziness.
OUZ′ing–lee– 3. rousingly.
4. carousingly.

Ū (you)

Single (Masculine) Rhymes

Primary or Secondary Accent Falls on Last Syllable; Imperfect Rhymes Are in Italics.

U– 1. oo, ooh, août [F.].
3. toodle-oo [slang].
BU– 1. boo, bu, boue [F.], bout [F.].
2. Abou, abu, aboo, *baboo, babu,* taboo, tabu, yabu, yaboo, debut, *zebu,* au bout [F.], bamboo.
3. bugaboo, peekaboo, marabou, âme de boue [F.], jusqu'au bout [F.], caribou.
CHU– 1. chew.
2. kachoo, *choo-choo* [slang], kerchoo, eschew.
3. catechu.
DU– 1. do, doo [Scot.], due, dew.
2. ado, adieu, subdue, bedew, redo, skiddoo [slang], *mildew,* chandoo, chandu, endew, endue, rendu [F.], *vendue,* indue, *Hindu,* undo, perdu, perdue, Purdue, fordo, foredo, misdo, outdo, *hoodoo,* to-do, *voodoo.*
3. billet-doux, derring-do, how-dy-do [coll.], honeydew, residue, underdo, overdo, overdue, well-to-do.
FU– 1. fu, fou [Scot. & dial. Eng.], fou [F.], feu, phoo.
2. mafoo, mafu, phoo-phoo.
GU– 1. goo, goût [F.].
2. ragout, bon goût [F.], burgoo, burgout, googoo.
3. mauvais goût [F.].
HU– 1. hoo, who, Hu.
2. ahu, *wahoo, Yahoo,* boohoo, yoohoo.
3. ballyhoo [slang].
JU– 1. Jew.
2. *baju* [Malay], bijou, *juju.*
3. acajou, kinkajou, sapajou.
KU– 1. coo, coup.
2. *aku, baku, cuckoo, coo-coo* [slang].
3. après coup [F.].
LU– 1. loo, Lu, Lou, blue, blew, flu, flue, flew, glue, clue, clew, clou [F.], slue, slew.
2. halloo, sky-blue, true-blue, *igloo,* unglue, tolu, *curlew, Lulu, Sulu, Zulu.*
3. ululu.
4. hullabaloo.
MU– 1. moo, moue [F.].

2. *emu,* immew, *limu, umu, mu-mu.*
NU– 1. new, knew, nu, Nu, gnu, nous [F.].
2. anew, *Danu,* canoe, renew, *venue, fire-new,* foreknew
3. ingénue, entre nous [F.], avenue, revenue, parvenu, hoochinoo, detinue, retinue.
4. Tippecanoe.
PU– 1. pu, pugh, pooh, poo [Scot. & dial. Eng.].
2. *napoo,* shampoo, rompu, pooh-pooh.
RU– 1. rue, roo, roux [F.], brew, bruh [Malay], drew, grew, grue, gru, crew, cru [F.], screw, sprew, sprue, true, strew, shrew, through, threw.
2. *garoo,* karroo, imbrue, withdrew, Peru, *froufrou,* accrue, *corkscrew, thumbscrew,* unscrew, untrue, bestrew, construe, guru.
3. kangaroo, buckaroo, gillaroo, wallaroo, wanderoo, potoroo, reconstrue, misconstrue, overstrew, overthrew.
SU– 1. sue, Sue, sou, Sioux, Soo.
2. ensue, pursue.
3. Daibutsu.
SHU– 1. shoo, shoe, chou [F.].
2. cachou, cashoo, cashew, *fichu, snowshoe, horseshoe.*
3. overshoe.
TU– 1. to, too, two, tu [L.], tout [F.], stew.
2. battue, tattoo, *Bantu, Gentoo,* lean-to, unto, hereto, thereto, whereto, *set-to,* surtout, virtu.
3. cockatoo, voilà tout [F.], *in situ* [L.].
VU– 1. vous [F.].
2. à vous [F.], *kivu.*
3. rendezvous, parley-voo [slang].
WU– 1. woo, Wu.
WHU– 1. whoo.
2. tu-whoo.
4. tu-whit, tu-whoo.
YU– 1. u, U, you, ewe, yew, few, phew, hue, hew, Hugh, q, Q, cue, queue, Kew, skew, lieu, mu, mew, smew, pew, spew, view, whew.
2. *bayou,* imbue, adieu, *curfew,* askew, *rescue,*

purlieu, review, revue, preview, *purview*.
3. w, W, double-U, I. O. U., feverfew, Elihu, barbecue, curlicue, retinue, interview.
ZŪ– 1. zoo, Zu.
2. kazoo, razoo, zoozoo.
4. Kalamazoo.

UB– 1. boob [slang], doob, jube, cube, Rube, rube [slang], tube.
2. *jujube*.
3. inner tube.
UCH– 1. ooch, hooch, cooch, mooch, mouch, smooch, smouch, pooch [all slang], brooch.
UD– 1. booed, chewed, dude, food, feud, hued, Jude, cued, queued, lewd, looed, blued, flued, flewed, glued, slued, slewed, mood, mooed, nude, snood, rude, rued, rood, brood, brewed, crude, screwed, prude, trued, shrewd, shood, shooed, stewed, thewed, viewed, wooed.
2. tabooed, imbued, eschewed, subdued, St. Jude, miscued, allude, elude, delude, prelude, illude, collude, *postlude*, unglued, preclude, seclude, include, conclude, occlude, exclude, almud, subnude, denude, renewed, shampooed, abrood, imbrued, home-brewed, unbrewed, accrued, unscrewed, obtrude, subtrude, detrude, retrude, intrude, protrude, construed, extrude, Mahsud, resued, pursued, *ètude*, reviewed, previewed, unwooed, exude, transude.
3. reimbued, unimbued, unsubdued, interlude, unrenewed, misconstrued, unpursued, hebetude, quietude, desuetude, mansuetude, consuetude, habitude, longitude, solitude, amplitude, lenitude, plenitude, magnitude, omnitude, torpitude, turpitude, nigritude, lassitude, crassitude, spissitude, dulcitude, latitude, rectitude, sanctitude, altitude, multitude, lentitude, aptitude, promptitude, certitude, fortitude, pinguitude, gravitude, servitude.
4. inquietude, disquietude, similitude, definitude, infinitude, decrepitude, solicitude, vicissitude, exactitude.
UDZ– 1. dudes, foods, feuds, Jude's, moods, nudes, snoods, roods, broods, crudes, prudes.
2. alludes, eludes, deludes, preludes, postludes, precludes, secludes, includes, concludes, occludes, excludes, denudes, obtrudes, subtrudes, detrudes, retrudes, intrudes, protrudes, extrudes, *ètudes*, exudes, transudes.
3. interludes, longitudes, solitudes, magnitudes, latitudes, altitudes, multitudes, aptitudes, certitudes.
UF– 1. oof, ouf, boof [loc.], bouffe [F.], goof, hoof, loof, poof, pouf, spoof, roof, proof, woof.
2. shadoof, behoof, aloof, reroof, reproof, *foolproof*, *fireproof*, disproof, thatch roof, Tartuffe, woof-woof.
3. cloven hoof, gable roof, waterproof, weatherproof, bulletproof.
4. opéra bouffe [F.].

UFT– 1. goofed [slang], hoofed, poofed, spoofed, roofed, woofed.
2. reroofed, unroofed, thatch-roofed.
3. cloven-hoofed, waterproofed, weather-proofed, bulletproofed.
UG– 1. boog [slang], fugue, fougue [F.], goog [slang], toug.
UJ– 1. huge, smoodge, rouge, Scrooge, scrouge, stooge [slang], vouge.
3. vermifuge, febrifuge, subterfuge.
UK– 1. uke [slang], duke, douc, gook [slang], juke, cuke [slang], Luke, fluke, snook, puke, spook, sook, tuke, stook, yeuk, yewk, yuk, yuke.
2. rebuke, chibouk, bambuk, caoutchouc, archduke, beduke, Chinook, charuk, peruke.
3. Hexateuch, octateuch, Pentateuch, Heptateuch.
4. bashi-bazouk.
UKS– *see* **ŪK**, plus " s " or " 's "; **1.** Fuchs.
UL– 1. buhl, fool, ghoul, gool [dial.], cool, school, mewl, mool, mule, pool, pule, spool, rule, drool, tool, tulle, stool, Yule.
2. *jambool*, *jambul*, befool, pilule [F.], *whirlpool*, slide rule, misrule, pasul, *toadstool*, *footstool*.
3. vestibule, Istambul, April-fool, molecule, ridicule, vermicule, verricule, reticule, Sunday school, swimming pool, wading pool, Liverpool, overrule.
ULZ– *see* **ŪL**, plus " s " or " 's "; **1.** gules, Jules.
UM– 1. boom, doom, doum, fume, ghoom, coom, coomb, loom, bloom, flume, gloom, plume, neume, spume, room, rheum, broom, brume, brougham, groom, grume, soum, tomb, womb, whom, zoom.
2. predoom, foredoom, perfume, legume, inhume, exhume, illume, *heirloom*, embloom, begloom, engloom, beplume, deplume, displume, simoom, *bedroom*, *tearoom*, *cloakroom*, *ballroom*, *barroom*, *storeroom*, *stateroom*, *courtroom*, *mushroom*, *bridegroom*, assume, subsume, consume, entomb, *costume*, resume, presume.
3. sonic boom, nom de plume, anteroom, reading room, dining room, drawing room, dressing room, living room, elbowroom, reassume, hecatomb, disentomb.
UMD– 1. boomed, doomed, fumed, loomed, bloomed, gloomed, plumed, spumed, roomed, broomed, groomed, tombed, zoomed.
2. predoomed, foredoomed, inhumed, exhumed, illumed, begloomed, engloomed, beplumed, deplumed, displumed, assumed, subsumed, consumed, entombed, *costumed*, resumed, presumed.
3. reassumed, preassumed, unassumed, unconsumed, unentombed, disentombed, unresumed.
UN– 1. boon, Boone, doon, dune, foon [slang], goon [slang], hewn, June, coon, loon, lune, moon, noon, spoon, rune, croon, prune,

strewn, soon, tune, toon, woon, wun, swoon.

2. baboon, bridoon, typhoon, buffoon, lagoon, dragoon, Rangoon, Calhoun, unhewn, jejune, cacoon, lacune, racoon, tycoon, cocoon, balloon, galloon, shalloon, walloon, doubloon, immune, simoon, commune, midnoon, forenoon, lampoon, tampoon, harpoon, impugn, oppugn, expugn, teaspoon, maroon, gambroon, gadroon, spadroon, quadroon, seroon, patroon, poltroon, quintroon, bestrewn, bassoon, monsoon, gossoon, attune, platoon, ratoon, spittoon, altun, entune, pontoon, spontoon, cartoon, festoon, aswoon.

3. rigadoon, barracoon, pantaloon, honeymoon, harvest moon, afternoon, tablespoon, macaroon, picaroon, octoroon, overstrewn, oversoon, Saskatoon, coquetoon, musketoon, importune, opportune, picayune.

4. intercommune, vinegarroon, inopportune.

ŪND– 1. duned, mooned, nooned, spooned, runed, crooned, tuned, wound, swooned.

2. Mahound, cocooned, ballooned, communed, impugned, harpooned, marooned, attuned, platooned, entuned, pontooned, untuned, cartooned, festooned.

3. pantalooned, honeymooned, unattuned, importuned.

ŬP– 1. boop [slang], dupe, Goop, hoop, jupe, coop, coup, scoop, loop, bloop [slang], cloop, sloop, noop [Scot. & dial. Eng.], snoop, poop, roup, drupe, droop, group, croup, scroop, troop, troupe, soup, supe [slang], stoop, stoep, stupe, stoup, swoop, whoop.

2. recoup, saloop, adroop, aggroup.

3. cock-a-hoop, Guadalupe, nincompoop, liripoop, loop-the-loop, paratroop.

ŬPT– 1. duped, hooped, couped, cooped, scooped, looped, snooped, drooped, grouped, trouped, stooped, swooped, whooped.

2. recouped, regrouped.

ŪR– 1. boor, dour, jour [F.], cour [F.], cure, lure, mure, moor, pure, poor, spoor, sure, tour, your.

2. endure, perdure, coiffure, bahur, nahoor, abjure, adjure, *injure*, bonjour [F.], conjure, secure, liqueur, concours, procure, obscure, allure, velure, velour, velours, colure, amour, unmoor, demure, immure, *tenure*, inure, impure, assure, cocksure, ensure, insure, unsure, *Ashur*, brochure, mature, *detour*, *contour*, gravure, huzoor, causeur.

3. perendure, abat-jour [F.], sinecure, resecure, insecure, pedicure, manicure, epicure, chevelure, condylure, blackamoor, belamour, Kohinoor, connoisseur, reassure, reinsure, coinsure, cynosure, ligature, tablature, amateur, premature, immature, climature, armature, signature, curvature, comfiture, confiture, forfeiture, garniture, furniture, portraiture, loquitur [L.], sepulture, garmenture, aperture, overture, coverture, voyageur.

4. affaire d'amour [F.], miniature, judicature, imprimatur, temperature, literature, expenditure, discomfiture, divestiture, investiture, autogravure, photogravure, rotogravure.

ŪRD– 1. gourd, cured, lured, moored, toured.

2. endured, perdured, coiffured, abjured, adjured, *injured*, conjured, secured, procured, uncured, obscured, allured, unmoored, immured, inured, assured, ensured, insured, matured, *detoured, contoured*.

3. unabjured, readjured, *reinjured*, resecured, unsecured, pedicured, manicured, unprocured, unobscured, unallured, uninured, reassured, self-assured, unassured, unmatured, unensured, uninsured.

ŪS– 1. use, deuce, douce, goose, juice, luce, loose, sluice, moose, meuse, mousse, noose, pouce, puce, russe [F.], Bruce, cruse, spruce, truce, trousse, Zeus.

2. abuse, caboose, adduce, traduce, educe, deduce, reduce, seduce, induce, conduce, produce, diffuse, profuse, *mongoose, verjuice*, excuse, *couscous*, unloose, recluse, occluse, vamoose [slang], burnoose, papoose, abstruse, disuse, misuse, obtuse, retuse, pertuse.

3. calaboose, reproduce, introduce, Syracuse, à la russe [F.], charlotte russe, Norway spruce, *Odysseus*.

4. superinduce, reintroduce, hypoteneuse.

ŪSH– 1. bouche, douche, louche [F.], mouche, smush [dial.], ruche, whoosh.

2. babouche, baboosh, debouch, bonne bouche [F.], barouche, farouche [F.], cartouche, cartouch.

3. Scaramouch, gobemouche [F.].

ŪST– 1. boost, deuced, goosed, juiced, joust, loosed, sluiced, meused, noosed, roost, spruced, truced.

2. adduced, traduced, educed, deduced, reduced, seduced, induced, conduced, produced, unloosed, reclused, vamoosed [slang], burnoosed, pertused.

3. untraduced, undeduced, unreduced, unseduced, uninduced, unproduced, reproduced, introduced.

4. superinduced, unreproduced, reintroduced, unintroduced.

ŪT– 1. Ute, Butte, boot, beaut [slang], hoot, jute, coot, cute, scute, scoot, loot, lute, flute, cloot, plute [slang], sluit, moot, mute, meute, smoot, newt, snoot, route, root, bruit, brute, fruit, croûte [F.], soot, suit, chute, shoot, toot, tute.

2. reboot, *freeboot*, unboot, refute, confute, argute, cahoot [slang], Paiute, acute, galoot [slang], salute, dilute, pollute, volute, immute, commute, permute, transmute, Canute, minute, cornute, depute, repute, impute, compute, dispute, *Rajput*, imbrute, cheroot, reroute, reroot, enroot, en route, unroot, uproot, *breadfruit, grapefruit, starfruit*, first fruit, recruit, en croûte [F.], choucroute [F.], nasute, dissuit, mis-suit, *lawsuit*, hirsute, pursuit, *offshoot, trapshoot, upshoot, outshoot*, skeet shoot, surtout, astute.

3. marabout, attribute, retribute, subacute, coûte que coûte [F.], prosecute, persecute, execute, baldicoot, bandicoot, absolute, resolute, dissolute, obvolute, evolute, involute, convolute, Malemute, comminute, disrepute, arrowroot, orrisroot, demisuit, birthday suit, parachute, bumbershoot [slang], overshoot, substitute, destitute, institute, constitute, prostitute.

4. electrocute, irresolute.

ŪTH– 1. booth, couth, sleuth, ruth, Ruth, truth, sooth, tooth, youth.

2. uncouth, Duluth, *thuluth*, vermouth, untruth, in sooth, forsooth.

3. polling booth, voting booth.

ŪTHD– 1. smoothed, soothed.

2. besmoothed, resmoothed, unsmoothed, resoothed, unsoothed.

ŪTHE– 1. booth, smooth, soothe.

2. besmooth, resoothe.

3. polling booth, voting booth.

ŪTHT– 1. sleuthed, toothed.

2. *gap-toothed, sharp-toothed.*

ŪV– 1. move, snoove, roove [Scot.], groove, prove, you've.

2. behoove, amove, remove, ingroove, approve, reprove, improve, disprove.

3. reapprove, disapprove.

ŪVD– 1. moved, grooved, proved.

2. behooved, ungrooved, approved, unproved.

3. unremoved, unimproved.

ŪVZ– *see* **ŪV**, plus " s " or " 's "; **1.** hooves.

3. horses' hooves.

ŪZ– *see* **Ū** through **ZŪ**, plus " s " or " 's "; **1.** ooze, use, booze, choose, fuze, fuse, guze, Hughes, skuse [dial. & coll.], lose, blues, muse, meuse, news, snooze, ruse, roose, bruise, Druse, cruise, cruse, trews, whose.

2. ill-use, misuse, abuse, effuse, refuse, refuze, diffuse, infuse, confuse, perfuse, transfuse, suffuse, accuse, excuse, amuse, bemuse, debruise, rebruise, peruse, chartreuse, masseuse, danseuse, contuse, enthuse.

3. disabuse, rediffuse, reinfuse, circumfuse, interfuse, retransfuse, reaccuse, reperuse, Vera Cruz, Santa Cruz.

ŪZD– 1. oozed, used, boozed, fused, skused [dial. & coll.], mused, meused, snoozed, roosed, bruised, cruised.

2. well-used, ill-used, unused, misused, abused, effused, refused, diffused, infused, confused, perfused, transfused, suffused, accused, excused, amused, bemused, debruised, rebruised, unbruised, perused, recruised, contused, enthused.

3. disabused, rediffused, reinfused, retransfused, reaccused, self-accused, unexcused, reperused, unperused, uncontused.

ŪZH– 1. luge, rouge, Bruges, vouge.

3. l'étoile rouge [F.].

Ū (you)

Double (Feminine) Rhymes

Primary or Secondary Accent Falls on Next to Last Syllable; Imperfect Rhymes Are in Italics.

U'a– 2. skua, luah, Lua.
3. ulua, atua.
4. punalua, Maunalua.
10. apologia pro vita sua [L.].

U'al– 2. dual.
3. eschewal, subdual, renewal, pursual, reviewal; *see also* **Ū'el.**

U'an– 2. duan, Siouan, Chouan.
3. Luchuan.

U'ans– 2. nuance.
3. eschewance, renewance, pursuance.

U'ant– 2. truant, suant.
3. pursuant; *see also* **Ū'ent.**

U'ard– 2. Seward, steward; *see also* **Ū'erd.**

UB'a– 2. juba, Cuba, kuba, Luba, Nuba, subah, tsuba, tuba.
3. Baluba, saxtuba.

UB'al– 2. Jubal, tubal.

UB'ee– 2. booby, cubi, looby, ruby.

UB'er– 2. goober, cuber, Khubur, suber, tuber, tubar.

UB'ij– 2. cubage, tubage.

UB'ik– 2. cubic.
3. cherubic.

UB'ing– 2. cubing, tubing.

UB'l– 2. Jubal, ruble, tubal.

UB'let– 2. cubelet, tubelet.

UB'rik– 2. lubric, rubric.

UCH'ee– 2. smoochy [slang].
3. Il Duce, Beluchi [It.], penuchi.
4. hootchy-kootchy [slang].

UCH'er– 2. blucher, moocher [slang], smoocher [slang].

UD'a– 2. Buddha, Judah, Nuda.
3. picuda, Bermuda.
4. barracuda.

UD'al– 2. udal, feudal.
3. paludal.

UD'ed– 2. snooded, brooded.
3. alluded, eluded, deluded, colluded, precluded, secluded, included, concluded, occluded, excluded, denuded, obtruded, subtruded, detruded, retruded, intruded, protruded, extruded, exuded, transuded.
4. uneluded, undeluded, unprotruded, unextruded, unexuded.

UD'ee– 2. boodie, feudy, moody, broody.
3. Yehudi, almude.

UD'ens– 2. prudence.
3. imprudence.
4. jurisprudence.

UD'ent– 2. prudent, student.
3. concludent, occludent, imprudent, protrudent.
4. jurisprudent.

UD'er– 2. lewder, nuder, ruder, brooder, cruder, shrewder, sudor [L.], Tudor.
3. alluder, eluder, deluder, includer, concluder, excluder, denuder, detruder, intruder, protruder, extruder.

UD'est– 2. lewdest, nudest, rudest, crudest, shrewdest.

UD'ik– 2. Sudic.
3. paludic.

UD'ing– 2. brooding.
3. abrooding, alluding, eluding, deluding, precluding, including, concluding, occluding, excluding, denuding, intruding, protruding, exuding, transuding.

UD'ish– 2. dudish, moodish, nudish, prudish, shrewdish.

UD'ist– 2. Buddhist, feudist, nudist, prudist.

UD'l– 2. boodle, doodle, coodle, noodle, nuddle [dial.], poodle, roodle, soodle.
3. caboodle [slang], flapdoodle [coll.].
4. Yankee-Doodle.

UD'lee– 2. lewdly, nudely, rudely, crudely, prudely, shrewdly, soodly [dial.].

UD'lz– *see* **ŪD'l–,** plus " s " or " 's "; 2. oodles [slang].

UD'ness– 2. lewdness, nudeness, rudeness, crudeness, shrewdness.

UD'o– 2. scudo, pseudo.
3. barbudo, picudo, escudo, testudo.
4. consuetudo [L.].

UD'or– 2. sudor, Tudor.

UD′u– 2. hoodoo, pudu, *to-do*, voodoo.

U′ee– 2. bowie, buoy, chewy, dewy, Dewey, phooey [slang], gooey [slang], hooey [slang], hui, cooee, Louis, louey [slang], bluey, blooey [slang], fluey, flooey, gluey, screwy, tui, stewy, thewy, viewy.
3. *mildewy*, St. Louis, chop suey.

U′el– 2. duel, fuel, jewel, newel, Reuel, gruel, cruel, crewel, shewel, tewel.
3. bejewel; *see also* **Ū′al.**

U′ent– 2. fluent.
3. confluent, perfluent; *see also* **Ū′ant.**

U′er– 2. ewer, chewer, doer, fewer, hewer, cooer, skewer, bluer, gluer, newer, ruer, brewer, screwer, truer, sewer, suer, shoer, tewer, stewer, viewer, wooer.
3. eschewer, wrongdoer, subduer, undoer, misdoer, outdoer, canoer, renewer, shampooer, bestrewer, ensuer, pursuer, horseshoer, tattooer, reviewer.
4. evildoer, overdoer, interviewer.

U′erd– 2. skewered, sewered, steward; *see also* **Ū′ard.**

U′est– 2. fewest, bluest, newest, truest.

U′et– 2. chewet, Jewett, bluet, cruet, suet.
3. revuette.

UF′a– 2. buffa [It.], chufa, gufa, goofa, goofah, luffa, loofah, stufa [It.].
4. catalufa.

UF′ee– oofy [slang], goofy [slang], spoofy [slang], roofy, woofy.

UF′er– 2. goofer [slang], hoofer [slang], spoofer, roofer.
3. aloofer.

UF′ing– 2. goofing [slang], hoofing [slang], spoofing, roofing, woofing.
3. waterproofing, weatherproofing, bulletproofing.

UF′less– 2. roofless, proofless.
3. reproofless.

UF′us– 2. goofus [slang], rufus, Rufus, rufous.

UG′a– 2. fuga [It.], muga, ruga.
3. Beluga, Cayuga.
4. Chattanooga.

UG′al– 2. bugle, fugle, fugal, jugal, frugal.
3. infrugal, unfrugal.
4. vermifugal, febrifugal.

UG′ee– 2. Bugi, boogie, boogey, boogy, luggie, rugae.
4. boogie-woogie.

UG′l– 2. bugle, fugle.

UG′ler– 2. bugler, fugler.

UG′ling– 2. bugling, fugling.

UG′o– 2. Hugo.
3. colugo, besugo [Sp.].

U′id– 2. fluid, druid.

U′ij– 2. brewage, sewage.
3. reviewage.

U′ik– 2. Buick.
3. toluic.

U′in– 2. ruin, bruin, sewen, sewin.
3. aruin.

U′ing– 2. booing, chewing, doing, dewing, hewing, cooing, cuing, bluing, blueing, gluing, cluing, clewing, sluing, slewing, mooing, mewing, spewing, ruing, brewing, screwing, trueing, strewing, suing, shoeing, whooing, stewing, viewing, wooing.
3. tabooing, debuting, imbuing, kachooing, eschewing, subduing, wrongdoing, *mildewing*, induing, undoing, misdoing, outdoing, voodooing, curfewing, boohooing, yoohooing, requeuing, *rescuing*, hallooing, rebluing, regluing, ungluing, recluing, reclewing, canoeing, renewing, shampooing, poohpoohing, accruing, rescrewing, unscrewing, bestrewing, construing, ensuing, pursuing, horseshoeing, tattooing, reviewing, previewing, rewooing.
4. peekabooing, evil-doing, underdoing, overdoing, ballyhooing, barbecuing, reconstruing, misconstruing, rendezvousing, interviewing.

U′is– 2. Lewis, Louis, brewis.
3. St. Louis.

U′ish– 2. Jewish, bluish, gluish, newish, shrewish, truish.
3. reviewish.

U′ist– 2. cueist.
3. canoeist, revuist.

UJ′ee– 2. fuji, Fuji, suji.
3. Mt. Fuji.

UK′a– 2. Uca, nucha, yuca.
3. cambuca, sambuca, palooka [slang], farruca, garookuh, verruca, festuca, bazooka.
4. noctiluca.

UK′al– 2. ducal, coucal, nucal, nuchal.
3. archducal.
4. noctilucal, Pentateuchal.

UK′ee– 2. fluky, snooky, spooky, rouky, sooky, Sukey, Yuki.
3. Kabuki, Belucki.

UK′er– 2. euchre, lucre, fluker, snooker, puker.
3. rebuker.
4. involucre.

UK′us– 2. fucus, fucous, leucous, mucus, mucous, rookus.
3. caducous.
4. noctilucous.

UL′a– 2. ula, boola [slang], Beulah, gula, Gula, goolah, hula, Lula, moola [slang], Eula, Zula.
3. bamboula.
4. Ashtabula, boola-boola, hula-hula.

UL′ee– booly, booley, duly, Dooley, coolie, coulee, coolly, bluely, newly, pooly, drooly, truly, tule, Thule.
3. patchouli, unduly, unruly, untruly.
5. iconoduly, Ultima Thule.

UL′er– 2. cooler, mewler, puler, pooler, spooler, ruler, drooler, tooler.
3. wine cooler, retooler.
4. ridiculer, water cooler.

UL′ess– 2. dewless, Jewless, flueless, clueless, pewless, screwless, viewless.
3. reviewless.

UL′est– 2. coolest, foolest.

3. damfoolest.

UL′ij– 2. Coolidge, schoolage.

UL′ing– 2. fooling, cooling, schooling, mewling, puling, pooling, spooling, ruling, drooling, tooling, stooling.
3. befooling, recooling, misruling, retooling.
4. overruling.

UL′ip– 2. julep, tulip.
3. mint julep.

UL′ish– 2. foolish, ghoulish, coolish, schoolish, mulish, pulish.
3. pound-foolish, tomfoolish.

UL′u– 2. ulu, hulu, Lulu, Tulu, Zulu.
4. Honolulu.

UM′a– 2. duma, pneuma, puma, Yuma.
3. mazuma [slang].
4. Montezuma.

UM′al– 2. brumal, tombal.

UM′an– 2. human, Newman, crewman, Truman.
3. inhuman, nonhuman, unhuman.
4. ultrahuman, superhuman, preterhuman; *see also* ŪM′en and ŪM′in.

UM′ee– 2. boomy, fumy, bloomy, gloomy, plumy, spumy, rheumy, roomy, broomy, groomy.
3. perfumy.

UM′en– 2. numen, rumen.
3. albumen, albumin, hegumen, legumen, legumin, acumen, illumine, bitumen.
4. catechumen; *see also* ŪM′an and ŪM′in.

UM′ent– 3. imbuement, eschewment, subduement, induement, renewment, imbruement, accruement.

UM′er– 2. boomer, doomer, fumer, humor, bloomer, plumer, roomer, rumor, groomer, tumor.
3. perfumer, ill-humor, illumer, assumer, consumer, entomber, costumer, resumer, presumer.

UM′erd– 2. humored, bloomered, rumored.
3. good-humored, bad-humored, ill-humored.

UM′id– 2. fumid, humid, tumid.

UM′ij– 2. doomage, plumage, roomage.

UM′ik– 2. humic, cumic, tombic.
3. costumic.

UM′in– 3. albumin, legumin, relumine, illumine; *see also* ŪM′an and ŪM′en.

UM′ing– 2. booming, dooming, fuming, looming, blooming, glooming, pluming, spuming, rooming, brooming, grooming, tombing, zooming.
3. predooming, foredooming, perfuming, inhuming, exhuming, illuming, assuming, consuming, entombing, resuming, presuming.
4. reassuming, unassuming, reentombing, disentombing, unpresuming.

UM′less– 2. boomless, doomless, fumeless, loomless, bloomless, gloomless, plumeless, spumeless, roomless, broomless, groomless, tombless, zoomless.

UM′let– 2. boomlet, plumelet, roomlet, groomlet, tomblet.

UM′or– 2. humor, rumor, tumor; *see also* ŪM′er.

UM′us– 2. dumous, fumous, humus, humous, plumous, spumous, brumous, grumous.
3. posthumous.

UN′a– 2. Una, luna, puna, Poonah, tuna.
3. lacuna, vicuna, Peruna, Fortuna.

UN′al– 2. dunal.
3. tribunal, lagoonal, lacunal, communal.

UN′ar– 2. lunar.
3. lacunar, sublunar, translunar.
4. semilunar, plenilunar, novilunar, interlunar, cassumunar.

UN′ee– 2. duny, luny, loony, Cluny, moony, puny, puisne, spoony, tuny, swoony.
3. festoony.

UN′er– 2. schooner, mooner, spooner, runer, crooner, pruner, sooner, tuner, swooner.
3. dragooner, lacunar, ballooner, sublunar, translunar, communer, lampooner, impugner, oppugner, harpooner, marooner, attuner.
4. semilunar, plenilunar, circumlunar, importuner.

U′ness– 2. fewness, blueness, newness, trueness.

UN′ful– 2. spoonful, tuneful.
3. balloonful, *teaspoonful*, untuneful.

UN′ik– 2. Munich, Punic, runic, tunic.

UN′ing– 2. mooning, nooning, spooning, crooning, pruning, tuning, swooning.
3. ballooning, communing, lampooning, impugning, oppugning, harpooning, attuning, retuning.

UN′is– 2. Eunice, funis, Tunis.

UN′ish– 2. moonish, spoonish.
3. buffoonish, balloonish, poltroonish.

UN′ism– 3. buffoonism, poltroonism.
4. opportunism.

UN′ist– 3. balloonist, lampoonist, harpoonist, bassoonist, cartoonist.
4. opportunist.

UN′it– 2. unit.
3. Anunit.

UN′less– 2. boonless, moonless, spoonless, runeless, tuneless.

UN′o– 2. uno [Sp.], Juno, Juneau, Bruno.

UN′um– 2. unum [L.].
3. jejunum.
6. e pluribus unum [L.].

UN′us– 2. Prunus.
3. fortunous, Portunus.

UN′yun– 2. union.
3. trade-union, reunion, nonunion, disunion, communion, trades-union.
4. labor union, excommunion.
5. intercommunion.

UP′a– 2. pupa, rupa, supa, stupa.
3. macupa [Tag.], arupa, ketupa.
4. kamarupa.

UP′ee– 2. kewpie, scoopy, loopy, snoopy, rupee, droopy, croupy, stoopy, swoopy, whoopee [slang].

UP′er– 2. duper, hooper, cooper, scooper,

looper, snooper, drooper, grouper, trooper, trouper, souper, super, stooper, stupor, swooper, whooper.

3. recouper, *mosstrooper*.

4. loop-the-looper, Oxford grouper, paratrooper.

ŪP'id– **2.** Cupid, Lupid, stupid.

ŪP'ing– **2.** duping, hooping, cooping, scooping, looping, snooping, drooping, grouping, trooping, trouping, stooping, swooping, whooping.

3. recouping, regrouping.

ŪP'ish– **2.** scoopish, loopish, snoopish, droopish, croupish, soupish, stoopish, swoopish.

3. Oxford groupish.

ŪP'l– duple, cupel, pupal, pupil, drupel, scruple.

3. subduple, quadruple, octuple, centuple, quintuple, septuple, sextuple.

ŪP'let– **2.** duplet, looplet, drupelet.

3. *quadruplet, octuplet, quintuplet, septuplet, sextuplet.*

ŪP'ment– **2.** groupment.

3. recoupment, aggroupment, regroupment.

ŪP on– **2.** coupon, jupon, yupon.

ŪR'a– cura [Sp.], lura, pleura, Mura, sura, surah.

3. ahura, tempura [Jap.], asura, caesura, flexura, datura, Keturah, vettura [It.], fattura [It.], bravura.

4. tambaroora, velatura, angostura.

5. appoggiatura, coloratura, fioritura [It.].

ŪR'al– **2.** Ural, dural, jural, lural, mural, neural, pleural, plural, rural, crural, sural.

3. subdural, procural, tellural, adneural, hypural, bicrural, caesural.

4. sinecural, intramural, extramural, antemural, intermural, interneural, commissural.

ŪR'ans– **2.** durance.

3. endurance, perdurance, procurance, allurance, assurance, insurance.

4. reassurance, reinsurance.

ŪR'ant– **2.** durant, jurant.

3. endurant, obscurant, assurant, insurant.

ŪR'at– **2.** curate, jurat, surat.

ŪR'ee– **2.** ewry, fury, houri, Jewry, jury, Curie, fleury, moory, Drury.

3. grand jury, de jure [L.]. Missouri.

4. counterfleury.

ŪR'er– **2.** curer, lurer, moorer, purer, poorer, surer, tourer.

3. endurer, abjurer, adjurer, obscurer, securer, procurer, allurer, demurer, inurer, impurer, assurer, ensurer, insurer, maturer.

4. reassurer, reinsurer, immaturer; *see also* **ŪR'or.**

ŪR'est– **2.** purest, poorest, surest.

3. securest, obscurest, demurest, impurest.

ŪR'ij– **2.** moorage, murage.

ŪR'ik– **2.** pleuric, neuric.

3. sulphuric, mercuric, telluric, caesuric.

4. dolichuric.

ŪR'im– **2.** Urim, Purim.

ŪR'ing– **2.** during, juring, curing, luring, mooring, spooring, touring.

3. enduring, abjuring, adjuring, conjuring, non-juring, recuring, securing, procuring, obscuring, alluring, unmooring, immuring, manuring, inuring, assuring, ensuring, insuring, maturing, retouring.

4. unalluring, resecuring, reassuring, reinsuring.

ŪR'ish– **2.** boorish, Moorish, poorish.

3. maturish.

4. amateurish.

ŪR'ist– **2.** jurist, purist, tourist.

4. manicurist.

5. caricaturist.

ŪR'lee– **2.** dourly, poorly, purely, surely.

3. securely, obscurely, demurely, impurely, maturely.

4. prematurely, immaturely.

ŪR'ment– **3.** abjurement, conjurement, securement, procurement, obscurement, allurement, immurement inurement.

4. reassurement, reinsurement.

ŪR'ness– **2.** poorness, pureness, sureness.

3. secureness, obscureness, demureness, impureness, cocksureness, matureness.

4. insecureness, immatureness.

ŪR'o– **2.** Uro, bureau.

3. maduro.

5. chiaroscuro.

ŪR'or– **2.** furor, juror.

3. adjuror, grand juror; *see also* **ŪR'er.**

ŪR'us– **2.** urus, Eurus.

3. anurous, Honduras, macrurous, Arcturus.

4. dolichurus.

US'a– **2.** Sousa, tuza.

3. Medusa, empusa.

4. Tuscaloosa, babirusa, Arethusa.

US'al– **3.** medusal, occlusal.

5. hypotenusal.

US'ee– **2.** goosy, juicy, Lucy, sluicy, moosey.

3. Debussy.

US'ens– lucence, nuisance.

3. translucence.

4. noctilucence.

US'ent– **2.** lucent.

3. adducent, traducent, abducent, reducent, conducent, producent, nonlucent, unlucent, translucent.

4. noctilucent, interlucent.

US'er– **2.** gooser, juicer, looser, sluicer, nooser, sprucer.

3. adducer, traducer, deducer, reducer, seducer, inducer, conducer, producer, unlooser, abstruser.

4. reproducer, introducer.

US'est– **2.** loosest, sprucest.

3. profusest, abstrusest.

US'ez– *see* **ŪS,** plus " s " or " 's ".

US'ful– **2.** useful, juiceful.

3. unuseful.

USH'a– **2.** fuchsia, Lucia.

3. Jerusha.

USH'al– **2.** crucial.

3. fiducial, minutial.
USH′an– 2. Lucian.
  3. Confucian, Aleutian.
  4. Lilliputian, Rosecrucian; *see also* **ŪSH′un.**
USH′un– 3. locution, ablution, pollution, dilution, solution, volution.
  4. attribution, retribution, distribution, contribution, execution, prosecution, persecution, allocution, elocution, collocution, absolution, dissolution, evolution, revolution, involution, convolution, resolution, imminution, diminution, comminution, substitution, destitution, restitution, institution, constitution.
  5. redistribution, ventrilocution, circumlocution, interlocution, electrocution, irresolution, circumvolution; *see also* **ŪSH′an.**
USH′us– 2. Lucius.
  3. astucious.
US′id– 2. deuced, lucid, mucid.
  3. pellucid, translucid.
US′ij– 2. usage.
  3. disusage, misusage, abusage.
US′ik– 2. fucic, glucic, mucic.
  3. ageusic.
  4. parageusic, anacusic.
US′ing– 2. loosing, sprucing.
  3. adducing, traducing, educing, deducing, reducing, seducing, inducing, conducing, producing, unloosing.
  4. reproducing, introducing.
US′is– 3. prosneusis.
  4. therapeusis, anacrusis.
US′iv– 3. abusive, deducive, seducive, inducive, conducive, effusive, diffusive, confusive, perfusive, transfusive, elusive, delusive, illusive, collusive, reclusive, seclusive, inclusive, conclusive, exclusive, obtrusive, intrusive, contusive.
  4. inconducive, inconclusive, unobtrusive.
US′lee– 2. loosely.
  3. diffusely, profusely, abstrusely, obtusely.
US′less– 2. useless, juiceless.
US′ment– 3. traducement, deducement, reducement, seducement, inducement, producement.
  5. superinducement.
US′ness– 2. looseness, spruceness.
  3. diffuseness, profuseness, recluseness, abstruseness, obtuseness.
US′o– 2. trousseau, whoso.
  3. Caruso.
  5. Robinson Crusoe.
US′om– 2. gruesome, twosome.
UST′ed– 2. boosted, roosted.
UST′er– 2. booster, fooster [Ir.], jouster, rooster, brewster, Brewster.
UT′a– 2. muta, tuta [It.].
  3. macuta, aluta, battuta [It.], Matuta.
  4. barracouta.
  5. Mater Matuta.
UT′al– 2. brutal.
  3. refutal, recruital.
UT′ant– 2. mutant, nutant.

3. commutant, disputant.
UT′ate– 2. scutate, mutate, nutate.
UT′ed– 2. booted, hooted, scooted, luted, looted, fluted, mooted, muted, rooted, bruited, fruited, sooted, suited, chuted, tooted, touted.
  3. *freebooted*, rebooted, unbooted, refuted, confuted, saluted, diluted, polluted, unlooted, immuted, commuted, transmuted, cornuted, deputed, reputed, imputed, computed, disputed, rerooted, rerouted, enrooted, unrooted, unrooted, uprooted, recruited, unsuited, voluted.
  4. executed, prosecuted, persecuted, undiluted, unpolluted, obvoluted, evoluted, revoluted, involuted, convoluted, recommuted, uncommuted, comminuted, undisputed, substituted, restituted, instituted, constituted, prostituted.
  5. unexecuted, reprosecuted, unprosecuted, unpersecuted, electrocuted, reinstituted, reconstituted, unconstituted.
UT′ee– 2. booty, bootee, beauty, duty, cootie [slang], cutie [slang], looty, fluty, muti, smooty, snooty, putti [It.], rooty, fruity, sooty, tutti.
  3. *freebooty*, Djibouti, Jibouti, agouti.
  4. tutti-frutti.
UT′en– gluten.
  4. highfaluten [coll.].
UT′er– 2. booter, fouter, hooter, cooter, cuter, luter, looter, fluter, mooter, Mutter [G.], muter, neuter, pewter, rooter, router, bruiter, fruiter, chuter, shooter, tooter.
  3. *freebooter*, confuter, accoutre, acuter, diluter, polluter, commuter, permuter, transmuter, Grossmutter [G.], minuter, imputer, computer, disputer, uprooter, recruiter, *peashooter*, *beanshooter*, *trapshooter*, *sharpshooter*, skeet shooter, astuter.
  4. coadjutor, executer, prosecuter, persecuter, substituter, restituter, instituter, constituter, prostituter.
  5. electrocuter; *see also* **ŪT′or.**
UT′est– 2. cutest, mootest, mutest.
  3. acutest, minutest, astutest.
UTH′er– 2. Luther, smoother, soother.
  3. uncouther.
UTH′ful– 2. ruthful, truthful, toothful, youthful.
  3. untruthful.
UTH′less– 2. ruthless, truthless, soothless, toothless, youthless.
UTH′ness– 2. smoothness, soothness.
  3. uncouthness.
UTH′som– 2. toothsome, youthsome.
UT′ij– 2. scutage, mutage, rootage, fruitage.
UT′ik– 2. mutic.
  3. scorbutic, toreutic.
  4. hermeneutic, therapeutic, pharmaceutic, diazeutic.
  5. antiscorbutic.
UT′il– 2. utile, futile, sutile.
  3. inutile, unfutile; *see also* **ŪT′l.**

UT′in– **2.** cutin, glutin.
3. Rasputin.
4. highfalutin [coll.].
UT′ing– **2.** booting, hooting, scooting, looting, fluting, mooting, muting, rooting, bruiting, fruiting, suiting, sooting, shooting, chuting, tooting.
3. *freebooting*, unbooting, refuting, confuting, saluting, diluting, polluting, commuting, permuting, transmuting, deputing, imputing, computing, disputing, rerooting, rerouting, recruiting, enrooting, unrooting, uprooting, *trapshooting*, skeet shooting.
4. prosecuting, executing, persecuting, highfaluting [coll.], convoluting, comminuting, parachuting, overshooting, substituting, instituting, constituting, prostituting.
5. electrocuting.
UT′ish– **2.** brutish, sootish.
UT′ist– **2.** lutist, flutist, fruitist.
3. computist.
4. absolutist, hermeneutist, therapeutist, pharmaceutist, parachutist.
UT′iv– **2.** fruitive.
4. coadjutive, persecutive, resolutive, evolutive, convolutive, substitutive, restitutive, constitutive.
UT′l– **2.** utile, futile, footle, rootle, brutal, sutile, tootle.
3. inutile, refutal, unfutile, recruital.
UT′lee– **2.** cutely, mutely, brutely.
4. acutely, minutely, astutely.
4. absolutely, resolutely, dissolutely, convolutely.
UT′less– **2.** bootless, rootless, fruitless.
3. reputeless.
UT′let– **2.** rootlet, fruitlet.
UT′ment– **3.** confutement, inbrutement, recruitment.
UT′ness– **2.** cuteness, muteness, bruteness.
3. acuteness, minuteness, hirsuteness, astuteness.
4. absoluteness, dissoluteness.
UT′o– **2.** Pluto, scruto, tutto [It.].
3. tenuto [It.].
4. assoluto [It.], risoluto [It.], sostenuto.
UT′or– **2.** suitor, sutor, tutor.
3. protutor.
4. executor, prosecutor, persecutor; *see also* **ŪT′er.**
UT′u– **2.** tutu, yutu.
UT′um– **2.** scutum, sputum.
3. verutum [L.].
UT′ur– **2.** future, puture, suture.
UT′us– **2.** Plutus, Brutus.
3. arbutus, scorbutus, computus.
UV′al– **3.** removal, approval, reproval, disproval.
4. disapproval.
UV′ee– **2.** movie, groovy.
UV′en– **2.** hooven, proven.
3. unproven, disproven.
UV′er– **2.** Hoover, louver, Louvre, mover, groover, prover.

3. Vancouver, remover, maneuver, approver, reprover, improver, disprover.
4. disapprover.
UV′erd– **2.** louvered.
3. maneuvered.
UV′ing– **2.** moving, grooving, proving.
3. removing, unmoving, approving, reproving, improving, disproving.
4. disapproving.
UV′less– **2.** moveless, grooveless.
UV′ment– **2.** movement.
3. approvement, improvement, disprovement.
U′ya– **2.** huia.
4. alleluia, hallelujah.
UZ′a– **2.** Musa, tuza.
4. Arethusa.
5. lallapalooza [slang].
UZ′al– **2.** musal.
3. refusal, perusal.
UZ′ans– **2.** usance.
3. misusance, recusance.
UZ′ant– **3.** accusant, recusant.
UZ′ee– **2.** oozy, boozy, choosy, choosey, doozy, newsy, snoozy, drusy, woozy.
UZ′er– **2.** oozer, user, boozer, chooser, doozer, fuser, loser, muser, snoozer, bruiser, cruiser.
3. abuser, refuser, diffuser, infuser, confuser, transfuser, suffuser, accuser, excuser, palouser, amuser, peruser.
UZ′ez– **2.** uses, oozes, boozes, chooses, fuses, loses, muses, snoozes, ruses, rooses, bruises, cruses, cruises.
3. misuses, abuses, refuses, diffuses, infuses, confuses, transfuses, suffuses, accuses, excuses, amuses, bemuses, peruses, masseuses, danseuses, contuses.
UZH′ee– **2.** bougie, rougy.
UZH′un– **2.** fusion, trusion.
3. effusion, diffusion, infusion, profusion, transfusion, suffusion, allusion, elusion, delusion, illusion, collusion, reclusion, preclusion, seclusion, inclusion, conclusion, occlusion, exclusion, obtrusion, detrusion, retrusion, intrusion, protrusion, extrusion, contusion, pertusion, Malthusian.
4. circumfusion, interfusion, self-delusion, reinclusion, reocclusion, disillusion.
UZ′ing– **2.** oozing, boozing, choosing, fusing, losing, musing, snoozing, bruising, cruising.
3. misusing, abusing, refusing, diffusing, infusing, confusing, transfusing, suffusing, accusing, excusing, amusing, bemusing, perusing, contusing.
4. interfusing, unaccusing, self-accusing, unamusing.
UZ′iv– **3.** accusive, amusive.
4. unamusive.
UZ′l– **2.** ouzel, foozle, goozle [dial.].
3. bamboozle, refusal, perusal.
UZ′ler– **2.** foozler, goozler [dial.].
3. bamboozler.
UZ′ment– **3.** accusement, amusement.

Ū (you)

❖

Triple Rhymes

U′a–bl– 3. doable, suable, stewable, viewable.
4. undoable, subduable, renewable, construable, pursuable, reviewable, unviewable.
5. unsubduable, unrenewable, unreviewable.
U′ant–lee– 3. fluently, truantly.
4. confluently, pursuantly.
UB′er–ans– 4. protuberance, exuberance.
UB–er–ant– 4. protuberant, exuberant.
5. unexuberant.
UB′er–us– 3. suberous, tuberous.
4. protuberous.
UB′i–a– 3. nubia, Nubia, rubia.
5. rabirubia.
UB′i–an– 3. Nubian.
4. Danubian.
UB′ik–l– 3. cubicle, cubical.
4. cherubical.
UB′it–us– 3. cubitus.
4. accubitus, decubitus, concubitous, concubitus.
UB′i–us– 3. dubious, rubious.
UB′ri–kate– 3. lubricate, rubricate.
UB′ri–us– 4. lugubrious, salubrious.
5. insalubrious.
UD′a–bl– 4. alludable, deludable, precludable, includable, concludable, denudable, protrudable, extrudable.
5. unincludable, unconcludable.
UD′in–al– 4. paludinal, testudinal.
5. longitudinal, attitudinal, altitudinal, aptitudinal.
UD′i–ness– 3. moodiness, broodiness.
UD′i–nize– 3. attitudinize, platitudinize.
UD′in–us– 4. paludinous, testudinous.
5. latitudinous, platitudinous, multitudinous, fortitudinous.
6. solicitudinous, vicissitudinous.
UD′i–o– 3. studio.
4. preludio.
UD′it–ee– 3. nudity, rudity, crudity.
UD′i–um– 3. studium.
4. preludium, postludium.
UD′i–us– 3. studious.

4. preludious, unstudious.
U′el–er– 3. dueler, fueler, jeweler, grueler, crueler.
U′el–est– 3. duelist, cruelest, crewelist.
U′el–ing– 3. dueling, fueling, jeweling, grueling.
4. refueling, bejeweling.
U′er–ee– 3. ewery, brewery.
U′i–ness– 3. dewiness, glueyness, screwiness.
U′in–us– 3. ruinous, bruinous, pruinous.
U′it–ee– 3. cruety, suety.
4. acuity, vacuity, circuity, annuity, strenuity, tenuity, congruity, fatuity, gratuity, fortuity.
5. assiduity, ambiguity, exiguity, contiguity, conspicuity, perspicuity, innocuity, promiscuity, superfluity, ingenuity, continuity, incongruity, perpetuity.
6. incontinuity, discontinuity.
U′it–iv– 3. fruitive, tuitive.
4. intuitive.
5. unintuitive.
U′it–us– 4. circuitous, fatuitous, gratuitous, pituitous, fortuitous.
UK′er–ee– 3. dukery, spookery.
4. caducary.
UK′ul–ent– 3. luculent, muculent.
UL′e–an– 3. joulean, Julian.
4. Herculean, cerulean.
UL′i–a– 3. Julia, thulia.
4. abulia.
5. parabulia, hyperbulia.
UL′ing–lee– 3. foolingly, coolingly, pulingly, droolingly, toolingly.
UL′ish–lee– 3. foolishly, ghoulishly, coolishly, mulishly.
UL′ish–ness– 3. foolishness, ghoulishness, coolishness, mulishness.
UL′it–ee– 4. credulity, sedulity, garrulity.
5. incredulity.
UL′i–um– 3. thulium.
4. nebulium, peculium.
UM′a–bl– 4. assumable, resumable, presum-

able, consumable.
  5. unassumable, unpresumable, inconsumable, unconsumable.
UM′a–blee– 4. presumably.
  5. inconsumably.
UM′e–fi– 3. humefy, tumefy.
UM′en–al– 3. noumenal.
  5. catechumenal; *see also* **ŪM′in–al.**
UM′er–al– 3. humeral, numeral.
UM′er–ee– 3. bloomery, plumery.
  4. perfumery, costumery.
UM′er–us– 3. humerus, humorous, numerous, rumorous, tumorous.
  4. unhumorous, innumerous.
UM′i–lee– 3. boomily, fumily, gloomily, rheumily, roomily.
UM′in–a– 3. lumina, numina, Rumina.
  4. alumina.
UM′in–al– 3. luminal, noumenal, ruminal.
  4. cacuminal, voluminal.
  5. catechumenal.
UM′in–ant– 3. luminant, ruminant.
  4. illuminant, nonruminant.
UM′in–ate– 3. luminate, ruminate.
  4. acuminate, cacuminate, illuminate, ferruminate.
UM′i–ness– 3. fuminess, bloominess, gloominess, pluminess, spuminess, roominess, rheuminess.
UM′ing–lee– 3. boomingly, doomingly, fumingly, loomingly, bloomingly, gloomingly, plumingly, spumingly, zoomingly.
  4. consumingly.
  5. unassumingly.
UM′in–us– 3. luminous, numinous.
  4. albuminous, leguminous, acuminous, aluminous, voluminous, bituminous.
UM′less–lee– 3. boomlessly, fumelessly, bloomlessly, gloomlessly, plumelessly, spumelessly, zoomlessly.
UM′ord–lee– 3. rumoredly.
  4. good-humoredly, bad-humoredly, ill-humoredly.
UM′or–us– 3. humorous, rumorous, tumorous.
UM′ul–ate– 3. cumulate, tumulate.
  4. accumulate.
  5. reaccumulate.
UM′ul–us– 3. cumulus, tumulus.
UN′a–bl– 3. tunable.
  4. impugnable, expugnable, untunable.
UN′er–ee– 3. lunary.
  4. buffoonery, cocoonery, sublunary, poltroonery.
  5. pantaloonery.
UN′i–form– 3. uniform, funiform, cuniform, luniform.
UN′ik–ate– 3. tunicate.
  4. communicate.
  5. excommunicate.
  6. intercommunicate.
UN′i–lee– 3. loonily, moonily, spoonily, swoonily.
UN′ing–lee– 3. mooningly, spooningly, crooningly, swooningly.

  4. ballooningly.
UN′ish–lee– 3. moonishly, spoonishly, swoonishly.
  4. buffoonishly, balloonishly, poltroonishly.
UN′it–ee– 3. unity, munity.
  4. triunity, jejunity, immunity, community, impunity.
  5. importunity, opportunity.
  6. intercommunity, inopportunity.
UN′it–iv– 3. unitive, punitive.
  4. communitive.
UN′less–lee– 3. moonlessly, tunelessly.
UN′yun–ist– 3. unionist.
  4. Reunionist, nonunionist, communionist.
UP′a–bl– 3. dupable.
  4. undupable, recoupable.
UP′er–ate– 4. recuperate, vituperate.
UP′er–ee– 3. dupery, coopery.
UP′i–al– 3. rupial, troopial, troupial.
  4. marsupial.
UP′i–er– 3. loopier, droopier, croupier, soupier.
UP′i–est– 3. loopiest, droopiest, soupiest.
UP′ing–lee– 3. scoopingly, loopingly, snoopingly, droopingly, troopingly, stoopingly, swoopingly, whoopingly.
UP′ish–lee– 3. loopishly, snoopishly, droopishly, croupishly.
UP′ul–us– 3. lupulus, scrupulous.
  4. unscrupulous.
UR′a–bl– 3. durable, curable.
  4. endurable, securable, incurable, procurable, assurable, insurable.
  5. unsecurable, uninsurable.
UR′a–blee– 3. durably, curably.
  4. endurably, incurably.
  5. unendurably.
UR′al–ee– 3. plurally, murally, rurally.
UR′al–ist– 3. pluralist, muralist, ruralist.
UR′al–izm– 3. pluralism, ruralism.
UR′at–iv– 3. durative, curative.
  4. indurative, depurative, muturative.
UR′et–ee– 3. surety.
  4. cocksurety, unsurety.
UR′i–a– 3. curia [L.].
  4. Manchuria, decuria, Lemuria, Etruria.
  5. glycosuria.
UR′i–al– 3. urial, curial, Muriel.
  4. figurial, augurial, mercurial, purpureal, centurial.
UR′i–an– 3. durian.
  4. Manchurian, tellurian, lemurian, Etrurian, Missourian, centurian, Arthurian.
UR′i–ate– 3. muriate.
  4. infuriate, luxuriate, centuriate.
UR′i–ent– 3. prurient.
  4. esurient, luxuriant, scripturient, parturient.
UR′if–i– 3. purify, thurify.
UR′ing–lee– 4. enduringly, alluringly, assuringly.
UR′i–o– 3. durio, curio, Thurio.
UR′ish–lee– 3. boorishly, poorishly.
  5. amateurishly.
UR′it–ee– 3. purity, surety.
  4. security, obscurity, demurity, impurity,

cocksurety, maturity, futurity.

5. insecurity, prematurity, immaturity.

UR′i–us– 3. furious, curious, spurious.

4. sulphureous, injurious, perjurious, incurious, uncurious, penurious, luxurious, usurious.

5. unpenurious.

US′a–bl– 4. unloosable, produceable.

5. unproduceable.

USH′i–a– 3. fuchsia, Lucia.

4. minutia.

USH′i–al– 3. crucial.

4. fiducial.

USH′i–an– 4. caducean, Confucian.

USH′un–al– 5. elocutional, evolutional, substitutional, institutional, constitutional.

6. circumlocutional.

USH′un–er– 5. executioner, resolutioner, revolutioner.

USH′un–ist– 5. executionist, elocutionist, resolutionist, evolutionist, revolutionist, constitutionist.

US′i–bl– 3. crucible.

4. adducible, traducible, educible, deducible, reducible, seducible, inducible, conducible, producible.

5. irreducible, unreducible, unproducible.

US′id–lee– 3. deucedly, lucidly, mucidly.

4. pellucidly.

US′if–er– 3. Lucifer, crucifer.

US′i–form– 3. luciform, nuciform, cruciform.

US′iv–lee– 4. abusively, conducively, effusively, diffusively, allusively, elusively, delusively, illusively, collusively, inclusively, conclusively, exclusively, obtrusively, intrusively, protrusively.

5. inconclusively, inobtrusively, unintrusively.

US′iv–ness– 4. abusiveness, conduciveness, effusiveness, diffusiveness, allusiveness, elusiveness, delusiveness, illusiveness, collusiveness, inclusiveness, conclusiveness, exclusiveness, obtrusiveness, intrusiveness, protrusiveness.

5. inconclusiveness, inobtrusiveness.

US′or–ee– 3. lusory.

4. elusory, delusory, prelusory, illusory, reclusory, conclusory, exclusory, collusory, prolusory, extrusory.

UT′a–bl– 3. lootable, mootable, mutable, scrutable, suitable, tootable.

4. refutable, confutable, commutable, permutable, transmutable, computable, disputable, inscrutable, unsuitable.

5. irrefutable, unrefutable, unconfutable, executable, prosecutable, incommutable, uncommutable, incomputable, undisputable.

UT′a–blee– 3. mutably, suitably.

4. immutably, permutably, transmutably, inscrutably, unsuitably.

UT′at–iv– 3. mutative, putative, sputative.

4. refutative, confutative, commutative, transmutative, imputative, reputative, disputative, sternutative.

5. uncommutative.

UT′e–al– 3. luteal, gluteal, puteal.

UT′ed–lee– 3. mutedly.

4. reputedly.

UT′er–ee– 3. bootery, pewtery, rootery, fruitery.

4. *freebootery.*

UT′e–us– 3. beauteous, duteous, luteous, gluteus.

UTH′ful–ee– 3. ruthfully, truthfully, youthfully.

UTH′ful–ness– 3. ruthfulness, truthfulness, youthfulness.

UTH′les–lee– 3. ruthlessly, truthlessly, youthlessly.

UTH′les–ness– 3. ruthlessness, truthlessness, youthlessness.

UT′i–fi– 3. beautify, brutify.

UT′i–ful– 3. beautiful, dutiful.

4. unbeautiful, undutiful.

UT′ik–al– 3. cuticle.

4. scorbutical, latreutical.

5. hermeneutical, therapeutical, pharmaceutical.

UT′in–ee– 3. mutiny, scrutiny.

UT′i–ness– 3. snootiness, fruitiness, sootiness.

UT′in–us– 3. glutinous, mutinous, scrutinous.

4. velutinous, unmutinous.

UT′iv–lee– 5. substitutively, constitutively.

UV′a–bl– 3. movable, provable.

4. removable, immovable, approvable, improvable, reprovable.

5. irremovable, unapprovable, irreprovable, unimprovable.

UV′i–al– 3. uveal, fluvial, pluvial.

4. alluvial, effluvial, diluvial, colluvial, exuvial.

5. postdiluvial.

6. antediluvial.

UV′i–an– 4. alluvian, diluvian, Peruvian, Vesuvian.

5. postdiluvian.

6. antediluvian.

UV′ing–lee– 3. movingly.

4. approvingly, reprovingly.

5. unapprovingly.

UV′i–um– 4. alluvium, eluvium, effluvium, diluvium, impluvium, compluvium.

UV′i–us– 3. pluvious, Pluvius.

4. Vesuvius.

6. Jupiter Pluvius.

UZ′a–bl– 3. usable, choosable, losable.

4. unusable, abusable, confusable, accusable, excusable, amusable, perusable.

5. unaccusable, inexcusable, unamusable.

UZ′at–iv– 4. accusative, recusative.

UZH′un–al– 3. fusional.

4. confusional, delusional, illusional, conclusional, intrusional.

UZ′i–bl– 3. fusible.

4. diffusible, infusible, transfusible, protrusible.

UZ′i–ness– 3. ooziness, booziness, chooziness, newsiness, snooziness, wooziness [slang].

ŎŌ (full)

see ŎŌ (good), following Ô (awe)

Ŭ (tub)

Single (Masculine) Rhymes

Primary or Secondary Accent Falls on Last Syllable; Imperfect Rhymes Are in Italics.

UB– 1. bub, chub, dub, hub, cub, blub, flub, glub, club, slub, nub, knub, snub, pub, rub, drub, grub, scrub, shrub, sub, tub, stub.
2. *hubbub*, *flubdub* [slang], *subshrub*.
3. sillabub, rub-a-dub.
4. Beelzebub.
UBD–1. dubbed, hubbed, cubbed, clubbed, glubbed, nubbed, snubbed, rubbed, drubbed, grubbed, scrubbed, shrubbed, subbed, tubbed, stubbed.
2. glub-glubbed.
UBZ– *see* **ŬB,** plus " s " or " 's "; **3.** mulligrubs [slang].
UCH– 1. Dutch, hutch, cutch, scutch, clutch, much, mutch, smutch, rutch, crutch, such, touch.
2. *nonesuch*, retouch.
3. insomuch, overmuch, inasmuch, forasmuch.
UCHD– 1. clutched, smutched, rutched, crutched, touched.
2. retouched, untouched.
UD– 1. bud, dud, cud, scud, Lud, blood, flood, mud, pud [coll.], spud, rud, crud, sud, sudd, shud, stud, thud.
2. *rosebud*, bestud.
UF– 1. buff, chuff, chough, duff, fuff, guff, huff, cuff, scuff, luff, bluff, fluff, clough, pluff [dial.], slough, sluff [dial.], muff, nuf [slang], nuff [slang], snuff, puff, ruff, rough, gruff, scruff, sough, suff [dial.], tough, tuff, stuff, whuff.
2. rebuff, Macduff, *handcuff* enough, cream puff, *dandruff*, *crossruff*.
3. counterbuff, fisticuff, powder puff, overstuff.
UFT– 1. buffed, chuffed, duffed, fuffed, huffed,

cuffed, scuffed, luffed, bluffed, fluffed, sloughed, muffed, snuffed, puffed, ruffed, roughed, soughed, tuft, stuffed, whuffed.
2. rebuffed, *handcuffed*, restuffed, unstuffed.
3. unrebuffed, candytuft, overstuffed.
UG– 1. ugh, bug, chug, dug, fug, hug, jug, lug, glug, plug, slug, mug, smug, pug, rug, drug, shrug, trug, tug, thug, vug.
2. *humbug*, *firebug*.
3. ladybug, tumblebug, doodlebug, bunnyhug.
UGD– 1. bugged, chugged, fugged, hugged, jugged, lugged, glugged, plugged, mugged, pugged, rugged, [dial.], drugged, shrugged, tugged.
2. *humbugged*, glug-glugged, undrugged.
UJ– 1. budge, fudge, judge, sludge, mudge, Mudge, smudge, nudge, pudge, rudge, Rudge, drudge, grudge, trudge.
2. adjudge, rejudge, prejudge, forejudge, misjudge, begrudge.
4. Barnaby Rudge [Dickens].
UJD– 1. budged, fudged, judged, sludged, mudged, smudged, nudged, drudged, grudged, trudged.
2. adjudged, rejudged, self-judged, welljudged, ill-judged, unjudged, forejudged, misjudged, begrudged, ungrudged.
UK– 1. buck, chuck, duck, cuck [obs.], luck, gluck, cluck, pluck, muck, Puck, ruck, truck, struck, suck, shuck, tuck, stuck.
2. *springbuck*, *prongbuck*, *roebuck*, *sawbuck*, *woodchuck*, lame duck, *potluck*, dumb cluck [slang], amuck, Canuck, *awestruck*, *moonstruck*, *sun-struck*.
3. waterbuck, Donald Duck, chuck-a-luck, panic-struck, thunderstruck, wonder-struck,

horror-struck, nip and tuck.

UKS— *see* **UK,** plus " s " or " 's "; **1.** dux, lux, flux, mux, crux, tux [slang].

UKST— 1. fluxed, muxed.
2. effluxed, refluxed.

UKT— 1. bucked, chucked, duct, ducked, clucked, plucked, mucked, trucked, sucked, shucked, tucked.
2. abduct, obduct, educt, deduct, induct, conduct, reluct, unplucked, eruct, instruct, construct, unshucked.
3. viaduct, aqueduct, fumiduct, circumduct, misconduct, usufruct, reconstruct.

UL— 1. dull, gull, hull, cull, scull, skull, lull, mull, trull, sull [dial.], stull, wull [dial.].
2. *seagull,* Mogul, ahull, dehull, école [F.], bricole, *numskull* [coll.], annul.
3. disannul.

ULCH— 1. gulch, cultch, culch, mulch.

ULD— 1. dulled, gulled, hulled, culled, sculled, skulled, lulled, mulled.
2. thick-skulled, dehulled, black-hulled, annulled.
3. disannulled.

ULJ— 1. bulge.
2. indulge, effulge, promulge, divulge.
3. reindulge.
4. overindulge.

ULJD— 1. bulged.
2. indulged, effulged, promulged, divulged.
3. reindulged, unindulged, undivulged.
4. overindulged.

ULK— 1. bulk, hulk, skulk, mulk, sulk.

ULKT— 1. bulked, hulked, skulked, mulct, mulked, sulked.

ULM— 1. culm, stulm.

ULP— 1. gulp, culp [slang], sculp, pulp.

ULPT— 1. gulped, pulped.
2. soft-pulped.
3. golden-pulped.

ULS— 1. bulse, dulse, dulce, mulse, pulse.
2. repulse, *impulse,* expulse, avulse, revulse, convulse.

ULST— 1. pulsed.
2. repulsed, avulsed, revulsed, convulsed.

ULT— 1. cult.
2. adult, incult, occult, penult, insult, consult, result, exult.
3. subadult, catapult, reinsult, reconsult.
4. antepenult.

UM— 1. um, homme [F.], bum, chum, dumb, gum, hum, come, scum, Lum, glum, plum, plumb, slum, mum, numb, snum, rum, rhumb, drum, grum, crumb, scrum, strum, thrum, some, sum, tum, stum, thumb, swum, yum.
2. *serfdom, kingdom, dogdom, dukedom, earldom, dumdum, begum,* Bonhomme, become, succumb, unplumb, benumb, *humdrum, threesome, wholesome, lonesome, awesome, toothsome, gruesome, twosome, tum-tum, yum-yum, Yum-Yum.*
3. tweedledum, Christendom, martyrdom, solidum, oppidum, orpheum, horreum, feefaw-fum, labium, stibium, cambium, cal-

cium, stadium, studium, ischium, silphium, lithium, cadmium, hafnium, opium, Arctium, vitium, otium, overcome, misbecome, colchicum, unicum, capsicum, cingulum, septulum, sertulum, crembalum, sugarplum, symbolum, pabulum, pendulum, minimum, quadrimum, optimum, maximum, labdanum, laudanum, platinum, labarum, cerebrum, kettledrum, *panjandrum, conundrum,* theorum, drearisome, wearisome, frolicsome, gamblesome, troublesome, meddlesome, quarrelsome, burdensome, cumbersome, bothersome, venturesome, debitum, placitum, cognitum, compitum, vacuum, menstruum, mutuum.
4. fee fi fo fum, ceruleum, castoreum, columbium, aerobium, exordium, sporangium, Eryngium, absinthium, agonium, euphonium, polonium, stramonium, ammonium, harmonium, opprobrium, delirium, tellurium, martyrium, gymnasium, potassium, Elysium, sestertium, consortium, nasturtium, caputium, deliquium, viaticum, chrysanthemum, molybdenum, aluminum, ad libitum, accubitum, acquisitum.
5. periosteum, equilibrium, polyandrium, hypochondrium, epigastrium, sacerdotium.

UMD— 1. gummed, plumbed, numbed, drummed, crumbed, strummed, thumbed.
2. ungummed, unplumbed.

UMF— 1. umph, humph, grumph [Scot.].
2. *triumph.*

UMP— 1. ump [slang], bump, chump, dump, gump, hump, jump, lump, flump, glump [slang], clump, plump, slump, mump, pump, rump, frump, grump, crump, trump, sump, tump, stump, thump, wump [slang].
2. high jump, bethump, *mugwump.*
3. overtrump.

UMZ— *see* **ŬM,** plus " s " or " 's "; **1.** Thrums.
2. *breekums, doldrums.*

UN— 1. un [dial.], bun, done, dun, Dunn, fun, gun, Hun, hon [slang], none, nun, pun, spun, run, sun, son, sunn, shun, tun, ton, stun, one, won.
2. well-done, ill-done, undone, foredone, outdone, begun, homespun, forerun, unrun, outrun, grandson, Whitsun, unwon.
3. honey bun, raisin bun, clarendon, overdone, underdone, unbegun, machine gun, Gatling gun, Sally Lunn, overrun, Tennyson, Atchison, Atkinson, Sheraton, Wellington, skimmington, Orpington, anyone, everyone, number one.

UNCH— 1. bunch, hunch, lunch, clunch [dial.], munch, nunch [dial.], punch, runch, brunch, crunch, scrunch.

UND— 1. bund, dunned, fund, gunned, mund, punned, sunned, shunned, stunned.
2. refund, unsunned, rotund.
3. moribund, cummerbund, machinegunned, verecund, rubicund, Rosamond, obrotund, orotund.

UNG— 1. bung, dung, hung, lung, flung,

clung, slung, pung, rung, wrung, sprung, strung, sung, tongue, stung, swung, young.

2. *geebung*, unhung, among, highstrung, *hamstrung*, unsung, betongue, *shantung*, *oxtongue*.

3. underhung, overhung, underslung, hereamong, thereamong, overstrung, mother tongue.

UNGD– 1. bunged, tongued.

2. black-tongued, thick-tongued, bell-tongued, sharp-tongued.

3. iron-lunged, leather-lunged, honeytongued, many-tongued, double-tongued, silver-tongued, trumpet-tongued.

UNJ– 1. lunge, longe, blunge, plunge, sponge.

2. expunge.

3. muskellunge.

UNK– 1. unk, unc [both slang], bunk, chunk, dunk, funk, hunk, junk, skunk, lunk [slang], blunk [slang], flunk, clunk [Scot. & dial.], plunk, slunk, monk, nunc, punk, spunk, drunk, trunk, sunk, tunk, stunk.

2. Mauch Chunk, quidnunc, undrunk, tree trunk, unsunk.

UNKT– 1. bunked, dunked, funked, junked, skunked, plunked, trunked, tunked.

2. defunct, injunct, conjunct, disjunct.

UNS– 1. once, bunce [slang], dunce.

UNT– 1. bunt, hunt, lunt, blunt, punt. runt, brunt, front, grunt, shunt, stunt, wont, wun't [dial.].

2. *staghunt*, fox hunt, affront, *bifront*, confront, *forefront*.

3. exeunt.

UNZ– *see* **ŬN,** plus " s " or " 's ".

UP– 1. up, dup [dial.], gup, hup, cup, scup, pup, sup, tup, yup [slang].

2. *windup*, hard up, *roundup*, *make-up*, *breakup*, *hiccough*, *hiccup*, *pickup*, *lockup*, *sunup*, *ripup*, *tipup*, *tossup*, *getup*, *letup*, *setup*.

3. up-and-up, loving cup, stirrup cup, buttercup.

UPT– 1. upped, cupped, pupped, supped, tupped.

2. abrupt, erupt, corrupt, disrupt.

3. interrupt, incorrupt, uncorrupt.

UR– 1. err, er, 'er, Er, Ur, burr, birr, churr, chirr, fer [dial.], fir, fur, her, cur, coeur, blur, slur, myrrh, smur, knur, per, purr, spur, sir, sur, shirr, stir, were, whir.

2. *nightchurr*, befur, defer, prefer, infer, confer, chauffeur, *furfur*, transfer, recur, incur, concur, occur, liqueur, demur, *larkspur*, *hotspur*, masseur, farceur [F.], susurr, deter, inter, hauteur, astir, Pasteur, bestir, restir, aver, rever.

3. cocklebur, butterbur, calaber, shillaber, caliber, calendar, calender, islander, lavender, provender, Lucifer, crucifer, Jennifer, conifer, dapifer, rotifer, aquifer, chronopher, pillager, villager, manager, tanager, onager, forager, vintager, cottager, ravager, voyager, voyageur [F.], dowager, integer, armiger, claviger, breviger, hardanger, challenger,

passenger, messenger, scavenger, harbinger, derringer, porringer, rapier, copier, massacre, sepulchre, odaler, victualer, chronicler, chiseler, traveler, leveler, hoveler, shoveler, wassailer, labeler, yodeler, quarreler, jeweler, gossamer, dulcimer, lorimer, customer, costumer, parcener, gardener, hardener, lengthener, strengthener, weakener, wakener, quickener, cheapener, deepener, sharpener, loosener, lessener, threatener, sweetener, shortener, fastener, hastener, chastener, listener, moistener, evener, scrivener, cozener, bargainer, almoner, commoner, summoner, coroner, ironer, reasoner, seasoner, poisoner, prisoner, northerner, southerner, easterner, westerner, *sojourner*, stuccoer, diaper, hanaper, worshiper, caliper, juniper, gossiper, galloper, walloper, jabberer, slumberer, numberer, sorcerer, slanderer, panderer, murderer, pilferer, chamferer, wagerer, staggerer, swaggerer, weatherer, furtherer, cornerer, naperer, scamperer, whimperer, whisperer, caterer, loiterer, shelterer, saunterer, barterer, plasterer, pesterer, roisterer, fosterer, blusterer, answerer, laborer, clamorer, conjurer, murmurer, usurer, venturer, lecturer, capturer, torturer, connoisseur, purchaser, silencer, licenser, trespasser, canvasser, harnesser, publisher, polisher, punisher, cherisher, nourisher, Britisher, vanquisher, accoucheur, amateur, marketer, bucketer, arbiter, forfeiter, surfeiter, scimiter, chapiter, Jupiter, warranter, disinter, frankfurter, *Winchester*, *Rochester*, harvester, sophister, sinister, presbyter, sandiver, caliver, gilliver, Gulliver, Oliver, miniver, *Andover*, *Passover*, journeyer.

4. Ambassadeur, ambassador, astronomer, tobogganner, coparcener, enlivener, developer, enveloper, embroiderer, encounterer, upholsterer, deliverer, maneuverer, conjecturer, adventurer, artificer, admonisher, relinquisher, restaurateur, Accipiter.

URB– 1. herb, gerb, curb, kerb, blurb, Serb, verb.

2. *potherb*, *suburb*, superb, acerb, perturb, disturb, *adverb*, reverb.

URBD– 1. herbed, curbed, verbed.

2. uncurbed, peturbed, disturbed.

3. imperturbed, unperturbed, undisturbed.

URCH– 1. birch, church, lurch, smirch, perch, search.

2. unchurch, besmirch, research.

URD– 1. urd, erred, bird, burred, Byrd, dird, furred, gird, heard, herd, curd, Kurd, blurred, slurred, purred, spurred, surd, shirred, turd, stirred, third, word, whirred.

2. *songbird*, *blackbird*, *halberd*, numbered, *snowbird*, *lyrebird*, *bluebird*, *lovebird*, befurred, inferred, conferred, transferred, begird, engird, ungird, unheard, *gooseherd*, recurred, concurred, occurred, demurred, absurd, deterred, interred, bestirred, restirred, averred, Cape Verde, *wayward*, *watchword*, *leeward*,

reword, *seaward, homeward, innward, onward, downward, upward, foreword, forward, hazard.*
3. myna bird, mockingbird, hummingbird, ladybird, undergird, overheard, massacred, sepulchred, reoccurred, disinterred, afterward, netherward.
4. cardinal bird.
ŬRF– 1. kerf, scurf, perf [slang.], serf, surf, turf.
3. hippocerf.
ŬRG– 1. erg, berg, burg, bourg.
2. exergue, *Goldberg, iceberg, Strasbourg, Pittsburgh.*
3. Heidelberg, Brandenburg, Edinburgh.
ŬRJ– 1. urge, dirge, scourge, splurge, merge, purge, spurge, serge, surge, verge.
2. submerge, emerge, immerge, asperge, resurge, deterge, absterge, diverge, converge.
3. demiurge, resubmerge, dramaturge, thaumaturge.
ŬRK– 1. irk, burke, Burke, dirk, girk, [slang], jerk, jerque, kirk, lurk, clerk, murk, smirk, perk, cirque, shirk, Turk, stirk, work, quirk, yerk.
2. *hauberk,* Dunkerque, berserk, *patchwork, woodwork, bridgework, clockwork, bulwark, guesswork, network, fretwork.*
3. handiwork, fancywork, needlework, openwork, waterwork, overwork, latticework.
ŬRKS– *see* **ŬRK,** plus " s " or " 's "; **2.** *steelworks, gasworks.*
ŬRL– 1. earl, erl [dial.], burl, birl, churl, furl, girl, gurl, herl, hurl, curl, skirl, merle, knurl, pearl, perle, purl, thirl, querl, swirl, twirl, whirl, whorl.
2. unfurl, becurl, uncurl, impearl.
4. mother-of-pearl.
ŬRLD– 1. burled, furled, hurled, curled, skirled, pearled, purled, world, swirled, twirled, whirled, whorled.
2. unfurled, becurled, recurled, uncurled, impearled, old-world.
3. underworld.
ŬRM– 1. berm, derm, firm, germ, sperm, term, therm, worm, squirm.
2. affirm, infirm, confirm, *Landsturm, silkworm, bookworm, glowworm, earthworm.*
3. pachyderm, reaffirm, disaffirm, isotherm, angleworm.
ŬRMD– 1. firmed, germed, termed, wormed, squirmed.
2. affirmed, confirmed.
3. reaffirmed, unaffirmed, reconfirmed, unconfirmed.
ŬRN– 1. earn, urn, erne, burn, Berne, churn, dern [dial.], durn [dial.], fern, herne, Hearn, kern, learn, pirn, spurn, tern, turn, stern, quern, yearn.
2. inurn, *sunburn, heartburn, cedarn,* adjourn, sojourn, relearn, unlearn, epergne, discern, concern, lucerne, Lucerne, attorn, *Saturn,* eterne, return, *nocturne,* inturn, interne, *downturn,* sauterne, *upturn, quartern,* astern,

eastern, cistern, extern, *sextern, leathern, northern.*
3. unconcern, sempitern, taciturn, overturn.
ŬRND– 1. earned, urned, burned, churned, learned, spurned, turned, sterned, yearned.
2. hard-earned, well-earned, unearned, *sunburned,* adjourned, sojourned, relearned, unlearned, discerned, concerned, returned, interned, *downturned, upturned.*
3. unconcerned, overturned.
ŬRNT– 1. burnt, learnt.
ŬRNZ– *see* **ŬRN,** above, plus " s " or " 's ";
1. Burns.
3. Robert Burns.
ŬRP– 1. urp [slang], burp, chirp, lerp, slurp, purp [dial.], turp, terp, twerp, twirp.
2. discerp, usurp, *Antwerp.*
ŬRPT– 1. burped, chirped, slurped.
2. excerpt, discerped, usurped.
ŬRS– 1. Erse, birse, burse, cherce [dial.], hearse, curse, nurse, purse, terce, terse, verse, worse.
2. imburse, disburse, rehearse, accurse, precurse, amerce, submerse, immerse, coerce, asperse, disperse, sesterce, averse, traverse, obverse, subverse, adverse, reverse, diverse, perverse, inverse, converse, transverse.
3. reimburse, intersperse, universe.
ŬRST– 1. erst, burst, first, Hearst, cursed, nursed, pursed, thirst, versed, verst, worst, wurst.
2. *sunburst,* disbursed, *outburst,* rehearsed, accursed, precursed, submersed, emersed, immersed, coerced, aspersed, dispersed, athirst, traversed, reversed, conversed, unversed.
3. reimbursed, unrehearsed, interspersed, untraversed, liverwurst.
ŬRT– 1. Bert, dirt, girt, hurt, curt, Kurt, skirt, blurt, flirt, nert [slang], pert, spurt, cert [slang], syrt, shirt, vert, wort, quirt, squirt.
2. begirt, *seagirt,* engirt, ungirt, unhurt, alert, inert, *expert,* assert, concert, exert, exsert, insert, *redshirt, Blackshirt, Brownshirt,* avert, obvert, subvert, advert, evert, revert, divert, invert, convert, overt, pervert, transvert, *madwort, ragwort, figwort, steepwort,* desert, dessert.
3. Adelbert, Ethelbert, Camembert, malapert, inexpert, preconcert, disconcert, intersert, undershirt, ambivert, retrovert, introvert, controvert, extrovert, pennywort, liverwort, motherwort.
ŬRTH– 1. earth, berth, birth, dearth, firth, girth, mirth, Perth, worth.
2. inearth, unearth, rebirth, unworth.
3. underearth, pennyworth, money's worth.
ŬRTS– *see* **ŬRT,** plus " s " or " 's "; **1.** Wirtz.
ŬRV– 1. curve, nerve, serve, verve, swerve.
2. recurve, *incurve, outcurve,* innerve, unnerve, observe, subserve, deserve, reserve, preserve, disserve, conserve.
3. unreserve.
ŬRVD– 1. curved, served, swerved.

2. unnerved, reserved, preserved, conserved.
3. undeserved, well-deserved, well-preserved, unpreserved, unconserved.
URZ– *see* **ŬR**, plus " s " or " 's "; **1.** furze.
US– 1. us, bus, buss, chuss [slang], fuss, guss, cuss, plus, muss, pus, Russ, Grus, truss, Sus, stuss, thus.
2. percuss, discuss, excuss, khuskhus, succuss, nonplus, *surplus*, untruss, *Cassius, Lucius, Brutus*.
3. harquebus, omnibus, blunderbuss, incubus, succubus, syllabus, *tremendous, horrendous*, hazardous, dubious, tedious, hideous, aqueous, igneous, carneous, corneous, impious, nucleus, copious, nacreous, cupreous, vitreous, gaseous, osseous, nauseous, lacteous, piteous, plenteous, bounteous, courteous, beauteous, luteous, niveous, envious, pluvious, abacus, repercuss, scandalous, libelous, cautelous, scurrilous, marvelous, frivolous, overplus, bibulous, flocculous, calculous, calculus, surculous, surculus, nodulous, scrofulous, cellulous, Romulus, cumulous, cumulus, granulous, querulous, garrulous, infamous, bigamous, blasphemous, venomous, *enormous*, amanous, bimanous, membranous, tyrannous, larcenous, ravenous, villainous, mountainous, verminous, acinous, acinus, *Maecenas*, hircinous, criminous, resinous, cretinous, sanguinous, ruinous, poisonous, consonous, gluttonous, dipnoous, dichroous, platypus, octopus, barbarous, nectarous, Tartarus, ludicrous, slumberous, tuberous, ulcerous, cancerous, ponderous, thunderous, dangerous, cankerous, humerus, onerous, viperous, Hesperus, prosperous, slaughterous, apterous, dexterous, pulverous, chivalrous, rancorous, nidorous, phosphorous, Phosphorus, valorous, dolorous, timorous, humorous, susurrus, susurrous, sinistrous, verdurous, fulgurous, sulphurous, murmurous, venturous, rapturous, torturous, Pegasus, covetous, halitus, halitous, aditus, fremitus, spiritous, transitus, riotous, vacuous, arduous, sensuous, fatuous, unctuous, fructuous, sumptuous, tortuous, mischievous, atavus, flexuous.
4. caduceus, polyphagous, analogous, homologous, amphibious, Aurelius, ingenious, calumnious, symphonious, uproarious, opprobrious, Tiberius, Americus, Leviticus, noctambulous, monoculous, tuberculous, unscrupulous, edentulous, didynamous, tridynamous, diaphanous, epiphanous, vertiginous, ferruginous, foraminous, contami-

nous, trigeminous, gelatinous, polygynous, polygenous, Antinous, ephemerous, polymerous, obstreperous, tetrapterous, preposterous, adventurous, edematous, velocitous, calamitous, precipitous, necessitous, innocuous, promiscuous, circumfluous, superfluous, impetuous, spirituous, tumultuous, presumptuous, voluptuous, incestuous, tempestuous.
5. heterologous, homogeneous, ignominious.
6. heterogeneous.
USH– 1. ush [slang], gush, hush, cush, lush, blush, flush, plush, slush, mush, rush, brush, crush, thrush, tush.
2. agush, ablush, aflush, reflush, *bulrush, onrush, outrush, tarbrush, clothesbrush*.
3. underbrush, hermit thrush.
USK– 1. busk, dusk, fusc, husk, cusk, musk, rusk, brusque, tusk.
2. embusk, adusk, subfusc, dehusk, *mollusk*.
UST– 1. bust, dust, dost, fust, fussed, gust, just, cussed, lust, plussed, mussed, rust, crust, trussed, trust, thrust.
2. combust, robust, adust, *gold-dust*, bedust, *stardust, august*, disgust, adjust, unjust, discussed, nonplussed, unmussed, encrust, betrust, entrust, untrussed, distrust, mistrust.
3. unrobust, readjust, coadjust, undiscussed.
UT– 1. ut, but, butt, phut, gut, hut, jut, cut, scut, glut, slut, mut, mutt, smut, nut, putt, rut, strut, shut, tut, what.
2. abut, rebut, *hagbut, catgut, woodcut*, recut, uncut, *haircut*, clear-cut, *crosscut*, besmut, *peanut, chestnut, walnut, doughnut, burnut, beechnut*, astrut, reshut, somewhat.
3. surrebut, scuttle butt, halibut, betel nut, hazelnut, butternut, coconut, occiput, Lilliput.
UTH– 1. doth.
2. *bismuth*.
3. azimuth.
UV– 1. of, dove, guv, gov [both slang], love, glove, shove.
2. hereof, thereof, whereof, above, truelove, reglove, unglove, *foxglove*.
3. turtledove, ladylove.
UVD– 1. loved, gloved, shoved.
2. beloved, ungloved.
3. unbeloved.
UX– *see* **ŬKS.**
UZ– 1. Uz, buzz, does, fuzz, guz, huzz, muzz, coz, was, 'twas.
2. abuzz, *humbuzz*, chauffeuse [F.], masseuse.
3. dear me suz [slang].
UZD– 1. buzzed, fuzzed, muzzed.

Ŭ (tub)

Double (Feminine) Rhymes

Primary or Secondary Accent Falls on Next to Last Syllable; Imperfect Rhymes Are in Italics.

UB′ee– 2. bubby, chubby, fubby [coll. Eng.], hubby, cubby, clubby, slubby, nubby, knubby, rubby, grubby, scrubby, shrubby, tubby, stubby.

UB′er– 2. dubber, hubber, lubber, blubber, flubber, glubber, clubber, slubber, snubber, rubber, drubber, grubber, scrubber, tubber, stubber.
3. *landlubber.*
4. moneygrubber.
5. India-rubber.

UB′erd– 2. Hubbard, blubbered, cupboard, rubbered.
4. Mother Hubbard.

UB′ing– 2. dubbing, hubbing, cubbing, blubbing, flubbing, glubbing, clubbing, nubbing, snubbing, rubbing, drubbing, grubbing, scrubbing, subbing [slang], tubbing, stubbing.
3. glub-glubbing.

UB′ish– 2. cubbish, clubbish, snubbish, rubbish, grubbish, shrubbish, tubbish.

UB′l– 2. bubble, double, hubble, nubble, rubble, trouble, stubble.
3. redouble.
4. hubble-bubble.

UB′ld– 2. bubbled, doubled, troubled, stubbled.
3. redoubled, undoubled, untroubled.

UB′lee– 2. bubbly, doubly, hubbly, knubbly, nubbly, rubbly, drubbly [dial.], strubbly, stubbly.

UB′ler– 2. bubbler, doubler, troubler.
3. redoubler.

UB′let– 2. doublet, knublet, shrublet, *sublet*, tublet.

UB′lik– 2. public.
3. republic, nonpublic, unpublic.

UB′ling– 2. bubbling, doubling, nubbling, troubling.
3. redoubling, untroubling.

UCH′ee– 2. duchy, clutchy, smutchy, touchy.
3. archduchy, grand duchy.

UCH′er– 2. Dutcher, scutcher, clutcher, smutcher, toucher.
3. retoucher.

UCH′ez– 2. hutches, scutches, clutches, smutches, rutches, crutches, touches.
3. retouches.

UCH′ing– 2. scutching, clutching, smutching, rutching, crutching, touching.
3. retouching.

UCH′on– 2. scutcheon.
3. McCutcheon, escutcheon.
4. inescutcheon.

UD′ed– 2. budded, cudded, scudded, blooded, flooded, mudded, spudded, crudded, studded, thudded.
3. rebudded, unbudded, bestudded, *starstudded.*

UD′ee– 2. buddy, cuddy, cuddie [dial.], scuddy, bloody, muddy, puddee, puddy, spuddy, ruddy, cruddy, cruddie [dial.], study.
3. brown study, *soapsuddy.*
4. fuddy-duddy, understudy, overstudy.

UD′eed– 2. bloodied, muddied, ruddied, studied.
3. unstudied.
4. understudied, overstudied.

UD′er– 2. udder, dudder, scudder, flooder, mudder, rudder, sudder, shudder.

UD′ij– 2. buddage, floodage.

UD′ing– 2. budding, cudding, scudding, blooding, flooding, mudding, spudding, crudding, studding, thudding.
3. rebudding, reflooding.

UD′l– 2. buddle, fuddle, huddle, cuddle, scuddle [Scot.], muddle, nuddle [dial.], puddle, ruddle, studdle.
3. befuddle, bemuddle.

UD′ld– 2. fuddled, huddled, cuddled, scuddled [Scot.], muddled, puddled, studdled [dial.].
3. befuddled, bemuddled.

UD′ler– 2. huddler, cuddler, muddler, puddler.

3. befuddler.
UD′let– **2.** budlet, floodlet.
UD′li– **2.** Dudley, cuddly, puddly.
UD′ling– **2.** fuddling, huddling, cuddling, scuddling [Scot.], muddling, puddling, studdling [dial.].
3. befuddling, bemuddling.
UD′son– **2.** Hudson, Judson.
UF′ee– **2.** buffy, fuffy [dial.], guffy [slang], huffy, cuffy, bluffy, fluffy, pluffy [dial.], sloughy, snuffy, puffy, ruffy, roughie, stuffy.
4. ruffy-tuffy.
UF′en– **2.** roughen, toughen.
UF′er– **2.** buffer, chuffer, duffer, guffer, huffer, cuffer, scuffer, luffer, bluffer, fluffer, pluffer [Scot.], slougher, muffer, snuffer, puffer, ruffer, rougher, gruffer, suffer, tougher, stuffer.
4. stocking stuffer.
UF′est– **2.** bluffest, roughest, gruffest, toughest.
UF′et– **2.** buffet, fuffit [Scot.], muffet, tuffet.
3. Miss Muffet.
UF′in– **2.** buffin, guffin [dial. & slang], cuffin, muffin, puffin.
3. *mumruffin.*
4. ragamuffin.
UF′ing– **2.** buffing, chuffing, duffing, huffing, cuffing, luffing, bluffing, fluffing, sloughing, muffing, puffing, roughing, ruffing, soughing, stuffing.
UF′ish– **2.** huffish, snuffish, puffish, roughish, gruffish, toughish.
UF′l– **2.** buffle, duffel, fuffle [Scot.], scuffle, muffle, snuffle, ruffle, truffle, shuffle, whuffle.
3. bemuffle, remuffle, unmuffle, beruffle, reshuffle.
4. double shuffle.
UF′ld– **2.** scuffled, muffled, snuffled, ruffled, shuffled.
3. bemuffled, remuffled, unmuffled, beruffled, unruffled, reshuffled.
UF′lee– **2.** bluffly, scuffly, muffly, snuffly, ruffly, roughly, gruffly, toughly.
UF′ler– **2.** scuffler, muffler, snuffler, ruffler, shuffler.
UF′ling– **2.** scuffling, muffling, snuffling, ruffling, shuffling.
3. bemuffling, remuffling, unmuffling, beruffling, reshuffling.
UF′ness– **2.** bluffness, roughness, gruffness, toughness.
UFT′ee– **2.** mufti, tufty.
UG′ee– **2.** buggy, fuggy, luggie, pluggy, sluggy, muggy, puggi, puggy, druggy.
UG′er– **2.** bugger, chugger, hugger, lugger, luggar, plugger, slugger, mugger, smugger, snugger, pugger, rugger, drugger, shrugger, tugger.
4. hugger-mugger.
UG′est– **2.** smuggest, snuggest, druggist.
UG′et– **2.** mugget, nugget, drugget.
UG′ing– **2.** bugging, chugging, fugging, hugging, jugging, lugging, glugging, plugging, slugging, mugging, rugging, drugging, shrug-

ging, tugging.
3. glug-glugging.
UG′ish– **2.** sluggish, muggish, smuggish, snuggish, puggish.
UG′l– **2.** guggle, juggle, smuggle, snuggle, puggle, struggle.
3. death struggle.
UG′lee– **2.** ugly, guggly, juggly, smugly, snugly, struggly.
3. *plug-ugly* [slang].
UG′ler– **2.** juggler, smuggler, snuggler, struggler.
UG′ling– **2.** guggling, juggling, smuggling, snuggling, struggling.
UG′nant– **3.** repugnant, oppugnant.
4. unrepugnant.
UG′ness– **2.** smugness, snugness.
UJ′ee– **2.** fudgy, sludgy, pudgy, smudgy.
UJ′er– **2.** budger, fudger, judger, sludger, smudger, nudger, drudger, grudger, trudger.
3. adjudger, rejudger, prejudger, misjudger, forejudger, begrudger.
UJ′ez– **2.** budges, fudges, judges, sludges, smudges, nudges, drudges, grudges, trudges.
3. adjudges, prejudges, misjudges, begrudges.
UJ′ing– **2.** budging, fudging, judging, sludging, smudging, nudging, drudging, grudging, trudging.
3. adjudging, rejudging. prejudging, forejudging, misjudging, begrudgng, ungrudging.
UJ′ment– **2.** judgment.
3. adjudgment, rejudgement, prejudgment, misjudgment.
UJ′on– **2.** dudgeon, gudgeon, bludgeon.
3. curmudgeon.
UK′a– **2.** bucca, pucka, pukka, yucca.
3. felucca.
UK′ee– **2.** bucky, buckie, ducky, lucky, plucky, mucky, tucky.
3. unlucky, Kentucky.
UK′er– **2.** bucker, chucker, chukker, ducker, clucker, plucker, mucker, pucker, trucker, sucker, succor, shucker, tucker.
3. *seersucker.*
4. Tommy Tucker.
UK′et– **2.** bucket, mucket, tucket.
3. Nantucket, Pawtucket.
UK′ij– **2.** pluckage, truckage, suckage.
UK′ing– **2.** bucking, chucking, ducking, clucking, plucking, mucking, trucking, sucking, shucking, tucking.
UK′ish– **2.** buckish, puckish.
UK′l– **2.** buckle, chuckle, huckle, muckle, knuckle, truckle, suckle, yukkel.
3. unbuckle, *parbuckle.*
4. honeysuckle.
UK′ld– **2.** buckled, chuckled, cuckold, knuckled, suckled.
3. rebuckled, unbuckled, *parbuckled.*
UK′ler– **2.** buckler, chuckler, knuckler, truckler, suckler.
3. *swashbuckler.*
UK′less– **2.** buckless, chuckless, duckless,

luckless, cluckless, pluckless, muckless, truckless, suckless.

UK'ling– 2. buckling, chuckling, duckling, knuckling, truckling, suckling.

3. rebuckling, unbuckling, *parbuckling*, *swashbuckling*.

4. ugly duckling.

UK'or– 2. succor; *see also* **ŬK'er.**

UK'see– 2. mucksy [dial.], puxy [dial.], pucksey [dial.], druxy.

3. Biloxi.

UKS'ez– 2. fluxes, cruxes.

3. effluxes, refluxes.

UKSH'un– 2. duction, fluxion, ruction, suction.

3. traduction, abduction, obduction, subduction, eduction, deduction, reduction, seduction, induction, conduction, production, affluxion, defluxion, influxion, obstruction, substruction, destruction, instruction, construction.

4. nonconduction, reproduction, introduction, manuduction, self-destruction, reconstruction, misconstruction.

5. superinduction, overproduction.

UKT'ans– 3. inductance, conductance, reluctance.

UKT'ed– 2. fructed.

3. abducted, deducted, inducted, conducted, obstructed, instructed, constructed.

4. unobstructed, misconstructed.

UKT'er– 2. ductor.

3. abductor, eductor, inductor, conductor, productor, obstructor, destructor, instructor, constructor.

4. nonconductor, introductor, manuductor, reconstructor.

UKT'il– 2. ductile.

3. inductile, productile.

UKT'ing– 3. abducting, deducting, inducting, conducting, obstructing, instructing, constructing.

4. nonconducting, misconducting, reconstructing.

UKT'iv– 3. adductive, traductive, deductive, reductive, seductive, inductive, conductive, productive, obstructive, destructive, instructive, constructive.

4. reproductive, introductive, manuductive, self-destructive, reconstructive.

UKT'or– *see* **ŬKT'er.**

UKT'ress– 3. seductress, conductress, instructress.

4. introductress.

UKT'ure– 2. structure.

3. substructure, constructure.

4. superstructure.

UK'us– 2. ruckus, succus.

UL'a– 2. bulla, mullah, nullah, sulla, Sulla.

3. Abdullah, medulla, cuculla, ampulla.

4. nulla-nulla.

UL'ee– 2. dully, gully, hully, cully, skully, sully, Tully.

UL'eed– 2. gullied, sullied.

3. unsullied.

UL'en– 2. mullein, mullen, sullen.

3. Cuchullin, McMullin.

UL'er– 2. duller, huller, color, culler, sculler, luller, mullar, muller, cruller.

3. medullar, dehuller, recolor, *tricolor*, discolor, miscolor, annuller, ampullar.

4. technicolor, versicolor, multicolor, watercolor.

UL'erd– 2. dullard, colored.

3. recolored, discolored, *rose-colored*, *flesh-colored*, *fresh-colored*, *wine-colored*.

4. multicolored, watercolored.

UL'et– 2. gullet, cullet, mullet.

3. surmullet.

ULG'ar– 2. Bulgar, fulgor, vulgar.

ULG'ate– 2. vulgate, Vulgate.

3. promulgate, divulgate.

UL'ij– 2. ullage, cullage, sullage.

UL'ing– 2. dulling, gulling, hulling, culling, sculling, lulling, mulling.

3. dehulling, annuling.

UL'ish– 2. dullish, gullish.

ULJ'ens– 3. indulgence, effulgence, refulgence, divulgence.

4. self-indulgence.

ULJ'ent– 2. fulgent.

3. indulgent, effulgent, refulgent, emulgent.

4. self-indulgent, interfulgent.

ULJ'er– 2. bulger.

3. indulger, promulger, divulger.

ULJ'ing– 2. bulging.

3. indulging, effulging, promulging, divulging.

ULJ'ment– 3. indulgement, divulgement.

ULK'ate– 2. sulcate.

3. inculcate, trisulcate.

ULK'ee– 2. bulky, hulky, sulky.

ULK'er– 2. bulker, skulker, mulker, sulker.

ULK'ing– 2. bulking, hulking, skulking, mulking, sulking.

ULP'ee– 2. gulpy, pulpy.

ULP'er– 2. gulper, pulper.

ULS'er– 2. ulcer.

3. repulser, expulser.

ULSH'un– 2. pulsion.

3. emulsion, demulsion, appulsion, repulsion, impulsion, compulsion, propulsion, expulsion, evulsion, revulsion, divulsion, convulsion.

ULS'ing– 2. pulsing.

3. repulsing, expulsing, convulsing.

ULS'iv– 2. pulsive.

3. emulsive, appulsive, repulsive, impulsive, compulsive, propulsive, expulsive, revulsive, divulsive, convulsive.

ULST'er– 2. ulster, Ulster, hulster.

ULT'ant– 3. insultant, consultant, resultant, exultant.

ULT'ed– 3. occulted, insulted, consulted, resulted, exulted.

ULT'er– 3. occulter, insulter, consulter, consultor, exulter.

ULT'ing– 3. occulting, insulting, consulting,

resulting, exulting.

ULT′iv– 3. consultive, resultive.

ULT′ness– 3. occultness, adultness.

ULT′ure– 2. culture, multure, vulture.
4. vegeculture, apiculture, pomiculture, sericulture, floriculture, agriculture, pisciculture, viticulture, horticulture, aviculture, sylviculture, boviculture.

ULV′er– 2. culver, hulver.

UL′yun– 2. scullion, mullion, rullion.
3. slumgullion.

UMB′a– 2. dumba, jumba, rumba [Sp.].
3. calumba, Columba.

UMB′el– 2. umbel, dumbbell.

UMB′ent– 3. accumbent, decumbent, recumbent, incumbent, procumbent, succumbent.
5. superincumbent.

UMB′er– 2. umber, cumber, lumbar, lumber, slumber, number.
3. encumber, renumber, outnumber.
4. disencumber, unencumber, overnumber.

UMB′l– 2. umbel, bumble, fumble, humble, jumble, scumble, mumble, rumble, drumble, grumble, crumble, tumble, stumble.
3. bejumble.
4. overtumble.

UMB′lee– 2. bumbly, fumbly, humbly, jumbly, mumbly, rumbly, grumbly, crumbly, tumbly, stumbly.

UMB′ler– 2. bumbler, fumbler, humbler, jumbler, mumbler, rumbler, drumbler, grumbler, crumbler, tumbler, stumbler.

UMB′ling– 2. bumbling, fumbling, humbling, jumbling, scumbling, mumbling, rumbling, grumbling, crumbling, tumbling, stumbling.
3. bejumbling.
4. overtumbling.

UMB′o– 2. umbo, gumbo, Jumbo.
3. columbo.
4. Mumbo Jumbo, mumbo jumbo.

UMB′ra– 2. umbra.
3. penumbra.

UMB′ral– 2. umbral, tumbrel.
3. adumbral, penumbral.

UMB′rus– 2. umbrous, cumbrous, slumbrous.
3. penumbrous.

UM′ee– 2. chummy [coll.], dummy, gummy, glummy, plummy, slummy, mummy, rummy, crumby, crummie, thrummy, tummy, thumby, yummy [slang].
3. gin rummy.
4. double dummy.

UM′el– 2. hummel, pummel, pommel, trummel [loc.].
3. bepummel.

UM′er– 2. dumber, gummer, hummer, comer, cummer, scummer, glummer, plumber, slummer, mummer, number, rummer, drummer, strummer, thrummer, summer, thumber.
3. *incomer, newcomer, latecomer,* succumber, midsummer.

UM′est– 2. dumbest, glummest, mummest, numbest.

UM′et– plummet, grummet, summit.

UM′ij– 2. chummage, plumbage, rummage, scrummage, summage.
3. rerummage.

UM′ing– 2. bumming, chumming, gumming, humming, coming, scumming, plumbing, plumming, slumming, mumming, numbing, drumming, crumbing, strumming, thrumming, summing, thumbing.
3. becoming, *incoming, oncoming,* forthcoming, succumbing, benumbing.
4. unbecoming, second coming, overcoming.

UM′is– 2. pumice, pummice, pomace.

UM′it– 2. plummet, grummet, summit.
3. consummate.

UM′lee– 2. dumbly, comely, glumly, plumbly, mumly, numbly, rumly.
3. uncomely.
4. troublesomely, cumbersomely.

UM′nal– 3. columnal, autumnal.

UM′ness– 2. dumbness, glumness, plumbness, numbness.

UM′ok– 2. hummock, drummock, stomach.

UM′oks– 2. hummocks, lummox, flommox [slang], glommox [dial.], stomachs.

UMP′ee– 2. bumpy, chumpy, dumpy, humpy, jumpy, lumpy, clumpy, plumpy, slumpy, frumpy, grumpy, crumpy, stumpy, thumpy.

**UMP′er– bumper, dumper, jumper, lumper, plumper, pumper, trumper, stumper, thumper.
3.** broad jumper, high jumper, *tup-thumper.*

UMP′et– 2. crumpet, trumpet, strumpet.

UMP′ij– 2. pumpage, stumpage.

UMP′ing– 2. bumping, dumping, humping, jumping, lumping, clumping, plumping, slumping, mumping, pumping, trumping, stumping, thumping.
3. *broad-jumping,* high-jumping. *tub-thumping.*
4. hurdle-jumping.

UMP′ish– 2. bumpish, chumpish, dumpish, humpish, jumpish, lumpish, plumpish, mumpish, frumpish, grumpish.

UMP′kin– 2. bumpkin, lumpkin, pumpkin.
4. Tony Lumpkin.

UMP′l– 2. rumple, crumple.

UMP′ling– 2. dumpling, rumpling, crumpling.
3. uncrumpling.

UMP′shun– 2. gumption.
3. assumption, subsumption, resumption, presumption, consumption.

UMP′shus– 2. bumptious, gumptious, scrumptious.

UMPT′iv– 3. assumptive, subsumptive, consumptive, resumptive, presumptive.

UMP′us– 2. compass, rumpus.
3. encompass.
4. gyrocompass.

UM′uks– 2. lummox, flummox [slang], glommox [dial.], stomachs.

UM′zee– 2. clumsy, mummsy.

UNCH'ee– 2. bunchy, hunchy, punchy, crunchy, scrunchy.

UNCH'er– 2. buncher, huncher, luncher, muncher, puncher, bruncher, cruncher, scruncher.
3. *cowpuncher*.

UNCH'ez– 2. bunches, hunches, lunches, munches, punches, brunches, crunches, scrunches.

UNCH'ing– 2. bunching, hunching, lunching, munching, punching, crunching, scrunching.

UNCH'on– 2. luncheon, nuncheon, sconcheon, puncheon, bruncheon, truncheon.

UND'a– 2. Lunda.
3. Balunda, rotunda.

UND'ane– 2. mundane.
4. inframundane, intramundane, extramundane, ultramundane, antemundane, supermundane, intermundane.

UND'ans– 3. abundance, redundance.
5. superabundance, overabundance.

UND'ant– 3. abundant, redundant.
5. superabundant.

UND'ed– 2. funded.
3. refunded, retunded, rotunded.

UND'ee– 2. undy, bundy, fundi, Fundy, gundy, gundi, Monday, Sunday.
3. Whitsunday.
4. salmagundi.

UND'er– 2. under, dunder, funder, plunder, sunder, thunder, wonder.
3. down under, hereunder, thereunder, refunder, asunder, dissunder, rotunder, enthunder.

UND'l– 2. bundle, mundle [dial.], rundle, trundle.
3. unbundle.

UND'ld– 2. bundled, trundled.
3. unbundled.

UND'ler– 2. bundler, trundler.

UND'let– 2. bundlet, rundlet.

UND'ling– 2. bundling, trundling.
3. unbundling.

UND'o– 3. secundo [L.].
5. basso profundo.

UND'rus– 2. thundrous, wondrous.

UND'um– 3. secundum [L.], corundum.
4. carborundum.

UN'ee– 2. bunny, dunny, funny, gunny, honey, money, punny, runny, sunny, tunny.

UN'eed– 2. honeyed, moneyed.

UN'el– 2. funnel, gunnel, gunwale, runnel, trunnel, tunnel.

UN'er– 2. dunner, gunner, cunner, punner, runner, shunner, tonner, tunner, stunner.
3. *rumrunner, gunrunner,* forerunner.
4. thousand-tonner, overrunner.

UNG'er– 2. hunger, monger, younger.
4. *warmonger, newsmonger, fishmonger, witmonger.*
4. ironmonger, fashionmonger, scandalmonger, gossipmonger, costermonger.

UNG'l– 2. bungle, jungle.

UNG'lee– 2. bungly, jungly.

UNG'us– 2. fungus.
3. mundungus.

UN'ij– 2. dunnage, gunnage, punnage, tonnage.

UN'ing– 2. dunning, funning, gunning, cunning, punning, running, sunning, shunning, tunning, stunning.
3. *rumrunning, gunrunning,* outrunning.
4. overrunning.

UN'ish– 2. bunnish, Hunnish, nunnish, punish, punnish.

UNJ'ee– 2. plungy, spongy.

UNJ'er– 2. lunger, blunger, plunger, sponger.
3. expunger.

UNJ'ez– 2. lunges, blunges, plunges, sponges.
3. expunges.

UNJ'ing– 2. lunging, blunging, plunging, sponging.
3. expunging.

UNJ'un– 2. dungeon.
3. Melungeon.

UNK'ard– 2. Dunkard, drunkard.

UNK'ee– 2. chunky, funky, hunky, junky, skunky, flunky, flunkey, monkey, punky, punkie, spunky.

UNK'en– drunken, shrunken, sunken.
3. unshrunken, unsunken.

UNK'er– 2. bunker, dunker, funker, hunker, junker, flunker, punker.
3. *mossbunker..*

UNK'et– 2. junket, tunket [dial.].

UNK'ish– skunkish, monkish, punkish.

UNK'l– 2. uncle, nuncle, truncal.
3. *carbuncle, peduncle, homuncle, caruncle.*

UNK'o– 2. bunco, junco.

UNK'shun– 2. unction, function, junction, punction.
3. inunction, defunction, adjunction, rejunction, injunction, conjunction, disjunction, compunction, expunction.
4. interjunction, interpunction.

UNK'shus– 2. unctious.
3. rambunctious, compunctious.

UNKT'iv– 3. abjunctive, adjunctive, subjunctive, conjunctive, disjunctive, compunctive.

UNKT'ure– 2. juncture, puncture.
3. conjuncture.
4. acupuncture.

UNK'um– 2. bunkum, Buncombe.

UN'less– 2. punless, runless, sunless, sonless.

UN'let– 2. punlet, runlet, tonlet.

UNSH'al– 2. uncial.
3. quinuncial, pronuncial.
4. internuncial.

UNST'er– 2. gunster, Munster, punster.

UNT'al– 2. puntal, frontal.
3. confrontal.
4. contrapuntal; *see also* ŬNT'l.

UNT'ed– 2. bunted, hunted, blunted, punted, runted, fronted, grunted, shunted, stunted, wonted.
3. affronted, bifronted, confronted, unwonted.

UNT'ee– 2. punty, runty, stunty.

UNT′er– 2. bunter, hunter, blunter, punter, fronter, grunter, shunter, stunter.
3. *head-hunter*, affronter, confronter.
4. fortune hunter.
UNT′ing– 2. bunting, hunting, punting, fronting, grunting, shunting, stunting.
3. *head-hunting*, affronting, confronting.
4. fortune-hunting.
UNT′l– 2. gruntle.
3. disgruntle; *see also* ŬNT′al.
UNT′ness– 2. bluntness, stuntness.
UNT′o– 2. junto, punto.
UN′yun– 2. onion, bunion, Bunyan, Runyon, trunnion.
UP′ee– 2. guppy, cuppy, puppy.
3. *hiccoughy, hiccupy*.
UP′er– 2. upper, cupper, kupper, scupper, crupper, supper.
UP′et– 2. scuppet, puppet.
UP′ing– 2. cupping, supping, tupping.
3. *hiccoughing, hiccuping*.
UP′ish– 2. uppish, cuppish.
UP′l– 2. couple, supple.
3. recouple, uncouple, unsupple.
UP′ler– 2. coupler, suppler.
3. uncoupler.
UP′let– 2. cuplet, couplet.
3. *quadruplet, quintuplet*.
UP′shun– 2. ruption.
3. abruption, eruption, irruption, corruption, disruption.
4. interruption, incorruption.
5. uninterruption.
UPT′ed– 3. irrupted, corrupted, disrupted.
4. interrupted, uncorrupted, undisrupted.
5. uninterrupted.
UPT′er– 3. abrupter, corrupter, disrupter.
4. interrupter.
UPT′est– 3. abruptest, corruptest.
UPT′ing– 3. erupting, corrupting, disrupting.
4. interrupting.
UPT′iv– 2. ruptive.
3. eruptive, irruptive, corruptive, disruptive.
4. interruptive, incorruptive.
UPT′lee– 3. abruptly, corruptly.
4. incorruptly.
UPT′ness– 3. abruptness, corruptness.
4. incorruptness.
UR′a– 2. gurrah.
3. goburra.
4. korumburra.
UR′al– 3. deferral, referral, demurral.
UR′ant– 2. currant.
3. demurrant, susurrant; *see also* ŬR′ent.
URB′al– 2. herbal, verbal.
3. biverbal.
URB′an– 2. urban, Bourbon, turban.
3. suburban.
4. interurban.
URB′ee– 2. derby, herby, blurby, verby.
3. Iturbi.
URB′er– 2. Berber, curber, blurber.
3. superber, perturber, disturber.
URB′id– 2. herbid, turbid.

URB′ing– 2. herbing, curbing, blurbing, verbing.
3. perturbing, disturbing.
URB′it– 2. sherbet, turbit.
URB′ot– 2. burbot, turbot.
URCH′ee– 2. churchy, lurchy, smirchy.
URCH′en– 2. urchin, birchen.
URCH′er– 2. bircher, lurcher, smircher, nurture, percher, searcher.
3. besmircher, researcher.
URCH′ez– 2. birches, churches, lurches, smirches, perches, searches.
3. besmirches, researches.
URCH′in– 2. urchin, birchen.
URCH′ing– 2. birching, churching, lurching, smirching, perching, searching.
3. besmirching, researching.
URD′ed– 2. girded, herded, curded, worded.
3. begirded, engirded, reworded, misworded.
URD′ee– 2. birdie, curdy, purdy, sturdy, wordy.
4. hurdy-gurdy.
URD′en– 2. burden, guerdon.
3. reburden, disburden.
4. overburden.
URD′er– 2. girder, herder, murder.
3. *sheepherder*, absurder.
URD′ing– 2. girding, herding, wording.
3. begirding, engirding, rewording, miswording.
URD′l– 2. girdle, hurdle, curdle.
3. begirdle, engirdle.
URD′lee– 2. curdly, thirdly.
3. absurdly.
UR′ee– 2. burry, durrie, firry, furry, gurry, hurry, curry, scurry, lurry, blurry, flurry, slurry, murrey, murry, purry, spurry, surrey, worry, whirry.
4. hurry-scurry.
UR′eed– 2. hurried, curried, scurried, flurried, worried.
3. unhurried, unworried.
UR′eez– 2. hurries, curries, scurries, flurries, worries.
3. snow flurries.
UR′el– 2. burrel, squirrel.
UR′ens– 3. transference, recurrence, incurrence, concurrence, occurrence, deterrence.
4. nonconcurrence, intercurrence.
UR′ent– 2. current, currant.
3. decurrent, recurrent, concurrent, percurrent, crosscurrent, demurrant, susurrant, deterrent.
4. undercurrent, intercurrent.
UR′er– 2. burrer, blurrer, purrer, spurrer, stirrer.
3. deferrer, preferrer, conferrer, transferrer, transferor, concurrer, demurrer, interrer, bestirrer, averrer.
URF′ee– 2. scurfy, murphy, surfy, turfy.
URG′al– 2. ergal, tergal, virgal.
URG′l– 2. ergal, burgle, gurgle, tergal, virgal.
URG′lar– 2. burglar, gurgler.

URG'o– 2. ergo [L.], Virgo.
3. a tergo [L.].
URG'us– 2. Fergus.
4. demiurgus, thaumaturgus, Thaumaturgus.
UR'ij– 2. courage, stirrage.
3. encourage, discourage, demurrage.
UR'ing– 2. erring, burring, churring, fur-ring, blurring, slurring, purring, spurring, shirring, stirring, whirring.
3. unerring, deferring, referring, preferring, inferring, conferring, transferring, recurring, incurring, concurring, occurring, demurring, deterring, interring, bestirring, averring.
4. disinterring.
UR'ish– 2. burrish, currish, flourish, nourish.
URJ'ee– 2. clergy, surgy.
4. metallurgy, dramaturgy, thaumaturgy.
URJ'ens– 2. mergence, vergence.
3. submergence, emergence, resurgence, insurgence, detergence, divergence, convergence.
URJ'ent– 2. urgent, surgent, vergent.
3. emergent, assurgent, resurgent, insurgent, detergent, abstergent, divergent, convergent.
URJ'er– 2. urger, berger, dirger, scourger, splunger, merger, purger, perjure, verger, verdure.
URJ'ez– 2. urges, dirges, scourges, splurges, merges, purges, verges.
3. emerges, asperges, converges.
URJ'id– 2. turgid.
3. energid, unturgid.
URJ'ik– 3. theurgic, energic, chirurgic, liturgic.
4. demiurgic, metallurgic, dramaturgic, thaumaturgic.
URJ'ing– 2. urging, dirging, scourging, splurging, merging, purging, surging, verging.
3. submerging, emerging, immerging, asperging, resurging, deterging, diverging, converging.
URJ'ist– 4. metallurgist, dramaturgist, thaumaturgist.
URJ'ment– 3. submergement, divergement, convergement.
URJ'on– 2. burgeon, surgeon, sturgeon.
URK'a– 2. furca, circa.
3. amurca, mazurka.
URK'al– 2. furcal, cercal.
3. novercal.
4. homocercal.
5. heterocercal.
URK'ee– 2. jerky, lurky, murky, smirky, perky, shirky, turkey, quirky.
URK'er– burker, jerker, jerquer, kirker, lurker, smirker, perker, shirker, worker.
3. nonworker, guessworker.
4. wonder-worker.
URK'in– 2. firkin, gherkin, jerkin, perkin.
URK'ing– 2. irking, jerking, lurking, clerking, smirking, perking, shirking, working, quirking.
3. hard-working, nonworking.
4. wonder-working.

URK'ish– 2. jerkish, clerkish, perkish, Turkish, quirkish.
URK'l– 2. cercle, circle, turkle.
3. encircle, excircle, novercal.
4. semicircle, homocercal.
URK'lee– 2. Berkeley, clerkly, circly.
URK'som– 2. irksome, murksome, worksome, quirksome.
URK'us– 2. cercus, circus, Quercus.
URL'ee– 2. early, burly, churly, girly, girlie, gurly, hurly, curly, murly, knurly, pearly, pirlie [Scot.], surly, Shirley, swirly, twirly, whirly.
4. hurly-burly.
URL'er– 2. birler, burler, furler, hurler, curler, pearler, purler, twirler, whirler.
URL'et– 2. burlet, pearlet, spurlet.
URL'in– 2. merlin, Merlin, murlin, purlin.
URL'ing– 2. birling, furling, herling, hurling, skirling, knurling, pearling, purling, sperling, sterling, thirling, swirling, twirling, whirling.
URL'ish– 2. churlish, girlish, pearlish.
URL'oin– 2. purloin, sirloin.
URL'u– 2. curlew, purlieu.
URM'a– 2. Irma, Burma, derma, syrma, Syrma.
4. pachyderma, terra firma.
URM'al– 2. dermal, thermal.
3. synthermal.
4. pachydermal, epidermal, taxidermal, hypodermal, hydrothermal, isothermal.
URM'an– 2. Burman, firman, Herman, German, germon, merman, Sherman, termen, termon.
URM'ans– 3. affirmance, confirmance.
4. disaffirmance.
URM'ee– 2. germy, spermy, wormy.
4. taxidermy, diathermy.
URM'eez– 2. Hermes, kermes.
URM'ent– 2. ferment.
3. affirmant, deferment, referment, preferment, determent, interment, averment.
4. disinterment.
URM'er– 2. firmer, murmur, termer, termor, wormer, squirmer.
3. affirmer, infirmer, confirmer, bemurmur, first termer.
4. second termer.
URM'ik– 2. dermic, thermic.
3. endermic.
4. pachydermic, epidermic, taxidermic, diathermic, geothermic.
URM'in– 2. ermine, termin, vermin.
3. determine.
4. redetermine.
URM'ind– 2. ermined.
3. determined.
4. redetermined, undetermined.
URM'ing– 2. firming, germing, terming, worming, squirming.
3. affirming, confirming.
URM'is– 2. dermis, kermis.
4. epidermis, endodermis, exodermis.
URM'ish– 2. skirmish, wormish.

URM'it– 2. hermit, permit.
URM'lee– 2. firmly, termly.
3. infirmly, unfirmly.
URM'os– 2. hirmos, spermous, thermos.
URM'un– 2. Berman, Herman, German, germen, germon, Sherman, termen, termon.
URN'a– 2. Smyrna, sterna.
3. taberna.
4. parapherna.
URN'al– 2. urnal, journal, colonel, kernel, sternal, vernal.
3. diurnal, hibernal, infernal, supernal, lucernal, maternal, paternal, fraternal, eternal, nocturnal, internal, external, hesternal, cavernal.
4. paraphernal, coeternal, diuternal, sempiternal, hodiernal, cothurnal.
URN'ant– 2. vernant.
3. alternant, secernent.
URN'ate– 2. ternate.
3. biternate, quaternate, cothurnate.
URN'ee– 2. burny, ferny, journey, pirnie, tourney.
3. enurny, attorney.
URN'el– 2. colonel, kernel; see also ŬRN'al.
URN'er– 2. earner, burner, churner, learner, pirner, spurner, turner, sterner, yearner.
3. adjourner, sojourner, returner, discerner.
URN'est– 2. earnest, Ernest, sternest.
URN'ing– 2. earning, urning, burning, derning [dial.], churning, learning, spurning, turning, yearning.
3. inurning, adjourning, sojourning, book-learning, discerning, concerning, returning, interning, upturning.
4. undiscerning, overturning.
URN'ish– 2. burnish, furnish.
3. reburnish, refurnish.
URN'ment– 3. adjournment, sojournment, secernment, discernment, concernment, attornment, internment.
URN'ness– 2. ternness, sternness.
3. asternness.
4. taciturnness.
URN'o– 3. inferno, Salerno.
URN'um– 2. sternum.
3. laburnum, Viburnum, alburnum.
URN'us– 3. cothurnus, Avernus.
UR'o– 2. burro, burrow, borough, furrow, thorough.
3. unthorough.
4. interborough.
URP'ee– 2. burpy, Burpee, chirpy, slurpy.
URP'er– 2. burper, chirper.
3. hyperper, usurper.
URP'ing– 2. burping [slang], chirping, slurping [dial.].
3. usurping.
URS'a– 2. Ursa, bursa, Byrsa, djersa.
3. vice versa.
URS'al– 2. ursal, bursal, cursal.
3. rehearsal, bicursal, succursal, dispersal, reversal, transversal.
4. interspersal, quaquaversal, universal,

partiversal; see also ŬRS'l.
URS'ant– 2. versant.
3. aversant, conversant.
URS'ee– 2. birsy [Scot.], mercy, nursy, Percy, pursy, Circe.
3. gramercy, Luperci.
4. controversy.
URS'er– 2. bursar, curser, cursor, mercer, nurser, purser, terser, verser, versor, worser.
3. coercer, disburser, rehearser, accurser, precursor, amercer, disperser, traverser, reverser, converser.
4. reimburser, intersperser.
URS'et– 2. tercet, verset.
URS'ez– 2. hearses, curses, nurses, purses, verses.
3. coerces, disburses, rehearses, accurses, precurses, amerces, submerses, immerses, asperses, disperses, traverses, reverses, converses.
4. reimburses, resubmerses, reimmerses, intersperses, universes.
URSH'a– 2. Persia, tertia.
3. inertia.
URSH'al– 2. tertial.
3. commercial.
4. noncommercial, uncommercial, sesquitertial, controversial.
URSH'an– 2. Persian, tertian.
3. Cistercian, lacertian.
4. sesquitertian; see also ŬRSH'un.
URSH'un– 2. version.
3. coercion, recursion, incursion, excursion, submersion, emersion, immersion, aspersion, dispersion, assertion, desertion, exsertion, insertion, concertion, abstersion, aversion, obversion, subversion, eversion, reversion, diversion, inversion, conversion, perversion.
4. interspersion, disconcertion, introversion, retroversion, extroversion.
5. animadversion; see also ŬRSH'an.
URS'ing– 2. cursing, nursing, pursing, versing.
3. coercing, disbursing, rehearsing, accursing, immersing, dispersing, traversing, reversing, conversing, transversing.
4. reimbursing.
URS'iv– 2. cursive.
3. coercive, decursive, recursive, precursive, incursive, discursive, excursive, immersive, aspersive, dispersive, detersive, abstersive, aversive, subversive, eversive, inversive, conversive, perversive, transversive.
4. introversive, extroversive.
URS'l– 2. birsle [Scot.], hirsel, nursle, tercel; see also ŬRS'al.
URS'lee– 2. tersely.
3. aversely, obversely, adversely, reversely, diversely, inversely, conversely, perversely, transversely.
URS'let– 2. purslet, verselet.
URS'ling– 2. nurseling, verseling.
URS'ment– 3. imbursement, disbursement, amercement.
4. reimbursement.

URS'ness– 2. terseness.
  3. averseness, adverseness, perverseness.
URS'o– 2. verso.
  3. concurso, reverso.
URS'on– 2. urson, person.
URST'ed– 2. bursted, thirsted, worsted.
URST'ee– 2. Kirsty, thirsty.
  3. *bloodthirsty*, unthirsty.
URST'er– 2. burster, thirster.
URST'ing– 2. bursting, thirsting, worsting.
URST'ling– 2. firstling, Hearstling.
URS'us– 2. Ursus, cursus, thyrsus, Thyrsis, versus.
  3. concursus, excursus, Melursus, adversus [L.], conversus, transversus.
URT'a– 2. Berta, Goethe, serta.
  3. Alberta, Elberta, Lacerta.
  4. Ethelberta.
URT'al– 2. curtal.
  3. consertal.
URT'an– 2. curtain, certain.
  3. encurtain, uncertain.
  4. overcurtain, overcertain; *see also* ŬRT'on.
URT'ed– 2. skirted, blurted, flirted, spurted, shirted, squirted, verted.
  3. alerted, asserted, deserted, exerted, inserted, concerted, *blackshirted, brownshirted,* averted, obverted, subverted, adverted, everted, diverted, inverted, converted, perverted, transverted.
  4. preconcerted, disconcerted, interserted, undiverted, introverted, controverted, extroverted, unperverted.
URT'ee– 2. cherty, cherte, dirty, Gertie, flirty, certie [Scot.], certy [Scot.], thirty.
URT'eez– 2. dirties, certes, thirties.
URT'er– 2. hurter, curter, skirter, flirter, spurter, squirter.
  3. *frankfurter,* asserter, deserter, exerter, inserter, concerter, averter, subverter, adverter, everter, reverter, inverter, converter, perverter.
  4. preconcerter, disconcerter.
  5. animadverter.
URT'est– curtest, pertest.
URTH'a– 2. Eartha, Bertha, bertha, Hertha.
URTH'ee– 2. earthy, birthy.
URTH'ee– 2. worthy.
  3. *seaworthy,* unworthy, *noteworthy, trustworthy, praiseworthy.*
URTH'en– 2. earthen, burthen.
URTH'less– 2. earthless, birthless, mirthless, worthless.
URT'in– 2. curtain, certain.
  3. encurtain, uncertain.
  4. overcurtain, overcertain; *see also* ŬRT'on.
URT'ing– 2. hurting, skirting, blurting, flirting, spurting, shirting, squirting.
  3. alerting, asserting, deserting, exerting, inserting, concerting, averting, subverting, reverting, diverting, inverting, converting, perverting.
  4. preconcerting, disconcerting, interserting, retroverting, introverting, extroverting.

URT'iv– 2. furtive.
  3. assertive, exertive, insertive, revertive, divertive, invertive, convertive.
  4. self-assertive, introvertive, extrovertive.
URT'l– 2. fertile, hurtle, kirtle, myrtle, Myrtle, spurtle, turtle, whortle.
  3. infertile.
URT'lee– 2. curtly, pertly.
  3. inertly, alertly, *expertly.*
  4. *inexpertly.*
URT'less– 2. hurtless, skirtless, shirtless.
URT'ness– 2. curtness, pertness.
  3. inertness, alertness, *expertness.*
URT'on– 2. burton, Burton, Merton.
  4. Gammer Gurton; *see also* ŬRT'an.
URT'um– 2. furtum [L.], sertum.
  3. assertum.
UR'us– 2. byrrus, churrus.
  3. susurrus, susurrous.
URV'a– 2. urva.
  3. conferva, Minerva.
URV'al– 2. nerval, serval, vervel.
  3. acerval, conferval, adnerval, minerval.
URV'ant– 2. fervent, curvant, servant.
  3. recurvant, observant, *maidservant,* conservant.
  4. inobservant, unobservant.
URV'ate– 2. curvate.
  3. recurvate, incurvate, tricurvate, acervate, trinervate.
URV'ee– 2. nervy, curvy, scurvy.
  4. topsy-turvy.
URV'er– 2. fervor, nerver, server, swerver.
  3. unnerver, observer, deserver, reserver, preserver, conserver.
  4. life preserver.
URV'id– 2. fervid.
  3. perfervid.
  4. topsy-turvied.
URV'il– 2. chervil, servile, vervel.
URV'ing– 2. Irving, curving, nerving, serving, swerving.
  3. unnerving, observing, deserving, reserving, preserving, conserving, unswerving.
  4. unobserving, undeserving, unconserving.
URV'less– 2. curveless, nerveless, serveless, verveless, swerveless.
  3. deserveless, reserveless, preserveless.
URV'us– 2. curvous, nervous.
  3. confervous, recurvous, unnervous.
URZ'ee– 2. furzy, jersey, kersey, Mersey.
URZH'un– 2. Persian, version.
  3. incursion, discursion, excursion, emersion, submersion, immersion, aspersion, dispersion, aversion, obversion, subversion, eversion, reversion, diversion, inversion, conversion, perversion.
  4. interspersion, introversion, retroversion, extroversion.
  5. animadversion.
USCH'un– 2. fustian.
  3. combustion, inustion.
US'ee– 2. fussy, Gussie, hussy, mussy.

4. overfussy.

US'el– 2. mussel, Russell, trussell; *see also* **ŬS'l.**

US'er– 2. busser, fusser, cusser, musser, trusser.
3. discusser, nonplusser.

US'et– 2. gusset, russet.

US'ez– 2. busses, fusses, cusses [coll.], plusses, musses, trusses.
3. discusses, nonplusses, untrusses.

USH'a– 2. Russia, Prussia.

USH'ee– 2. gushy, lushy, blushy, plushy, slushy, mushy, rushy, brushy, thrushy.

USH'er– 2. usher, gusher, husher, lusher, blusher, flusher, plusher, rusher, brusher, crusher, shusher.
3. fourflusher.

USH'est– 2. lushest, flushest, plushest.

USH'ez– 2. gushes, hushes, blushes, flushes, plushes, mushes, rushes, brushes, crushes, thrushes, tushes.
3. four-flushes.

USH'ing– 2. gushing, hushing, mushing, blushing, flushing, rushing, brushing, crushing.
3. unblushing, four-flushing, onrushing.

USH'un– 2. Russian, Prussian.
3. recussion, incussion, concussion, percussion, discussion, succussion.
4. repercussion.

US'ing– 2. bussing, fussing, cussing [coll.], mussing, trussing.
3. discussing, nonplussing, untrussing.

US'iv– 2. jussive, tussive.
3. concussive, percussive, discussive, succussive.
4. repercussive.

USK'an– 2. dusken, Tuscan.
3. molluscan, Etruscan.

USK'ee– 2. dusky, husky, musky, tusky.

USK'er– 2. husker, tusker.
3. *cornhusker.*

USK'et– 2. busket, musket.

USK'in– 2. buskin, ruskin, Ruskin.

USK'ing– 2. dusking, husking, tusking.
3. *cornhusking.*

USK'ule– 3. majuscule, minuscule, crepuscule, opuscule.

US'l– 2. bustle, duscle, hustle, justle, mussel, muscle, rustle, Russell, trussell, tussal, tussle.
3. *arbuscle,* crepuscle, opuscle, *corpuscle.*

US'lee– 2. muscly, rustly, thusly.

US'ler– 2. bustler, hustler, rustler, tussler.

US'ling– 2. bustling, hustling, muscling, rustling, tussling.

US'lz– 2. bustles, hustles, muscles, rustles, Brussels, tussles.

UST'a– 2. crusta.
3. Augusta.

UST'ard– 2. bustard, custard, mustard; *see also* **ŬST'erd.**

UST'ed– 2. busted, dusted, lusted, rusted, crusted, trusted.
3. combusted, bedusted, disgusted, adjusted, encrusted, entrusted, distrusted, mistrusted.

4. maladjusted.

UST'ee– 2. busty, dusty, fusty, fustee, fustie, gusty, lusty, musty, mustee, rusty, crusty, trusty.

UST'er– 2. buster, duster, juster, Custer, luster, bluster, fluster, cluster, muster, rustre, truster, thruster.
3. robuster, trust buster, adjuster, adjustor, *lackluster,* distruster, mistruster.
4. filibuster, readjuster, coadjuster.

UST'erd– 2. bustard, custard, lustered, blustered, flustered, clustered, mustered, mustard, rustred.
3. beflustered, unclustered.

UST'est– 2. justest.
3. robustest.

UST'ful– 2. gustful, lustful, trustful, thrustful.
3. disgustful, untrustful, distrustful, mistrustful.
4. overtrustful.

UST'ik– 2. bustic, fustic, rustic.
4. anacrustic.

UST'ing– 2. busting, dusting, husting, lusting, rusting, crusting, trusting, thrusting.
3. bedusting, disgusting, adjusting, encrusting, entrusting, distrusting, mistrusting.
4. readjusting, maladjusting, coadjusting, self-adjusting.

UST'is– 2. justice, Custis.
3. injustice.

UST'iv– 3. combustive, adjustive.

UST'lee– 2. justly.
3. robustly, augustly, unjustly.

UST'ment– 3. adjustment, encrustment, entrustment.
4. readjustment, maladjustment.

UST'ness– 2. justness.
3. robustness, augustness, unjustness.

UST'ral– 2. lustral.
3. lacustral, palustral.

UST'rate– 2. frustrate.
3. illustrate.

UST'rum– 2. lustrum, flustrum.

UST'rus– 2. lustrous, blustrous.
3. *lacklustrous.*

UST'us– 2. Justus.
3. Augustus.

UT'a– 2. gutta.
3. Calcutta.

UT'al– 3. abuttal, rebuttal.
4. surrebuttal; *see also* **ŬT'l.**

UT'ed– 2. butted, gutted, jutted, glutted, smutted, nutted, rutted, strutted.
3. abutted, rebutted.
4. unrebutted.

UT'ee– 2. butty, gutty, jutty, cutty, scutty, smutty, nutty, putty, puttee, rutty, ruttee, suttee.

UT'er– 2. utter, butter, cutter, scutter, flutter, glutter, clutter, splutter, mutter, nutter, putter, sputter, rutter, strutter, shutter, stutter.
3. abutter, rebutter, *woodcutter, stonecutter, meatcutter.*

4. bread-and-butter, peanut butter, surre-butter.

UT′erd– **2.** uttered, buttered, fluttered, muttered, sputtered, shuttered, stuttered.

3. unuttered, well-buttered, unfluttered.

UTH′er– **2.** other, mother, smother, brother, tother.

3. *grandmother*, another.

UT′ing– **2.** butting, gutting, jutting, cutting, glutting, smutting, nutting, putting, rutting, strutting, shutting.

3. abutting, rebutting, *woodcutting*, *stonecutting*, *crosscutting*.

UT′ish– **2.** sluttish, nuttish, ruttish.

UT′l– **2.** buttle, guttle, cuttle, scuttle, ruttle, subtle, suttle, shuttle.

3. abuttal, rebuttal, unsubtle.

4. surrebuttal.

UT′ler– **2.** butler, cutler, cuttler, scuttler, ruttler, subtler, sutler.

UT′ling– **2.** buttling, gutling [dial.], guttling, scuttling.

UT′on– **2.** button, glutton, mutton.

3. *bluebutton*.

5. bachelor-button.

UV′ee– **2.** covey, lovey.

4. lovey-dovey [slang].

UV′el– **2.** hovel, scovel, shovel.

UV′en– **2.** oven, sloven.

UV′er– **2.** hover, cover, lover, glover, plover, shover.

3. *windhover*, recover, uncover, discover, self-lover.

4. undercover, rediscover.

UV′ing– **2.** loving, gloving, shoving.

3. unloving, ungloving, self-loving.

UZ′ard– **2.** buzzard, huzzard.

UZ′ee– **2.** buzzy, fuzzy, hussy, huzzy, muzzy, wuzzy [slang].

4. fuzzy-guzzy, fuzzy-wuzzy.

UZ′en– **2.** dozen, cozen, cousin.

UZ′er– **2.** buzzer, nuzzer.

UZ′ez– **2.** buzzes, fuzzes, muzzes.

UZ′ing– **2.** buzzing, fuzzing, muzzing.

UZ′l– **2.** buzzle, guzzle, muzzle, nuzzle, puzzle.

3. bemuzzle, unmuzzle, bepuzzle.

4. crossword puzzle, jigsaw puzzle, Chinese puzzle.

UZ′ler– **2.** guzzler, muzzler, puzzler.

UZ′ling– **2.** guzzling, muzzling, nuzzling, puzzling.

3. bemuzzling, unmuzzling, bepuzzling.

UZ′n– **2.** dozen, cozen, cousin.

Ŭ (tub)

Triple Rhymes

Primary or Secondary Accent Falls on Second from Last Syllable; Imperfect Rhymes Are in Italics.

UB′a–bl– 3. clubbable, scrubbable, tubbable.
UB′er–ee– 3. blubbery, rubbery, scrubbery, shrubbery.
UB′er–er– 3. blubberer, slubberer, rubberer.
UB′i–er– 3. chubbier, grubbier, scrubbier, shrubbier, tubbier, stubbier.
UB′i–lee– 3. chubbily, grubbily, scrubbily, tubbily, stubbily.
UB′i–ness– 3. chubbiness, grubbiness, scrubbiness, *shrubbiness,* tubbiness, stubbiness.
UB′lik–an– 3. publican.
  4. republican.
UD′er–ee– 3. duddery, shuddery, studdery.
UD′i–er– 3. bloodier, muddier, ruddier, studier.
UD′i–est– 3. bloodiest, muddiest, ruddiest.
UD′il–ee– 3. bloodily, muddily, ruddily.
UD′i–ness– 3. bloodiness, muddiness, ruddiness.
UF′a–bl– 3. buffable, bluffable, ruffable.
  4. rebuffable, unruffable.
  5. unrebuffable.
UF′i–er– 3. huffier, fluffier, snuffier, puffier, stuffier.
UF′il–ee– 3. huffily, fluffily, snuffily, puffily, stuffily.
UF′i–ness– 3. huffiness, fluffiness, snuffiness, puffiness, stuffiness.
UF′ing–lee– 3. buffingly, huffingly, bluffingly, fluffingly, snuffingly, puffingly, stuffingly.
  4. rebuffingly.
  5. unrebuffingly.
UG′a–bl– 3. huggable, pluggable.
UG′er–ee– 3. snuggery, pugaree, druggery, thuggery.
UG′i–ness– 3. bugginess, slugginess, mugginess, pugginess.
UJ′er–ee– 3. drudgery, grudgery.
UK′er–ing– 3. puckering, succoring.
UK′i–ness– 3. luckiness, pluckiness, muckiness.
  4. unluckiness.
UK′shun–al– 3. fluxional, suctional.

4. inductional, reductional, conductional, productional, destructional, instructional, constructional.
UK′shun–ist– 3. fluxionist.
  4. productionist, obstructionist, destructionist, constructionist.
  5. reconstructionist.
UKT′i–bl– 4. deductible, conductible, productible, destructible, instructible, constructible.
  5. undeductible, indestructible, uninstructible.
UKT′iv–lee– 4. deductively, seductively, inductively, productively, obstructively, destructively, instructively, constructively.
  5. unproductively.
UKT′iv–ness– 4. seductiveness, productiveness, destructiveness, instructiveness, constructiveness.
  5. unproductiveness, reconstructiveness.
UKT′or–ee– 4. deductory, inductory, conductory.
  5. reproductory, introductory, manuductory.
UK′ul–ens– 3. truculence, succulence.
UK′ul–ent– 3. truculent, succulent.
UL′er–ee– 3. gullery, colory, skullery, scullery.
  4. medullary.
ULK′i–ness– 3. bulkiness, sulkiness.
UL′min–ant– 3. fulminant, culminant.
UL′min–ate– 3. fulminate, culminate.
ULS′if–i– 3. dulcify.
  4. emulsify.
ULS′iv–lee– 4. repulsively, impulsively, compulsively, revulsively, convulsively.
ULS′iv–ness– 4. repulsiveness, impulsiveness, compulsiveness, revulsiveness, convulsiveness.
ULS′or–ee– 4. compulsory, expulsory.
  5. uncompulsory.
ULT′a–bl– 4. insultable, consultable.
  5. uninsultable, unconsultable.
ULT′im–it– 3. ultimate.

4. penultimate.
6. antepenultimate.
ULT′ing–lee– 4. insultingly, exultingly.
ULT′ur–al– 3. cultural.
5. agricultural, floricultural, horticultural.
ULT′ur–ist– 3. culturist.
5. apiculturist, agriculturist, floriculturist, horticulturist.
UM′aj–er– 3. rummager, scrummager.
UM′ar–ee– 3. nummary, summary; *see also* **ŬM′er–ee.**
UMB′ens–ee– 3. cumbency.
4. decumbency, recumbency, incumbency.
UMB′er–er– 3. cumberer, lumberer, slumberer, numberer.
4. encumberer.
UMB′er–ing– 3. cumbering, lumbering, slumbering, numbering.
4. encumbering, unslumbering, outnumbering.
UMB′er–sum– 3. cumbersome, slumbersome, numbersome.
UMB′er–us– 3. slumberous, numberous.
4. unslumberous.
UMB′ling–lee– 3. rumblingly, tumblingly, stumblingly.
UM′er–ee– 3. chummery, flummery, plumbery, nummary, mummery, summary, summery.
UM′ing–lee– 3. hummingly, numbingly.
4. becomingly, benumbingly.
5. unbecomingly.
UMP′i–ness– 3. dumpiness, humpiness, jumpiness, frumpiness, grumpiness, stumpiness.
UMP′ish–ness– 3. dumpishness, lumpishness, mumpishness, frumpishness, grumpishness.
UMP′shus–lee– 3. bumptiously, scrumptiously.
UMP′shus–ness– 3. bumptiousness, scrumptiousness.
4. assumptiousness.
UMPT′iv–lee– 4. assumptively, resumptively, presumptively, consumptively.
UMPT′u–us– 3. sumptuous.
4. presumptuous, unsumptuous.
UN′a–bl– 3. punnable, runnable, shunnable.
UNCH′a–bl– 3. punchable, crunchable.
UND′ant–lee– 4. abundantly, redundantly.
6. superabundantly.
UND′er–er– 3. blunderer, plunderer, sunderer, thunderer, wonderer.
UND′er–ing– 3. blundering, plundering, sundering, thundering, wondering.
UND′er–us– 3. plunderous, thunderous.
UND′it–ee– 4. profundity, fecundity, jocundity, immundity, obtundity, rotundity.
5. moribundity, rubicundity, orotundity.
UN′er–ee– 3. gunnery, nunnery.
UNG′er–ing– 3. hungering, mongering.
4. *wordmongering, warmongering, newsmongering.*
5. scandalmongering, ironmongering.

UN′il–ee– 3. funnily, sunnily.
4. unfunnily.
UNK′shun–al– 3. unctional, functional, junctional.
4. conjunctional.
UNKT′iv–lee– 4. adjunctively, subjunctively, conjunctively, disjunctively.
UNK′u–lar– 3. uncular.
4. carbuncular, peduncular, caruncular, avuncular.
UNT′ed–lee– 3. huntedly, stuntedly, wontedly.
4. affrontedly, unwontedly.
UNT′ed–ness– 3. huntedness, bluntedness, stuntedness, wontedness.
4. affrontedness, unwontedness.
UNT′i–ness– 3. puntiness, runtiness, stuntiness.
UNT′ing–lee– 3. buntingly, huntingly, gruntingly, stuntingly.
UPT′iv–lee– 4. corruptively, disruptively.
5. interruptively.
URB′a–bl– 3. curbable.
4. uncurbable, perturbable.
5. imperturbable, indisturbable, undisturbable.
URB′al–ist– 3. herbalist, verbalist.
URB′i–al– 4. suburbial, adverbial, proverbial.
URD′er–er– 3. murderer, verderer.
URD′il–ee– 3. sturdily, wordily.
URD′i–ness– 3. curdiness, sturdiness, wordiness.
UR′ens–ee– 3. currency.
4. recurrency, concurrency.
UR′ent–lee– 3. currently.
4. recurrently, concurrently.
UR′id–lee– 3. hurriedly, flurriedly, worriedly.
UR′i–er– 3. burrier, furrier, hurrier, currier, courier, scurrier, purrier, worrier.
UR′i–ing– 3. burying, hurrying, flurrying, currying, scurrying, worrying.
UR′i–ment– 3. flurriment, worriment.
UR′ish–ing– 3. flourishing, nourishing.
4. unflourishing, unnourishing.
URJ′en–see– 3. urgency, vergency.
4. emergency, assurgency, insurgency, detergency, divergency, convergency.
URJ′er–ee– 3. perjury, purgery, surgery, vergery.
4. chirurgery.
URJ′ik–al– 3. surgical.
4. theurgical, energical, liturgical.
5. demiurgical, metallurgical, dramaturgical, thaumaturgical.
URK′i–lee– 3. jerkily, perkily, murkily.
URK′ul–ar– 3. furcular, circular.
4. tubercular, opercular.
5. semicircular.
URK′ul–ate– 3. circulate.
4. tuberculate, operculate, recirculate.
URK′ul–um– 3. furculum.
4. tuberculum, operculum.
URK′ul–us– 3. circulus, surculus, surculous.

4. tuberculous.
URL'i–er– 3. earlier, burlier, churlier, curlier, pearlier, surlier.
URL'i–est– 3. earliest, burliest, churliest, curliest, pearliest, surliest.
URL'i–ness– 3. earliness, burliness, curliness, pearliness, surliness.
URL'ish–ness– 3. churlishness, girlishness.
URM'an–ee– 3. Germany, verminy.
URM'at–iv– 4. affirmative, confirmative.
URM'in–al– 3. germinal, terminal.
4. adterminal, conterminal.
URM'in–ant– 3. germinant, terminant.
4. determinant, interminant, conterminant.
URM'in–ate– 3. germinate, terminate.
4. determinate, interminate, exterminate.
5. predeterminate, indeterminate.
URM'in–us– 3. terminus, verminous.
4. coterminous.
URM'it–ee– 4. infirmity, confirmity.
URN'a–bl– 3. burnable, learnable, turnable.
4. unburnable, unlearnable, returnable.
5. unreturnable, overturnable; *see also* ŬRN'i–bl.
URN'al–ee– 3. vernally.
4. infernally, eternally, internally, externally.
URN'al–ist– 3. journalist.
4. eternalist, externalist.
URN'al–ize– 3. journalize.
4. infernalize, eternalize, internalize, externalize.
URN'al–izm– 3. journalism.
4. infernalism, eternalism, externalism.
URN'ed–lee– 3. learnedly.
4. unlearnedly, concernedly.
5. unconcernedly.
URN'er–ee– 3. fernery, ternery, turnery.
URN'i–a– 3. hernia.
4. Hibernia, Calpurnia, Saturnia, evernia.
URN'i–an– 4. eburnean, Hibernian, Falernian, Saturnian.
URN'i–bl– 4. discernible.
5. indiscernible; *see also* ŬRN'a–bl.
URN'ish–er– 3. burnisher, furnisher.
4. refurnisher.
URN'ish–ing– 3. burnishing, furnishing.
4. refurnishing.
URN'it–ee– 4. modernity, maternity, fraternity, eternity, alternity.
5. sempiternity, taciturnity, diuturnity.
URN'it–ure– 3. furniture, cerniture.
UR'o–er– 3. burrower, furrower.
URP'en–tine– 3. serpentine, turpentine.
URP'i–lee– 3. burpily, chirpily, slurpily.
URP'i–ness– 3. burpiness, chirpiness, slurpiness.
URS'a–bl– 4. amerceable, traversable, reversable, inversable, conversable; *see also* ŬRS'i–bl.
URS'ar–ee– 3. bursary, nursery.
5. anniversary; *see also* ŬRS'or–ee.
URS'i–bl– 4. coercible, submersible, immersible, reversible, conversible.

5. incoercible, introversible; *see also* ŬRS'a–bl.
URS'i–form– 3. ursiform, bursiform, furciform, versiform.
4. diversiform.
URS'it–ee– 4. adversity, diversity, perversity.
5. university.
URS'iv–lee– 4. decursively, discursively, excursively, aspersively, dispersively, detersively.
URS'iv–ness– 4. coerciveness, discursiveness, excursiveness, detersiveness.
URS'or–ee– 3. cursory.
4. precursory, discursory, aspersory; *see also* ŬRS'ar–ee.
URTH'less–ness– 3. mirthlessness, worthlessness.
URT'i–bl– 3. hurtable.
4. unhurtable, insertable, avertible, subvertible, revertible, divertible, invertible, convertible, pervertible.
5. inconvertible, controvertible.
6. incontrovertible.
URT'is–ment– 4. advertisement, divertisement.
URV'a–bl– 3. curvable, servable, swervable.
4. observable, reservable, preservable, conservable, unswervable.
URV'at–iv– 3. curvative.
4. observative, reservative, preservative, conservative.
URV'ed–lee– 3. fervidly.
4. observedly, deservedly, reservedly.
5. undeservedly, unreservedly.
URV'ens–ee– 3. fervency.
4. observancy, conservancy.
URV'i–lee– 3. curvily, nervily, swervily.
5. topsy-turvily.
URZH'un–al– 3. versional.
4. excursional, reversional, conversional.
URZH'un–ist– 3. versionist.
4. excursionist, immersionist, aversionist, reversionist, conversionist.
US'a–bl– 3. mussable.
4. discussable.
5. undiscussable.
USH'a–bl– 3. hushable, flushable, brushable, crushable.
4. unhushable, uncrushable.
USH'i–lee– 3. gushily, mushily.
USH'i–ness– 3. gushiness, mushiness.
USH'ing–lee– 3. gushingly, blushingly, rushingly, crushingly.
USK'i–lee– 3. duskily, huskily, muskily.
USK'i–ness– 3. duskiness, huskiness, muskiness, tuskiness.
USK'ul–ar– 3. muscular.
4. majuscular, bimuscular, nonmuscular, unmuscular, minuscular, crepuscular, opuscular, corpuscular.
USK'ul–us– 3. musculus.
4. crepusculous, corpusculous.
UST'a–bl– 3. rustable, trustable.
4. adjustable.

5. readjustable, inadjustable; *see also* ŬST′i–bl.

ŬST′er–ee– **3.** blustery, flustery, clustery.

ŬST′er–er– **3.** blusterer, flusterer, musterer.

ŬST′er–ing– **3.** blustering, flustering, clustering, mustering.

ŬST′ful–ee– **3.** gustfully, lustfully, trustfully.
4. disgustfully, distrustfully, mistrustfully.

ŬST′i–bl– **4.** combustible.
5. incombustible, noncombustible, uncombustible; *see also* ŬST′a–bl.

ŬST′i–er– **3.** dustier, fustier, gustier, lustier, mustier, rustier, crustier, trustier.

ŬST′i–est– **3.** dustiest, fustiest, gustiest, lustiest, mustiest, rustiest, crustiest, trustiest.

ŬST′i–lee– **3.** dustily, fustily, gustily, lustily, mustily, rustily, crustily, trustily.

ŬST′i–ness– **3.** dustiness, fustiness, gustiness, lustiness, mustiness, rustiness, crustiness, trustiness.

ŬST′ri–us– **4.** industrious, illustrious.

ŬT′er–ee– **3.** buttery, guttery, fluttery, spluttery, muttery, puttery, sputtery, stuttery.

ŬT′er–er– **3.** utterer, butterer, flutterer, splutterer, mutterer, putterer, sputterer, stutterer.

ŬT′er–ing– **3.** uttering, buttering, guttering, fluttering, spluttering, muttering, puttering, sputtering, shuttering, stuttering.

ŬTH′er–er– **3.** motherer, smotherer.

ŬTH′er–ing– **3.** mothering, smothering, brothering, southering.

ŬTH′er–lee– **3.** motherly, brotherly, southerly.
4. unmotherly, unbrotherly.

ŬT′ing–lee– **3.** juttingly, cuttingly, struttingly.

ŬT′ler–ee– **3.** butlery, cutlery, sutlery.

ŬT′on–ee– **3.** buttony, gluttony, muttony.

ŬV′a–bl– **3.** lovable, shovable.
4. unlovable.

ŬV′el–er– **3.** hoveler, shoveler.

ŬV′er–ee– **3.** hovery, plovery.
4. recovery, discovery.

ŬV′er–er– **3.** hoverer, coverer.
4. recoverer, uncoverer, discoverer.

ŬV′er–ing– **3.** hovering, covering.
4. recovering, uncovering, discovering.

ŬZ′i–lee– **3.** fuzzily, muzzily, wuzzily [slang].

ŬZ′i–ness– **3.** fuzziness, hussiness, muzziness, wuzziness [slang].

Appendixes

Appendix I

---◆---

Publication

It may be taken as axiomatic that literature is written to be read, and that poets therefore customarily wish to publish their poetry. This chapter will deal with the practical questions that arise for the producing poet who seeks an outlet for his verse.

GAINING ASSURANCE

It is often a good idea for the inexperienced poet to join a class or a writers' group of some kind in order to get an unprejudiced reaction to his work. An advanced writing class is probably the best sounding board for a beginner; the instructor of such a course is usually highly trained in his field and gives responsible professional criticism to the members of his class. A writers' group or club is another possibility, but there is less assurance that its criticism will be on a sufficiently high level to be useful to the poet. Such a group can, however, often be of value on the practical level in the pooling of its members' experience and in surveying and discussing periodicals of various kinds.

READINESS FOR PUBLICATION

For the poet who has begun to write regularly, the question of readiness for publication invariably arises. If he has received encouraging reactions from his instructor or his group, or has analyzed his work thoroughly for himself, he is probably ready to submit his work for publication. The only way to tell for certain whether his poetry merits publication is to make a serious, sustained attempt, rather than a single, isolated submission. The writer must realize that only a small percentage of the material he submits to editors over a period of time is likely to be accepted for publication, and he must therefore prepare himself for the jolt of receiving rejection slips. Too many poets retire, feeling themselves worsted, after only one or two brushes with the realities of attempting publication.

Readiness for publication, then, implies confidence in the validity of one's work. It also implies a realization that the world is wide indeed, and that there are a good many other poets competing for every editor's attention. A certain modesty of expectation should be coupled with determination.

A young writer once read, in Louis Untermeyer's well-known anthology, of a poet who was launched upon a distinguished career by having a poem published in *The New Republic* magazine. The young writer immediately submitted her best and newest — the two adjectives are synonymous to most writers — poem to that magazine. When, contrary to all realistic expectations, it was accepted and promptly appeared in print, the writer secretly expected to wake up the next morning and find herself famous — Mr. Untermeyer *dixit!*

The poem, however, disappeared as easily as it appeared. The young poet never knew whether anybody read it; no critics stepped forward to welcome her to the ranks of American poetry; Mr. Untermeyer remained silent.

In other words, publication is pleasant, but it is a mistake to expect too much from it.

THE POET'S CARD FILE

Once the poet has begun to submit poetry for publication, it is a good idea for him to set up a card file in which to record the fortunes of his poems. A card should be made for each finished poem by typing (or writing) its title at the top and, for the poet's own information, the date or approximate date of its composition. Underneath the title will be recorded the name of the magazine to which the poem has been submitted, the date of submission, and in due course its rejection or acceptance. The card will probably look something like this after the passage of a little time:

```
THE QUARRY                               (1963)

    6/19/64, Satevepost - R  6/28
    7/1/64, Bitterroot - R  7/27
    8/2/64, Voices - R  9/8
    9/10/65, Messenger - A  11/5

                Published, Spring 1965
                (No payment)

(Reprinted, "Poetry of the Week,"
    New York Herald Tribune, 6/12/65)
```

This theoretical example assumes a rather full career for a poem, but it is reasonably typical of a successfully published one. There may be a good many cards for poems that never receive the accolade of an "A" for Accepted, after the final notation of submission, but if the writer is convinced the poem is a good one, he should not hesitate to keep on trying.

As the poet sends out more poems, he may find it convenient to separate the cards into four alphabetized divisions:

READY, the heading under which are filed poems that are finished and ready to submit, but not currently being circulated.

ACTIVE, under which are filed poems that are out on submission and from which no report has as yet been received.

ACCEPTED, under which are filed poems that have been accepted but are not yet in print. (Often there is a considerable time lag between acceptance and publication).

PUBLISHED, the final heading under which successful poems will come to rest, although even then there may be further notations if the poem is reprinted.

When a poem is returned by an editor as unsuitable for the needs of his magazine, the writer should scrutinize it for possible improvement before sending it out again.

THE POEM NOTEBOOK

Presumably the writer is keeping correct copies of all his poems in a loose-leaf notebook. These are his master copies, from which he will make the typed manuscripts to submit for publication.

WHERE TO SUBMIT POEMS

It is a good idea for the writer to acquaint himself with the market for poetry. He should remember that the magazines of the widest circulation and prestige receive very large numbers of unsolicited manuscripts for consideration every day. *Harper's Magazine*, which perhaps publishes two poems in a monthly issue, is said to receive about fifteen hundred verse manuscripts a month. *The Saturday Review*, *The New Republic*, *The Nation*, *Good Housekeeping*, and other large popular magazines receive thousands of manuscripts. The writer should not hesitate to try these markets if he has a poem or two that he thinks suitable for their pages, but he should be realistic about his chance of receiving an acceptance.

It is wise, therefore, to devote serious attention to the little magazines, and in particular to those devoted entirely to poetry. They are open to contributions by new poets, and most published poets first break into print in their pages. Many of them publish poetry of the very highest caliber, and any poet may be proud to have them publish his work. They are widely read by people whose major interest is poetry, and poems that appear in them are often reprinted in poetry columns and anthologies. A few of them, such as *Poetry, A Magazine of Verse*, are as distinguished in the field of poetry as the best among the general literary magazines and reviews.

In searching for possible markets for his poetry, the writer may well consider his local newspaper and any large newspapers in his area of the country. He may also wish to try the national newspapers, such as *The New York Times, The New York Herald Tribune*, and *The Christian Science Monitor*, all of which publish poetry.

The periodical room of a large public library is a good place to examine hard-to-find magazines. If a large library is not available to him, the writer can choose, from the list in this book, a few magazines that he thinks may be of interest to him. He can then order by mail copies of those publications that seem suitable.

A last resort — and one that many an inexperienced poet mistakenly settles for — is to submit poems blindly to magazines he has never seen. This can turn out to be a waste of time; the poet may find himself submitting his work to magazines that seldom or never publish his kind of verse. Worse, he may find himself with a poem accepted and printed in a magazine whose standards are totally incompatible with his own.

SELECTING POEMS TO SUBMIT

In looking over periodicals, the writer has probably already thought of several of his poems which might be appropriate for publication in one or two of them. Now he must seriously review the poems he has on hand and determine which ones he will submit to which magazines.

Two or three poems may be sent to advantage simultaneously. It is not wise to submit more than three at a time, except to the rare magazine which states as a matter of editorial policy that it is interested in larger selections from one poet. On the other hand, the poet should not hesitate to submit a single poem, particularly if it is an example of his best work.

SUBMITTING SEASONAL VERSE

Seasonal poetry is in demand, for magazines have found that material related to the time of year or to a particular holiday is popular with their readers. If the poems which the poet plans to submit are of a seasonal nature, he must be sure to submit them at the proper time, neither too soon nor too late for the market. The large magazines, in general, work two seasons ahead of the actual time of year. Thus, winter poetry should be submitted during the summer months, certainly by mid-August; spring poems are submitted in the autumn, summer poems in the winter, and autumn poems in the spring. If it is too late to submit a certain poem to a magazine, it may either be put away until the next year or submitted to a newspaper, since newspapers usually work only one season ahead at most. An autumn poem, for example, may be submitted to *The New York Times* late in August.

THE TYPESCRIPT

Each poem to be submitted should be typed with the author's name and address, single-spaced, in the upper left-hand corner of the paper. Paper of good quality and standard size (8½ by 11 inches) should be used. The typing should be neat; "erasable" bond can be a help to the poet who is not a very good typist, for erasures are easily made on it and corrections inserted unobtrusively.

The poem should be centered on the page; if it is short, it looks good if the balance is a little below the center. The poem may be double-spaced, with three spaces between the title and the body of the poem and two lines between stanzas. The author's name in the form he wishes to use for publication should be typed two spaces beneath the poem, slightly to the right, preceded by a hyphen. No other notations should be placed on the sheet, and certainly nothing about "first publication rights," "to be paid for at regular rates," or any similar reservations that amateur writers sometimes mistakenly include.

A dog-eared typescript should never be sent out; it confesses by its appearance that it has already passed through other hands and been rejected. A carbon copy is even worse; it suggests to an editor that he is a second or third choice, since somebody else obviously got the first copy.

In all these considerations, the guiding principle is that a manuscript must be well presented if it is to have a chance of acceptance. The editor's right to see a fair and clear copy is taken for granted, and any departure from that standard will make a bad impression. The writer should not be careless in any detail, but on the other hand he should not submit a manuscript that is made fancy or fussy in any way. A businesslike, clear, well-spaced typescript is all that is required. Less than that insults the editor. More, in the form of any decorations or frills, makes the poet seem amateurish.

In general, short poetry is the single exception to the rule that all manuscripts should be double-spaced. If a poem is long enough to run over a page in length, it may be double-spaced for the sake of ease in reading it. Single-spacing should be reserved for the short poem that looks better on a single page.

An example of how to place a poem on the manuscript page is shown separately.

THE COVERING LETTER

It is only courteous to send a covering letter with any manuscript, but it should be very brief; its only purpose is to submit the poems enclosed for the editor's consideration. It may include a brief statement of the writer's "credits" — that is, where he has published before — or it may state something short and to the point about the subject of the poem or poems being submitted.

The poet should not trespass upon the editor's good nature with a long, rambling personal letter. The editor is not running a column of advice to perplexed writers, and he will only be annoyed or antagonized by a long communication demanding special attention. An editor is a busy person who is vitally interested in finding publishable poems among the mass of material submitted to him, but he has no time to criticize the work of individual poets. The poet should simply submit his poems and let it go at that. If the first editor does not perceive their merit, perhaps the second editor will.

DUPLICATION OF SUBMISSIONS

No poem should be submitted to more than one publication at a time, because of the chance that both might accept it. This would involve the poet in a situation that would be worse than embarrassing. He should be well aware that the laws of copyright protect the publisher of any work against unlawful copying by any other publisher, and if he knowingly submits his poem to more than one periodical at a time, he lays them both open to such possible infringement. This would be a sort of literary bigamy on the part of the poet. If several magazines should accept the same poem, the writer would have to explain and withdraw his poem from all but one. What editor, discovering such a state of affairs, would wish to consider further work from this poet?

The same poem, if once refused, should not be submitted a second time to the same magazine. Editors have good memories, and they are quite rightly annoyed if the same poem turns up again. If a poem has been so completely rewritten, however, that it is for all practical purposes a new poem, it may be resubmitted. In that case it should be filed as a new poem, and a new card made for it in the poet's records.

Once a poem has been published, it should not be submitted to any other magazine. If a column of reprinted poetry or an anthology wishes to use it, the editor will write to the poet and to the magazine which published the poem originally to ask permission to reprint it. It is customary in this case to give permission for the reprinting of the poem.

The only time the poet may do anything further with the poem himself is when

Frances Stillman,
% Thomas Y. Crowell Company,
201 Park Avenue South,
New York, N.Y. 10003

A HILL LEGEND

Each evening it came again
  Over the hill,
A magical piping
  That took her will,

And she said, "That's love music--
  Who can it be?
There's someone out there
  A-calling me!"

Her pa went down
  On his knees to pray,
But she picked up her fiddle
  And slipped away.

Oh, she never came back,
  And the passing of years
Was lonesome, like love music
  Nobody hears.

But her kinfolk still,
  When the wild wind whines,
Hear a fiddling and piping
  Out in the pines.

                    ---Frances Stillman

Sample page as typed for submission to *The Saturday Evening Post*,
which published the poem.

he publishes a book of his own. Then he must get permission from the magazines where his poems have appeared to publish them in his book. Their permission should be acknowledged at the beginning of the volume.

THE STUDENT POET

The student poet should first devote his attention to contributing to his school or college literary magazine. Valuable experience in publishing and in editing can be gained from student publications, and the young writer is well advised to try out for the staff of his school magazine.

A few national or local poetry magazines have sections devoted to verse by young people, and these are of interest to the student. High school and sometimes younger students may also take part in certain local contests and in the national writing contests of *Scholastic Magazine*.

The college student may already be writing poems good enough to submit to national magazines of various kinds. In general, he is likely to have more success with poetry and little magazines than with the giants in the field.

There are several paperback books which collect college or "new" writing; the student should, by all means, submit his work to these.

ANTHOLOGIES

If the editor of an anthology asks a poet for the privilege of including one or more of his poems in a volume, this is a real compliment and, as has already been said, unless the writer has some reason to refuse permission, he may agree with pleasure.

A writer has real reason to refuse, however, if he is asked, as a condition for having his poem appear, to buy one or more copies of the book or to make a financial contribution to it. No bona fide anthology asks anything of an author but permission to use a poem. Unfortunately, a few money-making schemes masquerade in the guise of anthologies in which only the poet who pays is included. This does not produce an anthology of any real interest, since merit is obviously not the criterion for the selection of its contents. A poet may not receive much money, if any, for his work; but he should never, never pay to get it published.

THE BOOK OF POEMS

A poet's chance of getting a book of his poems published is greatly enhanced if he has first had a number of poems published in magazines. If he has already published his poems extensively in periodicals, he may wish to prepare a book manuscript and begin his campaign to have it published.

A poet who has advanced thus far in his career probably needs little advice concerning his projects. The editor of this book wishes him Godspeed and looks forward to seeing his first volume one day at the booksellers.

Appendix II

———————◆———————

Markets for Poetry and Verse

GENERAL MAGAZINES AND NEWSPAPERS

ADVENTURE MAGAZINE, 205 East 42 Street, New York 17, N.Y.

Monthly. Editor, Alden H. Norton. Uses some verse, about 20 to 25 lines long; "something lusty, adventurous, appealing to men." Pays $ .25 a line, on acceptance.

AMERICAN FORESTS, 919 17 Street, N.W., Washington 6, D.C.

Monthly. Published by American Forestry Association. Editor, James B. Craig. Short verse on outdoor subjects. Pays on publication.

AMERICAN LEGION MAGAZINE, 720 Fifth Avenue, New York 19, N.Y.

Monthly. Uses no serious poetry. Short humorous jingles used on the "Parting Shots" page, the editor of which is Mr. John Andreola. Pays $ 2.50 a line, on publication.

THE AMERICAN SCHOLAR, 1811 Q Street, N.W., Washington 9, D.C.

Quarterly. Editor, Hiram Haydn. Uses some very distinguished poetry. Pays $ 10 to $ 35, on acceptance.

ATLANTIC MONTHLY, 8 Arlington Street, Boston 16, Massachusetts.

Monthly. Editor, Edward A. Weeks. Uses one or two poems in each issue, as well as some light verse. Pays $ 150 a page of the magazine, on acceptance.

CHATELAINE, Maclean-Hunter Publishing Company, Ltd., 481 University Avenue, Toronto 2, Ontario, Canada.

Monthly. Editor, Mrs. Doris H. Anderson. Uses short verse. Pays on acceptance.

CHICAGO TRIBUNE, Tribune Tower, Chicago 11, Illinois.

Daily morning and Sunday newspaper. Uses verse in daily feature columns. Editor, "A Line O' Type or Two," or Editor, "In the Wake of the News." No payment.

THE CHRISTIAN CENTURY, 407 South Dearborn Street, Chicago 5, Illinois.

Weekly. Editor, Harold E. Fey. Uses some poetry of high quality.

THE CHRISTIAN SCIENCE MONITOR, 1 Norway Street, Boston 15, Massachusetts.

Daily evening newspaper. Address Editor, Home Forum Page. This page uses poems of high quality. Payment after publication.

COMMONWEAL, 232 Madison Avenue, New York 16, N.Y.

Weekly. Editor, Edward S. Skillin. Uses good poetry of various lengths. Pays $.40 a line, on acceptance.

GOOD HOUSEKEEPING, 57 Street at Eighth Avenue, New York 19, N.Y.

Monthly. Poetry Editor, Maureen O' Keefe. Uses short verse, both light and serious, on subjects of interest to women readers. Pays high rates, on acceptance.

HARPER'S BAZAAR, 572 Madison Avenue, New York 22, N.Y.

Monthly. Literary Editor, Alice S. Morris. Uses poems of high quality. Payment on acceptance.

HARPER'S MAGAZINE, 49 East 33 Street, New York 16, N.Y.

Monthly. Editor, John Fischer. Uses poems of high quality, preferably short. Some light verse. Payment on acceptance.

HARTFORD TIMES, 10 Prospect Street, Hartford 1, Connecticut.

Daily evening newspaper. Poetry Editor, Doris Smith ("The Poet's Corner"). Prefers short poems. No payment.

McCALL'S MAGAZINE, 230 Park Avenue, New York 17, N.Y.

Monthly. Address Poetry Editor. Uses poetry of high quality; subjects of interest to women readers.

THE NATION, 333 Avenue of the Americas, New York 14, N.Y.

Weekly. Address Poetry Editor. Uses poetry of high quality.

NEW REPUBLIC, 1244 19 Street, N.W., Washington 6, D.C.

Weekly. Address Poetry Editor. Uses poetry of high quality.

NEW YORKER, 25 West 43 Street, New York 36, N.Y.

Weekly. Address Poetry Editor. Uses serious poetry of high quality, as well as light and satirical verse.

NEW YORK HERALD TRIBUNE, 230 West 41 Street, New York 36, N.Y.

Daily morning and Sunday newspaper. Address Poetry Editor. Uses verse of high quality on the editorial page.

NEW YORK TIMES, 229 West 43 Street, New York 36, N.Y.

Daily morning and Sunday newspaper. Address Poetry Editor. Uses verse of high quality on the editorial page.

SATURDAY REVIEW, 25 West 45 Street, New York 36, N.Y.

Weekly. Poetry Editor, John Ciardi. Uses poetry of high quality; no fixed limit on length, "but short poems are easier for us to use." No translations. Payment on publication.

YANKEE, Dublin, New Hampshire.

Monthly. Address Poetry Editor. Uses poetry of high quality.

UNIVERSITY QUARTERLIES OF NATIONAL INTEREST; LITERARY AND LITTLE MAGAZINES

ANTIOCH REVIEW, The Antioch Press, Yellow Springs, Ohio.

Quarterly. Managing Editor, Paul H. Rohmann; Poetry Editor, Judson Jerome. Publishes 8 to 12 poems an issue, of any length. Prefers "modern treatment of significant themes." Pays $ 5 a page of the magazine, on publication.

APPROACH, 114 Petrie Avenue, Rosemont, Pennsylvania.

Editors, Albert and Helen Fowler. Poetry of page length preferred.

ARIZONA QUARTERLY, University of Arizona, Tucson, Arizona.

Quarterly. Editor, Fred C. McCormick.

CARLETON MISCELLANY, Carleton College, Northfield, Minnesota.

Quarterly. Editor, Reed Whittemore.

THE CAROLINA QUARTERLY, Box 1117, Chapel Hill, North Carolina.

Quarterly. Editor, Louis M. Bourne. Poetry of all lengths and forms. Pays $ 10 and up.

CHELSEA, P. O. Box 242, Old Chelsea Station, New York 11, N.Y.

Quarterly. Editors, Sonia Raiziss, Alfredo de Palchi (Poetry), Ursule Molinaro, Venable Herndon (Fiction). About half of each issue devoted to poetry, approximately 20 poets. No restrictions as to length, subject, or style; many translations.

CHICAGO REVIEW, University of Chicago, Chicago 37, Illinois.

Quarterly. Editor, Peter Michelson. Publishes serious poetry of any length, style, or subject; "serious" does not preclude either comedy or wit. Uses about 20 poems in each issue.

CITY LIGHTS JOURNAL, City Lights Books, 261 Columbus Avenue, San Francisco, California.

Annual in book form. Editor, Lawrence Ferlinghetti. Uses about six poems, preferably long, of any style or subject.

THE COLORADO QUARTERLY, Hellems 118, University of Colorado, Boulder, Colorado.

Quarterly. Editor, Paul Carter. Poetry up to 40 lines.

CONTACT, Box 755, Sausalito, California.

Bimonthly. Editors, Kenneth Lamott, Norman Disher, Evan S. Connell, Jr. Uses serious poetry of any length, style, or subject.

THE CREATIVE REVIEW, P. O. 564, Eugene, Oregon.

Quarterly. Editor, Glen Coffield. Prefers verse of 40 lines or less, "about living or any form of creativity."

EPOCH, 159 Goldwin Smith Hall, Cornell University, Ithaca, N.Y.

Issued three times a year. Editors, Baxter Hathaway and others. Uses 20 to 30 poems in each issue; no restrictions as to length, style, or subject. "We are interested only in poems of high literary quality."

FORUM, The University of Houston, Houston 4, Texas.

Editor, Donald W. Lee. Poems of high quality.

GEORGIA REVIEW, University of Georgia, Athens, Georgia.

Quarterly. Editor, W. W. Davidson. Uses five or six poems in each issue, preferably short; some light verse but mostly serious poetry. "We avoid the obscure." Receives about 2,000 poems a year. Pays $ .50 a line, on publication.

HUDSON REVIEW, 65 East 55 Street, New York 22, N.Y.

Quarterly. Editors, Frederick Morgan, Joseph Bennett, Mary Emma Elliott. Uses varying amounts of poetry, both light and serious, with no restrictions as to length, style, or subject; "only criterion, excellence." Pays $. 50 a line, on publication.

KENYON REVIEW, Box 127, Gambier, Ohio.

Quarterly. Editors, Robie Macauley, George Lanning. Publishes serious poetry, preferably under 50 lines, with no restrictions as to style or subject. "We use verse of high professional quality. Contributors include such poets as Robert Lowell, Robert Graves, Richard Wilbur, Randall Jarrell, William Stafford, and Delmore Schwartz." Pays $1 a line, on publication.

THE LITERARY REVIEW, Fairleigh Dickinson University, Teaneck, New Jersey.

Quarterly. Editors, Clarence R. Decker, Charles Angoff. Uses about 50 pages of poetry in each issue, both light and serious, with no restrictions as to length, style, or subject.

THE MASSACHUSETTS REVIEW, Memorial Hall, University of Massachusetts, Amherst, Massachusetts.

Quarterly. Editors, Jules Chametzky, John H. Hicks. Uses about 25 pages of poetry in each issue, with no restrictions as to length, style, or subject. Pays $ .20 a line, $ 3 minimun, $ 20 top, on publication.

MICA, 216 Northridge Road, Santa Barbara, California.

Quarterly. Editors, Raymond Federman, Helmut Bonheim. Uses 6 to 8 poems in each issue; likes "wit, human touch, non-academic."

THE MICHIGAN QUARTERLY, Alumni Memorial Hall, University of Michigan, Ann Arbor, Michigan.

Quarterly. Address the Editors. Short poems.

MIDSTREAM, 515 Park Avenue, New York 22, N.Y.

Quarterly. Published by The Theodor Herzl Foundation. Editor, Shlomo Katz. Uses two or three serious poems in each issue. Pays on publication.

THE MIDWEST QUARTERLY, Kansas State College, Pittsburg, Kansas.

Quarterly. Editor, Dudley T. Cornish. Serious poetry, with no restriction as to style or subject, not longer than 60 lines.

THE MINNESOTA REVIEW, Box 4068, University Station, Minneapolis 14, Minnesota.

Quality poetry with no restriction as to style, subject, or length. Pays on publication.

MUTINY, A Magazine of the Arts, Box 278, Northport, N.Y.

Issued three times a year. Editors, Jane Esty, Paul Lett. Uses 18 to 20 poems in each issue, with no restrictions as to length, style or subject. Pays $ .50 a line minimun, on publication.

THE NEW MEXICO QUARTERLY, The University of New Mexico Press, Albuquerque, New Mexico.

Quarterly. Editor, Roland Dickey. Uses about 10 poems in each issue, up to 30 lines in length, with no restrictions as to style and subject. Pays on publication.

NORTHWEST REVIEW, 129 Nestor, University of Oregon, Eugene, Oregon.

Quarterly. Editor, Edward van Aelstyn. Uses 10 to 16 poems in each issue. No restrictions on length, style, or subject. Pays $ 5 minimum for a poem, on acceptance.

THE OUTSIDER, 618 rue Ursulines, New Orleans 16, Louisiana.

Semiannual book periodical. Editors, Jon Edgar Webb, Louise Webb. Uses 20 or more poems in each issue, not more than 36 lines long. "No rhymed verse, no politics, no coffee house gibberish — but also no traditional poetry." Experimental and avant-garde. Prize awards.

PARIS REVIEW, 45-39 171 Place, Flushing 58, N.Y.

Quarterly. Editor, George A. Plimpton. Poetry Editor, X. J. Kenneddy. Uses 20 to 30 poems in each issue, with no restrictions as to length, style, or subject. Pays $ .35 a line (variable), on publication.

PRAIRIE SCHOONER, Room 219, Andrews Hall, University of Nebraska, Lincoln, Nebraska.

Quarterly. Editor, Bernice Slote. Uses 15 to 25 poems in each issue; no restrictions as to length, style, or subject. No payment.

QUARTERLY REVIEW OF LITERATURE, Box 287, Bard College, Annandale-on-Hudson, N.Y.

Quarterly. Editor, T. Weiss. No restriction as to length, style, or subject, but prefers experimental verse.

QUARTET, 1619 Potomac Avenue, Lafayette, Indiana.

Quarterly. Editors, Don Winkelman, Arnold Lazarus; Poetry Editor, B. P. Woodford. Uses about 10 to 15 poems in each issue; no restrictions as to length, style, or subject. No payment.

SAN FRANCISCO REVIEW, 2808 Laguna Street, San Francisco 23, California.

Annual. Editors, R. H. Miller, June Oppen Degnan, George Hitchcock. Poetry, long or short. Payment on publication.

SEWANEE REVIEW, University of the South, Sewanee, Tennessee.

Quarterly. Editor, Andrew Lytle. Uses 5 to 10 poems in each issue; no restrictions as to length, style, or subject. Pays $ .50 a line, on publication.

THE SOUTHWEST REVIEW, Southern Methodist University, Dallas 22, Texas.
Quarterly. Editor, Allen Maxwell. Prefers short poems. Pays $ 5 a poem, on publication.

TRACE, P. O. Box 1068, Hollywood, California.
Quarterly. Editor, James Boyer May; Associates, A. F. Franklyn, Milton VanSickle, G. E. Evancheck. Uses 15 to 20 poems in each issue; no restrictions as to length, style, or subject. Pays $ 3 minimum for verse-shorts, and from $ 5 to $40 for poems, after publication.

TRANSATLANTIC REVIEW, Box 3348, Grand Central Station, New York 17, N.Y.
Quarterly. Editor, J. F. McCrindle. Poetry Editors, George Garrett and B. S. Johnson. Uses 6 or 8 poems in each issue; prefers short poems; no restriction as to style or subject. Pays about $ 5 a poem, on publication.

THE UNIVERSITY OF KANSAS CITY REVIEW, University of Kansas City, Kansas City 10, Missouri.
Quarterly. Editor, Alexander P. Cappon. No restriction as to length, style, or subject. No payment.

VIRGINIA QUARTERLY REVIEW, 1 West Range, Charlottesville, Virginia.
Quarterly. Editor, Charlotte Kohler. Uses approximately 5 to 10 pages of poetry in each issue. No restriction as to length, style, or subject. Pays $.50 a line, on publication.

YALE REVIEW, 92-A Yale Station, New Haven, Connecticut.
Quarterly. Editor, J. E. Palmer. Uses a few exceptional poems. Payment on publication.

POETRY MAGAZINES

THE AMERICAN BARD, 1154 North Ogden Drive, Hollywood, California.
Quarterly. Editor, Edythe Hope Genee. Prefers poems of 24 lines or less; no restriction as to subject and style. Prize contests in each issue.

AMERICAN HAIKU, Box 73, Platteville, Wisconsin.
Semiannual. Publishes only haiku, from 120 to 180 in each issue. $ 55 in awards to the three best poets in each issue.

AMERICAN WEAVE, 4109 Bushnell Road, University Heights, Ohio.
Semiannual. Editor, Loring Williams. Poems up to 90 lines in length. "We get too many poems on death, sorrow, etc.; need good inspirational pieces." Cash prizes and book awards. Annual Chapbook Award provides publication of winner's poems.

BARDIC ECHOES, 1036 Emerald Avenue, N.E., Grand Rapids 3, Michigan.
Quarterly. Editor, Clarence L. Weaver. Official publication of The Bards, a poetry and music group of Grand Rapids; poetry of nonmembers is welcome.

THE BELOIT POETRY JOURNAL, Box 2, Beloit, Wisconsin.
Quarterly. Editors, Chad Walsh, Robert Glauber, David Stocking, Marion

Stocking, John Bennett, Bink Noll. Publishes poetry of high quality of any length, including very long poems. "We occasionally publish translations of foreign poetry (query us). Sometimes an entire issue is devoted to one long poem or to a series of poems centered around a theme (such as the special chapbook dedicated to Robert Frost). Mainly, we simply publish the best possible poetry of all poetic 'schools.' "

BITTERROOT, 5229 New Utrecht Avenue, Brooklyn 19, N.Y.

Quarterly. Editor, Menke Katz. Publishes serious poetry.

CANDOR MAGAZINE, 103 Clements Avenue, Dexter, Missouri.

Quarterly. Editor, Elvin Wagner. "Conventional type of poetry preferred, preferably 16 lines or less." Occasional prizes.

CARAVAN, Lamoni, Iowa.

Bimonthly. Editor, Helen Harrington. Prefers poems of social consciousness, relating man to his environment; 16 lines or less.

CARAVEL, a magazine of verse, 1065 Runnymede Street, East Palo Alto, California.

"Occasionally, which amounts to quarterly." Editor and Publisher, Ben Hagglund. Poetry of all lengths published, but considers 32 lines an ideal length. Prefers verse about people and places. Pays $ .05 a line.

THE CHAT NOIR REVIEW, 1368 N. Sedgwick Street, Chicago, Illinois.

Quarterly. Editor, Robert Herron Ingalls. Publishes serious poetry of all kinds and lengths.

CHOICE, P.O. Box 4858, Chicago 80, Illinois.

Semiannual. Editors, John Logan and Aaron Siskind. Publishes serious poetry of any length.

ELIZABETH, 103 Van Etten Blvd., New Rochelle, N.Y.

Semiannual. Editor and Publisher, James L. Weil; Associate Editor, Gloria R. Weil; Consulting Editors, Frederick Eckman, Gena Ford, Joseph Joel Keith, Felix Stefanile, Loring Williams. Prefers tight, modern style; 30 lines maximum preferred, though any length is considered.

EPOS, Crescent City, Florida.

Quarterly. Editors, Will Tullos and Evelyn Thorne. Poems of any length considered, but those of under 50 lines preferred. "No slant, no bias, no taboos. *Epos* is now in its 15th year and has never missed an issue . . . . we answer letters and report on manuscripts within one week."

ESSENCE, 91 Westerleigh Road, New Haven 15, Connecticut.

Semiannual. Editor, Joseph Payne Brennan. In general, poems of not over 25 lines are preferred; there are no restrictions as to style or subject. Receives submissions of well over 5,000 verses a year.

EXPERIMENT, 6565 NE Windermere Road, Seattle, Washington.

Issued occasionally. Editor, Carol Ely Harper. Poems of any length, preferably experimental and original.

FREE LANCE, A Magazine of Poetry and Prose, Editorial Office, 6005 Grand
Avenue, Cleveland 4, Ohio; Business Office, 2904 22 Street, Niagara Falls, N.Y.
   Semiannual. Editors, C. L. Jordan, Adelaide Simon, Russell Atkins, Helen
Collins. "Avant-garde poems preferred, but will consider any style."

THE GALLEY SAIL REVIEW, P.O. Box 4842, San Francisco 1, California.
   Semiannual. Editor, Stanley McNail. Verse of all kinds and lengths considered. Payment in contributor's copies.

GALLOWS, 3118 K Street, Eureka, California.
   Three or more issues a year. Editor, Jon T. Griffith. Verse of all lengths and
styles, but primarily free verse.

LYNX, 300 Broadway, Plainview, Texas.
   Semiannual. Editors, Paul Levine and Margaret Lee Johnson. Verse of any
length in "the modern idiom."

THE LYRIC, Christiansburg, Virginia.
   Quarterly. Editors, Ruby Altizer Roberts and John Nixon Jr. Verse of 40
lines or less preferred, traditional in technique. $ 600 yearly given in prizes
for the best poems in the magazine; also a college contest open to under-
graduate students in the United States or Canada, with $ 400 in prizes.

MIDWEST: A Magazine of Poetry and Opinion, 289 East 148th Street, Harvey,
Illinois.
   Quarterly. Editor, R. R. Cuscaden. Verse of all lengths and styles. "The
poems rejected most frequently by *Midwest* are those written by poets who
have not abandoned the idea that 19th-century poetry can still be written."

MIDWEST CHAPARRAL, 3302 East Lee, Tucson, Arizona.
   Semiannual. Editor, Mildred Nye Dewey. Prefers poems of 16 lines or less.
This magazine is the official journal of the "Regional Federation Chaparral
Poets," and uses only the poetry of members; query if interested.

NEW ATHENAEUM, Crescent City, Florida.
   Semiannual. Editor, Will Tullos. No poems of over 14 lines accepted; no
editorial slants or restrictions. All manuscripts reported on within one week.

OBERLIN QUARTERLY, Wilder Hall, Oberlin, Ohio.
   Quarterly. Editor, Robert Shaheen. Verse of any length considered, with
"a style which comes out of the poet, and subjects significantly presented."
Payment, $ .50 a line (subject to change).

OUTCRY, Box 8093, Foothill Station, Salt Lake City 8, Utah.
   Quarterly. Editor, Lee Holland; Associates, Alex Rode, Ron Connally.
Poems of any length, style, and subject matter considered.

PAN, 6 Issues of Poetry, R.F.D. 1, Housatonic, Massachusetts.
   Six issues in all. Editor, Alan Brilliant. Poems of any length, style, and
subject considered.

PASQUE PETALS, 924 S. Cleveland Avenue, Sioux Falls, South Dakota.
   Monthly. Editor, Adeline M. Jenney, Box 117, Valley Springs, South Dakota.

Official organ of the South Dakota State Poetry Society, in 38th year of publication. Has issued five anthologies; holds annual state high-school poetry contest.

POETRY, 1018 North State Street, Chicago, Illinois.

Monthly. Editor, Henry Rago. Publishes distinguished poetry of any length, any style. Pays $ .50 a line, on publication.

POETRY NORTHWEST, Parrington Hall, University of Washington, Seattle 5, Washington.

Quarterly. Editors, Carolyn Kizer, William Matchett, Nelson Bentley; Associate Editor, Robin Evans. "We prefer to consider groups of poems." Contributors receive 10 copies; prizes are awarded annually.

POETRY PILOT, 1078 Madison Avenue, New York 28, N.Y.

Monthly. A poetry news bulletin that publishes six to eight poems in each issue. Address poems to the poetry editor.

POETRY SCORE, General Delivery, Carmel, California.

Published irregularly. Editor, Jehanne Salinger Carlson. Prefers poems not longer than 50 lines, of any style.

QUAGGA, Box 7591, University Station, Austin 12, Texas.

Published irregularly. Editor, James W. Smith. Publishes good poetry of any length or style.

SCIAMACHY, 1096 Elm Street, Winnetka, Illinois.

Annual. Editor, Millea Levin. Prefers poems under 200 lines, modern or traditional in style. Also publishes translations of poetry from other languages, together with the original text.

SOUTH AND WEST, An International Literary Quarterly, 2601 South Phoenix, Fort Smith, Arkansas.

Quarterly. Editor, Sue Abbott Boyd. Poems of from 3 to 64 lines. "We are interested in originality more than perfection in form." Payment in copies and prizes.

THE SPARROW MAGAZINE, 103 Waldron Street, West Lafayette, Indiana.

Annual. Editor and Publisher, Felix Stefanile. Publishes poetry of any length, any style. (Also publishes the Vagrom chapbooks).

SPIRIT, A Magazine of Poetry, 232 Madison Avenue, New York 16, N.Y.

Bimonthly. Editor, John Gilland Brunini. The organ of The Catholic Poetry Society of America, *Spirit* publishes only the poems of members; query if interested. Considers poems of up to 200 lines, in any style.

TARGETS, Sandia Park, New Mexico.

Quarterly. Editor, W. L. Garner; Associate Editor, Lloyd Alpaugh. Publishes poetry of any length, any style. Pays $ 1 a page, on acceptance. Is looking for eight-page signatures by one poet, for which it pays $ 10 and 10 copies.

WISCONSIN POETRY MAGAZINE, 2821 E. Belleview Place, ⧣ 7, Milwaukee 11, Wisconsin.

Issued three times a year. Editor, A. M. Sterk. The official organ of the Wisconsin Poetry Foundation. Prefers poems "not too long," in any style. Prize awards.

THE WORMWOOD REVIEW, Box 111, Storrs, Connecticut.

Quarterly. Editor, Marvin Malone. Publishes poetry of from 4 to 250 lines, in any style, of any school. Pays three to six copies or $3 to $6, depending on length of poem.

Index

Index

"Abraham Lincoln Walks at Midnight" (Lindsay), 111
accent (*see also* meter):
  as determinant of meter, 4-5, 7, 12
  and natural pronunciation, 22-23
  and near-rhyme, 82-83
  and rhyme, 34-35
  and stress, distinction between, 88
accented-unaccented coupling, *see* imperfect rhyme
accent lines, 14
accent meter, 20-22
adjectives, use of, 116, 117
advertising verse, 4
Aeneid, The (Virgil), 7
alexandrine, 17, 45
allegory, 102-103
alliteration, 8, 33, 84, 87
American poetry, influence of, 80-81, 92
"Amoretti" (Spenser), 49, 50
amphibrachic meter, 12
amphimacer meter, 13
anapestic meter, 10
  and iambic, mixed, 12, 20
  line lengths in, 13, 14, 15, 16, 17, 18
  mood of, 23
  rhyme in, 34
Anglo-Saxon poetry, 8-9, 21, 84
animals, as subjects of poetry, 111
"Annabel Lee" (Poe), 18
anthologies, 364, 366
antibacchius meter, 13
Antony and Cleopatra (Shakespeare), 24
apostrophe, 122
Aristophanes, x, xiii, 33, 106
Arnold, Matthew, 92, 111
"Ars Poetica" (MacLeish), 110
art, as subject of poetry, 111
"Ash Wednesday" (Eliot), 107-108, 111
assonance, 33, 83-84, 86-87
Atsutada, 76
attitudes:
  moral viewpoint in, 93-94, 108
  and style, 112-113
  and subject treatment, 105-106

"Auctioneer of Parting, The" (Dickinson), 85
Auden, W. H., 21, 67, 106, 111, 118

bacchius meter, 13
ballad, x, 102
  accent meter in, 21
ballade, 51-57, 122
"Ballade of Good Counsel" (Chaucer), 54
"Ballade for Lost Childhood, A" (F. S.), 52
ballade royal, 54
"Ballad of François Villon, A" (Swinburne), 53
ballad line, 18-19
" Ballad of Prose and Rhyme, The " (Dobson), 55
"Ballad of Reading Gaol" (Wilde), 10
ballad stanza, 38, 42
"Ballad of William Sycamore, The" (Benét), x, 111
Banville, Théodore de, 69
"Barbara Allen," x
Basho (Matsuo Basho), 75
"Batter My Heart, Three-Person'd God" (Donne), 111
Baudelaire, Charles, 69
Beatitudes, 119
"Bells for John Whiteside's Daughter" (Ranson), 85
Benét, Stephen Vincent, x, 102, 111
Bentley, Edmund Clerihew, 79
Beowulf, ix
Betjeman, John, 106
Bible, the, xv, 80, 92, 119
Blake, William, 27, 114
blank verse, 32, 40, 70-72
"Blessèd Damozel, The" (Rossetti), 28
Boccaccio, 44
books, poetry, 364, 366-367
"Book of Songs," 33
"Brahma" (Emerson), 111
"Brignall Banks" (Scott), 29
Browning, Elizabeth Barrett, 51
Browning, Robert, x, 26, 80, 100, 115
"Buick" (Shapiro), 17
"Burnt Norton" (Eliot), 40
Buson, 75

Butler, Samuel, 101
"By the North Sea" (Swinburne), 84
Byron, George Gordon, Lord, xiii, 10, 14, 16, 19, 23, 44, 106, 111

"Caelica" (Greville), 17
caesura, 24
Campion, Thomas, 63
Canterbury Tales, The (Chaucer), x, 9, 16, 25, 38, 102
cantos, 30
Cantos (Pound), 101
"Captain Stratton's Fancy" (Masefield), 18
Carroll, Lewis, xiv, xv
Catullus, 7
Caxton, William, 9
"Centaurs, The" (Stephens), 69
chain rhyming, 33, 42, 64, 68-69
  in Spenserian stanza, 45, 49-50
chain verse, 69-73, 86
Chamisso, Adelbert von, 69
chant royal, 56-57
Chatterton, Thomas, 30
Chaucer, Geoffrey, x, 9, 16, 25, 29, 35, 38, 41, 44, 51, 54, 102
Chaucerian roundel, 59-60
"Children at Night" (F. S.), 60-61
Chinese poetry, 33
cinquain, 27-28, 76-77
"City Square, The" (F. S.), 60
classical poetry:
  meters of, 5-7, 11-13
  and rhyme concept, 32
  traditional forms of, 26, 41, 42-43, 73-74
Cléomadés, The (Le Roi), 58
clerihew, 79
clichés, 117, 118
closed couplet, 25-26
"Clothes" (F. S.), 70
Coleridge, Samuel Taylor, 28
consonance, 81, 85-86
consonant rhyme, 35, 81, 84-85, 87
consonant sound, in near-rhyme, 83-87
contractions, 117
couplet, 25-26
  in poem forms, 47, 48-49, 63, 64-65
  as rhyme scheme, 38
"Cow in Apple Time, The" (Frost), 111
Crapsey, Adelaide, 28, 76-77
Cretic meter, 13
Croi, Henri de, 51
cross rhyme, 40
curtal sonnet, 50

dactylic hexameter, 6-7, 9, 17, 18, 26
dactylic meter, 10-11
  line lengths in, 14, 15, 16, 17, 18, 19
  mood of, 23
  rhyme in, 34
  and trochaic, mixed, 20, 43
"Dance of Death, The" (Dobson), 56-57
Daniel, Arnaud, 70
Daniel, Samuel, 48
Dante, Alighieri, 41, 70

Davidson, John, 29
"Days" (Emerson), 121
"Death That Took Fair Helen" (F. S.), 68
De Rerum Natura (Lucretius), xii, 101
descriptive poetry, xi-xii
  subjects of, 101, 103-104
"Deserted Village, The" (Goldsmith), xii
"Destruction of Sennacherib, The" (Byron), 10, 14, 16, 19, 23
dialect verse, xv
"Dialogue, A" (Swinburne), 62-63
Dickinson, Emily, 15, 81, 85, 105
diction, 94, 115-118
didactic poetry xii, 103
dimeter, 14
dissonant rhyme, 81, 83, 86
distich, 26-27
Divine Comedy, The (Dante), 41
Dobson, Austin, 55, 56-57, 59, 65-66, 69, 70
"Dome of Sunday, The" (Shapiro), 84
Don Juan (Byron), xiii, 44
Donne, John, 35
Doolittle, Hilda (H. D.), 90
double ballade, 55
double-refrain ballade, 55
"Dover Beach" (Arnold), 92-93
dramatic poetry, x-xi
  subjects of, 101, 103
Drayton, Michael, 48
Drew, Elizabeth, 106
Dryden, John, 25, 106
Dunbar, William, 9
Dunciad, The (Pope), xiii
Dynasts (Hardy), 101

eight-line stanza, 29, 44, 51-52, 55, 57-58
elegy, 36, 104
"Elegy for Jane" (Roethke), 82, 85
eleven-line stanza, 30, 56
Eliot, T. S., 17, 40, 80, 93-94, 100, 107, 108, 109, 111, 116, 120, 122
Emerson, Ralph Waldo, 111, 121
end-stopped line, 24
end stress, 90
English poetry:
  development of, 8-9, 32, 41, 80
  meters of, 4-6, 9-11, 13
English sonnet, 48-50
English vocabulary, 35, 117
englyn, 77
enjambment, 25
envoi, 51, 52-53, 55-57, 71, 72
epic caesura, 24
epic line, 6-7, 9, 17, 18, 26
epic poetry, ix-x, 6-7, 30
  subjects of, 101-102
epigram, 26-27, 77, 78
  subjects of, 105
epitaph, 105
epitrite meter, 13
"Essay on Criticism, An" (Pope), 24
Essay on Man, An (Pope), xii, 26
Evangeline (Longfellow), 6, 11, 18, 23, 102
"Eve of St. Agnes, The" (Keats), 45

Everyman, 9
expository subjects, 101, 104-105

Faerie Queene, The (Spenser), 17, 29, 30, 45, 102
falling line, 91-92
"Father William" (Carroll), xv
feminine caesura, 24
feminine rhyme, 34-35, 38, 84-85
figures of speech, 119-122
Fitzgerald, Edward, 16, 42
five-line stanza, 27-28, 75, 76-77, 77-78
foot, feet (*see also* meter):
    in line lengths, 13-20
    meaning of, 6
    types of, 10-12
"Force That through the Green Fuse Drives the Flower" (Thomas), 94
foreign admixture verse, xv
Forster, E. M., 100
four-line stanza, 27, 42-43
"Four Quartets" (Eliot), 109
fourteeners, 30
"Four Trees upon a Solitary Acre" (Dickinson), 85
free verse:
    in history of poetry, 80-81
    meaning of, vii, viii, 22
    near-rhyme in, 82-87
    rhythm in, 88-92
    and subject matter, 114
    villanelle in, 95-96
French poetry:
    influence of, 7-8, 32, 41
    meter in, 17
    traditional forms of, 51, 56, 58-61, 63-66
Freud, Sigmund, 93, 108
Froissart, Jean, 51
front stress, 91-92
Frost, Robert, 26, 102, 111, 116, 120, 122
Fry, Christopher, 103

Gayley, Charles Mills, 104
"General William Booth Enters into Heaven" (Lindsay), 94
Gilbert, W. S., Sir, 36-37
Gilder, Richard Watson, 46
Godric, Saint, 8
Goldsmith, Oliver, xii
grammar, 118-119
"Grass" (Sandburg), 86-87, 89-90
Gray, Thomas, 111
Greek Anthology, 105
Greek poetry:
    meters of, 5-7, 11-13
    and rhyme concept, 32
    traditional forms of, 26, 41, 42-43, 73-74
greeting card verse, xiv
Greville, Fulke, Sir, 17
"Growing Up" (F. S.), 71-72
Guittone of Arezzo, 46

haiku, 75, 107
half-rhyme, 82
    variations of, 83-86

Hardy, Thomas, 18, 98, 101
Harper's Magazine, 361, 370
H. D. (Hilda Doolittle), 90
heptameter, 18-19
heroic couplet, 9, 25-26
heroic line, *see* iambic pentameter
hexameter, 17-18
    dactylic, 6-7, 9, 17, 18, 26
Hiawatha (Longfellow), 16, 80
Higginson, Thomas Wentworth, 85
Highet, Gilbert, 33
"Hippopotamus, The" (Eliot), 111
"Home Burial" (Frost), 102
Homer, ix, 6-7, 116
Hopkins, Gerard Manley, 8, 21-22
Horace, 7
Horatian ode, 74
Housman, A. E., x-xi, 39
Howard, Henry, Earl of Surrey, 48
Howard's End (Forster), 100
Hudibras (Butler), 101
Hugo, Victor, 69
humorous verse, xiv-xv, 105, 106
    forms in, 77-79
    rhyme in, 37-38
hyperbole, 122

iambic hexameter, 17, 45
iambic meter, 7, 10
    and anapestic, mixed, 12, 20
    in cinquain, 76-77
    line lengths in, 13, 14, 15, 16, 17, 18, 19
    mood of, 23
    rhyme in, 34
iambic pentameter, 9, 16, 17
    in traditional forms, 41-45, 52, 54, 68, 74
iambic tetrameter, 15, 43, 63
"I Am a Parcel of Vain Strivings Tied" (Thoreau), 14
Idylls of the King, The (Tennyson), x
Iliad (Homer), ix, 6
imagery, 74-76, 106-107
imperfect rhyme, xvii, 81, 82
    variations of, 83, 85-86
incantation, 4
"In Distrust of Merits" (Moore), 91
initial rhyme, 39-40
"In Memoriam" (Tennyson), 15, 109
"In Memory of W. B. Yeats" (Auden), 21
interlocking rhyme, *see* chain rhyming
internal rhyme, 39-40
"Intimations of Immortality" (Wordsworth), 74
"In Town" (Dobson), 70
inverted spelling-rhyme, 38
irregular ode, 74
"Is My Team Ploughing" (Housman), x-xi
"Isolation" (Arnold), 111
Italian poetry, 32, 35, 44
    sonnet forms of, 27, 28, 29, 45-47, 48

James I, King of Scotland, 9
Japanese poetry, 74-76
Jeffers, Robinson, 102
John Brown's Body (Benét), 102

Jonson, Ben, xiii, 9
"Journeys" (F. S.), 61
"Juggler" (Wilbur), 91
"July" (Dobson), 65-66

Keats, John, 29, 30, 45, 74, 102, 104, 107
Kipling, Rudyard, xiv
Kwokamu-Innobetto, Empress, 75
kyrielle, 63

"La Belle Dame Sans Merci" (Keats), 102
"Lacking Sense, The" (Hardy), 18
lai, 64-66
"Lake Isle of Innisfree, The" (Yeats), 111
"L'Allegro" (Milton), 122
Lamb, Charles, 27
landscapes, as subjects of poetry, 111
Langland, William, 8, 9
language:
    figurative, 119-122
    and poetic diction, 94, 115-118
    and rhyme, 35
Latin poetry:
    influence of, 41
    meters of, 5-7, 11
    and rhyme concept, 32
lay, 64
Lear, Edward, xiv, 78
Leaves of Grass (Whitman), 80
"Lenten Hymn, A" (Campion), 63
Leonard, William Ellery, 51
Le Roi, Adenès, 58
Lesbos, island of, 7
"Let No Charitable Hope" (Wylie), 111
light verse, xiv-xv, 105, 106
limerick, 77-78
Lindsay, Vachel, 94, 111
lines:
    ballad, 18-19
    in chain repetition, 69-72
    definition of, vii, viii
    epic, 6-7, 9, 17, 18, 26
    free-verse stress groups in, 89-92
    heroic, 9, 16, 17
    length of, 6, 13-20
    number of, in stanza forms, 25-30, 41-45
    pauses of, 24, 89
    refrain, 51-68 passin, 95-96
    run-on, 25
    scansion of, 22-23
litotes, 122
Little Willie, 79
"London" (Blake), 114
Longfellow, Henry Wadsworth, 6, 10, 11, 16, 18, 20, 23, 37, 80, 102
"Lotos-Eaters, The" (Tennyson), 24
"Louis XVI" (F. S.), 79
love, as poetic theme, 100
Lovelace, Richard, 28
"Lover Passes at Twilight, The" (F. S.), 77
"Love Song of J. Alfred Prufrock, The" (Eliot), 17, 93, 108
Lowell, Amy, 107
Lucretius, xii, 101

"Lycidas" (Milton), 36
"Lyke-Wake Song, A" (Swinburne), 26
lyric caesura, 24
lyric poetry, xii-xiii, 7
    attitude in, 113
    poem forms of, 45-51, 60-63, 64, 75-76
    stanza forms of, 25, 26, 27, 42-43
    subjects of, 101, 104-105

macaronic verse, xv
MacLeish, Archibald, 110
magazines, as poetry market, 361-363, 366, 374-378
magic, and poetry, 4, 7
Malay verse, 69
manuscript, preparation of, 363-365
markets, poetry, 361-363, 366, 369-378
Marlowe, Christopher, 9
masculine caesura, 24
masculine rhyme, 34-35
Masefield, John, 11, 18
Masters, Edgar Lee, 105, 111
Mayo, E. L., 84
"Melvin" (F. S.), 95-96
metaphor, 119-121
meter, 4-23
    classical, 5-7, 11-13
    definition of, viii, 4-5
    English, 4-6, 9-11, 13
    in humorous verse, 77-79
    line length in, 6, 13-20
    mixed, 12, 20-22
    and modernist forms, 88-89, 93-95
    and mood, 23-24
    outline of, 9-13
    rhyme in, 34
    scansion and pronunciation in, 22-23
    and syllable-count forms, 74-76
    in traditional poem forms, 45, 50, 52-54, 60, 63, 74
    in traditional stanza forms, 41-45
Methods and Materials of Literary Criticism (Gayler), 104
metonymy, 121-122
Millay, Edna St. Vincent, 120
Milton, John, ix-x, 16, 36, 109, 111, 122
    sonnet form of, 47-48
"Miniver Cheevy" (Robinson), 111
"Misconceptions" (Browning), 115
modern poetry, 80-96
    free verse, 22, 80-92, 95-96
    irregular forms in, 92-94
    near-rhyme in, 81-87, 94, 95
    rhythms of, 88-89, 94-95
    subject matter in, 100, 107-109, 114
    syllable counting in, 77
    traditional forms in, 81, 94-96
Molière, xiii, 106
molossus meter, 13
"Monna Innominata" (Rossetti), 51
monometer, 13-14
monosyllabic foot, 11
mood:
    and meter, 23-24

mood (cont.):
  in rhyme, 36-37
Moore, Marianne, 77, 91
Moore, Merrill, 51
morals, as poetic theme, xii, 100, 103, 105-106
"Mr. Flood's Party" (Robinson), 111
"Musée des Beaux Arts" (Auden), 111
"My Last Duchess" (Browning), 26, 100
"My Lost Youth" (Longfellow), 20
"My Papa's Waltz" (Roethke), 85

naga-uta, 76
narrative poetry, x, 25, 30
  subjects of, 101-103
Nash, Ogden, 38
near-rhyme, 40, 81-87, 94-95
"Never Seek to Tell Thy Love" (Blake), 27
newspapers, as poetry market, 362, 363, 369-370
"Night" (Shelley), 29
"Nightmare" (F. S.), 64-65
nine-line stanza, 29-30, 45
nonsense verse, xiv, 78
"Not Marble Nor the Gilded Monuments" (Shakespeare), 111

occasional verse, xiii-xiv
octameter, 19
octave, 29, 44
  in sonnet forms, 46-48
ode, 30, 73-74, 104
"Ode" (O'Shaughnessy), xii-xiii, 111
"Ode: Intimations of Immortality" (Wordsworth), 74
"Ode on the Death of a Favorite Cat" (Gray), 111
"Ode on Melancholy" (Keats), 107
"Ode on the Morning of Christ's Nativity" (Milton), 111
"Ode to a Nightingale" (Keats), 30, 74, 104
"Ode to Psyche" (Keats), 30
"Ode to the West Wind" (Shelley), 12, 42
Odyssey (Homer), ix, 6
"Old Familiar Faces, The" (Lamb), 27
"Old Man, The" (F. S.), 60
Omar Khayyám, 16, 42
one-line stanza, 25
"On His Blindness" (Milton), 47-48
"Only News I Know, The" (Dickinson), 15
"On the Naming of Cats" (Eliot), 111
onomatopoeia, 33, 122
O'Shaughnessy, A. W. E., xiii, 111
ottava rima, 44, 45
"Out of the Cradle Endlessly Rocking" (Whitman), viii

paeon, 13
Palgrave, Francis T., xii
pantoum, 69-70
Paradise Lost (Milton), ix-x, 16
parody, xiv-xv
"Patterns" (Lowell), 107
pauses, 89
  within line, 24

pentameter (*see also* iambic pentameter), 16-17
people, as subjects of poetry, 111
personification, 121, 122
Petrarch, Francesco, 70
Petrarchan sonnet, 45-47
" Pied Beauty " (Hopkins), 22
Pindaric ode, 74
plagiarism, 118
Poe, Edgar Allan, 18, 19, 39, 80, 92, 111
poem forms:
  and free verse, 88-92
  humorous, 77-79
  irregular, 92-94
  modern currents in, 80-81
  modernist-traditional, 81, 94-96
  and subjects, 113-115
  syllable-count, 74-77
  traditional, 45-74
poet (*see also* poetry):
  attitudes of, 105-106, 112-113
  influence of psychology on, 93-94, 108
  record files for, 110-111, 360-361
  submission of poems by, 359-366
poetic drama, x-xi
  subjects of, 101, 103
poetry:
  definition of, vii-viii
  historical development of, 3-9, 32-33, 41, 80-81
  kinds of, viii-xv, 101
  markets for, 361-363, 366, 369-378
  mood conveyance in, 23-24
  and prose, compared, 97
  publication of, 359-367
  revision of, 122-123
  style in, 112-123
  subjects of, 99-111
  truth in, 98-99
"Pool, The" (Mayo), 84
Pope, Alexander, xii, xiii, 24, 25, 26, 106
"Portrait of Mary" (F. S.), 39-40
"Postcard from the Volcano, A" (Stevens), 107
Pound, Ezra, 95, 98, 101, 106
"Preludes" (Eliot), 100, 120
pronunciation, xvii-xviii, 23
prosody:
  and rhythm, 3-4
  terminology of, vii-viii
"Psalm of Life" (Longfellow), 10
psychology, 93, 100, 108, 111
publication, 359-367
  markets for, 361-363, 366, 369-378
pyrrhic meter, 13

quantity:
  and free verse, 91-92
  as meter determinant, 5-6, 11-12
  and mood, 23-24, 36-37
quatorzain, 30
quatrain, 27, 69, 79, 105
  in traditional forms, 42-43, 48-49, 63, 67-68, 69-70, 77
quintet, *see* cinquain

Ransom, John Crowe, 85
"Raven, The" (Poe), 19, 39
"Recessional" (Kipling), xiv
refrain lines:
  as ballade feature, 51
  and chain linkage, 69-72
  in free-verse villanelle, 95-96
  in monometer, 14, 60-61
  in theme with variations, 50-51, 67-68
  in traditional forms, 51-68 *passinm*
religion, as subject of poetry, 111
religious poetry, 4, 32, 63
repetition (*see also* refrain lines):
  chain linkage by, 69-73
  as rhyme substitute, 70-71, 81, 86, 95-69
"Revenant, The" (F. S.), 67
rhyme, 32-40
  definition of, viii, 32, 33
  development of, 7-8, 32-33
  in humorous verse, 37-38, 77-79
  kinds of, 34-35, 39-40
  mood in, 36-37
  near-rhyme, 40, 81-87, 93-94, 95
  random, 39-40, 93-94
rhyme royal, 29, 44, 45
rhyme schemes, 38-40
  chain effect in, 68-69
  couplet, 25-26, 38
  in humorous verse, 38, 77-79
  irregular, 39-40, 93-94
  in traditional poem forms, 45-74
  in traditional stanza forms, 38-39, 42-45
rhyming dictionary:
  how to use, xvii-xviii
rhythm (see also meter):
  in prosody, 3-4
  stress-group, 88-92, 94-95
"Richard Cory" (Robinson), 111
"Rime of the Ancient Mariner, The" (Coleridge), 28
rising line, 90
Robinson, Edwin Arlington, 102, 111, 121
Roethke, Theodore, 82, 85
Romance of the Rose, x, 9
rondeau, 60-61
rondeau redoublé, 67-68
rondel, 58-60
"Rondel, A" (F. S.), 59
rondelet, 60
Rossetti, Christina, 51
Rossetti, Dante Gabriel, 28
roundel, 61-63
  Chaucerian, 59-60
rubai, 42
Rubaiyat of Omar Khayyám, 16, 42
"Runnable Stag, A" (Davidson), 29-30
run-on verse, 25

Saadi, 27
Sandburg, Carl, 86-87, 89
sapphic, 42-43
"Sapphics" (Swinburne), 43
Sappho, 7, 42
satire, xiii, 105-106

scansion, 22-23
science, as subject of poetry, 108-109
Scott, Walter, Sir, 29
"Sea, The" (Byron), 111
"Sea Fever" (Masefield), 11
seasonal poetry, 362-363
septet, 29, 44
sestet, 28, 43-44
  in sonnet forms, 27, 28, 46-48
sestina, 69, 70-73, 86
"Sestina" (Swinburne), 72-73
seven-line stanza, 29, 44, 54, 60
Shakespeare, William, x, 9, 16, 22-23, 24, 28,
  29, 35, 43, 44, 100, 101, 103, 111, 121
Shakespearean sonnet, 48-50
Shapiro, Karl, 17, 84, 100
Shelley, Percy Bysshe, 12, 29, 42, 120, 121
Sicilian octave, 44
Sidney, Philip, Sir, 9, 48, 99
simile, 119-121
"Sir Patrick Spens," x, 21, 38
Sitwell, Edith, 107
six-line stanza, 28, 43-44
Skelton, John, 9
slang, 116
"Snow-flakes" (Longfellow), 37
"Song" (Donne), 35
"Song" (H. D.), 90
Song of Hiawatha, The (Longfellow), 16, 80
sonnet:
  English, 48-50
  Italian, 27, 28, 29, 45-48
  sequences of, 50-51
  terza rima, 68
"Sonnet, The" (Gilder), 46
Sonnets (Shakespeare), 23, 35, 48-49, 121
Sonnets from the Portuguese (Browning), 51
"Soul Selects Her Own Society" (Dickinson), 85
Southey, Robert, xv
spelling rhymes, 35
  inverted, 38
Spenser, Edmund, 9, 102
  sonnet form of, 49-50
Spenserian stanza, 17, 29, 30, 45
spondaic meter, 11-12
Spoon River Anthology (Masters), 105, 111
sprung rhythm, 21-22
stanza, 25-31
  chain linkage in, 68-73, 86
  definition of, vii, viii
  line count definitions of, 25-30
  in modernist irregular forms, 94, 95
  set rhyme schemes for, 38-39
  of syllable-count verse, 74-77
  traditional forms of, 41-45
  in traditional poem forms, 45-75 *passim*
    ballade, 51-56
    ode pattern, 73-74
    sonnet, 45-51
  value of, 31
stanzaic ode, 74
Stephens, James, 69
Stevens, Wallace, 107, 120

"Stopping by Woods on a Snowy Evening" (Frost), 111, 116, 122
stress-group rhythms:
    and accent, distinction between, 88
    in Anglo-Saxon forms, 8
    in free verse, 90-92
    traditional-modernist use of, 94-95
style, 112-123
subject matter, 97-111
    finding of, 109-111
    and poem form, 113-114
    and publication, 362-363
"Surgeons Must Be Very Careful" (Dickinson), 105
Swift, Jonathan, 106
Swinburne, Algernon Charles, 26, 43, 53, 61-63, 72-73, 84
syllable-count poetry, 74-77
syllables (*see also* meter):
    length of, 5-6, 11-12, 23-24, 36, 91-92
    line-ending, and rhyme, 34-35
    stressed alliterative, 8, 22
    tonic accent pattern of, 4-6, 88
symbolism, 80, 102-103, 107-108
synechdoche, 121-122
syntax, 118-119

tailed sonnet, 50
tail lines, 14, 50, 64, 68
tanka, 75-76
Tate, Allen, 98
ten-line stanza, 30, 52-53, 74
Tennyson, Alfred, Lord, x, 15, 24, 80, 109
tercet, 27, 75
    in Italian sonnet, 27, 46
    in villanelle, 66-67, 95-96
terza rima, 27, 41-42
    chain-rhyming of, 42, 68-69
tetrameter, 15-16
theme lines, *see* refrain lines
themes, poetic, 93-94, 99-101, 108
theme with variations, 50-51, 67-68
"The Tide Rises, the Tide Falls" (Longfellow), 111
Thomas, Dylan, 94, 113
Thoreau, Henry David, 14
three-line stanza, 27, 41-42, 64, 66-67, 75
three-syllable rhyme, 34, 38, 84-85
"To Helen" (Poe), 111
"To Lucasta, going beyond the Seas" (Lovelace), 28
tonic accent, *see* accent
"To the Terrestrial Globe" (Gilbert), 36
traditional forms, 41-74
    and free-verse rhythms, 88-89
    modernist use of, 81, 92-96
    near-rhyme in, 87, 94-95
    and subject matter, 113-114
translations, xv, 75
tribrach meter, 13
trimeter, 15
triolet, 57-58
"Triolets of a Country-Hater" (F. S.), 58

triplet, *see* tercet
trochaic meter, 10
    and dactylic, mixed, 20, 43
    line lengths in, 13, 14, 15, 16, 17, 18, 19
    mood of, 23
    rhyme in, 34
trochaic pentameter, 16, 43
Troilus and Criseyde (Chaucer), 44
truncated line, 6
truth, in poetry, 98-99
"Tuft of Flowers, The" (Frost), 26
two-line stanza, 25-27
"Two Lives" (Leonard), 51
two-syllable rhyme, 34

unaccented rhyme, 81, 82
    variations of, 83, 85, 86
Untermeyer, Louis, 360
"Upon a Dying Lady" (Yeats), 111

Van Dyke, Henry, 54
Vaughan, Henry, 99
Venus and Adonis (Shakespeare), 28
Venus and Adonis stanza, 28, 43-44
vers de société, xiv
verse, definition of, vii
verse forms, *see* poem forms
"Verses on the Death of Dr. Swift, D. S. P. D." (Swift), 106
versification, definition of, viii
villanelle, 66-67
    in free verse, 95-96
Villon, François, 51, 116
virelai, 64-66, 69
Virgil, 7
Vision of Piers Plowman, The (Langland), 8, 9
"V-Letter" (Shapiro), 100
vowel rhyme, 81, 83-84, 86-87

"Wanderer, The" (Dobson), 59
"Warning, The" (Crapsey), 77
Welsh poetry, 77
Wesley, Charles, 43
Western Star (Benét), 102
"When Lilacs Last in the Dooryard Bloom'd" (Whitman), 90
"Whilst It Is Prime" (Spenser), 50
Whitman, Walt, viii, 80-81, 89-90, 92, 120
Wilbur, Richard, 91
Wilde, Oscar, 10
"With Rue My Heart Is Laden" (Housman), 39
words:
    in chain repetition, 69, 71-73, 86
    choice of, 115-122
Wordsworth, William, 24, 25, 47, 74, 98, 122
"World, The" (Wordsworth), 24, 25, 47
"Wrestling Jacob" (Wesley), 43-44
Wyatt, Thomas, Sir, 48
Wylie, Elinor, 111

Yeats, William Butler, 99, 107, 111, 113, 116, 118